Pop Culture in Asia and Oceania

Recent Titles in Entertainment and Society around the World

Pop Culture in Latin America and the Caribbean
Elizabeth Gackstetter Nichols and Timothy R. Robbins

Pop Culture in Asia and Oceania

JEREMY A. MURRAY
AND
KATHLEEN M. NADEAU, EDITORS

Entertainment and Society
around the World

ABC-CLIO™

An Imprint of ABC-CLIO, LLC
Santa Barbara, California • Denver, Colorado

Library of Congress Cataloging-in-Publication Data

Names: Nadeau, Kathleen M., 1952- editor of compilation. | Murray, Jeremy A., editor of compilation.
Title: Pop culture in Asia and Oceania / Jeremy A. Murray and Kathleen M. Nadeau, editors.
Description: Santa Barbara, California : ABC-CLIO, an imprint of ABC-CLIO, LLC, [2016] | Series: Entertainment and society around the world | "This book is also available as an eBook"—Title page verso. | Includes bibliographical references and index.
Identifiers: LCCN 2016025602 (print) | LCCN 2016028895 (ebook) | ISBN 9781440839900 (hardback : acid-free paper) | ISBN 9781440839917 (electronic)
Subjects: LCSH: Popular culture—Asia. | Popular culture—Oceania. | Asia—Civilization. | Oceania—Civilization. | Asia—Intellectual life. | Oceania—Intellectual life. | Asia—Social life and customs. | Oceania—Social life and customs.
Classification: LCC DS12 .P55 2016 (print) | LCC DS12 (ebook) | DDC 306.095--dc23
LC record available at https://lccn.loc.gov/2016025602

ISBN: 978-1-4408-3990-0
EISBN: 978-1-4408-3991-7

20 19 18 17 16 1 2 3 4 5

This book is also available as an eBook.

ABC-CLIO
An Imprint of ABC-CLIO, LLC

ABC-CLIO, LLC
130 Cremona Drive, P.O. Box 1911
Santa Barbara, California 93116-1911
www.abc-clio.com

This book is printed on acid-free paper ∞

Manufactured in the United States of America

For Buster and Pearl
—K. N.

For Katherine and Alexander
—J. M.

Contents

Preface

This volume aims to introduce the general reader to various forms of popular culture in Asia and Oceania. Our volume in this series includes topics related to East Asia, South Asia, Southeast Asia, Central Asia, as well as the Pacific islands of Oceania, including Australia and New Zealand, but does not include western Asia, or what is sometimes referred to as the Middle East. The people within the broad geographical regions that are included here comprise about a half of the world's total population of 7 billion. This presents us with the mighty task of introducing half of the world's popular culture in just one volume. Some countries and regions, and some topics, have been allocated greater attention and detail than others, which is sometimes based on population, sometimes on regional influence, and sometimes on the availability of expertise and information. Naturally, we were forced to make many difficult decisions of inclusion and exclusion for the volume, since a project of this scope could easily include dozens of books full of rich and fascinating materials.

In planning this volume, we recognized the limitations of our own expertise, and so we reached out to colleagues with experience and deep knowledge of the many topics that we hoped to cover. We are extremely grateful to the many scholars who were willing to write entries based on their specialization. The nearly 100 experts included in this volume undertook the challenge of distilling an enormous amount of their own research and knowledge on one or more topics that many of them have spent years studying, and they turned this into contributions averaging only about 1,000 words. Some of the contributors have written many articles and books on their respective topics, and for this project, they have provided the reader with a concise and fascinating glimpse into their expertise. Our cohort of contributors here includes both very new and very experienced scholars; some authors are prominent leaders of their respective fields, and others have just embarked on their academic careers. We hope that the result of these many voices coming together is informative, dynamic, and compelling. While we certainly could not hope to cover all topics under the broad heading of popular culture in Asia and Oceania, we do hope that the reader's understanding of the topic is enriched and that the reader is inspired to pursue some of these subtopics further and in more detail.

It has been our great pleasure to compile this book and also contribute some of our own entries. We thank all contributing authors for their time, effort, and expertise. We also wish to thank our editor, Kaitlin Ciarmiello and ABC-CLIO for making this book possible. Thanks to Ellen Rasmussen, media editor at ABC-CLIO for her work on image research, and thanks to the production team at Amnet, including project manager Jennifer Crane and copyeditor Melissa Churchill, for their excellent work.

We hope that the reader finds both enjoyment and edification in these pages.

Chronology

1167–1227	Rise of Mongolian wrestling contests under Genghis Khan
1603–1868	Japan's Tokugawa Shogunate founds *gendai budo* or *shinbudo*
1815	Artist Katsuhika Hokusai popularizes term "manga"
1859	Official codification of Australian-rules football
1860	Jigoro Kano introduces modern style of judo ("yielding/gentle way")
1867	Manila Jockey Club is established in the Philippines
1873	Horace Wilson introduces baseball to students at Kaisei-ko, now Tokyo University
1895–1945	Japanese colonization of Taiwan
1897	Baseball introduced to Taiwan
1898	Emilio Aguinaldo declares Philippine independence from Spanish colonialism
1898	Spain cedes Philippines to United States
1899–1901	Boxer uprising in China
1908	Inaugural beauty pageant in the Philippines
1913	Rabindranath Tagore becomes first Asian Nobel laureate
1918–1991	Period of Soviet Central Asia
1920	Indian activist B. R. Ambedkar mobilizes masses to outlaw "untouchability"
1934	National agency of Philippine Charity Sweepstakes Office created
1945	Sukarno proclaims independence, becoming president of Indonesia
1945	Founding of Democratic Republic of Vietnam
1945	Taiwan taken over by Republic of China government
1946	United States grants Philippines independence
1948	Burma gains independence from Britain

1949	Communists win the civil war in China and Nationalists move to Taiwan
1949	End of Hollywood Empire in China
1950–1976	Chinese propaganda songs replace outlawed Tibetan national songs
1951	Akira Kurosawa's *Rashomon* becomes world famous at Venice Film Festival
1952	Yvette Williams is first female Olympic gold medalist for New Zealand
1953	Armistice ends Korean War and divides North and South Korea
1953	Central Newsreel and Documentary Film School founded (Communist China)
1954	Philippines wins bronze medal at World Basketball Championships in Brazil
1956	China airs first annual New Year Spring Festival Television Gala
1956	Ali Akbar College of Music established in Calcutta (Kolkata)
1957	Federation of Malaya gains independence from the British
1957	Opening of the first Vietnamese film journal, *Điện Ảnh* (*Cinema*)
1959	China dissolves the government of Tibet
1962	First public Indonesian-wide TV broadcast shows Fourth Asia Games in Jakarta
1962	Ne Win sets up military government in Burma
1965	Singapore becomes an independent state
1965	Ferdinand Marcos elected president of Philippines
1966	Taiwan is the second-largest film-producing nation in the world
1966–1976	Chinese Cultural Revolution
1967	Amar Chitra Katha (Immortal Picture Stories) dominates comic series in India
1967	Suharto named president and turns Indonesia into a police state
1968	Yasunari Kawabata (Japan) wins Nobel Prize for literature
1970	Inauguration of New Year Cinema in China
1970	Japanese youth fashions go global

1970	*Yaoi*, gay manga and animation from Japan, is globally popular
1971	Bangladesh independence declared from Pakistan
1973	F. Sionil Jose finishes Rosales novels (*Mass*, *The Pretenders*, *My Executioner*)
1975–1987	Reunification marks a new era in Vietnamese national cinema
1976	Death of Mao Zedong
1977	Female college students allowed to wear jeans in class in Japan
1977	Australian Colleen McCullough's *The Thorn Birds* is an international best seller
1980	Historical Television Dramas launches in China
1980	Guang Chunlan (Maoist Uyghur) Xinjiang's leading female filmmaker
1982	Jet Li in *The Shaolin Temple* becomes an instant international martial arts icon
1982–1988	Taiwan New Cinema Movement
1983–2009	Civil war in Sri Lanka
1984	Cui Jian pioneers rock and roll in China
1985	Sino-Japan *weiqi* match replaces earlier friendly contests
1986	People Power Revolution peacefully overthrows the Marcos dictatorship
1986	Corazon Aquino elected president of Philippines
1987	Establishment of the New Zealand film industry
1988	Ne Win steps down, but military continues to rule Burma repressively
1989	Burma renamed Myanmar
1989	China cracks down on Tiananmen Square protests
1990	Return of Hollywood films to China
1991	Aung San Suu Kyi wins Nobel Peace Prize
1991	Film *Tiananmen*, by Shi Jian, fails to pass government censorship
1991	*The Theory of Music* written for North Korean state to censor national songs
1991	Voice of America launched in Tibetan

1992	Fidel Ramos succeeds Aquino as president of Philippines
1992	K-pop style introduced by Seo Taiji & Boys
1994	First Internet connection in China
1994	Kenzaburo Oe (Japan) wins Nobel Prize in Literature
1994	*Once Were Warriors*, first Maori film set in the city, is also highest-grossing film
1995	Australian actor Mel Gibson wins Academy Award for *Braveheart*
1995	Nobel Prize candidate Pramudya Ananta Toer wins Magsayay Award
1997	Arundhati Roy wins Booker Prize for *The God of Small Things*
1997	Singapore becomes one of the world's strongest economies
1998	Ayu Utami's controversial novel *Saman* explores alternative sexualities in Indonesia
1998	Amartya Sen wins Nobel Prize in Economics
1998	Pro-democracy movement prompts Suharto to leave presidential office
1999	High-schooler Han Han wins New Concept Writing Competition in China
1999	First edition of Tharoor Shashi's *The Great Indian Novel*
2000	Gao Xingjian (China) wins Nobel Prize in Literature
2001	Megawati Sukarnoputri elected president of Indonesia
2001	Globalization and industrial restructuring of China
2002	East Timor celebrates independence from Indonesia
2002	Yu Hua become first Chinese author to win the James Joyce Foundation Award
2003	Mongolian sumo wrestler Dolgorsüren Dagvadorj ranked *yokozuna* in Japan
2004	Munir, Indonesian civil rights activist/martyr, poisoned onboard Air Garuda
2006	Muhammad Yunus (Bangladesh) wins Nobel Peace Prize
2008	Art critic Li Xianting founds Li Xianting Film School
2008	Dhondup Wangchen jailed for interviewing Tibetans about Beijing Olympics

2008	China's Ministry of Health declares Internet addiction a clinical disorder
2009	Kenichi Kakutani founds Japan's first women's professional baseball league
2010	Women's soccer introduced in South Asian Games, hosted in Dhaka, Bangladesh
2010	*If You Are the One*, a dating show in China, becomes instant national hit
2010	Liu Xiaobo (China) wins Nobel Peace Prize
2011	March 11 (3.11) tsunami engulfs Japan, causing some 16,000 lives lost
2012	Australian Rugby League Commission is formed
2012	South Korean song "Gangnam Style" goes global
2012	Mo Yan (China) wins Nobel Prize in Literature
2012	Mike Sui's *12 Beijingers* goes global on Chinese Youku
2013	Manny Pacquiao becomes global boxing icon
2013	Li Na wins Australian Open Cup
2014	China's State Council lifts ban on console sales in the Shanghai Free Trade Zone
2014	Shiralijan of Flying Tigers wins Chinese Basketball Association championship
2014	Heavy metal promoted by Joko Widodo, incoming president of Indonesia
2014	Kumar Sangakkara leads Sri Lanka to its first ICC World Championship
2013	Inbee Park dominates women's golf, winning fifth Grand Slam title
2015	Popular Hong Kong TV series *Hakka Sisters* airs on the worldwide Internet
2015	Jakarta hosts International Social Media Week Conference
2015	Nepal's deadliest earthquakes hit the Gorkha region
2016	Google's AlphaGo computer program defeats *weiqi* world champion, Lee Sedol

Introduction

What Is Popular Culture?

Popular culture is not easy to define, and many would disagree about exactly what it is. It changes from one era to the next, and time may reveal a hit song, a pulp novel, or a fashion fad to be more enduring than once expected. But a point of departure for this exploration is that *pop culture is fun*. By its very definition, popular culture is defined as such because many people like it. Some may sniff at the term "popular culture," thinking it less worthy or sophisticated than whatever constitutes the equally vague label of "high culture." Likewise, some may believe that pop culture is mass-produced and mass-marketed trash that will not stand the test of time, never to be enshrined in museums or celebrated in concert halls. But still, as a people, we consume it and enjoy it, or else it would not qualify to be labeled as popular culture. We categorize things as being part of popular culture first by the preference of a large group of people and commercial success.

Defining popular culture with precision, though, is difficult for academic experts, cultural critics, and most anyone else. There is widespread disagreement about precisely how we should think and write about popular culture. Is it necessarily lowbrow or vulgar in contrast to the kind of art and music found in galleries and symphony halls? Some kinds of popular culture of the past, like jazz, early cinema, and various types of provocative theater and visual art, were criticized as cultural trash in their day, but the passing of time has revealed them to be generally accepted as being among humanity's highest achievements. Trying to clearly define popular culture is like trying to hit a moving target.

What we call "popular culture" is a fluid category that shifts and changes with time. Scholars of anthropology and other fields wrestle over the definition of popular culture. Some choose to link it to mass production beginning in the Industrial Revolution. This, in turn, links popular culture to Western civilization (western Europe and the United States), which is not necessarily suitable for our volume. Was the popular culture of Asia and Oceania waiting to be ignited by the 18th- and 19th-century mechanization of production in the West? Certainly not. Indeed, tracking the movement of products and cultural motifs many centuries earlier along the Eurasian land routes (sometimes called the Silk Roads), and later the interactions following the Arab Muslim conquests and the Crusades, reveals trends that turn this idea on its head. Many forms of popular culture, from music to fashion and storytelling in the form of puppet shows and village-level cultural performance arts, were only ignited in the West after Europeans were introduced to the more sophisticated songs and visual ways of dramatizing various art forms of western, southern, and eastern Asia. Art, music, dance, sport, and literature were all being produced by and for the people of Asia and Oceania long before modernization or mass production in the West. And so as we embark on an exploration of popular culture in Asia and Oceania, we should be wary of definitions that are constructed in the West and privilege a Western narrative with little consideration for global and historical realities. Likewise, we should be aware of the complexity of global cultural flows of ideas, even before the phenomena of industrialization and globalization in recent years.

One simple way to proceed is by taking the words "popular" and "culture" separately. "Popular" can mean of or relating to the people, broadly defined, and can also mean something that is particularly enjoyed by a large group of people. "Culture" can mean a total or holistic view of human intellectual and artistic production, sometimes within a defined group of people (like a country, an ethnic group, or a time period), and it can also mean a refined or high-minded category of this kind of artistic or intellectual endeavor. Bringing these terms together starts us off with quite a broad definition, one that aims to escape the overly simple definitions of popular culture. A Mongolian festival with ancient traditions featuring competitions of horsemanship and wrestling qualifies as popular culture here; a Chinese singing competition featuring teen idols and text-message voting does as well; so to do the cinemas of Akira Kurosawa of Japan and Baz Lurhman of Australia, the martial arts, video-game addiction, Bollywood stars, and much more. Our embrace of a deliberately broad definition of popular culture has allowed us to include a rich collection of entries in this volume that comprise a textured and complex portrayal of the cultures of Asia and Oceania, with an emphasis on recent developments and longer trends that have shaped current cultural landscapes.

The Political Context

In this short introduction, we naturally are unable to provide a thorough historical and political situation for the reader that covers all areas treated in this volume. We hope that the attentive reader will be able to glean much of that history and political context from the entries included here, but these short notes will provide some basis of how these factors specifically can affect the creation and consumption of popular culture. For a thorough history and political background of Asia and Oceania, please see our suggested further readings at the end of this introduction.

Popular culture, like all culture, is influenced by political, economic, geographic, and social factors. Today, as in the past, powerful political and economic forces control networks of communication that distribute music and visual media, sometimes encouraging cultural production and distribution and sometimes forbidding it. In America, we consider our realm of popular culture production to be free of political meddling, and this is true in a relative sense, although perhaps constrained by the sometimes-conservative inertia of powerful advertisers and media conglomerates. But there are many countries, including some in Asia and Oceania, where artists and intellectuals who articulate bold critiques of their political leaders and institutions run the risk of censure, imprisonment, or worse.

If an artist's work is subversive and aims to explicitly undermine a powerful entity or individual, like a government or a political figure, in many political environments, that work will generally not enjoy mass-marketed distribution. In many countries, the government controls and regulates the airwaves, as it controls other infrastructure. Powerful advertisers are cozy with powerful politicians, which can mean limited access and often danger for those who speak with subversive voices, even in an Internet world. If, on the other hand, an artistic writer or filmmaker praises those in power and is seen by all as a shill or a toady, that individual's work may be poorly received by the public and criticized as artificial and inauthentic.

Besides the extremes of the political spectrum, expressions of popular culture in literature, film, music, sports, and other realms that do not criticize or endorse political institutions and individuals can naturally be very popular around the world in a way that is largely unfettered. Sports, for example, are generally viewed as being apolitical, though individuals may choose to express political views or protests in various ways. Fans of one team or another may clash over the results of a contest, and sometimes these rivalries erupt in violence. Also, in the context of venues like the Olympics or the FIFA (*Fédération Internationale de Football Association*) World Cup, the governing bodies of these competitions can significantly influence politics in deciding which country or city will host an event. Within that country, citizens sometimes protest the expenditures involved in hosting the Olympics or the World Cup, especially in countries that must spend lavishly on new construction projects exclusively for the event. Local people, especially poor vendors and settlement communities, may be displaced for the sake of creating a clean and opulent national image. South Korea, in hosting the 1987 Olympics, not only forcibly relocated poor communities and forbade poor vendors from doing business at the site but also banned restaurants from selling dog soup, a local favorite, due to international outrage. Yet, while dogs are often a protected animal in the West, the cow (India), water buffalo or *carabao* (Indonesia and the Philippines), and peacocks (Korea) are considered revered national treasures. By way of the South Korean example, in preparation for the 1988 Winter Olympics, an ancient sacred mountain (Mount Gariwang), home to protected species and ancient oak trees considered national treasures, was mowed down despite the international movement of concerned environmental protesters. Gearing up for the 2016 Olympics, Brazil, similarly, has forcibly removed thousands of *favela* residents from the game sites.

In recent years, in the People's Republic of China, South Africa, Russia, and Brazil, the hosting of the Olympic Games has been a deeply dividing political issue. The glory of hosting such a global event is outweighed, in the view of many opponents, by the fact that essential infrastructure and other urgent domestic spending will be cut or abandoned in favor of building a stadium or facility that may be used only for a month or two and then left to crumble for lack of demand after the event. Issues like these, plus scandals relating to corruption and bribes, doping and other substance abuse, controversial statements, and racism, can make the popular culture of a sporting world a realm of high political stakes.

Popular music is often thought of as a frothy realm of the latest hit songs, but it can also include subversive messages that criticize the status quo. In China, the music of Cui Jian inspired a generation in the 1980s. In Japan, Indonesia, Australia, and almost every culture, popular music can become a powerful venue for protests of all kinds, whether lighthearted or sincere and arresting. Cinema and literature generally feature narrative storytelling, which always has the potential to be explicitly or implicitly political in nature. The stories that artists choose to tell can both reflect a cultural climate and also inform an audience. Writers of all kinds have historically challenged readers with powerful critiques of society that can be general or specific in their targets.

In these and many other contexts, the audience does well to consider the political and cultural context out of which a song, a poem, a painting, a novel, or an athlete emerges. Consider what industry forces bring a pop singer to your attention and what the message of that song is. Think about what films succeed at the box office and why. Weigh the stakes of international sports competitions not only on the field but also in national and regional economies. These considerations may shape the way you encounter popular culture and help provide a deeper political context for its production and consumption.

Globalization and Global Popular Culture

We are constantly reminded that the world is more closely connected than it has ever been. From new media to multinational entertainment conglomerates that distribute products to eyes and ears around the world, popular culture is shared more than ever across greater distances and greater numbers of people. This is a continuation of connections that have been building for decades and perhaps centuries, facilitated by technology and profit motives. The results of increasing connections across space are varied. Sometimes these connections increase access to information and entertainment, and in so doing, empower the people who gain that access. Sometimes the new networks and avenues of cultural access mean that a small number of well-placed and powerful entertainment juggernauts are facilitated in the distribution of their products to an ever-expanding audience.

As with the example of blockbuster American films like the Fast and Furious or Transformers franchises, foreign audiences like those of Asia and Oceania welcome this most popular of American pop culture, even though it is generally not the most critically acclaimed or culturally significant art in its medium. Of course this gives rise to a cyclical question: massively popular and perhaps lowbrow American fare is exported with the powerful marketing forces of huge studios, and audiences in turn consume the products that are played in their theaters. Is it the preference of the audience that demands these films, or is it simply limited choice in film selections? Sometimes the films are chosen by market demand, but sometimes in certain countries there are governmental quotas on foreign films, and only approved Hollywood films are imported and screened publicly, based on concerns of either censors or those who would protect domestic film production.

In the case of the record-setting *Furious 7* (2015), from the Fast and Furious franchise, the film involved both American and Chinese producers and distributors and an Australian director born in Malaysia, James Wan. The partnership between American and Chinese distributors was naturally a crucial factor in the film's record-setting performance in Chinese theaters, and these mechanics are as important, if not more important, than Chinese audiences' taste in our assessment of the film's box-office performance and critical reception in China. Some American productions, such as *Iron Man 3* (2013), even feature characters played by Chinese actors, inserted in scenes that are featured only in the version of the film screened to Chinese audiences. While this phenomenon has largely been a characteristic of feature films, it indicates an interesting development in multinational corporate cooperation in productions with huge budgets that aim for maximum global audiences. As this trend percolates into the worlds of television, radio, and film throughout Asia and Oceania, it seems that globalization is not necessarily always a harbinger of diversity and richer cultural exchange and awareness. Increased multinational cooperation and globalization can also lead to a more homogenized and, perhaps, culturally insubstantial product.

The homogenizing of popular culture on a global scale is a relatively recent phenomenon. This may be popular culture at its least compelling. If this is the direction of global culture, it seems to be the true product of both the efficiency of the age of industrialization combined with the glossy sheen of the age of information— mass-marketed popular culture diluted beyond any recognizable cultural substance. Perhaps this is a pessimistic view of a shared global experience of cultural fare that is not intended to do anything more than to briefly entertain and divert an audience, but still it threatens to eclipse more regionally diverse cultures.

But a more optimistic view would highlight other trends, like the democratization of the production of popular culture in the form of new media and the relative affordability of production and distribution of content in many formats. From YouTube sensations to all kinds of Web sharing of constantly expanding cultural content, people have a potential audience of billions for their artistic expression. Efforts at cultural preservation and increased online availability of global cultural content are also vital to this process, and people around the world can learn about distant peoples and places through online interactions that can potentially be more holistic and immersive than written content alone. An Internet sensation in Korea may sweep the world, like Psy's "Gangnam Style"; a high-school student in America may learn about *kabaddi* for a school report and start a club for the sport in her hometown; an online video of the Maori *haka* may inspire viewers on the other side of the world; video-game enthusiasts in 10 different countries may become acquainted through a shared online game; an aspiring Australian actor may land a part in Hollywood via a video-chat audition from Sydney; an artist may give voice to a political or social issue in artwork available for global consumption even though that same expression is outlawed in her home country. The terrain of popular culture today is shifting and dynamic, and this volume hopes to provide the reader with some understanding of short-term and long-term phenomena on a global landscape.

Orientation to This Volume

Assembling this volume included difficult decisions about what we could include and what we would not be able to cover. Certain categories and broad topics are included while others have been excluded. In eight categories and about 100 entries, many topics are covered here, though naturally we have not been able to cover all topics exhaustively. Some regions have received less attention than others, but we hope to still be able to point the interested reader to relevant materials and topics that are covered less thoroughly here. The volume is divided into eight main sections in the following order: popular music; books and contemporary literature; cinema; television and radio; Internet and social media; sports; video games; and fashion and couture.

While the purview of our volume includes the popular culture of half the world's population, there are naturally many topics and areas that we are not able to treat thoroughly or at all in the confines of one volume. Food and foodways (a social science term referring to the production and consumption of food, especially within a given cultural context) comprise a fascinating realm for understanding popular culture around the world, and the diverse cuisines of Asia and Oceania are well worth both intellectual and gastronomical exploration! Architecture is another fascinating expression of regional aesthetics and culture that provides the visitor with a town or city's flavor. Visual art of all forms is an important realm of culture, from graffiti to sculpture to painting to art installations that push boundaries and can provoke visceral reactions in the viewer. The theater and performance arts also make up a vital and exciting realm of culture, from street performers to opera to shadow puppetry to rituals that blur the boundaries between dramatic performance and spiritual possession. We regret that we have not been able to include any of these topics in the current volume, but we encourage the reader to explore them further.

Our entries each include a "Further Reading" section for the curious scholar, and our general bibliography also will be helpful for continued explorations. The entries that are included here can only serve as an introduction to an expansive subject that we encourage the reader to explore further. In each entry, an expert author has distilled a great deal of information into a relatively small package averaging 1,000 words, sometimes summarizing years of research and hard-won experience into each paragraph. The nearly 100 authors gathered in this volume have lived and traveled extensively in the regions that they write about. We hope that their passion and enthusiasm will be conveyed to the reader as you encounter the cultures of Asia and Oceania in these pages.

Jeremy A. Murray and Kathleen M. Nadeau

Further Reading

D'Arcy, Paul. 2008. *People of the Sea: Environment, Identity, and History in Oceania*. Honolulu: University of Hawai'i Press.

Denoon, Donald, Philippa Mein-Smith, and Marivic Wyndham. 2000. *A History of Australia, New Zealand, and the Pacific: The Formation of Identities*. Boston: Wiley-Blackwell.

Golden, Peter B. 2011. *Central Asia in World History*. Oxford, UK: Oxford University Press.

Murphey, Rhoads. 2014. *A History of Asia*. 7th ed. New York: Pearson.

Chapter 1: Popular Music

Introduction

Popular music in Asia and Oceania consists of many different and changing forms and styles. Music springs from the heart and soul of an individual or group in relation to their personal experiences in the context of the societies, cultures, and histories in which they live and find their sense of being and becoming in the world. Musical creations are influenced by local, global, and transnational flows of delightful sounds and songs that inspire new innovations that take root in culturally unique ways. Popular music in Asia and Oceania, as elsewhere around the world, is a wonderful invention with a long history of its own that is intertwined with the changing modern world and the ancient indigenous musical styles of the richly diverse local communities, societies, and individuals who compose them.

In Asia, generally, popular music is a product of centuries of circulating influences coming from indigenous communities and ancient Indian and Chinese civilizations as well as the European colonizers and, more recently, the dominant global music industry. Indigenous popular musical performances often embody the playing of various kinds of original local musical instruments. Many indigenous communities continue to reinvent and innovate upon earlier musical and cultural ritual performances that began by listening to scores of songs sung by birds and other living beings of the forests, and the sounds of the natural environment, imitating them as a way to honor them. The culturally and historically different local peasantries around the wider region have also left a rich legacy of popular musical folk traditions that continue to be drawn upon today. Popular musical forms are locally varied, ranging from highly ornate and choreographed performances such as those displayed in Balinese dance rituals to the freewheeling, creative styles of Korean farmers or, more broadly, everyday people singing out their sentiments. The great civilizations that introduced Hinduism, Buddhism, Confucianism, and Islam to communities along the Silk Roads and everywhere around the mainland, reaching the islands of Southeast Asia as early as the first millennium of the New Common Era, continue to have a formative influence on the global music industry. These rituals, religions, and philosophies, replete with their musical ways of telling stories, have everywhere intertwined with indigenous traditions to come up with fresh expressions. The great Asian world religions, together with Christianity brought by the colonizers, continue to shape and be shaped by the music industry today. Contemporary Asian youth culture and music has become a global phenomenon, attracting an enormous international following. Indie pop; Punjabi rap; Bollywood film music; Chinese, Japanese, and Korean pop; traditional country or folk music; and Muslim secular and religious music have been and continue to be important means of instrumentation, rhythmic movements, vocal techniques, sweet melodies, and visual expressions of Asian popular music.

By contrast, pop music in Australia and New Zealand mainly emerged in tandem with jazz, soul, country, and rock and roll in the United States and Western Europe beginning in the 1950s. Australia and New Zealand have developed into Western democratic countries, since British colonization strongly encouraged immigration from Europe. Prior to the coming of European settlers, Australia was home to the Aboriginal communities, and New Zealand to the Maori people. Both indigenous groups, like Native Americans in the United States, make up the minority populations of their own countries today. However, indigenous musicians and singers continue to have a strong presence and a large following in the pop-music world. Pop music also provides a forum for the promotion of human rights and indigenous rights around the world.

The following entries offer the reader a fascinating look at the rich and culturally diverse ways in which popular music in Asia and Oceania have developed and acquired an international audience. They provide culturally rich and informative discussions on the rise of South Asian pop songs, which have emerged out of a complex structure of cinema production that includes musical scores and composition, actresses and actors, singers and dancers, choreographies and cinematography, K-pop, and Australian rock, among other pertinent pop expressions, into the 21st century.

Kathleen M. Nadeau and Jeremy A. Murray

Further Reading

Battieste, Lejarie. 2007. "Music, East Asia and Oceania." In *The Greenwood Encyclopedia of World Popular Culture, Volume 6: Asia and Pacific Oceania*. Ed. Gary Xu and Vinay Dharwadker, 203–211. Westport, CT: Greenwood Press.

Booth, Gregory, and Bradley Shope, eds. 2014. *More than Bollywood, Studies in Indian Pop Music*. New York: Oxford University Press.

Fuhr, Michael. 2016. *Globalization and Popular Music in South Korea: Sounding Out K-Pop*. New York: Routledge.

ALTERNATIVE MUSIC SCENES, CHINA

Contemporary Chinese alternative music scenes include the music, people, places, and events associated with China's rock-based music over the past 30 years. While it first appeared in the mid-1980s as a nonconformist music genre, Chinese rock developed into a subculture in the 1990s. By the 2000s, it had transformed into smaller music circles in terms of subgenres. It has become a popular part of urban youth culture in the 2010s.

The launch of government-sponsored, nationwide reform in the late 1970s marked an important and abrupt change in the history of the People's Republic of China. Before that, socialist China cut off cultural input from most Western countries. In the wake of Mao's death in 1976, China became increasingly active in international cultural and economic exchanges and loosened state control over domestic public culture. In the 1980s, semilegal imports of popular music (most of which came from Taiwan and Hong Kong) and local production quickly found a place in the daily entertainment of Chinese citizens. Yet in this period, the reforms the state permitted in political and cultural domains were notably stricter than in the economic sphere. Bureaucracies of various kinds still exerted powerful supervision over local popular culture by restricting what could be produced and sold and what appeared in mass media.

The first wave of Chinese rock music emerged amid these social trends in the late 1980s. Its most representative figure was Cui Jian (1961–), who was widely acknowledged as the godfather of Chinese rock. He was the first musician in China to establish a distinct, rebellious way of conveying ideas through what contemporaneous commentators called *yaogun* (摇滚), a Chinese translation of "rock and roll" that soon received broad acceptance. Unlike popular Chinese songs of the time, nascent rock music like Cui Jian's was less familiar to Chinese listeners who had, in the relatively closed political and cultural climate of the 1960s and 1970s, missed the sweeping transnational popularity of this cultural form. The absence of a Chinese rock culture, however, granted rockers in the late 1980s a space for freer and more diverse modes of composition. At the same time, the "delayed" emergence of rock music in China turned its local production into a more culturally specific process in which *yaogun*, as a genre, was an expression not only of its musicality but also its social connotations.

Specifically, rock music's Chinese pioneers considered it a form of "authentic self-expression and emotional release in the face of oppression," according to the scholar Andrew Jones (1992, 91). This radical understanding means that songs assembled by the mainstream and state-supported popular-culture industry were artificial in terms of content, production, and ways of performing. The "oppression" refers to various forms of restrictions in late 1980s' Chinese society, where the internal tensions of the decade-long social reform had affected the everyday life of ordinary citizens. Many pro-rock critics have argued that in sharp contrast to Chinese popular songs, rock music encouraged reflexive listeners by bravely engaging them with concrete social reality. Such interpretations may exaggerate the avant-garde side of rock music by oversimplifying its effects on its audience. Yet it would be fair to say that rock music at its inception in the late 1980s offered an alternative and compelling approach to social issues through passionate, individualistic expression.

While songs like Cui Jian's "Nothing to My Name" (1987) received nationwide attention, by the early 1990s *yaogun* was an elite subculture. The majority of active fans consisted of a small circle of young intellectuals, college students, and foreigners residing in Beijing. Significant figures and bands in this period included Black Panther, Dou Wei, He Yong, Tang Dynasty, and Zhang Chu.

It is often believed that the Beijing rock scene began to lose its avant-garde appeal in the early 1990s, not long after the government crushed the Tiananmen student protest in 1989. This is because a nationwide cynicism that individual efforts could ever shake the state's iron fist emerged subsequent to the movement and stifled the acceptance of rock ideology. De Kloet's (2010) research challenges this fundamental assumption of "rock as means for resistance" by showing that since the early 2000s, rock has greatly diversified from its earlier monolithic ideology. It now has a clearer musical and social classification divided into *scenes*, such as heavy metal, punk, or folk rock. In other words, rock subculture has not *declined* but *transformed*.

Global music products smuggled in through unlicensed conduits were a feature of China's underground music world in the 1990s and early 2000s. Disposed of by overseas markets as shopworn items, tapes and CDs, many of which had been purposefully defaced, were imported as waste by coastal traders, who would later screen off usable pieces and resell them to domestic dealers. Roundabout input, as such, was invaluable for pre-Internet Chinese musicians, for it greatly enriched

Punk Rock in China (SMZB)

During the 1990s, punk rock made its way into China. The Sex Pistols, the Ramones, the Clash, and other pioneers of the genre heavily influenced the inception of the scene within China. In 1996 one of China's first punk-rock bands emerged out of Wuhan. Members Wu Wei and Zhu Ning formed the group SMZB to express what it meant to live in some of the country's most transformative years under Deng Xiaoping's economic reforms. SMZB's sheer energy garnered both admiration and confusion, but through the past two decades, the band has developed a loyal fan base and established Wuhan as a hub for Chinese punk rock. Their sometimes politically driven songs have caused the band's set lists to be curtailed and their music to be censored online. However, SMZB is still active and serves as a model for Chinese punk rock.

Jason Brown-Galindo

their music repertoire, which otherwise would not be established in China's undeveloped local markets. Yet this process was compressed in time and fragmented in space. Music that had accumulated over the past few decades in other parts of the world suddenly appeared in China without having been classified by critics, marketers, or other "tastemakers." Marked with this collective experience, rockers of the time were dubbed the "cut generation" (打口一代).

Notwithstanding the emergence of subscenes, alternative music in China generally maintained its underground status into the late 2000s. This situation coexisted with an antimainstream ethos that could easily be found in contemporary publications. Rock-oriented outdoor music festivals were rare, but there was the annual Midi Festival (2002–). Some influential bands and musicians in the early to mid-2000s were Brain Failure, Hang on the Box, Muma, New Pants, PK14, Second Hand Rose, Top Floor Circus, Twisting Machine, Wild Children, Xie Tianxiao, Yaska, and Zuoxiao Zuzhou.

Since the late 2000s, once-marginalized underground rock has gained acceptance in popular culture under a new term: "independent music" (独立音乐). Most participants in the independent music scene were born after 1985, grew up in China's emerging urban middle-class families, and attended college as part of the ever-expanding post-1999 population of students in higher education. The increasing popularity of independent music has been accompanied by hipster-like independent cultures that have been overtly incorporated into urban landscapes

A young man dances at the 2006 Midi Music Festival in Beijing, China. The festival, hosted by the Midi School of Music since 1997, includes a wide range of local and foreign musical acts in many genres, and often includes environmentalist messages. (AP Photo/EyePress)

and commercial arrangements. The Drum Tower area in Beijing is an example of such an urban space. TV programs in the 2010s have also extended the fame of some underground musicians to a broader audience. Since 2007 the Chinese government has been employing a top-down policy of developing "cultural and creative industries" nationwide. Regardless of its original intention, this new policy has contributed to the growing incorporation of alternative music scenes into mainstream culture. The number of outdoor music festivals, for example, has skyrocketed at a rate unexpected by many older rock fans. An index of related bands and musicians includes Carsick Cars, Chui Wan, Hang Gai, Hedgehog, Joyside, Miserable Faith, Omnipotent Youth Society, Queen Sea Big Shark, Re-TROS, and Snapline.

Independent music is not a musical innovation per se. Instead, its prevalence reflects how contemporary Chinese urban youth attempt to pursue an independent status in their everyday lives through cultural activities. Compared to its predecessor, underground rock, independent music is associated less with a grand narrative that emphasizes collective "resistance" either metaphorically or practically. Nor do its advocates merely hunger for fun by engaging with the scenes. Rather, young participants are more inclined to start their resistant acts in their personal lives and less interested in performing to seize power from existing authorities. The kind of independence they embrace is a disposition balanced between entertainment and seriousness that is cultivated through music.

Shan Huang

See also: Public-Square Dancing, China (Chapter 6: Sports); Small-City Music, China

Further Reading

Baranovitch, Nimrod. 2003. *China's New Voices: Popular Music, Ethnicity, Gender, and Politics, 1978–1997.* Berkeley: University of California Press.

de Kloet, Jeroen. 2010. *China with a Cut: Globalisation, Urban Youth and Popular Music, IIAS Publications Series Monographs.* Amsterdam: Amsterdam University Press.

Groenewegen-Lau, Jeroen. 2014. "Steel and Strawberries: How Chinese Rock Became State-Sponsored." *Asian Music* (Winter/Spring): 3–33.

Huang, Shan. 2014. *Independence at Large: Contemporary China's Alternative Music Scenes and the Cultural Practices of Post-Socialist Urban Youth.* MA thesis, University of South Carolina.

Jones, Andrew F. 1992. *Like a Knife: Ideology and Genre in Contemporary Chinese Popular Music, Cornell East Asia Series.* Ithaca, NY: East Asia Program, Cornell University.

ARIRANG: KOREAN FOLK SONG

All Koreans know some variation of a folk song that is generically called "Arirang." There are so many regional derivations that it is somewhat misleading to think of Arirang as one song. Many Korean folklorists, musicologists, and literary scholars have studied Arirang, identifying some 50 regional versions with thousands of lyrical variations. All it really takes to qualify as an Arirang song is the nonsensical refrain "*Arirang, arirang, arariyo*" (or Chindo Arirang's "*Ari arirang, suri surirang*"). Although some argue that the song is of ancient origin, others contend that it is a relatively modern song that originated no earlier than the mid-19th century. The best-known "standard" ("*ponjo*") "Arirang" originated as a song for a silent film, derived from a regional folk song sung by residents in Kyŏnggi Province, where the capital city of Seoul is located.

Regardless of its age or origins, there is no doubt that Koreans regard Arirang as their national song. It is not uncommon for Korean expatriates to name their restaurants or businesses Arirang; there is even a television network called Arirang TV, which broadcasts in English to promote Korean culture among international audiences. The term "Arirang" itself is difficult to define and translate into English. Most folklorists now agree it is just a nonsensical word, like "hey diddle diddle." Moreover, people around the world recognize the melody of the "standard" version, which has been adapted for school orchestras and choirs. Khmer street musicians in faraway Cambodia play "Arirang" on their traditional instruments to welcome the thousands of Korean tourists who flock there to see the ancient Angkor complex.

There are compelling reasons to claim that some Arirang songs originated as work songs, not the least of which is a call-and-response structure that is common to most versions. A leader sang a verse, with lyrics that might either be long established or improvised on the spot, and the rest of the work crew would join in for the refrain. One of the appeals of this song form was that it lent itself to the extemporaneous expression of one's immediate thoughts, concerns, and feelings. It also made Arirang songs versatile, as they could express the sorrow of lost love, separation from family or home village, confusion and disorientation during times of rapid change, or the unjust treatment of common people by political elites.

A May 31, 1894, article in the Japanese *Yūbin hōchi* newspaper was the first foreign account of an Arirang song, whose lyrics were unambiguously anti-Japanese ("Life in Inch'ŏn and Chemulp'o is good, but we can't bear being persistently burned by the Japanese"). In 1896 Homer Hulbert (1863–1949) published a melodic transcription of what is now called "old" (*kujo*) Arirang in an American missionary newsletter. In the 1910s, Koreans, Japanese, and foreign missionaries published some folk-music anthologies that included Arirang songs. But the best-known Kyŏnggi version burst onto the national consciousness as the theme song of a 1926 silent film entitled *Arirang* by Na Ungyu (1902–1937). Filmgoers received a printed program with lyrics and a melodic score so that they could sing the song together as the film ended. Na claimed to have heard students singing it while he was in prison with them. His version—arranged in a 3/4 waltz meter rather than the traditional *semach'i* rhythm (3:3:4 beats, sometimes rendered as 9/8 meter)—was among the first of many arrangements that conformed to Euro-American popular song structures. It became the basis for numerous subsequent recorded versions and written arrangements in the latter half of the colonial period.

Arirang, arirang, arariyo
I go over the Arirang hills.
There are no stars in the clear sky,
In my breast are many thoughts.
[Refrain]
The one who abandoned me
Will be footsore before s/he goes ten li [5,000 meters].
[Refrain]
There are many stars in the clear sky,
And many griefs in life in this world.

During the 30-year colonial occupation of Korea by Japan (1910–1945), some Arirang songs expressed resentful nationalist sentiments toward the Japanese presence.

Arirang, arirang, arariyo
Friends, wake up from your shallow dream.
The crimson sun [representing Japan] *is rising over Arirang Hill*
With two arms stretched wide (Kim and Wales 1941, vii).

In his memoir, the communist revolutionary Kim San (Chang Chi-rak, 1905–1938) wrote that Arirang "symbolizes the tragedy of Korea. Its meaning is symbolic of constantly climbing over obstacles only to find death at the end. It is a song of death and not of life" (Kim and Wales, 6). Yet despite such hyperbole, like black American blues and other sorrow songs, Arirang has provided a means for people both to name and face the source of their suffering—and to transcend it.

Sorrow, sentimentality, indignation, and a sense of bitter irony pervade many Arirang songs, but they are not all so glum. A 1935 arrangement for piano and voice by An Ikt'ae (1906–1965) calls for *allegretto gioco ben ritmo* (a cheerful, playful rhythm). Arrangements for symphony orchestras, solo instrumentalists and singers, jazz combos, and rock bands frequently use the melody to create a more festive mood.

By the 1930s "Arirang" was a popular song outside the Korean peninsula. Koreans migrated to northeast China (Manchuria), Russia, and Mongolia, where many ethnic Koreans remain today. They brought Arirang with them, and it became so well known in China that some Chinese claim it as part of their cultural heritage. It was also prominent in the repertory of interwar Japanese popular music; thus it was well known throughout Japan's Asian empire, in Taiwan, Manchuria, and eventually Southeast Asia. Japanese songsmiths produced a staggering number of recorded arrangements between 1931 and 1945, indicating that Arirang had become a marketable "brand" of popular music in imperial Japan. The musical settings for these arrangements were quite diverse: for instance, a 1932 Nippon Columbia version featured the famous chanteuse Awaya Noriko (1907–1999) duetting with Korean singer Ch'ae Kyuyŏp (1906–1949), accompanied by the Meiji University Mandolin Orchestra.

Since 1945 the Korean peninsula has been divided into two competing states, the socialist Democratic People's Republic of Korea (DPRK) in the north and the Republic of Korea (ROK) in the south. An armistice ended the Korean War in 1953, but technically they are still in a state of war, and hostility between them is strong. Nevertheless, most Koreans long for a political reunification. Arirang is one of the few cultural aspects that both North and South Korea continue to share; there is even an Arirang promoting reunification (*t'ong-il*) of the peninsula, which sounds like modern synthesized Asian pop music instead of a folk song. Arirang is often played during high-level diplomatic exchanges between the DPRK and ROK.

Arirang has become an important symbol of Korean national identity. Many scholars romanticize it as an archive of Korean historical experience, an expression of the national essence (*kuksu*), and a cultural treasure that links all ethnic Koreans—in the peninsula and abroad—to one another. Having been in imperial China's shadow for centuries, Japanese colonial subjects for decades, and combatants in the Cold War's first serious military engagement, Koreans cling strongly to aspects of their culture that are distinctive. Recent Chinese claims to the Arirang song thus offend Koreans considerably, although China's recognition of the importance of this folk song is also indicative of Arirang's ethnomusicological value and historical significance.

E. Taylor Atkins

See also: P'ansori: Korean Narrative Singing; Popular Music, North Korea

Further Reading

Ahn Eaktai [An Ik-t'ae]. 1935. *The First Manifestation of the Korean Music by Eaktai Ahn from Korean Life for Voice and Piano*. Philadelphia: Elkan-Vogel.

Atkins, E. Taylor. 2007. "The Dual Career of 'Arirang': The Korean Resistance Anthem That Became a Japanese Pop Hit." *Journal of Asian Studies* 66, no. 3 (August): 645–687.

Dunbar, Jon. 2012. "Arirang, Korea's Unofficial Anthem." April 5. www.korea.net/NewsFocus /Culture/view?articleId=99813. Accessed April 22, 2015.

Kim San and Nym Wales. 1941. *Song of Ariran: The Life Story of a Korean Rebel*. New York: John Day.

Kim Yeon Gap. 2012. *The Culture of Arirang*. Seoul, KR: Jimoondang.

Sheen Dae Cheol, ed. 2013. *Arirang in Korean Culture and Beyond: Arirang from Diverse Perspectives*. Seoul, KR: Academy of Korean Studies Press.

Discography

Kuktan Arirang. 2004. *Arirang: Korean Song and Dance Ensemble*. Smithsonian Folkways /Monitor Records 430.

Various artists. 2005. *Ariran no nazo* [The Enigma of Arirang]. King Records 3230.

Various artists. 2003. *Kita to minami no Ariran densetsu—Ariran no rūtsu o tazunete* (Japanese title); *Puk, nam Arirang ŭi chŏnsŏl* (Korean title) [The Legend of Arirang, North and South—Searching for the Roots of Arirang]. King/Synnara: KKCC 3005.

CONTEMPORARY POPULAR MUSIC, CHINA

The term "Chinese popular music" often refers to music circulating in pan-Chinese areas, including China, Taiwan, Hong Kong, and overseas communities, with lyrics written in Chinese languages (Mandarin, Cantonese, Taiwanese, Hakka, etc.). Contemporary Chinese popular music in this entry has a smaller coverage: it applies more specifically to Mandarin popular songs that have had nationwide influence on mainland China since the late 1970s. The following text introduces how, over the past four decades, popular music in China has become a widely recognized music category that shares a number of similarities with its counterparts elsewhere while maintaining its local specificities. Particular attention is paid to the social context in which this music emerged and became accepted as a form of popular culture.

In the first three decades of the People's Republic of China (PRC) from 1949 to 1979, Chinese society was imbued with political campaigns in which cultural forms such as film, music, and literature were treated as objects of political governance. State censorship over music was exerted in a top-down manner, reaching its height during the Cultural Revolution (1966–1976). Most songs circulating in public domains were sanctioned as either beneficial for, or having no harm to, the nation-building and political projects led by the Chinese Communist Party (CCP). The repertoire of music shared by nationwide listeners was relatively small.

Deng Xiaoping's (1904–1997) national "reform and opening" program launched in the late 1970s marked an important moment in the history of the PRC. Since the initiation of this policy, the state has showed greater tolerance to "unorthodox" cultures either imported from abroad or generated locally. Yet the state's role as a strong censor has been largely maintained through the intervening years up to the time of writing, though not in a completely consistent capacity or tone. In the 1980s, what arrived in the field of music perhaps most significantly was the massive circulation of Taiwan and Hong Kong popular music. These songs were primarily imported through unofficial conduits and then duplicated locally through nascent popular media technologies such as recorders and tapes. These forms of popular music were notably influential due to their linguistic, aesthetic, and cultural accessibility, which quickly conquered mainland audiences. Until that point, mainlanders had largely been blocked off from pan-Chinese popular music from outside China since 1949. Intriguing work such as Teresa Teng's music sung with her remarkably soft voice also inspired some mainland musicians, who now had a revived idea of how real popular music might sound.

Notwithstanding the ideological objection toward some of this new music found in some of the bureaucracies for state-affiliated musicians, Hong Kong- and Taiwan-based popular music, as well as the domestic creations they inspired, had phenomenally changed the music repertoire of China's post-Mao generation growing up in the 1980s and 1990s. These pieces reshaped the everyday listening experience in the PRC and obtained national popularity in Chinese social life. This presented a challenge that the state-produced propaganda music, which gradually lost its political significance, could no longer compete with.

By the end of the 1990s, Chinese popular music had become a solid medium for reflecting, articulating, and producing social meaning. It had opened, for example, a thriving public space for the negotiation of broad social issues such as gender, ethnicity, and politics. New forms of social activities had been established around this music. For instance, Karaoke Television (KTV), a form of group-oriented pastime in which participants sing popular songs together in private rooms, had grown to be extremely prevalent in broad social settings ranging from business team-building exercises to recreational gatherings. Popular music had played a huge role as well in shaping young listeners' inner worlds at a very personal level. Love-themed songs, the dominant type, were particularly important in modeling listeners' understanding of intimate relationships. An increasingly diversified pool of subgenres was also strongly linked with the identity politics of urban youth growing up in a globalizing China. Musicians like Cui Jian, for example, were hugely important in both reflecting and influencing the ideas, anxieties, and values of the generation of Chinese young people who came of age in the 1980s and beyond.

From the mid-1990s onward, China has been the biggest market for the popular-music industry based in Hong Kong and Taiwan. The transnational creation of music, stardom, and profits was seized in the hands of a few companies. Fan culture was quickly developed in the 1990s, when the "popular singer" became a new kind of social character that was open to flexible packaging from the perspective of marketing logic. The exceptionally famous singer Faye Wong (Wang Fei) exemplifies such dynamics of star production. A few years after she started a career in China, Beijing-born Wong was signed to a Hong Kong record company that essentially transformed her both personally and professionally, casting her in a way that was not culturally specific to her mainland roots. Working on her image in this way has helped to attract a larger audience from the pan-Chinese and global communities.

Beyond the updates regarding musical pieces, what the 2000s witnessed foremost was the vigorous marriage between mass media and grassroots participation. In 2005 the *Super Girl Contest*, a televised singing contest modeled on the original British television competition *Pop Idols*, became a major public event due to the exceptionally large audience it attracted. Li Yuchun won the contest with her unique performance style, but, more decisively, she won not simply based on the votes from professional commentators but rather from the vast number of text-messaging (SMS) ballots from a participatory viewing audience. She and some of her competitors who also had huge fan bases were signed to leading record companies after the contest. In 2013, Li went on to win the Best Worldwide Act award in the MTV Europe Music Awards, and is known internationally as Chris Lee. Although the *Super Girl Contest* in its original form did not last long, it greatly inspired a new model of idol/pop singer production that strategically incorporated grassroots and nonmainstream singers into the popular-music industry via powerful mass media. In the 2010s, a variety of TV shows have successfully furthered this tactic through different arrangements. With the prosperity of such programs, popular music in China today has become something more viewer friendly and interactive, formulating a manner of appreciation in which listening is heavily situated in, if not surpassed by, visual and verbal presentations.

In the 2010s, the once-marginalized rock-based alternative music has shown a great tendency to be an aspect of popular urban culture, especially among youths. The underground music circle's growing awareness of professionalism, the growing number of middle-class urban youth with middlebrow cultural preferences, and the state's proactive role in promoting "cultural and creative industries" are some factors that have cultivated this new trend.

Shan Huang

See also: Alternative Music Scenes, China; TV Singing Competitions, China (Chapter 4: Television and Radio)

Further Reading

Baranovitch, Nimrod. 2003. *China's New Voices: Popular Music, Ethnicity, Gender, and Politics, 1978–1997.* Berkeley: University of California Press.

de Kloet, Jeroen. 2010. *China with a Cut: Globalisation, Urban Youth and Popular Music.* Amsterdam: Amsterdam University Press.

Groenewegen-Lau, Jeroen. 2012. "China Music Mappings." www.culturalexchange-cn.nl /mapping-china/music. Accessed March 17, 2016.

Groenewegen-Lau, Jeroen. 2014. "Steel and Strawberries: How Chinese Rock Became State-Sponsored." *Asian Music* (Winter/Spring): 3–33.

Jones, Andrew F. 1992. *Like a Knife: Ideology and Genre in Contemporary Chinese Popular Music.* Ithaca, NY: East Asia Program, Cornell University.

Moskowitz, Marc L. 2010. *Cries of Joy, Songs of Sorrow: Chinese Pop Music and Its Cultural Connotations.* Honolulu: University of Hawai'i Press.

ETHNIC MUSIC, CHINA

In a broad sense, all music can be described as ethnic, given that every musician belongs to an ethnic group. However, in popular classification, ethnic music generally denotes music that is considered to capture the cultural flavor of an ethnic minority, with particular reference to vocal delivery, language, instrumentation, scale, and rhythm. Thus in China the many folk musics of the country's 55 officially designated ethnic minorities (*shaoshu minzu*, lit. "minority nationalities") are marked as ethnic. In contrast, the various folk musics of the majority Han, who account for over 90 percent of the population, are generally not understood or classified in terms of ethnicity.

Ethnic folk music experienced mixed fortunes during the early decades of the People's Republic of China (PRC). The nation's cultural policy demanded that artistic works reflect the lives of the masses, thus bringing new prestige to many folk practices, including music, but with the further demand that all such works serve political needs. In line with this policy, professional musicians were sent to live with the masses, study their folk practices, and then produce folk-flavored compositions with political content for mass consumption.

Minority folk practices became popular targets for this process of song collection, adaptation, and popularization for a number of reasons. Firstly, the Han appraisal of minorities was—and continues to be—ambivalent, regarding them on the one hand as primitive, backward, and sexually immoral, but on the other hand as exotic, romantic, and artistic. The latter positive perception meant that minority musical elements could bring instant exotic flavor to revolutionary songs such as "The Rising Sun Never Sets on the Grasslands" and "Xinjiang Is Good," as well as the popular film musical *Third Sister Liu* with its rural setting among the Zhuang minority.

Secondly, initial PRC ethnic policy was one of reconciliation toward minority groups, many of whom dwelled in strategically important border regions and whose support was thus vital to China's territorial integrity. Incorporating minority musical elements into the socialist canon was a means of drawing minorities into an official image of the nation as politically united but tolerant of cultural difference. This image of a harmonious multiethnic nation continues to be promoted in contemporary China on shows such as the Spring Festival Television Gala, which invariably features a song-and-dance medley performed by a small army of smiling (and predominantly female) performers in various minority costumes.

Third, the association of ethnic minorities with the romantic and the exotic provided a means for the exploration of themes that would otherwise have been condemned as bourgeois. So while 1930s love songs from Shanghai were condemned as decadent "yellow music" (with yellow implying pornographic or morally deviant), the film musical *Five Golden Flowers* was a huge hit in 1959, with its gentle tale of minorities, festivals, and romance, albeit with a cast of characters who were impeccably dedicated to building socialism amid the picturesque scenery of southwest China.

The popularization of minority musical forms in the PRC provided new opportunities for minority artists, who were recruited into new state-run cultural institutions such as the Central Nationalities Song and Dance Troupe, established in 1952. However, popularization also brought appropriation, as music professionals adapted elements of minority folk songs, particularly lyrics, in ways that conflicted with local sensibilities. For example, controversy surrounds the legacy of Wang Luobin, a Han composer who produced numerous nationwide hits based on the folk melodies of minorities in northwest China. Critics have argued that his adaptations constitute copyright theft and that the Mandarin lyrics of his adaptations reduce minorities to exoticized and sexualized objects for Han consumption.

Whereas the first 17 years of the PRC were relatively tolerant of ethnic difference, the emphasis of the Cultural Revolution (1966–1976) was upon the assimilation of minorities into a singular proletarian culture. Minority folk practices themselves received short shrift, yet the utilization of minority musical elements in revolutionary genres continued to be popular with both composers and audiences. Such elements appeared not only in revolutionary songs, such as "The Zhuang People Sing a Song about Chairman Mao," but also in other cultural products featuring music, such as the stage musical *Red Hawk of the Grasslands*. Although earlier PRC representations of minorities—including the aforementioned *Five Golden Flowers*—were banned as politically incorrect, and new compositions increasingly focused on eulogizing China's leader, Mao Zedong (1893–1976), composers continued to enjoy greater scope for artistic expression through the inclusion of minority musical elements.

Since the end of the Cultural Revolution, an audience has emerged for increased authenticity in the performance of folk music, particularly that of ethnic minorities. In line with this demand, the prestigious China Central Television (CCTV) Young Singer Competition created a new singing category in 2006 named *yuanshengtai* (lit. "original ecology" but better understood as "cultural authenticity"). This category mainly featured minorities singing in their own languages accompanied by traditional acoustic instruments, although it was also open to Han folk singers.

The rise of *yuanshengtai* has gone hand in hand with an explosion in domestic tourism. Rather than watch staged performances of ethnicity on television, urban Chinese now have the time and money to visit distant regions and experience ethnic practices firsthand. One famous destination for ethnic tourism is the old town of Lijiang in China's southwestern Yunnan Province, which is known for its Naxi minority culture, including so-called "Naxi Ancient Music." A performance of this genre for visitors to Lijiang typically comprises an ensemble of elderly musicians performing in solemn, nonvirtuosic heterophony; that is, each musician adds personal variations to a single melodic line to create a richly textured sound. This practice of heterophony is common in regional Han instrumental music, and indeed "Naxi Ancient Music" was once a part of Han-derived ritual in Lijiang, but the current name glosses over these details in favor of emphasizing the ethnic dimension.

While domestic tourists have traveled to minority regions in recent decades, minority musicians have traveled overseas to perform at international cultural events. For example, the two-part choral "Big Song" genre of the Dong minority was performed in Paris in 1986 and subsequently in numerous other foreign cities. Such overseas performances have served to promote both national image and regional tourism. Dong Big Song, for example, has helped bolster the national image by "disproving the biased belief in the world of Western music that Chinese folk music lacks multi-part choral singing" (Kaili Evening News 2000, 5).

Minority musical elements and musicians have also featured prominently in contemporary nonrevolutionary music genres, including mainstream pop, electronica, and rock music. Singer and writer Wu Hongfei has even claimed that Chinese rock-music history is a history of ethnic minority music. But such a claim simplifies a complicated issue when Chinese rock includes not only minority musicians who incorporate minority forms (e.g., the Mongolian throat-singing folk rock of Hanggai) but also Han who represent minority culture (e.g., the Tibetan-tinged rock of "Return to Lhasa" by Zheng Jun) and minorities whose music lacks overt expressions of ethnicity (e.g., Cui Jian). In fact, in a country where ethnically unmarked Han enjoy *yuanshengtai* while urban-based minorities enjoy hip-hop and pop, it is becoming increasingly difficult to determine what can and cannot be classified as ethnic music.

Paul Kendall

See also: Alternative Music Scenes, China; Popular Music, Mongolia; Popular Music, Uyghur

Further Reading

Baranovitch, Nimrod. 2003. *China's New Voices: Popular Music, Ethnicity, Gender, and Politics, 1978–1997.* Berkeley: University of California Press.
Clark, Paul. 2008. *The Chinese Cultural Revolution: A History.* Cambridge, UK: Cambridge University Press.
Harris, Rachel. 2005. "Wang Luobin: Folk Song King of the Northwest or Song Thief? Copyright, Representation, and Chinese Folk Songs." *Modern China* 31, no. 3: 381–408.
Kaili Evening News 凯里晚报. 2000. "侗族大歌入选央视春节晚会 [Dong Big Song Selected for Spring Festival TV Gala]." November 17.
Rees, Helen. 2000. *Echoes of History: Naxi Music in Modern China.* Oxford, UK: Oxford University Press.
Sina.com.cn. 2009. "吴虹飞：中国摇滚史其实是少数民族音乐史 [Wu Hongfei: The History of Chinese Rock Is Actually the History of Ethnic Minority Music]." March 27. http://ent.sina.com.cn/y/2009-03-27/14012441964.shtml. Accessed May 28, 2015.

FOLK SONGS, INDIA

Folk songs embody the raw emotions of almost every aspect of human life. Although in the current phase of globalization a vast impact of bourgeois and elite cultures is visible on folk songs, and under the postmodern conditions it becomes difficult to extricate folk from elite culture, still folk songs are quite popular in India and have a motivating force. In elite culture, we see that trends and fashions are coming closer to many folk artifacts, and the intelligentsia is fascinated or forced to listen to the folk under the pressures of alternative modernity. Folk songs are closer to folk spirit, in comparison to other folk genres like folktales, folk sayings, folk drama, and so on. The reason is nothing but the poignant appeal of folk songs due to their rhymes and content. Folk literature, handed down through the generations, consists of a rich body of creation myths, folktales, animal stories, rhymes, songs, riddles, and proverbs in which the spoken word is closely connected with specific images, dance enactment, song cycles, symbolic acts, and plays.

Folk songs are often found in agrarian societies. For a country like India, where agriculture is the main occupation of the people, the importance of folk songs becomes exceedingly significant. The rich cultural traditions also add value to it. The folk songs in the Indian milieu are no longer considered negative or backward artistic expression. We find a discourse of the marginalized people in them. They are unique in their capacity to help us look at the patterns of life from an alternative perspective. They have also shown a mild criticism of authority, hegemony, and torture, but have never shown the destructionist motif. Folk songs reflect on traditional knowledge, wisdom, convention, practices, and ways of the people as collected and continued through oral tradition. These songs are always fresh, raw, noncanonical, agrarian, and popular in their locality and especially in folk subculture, having a unique mass culture.

Indian folk songs can be divided into folk lyrics and folk ballads. Folk ballads may be divided further into three categories: (1) the traditional secular ballads or incidental ballads, (2) the traditional mythological and religious ballads, and (3) the minstrel ballads (both traditional and contemporary). Among these, traditional mythological ballads have prime importance. The traditional secular ballads elucidate the cult of the Indian ethos and lofty human values. The incidental ballads highlight many events of national importance in Indian history—national, contemporary, and mythological. The *Alha* and other genres of songs especially in the *Raso grantha* come under this category. The traditional mythological and religious ballads present the tradition of Hinduism, especially focusing on its practical aspects. They sing the glory of religious personalities, saints, gods, and goddesses. They also present the rich composite culture of India in Sufi, or Muslim mystic, songs. The minstrel ballads became popular in the middle ages of Indian sociopolitical history. The court poets started these ballads, and the tradition continues even today. In political rallies, supporters of a political leader are often found singing the glory of the leader or the political party in a hyperbolic way with quite visible conceits and imagery.

Folk lyrics may be broadly categorized as *samskara* lyrics, age lyrics, season lyrics, *vrata* (fasting) lyrics, deity lyrics, labor lyrics, and caste-based lyrics. Since India is a country of numerous dialects and traditions, it is neither appropriate nor possible to discuss in detail a particular folk song or lyric; rather, here we will focus on providing genre-based characteristics of the folk songs. The thoughts and emotions are largely similar in the various lyrics; the only perceptible difference is that of language.

The Sanskrit word *samskara* means to prepare or to make perfect, and it generally refers to a major ritual in one's life, as in a purification ritual. The *samskara* lyrics provide the foundation of Indian folk belief and religion. These lyrics enshrine popular culture of one Indian holistic view of life. In general, the subdivisions are birth *samskara* lyrics (sung at the time of child birth); *mundana samskara* lyrics (sung at the time of first shaving of the hair on the child's head); *yagyopaveeta samskara* lyrics (sung on the occasion of offering the sacred thread of Hinduism to a child, traditionally the beginning of education); marriage *samskara* lyrics (called marriage *sangeet* in popular usage, sung before and after the marriage ceremony); *gamana samskara* lyrics (sung as the bride moves from the parental home to the home of the husband); and the lyrics of last ritual. Indian philosophy has provisioned for four *ashrama* in human life: the *brahmacharya*, the *grahastha*, the *vanaprastha*, and the *sanyas*. When a person dies after completing a long and perfect life, in some cases songs are sung. Indian Hindu tradition marks 16 *samskaras* beginning from the time of conception to the last day of life in the world. In the life of householders (the *grahastha*), these *samskara*-based lyrics have great importance. They prevent human life from becoming monotonous and relate to the philosophy of life as a complete whole and to seeing it not in fragments but in unity and coherence.

In a traditional Indian way of life, there are also popular lyrics suitable for different life stages. From early childhood until old age there are cradle lyrics, childhood lyrics, youth lyrics, and devotional lyrics (bhajan). India is a miniature world in itself, and the Indian way of life reflects a keen environmental awareness. The tropical climate of the country holds rich fascination with its changing seasons, and that has given rise to a set of season lyrics. The season lyrics include Kajali, Hindola, Faag, Holi, Charakhi, Bindiaya, and others, and they add to the festivities of the seasons. Among the season-based folk lyrics, *baramasa* is popular in almost every part of India. Its theme revolves around the separation of the lover from his or her beloved and its effect on the personalities and actions of the characters concerned. In Indian literature, seasons are depicted normally in two forms: *rituvarnana* and *baramasa*. The condition of togetherness and union of the lover and the beloved is depicted in *rituvarnana* and that of separation in the *baramasa*. In the *rituvarnana*, the poet divides the year in three or six time slots as different *ritus*, and in *baramasa*, the year is analyzed in 12 months. The correlation of season and psyche is reflected through the narrative of *baramasa*. In *baramasa* the characteristics of season work as the catalyst in affecting the psyche of the beloved, and in associating herself with nature, she translates her anxiety, separation, and the good past days spent in union. The narration of *baramasa* depicts the circularity of the Indian concept of time.

The *vrata* lyrics are another significant branch of folk lyrics. For many, the Indian lifestyle is grounded in spirituality. For purging the soul from a spiritual and religious point of view and for keeping the metabolism at peace from a medical point of view, *vrata* (fasting) has been prescribed for different days of the year. Different days meant for *vratas* have certain stories and songs associated with them that are performed mostly in the evening. Deity lyrics are sung in the eulogy of the gods. In large part they are addressed to Shiva Ji, Sri Rama, Sri Krishna, goddess Durga Ji and her different forms, goddess Parvati Ji, Hanuman Ji, and others. Labor lyrics are meant for easing stress and fatigue while performing different kinds of work in farms, fields, and production houses. The caste-based lyrics are almost obsolete today, since the division of caste and creed is discouraged, but we cannot ignore the existence of *kahar* (the palanquin-bearer) songs, *mallah* (rover) songs, *aheer* songs, *lodhis* songs, and others that are reminiscent of these social divisions.

Folk lyrics are quite relevant in the contemporary context because they carry the tradition, glory, and prosperity of folk wisdom to readers and listeners who are unaware of their value. They are also useful in establishing healthy cultural relationships among different groups within the nation and beyond national boundaries because ultimately they speak the language of love and equality. The studies of folk lyrics provide a storehouse of information and value to other disciplines of knowledge, like sociolinguistics, social anthropology, demography, literature, and philosophy.

Ravindra Pratap Singh

See also: Musicians, India

Further Reading

Borrow, George. 1982. *The Ballads of All Nations*. London: Alston Rivers Ltd.
Singh, R. P. 2012. "Representative Folk Literature of Hindi Speaking North India." *Spark International Online Journal* 4, no. 8 (August).

HEAVY METAL, PUNK, AND INDIE MUSIC, INDONESIA

On October 20, 2014, Joko Widodo or "Jokowi" (1961–) was elected the seventh president of Indonesia. During his campaign, the mainstream media was particularly obsessed with his love of heavy-metal music. His campaign team enabled this media attention to raise his popularity among young voters. Jokowi became Indonesia's media darling overnight as he donned T-shirts from such bands as Napalm Death and Lamb of God, all while flashing the hand gesture of a horned devil. An all-star list of international metal bands even endorsed his presidential campaign and offered congratulations to Jokowi after his win (Resky 2014). The popularity of independent, alternative, underground music in Indonesia—heavy metal, punk, indie, rap, and reggae, to name just a few genres—seems to be growing exponentially across Indonesia as a result of mainstream media attention. Independent music in Indonesia, however, has a much more subterranean history, strongly influenced by imported rock music of the 1970s, the growth of community networks and independent media outlets in the 1980s and 1990s, and the development of independent record labels in the 1990s until today. In this article we will look at the major trends in independent music over the past 40 years in Indonesia, paying particular attention to the bands, media outlets, and record labels that built and sustain the independent music scene in Indonesia.

The seeds of independent music in Indonesia began in the 1970s. The pioneers of rock—God Bless (1975), Gank Pegangsaan (1970), and Giant Step (1971)—found initial fame by covering the music of British bands such as Deep Purple, Black Sabbath, Genesis, and the Rolling Stones. Indonesian audiences also saw an influx of foreign music magazines at the same time. *Aktuil*, first published in Bandung on June 6, 1967, was one of the first magazines to write about global music trends together with Indonesian bands. The magazine only lasted until 1986 but had already established a cult following and was considered by many to be "required reading" for independent music lovers. The magazine opened channels to music networks abroad where there was otherwise little access to such information and even brought foreign bands to Indonesia. In 1975 the magazine organized a surprise concert by Deep Purple in Jakarta. At that time, popular musical performances of any variety were rare, let alone from international bands.

The formation of independent music communities became an identity marker for many music fans looking to create alternative music scenes. In the late 1980s and early 1990s, some underground communities started forming around common musical interest: the punk communities Young Offender, South Sex, and Slumber in Jakarta; the metal community at Ujung Berung Rebel in Bandung; and reggae communities at Bruna Bar on Kuta Beach in Bali. Regardless of musical genre, they were all interested in creating new social spaces. What began as informal hangouts often developed into cafés and restaurants established to host independent music shows. Poster Café, Pid Pub, and Nirvana Café in Jakarta were hubs for underground music events in the 1990s. Today you can find The Jaya Pub in Jakarta, which hosts Superbad!, a monthly live music event featuring independent bands from across Indonesia.

The creation of alternative forms of media to access information about independent music also developed out of these underground music communities. Mainstream magazines of the 1980s and early 1990s were replaced by a huge network of fanzines in the mid- to late 1990s. Produced by and for independent music communities, part of the rapid growth of fanzines had to do with the ease with which they could be photocopied and distributed en masse at a low cost. *Brainwashed Zine* is one of the most notable underground music fanzines of the 1990s, created by Wendi Putranto (1971–) in Jakarta in 1996. Fanzines were distributed alongside other independent creative industries, such as clothing companies that also sold independent music. Alternative economies also developed alongside independent music, including especially the creation of more independent record labels.

Up until the 1990s, there was very little information about how to produce music on a larger scale. Many independent musicians were fed up with the limited range of musical styles represented by mainstream popular music, so they formed their own small-scale record labels to produce their own music. Fast Forward Records (FFWD, 1999) was one of the first independent record labels in Indonesia. In addition to releasing independent bands, they also organized the promotion, marketing, media management, production, and event organizing for musicians. Many of the biggest names in independent music in Indonesia started their careers with FFWD: Mocca (indie-pop, 2002), Homogenic (electro-pop, 2004), and The SIGIT (hard rock, 2006).

Community networks developing across a variety of musical genres have always been a feature of independent music in Indonesia. Sharing information through informal networks gave many musicians a point of reference to start their own bands and produce their own music in response to global musical influences. We will end by looking briefly at three contemporary bands—Superman Is Dead, Seringai, and White Shoes and the Couples Company—who grew out of the independent music scene to find national and international success.

Superman Is Dead (1995) is a punk band from Bali influenced by Social Distortion, NOFX, and Green Day. Their early albums were released independently on cassette in the late 1990s and early 2000s. They later gained wider audiences by signing with the major label Sony Music Records from 2003 until the present. They are best known for bringing punk music to mainstream audiences in Indonesia.

Seringai (2002) is a heavy-metal band from Jakarta, influenced by Black Sabbath, Motorhead, and Black Flag. They released a total of five albums, all of which were independently produced by band members. They have a cult following of fans who call themselves Serigala Militia (The Wolf-Pack Militia). They are an example of a band that was able to build a strong alternative economy to support their music. They started their own record label and production house, called High Octane (2004), and opened a record store in Jakarta where they also sell their own clothing line, called Lawless (2010). Today they are considered the contemporary veterans of the independent music scene in Jakarta and still actively promote independent music in Indonesia through radio (GenFM) and music journalism (*Rolling Stone* magazine, Indonesia).

White Shoes and the Couples Company (2002) is an indie-pop band from Jakarta who formed out of a group of friends studying music at the Institute Kesenian Jakarta (Jakarta Arts Institute, IKJ). Their music draws from more local influences, especially Indonesian movie soundtracks from the 1930s through the 1970s. In addition to releasing their first album with the independent record label Aksara in 2005, they also created their own label, Pura-Pura Records, to produce their 2010 album. They have had a great deal of international success, signing a contract with the Chicago-based independent record label Minty Fresh (2007) and touring in the United States, playing concerts at South by Southwest Music Festival in Austin, Texas, (2008) and Amoeba Records in San Francisco, California (2008).

Megan Robin Hewitt

See also: Protest Music, Indonesia

Further Reading

Baulch, Emma. 2007. *Making Scenes: Reggae, Punk, and Death Metal in 1990s Bali*. Durham, NC: Duke University Press.

Bodden, Michael. 2005. "Rap in Indonesian Youth Music of the 1990s: 'Globalization,' 'Outlaw Genres,' and Social Protest." *Asian Music* 36, no. 2: 1–26.

Rezky, Muhammad. 2014. "World Musician Metal Bands Congratulate Jokowi." *Bubblenews*. August 12. www.bubblews.com/news/5573390-world-musician-metal-band-into-congratulates-039039jokowi039039. Accessed June 1, 2015.

Wallach, Jeremy. 2005. "Underground Rock Music: And Democratization in Indonesia." *World Literature Today* 79, no. 3: 16–20.

Wallach, Jeremy. 2008. *Modern Noise, Fluid Genres: Popular Music in Indonesia, 1997–2001*. Madison: University of Wisconsin Press.

HIP-HOP, JAPAN

While Japanese hip-hop remains on the margins of a music industry dominated by J-pop, it has nonetheless exerted great cultural influence in Japan and elsewhere. A stroll through youth districts in Japanese cities reveals walls covered with graffiti

DJ Krush

DJ Krush (ISHI Hideaki, 1962–) is perhaps Japan's best internationally known hip-hop DJ, noted for his atmospheric tracks. Coming from humble origins, he was inspired to become a DJ after seeing a screening of *Wild Style* in 1983. He began performing in Tokyo's Yoyogi Park on Sundays and formed the Krush Posse with DJ Muro and other artists in 1987. A solo artist since 1992, Krush gained acclaim for his improvisatory skill with turntables as a live instrument, trading licks with musicians like the late jazz guitarist Ronny Jordan. Beginning with his inclusion of a *shakuhachi* flute in "Only the Strong Survive" (1995) with American rapper C. L. Smooth, Krush is noted for his use of Japanese instruments; he has worked with such prominent musicians as *shakuhachi* player Morita Shūzan, *taiko* (drums) player Naitō Tetsurō, and *tsugaru shamisen* (folk banjo) master Kinoshita Shin'ichi. He also incorporates the Japanese aesthetics of imperfection, expressed in timing and pitch differences, and *ma* (space) into his tracks.

Noriko Manabe

and fans dressed in hip-hop fashion. Japanese DJs (e.g., DJ Krush), breakdancers, and hip-hop fashion chains enjoy global recognition, while Japanese DJs have won top prizes in the World DMC DJ Championships (e.g., DJ Kentaro, DJ Izoh, Kireek).

Hip-hop in Japan is said to have started in 1983 with the screening of Charlie Ahearn's *Wild Style*, but it is better understood as a continuation of Japanese interest in black music, which stretches back to jazz in the early 1900s and R&B and disco in the 1960s and 1970s. The techno-pop group Yellow Magic Orchestra arguably recorded the first rap recording: "Rap Phenomena" (1981), a pun on hearing nonexistent noises and the growth of rap music. In the 1980s, hip-hop grew in both trendy clubs with university-educated rappers like Itō Seikō and in pedestrianized Yoyogi Park on Sundays with more working-class artists like B-boy Crazy-A and DJ Krush. Rap became commercially successful in 1994, with the party-time rap of Scha Dara Parr and East End x Yuri. The underground scene at the time was featured in the Thumpin' Camp concert in Tokyo in July 1996, including King Giddra, Rhymester, Buddha Brand, ECD, Muro, and others. The landmark event served as an inspiration to younger generations of rappers.

Aesthetics of Japanese Hip-Hop

Discussions of Japanese hip-hop can often begin with assumptions of copycat imitation, and the appearance of performers and fans in baggy pants, baseball caps, chains, and occasional overtanning would encourage this view. Nonetheless, hip-hop in Japan is its own thriving culture, and aspects of its culture and language make straight imitation of American hip-hop impossible. The aforementioned mid-1990s generation of rappers was instrumental in formulating the aesthetics of Japanese rapping. American rappers vary the rhythm of their flows by exaggerating stress accents (e.g., FIGHT the POW-ers that BE); Japanese lacks these stress accents, and all syllables are pronounced with the same length and loudness. In addition, Japanese poetry typically does not have end rhymes, as most sentences end with auxiliary verbs (e.g., "have" in English) like -desu and -masu. K Dub Shine of the crew King Giddra developed a technique whereby he formed lines of verse of sentence fragments ending with a key noun, verb, or adjective, giving infinite rhyming possibilities. This rhyming scheme was widely adopted among Japanese rappers. As the practice of Japanese rap was established, some rappers, like Boss of Tha Blue Herb, cultivated flow reminiscent of spoken word. Meanwhile, DJs like DJ Krush began to incorporate Japanese instruments (e.g., shakuhachi flute) and aesthetics (ma, space, and wabi-sabi, deliberate imperfection) into their works, most famously in his album Jaku. Tracks can be musically eclectic, drawing not only from R&B and jazz but also traditional Japanese music, anime theme songs, "world" music, and vintage movie soundtracks.

Hip-Hop and Sociopolitical Critique

While a number of Japanese rappers are alumni of elite universities, rappers of rougher backgrounds have been garnering much attention, particularly as Japan's long-running financial crisis led to severe declines in economic opportunities for youth and the working class by the early 2000s. The crew MSC told tales of exhausted laborers, criminals, and drug deals. Anarchy, a former gang leader from the Kyoto housing projects, gained critical acclaim with his painful autobiographical stories of growing up without a mother in a drug-infested environment. Shingo Nishinari takes his stage name from Nishinari, Japan's largest gathering place for day laborers—typically old men, many living in makeshift homes under shantytown conditions. Songs like "Ill Nishinari Blues" encapsulate scenes from this difficult life. Dengaryu⁻, a rapper from Yamanashi Prefecture (home of Mount Fuji), has critiqued economic depression in the regions ("Ice City") and national energy policies ("Straight Outta 138").

The triple disaster of earthquake, tsunami, and nuclear accident on March 11, 2011, called "3.11," incited many Japanese to protest government policies, and hip-hoppers were at the forefront of these protests. An antinuclear demonstration in the bohemian Tokyo neighborhood of Kōenji on April 10, 2011, drew as many as 15,000 people, attracted by the passionate rapping of female rapper Rumi and reggae pioneer Rankin Taxi, among others. Often featuring trucks loaded with speakers and amplifiers, antinuclear demonstrations grew to crowds as large as 200,000 people in a demonstration in Tokyo's central government district of Kasumigaseki on July 29, 2012. As anger over the lack of change in nuclear policy grew, the performance style shifted from musicians and rappers performing prepared songs to a more participatory format, whereby rappers like ECD, Akuryō, and ATS exchanged antinuclear slogans like, "We oppose restarting [nuclear power plants]," with the protesters in a call-and-response pattern, all to the beats of an R&B track.

This style of rapping slogans with the protesters has been adopted in other Japanese cities and in subsequent movements. In December 2013, the Secrets

Protection Law was passed. This law, among other issues, made it a criminal act for third parties (such as journalists) to press inappropriately for information on state secrets from government officials, although one would not know what the state secrets were. In July 2014, Prime Minister Abe and his Cabinet voted to reinterpret the Constitution, which had forbidden war except in cases of Japan's self-defense since the end of World War II, to allow fighting overseas alongside allies, even if Japan itself had not been attacked; the Security Bills, which made such troop deployment legally possible, were passed amid massive and frequent protests in September 2015. Those protests were filled with the sound of rap and hip-hop: the Students Against the Secrets Protection Law (SASPL) and their successor group, Students Emergency Action for Liberal Democracy (SEALDs), adopted the syncopated cadence of rap to deliver slogans like, "Tell me what democracy looks like," previously heard in the 1999 protests against the World Trade Organization meeting in Seattle and Occupy Wall Street, and its Japanese translation, "*Minshushugi tte nanda?*" Their calls and responses were picked up by teenagers and grandmothers alike. Another popular call pattern improvised on a classic rap gesture:

Rapper:	I say "*kenpō*" [constitution], you say "*mamore*" [protect].
	Kenpō!
Protesters:	*Mamore*!
Rapper:	*Kenpō*!
Protesters:	*Mamore*!

While Japanese rap lyrics are overwhelmingly about daily life, hip-hoppers have also released a number of political recordings, both informally in cyberspace and through commercial release. The bilingual rapper Shing02, who joined the hip-hop community while a student at the University of California at Berkeley, has been a consistent sociopolitical commentator and antinuclear activist, having worked on the multimedia project Stop Rokkasho (against the nuclear fuel recycling plant Rokkasho) with famed Japanese composer Sakamoto Ryūichi. He teamed with Hunger, a rapper from tsunami-hit Sendai, to criticize the pronuclear slant in media coverage in "The Revolution Will Not Be Televised" (2011), in which they take Gil Scott-Heron's track and premise of the media as a distortive presenter of dominant (white) views about African Americans and apply it to the Japanese case, where the media has broadcast primarily the official views of the nuclear industry and the government. Shing02 has also released songs and videos on many other topics, including "Nihonkoku kenpō" ("Japan's Constitution," 2015), a 22-minute epic on the history and current controversy regarding the Constitution and entertainment law that restricts dance clubs.

Not all Japanese hip-hop is liberal. As David Morris and Dexter Thomas have noted, Zeebra and K Dub Shine of King Giddra both pronounced nationalist views, although K Dub Shine has advocated for proper constitutional amendment rather than the Cabinet-level reinterpretation of the constitution employed by the Abe administration to pass the Security Bills. One rap crew that spews neonationalist rhetoric is Arei Raise, whose song "Kyōji" ("Pride," 2007) calls the Pacific War a "holy war" that was "noble and grand." The video is shot in Yasukuni itself. Show-K released "Nihonjin Stand Up!" (2010), a rant against China in the wake of the Senkaku Islands fishing incident. In the run-up to the passing of the Security Bills, Show-K released several songs advocating for militarization, including "Teikoku kenpō" ("Imperial Constitution," 2015), a response to Shing02's song.

In a country dominated by commercial pop, hip-hop offers a potential alternative of self-authored tracks about real life. Hip-hop's reputation as a frank expression has made it an ideal vehicle for protests against government policies and societal injustice. This frankness has also made it a vehicle for neonationalist and racist rhetoric. And then, of course, it's also simply party music.

Noriko Manabe

See also: K-pop

Further Reading

Condry, Ian. 2006. *Hip-Hop Japan: Rap and the Paths of Cultural Globalization.* Durham, NC: Duke University Press.

Manabe, Noriko. 2006. "Globalization and Japanese Creativity: Adaptations of Japanese Language to Rap." *Ethnomusicology* 50, no. 1 (Winter): 1–36.

Manabe, Noriko. 2015. *The Revolution Will Not Be Televised: Protest Music After Fukushima.* New York: Oxford University Press.

K-POP

K-pop is a popular music genre from South Korea that combines and uses hip-hop, pop, rock, and electronic and audiovisual elements. In the West, the artistic ideal is one of solitary genius—the singer, songwriter, multi-instrumentalist—but in the K-pop world the goal is not the artistic expression of individuals but rather the collective production of the ideal product. This leads some to dismiss K-pop as a monolithic money-driven manufactured approach to artistic creation, yet the highly skilled teams of producers, directors, videographers, photographers, songwriters, audio technicians, choreographers, costume designers, and stylists that create the final amalgamation of audio, video, and live performance are no less artists, even though the final product is performed by K-pop stars, called idols, that may have had little input into the production process.

One reason frequently given for this team approach is to recoup the investment the agencies make in K-pop stars, because agencies spend years molding each idol before debut. In most of the world, stars are expected to struggle to attain the necessary training and attract attention on their own until they are discovered. In K-pop, however, worldwide auditions are held to find the raw material; these young recruits are then sculpted into polished stars through years of company-funded training in dance, singing, interview skills, foreign languages, and more. They cannot rely on becoming megastars due to something as basic as phenomenal vocal technique, as the expectation of the audience is for much more than talent in a single area. In fact, many K-pop stars are heavily autotuned, but they can be phenomenally successful through a combination of talent, training, and charisma—because modeling for top brands and appearances on television shows earns more than sales of units of music (MP3 files, CDs).

Control over K-pop artistry is concentrated in the teams assembled by top entertainment agencies, such as SM, YG, and JYP Entertainment. Sooman Lee, the "SM" of SM Entertainment, transitioned from singer and radio DJ to music mogul. SM Entertainment came first and demonstrated how a training system, keen attention to a formula, and hard work could turn random teenagers into superstars. SM Entertainment, more than 20 years after it emerged on the music scene in Korea, is still the largest music entertainment agency; this is attributed to micromanagement, keeping a finger on the changing pulse of Korean tastes, and a willingness to try new approaches. At times this method of management is criticized by Korean and international fans, with rumors of 1,200-calorie diets, a lack of access to cell phones, and bans on dating coupled with contracts, frequently called "slavery contracts," with durations of seven years or even more.

Each of the major entertainment groups is somewhat different—YG Entertainment has positioned itself as the label where artists express their individuality with more abandon. The YG artists, such as Psy, Big Bang, and 2NE1 seem to standout for spectacle rather than something as ordinary as physical beauty. Perhaps the YG owner, Hyunsuk Yang, formerly a member of the groundbreaking Seo Taiji and Boys, has preserved respect for the sort of rebellion he himself showed when young. Jinyoung Park (head of JYP Entertainment) is the only one of the major studio heads that continues to perform, with releases coming out each year. He is closely involved with his groups, such as 2PM, the Wonder Girls, and Miss A, personally providing artistic direction in music and encouragement for acting. This is indicative of a trend toward inclusion of idol stars in productions from musicals to TV dramas to top-grossing movies—indicating a future in which celebrity is celebrity, without limit on spheres of activity.

In 2012, South Korean rapper, Psy, released his infectious hit, "Gangnam Style," which went on to become a truly global phenomenon, and the most viewed video on YouTube. Here, Psy performs the song on NBC's *Today* show in New York in 2012. (Jason DeCrow/Invision/AP Images)

Although there is a creative core in K-pop, there are elements that make the formulas employed by the various entertainment agencies visible. Musically K-pop is catchy and incorporates effective hooks that stick in the listener's mind. The international world is welcomed as the biggest stars frequently release a version of the song in Chinese and/or Japanese. For nearly two decades the K-pop refrains, regardless of the song's language, have included words and phrases in English, and some groups have tried to break into the English market (such as Se7en, BoA, and the Wonder Girls). Further, genre boundaries common in Western popular music are completely absent. Most top K-pop stars are part of genre-dimorphic groups that release tracks in multiple genres including electronic dance, hip-hop, rap, R&B, reggaeton, jazz, and crooning slow ballads. K-pop is consumed and becomes popular through performance on screen; this means that the physical appearance of stars—ranging from their symbiotic role with high-end fashion to pressure for cosmetic surgery—is important. The stars are conventionally attractive and representative of the increasingly intensified commodification of the body in Korea. Yet, unlike musical stars in other regions, they remain relatively scandal free—until recently something as mild as marijuana use was enough to be dismissed from a company. Idol stars can play young and innocent (dressed in pastels and bright colors, with a chirp in their voices) or be tough (boy groups) or sexy (girl groups), and they may shift back and forth across this border between one release and the next.

K-pop elements come together in live performances, most often on weekly television shows that feature top acts performing their recently released songs—these are dubbed "comebacks" because the group is coming back to perform after not releasing a song for a few months. Each major channel has its own show, and the most sought-after idol groups will perform the same song four nights a week for the first three weeks or so after the song is released. Fans around the world can watch these performances, as well as music videos, online. K-pop has increasingly become a visual spectacle where the popularity of release can be measured in YouTube views (more than 5 million in the first week is standard for the top groups). The visual elements of K-pop music videos, therefore, are evocative, unforgettable, and at times disturbing, with symbolic references drawn from an international palate. These spectacular and widely popular music videos and the live performances most often emphasize dance. Dance, particularly the spectacle of highly synchronized reproduction of extremely complicated choreography, has become a top selling point for domestic and international fans. The dance motions necessary for an arresting live performance alternate between easy enough to attract complete novices, as in "Gangnam Style," and complex enough to wow professional dancers (often by the same groups, although SHINee, BoA, and EXO are particularly praised for their dances).

The choreography featured in K-pop, however, just like the music, songs, fashions, and even the cast in music videos, is increasingly imported from abroad or recorded overseas, with top studios forming symbiotic relationships with dozens of individual artists and artistic teams capable of collectively producing the most technically sophisticated product possible. Because K-pop stars are manufactured under the strong artistic vision of management companies that are willing to hire the top talent from anywhere in the world, the mystery is not how they produce such excellent products but rather how long the "K" in K-pop will maintain significance.

CedarBough T. Saeji

See also: The "Gangnam Style" Fad (Chapter 5: Internet and Social Media)

Further Reading

Epstein, Stephen, with James Turnbull. 2014. "Girls' Generation? Gender, (Dis)Empowerment, and K-pop." In *The Korean Popular Culture Reader.* Ed. Kyung Hyun Kim and Youngmin Choe, 314–336. Durham, NC: Duke University Press.

Epstein, Stephen, and Rachael Miyung Joo. 2012. "Multiple Exposures: Korean Bodies and the Transnational Imagination." *The Asia-Pacific Journal* 10, no. 33.

Howard, Keith. 2006. *Korean Pop Music: Riding the Wave.* Folkestone, UK: Global Oriental.

Lie, John. 2015. *K-pop: Popular Music, Cultural Amnesia, and Economic Innovation in South Korea.* Los Angeles: University of California Press.

Russell, Mark James. 2008. *Pop Goes Korea: Behind the Revolution in Movies, Music, and Internet Culture.* Berkeley, CA: Stone Bridge Press.

MUSICIANS, INDIA

The rich cultural heritage of Indian musicians goes back to earlier times and has produced eminent singers, composers, and instrument players down the centuries. Under the Delhi Sultanate and the Mughals, the Indian subcontinent witnessed two great musicians: the poet Amir Khusrau (1253–1325) and Miyan Tansen (1506–1589). In the last three to four decades, Indian musicians have catapulted into national and international fame. They have incorporated different styles, such as Hindustani, Carnatic, *qawwali*, *gzagals*, folk, jazz, rock, pop, reggae, and others. The songs from Bollywood are very much appreciated by Indians and the diasporic community. The songs and beats of musical instruments reverberate in the drawing rooms of residences, streets, bazaars, secular and religious festivals, ceremonies, and marriage *pandals*. The recorded works appear on records, audiocassettes, CDs, and TV music channels. If there is a live performance by a musician, crowds throng in. One cannot imagine a pop culture of India without musicians. All types of singers and players of musical instruments, such as *sarod*, flute, *sarangi*, *veena*, tabla, *sahnai*, and others have carved a niche in the popular culture of India.

In the popular culture of India, the playback singers, singers who prerecord songs for actors to use in movies, have a unique identity of their own. The sonorous, melodious, and enchanting voices of scores of Indian singers have enthralled listeners. Dominating the Indian musical scene for more than six decades, the younger sister of Lata Mangeshkar, Asha Bhonsle (1933–), has entertained generations of Indians through her Bollywood songs. She is equally at ease with *bhajans* (devotional songs), *ghazals*, and pop. Alisha Chinai (1972–), known as India's Madonna, is a talented pop artist and "Queen of Indian Pop." Her haunting and husky voice revolutionized pop music and heralded a new era. Adnan Sami (1973–) is a notable Indian pop musician whose music videos sell like hotcakes. His single "Lift Kara Do" has never lost its charm. Remo Fernandes (1953–), of the earlier era, amalgamated rock and Indian music. Usha Uttup inspired a generation of singers, and her number "Hare Rama Hare Krshna" is evergreen. Xenia (1980–) became another pop sensation with her album *Meri ada*. Since the 1980s, Alka Yagnik has been a well-known playback singer. Lata Mangeshkar, Kishore Kumar, Hemant Kumar, Mohammed Rafi, Mukesh, Talat Mahomud, and others have become part of the Indian music scene with their memorable songs being listened to almost daily through radio, TV, and CDs. A. R. Rahman (1966–), known as Dileep Kumar before his conversion to Islam, is dominating the Indian music world as a singer, music composer, and songwriter. Winner of two Academy Awards, two Grammy Awards, and a Golden Gobe, Rahman has held sway over the Indian music scene for the last two and a half decades. Film director Shubha Mudgal (1959–), *bhajan* singer Anuradha Paudhwal (1954–), *ghazal* singers Jagjit Singh (1941–) and Pankaj Udhas (1951–), bhangra disco king Daler Mehndi (1967–), and Punjabi folk singer Gurdas Mann (1957–) are some of the prominent musicians of present-day India. Popular TV programs like *Sa re gama* have brought members of the upcoming generation of singers, including Sonu Nigam, Kalpna Yagnik, Shreya Ghosal, Rituraj, and others, to the forefront.

Instrumentalists, composers, gurus, and *ustads* (masters) have taken Indian music not only to individual homes but around the world. Vocal forms like *khayal* and *thumri*, Hindustani as well as Carnatic musical traditions, folk singing and others are quintessential aspects of the Indian musical tradition. There has been a fusion of Indian and Western musical instruments, with violin, trumpet, guitar, saxophone, mandolin, clarinet, and organ being used in Indian popular and classical music. Pandit Hariprasad Chaurasia is a well-known classical musician, and his renderings on the flute are second to none. The *bhajans* of M. S. Subbulakshmi enthrall listeners. Amjad Ali Khan is a well-known *sarod* player. Ravi Shankar, exponent of the sitar and composer of Hindustani classical music; the renowned *sarod* player Ali Akbar Khan; tabla virtuoso Zakir Hussain; *shehnai* maestro Bismillah Khan; violinist, composer, and conductor L. Subramaniam; and others have put India on the international map musically.

From the chanting of Vedic hymns to singing in the courts of royalty, Indian musicians have come a long way in becoming an intrinsic part of contemporary Indian pop culture.

Selected Biographies of Indian Musicians

Mangeshkar, Lata (1929–)

The doyenne of Indian singers, Lata Mangeshkar has dominated the Indian musical scene for more than half a century. This "Nightingale of Bollywood" was born in Indore, Madhya Pradesh, on September 8, 1929, to Shevanti Mangeshkar and Dinanath Mangeshkar, a notable classical singer and owner of a theater company. Her siblings, such as brother Hridaynath Mangeshkar and sisters Asha Bhosle, Usha Mangeshkar, and Meena Mangeshkar, are also noted personalities in Indian music. Lata's father was a guru in her childhood, imparting lessons in singing and acting. After his death, Lata came under the care of a close family friend, Vinayak Damodar Karnataki, from the age of 13. Her acting and singing career blossomed. Her first acting assignment was in the movie *Pahili mangalagaur*, released in 1942. But Lata took more interest in singing, and she recorded her first film song in Vasant Joglekar's Marathi cinema *Kirti hasaal*. In 1945 Lata sang a prayer, "Mata tere charnon mein" ("Mother at Your Feet"), in the movie *Badi maa*. She struggled for about five years to establish herself as a playback singer. Lata recorded her first Hindi song in the film *Aap ki sewame* in 1947. She never looked back and went on to establish herself as a notable singer. Another reputed singer, Noorjehan, had left for Pakistan after the Indian subcontinent was partitioned in August 1947. Lata was the unchallenged singer developing her own style, which has never diminished. Her mentors during her early career were Aman Ali Khan, Amanat Khan, Tulsidas Sharma, Ghulam Hyder, Anil Biswas, and Kundanlal Saigal. Lata was catapulted into fame after the release of Ghulam Haider's film *Majboor* in 1948, in which she sang "Dil mera toda" ("Broke My Heart"). The next year, her songs in four hit films, *Mahal*, *Barsaat*, *Dulari*, and *Andaz*, made her immensely popular. These immortal songs, such as "Ayega aanewala," "Meri lal dupatta," and others are still enthralling lovers of classical music. Purity, sharpness, suppleness, clarity, high-pitched tones, and lyrical notes were hallmarks of her songs. The trend of nasal voices produced by singers such as Noor Jehan, Shamshad Begum, and Zohrabai Ambalewali became passé. Lata's particular falsetto voice changed the style of playback singing in the Indian film industry.

In the 1950s, Lata worked with prominent music directors such as Kalyanji-Anandji, Khayyam, Shankar-Jaikishan, Naushad, Hemanta Kumar, and S. D. Burman and left for posterity haunting and charming songs from memorable movies like *Baiju bawra* (1952), *Shree 420* (1955), *Chori chori* (1956), *Devdas* (1955), and *Madhumati* (1958). She never looked back, and Lata's popularity has increased as the years have passed. Lata was the unchallenged queen of the movie world of Mumbai. Without her songs, the hits of the 1960s would have been drab and prosaic. The superhit movie *Mughal-e-azam* was made more memorable with her song "Pyar karna to darna kiya" ("Why Afraid If You Love"). She churned out evergreen songs such as "Aap ki nazron ne samjha" ("Your Looks Understood," *Anpadh*, 1962), "Lag ja gale" ("Let Us Embrace," *Woh kaun thi?*, 1964), "Gata rahe mera dil" ("My Heart Goes on Singing," *Guide*, 1965), "Tu jahaa chalega, mera saya sath hoga" ("Whenever You Go, My Shadow Will Follow," *Mera saaya*, 1966), "Hothon pe aisi baat ayi" ("Some Words Came by the Lips," *Jewel Thief*, 1967), and others. Lata also sang in movies such as *Pati patni* (1966), *Abhilasha* (1969), *Bhoot bangla* (1965), and *Baharon ke sapne* (1967), with R. D. Burman as music director. She also sang for Bengali and Marathi cinemas. Her nonfilm song "Aye mere watan ke logon" ("Oh! People of My Country"), sung during the Sino-Indian War of 1962, aroused a patriotic fervor and brought tears to many, including the Indian premier, Jawaharlal Nehru. In the 1970s, Lata's fame reached greater heights with memorable songs such as "Rangeela re" (*Prem pujari*, 1970), "Khilte hain gul yahaan" (*Sharmelee*, 1971), "Inhi logo ne" (*Pakeeza*, 1972), and "Piya bina" (*Abhiman*, 1973). The movies *Kati patang* (1971), *Amar prem* (1972), *Caravan* (1972), and *Aandhi* (1975) became box-office hits with her songs. Lata gained international fame and performed superbly at London's Royal Albert Hall. She also gave a concert in the United States. A new generation of music directors, such as Rajesh Roshan, Anand-Milind, Anu Malik, and A. R. Rahman, were making their presence felt in Bollywood. Their movies appealed to people with their excellent direction, story lines, and Lata's haunting music. The songs from Yosh Chopra–directed movies, such as *Chandni* (1989), *Lamhe* (1991), *Darr* (1993), *Yeh dillagi* (1994), *Dilwale dulhaniya le jayenge* (1995), *Dil to pagal hai* (1997), *Mohabbatein* (2000), *Mujhse dosti karoge* (2002), and *Veer zaara* (2004), became extremely popular. She also sang many *ghazals* with Jagjit Singh. Her *ghazal* album entitled *Saadgi* (2007) contained outstanding numbers. She does not like remix albums, which have become trendy these days. Lata also laments the deterioration of Bollywood music in which singing has become secondary and musical instruments primary. Lata was not successful when she began to produce films, including *Kanchan* (1950), *Jhaanjhar* (1953), and *Lekin* (1990). Her launch of a perfume brand called Lata Eau De Parfume (1999) and design of a jewellery collection, Swaranjali (2005), were also not that successful. She has established a hospital in Pune in western India commemorating her departed father. Lata loves watching cricket. Diamond is her favorite gem.

In her lifetime, Lata has been the recipient of many honors and awards. She has won laurels such as a platinum record for EMI London, Filmfare Awards (1959, 1963, 1966, and 1970), Padma Bhushan (1969), Dadasaheb Phalke Award (1989), and Padma Vibhushan (1999). In 2001 Lata won India's highest civilian award: the Bharat Ratna. She was a member of India's lower house of parliament, Rajya Sabha, in 1999. Lata was featured in the *Guinness Book of World Records* for singing 30,000 songs between 1948 and 1987. She can sing with equal ease in about 20 Indian languages, and her solos and duets have mesmerized millions of people. The reigning melody queen, Lata Mangeshkar still captivates people with her hypnotic songs. She has become an institution and an iconic figure.

Shankar, Ravi (1920–2012)

Ravi Shankar, the famous sitar maestro, was born on April 7, 1920, in Varanasi, Uttar Pradesh. A disciple of Ustad Allauddin Khan (1862–1972), he struggled hard to be an accomplished sitar player. In 1936 he left brother Uday Shakar's dance troupe and came to Maihar to apprentice under his guru, Ustad Allauddin Khan. The *guru-sisya parampara* (teacher-disciple tradition) is at the root of Indian music. He began his musical career in Mumbai (Bombay) in 1944. Working for the HMV Company, Ravi Shankar provided musical scores to movies and ballets. He was the music director of government-owned All India Radio in the 1950s.

Ravi Shankar became well known in India and abroad, making the audience spellbound by his sitar playing. The West applauded his compositions. Ravi Shankar collaborated with prominent musicians like Ali Akbar Khan (1922–2009), Pundit Chatur Lal (1925–1965), George Harrison (1943–2001), Yehudi Menuhin (1916–1999), Jean Pierre Rampal (1922–2000), and Phillip Glass (1937–). He composed music for highly successful films, such as Satyajit Ray's *Apu Triology* and Richard Attenborough's *Gandhi*. His performances at the Monterey Pop Festival, Woodstock Festival, Royal Festival Hall, and Concert for Bangladesh were watched by millions around the globe. His daughters, Norah Jones (1979–) and Anoushka Shankar (1981–), have become an accomplished singer and a sitar player, respectively. Anoushka penned a biography about her father, *Bapi—The Love of My Life* (2002), which threw light on Ravi Shankar's life and times. He was awarded with many honors, such as Padma Vibhushan (1981), Magsaysay Award (1992), Bharat Ratna (1999), Commander of the Legion of Honour of France (2000), Honorary Knight Commander of the Order of the British Empire (2001), and others.

The *numero uno* of Indian music, Ravi Shankar's performances always drew packed audiences.

Bismillah Khan (1916–2006)

Bismillah Khan, world-renowned *shehnai* maestro, was born at Dumraon, Bihar, on March 21, 1916, into a family of musicians. His guru was his uncle Ali Baksh "Vilayatu," the *shehnai* player of Varanasi's Vishwanath temple. Bismillah Khan made the Indian musical instrument the *shehnai* famous, and, in fact, his name became synonymous with it. Originally associated with ceremonial occasions, the *shehnai*, a double-reed aerophonic instrument made of wood with six to eight holes, found a place in concert halls because of Ustad Bismillah Khan.

Music became the soul of Ustad's life, transcending religious barriers. Although a Shia Muslim, he was a devotee of Saraswati, the Hindu goddess of knowledge. He resided in the Hindu holy city of Varanasi, playing on the banks of the Ganga River and at the temples. The Khan Saheb had the rare honor of playing *shehnai* on the eve of Indian independence at Red Fort while the national flag was being unfurled. He provided *shehnai* music for films like *Sanaadi appanna* and *Goonj uthi shehnai*. In 1966 he was in Edinburgh, and the next year he played in the United States, captivating the audience. His *jugalbandi* (duet) with sitar maestro Vilayat Khan (1928–2004) and *sarod* player Amjad Ali Khan (1946–) became immensely popular. The *shehnai jugalbandi* of Ustad and disciple Bageshwari Qamar, the first female *shehnai* player of India, in 1994, enthralled music lovers with their *todi* (morning), *madhuwanti* (evening), and *yaman* (night) *ragas*.

The *shehnai* virtuoso's death on August 21, 2006, in Varanasi was an irreplaceable loss to Indian music.

Ali Akbar Khan (1922–2009)

Ustad Ali Akbar Khan, the renowned *sarod* player and composer, was born at Shivpur, Bangladesh, on April 14, 1922. His parents were Madina Begum and

Baba Allauddin Khan (1862–1972), a noted musician and founder of Senia Maihar Gharana. The family had about 400 years of tradition in Indian classical music. His forte was playing the *sarod*, the 25-stringed musical instrument played with a bow. Like his father, he became the court musician of Maharaja of Jodhpur. In 1955 Khan was in the United States at the invitation of Yehudi Menuhin (1916–1999) and was helping to make Indian classical music immensely popular. He had composed musical scores for well-known films like Satyajit Ray's (1921–1992) *Devi* and Bernardo Bertolucci's (1940–) *The Householder* and *Little Buddha*. Khan performed *jugalbandi* (a duet) with Ravi Shankar (1920–2012), Nikhil Banerjee (1931–1986), L. K. Subramaniam (1947–), and Vilayat Khan (1927–2004). His son Aashish Khan (1939–) is an accomplished *sarod* player.

Ustad Khan produced many disciples who kept up the tradition of the guru. His Ali Akbar College of Music in Calcutta (Kolkata), established in 1956, is a premier institution of Indian classical music. He opened similar institutions in the United States and Switzerland. Ustad Khan toured extensively, giving musical performances all over the world. Living in the United States since 1968, the Swara Samrat (Emperor of Melody) was awarded the Padma Vibhushan (1989), MacArthur Genius Grant (1991), and National Heritage Fellowship (1997).

Patit Paban Mishra and Sangita Babu

See also: Folk Songs, India; *Lavani* Dance and Film (Chapter 3: Film)

Further Reading

Avtar, Ram. 1987. *History of Indian Music and Musicians*. New Delhi: Pankaj Publications.
Dwyer, Ralph, and Christopher Pinney, eds. 2001. *The History, Politics and Consumption of Public Culture in India*. New Delhi: Oxford University Press.
Kasbekar, Asha. 2006. *Pop Culture India! Media, Arts, and Lifestyle*. Santa Barbara, CA: ABC-CLIO.
Massey, Reginald. 1977. *The Music of India*. New York: Crescendo Publishers.

P'ANSORI: KOREAN NARRATIVE SINGING

P'ansori is a distinctive Korean art in which a singer (*kwangdae* or *sorikkun*) tells an epic tale interspersed with musical passages accompanied only by a drummer (*kosu*). There are narrative song traditions in neighboring China and Japan, but they look and sound quite different from the spartan performance style of *p'ansori*. Since about 70 percent of Korean vocabulary is Sino-Korean (words of Chinese origin, written with Chinese characters), it is notable that there are no ideographs for *p'ansori*; the word is written only in *han'gŭl*, the Korean phonetic script. The term combines *p'an* ("a place where people gather") with *sori* ("sound"). Originating as a folk art performed in open-air public spaces, *p'ansori* gradually migrated indoors to intimate aristocratic salons and is now performed in major concert halls as a refined art. In 1964 the government of the Republic of Korea enshrined *p'ansori* as a National Intangible Cultural Property, and in 2003 the United Nations

Educational, Scientific and Cultural Organization (UNESCO) designated it as a Masterpiece of the Oral and Intangible Heritage of Humanity. Many Koreans regard it as an art form that expresses the national essence of their country.

One theory of *p'ansori's* origins suggests that it developed from the songs of shamans, spirit mediums who communicated with the folkloric gods of Korea through ritual music and dance. By the 18th century, *p'ansori* had taken the basic form it has today. It was performed in outdoor markets and other public spaces (*madang*) where Korean commoners gathered. Performers sang from a repertoire of 12 narratives (*madong*), but the best ones improvised and varied their melodies, embellishing the stories as they saw fit. *P'ansori* narratives were generally tragicomic and satirical, mixing dramatic accounts of heroism and villainy with wry humor and wordplay.

Under the rule of the Yi dynasty (1392–1910), Korea was a rigidly stratified society. At the top were the *yangban*, scholar-officials who were highly educated in classical Chinese learning and worked as government officials and administrators. The second group was the *chung-in*, people who lived in towns and had special technical skills; they provided a variety of services for the government as military officers, craftspeople, musicians, and physicians. Next were the *sangmin*, commoners who worked as farmers, laborers, fishers, and merchants. At the bottom of the hierarchy were the *ch'ŏnmin*, "vulgar" or "base" people. Early *p'ansori* singers and their accompanists were included in this lowly group, although their audiences consisted of *chung-in* and *sangmin*. Thus, in its early days, *p'ansori* was considered popular culture: it was for common people's entertainment and was generally disparaged by elites.

However, in the mid-19th century, *p'ansori* became a more "respectable" art, due to the patronage of nobles like Sin Chaehyo (1812–1884). An instrumental musician rather than a singer, Sin whittled the repertoire of 12 *madong* down to five, each of which he revised and standardized to create narratives that promoted one of the five fundamental relationships (*oryun*) emphasized in Confucian philosophy:

1. *Song of simch'ŏng*: Parent/child, filial piety
2. *Song of ch'unhyang*: Husband/wife, conjugal fidelity
3. *Song of hŭngbu*: Elder brother/younger brother
4. *Song of chŏkpyŏk*: Ruler/ministers, generals/soldiers
5. *Song of sugung*: Friends of equal status

Sin's efforts to make *p'ansori* a vehicle for promoting official orthodoxy remain controversial to this day. *P'ansori* had long been a vehicle for satire, a way for commoners to criticize the *yangban* for their pretentiousness, hypocrisy, greed, and indifference to the people's welfare. Much of the satire, double entendre, and wordplay remain, but they were probably sharper and more prominent in earlier versions than they are now. Modern singers earn acclaim for their improvised and individual interpretations of the five canonical works Sin Chaehyo selected.

Sin is famous for another innovation: his protégé Chin Ch'aesŏn (1847–?) was the first female *p'ansori* singer. By the late 19th century, top singers of both sexes were performing in elite salons and even the Yi royal palace. Despite *p'ansori* singers' lowly social status, the art itself had earned esteem, and the best singers could be handsomely rewarded.

Another major change for the art occurred in the first decade of the 20th century, when a national theater opened in Seoul. Several entertainers formed troupes to modernize *p'ansori* as a theatrical form. Instead of one singer handling all of the narration and characters' voices, now roles were assigned to individual actors. The vocal style of this new kind of performance—*ch'anggŭk* ("singing theater")—retained the raw, throat-splitting emotion of *p'ansori*, but audiences were thrilled by the new format, especially the titillating presence of women on stage. *Ch'anggŭk* is perhaps more popular with the general public today, but it does not quite have the artistic status of original *p'ansori*, which demands tremendous artistry and stamina from one performer.

During the period of Japanese colonial rule (1910–1945), recording companies produced *p'ansori* records for general purchase, documenting the styles of some of the most esteemed singers of the past. During World War II, new regulations and censorship imposed hardships on performers, as did the later Korean War. State patronage after 1964 helped revive the art, and some dissidents wrote new libretti (such as Kim Chiha's *Five Bandits*) to protest against government dictatorship in South Korea.

The four most important elements of a *p'ansori* performance are singing (*ch'ang*), narration (*sasŏl* or *aniri*), dancing (*pallim*), and dramatic (*nŏrŭmsae*) gestures. The only "prop" besides the drum is the singer's paper fan, with which she or he adds dramatic emphasis by pointing or waving it open and closed. Drummers play set rhythmic patterns (*changdan*) but creatively vary them to suit the texts, melodies, and emotional content. *P'ansori* singing is known for its raw, rough vocal quality rather than purity of tone and for the melismatic bending of pitches over a single syllable (not unlike black American blues, R&B, and gospel singing). To attain the harsh rasp of *p'ansori* vocals, singers are said to have trained on wooded mountains, trying to sing louder than the sounds of nature, and to have spit up blood from straining their vocal cords. Women singers train to achieve the same rough vocal texture men have, essentially defeminizing their voices.

The most important aspect of *p'ansori* aesthetics is the emotion conveyed via this dramatic vocal style. Much like Americans prize "soul" in blues and R&B singing, Koreans expect the expression and cathartic release of what they call *han*. *Han* basically means "indignant sorrow": it is grieving or sadness caused by an identifiable person, event, or circumstance; it is misery caused by injustice, beyond the control of the aggrieved party. Koreans regard *p'ansori* as the ultimate musical expression of *han*, because its narratives highlight the tragic absurdity and injustice of life, explicitly *naming* the source of the characters' grief, with which audiences identify.

Although television and pop music have reduced the audience for traditional arts, in the 1990s two films by Im Kwŏnt'aek (*Sŏp'yŏnje* and *Chunhyang*) raised the profile and appreciation of *p'ansori* among the general public, who recognize it as a uniquely Korean art form.

E. Taylor Atkins

See also: Arirang: Korean Folk Song

Further Reading

Jang, Yeonok. 2014. *Korean P'ansori Singing Tradition: Development, Authenticity, and Performance History*. Lanham, MD: Scarecrow Press.

Park, Chan E. 2003. *Voices from the Straw Mat: Toward an Ethnography of Korean Story Singing*. Honolulu: University of Hawai'i Press.

Pihl, Marshall R. 1994. *The Korean Singer of Tales*. Cambridge, MA: Harvard University Press.

Um, Haekyung. 2013. *Korean Musical Drama:* P'ansori *and the Making of Tradition in Modernity*. Aldershot, UK: Ashgate.

Willoughby, Heather. 2000. "The Sound of Han: P'ansori, Timbre and a Korean Ethos of Pain and Suffering." *Yearbook for Traditional Music* 32: 17–30.

Discography

Jung Jung Min [Chŏng Chungmin]. 2007. *Voyager Series—The Art of Pansori*. Columbia River Entertainment Group 0140208.

Kim So-hee [Kim Sohŭi]. 1989. *P'ansori—Korea's Epic Vocal Art and Instrumental Music*. Nonesuch 7559720492.

PINOY JAZZ, PHILIPPINES

Jazz came to the Philippines by way of American nationals and returning Filipinos who came to the country during the American colonial period (1898–1946). The phonograph together with 78-rpm recordings of American music like jazz, swing, Dixieland, foxtrot, and blues were brought into the country, thereby providing a new listening experience that was modern and cosmopolitan. Furthermore, the American introduction of music recording paved the way for local artists to reach a bigger audience.

The singer Maria Evangelista Carpena (1886–1915) is considered the first Filipino recording artist. Her recording of the song "Ang maya" ("The Sparrow"), composed by Jose Estella (1870–1943) with lyrics by dramatist Severino Reyes (1861–1942) under the American label Victor Records, was issued around 1908–1909. American Tin Pan Alley songs gave inspiration to Filipino composers like M. Nazario, who wrote "Manila Boxing Rag" in 1914, and Jose Estella with several songs, namely "California: March" in 1899, "Germinales" circa 1908, "Manila Carnival Rag" in 1914, and "Visayan Moon" in 1922. Noted composer Francisco Santiago was obviously influenced by the music of the time when he wrote "Balintawak: Filipino Fox-Trot" in 1920. In 1921 pianist Luis Borromeo (ca. 1879–1939) of Cebu came home after six years of musical stints in vaudeville theaters in the United States of America (1915–1921). His concerts in Cebu, Iloilo, and Manila featured a mixed repertoire of early jazz, opera, and classical songs, including Filipino art songs (*kundiman*). He eventually formed his own vaudeville troupe, named Borromeo Follies of 1924, which presented an amalgamation of music, dance, short plays, and comedies. Borromeo dominated the local cultural scene, which earned him the title "King of Jazz" in the Philippines.

Big bands playing in dance halls, theaters, cabarets, and hotels as well as at social events and town celebrations flourished in the 1930s. Among the favorites were Shanghai Swing Masters, Pete Aristorenas Orchestra, Cesar Velasco Band, Tirso

Cruz Orchestra, Mabuhay Band, and Mesio Regalado Orchestra. Radio became the medium to air jazz music, and local artists performed live at broadcast time. Mike Velarde (1913–1986), composer of the popular "Ugoy-ugoy Blues" in the mid-1930s, was a featured musician in two weekly radio shows, *Sunrise Program* in the morning and *Stardust Program* in the evening. Here he sang and played jazz arrangements on the piano. He formed a jazz band named Mike Velarde's Jazztocrats. Lito Molina (born Exequiel Siauingco Molina, 1929–), dubbed the "Father of Philippine Jazz," started playing professionally with various bands in the 1940s. He joined the Pete Aristorenas Orchestra in 1949 and by 1955 formed the Jazz Friends, which was active in the concert scene until the 1980s. Angel Peña (1921–2014), a music stalwart both in jazz and classical music, was a composer, arranger, and bass player. His jazz piece "Bagbagtulambing" made a mark in the local repertoire when it was performed in 1956 for a university fraternity annual concert. Likewise, his "Concerto for Jazz Quartet and Orchestra," which premiered in 1981 at the 75th anniversary of Filipino presence in Hawaii, perhaps best exemplified his creativity in fusing two contrasting genres of jazz and classical music into a composition. Bobby Enriquez (1943–1996) was undeniably the most exciting Filipino jazz piano virtuoso of his time. A child prodigy, he was self-taught and started playing jazz professionally at the age of 14. He left home and traveled to pursue a music career in Manila, Southeast Asia, Hong Kong, Taiwan, and Honolulu, eventually landing in the U.S. mainland, where he achieved international recognition as "the Wildman." His being a martial artist enhanced the showmanship, precision, and speed he displayed on the piano.

When considering jazz in the Philippines, one needs to make mention of the Katindig clan, with Romy Katindig, Eddie Katindig, Roland "Boy" Katindig, Henry Katindig, Tateng Katindig, and Maria Katindig-Dykes, who are all practitioners of jazz. A young breed of musicians who continue the creation of Pinoy jazz include the Ugoy-ugoy Band, led by Bond Samson (born James Samson, 1965–), RiaVillena-Osorio (1980–), and Jesper Colleen Mercado (1988–).

Felicidad A. Prudente

See also: Pinoy Pop, Philippines; Pinoy Rap, Philippines; Pinoy Rock, Philippines

Further Reading

Keppy, Peter. 2013. "Southeast Asia in the Age of Jazz: Locating Popular Culture in the Colonial Philippines and Indonesia." *Journal of Southeast Asian Studies* 44, no. 3: 444–464.

Quirino, Richie. 2004. *Pinoy Jazz Traditions.* Pasig City, PH: Anvil Publishing, Inc.

Walsh, Thomas P. 2013. *Tin Pan Alley and the Philippines: American Songs of War and Love, 1898–1946, A Resource Guide.* Lanham, MD: The Scarecrow Press, Inc.

PINOY POP, PHILIPPINES

Filipino popular music, commonly called "Pinoy pop" or "P-pop," is a broad genre that encompasses various types of songs and themes, such as ballads, novelty songs, inspirational songs, and fusion of indigenous and contemporary idioms.

The term "Pinoy" is a colloquial term for Filipino that is often used to give Filipino pop artists their own identity. Pinoy pop uses the Filipino language and other local languages such as Tagalog, Cebuano, Ilocano, and Kapampangan. English is also used as well as the mixing of English with Tagalog words, called "Taglish."

Songs in the Pinoy pop genre are conceived, created, and/or performed by local artists often identified with the Organization of Professional Filipino Singers (*Organisasyon ng Pilipinong Mang-aawit*, OPM). The organization is closely linked with local recording studios and the Philippine Association of Record Industry (PARI), which disseminates music for entertainment and economic gain. Leaders of OPM are practicing musicians themselves. The Apo Hiking Society, with the trio of Jim Paredes (1951–), Boboy Garovillo (1951–), and Danny Javier (1947–), have been pioneering advocates of OPM together with Mitch Valdes (1951–), Celeste Legaspi (1950–), Jose Mari Chan (1945–), and Gary Valenciano (1964–). Current OPM president Ogie Alcasid (born Herminio Jose Lualhati Alcasid Jr., 1967–) is himself an accomplished singer-songwriter with multiawarded songs such as "Pangarap ko ang ibigin ka" ("My Dream Is to Love You"), "Kailangan kita" ("I Need You"), and "Kung mawawala ka" ("If You Are Gone").

Songwriting competitions contribute to the development of local talents in creating modern-day pop songs. The Metro Manila Popular Music Festival, better known as Metropop, served to discover new artists and launch the music careers of composers and singers from its inception in 1978 until it ended in 1985. It was later revived with a new name, Metropop Song Festival, in 1996 and continued until 2003. The festivals produced enduring songs like "Anak" ("Child") by Freddie Aguilar (1953–), "Kay ganda ng ating musika" ("How Beautiful Is Our Music") by Ryan Cayabyab (1954–), "Be My Lady" by Vehnee Saturno (born Venancio Saturno, 1954–), and "Salamat, salamat musika" ("Thank You, Music") by Gary Granada (1960–).

Another songwriting and music video competition is the Himig Handog (Song Offering), which ran in 2000 until 2003 and was later revived in 2013. Each year Himig Handog has revolved around a title and theme, such as "Himig handog sa bayang Pilipino" ("Song for the Filipino Nation") in 2000, "Makabagong kabataan" ("Modern Youth") in 2001, and "P-pop Love Songs" in 2013, which produced hit songs like "Nasa iyo na ang lahat" ("Everything Is with You") by Jungee Marcelo and "This Song Is for You" by Jude Thaddeus Gitamondoc (1978–).

A more recent development in songwriting competitions is the Philippine Popular Music Festival, or Philpop, spearheaded in 2012 by well-known composer-arranger Ryan Cayabyab. Philpop's goal is to encourage more experimentation while also appealing to a wider audience. So far, it has discovered new talents such as Karl Vincent Villuga (1985–) for "Bawat hakbang" ("Each Step") in 2012 and the duo of Thyro Alfaro (1991–) and Yumi Lacsamana (1988–) with "Dati" ("In the Past") in 2013.

Felicidad A. Prudente

See also: Pinoy Jazz, Philippines; Pinoy Rap, Philippines; Pinoy Rock, Philippines

Further Reading

Japitana, Norma L. 1977. "The Acceptance of the Filipino 'POP' Music." In *Sandiwa: National Music Festival*. Manila, PH: Folk Arts Theatre.

Santos, Ramon. 1994. *MUSIKA: An Essay on the American Colonial and Contemporary Traditions in Philippine Music*. Manila: Cultural Center of the Philippines.

PINOY RAP, PHILIPPINES

Filipino rap, also known as Pinoy rap, uses English, Filipino, and other Philippine languages such as Tagalog, Ilocano, Sebuano, Chavacano, and Taglish (a mix of English and Tagalog words). Igorot rap, from the Cordillera region and using the Ibaloi language, was released in 2008 by Gwyneth Recording Studio. Delivered in a half-spoken, half-sung, rhythmic manner, Pinoy rap tackles varied themes from seemingly trivial topics to serious ones, especially about love and sex. It is often rendered in storytelling style and characterized by irreverent and humorous wordplay. Pinoy rap is supported by an ostinato beat to provide a rhythmic drive and/or repetitive harmonic progression in moderate tempo. Other times, familiar popular melodies are appropriated to serve as points of interest. For example, the tune of the Beatles' "Yellow Submarine" is borrowed in the rendition of a Pinoy rap entitled "Sinabmarine" by Andrew E.

"Na onseng delight" ("Scammed Delight"), in 1980, is the earliest recorded Pinoy rap, released by Wea Records. It gives advice on materialism and has been attributed to Dyords Javier (born George Javier). About the same time, pioneering rapper Vincent Daffalong released an Alpha Record album entitled *Okay sa-rap* (*Okay with Rap*), including the song "Mahiwagang nunal" ("Miraculous Mole"), which talks about Filipino beliefs on moles.

Pinoy rap entered the mainstream through matinee idol Francis M (born Francis Magalona, 1964–2009), with his debut rap album entitled *Yo!*, which included "Mga kababayan ko" ("My Countrymen"). Expressing his love of country as a Filipino, Francis M used both English and Tagalog. Another early exponent of Pinoy rap is Andrew E (born Andrew Espiritu, 1967–) who gave Filipino listeners his blunt yet funny advice with a rap in 1990 entitled "*Humanap ka ng panget*" ("Look for Someone Ugly").

By mid-1995, Andrew E founded a rap recording label called DongaloWreckords, where he produced new talents like Salbakuta with a debut single entitled "Stupid Love." Some female rappers also rose to popularity, like MC Lara (born Glenda Resureccion), Lady Diane, and Julie Ann San Jose (1994–), who was paired with Elmo Magalona (1994–), son of Francis M, who passed away in 2009.

Gloc 9 (born Aristotle Pollisco, 1977–) is undeniably the most highly acclaimed Filipino rapper in the country today. An award-winning artist, he paid tribute to his mentor Francis M with "Alalay ng hari" in 2012. For the most part, Gloc 9 songs tackle social issues such as poverty, corruption, and patriotism. Among the prominent rap songs with relatively wide viewing on YouTube are Bass Rhyme Posse's "Buhay estudyante" ("Student Life"), Mastaplann's "Is It Tyme," Death Threat's "Gusto kong bumaet" ("I Want to Be Good"), Legit Misfitz "Air chinelas" ("Slippers"), Chavacano group Rapasia's "Hoy! Tsismosa" ("Hey! Gossiper"), and Greyhoundz' "Ang bagong ako" ("The New Me"). It is important to mention that Pinoy rap is used as a medium of expression among Filipino American youth to articulate their culture and identity.

Rap contests are much-awaited events among amateur rappers. Known as Fliptop battles or simply Fliptop, they involve two rappers throwing invectives at each other within a time limit. Coming from the word "flip," it means to toss back the insults to the competitor. A panel of judges selects the winner after three rounds. The aim of Fliptop participants is to discredit the competitor's viewpoint by insulting him with offensive words and vulgar phrases. The recitation of rap is unaccompanied and thus more flexible with loose rhythm and structure. Local rappers generally use the Filipino language; English is employed when competing with international participants. Fliptop audiences laugh, jeer, and clap as the battle progresses. Each member of the panel of judges explains how he or she voted at the end of the battle. A referee is present to maintain order. Fliptop events are uploaded on the website Fliptop-Battle.com, which was founded in 2010 by rapper Anygma (born Alaric Riam Yuson, 1989–). It is one of the most subscribed-to sites in the country today and is shared on YouTube as well.

Felicidad A. Prudente

See also: Pinoy Jazz, Philippines; Pinoy Rap, Philippines; Pinoy Rock, Philippines

Further Reading

Bass, Angela. 2010. "Hip-Hop: It's the Dash in "Filipeanut-American." *Berkeley Journalism.* http://escholarship.org/uc/item/2n87c0zn. Accessed November 26, 2015.

Santos, Ramon. 1994. *MUSIKA: An Essay on the American Colonial and Contemporary Traditions in Philippine Music.* Manila: Cultural Center of the Philippines.

PINOY ROCK, PHILIPPINES

Pinoy rock is a term that encompasses diverse sounds and styles to include pop rock, punk, new wave, heavy metal, ska, reggae, and alternative rock. It is a hybrid music, with American and British bands serving as models or a springboard toward the creation of local sounds. For example, early American and British musicians in the late 1950s that had an impact on the local scene were Elvis Presley, Cliff Richard, the Shadows, and the Ventures, to name a few. As in the rest of the popular-music world, the 1960s was dominated by the Beatles. Pinoy rock is best identified with the use of the Filipino language and other native tongues, such as Tagalog, Cebuano, and Kapampangan. The English language is likewise used.

Considered a pioneer in Pinoy rock bands, Ramon "RJ" Jacinto (1945–) is a musician, entrepreneur, and founder of radio station DZRJ, which introduced rock music to Filipino listeners in the 1960s. He is also known for his band RJ and the Riots, which initially played the latest rock music from abroad. A legendary Pinoy rock group is the Juan dela Cruz Band, which was formed in 1968 by Wally Gonzalez and later joined by singer-drummer Joey "Pepe" Smith (1947–) and bassist Mike Hanopol (1946–). In 1973 the group premiered their original song "Himig natin" ("Our Hymn"), which to this day is considered *the* Pinoy rock anthem. The name "Manila sound" emerged in the 1970s, with songs composed by the Hotdogs, a band formed by brothers Dennis and Rene Garcia together with Louie Nepomuceno and Tito del Rosario. They gained popularity with their light and short melodic phrases, which characterized their compositions, such as "Manila," "Ikaw ang Miss Universe" ("You Are Miss Universe"), and "Annie Batungbakal." Most of the Hotdogs' songs tell about Filipino lifestyles in a fun and humorous way.

Under martial law in the 1970s, Philippines produced folk rock bands and singers who were at the forefront of political demonstrations and protests. Social commentary songs animated the music scene with performances of bands and musicians during rallies, like Asin, The Jerks, Grupong Pendong, Sampaguita, Jess Santiago, and Paul Galang. The 1978 debut album of Asin (meaning "salt"), formed by Mike Pillora Jr. and Cesar Bañares Jr. and later joined by Lolita Carbon and Pendong Aban Jr., introduced the use of indigenous musical instruments such as gongs (*kulintang*) and bamboo Jew's harps (*kubing*) in the song "Ang bayan kong sinilangan" ("The Country Where I Was Born"). Other artists followed suit, like Heber Bartolome (1948–), Joey Ayala (1956–), Grace Nono, and Bob Aves; they, together with Asin, are considered exponents of what is labeled today as "alternative music" and features the use of folk instruments and materials.

The progressive band called The Jerks, formed in 1979 by Chicoy Pura and guitarist Jun Lopito, likewise made a mark in the Pinoy rock scene with their nationalistic songs, particularly "Reklamo ng reklamo" ("Complaining Incessantly"), which won the 1998 NU Rock Awards for Best Album and the 1998 Katha Award for Best Rock Song. New socially relevant songs by composers like Noel Cabangon (1960–) carry on the tradition with street concerts and campus tours around the country.

Pinoy rock bands prevailed in the 1980s and 1990s with The Dawn, Introvoys, AfterImage, Eraserheads, and Rivermaya among the most prominent. Songs such as "Enveloped Ideas" (1986) by The Dawn and "Line to Heaven" (1993) by the Introvoys continue to be heard in retro concerts today. Commercially successful songs of AfterImage included "Habang may buhay" ("While There's Life"), "Next in Line," and "Mangarap ka" ("You Dream"). The group was named Artist of the Year by NU Rock Awards in 1994 and followed that up with a 1995 Awit Award for Album of the Year for their second album, entitled *Tag-ulan, tag-araw* (*Rainy Day, Summer Day*).

The Eraserheads formed in 1989 with members Ely Buendia (1970–), Raimund Marasigan (1971–), Buddy Zabala (1971–), and Marcus Adoro (1971–). They stood out as the most influential and multiawarded group of the late 1990s, receiving the Viewer's Choice Award for Asia from the 1997 MTV Video Music Awards. Their debut album, entitled *Ultraelectromagneticpop!*, was a smash hit in 1993 and was NU Rock Awards Album of the Year in 1994. Many more awards followed, namely the Guillermo Memorial Award, Awit Awards, and Katha Music Awards. Eraserheads disbanded in 2002, and the band was honored with the Hall of Fame Award at the NU Rock Awards in 2003.

Another multiawarded band is Parokya ni Edgar, which was formed in 1993. Led by vocalist Alfonso "Chito" Miranda Jr. (1976–), they continue to earn recognition. Among their awards are the NU Rock Award for Best New Artist in 1996 and three-time Artist of the Year in 1999, 2000, and 2003. The song "Mr. Suave" earned three Awit Awards in 2004 for Record of the Year, Best Music Video Performance, and Best Novelty Recording, while "Paki-usap lang" ("Please Let Us Talk) was Best Song of the Year in 2011. They also won an MTV Video Music Award, the International Viewer's Choice Award for MTV Southeast Asia for "Harana" ("Serenade") in 1999. Local media call Parokya ni Edgar the "National Band of the Philippines" (*Pambansang banda ng Pilipinas*) for these achievements. Sharing the title is Rivermaya, which continues to be a leader in the Pinoy rock scene. Formed in 1994, the group is currently composed of Mark Escueta (1976–), Mike Elgar (1976–), Ryan Peralta, and Norby David. Their album *Free* was Best Album of the Year at the NU Rock Awards in 2000. Among the most popular of Rivermaya songs on YouTube, with more than 2 million views, are "Himala" ("Miracle"), "Kisapmata" ("Blink of an Eye"), "Liwanag sa dilim" ("Light in the Dark"), "Your Song," and "Okay lang ako" ("I'm Okay"). They were also commissioned to compose the Southeast Asian Games athletes' anthem, entitled "Posible" ("Possible"), in 2005.

The underground scene received some attention in the 1990s with amateur bands playing at selected music bars like Club Dredd (formerly Red Rocks) and Kampo, both located in Quezon City and Sazi's (formerly Mayric's) in Manila. In addition, the advocacy of radio station NU107.5 to provide airtime to unknown bands gave further rise to Pinoy rock groups with a wide array of musical substyles, such as hard rock, heavy metal, alternative rock, indie rock, punk rock, alternative punk, grunge, and the like. Promising rock bands continue to emerge in the local scene; among them are Pupil (formed by multiawarded artist Ely Buendia in 2005), Urbandub, Itchyworm, AgawAgimat, and the all-female band Tribal Fish, to name a few.

Felicidad A. Prudente

See also: Pinoy Jazz, Philippines; Pinoy Pop, Philippines; Pinoy Rap, Philippines

Further Reading

Anonymous. 1989. "Interview: Heber Bartolome." *Notes* 1: 31–37.
Santos, Ramon. 1994. *MUSIKA: An Essay on the American Colonial and Contemporary Traditions in Philippine Music.* Manila: Cultural Center of the Philippines.

POPULAR ALBUMS, AUSTRALIA

The 10 best-selling albums in Australia, as certified by the Australasian Recording Industry Association (ARIA) as of 2016 are, in order:

1. *Bat Out of Hell* (1977) by American singer-songwriter Meat Loaf, with sales of 1,750,000 nationally
2. *Whispering Jack* (1986) by Australian singer-songwriter John Farnham
3. *Brothers in Arms* (1985) by British rock band Dire Straits

4. *Gold: Greatest Hits* (1992) by Swedish rock group ABBA
5. *Thriller* (1982) by American vocalist, songwriter, and performer Michael Jackson (1958–2009)
6. *The Best of ABBA* (1975) by ABBA
7. *Come On Over* (1997) by Canadian Shania Twain
8. *Innocent Eyes* (2003) by Australian singer-songwriter and actor Delta Goodrem
9. *Greatest Hits* (1982) by British rock group Queen, with 1,050,000 copies sold
10. Sharing 10th place with over 980,000 units sold in Australia are four albums: *The Dark Side of the Moon* (1973) by British band Pink Floyd, *Grease: The Original Soundtrack from the Motion Picture* (1978) by various artists, *Jagged Little Pill* (1995) by Canadian Alanis Morissette, and *21* (2011) by British singer-songwriter Adele

Triple J's Hottest 100

Hailed as the world's largest "musical democracy," the Hottest 100 is a music poll that has been run by Triple J, the youth arm of federally funded Australian Broadcasting Corporation (ABC), since 1989. The poll began as a list of listeners' all-time favorite songs, but, realizing that these were unlikely to shift significantly each year, the station relaunched the poll in 1993 to count down the favorite songs of that calendar year only. The annual countdown is held on Australia Day (January 26) each year. Since the 1990s, Hottest 100 parties have become part of the national tradition for many young Australians. The poll provides the soundtrack and the momentum for these parties.

Although the countdown features songs from around the world, its coincidence with one of Australia's national holidays—together with the fact that it is run by the national broadcaster, which has a specific charter to promote Australian identity and culture—results in fervor for and promotion of Australian artists who succeed in placing in the poll. Between 1993 and 2014, 11 Australian artists have won the No. 1 spot. The first Australian song to win was Spiderbait's "Buy Me a Pony" in 1996; the most recent was Chet Faker's "Talk Is Cheap" in 2014.

Triple J's musical programming focuses on predominantly "alternative" or independent musicians rather than mainstream pop artists, which results in a hit list very different to mainstream charts for pop music. This programming has also led to allegations of "hipsterism" and musical snobbery as well as criticisms against the poll's lack of gender diversity. In January 2015, a social media campaign to win American pop artist Taylor Swift a place in the Hottest 100 for 2014 was launched by a humorous article on global media site BuzzFeed, despite the fact that her music had never received airtime on Triple J. Swift's hit pop song "Shake It Off" was ultimately disqualified. In an official statement, Triple J praised Swift's music and successful career but highlighted that her entry—which researchers projected would reach the No. 12 slot—would have ousted a local independent artist and would not have accurately represented the station's hits and thus would not be in the spirit of the poll.

Jessica Carniel

Other best-selling albums in Australia performed by Australian artists include *Back in Black* (1980) by AC/DC, the self-titled album *Savage Garden* (1997) by Savage Garden, *Don't Ask* (1994) by Tina Arena, and *Recurring Dream: The Very Best of Crowded House* (1996) by Australian/New Zealand band Crowded House.

Australian plumber John Farnham's (1947–) career as a pop singer began in 1967 with the novelty song "Sadie (The Cleaning Lady)," with No. 1 hit singles following in four successive decades. Delta Goodrem was an actress on Australian popular television soap opera *Neighbours*, winning a Logie Award for Best New Talent before turning to a music recording career at age 15. She also starred in the movie *Hating Alison Ashley* (2005) and featured as a coach on Australian talent series *The Voice: Australia* in 2012. Tina Arena began her showbiz career at age seven on the television series *Young Talent Time* (1971–1988, 2012) and after a successful solo career and album sales over 8 million, she returned as a judge on the 2012 revival of the iconic show.

Best-selling Singles in Australia

Best-selling singles in Australia include "Party Rock Anthem" (2014) by LMFAO with 1,050,000 units sold, "Candle in the Wind 1997 (Goodbye England's Rose)" (1997) by Sir Elton John, "Somebody That I Used to Know" (2011) by Australian artist Gotye (featuring Kimbra), "Moves Like Jagger" (2014) by Maroon 5 (featuring Christina Aguilera), "Sexy and I Know It" (2014) by LMFAO, and "Roar" (2014) by Katy Perry. Songs that have sold over 630,000 copies in Australia include "Gangnam Style" (2013) by Psy, "Battle Scars" (2013) by Australian singer-songwriter Guy Sebastian (featuring Lupe Fiasco), "Blurred Lines" (2014) by Robin Thicke (featuring T.I. and Pharrell), "Call Me Maybe" (2013) by Carly Rae Jepsen, "Happy" (2014) by Pharrell Williams, and "Love the Way You Lie" (2013) by Eminem (featuring Rihanna).

Notably, the solo hit single "Chandelier" by Adelaide singer-songwriter Sia (born Sia Kate Isobelle Furler, 1975–) went four times platinum, selling 280,000 copies in Australia. At the 2015 APRA (Australasian Performing Rights Association) Awards, Sia was named Australia's top songwriter for the third consecutive year. Sia has written songs for Rihanna, Beyoncé, Britney Spears, Christina Aguilera, and Katy Perry.

Belgian-born Australian singer-songwriter Gotye (born Wouter "Wally" De Backer, 1980–) was a member of the Melbourne-based alternative indie-pop band The Basics before embarking on a solo career, finding worldwide success with the song "Somebody That I Used to Know" (2011) with New Zealand singer Kimbra Lee Johnson.

Born in Malaysia in 1981, Guy Sebastian's family relocated to Melbourne and later Adelaide, Australia. In 2003 Sebastian was the first winner of the *Australian Idol* television series (2003–2009), and from 2010 to 2012 he was a judge on the Australian vocalist talent-scouting series *The X Factor*. His career includes six No. 1 singles and two No. 1 albums, with album sales of 1,150,000. Sebastian was also announced as Australia's first official entry in the Eurovision Song Contest in 2015.

Iconic Australian Popular Songs

In 2011 *Australian Geographic* magazine proposed a list of the 15 most iconic Aussie songs of all time. The list includes "True Blue" (1981) by folk singer John Williamson, exploring icons of Australian culture, including mateship (loyalty to friends), cockatoos (a type of Australian bird that makes a particularly annoying screech), sponge cake (a crucial ingredient in lamingtons, a traditional homemade Australian snack cake similar to Hostess Twinkies), "smoko" (a cigarette break during work), Vegemite (a savory spread eaten on toast or in sandwiches and made of yeast extract derived from the beer-making process). "Down Under" (1980) by Men at Work also includes classic Aussie iconography, namely references to a run-down Volkswagon Kombi van (a traditional surfer's vehicle), Vegemite sandwiches, and flowing beer and vomit (i.e., to "chunder" means to vomit). "Khe Sanh" (1978) by pub rock band Cold Chisel conveys the reminiscences of an Australian Vietnam War (1955–1975) veteran suffering from posttraumatic stress disorder and drug abuse, with thematic similarities to the Bruce Springsteen song "Born in the USA" (1984).

In 2001, to celebrate APRA's 75th anniversary, 100 members of APRA also voted for the top 30 ("best and most significant") Australian songs (from 1926–2001), a list that included "Friday on My Mind' (1966) by The Easybeats; "Eagle Rock" (1971) by Daddy Cool; "Down Under" (1980) by Men at Work; the humorous "Pub with No Beer" (1957) by Australian country singer Slim Dusty; "Long Way to the Top" (1975) by AC/DC, about the numerous lifestyle problems involved in attaining success for a rock band; "Beds Are Burning" (1987) by Midnight Oil, a political protest song about Australian aboriginal land rights; and the Australian aboriginal-language protest song "Treaty" (1991) by indigenous band Yothu Yindi.

Notably, the lead singer of iconic Australian rock band Midnight Oil (1973–2002), environmental activist Peter Garrett, was also elected to the House of Representatives (the lower house of the bicameral Parliament of Australia) from 2004 to 2013, and in 2003 was granted membership of the Order of Australia "for service to the community as a prominent advocate for environmental conservation and protection, and to the music industry" (Australian Government 2003). In 2012 the members of Yothu Yindi were also inducted into the ARIA Hall of Fame, performing their hit single "Treaty" (1991).

J. T. Velikovsky

See also: Popular Transmedia, Australia (Chapter 5: Internet and Social Media)

Further Reading

"APRA's Ten Best Australian Songs." 2001. www.debbiekruger.com/pdfs/apratenbest.pdf. Accessed March 28, 2016.

Dale, D. 2010. *The Little Book of Australia: A Snapshot of Who We Are*. Crows Nest, AU: Allen & Unwin.

Australian Government. 2003. "It's an Honour: Australia Celebrating Australians." http://www
.itsanhonour.gov.au/honours/honour_roll/search.cfm?aus_award_id=1043291&search
_type=advanced&showInd=true. Accessed March 28, 2016.
National Geographic. 2011. "Iconic Aussie Songs." www.australiangeographic.com.au/blogs
/ag-blog/2011/01/top-10-classic-aussie-songs. Accessed March 28, 2016.

POPULAR MUSIC, MONGOLIA

Music and politics have often been linked in 20th-century Mongolia. Despite the country's relative isolation after its socialist revolution in 1921, Mongolia was exposed to Western popular music, especially starting in the late 1950s. Mongolians who traveled to the West smuggled in records or tapes, and students and officials who traveled to the Soviet Union or Eastern Europe in the 1960s and 1970s were, in addition, introduced to Western popular music from their socialist allies. Young people in particular knew the music of such bands as the Beatles and the Rolling Stones, which also ushered in an interest in Western hair and clothing styles.

Recognizing the attraction of Western rock music and hip-hop and such accoutrements as dungarees, the Mongolian authorities attempted to co-opt these potentially subversive musical forms. They selected and supported a group of bands, including Soyol Erdene (Cultural Jewel) and Bayan Mongol (Rich Mongolia), which acquiesced to the government's and the socialist Mongolian People's Revolutionary Party's agendas and choice of venues. If the bands and performers agreed to such limitations, the government provided specific benefits, including salaries, opportunities to record, and concerts. Their repertoire would include romantic songs but also evocations of the Mongolian countryside and messages concerning socialism and current political campaigns. Their musical instruments ranged from brass, electric organ, and bass to guitar and drums.

Yet as *perestroika* (or "restructuring of the economy") and *glasnost* (or "openness and greater freedom of expression") gained favor in the Soviet Union with the rise of Mikhail Gorbachev in 1985, these trends reached Mongolian political and social life and reverberated in the musical scene. New groups, which did not necessarily abide by government dictates, arose. They claimed influences from an astonishing variety of singers, including Bon Jovi, Whitney Houston, ABBA, and Rod Stewart, among others. Khonkh (Bell), one of these groups, performed at the demonstrations from December 1989 to March 1990, which culminated in the collapse of socialism and the one-party political system. Their songs became somewhat of an anthem of the large contingents of youth who helped bring down the government.

The euphoria that attended the successful overthrow of the government quickly eroded, with a disastrous economic collapse in the early 1990s and the ensuing elimination of state subsidies. Because rural areas could not afford to pay performers, bands were limited to the capital city of Ulaanbaatar. The musicians themselves faced enormous challenges. Rents for sound equipment, concert halls, and musical instruments all skyrocketed, and lax enforcement of government copyright laws impinged upon musicians' incomes. The earlier government support vanished, compelling performers to manage their own finances, set up their own concerts, and obtain their own equipment, while, at the same time, finding venues for rehearsals and working on their own compositions.

On the other hand, musicians had greater freedom. Bands could select their own names. A hard-rock group called itself Kharanga, which is a gong used in Buddhist monasteries. The designation Chinggis Khan—also the name of Ulaanbaatar's airport, a hotel, a vodka, Ulaanbaatar's main square, a beer, and numerous other objects—was used by a popular group. Performers joined together to form a Mongolian Singers' Union in 1998, and an annual award ceremony for music, known as the Pentatonic, garnered additional publicity, making popular stars out of Sarantuya (or Saara), Jargalsaikhan, Oyunaa, and Ariunaa, who called herself the "Mongolian Madonna." In addition, the second or third generation of several traditional musicians actually experimented with or became totally identified with rock music. Nightclubs and bars often supplanted concert halls as venues for popular music.

The most significant development has been the sponsorship of businesses and political parties. Companies that wish to cater to a youth market have recognized the value of rock groups in advertising their products. Firms selling clothing, cars, liquor, and beauty and health products have provided the funds needed by the bands, which profit from the relatively small segment of the population that has prospered and can afford the luxury products purveyed by these businesses. Politicians who seek to attract young people have recruited popular bands to perform at campaign rallies and in advertisements.

The question that confronts these performers concerns their branding. How can they borrow foreign musical forms and yet retain their Mongolian heritage and identity? Is it sufficient to perform songs about Mongolian heroes, pastoral lifestyle, or romances relating to herders? A few musicians have attempted to overcome criticism that they adhere to Western musical styles and ignore Mongolian traditions by incorporating Mongolian songs and musical instruments in their performances. Throat singing and horse-head fiddle playing, two practices that reflect Mongolian traditions and are often portrayed as national symbols, are mixed with a variety of rock music forms. Some performers don Mongolian clothing, including the *deel*, a long robe made of fur-lined sheepskin with a sash, and one even dressed like one of Chinggis Khan's soldiers. Is this sufficient as an affirmation of Mongolian history and heritage?

A few performers went to extremes in adopting the Western rap medium and linking it to greater pride in Mongolian national concerns. Although their themes touched on government corruption, inequality, and other social ills, they tended to emphasize love and its vagaries. They incorporated Mongolian folk music and melodies in their dances, songs, and performances, but their appearance often overshadowed their themes and music. Punk hair, pierced ears and other body parts, tattoos, jewelry, and outlandish clothing attracted considerable attention, and the rap lyrics, spoken or sung aggressively, with occasional pornographic content, perhaps had a greater effect on their audiences than their social critiques. A commercialized and popularized form of gangsta rap has also been introduced. Concerts and videos, which actually reach a wider audience, have made these rappers better known among Mongolian youth. However, some critics have asserted that gangsta rap has little resonance with Mongolian society and merely imitates American groups. They state that the gangsta rappers have not had the same ghetto experiences as their American counterparts, as most of the Mongolian performers come from middle-class backgrounds. The controversy about the authenticity of the songs they produce continues to swirl in music circles. Similarly, the relation of hip-hop to Mongolian culture has also been questioned. Is it an artificial form imported from the West, or can it reflect the genuine Mongolian heritage?

Traditional folk music had posed problems during the socialist era. The principal musical instruments and forms, the horse-head fiddle (*morin khuur*), the long song (*urtiin duu*), and the short song (*bogino duu*), dealt with pastoral life, love, religion, and the unique Mongolian heritage and history. Yet socialism demanded a link between politics and music and the other arts. Music had to represent the interests of the formerly oppressed social classes. The socialist government devised a plan for using traditional songs and musical instruments to foster nationalism and the interests of the state, selected specific songs, and supervised the content of lyrics. Performers adhered to these ideological objectives and received government patronage. Similarly, the state supported throat singing, or overtone singing (*khömii*), as long as it abided by government strictures. It also included the approved music and lyrics in classes at schools and universities.

The collapse of socialism in 1990 reduced or, in some cases, eliminated government subsidies and created difficulties for singers and musicians. Foreigners initially helped to preserve throat singing, long songs, and *morin khuur* orchestras. Japanese, Korean, and Western producers and impresarios have invited a few of the leading performers to give concerts abroad. Later, Mongolian companies and political parties began to provide funds for some ensembles, allowing them to survive.

Morris Rossabi

See also: Popular Music, Uyghur

Further Reading

Marsh, Peter. 2006. "Global Hip-Hop and Youth Cultural Politics in Urban Mongolia." In *Mongolian Culture and Society in the Age of Globalization*. Ed. Henry Schwarz, 127–160. Bellingham, WA: Center for East Asian Studies, Western Washington University.

Marsh, Peter. 2009. *The Horse-Head Fiddle and the Cosmopolitan Reimagination of Tradition in Mongolia*. London: Routledge.

Pegg, Carole. 2001. *Mongolian Music, Dance, & Oral Narrative*. Seattle: University of Washington Press.

Rossabi, Morris. 2005. *Modern Mongolia: From Khans to Commissars to Capitalists*. Berkeley: University of California Press.

POPULAR MUSIC, NORTH KOREA

Popular music is everywhere in North Korea, officially called the Democratic People's Republic of Korea (DPRK). It is played in homes and public spaces, and North Korean people of all ages adore certain songs more than others, just like people do in other parts of the world. North Korea's popular music is a large artistic production, but it is not driven by commercialism, which is a key distinction. Rather, the government, schools, and the Korean Workers' Party (the ruling party) cooperate to produce music, while keeping in mind the taste of the public and the political climate. Music is free to all, but North Korea's production system censors the content of both music and performance (but all popular music is, to an extent, censored). The popularity of a song is determined not so much by sales but by public response, and some performers even achieve the status of stardom. Because of the state's involvement, North Korea's popular music is different from the market-based popular music more common in the world, but it is similar in that the public ultimately chooses what songs to enjoy, despite the censorship. At the same time, outside the official world, through private networks, the people of North Korea enjoy bootleg music from unexpected places like South Korea, the United States, and Europe.

Popular music in North and South Koreas is called *taejung kayo*, which means "song of the masses." Immediately after the Korean peninsula was divided in 1945 by the Soviet Union (occupying the northern half) and the United States (occupying the southern half), the nascent North Korean state began commissioning music for the ordinary people. This activity became more systematic after the DPRK was established in 1948. The government reorganized the artistic world and supported artists to create a new socialist future. Many songwriters and singers started their careers during the colonial period (1910–1945), when Korea was a colony of the Japanese Empire. Some were sent to the Soviet Union to further their study. In the beginning, the artists of North Korea's musical landscape were a diverse group, ranging from those who loudly supported the socialist regime to those who were forced to stay in the country. The diversity soon disappeared as the artistic ideology of socialist realism dictated what music was best for a country facing revolutionary changes. Music was now to be produced with two aims: reflect the experience of ordinary people and motivate the nation with revolutionary messages.

An interesting case is the life of the composer Kim Sunnam (1917–1983; Kim is the family name, which is written first in East Asia). Kim was born in Seoul during Korea's colonial period and went to Japan as a young adult to study music, where he became interested in writing music containing radical, leftist ideas, or what can be termed "proletarian music." As a member of a socialist party in Seoul, he moved northward to North Korea in 1945 when the peninsula became divided. In 1952 he went to the Soviet Union to study the music of socialism pioneered by the Russian composer Dmitri Shostakovich (1906–1975), who recognized Kim's talent. Kim's career in North Korea, however, was tumultuous, as he fell out of favor with the dominant Kim Il Sung faction. He was reinstated in the 1960s, but Kim Jong Il (Kim Il Sung's son and the next leader) also saw Kim Sunnam as unfit and banned his music in the 1970s. In the past two decades, his music has received more recognition in South Korea. His music ranges from folk songs and operas to symphonies and complex modernist compositions, some of which can be sampled on the Internet. The song "Sanyuhwa" ("Mountain Flower"), based on the poem of Kim Sowŏl, is especially gorgeous.

As a system supported and censored by the government, North Korea's popular music today is officially guided by a body of music theory written by Kim Jong Il. *The Theory on Music*, written in 1991, outlines what role music plays for the nation, what message it should give to the people, and which style is best for the national situation. Kim Jong Il's music theory, in turn, is based on the ideological philosophy of the founding leader Kim Il Sung, which is called Juche (*Chuch'e*). Juche's main idea is self-reliance, and this idea applies to the individual, the nation, and the state. All music in North Korea is hence Juche music, with the aim of spreading the message of self-reliance. Performers, too, are considered human vehicles of delivering the principles of Juche. They are discovered while they are children and begin their afterschool training at special art institutions. The Children's Palace in the capital city of Pyongyang is the best of these institutions. The often-sensationalized images of children singing, dancing, and playing instruments in perfect, robotic harmony are usually the images of children from this school. Collective performance is indeed emphasized, but it would be incomplete to see institutions like Children's Palace and precocious North Korean performers simply as instruments of the state and the party. Many countries recognize gifted children and have both public and private institutions for supporting their talent.

North Korea's most popular musical act in the 21st century is the all-women group Moranbong Akdan, known in English as Moranbong Band (*moranbong* means "peony hill," a historical place in central Pyongyang, and *akdan* means "band"). The band consists of 18 women who sing, dance, and play various instruments. They are all virtuosos. From percussion and guitar to violin and vocals, Moranbong Band is a complete (self-reliant!) entertainment package that can handle an array of musical genres. They hold dozens of concerts a year and even tour other countries. Their performance includes rock operas with a full-sound, four-piece song-and-dance routine and a cappellas. The members were trained in government-run arts programs from childhood and were selected by the country's leadership, which included the current leader Kim Jong Un (son of Kim Jong Il). In fact, performing for North Korea's wealthy and powerful is an important job of the band.

Moranbong Band's overall sound is undoubtedly modern and Western, and yet the content of nationalism and their melodramatic style render their final product uniquely North Korean. Since their debut in 2012, Moranbong Band has had a string of hits, including "Fluttering Red Flag," "Without a Break," and "Let's Learn." (Their live concerts can easily be found on the Internet.) The song "Let's Learn" was a big hit. The song is sung by five members who also perform a choreographed dance. To some, the effect is a little campy, but to turn away from the audiovisual spectacle is difficult: the audience is drawn to the performers. Regardless of the national context, and whether one agrees with the message or not, "Let's Learn" as popular music deploys its power to momentarily erase personal and cultural differences, quickly reaching the universal human sensation of enjoyment.

Cheehyung Harrison Kim

See also: Movies, North Korea (Chapter 3: Film)

Further Reading

Armstrong, Charles K. 2003. *The North Korean Revolution, 1945–1950*. Ithaca, NY: Cornell University Press.

Cumings, Bruce. 1997. *Korea's Place in the Sun: A Modern History*. New York: W. W. Norton.

Frank, Rüdiger, ed. 2010. *Exploring North Korean Arts*. Vienna, AT: Verlag für Moderne Kunst.

Kim, Cheehyung. 2012. "Total, Thus Broken: *Chuch'e Sasang* and North Korea's Terrain of Subjectivity." *The Journal of Korean Studies* 17, no. 1: 69–96.

POPULAR MUSIC, TIBET

Tibetan pop music first emerged in the 1980s and can be described as an assortment of Tibetan melodies played on Western instruments. It was initially inspired by sounds from China, Hong Kong, and Taiwan and gradually evolved into a unique style with distinct features, such as the rise from low to high pitch, the long-held pitch, and the incorporation of traditional Tibetan instrumentations. Like pop music everywhere, Tibetan pop also includes elements of a variety of musical genres, including rock, ballad, dance, pop-folk, and, more recently, rap. The lyrics can be Tibetan or Chinese. Unlike Western pop music, which is identified mainly with the younger generation, Tibetans of all ages listen to the Tibetan equivalent. Prominent singers include Yadong, Kunga, Tsewang Lhamo, and Sherten.

From the early 1950s onward, music has been used in China by the state as a way of promoting nationalism or to advance certain political ideas. This has been particularly true in the Tibetan areas, where until well into the 1980s almost all permitted songs and music celebrated themes such as the "liberation" of Tibet or expressed the "joy of the Tibetan people" at being united with China. These highly politicized songs were often performed by Tibetan singers, among whom the most prominent was Tseten Dolma, who performed at official concerts and events throughout China, becoming a persuasive representation for many Chinese of Tibetans' gratitude to the Communist Party.

Very often, these propaganda songs incorporated Tibetan tunes or themes, or were traditional folk songs rewritten with socialist lyrics, accompanied with Western instrumentation. Songs of this kind were omnipresent during the Cultural Revolution (1966–1976), when songs about the party, revolutionary spirit, and collective unity were broadcast everywhere on a daily basis. As early as the 1930s, Chinese musicians had composed songs with Tibetan tunes or Tibetan themes, part of a conscious attempt to incorporate the Tibetans within the Nationalist

Party's conception of a multiethnic China. The PRC government was thus continuing the same use of music as a medium to propagate certain ideologies and values. But for Tibetans, whether or not they agreed with the content of such songs, for many it would have been the first time that they had heard such renditions of their traditional folk songs.

With the death of Mao Zedong in 1976 and the rise of Deng Xiaoping as China's paramount leader, Tibet also witnessed a period of reform. Certain sociopolitical changes were permitted, and Tibetan culture, religion, and language began to revive. The loosened policy enabled a resurgence of Tibetan identity and values, which could also be seen in the music scene. Two singers, Jampa Tsering and Dadron, were prominent in developing Tibetan-style pop music. The new form showed some influences from *gangtai* music—a Chinese compound term formed from the names of Hong Kong (Xiang*gang*) and *Tai*wan—which counted Deng Lijun, a Taiwanese singer, as one of the main representatives. The *gangtai* style features slow-paced, soft vocals in Chinese accompanied by Western instruments.

What was new about Jampa Tsering and Dadron's music was their assertion of "Tibetanness" in their songs. Most of their songs were sung in the Tibetan language, and the theme of their songs concerned the beauty of the Tibetan land and pride in the Tibetan culture. Furthermore, to emphasise her Tibetan identity, Dadron always performed on stage wearing her traditional Tibetan dress.

Most importantly, these songs did not contain any eulogies to the Communist Party or the Chinese state. Unlike the propaganda songs Tibetans had heard until then, these songs expressed individual feelings and longings that had long been suppressed, especially during the Cultural Revolution. Tibetans could identify with these songs, both in terms of values and experiences. Dadron, in particular, became well known throughout Tibet, but her career came to an end when she fled Lhasa for exile in 1992. The emergence of Tibetan pop was thus related to a motivation to create music that was Tibetan in values and modern in style.

After Dadron's flight to India, Tibetan singers from the former Tibetan provinces of Kham and Amdo—incorporated nowadays within the Chinese provinces of Sichuan, Gansu, Qinghai, and Yunnan—dominated the musical landscape. This shift in musical production to the peripheral areas may be explained as follows. From 1987 to 1989, Lhasa saw a series of large-scale pro-independence demonstrations that ultimately led to the imposition of martial law in March 1989. In 1992 Chen Kuiyuan, an ethnic Chinese official, became the party secretary of the Tibet Autonomous Region (TAR) and introduced more restrictions on religious and cultural freedom. Under such harsh conditions, it was hardly possible to produce any creative work. Another factor was the technological possibilities of the 1990s, which led to a further innovation in the Tibetan musical world: the making of music videos. Yadong, a native from Derge (Sichuan Province) and among the best-known Tibetan performers, for example, took advantage of this and was one of the first to produce music videos that depict colorful Tibetan festivals or picturesque Tibetan scenery.

The economic surge of the 1990s, which saw the emergence of record companies and new investors, also played a part in the emergence of new performers.

At the same time, Tibet became a favorite tourist destination for many Chinese urbanites as part of a general "Tibet fever" that spread throughout mainland China in the 1990s. Many Tibetan performers thus began to sing in Chinese to reach this audience. The lyrics of Yadong's two best-known songs, "Qingzang gaoyuan" ("The Tibetan Plateau") and "Xiangwang shenying" ("Yearning for the Divine Eagle"), for example, are in Chinese. All this meant that Tibetan pop music was disintegrating at the center but was revived from the periphery.

The singers who became known in the 1990s and 2000s include Yungdrung Gya (Chinese: Rongzhongerjia), Dechen Wangmo, Jamyang Dolma, Jamyang Kyi, and Chunshol Dolma.

In the late 1990s, another female vocalist appeared in the music scene. She went on to produce many hits and topped the charts in mainland China several times: Han Hong. Half Tibetan and half Chinese, she only sings in Chinese, but many of her early hits included Tibetan themes. Han Hong is still extremely popular in mainland China, but her popularity within the Tibetan audience cooled down after she started appearing in officially organized events and singing songs with propaganda contents, such as "Tianlu" ("Heavenly Road"), a ballad that celebrated the opening of a railway to Tibet in 2006.

In 2008 Tibet saw again large-scale protests and, since 2009, a wave of self-immolations in protest against Chinese rule. This defiance has been reflected in music production of that time, with many singers choosing bolder themes that assert their Tibetan identity and their political loyalties. Lyrics referring to the importance of the Tibetan language, urging Tibetans to maintain unity, and asserting pride in one's own culture started to come out of Tibet. Many singers also explicitly reverted to singing in Tibetan so as to promote their own language. Some singers even went further and referred to the self-immolations, Tibetan independence, or the Dalai Lama. At least 10 singers are known to have been arrested for having expressed views and sentiments that were deemed subversive by the Chinese authorities.

Popular music has thus become a channel to express dissent and to voice the hopes and aspirations of the Tibetan people in a context where direct expression is often dangerous or unpredictable. Whether as a form of cultural assertion or as an arena for political expression, Tibetan pop continues to develop as a diverse and vibrant art form.

Yangdon Dhondup

See also: Cinema, Tibet (Chapter 3: Film)

Further Reading

Dhondup, Yangdon. 2008. "Dancing to the Beat of Modernity: The Rise and Development of Tibetan Popular Music." In *Tibetan Modernities: Notes from the Field on Cultural and Social Change*. Ed. Robert Barnett and Ronald Schwartz, 285–304. Leiden, NL: Brill.

Diehl, Keila. 2002. *Echoes from Dharamsala. Music in the Life of a Tibetan Refugee Community*. Berkeley: University of California Press.

Tibet Information Network (TIN). 2004. *Unity and Discord: Music and Politics in Contemporary Tibet*. London: Tibet Information Network.

POPULAR MUSIC, UYGHUR

Uyghurs live primarily in the Xinjang Uyghur Autonomous Region of China. Music is one of the most highly valued parts of their popular culture. Nearly all events, public and private, include it in one form or another. Music, more than any other cultural genre, is what brings Uyghur traditions into the present and carries them into conversation with a diverse array of cosmopolitan cultural expressions. Over the past several decades, beginning with the professionalization of Uyghur "classical" music in the form of the 12 *muqam* and other folk genres, oral traditions have become a prominent source for use in popular music. Musicians have melded flamenco, blues, rock, and hip-hop styles with older local traditions in order to create a rich, Uyghur soundscape.

The Uyghur 12 *muqam* (hereafter, *muqam*), related to the improvisational, mode-based *maqam* found throughout the Muslim world, are often regarded as the classical music of the Uyghurs. Among contemporary Uyghurs, *muqam* refers to large, multihour "suites" of song, instrumental music, and dance set to both classic poetry and folk texts that have been edited continuously since the mid-20th century and made into a symbol of Uyghur history and identity. Professional *muqam* ensembles throughout Xinjiang, influenced by a push to combine "the local" with "the international" and "the Western," stage formal concerts in performance halls, performing in a grandiose style meant to represent the greatness of Uyghur music throughout the region, China, and the world. Individual musicians playing informally at social events, however, often perform *muqam* using texts that the ensembles have long discarded, singing and playing in a style fundamentally different from that which is on stage. Many see the *muqam*, particularly in its uninstitutionalized forms, as a type of "classical folk" music, part and parcel of other forms of music and cultural expression. Folk song, for its part, remains an important part of Uyghur musical life, sometimes staged but far more frequently performed in private gatherings among family and friends. Numerous regional styles of folk song, along with a broadly shared, pan-Uyghur repertoire numbering in the hundreds, are alternatingly playful and mournful, sometimes singing the whims of romantic love while at other times commemorating important historical events and/or ruminating on the pains of being separated from one's homeland.

Muqam and folk song play important roles in the contemporary Uyghur popular music scene and in several ways. One is through the setting of *muqam*-inspired melismas—which many people identify as a style unique to and producible only by Uyghurs—and texts in the melodies of newly composed songs. The work of Abdulla Abdurehim (1969–), "the King of Uyghur Pop," who has been performing since the 1990s, defines this style. Möminjan Ablikim (1976–), Shir'äli Ältekin (1976–), and countless younger performers are continuing to perform in this style, sometimes even singing *muqam* excerpts to the accompaniment of pop beats, working to develop a uniquely Uyghur form of popular musical expression. Folk song, similarly, is often set to driving, electronic beats on the keyboard and other electronic instruments. These forms of folk date back to the 1980s and are still wildly popular at weddings and in clubs throughout Xinjiang. The boundaries between genres are not hard and fast: single performers include *muqam*, folk song, and composed songs on their albums, a fact true of "traditional" performers such as Ayshigül Muhämmäd (1970–), Sänubär Tursun (1971–), and Abduqadir Yareli (1979–) as much as of more strictly "pop" artists.

Western pop music styles entered the Uyghur soundscape in the 1980s in the figure of Äkhmätjan (1969–1991), the first Uyghur rock star. A child prodigy and master of traditional Uyghur instruments, he discovered electric guitar and the rhythms of Turkish folk rock at the age of 17. Combining his previous training in Uyghur classical and folk music, over the next few years he transformed traditional Uyghur musical forms into rock operas by transposing them onto electric guitar. Although he died at the age of 22 from a heroin overdose, his legacy had a profound effect on later musicians, many of whom had only watched video recordings of his performances on grainy VHS cassettes.

One of the musicians who rose to prominence after Äkhmätjan was Äsqär Mämät (1964–), a Uyghur singer who moved to Beijing and was influenced by Han rockers such as Cui Jian (1961–). As one of only a few Uyghur musicians consciously writing and performing for cosmopolitan and non-Uyghur audiences, Äsqär had a tremendous effect on Uyghur musicians who followed him in breaking from more conventional forms of Uyghur music. For instance, in the early 2000s, one of the guitarists in Äsqär's band, Ärkin Abdulla (1978–), began to mix particular traditional compositional forms, rhythms, and instrumental arrangements with the novo flamenco stylings of the Gypsy Kings. By the end of the decade, he was the most famous flamenco guitarist in China. Ärkin sang many of his songs in Chinese and became an inspiration for a generation of young, urbane Uyghur men and women to build their identities through Turkish and European borrowings. The Uyghur blues singer Pärhat Khaliq (1982–) also followed this model by building up his persona first as a Uyghur singer in the German rock scene and then finding a nationwide following as a finalist on the TV show *The Voice of China* in 2014.

One of the more recent phenomena to emerge was the arrival of hip-hop music and fashion. One of the first crews to receive a large measure of success among urban Uyghur youth was the group Six City (Altä Shähär). Many of their most popular songs were remixes of folk songs set to hip-hop rhythms with hooks built out of the original melodies. More than anything, disenfranchised youth from the cities seemed to identify with the attitude of defiance and refashioned dignity that comes from hip-hop comportments. Another major figure in the new pop scene is the self-styled singer Ablajan Awut Ayup (1984–). Mixing influences like Michael Jackson, Justin Bieber, K-pop, and mainstream Chinese pop with Uyghur poetry, Ablajan has become popular with young listeners, for whom he projects an image of success and sophistication that many find enticing.

Uyghur musicians draw on tradition in order to produce shared visions of both the past and the future. Popular musicians draw on the past (*muqam*, folk song, other oral forms) as a source of compositional creativity that appeals to a mass Uyghur audience; traditional performers seek to modernize their performance idioms, bringing them in line with international standards; flamenco and blues guitarists actively traditionalize their music as a way of bringing tradition into conversation with otherwise unconnected musical genres. As scholars have suggested, Uyghur music enables Uyghurs from diverse locations to identify with each other through a shared musical experience. Furthermore, others have argued, the way musicians meld elements of Uyghur musicality to Western classical music standards and new genres such as hip-hop and flamenco builds a sense of cosmopolitan and transnational belonging.

Darren Byler and Elise Anderson

See also: Alternative Music Scenes, China; Ethnic Music, China; Popular Music, Mongolia

Further Reading

Harris, Rachel. 2001. "Cassettes, Bazaars and Saving the Nation: The Uyghur Music Industry in Xinjiang, China." In *Global Goes Local: Popular Culture in Asia*. Ed. Tim Craig and Richard King, 265–83. Vancouver, CA: University of British Columbia Press.

Light, Nathan. 2008. *Intimate Heritage: Creating Uyghur Muqam Song in Xinjiang*. Berlin: Lit Verlag/Transaction Publishers.

Smith-Finley, Joanne N. 2013. *The Art of Symbolic Resistance: Uyghur Identities and Uyghur-Han Relations in Contemporary Xinjiang*. Leiden, NL: Brill Press.

Wong, Chuen-Fung. 2013. "Singing Muqam in Uyghur Pop: Minority Modernity and Popular Music in China." *Popular Music and Society* 36, no. 1: 98–118.

PROTEST MUSIC, INDONESIA

One of the functions of music is as a form of communication. It can be used to express ideas and feelings. Indonesia has an abundance of political music. This has something to do with the long history of Indonesia, in which there was often a lack of freedom of speech. Indonesia has experienced repression under both colonialism and independent nationhood. Freedom of speech was uncommon, as public presses and medias were under surveillance and censored by the government until the late 1990s. Dissatisfaction and protest were expressed in some of the songs written by Indonesian musicians.

Protest lyrics were sometimes expressed in a mild way, almost like complaining more than protesting, for example, "someone was shot to death" and "so many greedy people in my home country." However, some others were braver in expressing their protest.

In the late 1990s, student protests were happening all over Indonesia, so that finally the president, Soeharto, had to step down after ruling Indonesia for more than 30 years, since 1965. Protest songs sung by student protesters served to inspire and encourage them to complete their mission.

Some well-known musical groups and musicians noted as singers of protest songs are Iwan Fals, SWAMI, Harry Roesli, and Efek Rumah Kaca. Efek Rumah Kaca wrote a song that was related to the killing of Munir, who was murdered

The Indonesian singer-songwriter Iwan Fals has been compared to the American icon of folk music, Bob Dylan. His hugely popular music includes love ballads set to beautiful melodies, but also songs of social criticism and protest. (Jeff Aries/ZUMA Press/Corbis)

for his activities working in a nongovernmental organization (NGO) that was promoting human rights. The song told a story of strength and belief in the power of human righteousness in the face of social injustice that can never be stopped by anyone, including the military.

Iwan Fals is a well-known singer who often sings about the social and political situation. He is very sensitive to people's problems, and many of his songs exasperate the authorities. Some well-known songs he has written are "Umar Bakri" (a name of a teacher living a simple, humble life), "Aku penyanyi jalanan" ("I Am the Street Singer"), "Air mata api" ("Tears of Fire"), "Badut" ("Clown"), "Balada orang-orang pedalaman" ("Hinterland People Ballad"), "Balada pengangguran" ("Jobless People Ballad"), "Bangunlah putra-putri pertiwi" ("Wake Up, Children of the Nation!"), "Bento" ("Stupid"), "Demokrasi otoriter" ("Authoritarian Democracy"), and many more.

SWAMI is a band that sang a very powerful song entitled "Bongkar" ("Demolish!" Or it could have another meaning: "Uncover!"). People believe that it was written by one of the musicians of SWAMI, Iwan Fals, because he has been well known for his protest songs for a long time in Indonesia. "Bongkar" is a song of protest against the government being ruled by people who were thought to be too powerful and exerted complete control over the nation's assets. Iwan was inspired to write this song by the situation of the government planning to flood a whole village in Kedung Ombo to make a new dam.

"Bongkar" was sung by many protesters for many years and continues to be sung today. The lyrics are such an inspiration for protesters: "(Now) we have to go down the street, to knock down the satans who are standing in open wide straddled legs."

Protest songs became very common after the late 1970s, during the Soeharto era. One example of a protest song, in 1978, is "Aje gile," which was written in a very straightforward and brave lyrical style by Mogi Darusman. His genre of songwriting is associated with rock music. He was not alone at that time. There were several others who had sociopolitical protest themes in their songs, such as Remy Sylado and Harry Roesli, who severely objected to the culture of corruption in

Soeharto's era. In 1978 musical artist Mogi Darusman wrote "Rayap-rayap" ("The Termites"), a satirical song about corrupt people that was banned by the attorney general under the command of Soeharto. This is one of the lyrics of the song: "*Kau tahu rayap-rayap / makin banyak di mana-mana / di balik baju resmi / merongrong tiang negara*" ("You know the termites / there are so many everywhere / behind the formal attire / eating the pillar of the country").

However, not all music in Indonesia at that time had protest lyrics; some others enjoyed "normal" songs, such as those sung by the pop bands Koes Plus, Favorite Group, D'Lloyd, The Mercy's, and Panbers, who were very popular at that time. Meanwhile, student protest songs proliferated, triggered by Soeharto wanting to continue to rule the country by decree and by his national policy of development and modernization by using foreign loans.

Soeharto responded to the student protests by applying "campus life normalization" and "students coordination body." These policies meant that the military was free to go into campuses, and student protesters were sent to prisons. Later, Iwan Fals wrote songs for those students who were forcibly relocated to faraway frontiers and those who were sent to jails. His songs were famous in the 1980s and were still being sung by many student protesters into the late 1990s.

Many rock songs in Indonesia have adopted protest lyrics, such as in "Bromocorah" ("Criminals"), "Nyanyian khalayak" ("The Song of [Common] People"), "Ken Arok" (the name of a king in the old kingdom in East Java), and "Philosophy Gang" by Harry Roesli. Then there was Leo Kristi and his songs "Nyanyian cinta" ("The Song of Love"), "Nyanyian tanah merdeka" ("The Song of a Free Land"), and "Nyanyian malam" ("The Song of Night"). Kristi mainly wrote folk songs and country-style music. In his songs he talked about the burden and sorrow of the Timorese: "Stiff dead bodies / Between altars and benches / The savanna grass has become red / Cattles are gone / Relatives are gone / I don't know where they are."

Meanwhile, Indonesian pop musicians began to follow the lead of their rock counterparts by embracing protest lyrics, such as in songs by Bimbo (e.g., "Kenapa hutanku kau bakar" ["Why Did You Burn My Forest?]," "Lestarikan Indonesia" ["Preserve Indonesia"], "Abang Becak" ["Becak Driver"], "Tante Sun" ["Aunty Sun," in which they satirized the First Lady of Indonesia at the time]) and Keenan Nasution ("Negeri cintaku" ["My Beloved Country"]). In this song he wrote, "*Hei kaum muda masa kini, kita berantaslah korupsi / Jangan membiarkan mereka menganiaya hati kita*" ("Young people, let's stop corruption / Don't let it torture our heart"). One of the writers was Erros Djarot. He had other songs with protest lyrics, but he also sang from a broad spectrum of genres.

These days many protest songs still exist because the situation remains while the cases change from one to another. Some of the old protest songs are still used by protesters because of their special ability to boost the fearlessness of the singers when they sing the song together. One of them is "Bongkar" by Iwan Fals. His main power is the poetical strength of his lyrics that no one has yet been able to match.

Myrtati Dyah Artaria

See also: Pramoedya Ananta Toer (Chapter 2: Books and Contemporary Literature)

Further Reading

Gitomartoyo, W. 2009. "Kupu-Kupu Malam." *Rolling Stone Indonesia* 32, no. 12: 71.

Kurniasari, T. 2010. "Iwan Fals Returns to His Roots." *The Jakarta Post.* June 27. www
.webcitation.org/6B3Hu7Mex. Accessed September 29, 2012.

Wallach, Jeremy. 2003. *Modern Noise, Fluid Genres: Popular Music in Indonesia, 1997–2001.*
Madison: The University of Wisconsin Press.

Woodrich, Chris. 2013. "Lilis Suryani's 'Gang Kelinci' as a Reflection of Social Realities in
Indonesia (1957–1965)." *Diglossia* 4, no. 2: 73–83.

PUNJABI RAP, REMIX, AND BHANGRA

The definition of "bhangra" has been modified over the last 40 years. It is influenced by rural traditions in India and Punjab that still continue today. Originally, bhangra was described as a type of folk dance with songs performed by groups of men celebrating their crop harvests. With simple musical accompaniments such as the *dhol* (a barrel drum) and *toombi* (a single-stringed instrument), dancers thrust out their chests with pride, gyrate their shoulders, and even perform acrobatic feats to enjoy the rewards of their labor in the fields.

The history of bhangra reveals that the dance may have originated during the time of the wars with Alexander. However, we are still not sure whether it existed before 500 years ago. During the 14th and 15th centuries, wheat farmers of Punjab danced and sang songs about village life in their leisure time and as they worked in the fields. Eventually, this folk form became part of the harvest celebrations popularly known as the Baisakhi festival. This festival is celebrated every April 13 with great pomp and splendor. Today this dance form is found among people from all levels of class and education. It is a popular form of entertainment performed at weddings, parties, and other social functions.

Because of its ethnic background, bhangra carries a unique authenticity and strong cultural origin, a frame within which it is represented. Bhangra is usually sung in the Punjabi language, which has a Sanskrit base and is a mix of Hindi and Urdu, which are the national languages of India and Pakistan. Punjabi is also the official language of the Sikh community in India. Bhangra was gradually reinvented during the mid-1960s and 1970s in the United Kingdom to the extent that its lyrics, rhythms, and dance styles influenced the music of India, especially the songs produced for Bollywood films.

As Punjabis migrated across the world, bhangra followed suit. At the turn of the 20th century, it spread throughout the British Commonwealth in the "old" (exclusive) diaspora, during the British Raj period, and then, some 50 years later, around the world. Following this pattern, bhangra has gained symbolic status as an element of the Punjabi "community." New bhangra creations—referred to as "post-bhangra" or the "bhangra remix"—stretch across boundaries as modern cultural forms. These modern forms of bhangra also exist transnationally between

South Asian Americans, South Asian Australians, and South Asian British, as bhangra music is created and heavily consumed in each of these communities.

The British South Asian crossover film *Bend It Like Beckham* boasts of a popular soundtrack that contains foot-tapping bhangra numbers as it connects bhangra to soccer and celebrations. These days, popular bhangra ringtones are downloaded to mobile phones, and bhangra dolls are bought and sold on eBay. In Britain and Australia, bhangra dance classes have taken over established aerobic routines. A recent song by the group Bhangra Knights was used in a highly successful advertising campaign for Peugeot automobiles. The advertisement became so popular that the full song from Bhangra Knights was listed as one of the most popular songs in Britain and ranked high on popular music charts across the world.

In recent years, bhangra has changed from being merely a dance form to a stylish form of music. Its music has evolved as it has gained international recognition over the years. From being a traditional folk form of Punjab, bhangra has been reinvented and now incorporates elements of rap, hip-hop, and other Western forms of music.

In recent years, the rustic, raw sound of the *dhol* has been supplemented with contemporary musical styles. Bhangra has been fused with disco, reggae, techno, house, and jungle beats. The most famous fusion, perhaps, is with hip-hop and rap. The tipping point was when well-known Indian Punjabi rapper Jay-Z threw in a verse of "Mundiya to bach kerahi" by U.K. artist Punjabi MC in his song "Beware of the Boys" in 2004. That was the culmination of bhangra going mainstream.

Bollywood is the most popular Indian film industry, based in Mumbai, in the state of Maharashtra in India. A lot of song and dance is incorporated into Bollywood movies. Many musicians began their careers by writing songs for Bollywood movies.

In 2008 Snoop Dogg rapped in the title song of the Bollywood movie *Singh Is King*. This is a good example of the fusion of hip-hop and bhangra and American artists recognizing the appeal of hip-hop in India.

Bohemia is a Punjabi rapper who moved to San Francisco when he was 14. Later on he established a recording label in Oakland after he was heard rapping in Punjabi. He brought in a new culture in 2003 with his debut album *Vich pardesan de* (*In the Foreign Land: Desi Rap*, traditional Indian rap). It was easier for him to relate to the roots of hip-hop because of his youth spent adapting to the streets of America.

Hard Kaur (her name translates as Hard Core) is the first Indian female MC who became famous across Bollywood and internationally for her rap music. She was born in India but moved to England when she was 20. She has sung Punjabi rap songs for many Bollywood movies and has ventured into the American hip-hop industry as well. In 2010 she worked with Eminem's group D12 to produce a rap song called "Desi Dance" (Indian traditional dance). The song is in English, but the lyrics emphasize a connection between India and America. The song is dedicated to the women of South Asia.

Hard Kaur, whose music is highly influenced by bhangra, has an image that falls somewhere between a spiky punk and a Bollywood heroine. Her latest album, entitled *Supawoman* (released by Saregama Records), resonates with her sharp, deep voice and reveals a specific medium of hip-hop and rap within its beats. The lyrics in her songs portray a tough, independent woman as she criticizes British racism and encourages women to make their own choices. Her songs celebrate the fact that she has the power to question her culture's sexual rules and roles. This is the core of the appeal found in her music.

Bally Sagoo, who hailed from Birmingham, was one of the first Indians to have created a mark in remixes. He was fondly referred as the Quincy Jones of British Asian music. In an interview with *Time* magazine, Sagoo described his music as "a bit of tablas (Indian drums) and a bit of the Indian sound, but ring on the bass lines, the funky drum (*dhol*) beat and the James Brown samples." In 1991 he compiled *Star Crazy*, which popularized bhangra across the world. It also included a remix of Pakistani *qawwali* (Sufi songs). The famous singer Nusrat Fateh Ali Khan's sublime voice fitted effortlessly into the bhangra rhythms, Hollywood strings, and Latin vibes. Sagoo also opened the Michael Jackson concert in Mumbai with his famous song "Dil cheez" ("My Heart"), which reached No. 12 in the U.K. charts in 1996.

During this time Apache Indian (Steven Kapoor) took to reggae, influenced by his Afro-Caribbean school friends. Today Apache is an international ambassador for bhangra. He is a famous name to reckon with in the reggae circuit, not only in India but among young British Asians.

Bhangra has traveled far and wide over the past 30 years, from being the music of the Punjabi farmers to the "Golden Age" of British bands such as Alaap and Heera to today's fusions of hip-hop. For many Sikh populations settled in different parts of the world, bhangra brings back memories of home and provides comforting consolation. Bhangra remixes are associated with the Punjabi culture yet have appealed to many outside, transcending race, gender, class, and economic backgrounds. We can almost view the acceptance of bhangra remixes as performed in clubs and the *desi* (traditional Indian) music scene from an intersectional lens where many individuals are drawn toward the Punjabi culture knowingly and unknowingly. In spite of the many new subgenres that have developed around bhangra and the fact that it is continuously evolving into exciting new forms, bhangra is here to stay. In the Punjabi language, the bhangra catchphrase says it all: "*Chak de phattey* [Tear up the floorboards] and rock the house!"

Susannah Malkan

See also: Heavy Metal, Indie Music, and Punk, Indonesia

Further Reading

Asian American Music. 2013. "MC Rajinder Singh, Being Young, Brown and Hip." June. https://asianamericanmusicatumd.wordpress.com/2013/12/03/mc-rajinder-singh-being-young-brown-and-hip. Accessed May 20, 2015.

Courtney, David. 2015. "Bhangra: Music and Dance from the Punjab." http://chandrakantha.com/articles/indian_music/bhangra.html. Accessed May 18, 2015.

Mittal, Tusha. 2006. "Bhangra Beats: Punjabi Dance Plays Differing Roles in Traditional, Fusion, Hip-Hop World." http://indianewengland.com/ME2/dirmod.asp?sid=CE2F99 5870CF4FAF8C5DE30FDFDF3B05&nm=Main&type=Publishing&mod=Publications% 3A%3AArticle&mid=8F3A7027421841978F18BE895F87F791&tier=4&id=BD5757 2B3F2245F5908C976E7834BB6E. Accessed May 17, 2015.

Steward, Sue. 2007. "Bhangra Spreads Its Empire." www.theguardian.com/music/2007/oct /14/urban. Accessed May 18, 2015.

SMALL-CITY MUSIC, CHINA

China's breakneck urbanization has been extensively reported by English-language media, as have some of the musical activities that have emerged from its big cities, particularly rock music in Beijing and dance music in Shanghai. However, urbanization has also produced hundreds of smaller cities whose names are barely known beyond China, each of which contains 100,000 or so citizens and their accompanying musical practices. Located in southwest China, Kaili is one such city and serves here as an example for the description of everyday musical practices in small Chinese cities. Just as Kaili would be missed from most tours of urban China, everyday music making within the city could also be easily missed, hidden as it is by the high-decibel sounds of piped music, construction, and traffic. Yet music making in the city is multiple and diverse, including unison park singing, multipart indoor choirs, open-mike nights, ethnic instruments, university music courses, guitar gatherings, and a cappella music. This entry introduces some of these musical practices, and their position within the wider aural and visual environment of the city, by recounting a series of observations made in Kaili during 2011 and 2012.

Every morning around 9:00 a.m., a number of middle-aged and elderly people gather as an informal choir on the summit of Apple Hill Park, where they sing from a repertoire that ranges from old revolutionary songs and classic movie theme tunes to contemporary R&B. This wide repertoire is given a certain aesthetic coherence by the group's simple format of unison singing mainly accompanied by *erhu* (two-stringed fiddle). The choir's position at the summit of the park separates its musical sound from the sounds of the busy avenues below. For many singers, the park summit is an important stop on their morning exercise itinerary; they climb the hill, do calisthenics, sing to exercise their lungs, then descend into the city to go about the rest of their day.

Most of the choir members are retired. With a relative abundance of free time, they participate in music groups across the city. These groups are tucked away in rooms within larger buildings or compounds, making them visually and aurally undetectable from the street. For example, a second choir is based in an official "culture center," which is itself situated within the compound of the local finance bureau. A third choir is located in the building of the local labor union, a somewhat functionally defunct institution that has resorted to renting out its rooms. In contrast to the Apple Hill Park choir, both of these indoor choirs sing in multipart harmony, and their teachers place heavy emphasis on vocal technique and pronunciation. While singing is a form of exercise at Apple Hill Park, it is a form of educational self-improvement at these indoor choirs.

During the evening, Kaili's pavements are at their busiest, as people stroll among a sea of commerce and piped music. An example of the latter emits from a centrally located bus stop. It is a fairly ordinary bus stop by local standards but unique by global standards; the major bus stops of the city have been constructed according to the markers of the Miao, a local ethnic group, and so their pillars are topped with representations of silver headdresses. Somewhat incongruously, speakers embedded within the roof of the bus stop are playing a mixture of English- and Chinese-language pop music, as broadcast by the local radio station, with a distinct lack of Miao ethnic flavor.

The pavement widens near the bus stop as it meets an entrance into Zhongbo Plaza, a mazelike, two-level pedestrianized shopping area. A group of middle-aged and elderly people are ballroom dancing here in male-female and female-female pairs. They have set up their own sound system, which blasts out a curious selection of tracks: a dance version of "Nanniwan," a revolutionary classic that borrows from northwestern Chinese folk traditions; a Miao-style pop song performed by the famed local singer Ah You Duo; and a Mandarin version of "Jimmy Jimmy Jimmy Aaja," a song from the 1982 Indian movie *Disco Dancer*.

Located beyond the dancers and within Zhongbo Plaza is Bright Star, a multi-purpose entertainment venue that holds an open-mike night every evening. Those who brave the open-mike stage generally choose to sing Chinese-language pop songs from the last 30 years or so, but once again, their music making is aurally and visually hidden. To reach the stage, a visitor leaves the bustle of Zhongbo Plaza to pass through Bright Star's small street-level entrance and descend an escalator, only to encounter the high-decibel environment of an arcade zone below, with the open-mike stage located beyond. Particularly audible is the Japanesque electro-pop hit "Dragostea din tei," from the Moldovan pop group O-Zone, which plays from the dance machines at the front of the arcade.

The entirety of Kaili's city center is easily accessible by foot, but the center does not encompass the entirety of musical life in the city. At the end of one bus route lays Longtouhe Village, on the western outskirts of the city. The bus has speakers embedded in its roof, and the young driver is taking advantage of them to play a mixture of hip-hop and pop. At Longtouhe Village, heavy-goods vehicles are lumbering their way toward mines and factories outside of the city. There are also vehicles being repaired at the side of the road, so that the combined sounds of maintenance work and traffic make this another unlikely site for musical activity. And yet, most Friday and Saturday evenings, a group of local women gather outside one of their houses to dance to the *lusheng*, a six-pipe wind instrument that features prominently in the folk music of the Miao and other local ethnic groups. On a good day, they have a male *lusheng* player to accompany them. On other days, they use a stereo system. These dancers only wear the silver Miao headdresses depicted by Kaili's aforementioned bus stops when performing at annual *lusheng* festivals and other special occasions.

A second bus route takes students to the new campus of Kaili University in the still-undeveloped "development zone" of the city. There is a local joke that the university's students "*kaimen jianshan*," a phrase that usually means "to get to the point" but is used here in its literal sense of "opening the door to see mountains" to describe the remote and mountainous location of the campus. Unsurprisingly, some students complain about the lack of atmosphere and activity on the campus. Indeed, some parts are so quiet that cicadas can be heard at night. However, the music department—isolated at the back of the campus—produces an array of Miao song, bel canto, *lusheng*, and piano, while the hipper students gather between classes to play guitar at a small café selling Taiwanese bubble tea. After classes, an American teacher guides an extracurricular a cappella group, who sing songs in Chinese, English, and even both languages together in a medley arrangement of Savage Garden and Jay Chou, one of Taiwan's biggest stars.

First impressions are misleading for both the university and the wider city. There is a diversity of musical practices in Kaili, but such practices are easily hidden by the high-decibel environment of contemporary urban China.

Paul Kendall

See also: Alternative Music Scene, China

Further Reading

Chau, Adam Yuet. 2006. "Drinking Games, Karaoke Songs, and 'Yangge' Dances: Youth Cultural Production in Rural China." *Ethnology* 45, no. 2: 161–172.

Finnegan, Ruth H. 1989. *The Hidden Musicians: Music-Making in an English Town*. Middletown, CT: Wesleyan University Press.

Rees, Helen. 1995. "The Many Musics of a Chinese County Town: A Case-Study of Co-Existence in Lijiang, Yunnan Province." *Asian Music* 27, no. 1: 63–102.

Chapter 2: Books and Contemporary Literature

Introduction

Popular literature in Asia and Oceania needs to be understood contextually in relation to the specific histories, societies, and the world in which individual writers live. Many local writers—like two Nobel Prize laureates, Burmese opposition politician Aung San Suu Kyi (1945–) and the national hero of India and Bangladesh Rabindranath Tagore (1861–1941)—are social critics who give voice to the voiceless by exposing the injustices of colonization, imperialist domination, and dictatorship. In countries where the press is heavily censored, such as Myanmar (Burma), Cambodia, Indonesia, North Korea, and modern-day China to a large degree, writers and poets seem to subtly elaborate novels and prose that are fictitious yet deeply anchored in local histories and the issues of the times. Characters in their stories mainly represent ordinary people whose anguish and frustration with their complicated situations in the midst of political corruption and poverty have brought them to rebel against an unjust system that takes advantage of the less fortunate and wreaks havoc on the natural environment.

Pramoedya Ananta Toer (1925–2006), Nobel Prize candidate of Indonesia, wrote many novels from prison. He would memorize and tell his new stories in segments, day by day, to fellow inmates who were eager to hear them. Later, from his cell, he wrote and smuggled them out on pieces of paper. In 1992 Toer's *This Earth of Mankind* was banned by the Indonesian government because it sympathized with the local Chinese community. Others, like Shashi Tharoor (1956–) of India, have produced spectacular novels patterned after Hindu mythology. He renamed archetypical characters in ancient Hindu epic adventure stories to represent modern political and historical figures in *The Great Indian Novel*, which retells the history of India from colonialism to independence and the partition of India and Pakistan.

Philippine novelist Jose Sionel (1924–), similarly, writes about colonialism and the social inequities of class struggle. His most famous novel, *Mass*, which was made into a movie and became a big local hit onscreen in 2011, tells a story with the message that children are not guilty for the shortcomings of their parents. The main characters are young adults and college students participating in the popular protest movement against the Marcos dictatorship and, at the same time, the Philippine government's backing of the United States' involvement in the Vietnam War in the early 1970s. It is a story of young idealists in the nationalist struggle for Philippine liberation from neocolonial governmental structures. One of the leading protagonists is a young college student struggling for greater social equality and justice who rose up against her own wealthy family, who favored the dictatorship.

More broadly, East Asian literature and South Asian literature cover many centuries and have influenced nearby literary traditions in Central Asia and Southeast Asia. East Asian literature is often critically intertwined with Confucian philosophy and history. In early China and today, poetry has provided writers a way to subtly and indirectly speak and even sing about matters that might otherwise be censored for directly challenging the powers that be. Many local contemporary writers have composed novels about pivotal moments that changed history, such as the tragic excesses of Maoist China (1949–1976) and the cultural struggles of post-Mao China. Authors like Nobel laureates Mo Yan (1955–) and Gao Xingjian (1940–) wrestle with issues of Chinese cultural identity in their writing in very different ways. Contemporary popular East Asian literature also provides a basis for narratives in films, television, and dramatic performances.

In Oceania, Australian Aborigine and New Zealand Maori writers often write about past and present issues that continue to pass through their own lives. Indigenous nationalist novelists and poets commonly write in relation to their own societies and experiences from their own culturally diverse and different points of view. Whether male or female, local literary writers in Asia and Oceania often write against the grain in ways that are different from those of Western writers.

However, the majority populations of Australia and New Zealand have been strongly influenced by Anglophone and European traditions. Like New England in the United States, both countries are former colonies of Great Britain, which mainly, then, encouraged English and Western Europeans to migrate and settle down to make their families and homes there. Aussie and Kiwi writers produce works that often are written for an international audience, especially British and North American English-speaking readers. Even so, they tend to incorporate pride of heritage and a sense of having a national identity into their works. Many contemporary and popular science-fiction books, novels, detective stories, and thrillers, attracting an international readership, have come out of Australia and New Zealand, especially since the late 20th century and into the new millennium.

Alongside the more serious genres of literature in Asia and Oceania, popular voices also produce materials like comic books and cartoons and other more lighthearted fare. The broad category of literature includes both the high-minded literary pursuits of Nobel laureates and the frothier entertainment of pulp fiction and comics. But the line between literature and pop fiction is not always clear, as some of the entries in this section demonstrate.

Kathleen M. Nadeau and Jeremy A. Murray

Further Reading

Aung San Suu Kyi. 1991. *Freedom from Fear and Other Writings*. New York: Penguin Books.
Dalle, Eric. 2007. "Literature, East Asia and Oceania." In *The Greenwood Encyclopedia of World Popular Culture, Volume 6: Asia and Pacific Oceania*. Ed. Gary Xu and Vinay Dharwadker, 161–171. Westport, CT: Greenwood Press.
Tharoor, Shashi. 1989. *The Great Indian Novel*. New York: Arcade Publishing.
Toer, Pramoedya Ananta. 1975. *This Earth of Mankind*. New York: Penguin Books.

COMIC-BOOK HEROINES, PHILIPPINES

In the Philippines, an archipelago made up of 7,107 islands with a rich cultural history and egalitarian politics before it was colonized by Spain and America, you will find a female superhero who reigns supreme over other comics or *komiks* (folk and super) heroes. Her name is Darna. In contemporary times, she is now joined by another heroine, this time made popular by graphic novel. Her name is Alexandra Trese.

The stories of Darna and Trese are unique when compared to the popularity of male superheroes in most Western countries. Their popularity rests on the fact that they have not only managed to capture the imagination of Filipinos but have also evolved and adapted to continue to embody the aspirations of the Filipino people.

Darna

In the pantheon of local folk and fictional heroes, no one has ever come close to the popularity that Darna has achieved. Apart from her beginnings in *komiks*, she already has 13 commercially successful movies under her belt, three live-action television series (1997, 2005, 2009), two ballet productions (1997 and 2003), an animated series (1986), a number of television advertisements, and a successful transition from the humble *komiks* that was initially targeted at and consumed by the Filipino-speaking masses to the more contemporary, all-English comic book (released by Mango Comics in 2003) that was aimed at the more middle-class market.

Darna came from the mind and design of Mars Ravelo, considered one of the most prolific and highly revered *komiks* writers in the Philippines. Darna first appeared in *Pilipino Komiks* on May 13, 1950. She was first illustrated by Nestor Redondo—another *komiks* icon—who drew the image of Darna in clean but powerful and graceful lines.

People familiar with Darna's physical appearance would quickly point out her similarity to DC Comics' Wonder Woman (who first appeared in 1941). However, Ravelo's idea for Darna came from the Superman comics of the American soldiers. Ravelo wanted to depart from the typical male-centered superheroes of the United States, so he created a female superhero patterned after his mother, who had taken care of him alone after the death of his father. Popular stories trace the name of Darna to Ibong Adarna, a mythical and magical but elusive bird with healing powers from a 17th-century Filipino epic. However, others say that the choice of Darna and her female alter ego, Narda, was conceived for anagram purposes.

Despite the many variations of her story in different platforms, Darna's story in *komiks* started when a young orphan girl named Narda was playing with her younger brother, Ding, and saw a falling star. Investigating where it landed, Narda found a white, glowing stone from the crash site. Afraid of being questioned by her playmates about her discovery, she swallowed the stone and was immediately overcome by a strange sensation and a flood of images of planets and alien races that caused her to lose consciousness. Upon waking up in their home, Narda confided to her *lola* (grandmother) Asay and Ding about the mysterious stone that she'd swallowed, upon which was written the word "Darna." Upon uttering the name, Narda was transformed into a tall, powerful woman from the planet Marte. Now transformed, Darna explained that she was sent to Earth to defend it from the forces of darkness and hatred. She told them that if they wanted Narda to come back, she just needed to shout her name and she would transform again.

In her original *komiks* narrative, Darna possesses the powers of flight, super strength, super speed, and indestructibility to all man-made weapons. Darna is a character that is an amalgam of all things Filipino: her characterization shows the empowered position of women in precolonial Filipino society, and her costume is a combination of symbols found in the Philippine flag and in the costume of several ethnolinguistic groups (especially the loincloth). Further, the concept of the white stone harkens back to the Filipinos' belief in the *agimat* (amulet) whose bearer must possess the virtue of pure heart and noble intention in order to wield its power.

Alexandra Trese

Unlike Darna, Alexandra Trese is a relatively new heroine in the landscape of comic-book heroines in the country. While not yet in the same league as Darna in terms of enduring appeal, mainstream popularity, or even scholarly inquiry, Alexandra Trese is a rising star in the pantheon of contemporary superheroes as evidenced by the number of stories already produced (six books from 2008 to 2014 and counting) and accolades.

The Trese series is written by Ferdinand Benedict "Budjette" Tan and drawn by Jonathan "Kajo" Baldisimo and was first published independently by Alamat Comics before Visprint Incorporated turned it into a graphic novel. Trese belongs to the horror/crime genre and is similar in characterization and scope to *Kolchak: The Night Stalker* and *The X-Files*. In the afterword of the first volume of the series, Tan traced Trese's origins to a short-lived radio show in the Philippines called *The World of the Unknown*, which was inspired by shows such as *Twilight Zone* and *Tales from the Crypt*. In its evolution from a radio program to comics, Tan opted to make the lead character a woman named Alexandra Trese, the youngest of the six children of Anton Trese (who was the protagonist in the radio program). Initially, the stories were designed to be self-contained (one-shot stories) and followed Warren Ellis's "pop comics" style, which serves to create comic books that can be read and understood by non-comic-book fans. It was only in the third book that Tan and Baldisimo decided to expand it into a mythology.

The graphic novel follows the story of Alexandra Trese, owner of a bar named The Diabolical and a police consultant for unexplained and supernatural events. Each book is episodic in nature, mirroring the format of television serials, and the stories are culled from popular stories and urban legends, and even recognizable public figures, and feature familiar places and streets in Metro Manila.

Trese is a *babaylan-mandirigma* (shaman-warrior) garbed in a black button-down, Chinese-inspired trench coat. She wields a magical *kris* (knife) called *sinag* (light), a short sword with wavy edges that was inspired by an actual weapon used by an ethnolinguistic group from Mindanao—the Maranaws. She also possesses psionic abilities, in particular energy healing, mediumship, and divination. She is joined in her fight by a police officer named Captain Guerrero, the mysterious, mythical, and powerful *kambal* (twins), and a host of creatures derived from lower Philippine mythology.

Cherish Aileen A. Brillon

See also: Manga

Further Reading

Brillon, Cherish Aileen A. 2007. *Manufacturing a GMA Telefantasya: A Political Economy Case Study of Darna.* Graduate thesis, University of the Philippines.

Cueto, Eric. *Mars Ravelo.* http://marsravelosdarna.wix.com/marsravelosdarna/article#!. Accessed March 24, 2016.

Darna Lives. http://darnalives.blogspot.com. Accessed March 24, 2016.

Flores, Emil. 2007. "Comics Crash: A Survey of Filipino Comics and Its Quest for Legitimacy." *Journal of English Studies and Comparative Literature* 7, no. 1: 46–58.

Lent, John A. 2009. *The First One Hundred Years of Philippine Komiks and Cartoons.* Tagaytay City, PH: Yonzon Associates.

Mars Ravelo Superheroes. http://marsravelosuperheroes.tripod.com. Accessed March 24, 2016.

Pilipino Komiks. http://pilipinokomiks.blogspot.com. Accessed March 24, 2016.

Roxas, Cynthia, and Joaquin Arevalo Jr. 1985. *A History of Komiks of the Philippines and Other Countries.* Quezon City, PH: Islas Filipinas Publishing Co., Inc.

Trese. http://tresekomix.blogspot.com. Accessed March 24, 2016.

COMIC BOOKS, INDIA

Amar Chitra Katha (Immortal Picture Stories) has been the dominant comic-book series in India since its inception in 1967. Discussing his decision to found this series, Anant Pai (1929–2011) stated, "Believe it or not, I was never a comic buff myself, not until I started to make them! But my nephews read [foreign] comics and were just fascinated by them. Seeing their interest, I got the idea to create comic books on Indian culture. Now I am the 'Father of Indian Comics'"

(McLain 2009a, 24). In the early 1960s, Anant Pai recognized not only how popular imported Western comic books were with Indian children but also the potential
of the comic-book medium for teaching Indian history and Hindu mythology to
children. Greatly concerned that the millions of middle-class Indian children being
educated in English-language schools were losing touch with their own heritage,
Pai decided to found a comic-book series that would rival the imports by featuring
Indian heroes and story lines. To date, over 440 titles have been published in the
Amar Chitra Katha series, and more than 90 million issues have been sold. For
several generations of Indians, the Amar Chitra Katha series has been foundational
to defining what it means to be Indian and Hindu. And for Indian comics creators,
the Amar Chitra Katha series has been so omnipresent that they have all had to
grapple with its legacy.

The first comic book in the Amar Chitra Katha series, *Krishna* (published in
1969), featured stories of the Hindu god Krishna drawn from classical Hindu
mythological scriptures and inaugurated the birth of the Indian comic-book
industry. After a handful of comic issues featuring other divine heroes from
Hindu mythology, Anant Pai decided to add historical Indian heroes into the mix,
beginning with the medieval Indian king Shivaji (1971) and eventually incorporating modern freedom fighters including Subhas Chandra Bose (1975) and
Mahatma Gandhi (1989). The publisher of the series, Mumbai-based India Book
House, marketed the comic books to Indian parents and educators as "the route
to your roots," emphasizing that the comics would complement and enhance
both religious and secular education. Anant Pai envisioned his series as the van-
guard of national integration, claiming that Amar Chitra Katha promotes unity in
diversity by featuring heroes and stories from different regions of India and from
India's different religious communities. However, scholars have emphasized that
the national integration promoted through this series aligns in several significant
ways with Hindu nationalist ideology, presenting a vision of India and Indianness
that is Hindu at its core. Frances Pritchett, for instance, provides a taxonomy of
the heroes featured in this series in an important essay and concludes that despite
its slogans to the contrary, Amar Chitra Katha will not appeal to all Indians, for
"readers who happen to be of the wrong gender, the wrong politics, or the wrong
religion will find themselves only scantily represented in what is ultimately a vision
of the future at least as much of the past" (Pritchett 1995, 104).

Several additional comic-book brands arose in the 1980s in the aftermath of
Amar Chitra Katha's noteworthy marketing success. One of the first new series to
be launched was again founded by Anant Pai and published by India Book House.
Tinkle debuted in 1980 and targeted English-language readers ages eight and
younger who could grow into Amar Chitra Katha. This monthly comic featured
multiple short, humorous stories in each issue and a recurring cast of fictitious
Indian characters. Today both Tinkle and Amar Chitra Katha have been acquired
from India Book House by the start-up company ACK Media.

The founders of other new comic-book brands in the 1980s each had to grapple
with the question of what it meant to create Indian comic books in the aftermath of

the precedent set by Amar Chitra Katha. What sorts of heroes should be featured? What kinds of stories should be told, and what sources should they be drawn from? What kinds of artistic styles should be utilized? Some founders followed closely in the footsteps of Amar Chitra Katha. Dreamland Publications, for instance, was a New Delhi–based publisher of children's books that began its own series of mythological comics in the early 1980s in an effort to compete for the market. Like Amar Chitra Katha, Dreamland Publications also drew upon the wealth of stories from Hindu mythology, including the *Ramayana* and *Mahabharata* epics, for inspiration. These comics share in common with Amar Chitra Katha not only their grounding in Hindu mythology but also the slippage between the concepts of "Hindu" and "Indian."

Other founders chose to actively deviate from the Amar Chitra Katha model. One example is Raj Comics, founded in 1984 by the brothers Sanjay, Manish, and Manoj Gupta and published by the New Delhi–based publisher Raja Pocket Books. These brothers decided to feature heroes who were ethnically and geographically Indian but were not figures from Hindu mythology or Indian history. Instead, they featured fictive Indian superheroes with amazing superpowers: Nagaraj, Shakti, Super Commando Dhruva, and Super Indian are some of the most popular superheroes in this series, which now includes over 5,000 titles.

In the first decade of the 21st century, a new generation of comic-book creators arose in India, all of whom had grown up reading Amar Chitra Katha comics. As they founded new comic-book brands, some continued to model their heroes, stories, and images upon Amar Chitra Katha. An example can be seen in the Chitra Kathayain series published by the New Delhi–based Rohan Book Company, which created issues featuring the same mythological and historical Indian heroes, stories, and images previously featured in Amar Chitra Katha. Others remained grounded in Hindu mythology for their story inspiration but sought to revise the artistic style to incorporate a more overt superhero visual aesthetic. An example can be seen in the Vimanika Comics series founded by Karan Vir Arora in Mumbai in 2008. Unlike the more traditional adolescent and smooth-limbed deities featured on the cover of Amar Chitra Katha's *Krishna* and other titles, the Hindu deities featured in Vimanika Comics are downright bursting with muscles. Still others radically rethought the earlier precedent. Vivalok Comics, published by the Viveka Foundation in New Delhi, created an alternative version of the Indian hero, one that centers on celebrating the diversity of India's many local traditions. Its founder and editor, Rukmini Sekhar, described this series as encompassing a unique Indian aesthetic centered on "smallness" in an effort to present a pluralistic society featuring Indian heroes that care about social and environmental justice and come from both Hindu and Muslim, high-caste and low-caste, male and female, rural and urban backgrounds.

Beyond comic books, India also has a rich variety of comic genres, including comic strips, political cartoons, and graphic novels. India's history of political cartoons dates to the 19th century, when political cartoons were published in major Indian newspapers and vernacular publications such as *Urdu Punch* and

Hindi Punch. In the 20th century, many Indian comic strips or "funnies" were also featured in Indian newspapers and magazines. The long-running monthly children's magazine *Chandamama*, founded in 1947, included a mix of stories, games, and comic strips featuring Indian characters and was especially popular for its comic illustrations.

In the 21st century, the graphic novel is starting to rise in India, with several small publishing houses printing graphic novels on a wide number of different themes, from serious political issues, as in Vishwajyoti Ghosh's *Delhi Calm*, Naseer Ahmed and Saurabh Singh's *Kashmir Pending*, and Orjit Sen's *River of Stories*; to existential meditations upon contemporary life in urban India, as in Appupen's *Moonward* and Sarnath Banerjee's *Corridor*; to critical rethinkings of classical Hindu mythology, as in Samhita Arni and Moyna Chitrakar's *Sita's Ramayana*.

Karline McLain

See also: *Mahabharata* and *Ramayana* (Chapter 4: Television and Radio); Tharoor, Shashi

Further Reading

Lent, John A. 2004. "India's Amar Chitra Katha: Fictionalized History or the Real Story?" *International Journal of Comic Art* 6, no. 1: 56–76.

Lent, John A. 2009. "An Illustrated History of Indian Political Cartooning." *International Journal of Comic Art* 11, no. 2: 3–25.

McLain, Karline. 2009a. *India's Immortal Comic Books: Gods, Kings, and Other Heroes.* Bloomington: Indiana University Press.

McLain, Karline. 2009b. "Vivalok Comics: Celebrating All That Is Small in India." *International Journal of Comic Art* 11, no. 2: 26–43.

McLain, Karline. 2014. "*The Gandhi Story*: An Official Indian Comic Book History of the Mahatma." *International Journal of Hindu Studies* 18, no. 3: 291–325.

Pritchett, Frances W. 1995. "The World of Amar Chitra Katha." In *Media and the Transformation of Religion in South Asia*. Ed. Lawrence A. Babb and Susan S. Wadley, 76–106. Philadelphia: University of Pennsylvania Press.

Rao, Aruna. 2001. "From Self–Knowledge to Super Heroes: The Story of Indian Comics." In *Illustrating Asia: Comics, Humor Magazines, and Picture Books*. Ed. John A. Lent, 37–63. Honolulu: University of Hawai'i Press.

JOSE, FRANCISCO SIONIL (1924–)

F. Sionil Jose is a prolific English-language Philippine writer. He has received many honors for his writing, most notably the Chevalier dans l'Ordre des Arts et Lettres conferred by France in 2000, the designation as National Artist for Literature conferred by the Philippines in 2001, and the Pablo Neruda Centennial Award in 2004. His fiction has given voice to Philippine history, and in his thought-provoking and sometimes trenchant journalism over the past 65 years he has held a mirror to Philippine cultural and political life, taking to task not only Filipino economic elites but also those of other countries who have sought their own advantage.

Jose was born to a landless peasant family in the town of Rosales in the northern Philippine province of Pangasinan, in the Philippine Islands, then a dependent colony of the United States. The 1930s in Pangasinan was a time of widening gaps between the rich and the poor, a situation that was common in much of the less-developed world due to the Great Depression. Added to this was the bombing and then invasion of the Philippine islands by the armed forces of Imperial Japan in 1941–1942, just after Jose's 17th birthday, and the four years of brutal repression that followed. The result was the formation in this young man of an abiding skepticism of the motives of people in power and resentment of both political corruption and the social conditions that foster inescapable poverty. As a novelist and essayist, Jose has returned many times to these themes.

Entering college at the University of Santo Tomas in Manila, in the first class since the campus reopened in 1946 after years of serving as an internment camp for foreign internees, Jose came under the influence of Paz Latorena (1908–1953), a literature professor and one of the country's first generation of writers in English. While still in college, he wrote for *The Commonweal*, a national Catholic weekly in Manila, and worked as assistant editor for the United States Information Service. Upon leaving Santo Tomas, he took up journalism at the English-language newspaper *Manila Times*, where he worked until 1960, becoming managing editor of its Sunday magazine. He also edited *Comment*, a quarterly magazine, from 1956 to 1962, and *Progress*, an annual publication of the *Manila Times*, from 1958 to 1960.

In 1957 Jose organized the Philippines chapter of PEN (Poets, Essayists, Novelists), the international organization that works to promote literature and protect writers from government interference. He left the Philippines in 1961 to become managing editor of the weekly *Asia Magazine* in Hong Kong and afterward worked in Sri Lanka as information officer for the Colombo Plan, an organization established to enable technology transfer from developed nations to the Asian developing world. Returning home in 1965, he received a grant from the Congress for Cultural Freedom, an international organization of mostly left-leaning academics, public intellectuals, and writers, which enabled him to establish a publishing house and a bookshop. He named the bookshop Solidaridad in homage to the newspaper published in the late 1800s by Filipino students in Europe advocating for just treatment of Filipinos by the Spanish colonial government, including representation in the Cortes Generales, the Spanish parliament. The bookshop displayed Asian art and made available books from abroad as well as literature in English by Filipino and other Asian writers. A stop at Solidaridad on Padre Faura Street in the Ermita section of Manila became essential for intellectuals and diplomats visiting from abroad as well as aspiring Filipino academics and American expats. Together with the regular PEN meetings held in its upstairs room and the welcoming atmosphere extended by Jose and his wife, Tessie, Solidaridad made F. Sionil Jose the most influential cultural figure of the modern Philippines.

The grant that established the bookshop also enabled Jose to fulfill a long-held dream—to publish a magazine that mattered, a magazine of thought that could be a guide for national leaders. Thus *Solidarity* was born, a monthly magazine that sought to publish the most informative articles on Asian and Philippine policy, development, history, and literature. The magazine took on the "big" topics of the day and was unflinching in its defense of the poor and opposition to the moral rot that caused their oppression. *Solidarity* was published from 1966 through 1977 and later from 1983 to the end of martial law in 1986. Jose often tells the story of how, during nightly curfew in the martial-law years, when only police were out in the streets, his office at Solidaridad Bookshop was ransacked and his files searched. No money or valuables were taken but, tellingly, his fountain pen was smashed—evidently as a not-so-subtle warning that his writings against the martial-law government and powerful economic interests would not be taken lightly!

During the martial-law period, Jose continued to advocate on behalf of the land-less poor, joining forces for a few years with his Pangasinan province-mate and land-reform advocate Conrado Estrella (1917–2011), who served as secretary of agriculture in the cabinet of President Ferdinand Marcos (1917–1989). At this time, also, Jose was completing the five-novel sequence known as the Rosales Saga due to the story being centered on the people of the town of Rosales in Pangasinan, the place of Jose's early upbringing. The first of these, *The Pretenders*, was self-published by Solidaridad in 1962. The others followed sporadically as Jose wrote while engaged in his other pursuits, so that the second, *Tree*, came out 16 years later in 1978, followed quickly by *My Brother, My Executioner* (1979), *Mass* (1982), and *Po-on* (1984). Three were originally published by Solidaridad Publishing House, one by a press in Amsterdam, and one by another Manila-area press, New Day Publishers, because its editor, Gloria Rodriguez (1928–), importuned Jose to allow her press to publish it. All have also been published internationally, translated into 22 languages, in Jakarta, Lisbon, Moscow, Hanoi, Prague, Tokyo, Sydney, Stockholm, Taipei, Amsterdam, Copenhagen, and Bonn. Altogether, Jose's literary output to date encompasses the five Rosales novels, eight other novels, two novellas, five collections of short stories, six collections of essays, a collection of poetry, and a children's book. He also edited two anthologies of short stories by other authors. Besides this, Jose continues to write, notably his "Hindsight" column in the *PhilStar*, the digital edition of the *Philippine Star* newspaper, which serves as his blog.

The Rosales Saga spans modern Philippine history, detailing the humiliating effects of colonial rule by Spain and the United States, plus the years of Japan's occupation, followed by equally oppressive Filipino elites. Though not published in chronological order, the beginning of the historical narrative stretches from the execution of three native priests by the Spanish colonial powers in 1872 to the imposition of martial law a century later. In an interview with Laurence D. Stifel, an international development consultant with whom Jose had a long friendship, Jose summarized his views encapsulated in the Rosales novels: "The collaboration with predatory rulers, whether Americans, Spaniards, Japanese or our own oligarchy has continued through generations. . . . It was wrong to collaborate with the Spaniards, the Japanese, the Americans; is collaboration with the rapacious native elite any less wrong?" (Bernad 1991, 274).

Jose's writing is not without controversy. In an op-ed essay published in 1988 on the anniversary of the American deployment of the atom bomb on Hiroshima, he wrote from memory "of what it was like in the Philippines during the . . . years of Japanese occupation [which] amounted to the most atrocious form of colonialism Southeast Asia ever experienced" (Jose 1988). He advanced the thesis that far from being a victim, Japan's postwar economic machine in its "euphoric narcissism" was sweeping through Southeast Asia, "laying waste our weak societies and ravaging our unprotected environment." This critique of Japan as a "massive vacuum cleaner" was not new in Southeast Asia, and Filipinos in particular have long resented that the United States helped rebuild Japan while offering little assistance to the Philippines, which had been devastated by the war and particularly by the American "liberation." But that Jose penned this essay from Kyoto, where he had just finished a six-month fellowship as a research scholar, seemed exceptionally confrontational.

In June 2015, in the context of China's advances on islands in the South China Sea claimed by several nations, including the Philippines, Jose predicted in his *PhilStar* blog that an armed conflict with China is coming and asserted that Filipino ethnic Chinese can be expected to take sides against the Philippines. This rambling essay opened an old wound in Philippine political life, and the column was met with numerous rejoinders.

Roger J. Bresnahan

See also: Popular Literature, Philippines

Further Reading

The five novels of the Rosales Saga were republished as three novels by The Modern Library (New York): *Dusk* (1998), containing *Po-on*; *Don Vicente* (1999), containing *My Brother, My Executioner* and *Tree*; and *The Samsons* (2000), containing *The Pretenders* and *Mass*.

Bernad, Miguel A., ed. 1991. *Conversations with F. Sionil Jose*. Quezon City, PH: Vera-Reyes.

Bresnahan, Roger J., ed. 1990. *Conversations with Filipino Writers*. Quezon City, PH: New Day Publishers.

Jose, F. Sionil. 1988. "After Hiroshima: The Second Coming." *New York Times International Edition* (August 6): 15.

Jose, F. Sionil. 2011. *Gleanings from a Life in Literature*. Manila, PH: Santo Tomas University Publishing House.

Jose, F. Sionil. 2015. "A Memoir of War (Then) and China (Now)." June 7. *Hindsight* (blog). *The Philippine Star* (digital edition). http://www.philstar.com/sunday-life/2015/06/07/1462943/memoir-war-then-and-china-now. Accessed March 24, 2016.

Morales, Aldredo T. 1989. *F. Sionil Jose and His Fiction: The Filipino's Journey to Justice and Nationhood*. Quezon City, PH: Vera-Reyes.

LITERATURE, DALIT

Dalit literature includes the prose, plays, and poetry written by members of India's formerly untouchable caste communities. These works frequently—though not exclusively—address Dalit struggle and resilience amid ongoing caste discrimination, relying on their activist content and style to challenge oppression. The identifier "Dalit," meaning "oppressed" or "broken people" in Marathi, was first used in the 19th century. When the political leader and activist Dr. B. R. Ambedkar (1891–1956) mobilized fellow untouchables to fight for political power, human dignity, and the outlawing of untouchability in the 1920s, people embraced the term to signify their identity as one born of struggle and resilience amid caste discrimination.

The traditional Brahminical social code that led to the practices of untouchability was comprised of four *varnas* or castes based on occupation. The pundits, Brahmin priests, held the highest position. They were followed by the Kshatriyas, who were royalty or warriors; Baniyas, who worked as merchants or agricultural workers; and Shudras, who held manual labor jobs. Historically, Dalits, as Shudras, were deemed the lowest caste because their jobs as butchers, leather workers, human-waste collectors, and corpse clearers were believed to make them ritually impure. Consequently, their touch was treated as spiritually contaminated, leading the supposed higher castes to ostracize Shudras as outcastes, denying them basic human rights. Accordingly, Dalit writing chronicles their oppression as well as their resilience in protesting violence and discrimination. With an activist sensibility, this literature grants a voice to the silenced to fuel the Dalit fight for equality. While it emphasizes the spiritual and cultural traditions that distinguish Dalits from their upper-caste Hindu oppressors, it also stresses that Dalits are legitimate Indian citizens who, as part of Indian cultural history, are entitled to legal protection and political representation.

Much of Dalit tradition, even today, is expressed through oral stories or folk songs. The first written texts date back to Buddhist literature, Tamil Siddhas, and Bhakti poets from the medieval period. These writings sought to liberate individuals from the Brahminical structures of caste. Some identify the essays and political tracts by Dr. Ambedkar—written between the 1920s and the 1950s—as the beginning of a second stage of Dalit writing. Influenced by his encounters with African American activists of the Harlem Renaissance during his graduate studies at Columbia University, Ambedkar's work addressed the sociopolitical plight of Dalits, the place of Marxism in Dalit resistance, and critiques of Vedic religious scriptures that perpetuated casteism. His final work explored how and why Dalits should renounce Hinduism in favor of Buddhism to free themselves from being defined by caste. Although his writing was primarily sociological or political, it inspired a body of critical, philosophical texts that trace Dalit discourse and intellectual tradition that, in turn, informs much of the literary production from the post-Ambedkar years to the present.

The term "Dalit literature," as we know it today, first emerged as a formal category at the Maharashtra Dalit Sahitya Sangha Conference (Maharastra Dalit Literary Society) of 1958, held in Mumbai (Bombay). Initially, writers published in Indian vernacular languages such as Marathi, Hindi, Tamil, Gujarati, and many others. When Mulk Raj Anand and Eleanor Zelliot published an anthology of Marathi

Dalit writing translated into English in 1992, and Dalits themselves began to write in English, it heightened awareness of the Dalit experience within the international community, which in turn launched these works into the mainstream. Some critics maintain that it was this international attention that dissolved the initial resistance of Indian presses to publish these texts.

Many Dalit writings from the Ambedkar period or shortly after it were autobiographical. Critics and historians attribute this to the need for writers to break long-imposed silences by speaking out against their struggle amid the violence and degradation inflicted upon them. *Joothan* by Valmiki, written in Hindi, and *The Outcaste* by Jadav, written in English, are among the first and most famous of this genre. Such accounts might be read as ones that simultaneously opened spaces for Dalits to assert their own agency while raising public awareness of their fight for justice within society.

These accounts were followed by fiction and poetry that increasingly represented the sociocultural, economic realities faced by Dalits and their political aspirations around securing equality and dignity. Writers relied on what critics call an aesthetics of opposition to craft a distinctively Dalit voice through which to assert their legitimacy and equality. For instance, strategies of narrative interruption, subversion of conventional and canonical literary tropes, and provocative language and content representing Dalit experience and resilience are some of the most distinctive characteristics of this literary tradition. Negative critiques of Dalit writings maintain that its representations of filth, violence, or the grotesque through its imagery detract from its literary and aesthetic excellence. In an interview published in *Akrosh*, Gujarati poet Neerav Patel counters such critiques, explaining that while the images may be unsettling, Dalit writers who expose and condemn the realities of oppression by controlling how Dalit experience is narrated reclaim lost power and agency for themselves and the Dalit community.

While these practices challenge, and even overturn, practices associated with the Indian literary canon, they press for acknowledgment by it through canonical restructuring that acknowledges Dalit voices by integrating them into India's literary discourse. Common themes of modern Dalit writing include caste discrimination, social marginalization, and violence against Dalit women. But they also include accounts of resilience, activism, and celebrations of Dalit culture. Given that the Dalit liberation movement began in Maharastra, the first modern Dalit literature was authored in Marathi by figures such as Baburao Bagul and Namdeo Dhasal, who went on to form the Dalit Panthers Movement. Subsequently, texts emerged in other languages and covered experiences specific to their local communities in addition to the global issues mentioned above. For instance, Gujarati Dalit literature, which emerged a bit later in the 1970s and 1980s, addressed questions of reservation for Dalits, a system similar to affirmative action legislated by the Indian government. Hindi-language writer Valmiki devoted his autobiographical work *Joothan* to sharing his story of overturning his internal struggle against a system that ruthlessly challenged his human rights and dignity to lay out a plan to liberate his people from deeply entrenched oppression. The Tamil activist writer

Bama explores casteism in the Christian Dalit communities through a combination of folk narrative and a poetics of protest that challenges patriarchy inflicted from within the caste and from outside it.

Novels such as Mulk Raj Anand's *Untouchable* (1935) and the short stories of the Bengali anti-bond-slavery activist Mahasweta Devi—introduced to Western readers through translations by Gayatri Spivak—raised an awareness of Dalit experience among academic audiences. But one can make the case that Arundhati Roy's Booker Prize–winning novel *The God of Small Things* (1998), her subsequent activist writings and campaigns, and Danny Boyle's Oscar-winning film *Slumdog Millionaire* (2008)—based on Vikas Swarup's novel *Q and A*—have played a major role in bringing awareness of Dalit human rights issues into the popular consciousness. These works have raised questions about whether texts like these, authored by non-Dalits, ought to count as Dalit literature. The general feeling among writers who are Dalit appears to be that these texts differ from their own because they can only narrate caste experience from the outside. Despite this perceived gap and the relatively few negative critiques of these texts, they are accepted as sources that promote productive dialogue, and their writers are accepted as supporters of Dalit liberation.

Sejal Sutaria

See also: Women Writers, India

Further Reading

Anand, Mulk Raj, Ed Mulk, Raj Anand, and Eleanor Zelliot. 1992. *An Anthology of Dalit Literature (Poems)*. New Delhi: South Asia Books.

Gajarawala, Toral Jatin. 2012. *Untouchable Fictions: Literary Realism and the Crisis of Caste*. New York: Fordham University Press.

Paswan, Sanjay, and Pramanshi Jaideva. 2002. *Encyclopedia of Dalits in India: Movements*. New Delhi: Kalpaz Publications.

Randhawa, Harbir Singh. 2010. *Dalit Literature: Contents, Trends and Concerns*. New Delhi: Sarup Books.

LITERATURE, POST-1990, CHINA

Chinese literature and culture since the 1990s can best be understood in the historical context of two crucial turning points. The first is the globalization process set in motion by Deng Xiaoping's (1904–1997) economic policies during the New Era (*Xin shiqi* 新時期, 1979–1989), a marked shift from China's state-planned economy in the 1950s–1970s toward a market economy. The second turning point occurred on June 4, 1989, during the Tiananmen Square massacre in Beijing and its aftermath, which brought the 1980s atmosphere of intellectual freedom and optimism (referred to as Culture Fever or *wenhua re* 文化熱) to a halt. By the early 1990s, elite literature, represented by the root-seeking (*xungen* 尋根) and avant-garde (*xianfeng* 先鋒) movements, gave way to more popular forms of literature, partly as a result of the decrease in government subsidies for state literary institutions like the Chinese Writers Association. One example of the proliferation of popular literature is the work of Wang Shuo (王朔, 1958–), whose hooligan literature (*pizi wenxue* 痞子文學) depicting sex and violence mocked the very idea of elite literature by adopting a colloquial language and humorous writing style.

The career trajectories of Yu Hua (余華, 1960–) and Su Tong (蘇童, 1963–) also illustrate how literature and popular culture became increasingly aligned. Two of the most internationally recognized contemporary Chinese writers, their work first became known largely due to director Zhang Yimou's critically acclaimed film adaptations of Yu Hua's *To Live* (*Huozhe* 活著 novella, 1993; film, 1994) and Su Tong's *Wives and Concubines* (*Qiqie chengqun* 妻妾成群 novella, 1987; *Raise the Red Lantern*, *Da hong denglong gaogao gua* 大紅燈籠高高掛 film, 1992). While their earlier writing was experimental in style, they later adopted a realist style more accessible to readers. Along with Mo Yan (莫言, 1955–), whose novel *Red Sorghum* (*Hong gaoliang jiazu* 紅高粱家族, 1986) was made into a film in 1987 also directed by Zhang Yimou, contemporary Chinese fiction in translation finally attained world recognition by the mid-1990s.

During this same period, feminist literature (*nüxing wenxue* 女性文學) underwent significant developments as women writers started writing about the personal experiences of individual women. Authors like Wang Anyi (王安憶, 1954–) and Tie Ning (鐵凝, 1957–) had already explored women's psychology in the late 1980s and addressed issues such as sexual love and gender relations, but in the 1990s there was a new focus on female subjectivity. Same-sex love, a common theme in women's writing in the 1920s and 1930s, resurfaced in stories like Chen Ran's (陳染, 1962–) "Breaking Open" ("Pokai" 破開, 1995). These narratives are characterized by their attention to personal exploration and expression and their innovative form, such as the calling up of repressed memories and fragmentation. Avant-garde novels

Zhou Weihui, or Wei Hui, shot to fame with her controversial novel *Shanghai Baby* (1999), which follows the love affairs of an aspiring author in Shanghai, and was banned in China. She is seen here in Cannes, France, in 2006, promoting the film version of the book. (dpa Picture Alliance Archive/Alamy Stock Photo)

like Chen Ran's *A Private Life* (*Siren shenghuo* 私人生活, 1996) and Lin Bai's (林白, 1958–) *A War of One's Own* (*Yigeren de zhanzheng* 一個人的戰爭, 1994), as well as Wang Anyi's historical saga *Song of Everlasting Sorrow* (*Changhen ge* 長恨歌, 1996), all depict how female identity and individuality are shaped by social and cultural forces. By the late 1990s, one popular subcategory of women's literature that emerged was the genre of body writing (*shenti wenxue* 身體文學). The beauty writers (*meinnü zuojia* 美女作家) garnered controversy through their frank depiction of drugs and sexual promiscuity, and their cosmopolitan view of youth culture, most notably in Wei Hui's (衛慧, 1973–) *Shanghai Baby* (*Shanghai baobei* 上海寶貝, 1999) and Mian Mian's (棉棉, 1970–) *Candy* (*Tang* 糖, 2000), both of which were widely translated.

The Nobel Prize in Literature also contributed to the international recognition of contemporary Chinese literature, beginning in 2000 when the experimental playwright and author Gao Xingjian (高行健, 1940–) became the first Chinese-born author to receive the award. In the 1980s, he established his reputation with a series of absurdist plays, including *Bus Stop* (*Chezhan* 車站, 1983) and *Wild Men* (*Yeren* 野人, 1985), before publishing his semiautobiographical experimental travel narrative *Soul Mountain* (*Lingshan* 靈山) in 1990. In 2012 the author Mo Yan, whose work reconstructs rural folk culture and is grounded in the body's physical needs, was also awarded the Nobel Prize in Literature. His trademark narrative mode of "strange realism" (*guaidan xianshi zhuyi* 怪誕現實主義) is most evident in his satirical novels, such as *The Republic of Wine* (*Jiu guo* 酒國, 1992), *Big Breasts and Wide Hips* (*Fengru feitun* 豐乳肥臀, 1995), and *Life and Death Are Wearing Me Out* (*Shengsi pilao* 生死疲勞, 2006). In the last decade, critical realist novels that explore contemporary social issues make up another genre of literature that has received critical acclaim in China and overseas. For example, Yan Lianke's (閻連科, 1958–) *Dream of Ding Village* (*Ding zhuang meng* 丁莊夢, 2006) was inspired by a scandal in rural Henan in which villagers selling blood were contaminated with AIDS, leading to a major outbreak in the province.

A literary group that has made a significant impact on popular culture is the post-1980s (*baling hou* 八零後) generation of writers represented by celebrities such as the novelist-blogger Han Han (韓寒, 1982–) of *Triple Door* (*San chong men* 三重門, 2000) fame and young-adult novelist and filmmaker Guo Jingming (郭敬明, 1983–), whose best-selling *Tiny Times* (*Xiao shidai* 小時代) series has been a huge commercial success in both book and film form. Together with writers like Chun Sue (春樹, 1983–) and Zhang Yueran (張悅然, 1982–), the post-1980s group has given a voice to the previously ignored younger generation of writers.

The genre of literature that has seen the most dramatic upsurge in popularity in China since the 1990s, however, is Internet literature (*wangluo wenxue* 網絡文學). Chinese Internet writers known as *xieshou* (寫手) produce literature intended to be read on screen, and the most popular writers have cultivated legions of fans known as netizens or *wangyou* (網友). *Under the Banyan Tree*, whose site at rong-shuxia.com originated in 1997, is arguably the most well-established website for

Tsai Chih Chung (1948–)

Born in rural Taiwan, Tsai started as a cartoonist in Taipei at the age of 15 and saw early success in film animation, creating *Lao Fuzi* (*The Old Master*, 1981). Tsai's fame today rests on his comics about traditional Chinese culture. Captivated by the wit and wisdom of the Daoist classic *Zhuangzi*, he published *Zhuangzi Speaks: The Music of Nature* (1986). Its phenomenal success led to comic versions of *Laozi* and Confucius soon after. Tsai uses phrases from the original texts along with his own words to convey ancient ideas, but his genius is most evident when his sharply drawn figures and their worldviews come alive in the frame of a comic strip, even without words. Buddhism, Chinese history, classic novels, and popular tales have all been retold through Tsai's work. With more than 40 million comics sold, plus English editions, Tsai is a globally admired master of his art.

Desmond Cheung

Internet literature written in Chinese, and some of its earliest writers included those publishing under the pen names Li Xunhuan (李尋歡), Annie Baby (安妮寶貝), and Ning Caishen (宁財神). Internet novels, such as Murong Xuecun's (慕容雪村, 1974–) 2004 novel *Chengdu, Please Forget Me Tonight* (*Chengdu, jinye qing jiang wo yiwang* 成都，今夜請將我遺忘, 2002) have made it into print and gone on to receive literary recognition in translation. Beginning around 2000 with the inception of poetry forums such as poemlife.com, the Internet also became the creative space for poetic innovation. Groups like the School of Rubbish (Laji pai垃圾派) and its predecessor the Low Poetry Movement (Di shige yundong 低詩歌運動) have challenged the prevailing notions of poetry as a sacred and elite art form. Finally, in the last decade, the category of sinophone literature (*huayu wenxue* 華語文學) has drawn attention to the question of what constitutes Chinese literature, raising questions about the relationship between cultural production in mainland China and Hong Kong, Taiwan, and overseas.

Angie C. Chau

See also: Han Han (Chapter 5: Internet and Social Media); Hua, Yu; Literature, Taiwan; Literature, Tibet; Literature, Uyghur

Further Reading

Chi, Pang-yuan, and David Der-wei Wang, eds. 2000. *Chinese Literature in the Second Half of a Modern Century: A Critical Survey*. Bloomington: Indiana University Press.

Hockx, Michel. 2015. *Internet Literature in China*. New York: Columbia University Press.

Hong Zicheng. 2007. *A History of Contemporary Chinese Literature*. Trans. Michael M. Day. Leiden, NL: Brill.

Inwood, Heather. 2014. *Verse Going Viral: China's New Media Scenes*. Seattle: University of Washington Press.

Lau, Joseph S. M., and Howard Goldblatt, eds. 2007. *The Columbia Anthology of Modern Chinese Literature*, 2nd ed. New York: Columbia University Press.

Shih, Shu-mei. 2007. *Visuality and Identity: Sinophone Articulations across the Pacific*. Berkeley: University of California Press.

Zhang, Xudong. 1997. *Chinese Modernism in the Age of Reform: Cultural Fever, Avant-Garde Fiction, and the New Chinese Cinema*. Durham, NC: Duke University Press.

LITERATURE, TAIWAN

The literature of Taiwan is as diverse as the island's historical and political experiences. Take, for example, the brilliant novel *Orphan of Asia* by Taiwanese author Wu Zhuoliu (1900–1976). First published in 1946, *Orphan* depicts the life of a young man named Hu Taiming who struggles with issues of Taiwanese identity. Hu Taiming is legally a member of the Japanese Empire under Japanese colonialism (1895–1945), but he is treated as a second-class citizen in his own homeland; he identifies with mainland Chinese with whom he shares an ethnic heritage, but he is rejected by his mainland Chinese counterparts when he studies abroad in Japan. When he falls in love with a Shanghainese woman while working on the mainland, he is unable to fully participate in local politics because he is considered a foreigner. Thus, the protagonist Hu Taiming is truly an orphan of Asia. Like Taiwan, he is at once an integral participant in Asian history, yet at the same time his voice is drowned out by competing voices that metaphorically speak louder than, or speak for, him.

Literature in Taiwan before Japanese occupation was marked by the interaction between Aboriginals of Austronesian descent who peopled the island and residents of the mainland who migrated to the island during the Ming dynasty (1368–1644). Taiwan entered official records when it was incorporated as a province of Fujian, located on the mainland, in 1683. To the governors of Beijing, Taiwan was a remote frontier outpost for the following 200 years. In 1895 the island was ceded to Japan by the Qing government in China.

The imprint of 50 years of Japanese colonization on Taiwanese literature is evident in numerous ways. In the 1920s the Taiwanese New Literature Movement included writers such as Lai He (1894–1943) and Yang Kui (1906–1985), who debated the use of classical Chinese modes of expression in an age of modernization, discussed whether or not it was best to write in Taiwanese vernacular, and navigated a number of concerns: Western notions of democratic governance, identification with Han Chinese on the mainland, and anti-imperialism. In 1931 the colonial government cracked down on the Taiwanese New Literature Movement and its advocates.

A second generation of writers, who had come of age within the Japanese educational system, emerged in the 1930s. They described both the advantages and disadvantages of living under foreign rule—unlike the first generation of writers who focused on the harsh yoke of colonization. Writers who studied abroad in Japan were influenced by both Japanese written modes as well as Western artistic concepts. A nativist movement, which advocated for the protection of local traditional and agrarian culture in Taiwan as a form of resistance against

Japanese assimilation and modernization, was endorsed by Huang Shihui (1900–1945) and Guo Qiusen (1904–1980). From 1937 to 1945, Taiwanese writers were divided by the government into pro- and anticolonial camps, and Chinese-language sections were banned in newspapers and magazines.

KMT (Kuomintang, Guomindang, Nationalist Party) rule in Taiwan began with retrocession in 1945 and was followed by the violent February 28 Incident of 1947, the KMT retreat to Taiwan in 1949, and the subsequent "White Terror" as the government censored local dissent, alignment with the "free world" during the Cold War, and the eventual decline of Taiwan's international recognition after losing representation in the United Nations in 1971. As we can see, each chapter in the KMT history of Taiwan, just like Taiwan's historical trajectory throughout the 20th century, was quite brief; as a result, a complex process of acceptance, rejection, and adaptation of various influences shaped the experiences and ideas presented in Taiwan's literature. Some ruptures with the past were more intense than others. For example, middle-aged writers during the initial stages of Nationalist rule in the 1950s were hampered by the replacement of Japanese with Mandarin Chinese as the official language.

After 1945 the Nationalist regime promoted traditional culture, including classical poetry, which as Michelle Yeh has written, maintained the conventional meter and rhythm of its 3,000-year tradition as a "sister art" to calligraphy and painting. Realistic writing avoided references to class consciousness or other left-wing elements ascribed to the May Fourth Movement in China, while writings that focused on the private life, including nostalgic reflections of the mainland, received approval by the state, as did writings with anticommunist, pronationalist themes. In the late 1950s and early 1960s, a collection of writers, including authors Wang Wenxing (1939–) and Bai Xianyong (1937–), employed modernist writing techniques, such as obscure language and reflections on metaphysical dilemmas. These writers displayed a "double alienation" from the writing tradition on the mainland and from the physical geography of the mainland that was their home. An important part of the modernist literary movement in Taiwan was the journal *Xiandai wenxue* (*Modern Literature*, 1960–1973). Founded by Taiwan university students, the journal also published translations of Western authors, such as Franz Kafka, James Joyce, and Virginia Woolf.

Modernist writing contrasted with the work of nativist writers of the 1970s. The "revival" of the nativist literature movement reflects a transitional period as writers conveyed the experience of local Taiwanese whose perception of history and society differed from that of the mainlanders who immigrated to the island in 1949 following the Nationalist defeat by the Communists. Angelina Yee, in her article "Constructing a Native Consciousness: Taiwan Literature in the 20th Century," summarizes the nativist point as it was positioned against: (a) Western values such as capitalism, materialism, and imperialism, (b) the repressive, minority KMT Nationalist government, and (c) the oppressive mainland Chinese government. Authors of the nativist movement include Wang Tuo (1944–), Yang Qingchu (1940–), Chen Yingzhen (1937–), and Wang Zhenhe (1940–). In 1972,

Huang Chunming, National Treasure

What does it take to become a national treasure in Taiwan? For Huang Chunming, it has taken five decades of innovative, humane, and often pioneering fiction, the creation of a venue and style of contemporary drama, ceaseless attention to and involvement in humanitarian enterprises, and a love of place and people.

Born in rural Taiwan in 1935, Huang was one of a coterie of writers and artists with close ties to the generally impoverished Taiwanese countryside and its people, whose work has often been labeled "nativist" but at core can be considered a form of compassionate realism.

Huang began writing short fiction in the 1950s as a student in a small college in eastern Taiwan. His stories gained popularity with readers eager for tales of small-town and rural Taiwan, particularly as a counterpoint to the more "elevated," urban-based stories by university-trained, Western-oriented writers. As his career progressed and his renown expanded in the wake of such masterpieces as "Fish" ("Yu") and "The Gong" ("Luo"), he added urban settings and themes to his substantial oeuvre. That included fiction that attacked the corrosive effect of global capitalism and slavish attitudes toward the West, powerful stories like "The Two Sign Painters" ("Liangge youqi jiang"), in which the city defeats and demeans "migrants" from the countryside.

Huang Chunming's immense and varied contributions to Taiwanese culture and popular institutions, including children's theater, have been acknowledged by his anointment as a National Treasure. His work, translated into many languages, has also made him an acclaimed international literary figure and a cultural ambassador of his Taiwanese home.

Howard Goldblatt

differences between modernist and nativist writers were at the heart of the "New Poetry" debates, in which nativist criticism was directed toward the modernists for not using traditional Chinese techniques or Taiwan's local dialects in their writings. The debates culminated in 1977–1978, following a government-organized conference in 1977 entitled "The Symposium of Literary Workers," during which attacks on nativist literature took center stage.

In 1987, a watershed year in Taiwan, martial law, which had been established in 1947, was finally abolished. After 1987 and the formation of an opposition party (the Democratic Progressive Party), Taiwan's "baby boom" generation no longer needed to actively engage in political discussions. Instead, literature was characterized by problems of Taiwan's middle-class, relaxed moral standards and liberated sexual views. Today's literature is multifaceted and includes digital media, postmodern trends, ecoliterature, feminist works, science fiction, and LGBT fiction. In addition, authors have stressed their unique cultural identity upon the reopening of communication with China. The diversity in Taiwan's literature is thus not merely the result of Taiwan's incorporation into global trade networks but, as scholar Fangming Chen writes, "aspirations for liberation did not have to wait until the introduction of postmodern thought into Taiwan; rather, it was precisely the end of martial law that enabled previously suppressed desires to be unbound" (Chen 2007, 45).

In Taiwan of the 1990s to the writing of today, we find, as Fran Martin has written in the context of sexual knowledge, "critical and selective appropriations and reworkings of terms and concepts that originated elsewhere" and at home (Martin 2003, 23). Short stories such as Zhu Tianwen's (1956–) "Fin de Siècle Splendor" and Qiu Miaojin's (1969–1995) "Letters from Montmartre" radically interrogate not only the difference between nativism and modernism, or colonial and postcolonial experience, but the nature of these long-standing ideas and divisions. Today's literature in Taiwan continues to open up new fissures and fault lines as it recovers the past and contemplates the future.

James Wicks

See also: Cinema, Taiwan (Chapter 3: Film)

Further Reading

Chang, Sung-sheng, Michelle M.-H. Yeh, and Mingru Fan. 2014. *The Columbia Sourcebook of Literary Taiwan*. New York: Columbia University Press.

Chang, Yvonne Sung-sheng. 2004. *Literary Culture in Taiwan: Martial Law to Market Law*. New York: Columbia University Press.

Chen, Fangming. 2007. "Postmodern or Postcolonial? An Inquiry into Postwar Taiwanese Literary History." In *Writing Taiwan: A New Literary History*. Ed. David Der-wei Wang and Carlos Rojas, 26–50. Durham, NC: Duke University Press.

Lau, Joseph S. M., and Howard Goldblatt, eds. 2007. *The Columbia Anthology of Modern Chinese Literature*. New York: Columbia University Press.

Martin, Fran. 2003. *Situating Sexualities: Queer Representation in Taiwanese Fiction, Film and Public Culture*. Hong Kong: Hong Kong University Press.

Yeh, Michelle, and N. G. D. Malmqvist. 2001. *Frontier Taiwan: An Anthology of Modern Chinese Poetry*. New York: Columbia University Press.

LITERATURE, TIBET

Tibetan literature is often associated with Buddhism. This was certainly valid for pre-1950s Tibet, which, in view of its small population, ranked among the most active centers of Buddhist textual production in Asia. But with the Chinese takeover, Tibetan literature underwent tremendous changes. While Tibetan popular literature per se is still slow to emerge, Tibetan writers have creatively inaugurated genres in a few decades: realism, magic realism, biofiction, as well as free-verse poetry and the novel. Moreover, Tibetan literature is now increasingly written in Chinese and English, enlarging its potential readership and diversifying the Tibetan literary spectrum.

In the 1950s, Tibet's military takeover by the newly founded People's Republic of China (PRC, f. 1949) introduced new cultural and literary standards. The translation of Mao's works and Marxist-Leninist classics into Tibetan by educated lamas and monks paved the way for new literary styles and lexicon. Another radical change occurred in the late 1970s and early 1980s: a new generation of Tibetans, grown up during the Cultural Revolution (1966–1976), educated by clerics who had survived the Maoist frenzy, and increasingly familiar with Chinese modern literature, set to inventing a modern fictional and poetic literature in the Tibetan language, under the watchful Chinese state's ideological guidance. The first Tibetan-language free-verse poem, "Waterfall of Youth" ("*Lang tsho'i rbab chu*"), was written in 1983 by Dondrup Gyal (Don grub rgyal, 1953–1985), the hero of this new literature. Claiming that Tibetan youth should shape their future in their radically changed environment in the same way as poetry was to evolve by adopting new styles, his poem enabled the emergence of underrepresented categories of writers (high-school students, laypersons, women authors). The multisecular, complex rules that had dominated poetic writing in Tibet began to lose their grip. Free-verse poems filled state-funded literary magazines, still the only venue for literary creation in the 1980s. Realist fiction appeared concurrently, with hundreds of short stories set in a Tibetan background, replete with realistic dialogues, an all-knowing narrator, a plot, ordinary heroes, and clear and realistic time and space frames. Langdun Paljor's (Glang mdun dpal 'byor, 1941–2014) *The Head Turquoise* (*Gtsug gyu*), the first full-length Tibetan novel, was published in Lhasa in 1985. It portrayed the plight of a servant victim of the hypocrisy and corruption of the Tibetan Lhasa elite in pre-1950 Tibet. In spite of its heavy political subtext, in tune with some 1980s literary creation, the novel was a huge success due to its minute depiction of Lhasa's "old society" from within.

In the 1990s, Chinese leaders encouraged economic liberalization. State monopoly on Tibetan literature was partially lifted: independently run magazines diversified their literary offering, a trend that increased in the 2000s and 2010s. The major innovations to be noted are the "new versification" by the popular poet Sengdor (Seng rdor, 1980–), the emergence of women writers with the publication in 2014 of *Cheese* (*Phyur ba*) by Khamo Gyal (Mkha' mo rgyal), the first women's novel, and the increase in the number of novels published (totaling around 30 in 2015). The most successful—and controversial—of novelists, with five published works to date, is Tsering Dondrup (Tshe ring don grub, 1961–), who throughout his 30-year writing career has taken great delight in targeting both greedy Tibetan lamas and corrupt Chinese cadres. Between 2009 and 2014, a state-run publishing house launched the 25-title collection Tibetan Writers of the Twenty-First Century. Starting with an initial print run of 2,000, best sellers reached 10,000 copies, a high figure considering there are only 6 million Tibetans, and only half of them are literate. But the all-time best seller among contemporary Tibetan texts is doubtlessly *The Joys and Sorrows of the Naktsang Boy* (2007), the autobiography of Naktsang Nülo (Snags tshang nus blo, 1949–), with an estimated 40,000 circulating (mostly illegal) copies. With its heavy use of the northeastern Amdo Tibetan dialect and its so-far unique Tibet-centered depiction of the violent Sino-Tibetan war in the 1950s, it comes close to a Tibetan version of popular literature. Due to its sensitive political content, though, the book was banned in 2009.

But if one takes "popular" as meaning both "nonreligious" and "widespread," mention should be made of the centuries-old epic *Gesar* (*Ge sar*), featuring its eponymous semilegendary hero. Gesar's voluminous and numerous episodes (possibly over 100, some containing up to 1,000 printed pages) are still popular, especially in nomadic communities (now dwindling due to imposed settlement policies) where bards can still be found, and the epic is infusing contemporary literary, musical, drama, and film creation.

Several factors contribute to the dearth of popular literature per se in Tibet: a still-low literacy rate (ca. 50 percent), an overwhelmingly rural population (ca. 80 percent), a lack of urban life with Tibetan characteristics (towns are Chinese), a prestigious and ancient literary tradition that may stifle innovation, the still-prevalent view that literature belongs to the realm of the sacred, making "popular literature" an oxymoron, the still-important gap between spoken and written Tibetan, the scarcity of commercial bookshops, the ban on Tibetan private publishers, the tight scrutiny of Tibetan authors by Chinese authorities, and evidently the declining state of Tibetan language in public space. As a consequence, such genres as romantic novels, cartoons, and mystery and detective stories are still unheard of in the Tibetan language.

China's takeover of Tibet has led to the recent adoption of Chinese as a literary language, a classical colonial case of diglossia. Two Sinophone half-Tibetan authors have proven quite popular both among Chinese readers and internationally: Tashi Dawa (1955–), who introduced magic realism to Tibetan literature, and Alai (1959–), whose use of Tibet is controversial among Tibetans (Kyabchen Dedrol 2009). In exile, where an estimated 3 percent of the Tibetan population lives, little literature is produced, and English prevails. The most popular work produced in exile so far is the prize-winning *The Mandala of Sherlock Homes*, by Jamyang Norbu (1999), in which the famous detective sets out to solve mysteries in a Tibet that is coveted by China, Russia, and the British alike.

In fact, the association between Tibet and popular literature is most visible in world popular literature best sellers, where Tibet serves as mostly a catchy backdrop: *Lost Horizons* (1933) by James Hilton, *Tintin in Tibet* (1960) by Hergé, and lately *Tibet Code* (2008) by He Ma. Still, the translation of two episodes of Harry Potter and of Antoine de Saint-Exupéry's *The Little Prince* into Tibetan, in the early 2010s, may open new literary perspectives and inspire Tibetan writers to develop a much-awaited indigenous popular literature in the Tibetan language.

Françoise Robin

See also: Cinema, Tibet (Chapter 3: Film)

Further Reading

Hartley, L., and P. Schiaffini, eds. 2008. *Modern Tibetan Literature and Social Change.* Durham, NC: Duke University Press.

Kyabchen, Dedrol. 2009. "Alai on Tibetan Language." *Tibet Web Digest.* May 31. http://tibet webdigest.com/alai-on-tibetan-language. Accessed May 19, 2015.

Robin, F. 2009. "The Tibetan Novel: Still a Novelty. A Brief Survey of Tibetan Novels Since 1985." *Latse Library Newsletter* 6: 26–45.

Stewart, F., H. J. Batt, and T. Shakya, eds. 2000. *Mānoa* 12/2 *Song of the Snow Lion. Tibetan Contemporary Literature*. Honolulu: University of Hawai'i Press.

Stoddard, H. 1996 [1994]. "Tibetan Publications and National Identity." In *Resistance and Reform in Tibet*. Ed. R. Barnett and S. Akiner, 121–156. Delhi: Motilal Banarsidass.

LITERATURE, UYGHUR

In any treatment of Uyghur literature, the first task is determining the starting point. A nomadic tribe called the Uyghurs entered the historical record in the sixth century and within 200 years had established a powerful empire. The ninth century saw the Uyghurs' political fortunes decline, but in subsequent centuries Uyghurs were employed as scribes in the Mongol and Chinese empires, and in parts of Eurasia they acquired a reputation for learning. Beginning in the 10th century, Islam began to take hold in the region we now know as Xinjiang, the Uyghur homeland; and by the 16th century nearly all of the people we now think of as Uyghurs had become Muslim.

With the coming of Islam, Uyghur literature was transformed, with Persian poetic genres replacing native forms and the vertical Uyghur script abandoned in favor of a modified Arabic orthography. The name Uyghur also gradually fell into disuse, as the culture and identity of the region's peoples was reoriented by membership in the broader Islamic community. China's 18th-century conquest of the region added another layer of complexity to regional identities. It was only in the 20th century, as social and political change profoundly altered Central Asian life, that "Uyghur" gained currency again as the preferred designation for a contemporary people. It is with this era of change, in which the term "Uyghur" once more came to denote a living literature, that the below discussion will begin.

In the decades before and after the 1917 Bolshevik revolution, Central Asian communities were radically reshaped by ideas and practices we now identify with modernity: nationalism, socialism, mass education, and the bureaucratic state. Local reformers and Bolshevik planners recognized various Central Asian groups—Uzbeks, Kazakhs, Tajiks, and others—as Soviet nationalities. The Uyghurs were among the smaller groups thus recognized in the USSR; but at the same time, they were defined as part of a much larger national group including millions of brethren across the Chinese border in Xinjiang.

In the Soviet Union as elsewhere, a key part of the nation-building process was the codification of national languages and literatures. Central Asian communities had for centuries shared a common literary canon, written in Persian as well as Chaghatay, the literary lingua franca of Turkic Central Asia. Once modern languages like Kazakh, Uzbek, and Uyghur had been standardized from the spoken dialects of their respective communities, fragments of this common canon were adopted by the new nations as their ancestral literary heritage. Each national literature also absorbed parts of the oral literature transmitted locally over the centuries. And across

Central Asia, a new generation of writers made their respective national languages the vehicle for a new literature that was "national in form, socialist in content."

Modern Uyghur literature was no exception. In the 1920s, Soviet Uyghur literature textbooks began to shape a national canon around classical Central Asian poets, oral literature from the Uyghur region, and a cohort of young Uyghur writers schooled in Soviet literary technique. Till the mid-1930s, though, this literature was largely confined to the Soviet Uyghur community; the much larger population in Xinjiang had little access to Soviet publications, which Xinjiang's rulers considered a potential threat to the province's stability. All this changed after 1933, as the Xinjiang government under Sheng Shicai reversed course and aligned closely with the USSR, while still acknowledging nominal allegiance to China. Soviet advisers and publications poured into Xinjiang, bringing with them the notion of a modern Uyghur nation and language as well as a Uyghur literature that had already developed an orthography, style, and canon. The relatively small Soviet Uyghur community thus had an outsized influence on the development of 20th-century Uyghur literature; and from the mid-1930s through the late 1950s, the literatures of the Chinese and Soviet Uyghur communities developed in tandem. A cohort of young writers from Xinjiang was soon added to the Uyghur canon: the poet Lutpulla Mutellip (1922–1945), the dramaturge Zunun Qadiri (1912–1989), and many others.

Stalin's 1937 purge wiped out much of the original cohort of Uyghur literati in the USSR, and Sheng soon extended the purge into Xinjiang, imprisoning and executing numerous writers and intellectuals. Yet while Uyghur literature limped along in the USSR for a time, it continued to flourish in Xinjiang, despite Sheng's penchant for purges. By 1944 the Chinese Nationalist Party had regained control of Xinjiang, kicked out the Soviet advisers, and sent Sheng packing. But the USSR was not easily deterred, and in late 1944 a Soviet-backed insurrection resulted in the founding of the separatist Eastern Turkestan Republic (ETR) in northern Xinjiang. While Uyghur literature in southern Xinjiang took a more nationalist turn, writers in the ETR maintained the socialist outlook and style of their Soviet patrons. After 1949, as Xinjiang and the ETR were integrated into the new People's Republic of China, former ETR literati, already seasoned in a socialist literary milieu, became prominent in the new cultural establishment of socialist Xinjiang.

Uyghur literature in the early years of Chinese Communist Party rule in Xinjiang continued along much the same lines as Soviet-inspired Uyghur literature of the previous three decades. Young poets discarded complex ancient meters and ornate Persian vocabulary in favor of a popular style that the newly literate could easily understand. Uyghur prose fiction, still in its infancy, took baby steps as writers extolled the achievements of socialism in short stories and novellas. The rapidly evolving new Uyghur canon was promulgated in schools throughout the province as literacy continued to spread. Uyghur literature textbooks in Xinjiang typically included a few Soviet Uyghur authors, and vice versa.

In the late 1950s, Sino-Soviet relations took a turn for the worse, and by the 1960s cultural exchange between the two countries had ceased. As Chinese policies continued to radicalize, Soviet officials lavished support on Uyghur official culture in an effort to win hearts and minds on both sides of the border. Tens of thousands of Uyghurs left China for the USSR, including a substantial number of writers and intellectuals, whose presence greatly enriched Soviet Uyghur literature in the following decades. In 1963 Xinjiang's border with the USSR was sealed, not to be reopened for two decades. Uyghur literature was now split in two.

Uyghur literature in the USSR carried on with renewed vigor and ample state support. Particularly notable was an efflorescence in prose fiction, much of it focusing on themes from Uyghur history. Meanwhile, spiraling radicalism in China culminated in the Cultural Revolution (1966–1976), which saw the condemnation of nearly all the country's intellectuals, living and dead. Uyghur writers were no exception, and Uyghur literature during the Cultural Revolution was reduced largely to strident revolutionary slogans wrapped in the flimsiest of literary garments.

The end of the Cultural Revolution and the beginning of China's reform era saw the rapid resurgence of Uyghur literature in China. Three decades of Maoist cultural policies were substantially rolled back, and long-suppressed literary energies burst forth in a remarkable outpouring of creativity, a phenomenon echoed across China. Uyghur prose fiction in Xinjiang finally hit its stride, with numerous novels appearing each year by the mid-1980s. Literary translation had a substantial impact, with foreign and Chinese works in all genres published in accessible Uyghur editions. In the mid-1980s, works encountered in translation helped spark a modernist movement in Uyghur poetry that remains vibrant today.

A key development in reform-era Uyghur literature has been the publication of much of the classic Central Asian literary corpus. Most of these works had previously circulated in Xinjiang only in manuscript form and were restricted and even burned during the Mao era. The reform-era publication of these works, often in modern Uyghur adaptations, has had a tremendous effect on contemporary poetry, as many poets—including some modernists—have incorporated themes, styles, and vocabulary from the classical canon.

The USSR's disintegration into independent states meant an end to Moscow's patronage of Uyghur culture, and Uyghur literature in the new Central Asian republics has gradually ebbed in vitality. The breakup of the Soviet Union and the Tiananmen incident spooked Chinese authorities, and state cultural control has progressively tightened in Xinjiang since the mid-1990s. At the same time, the proliferation of personal computers and the Internet has broken the near-monopoly that official cultural organs had enjoyed on modern Uyghur literature from the very beginning. This technological shift has given new energy to a literature that might otherwise be struggling under the weight of rapid social change. Even as Chinese-language schooling increasingly replaces mother-tongue education in Xinjiang, the Internet has helped enable the flourishing of a vibrant and varied contemporary literature in Uyghur.

Joshua L. Freeman

See also: Cinema, Uyghur (Chapter 3: Film)

Further Reading

Abdushükür Turdi, Lyu Bin, and Azad Rehmitulla Sultan, eds. 2006. *Uyghur edebiyati tarixi* [*A History of Uyghur Literature*]. 5 vols. Beijing: Milletler neshriyati.

Brophy, David. 2016. *Uyghur Nation: Reform and Revolution on the Russia-China Frontier.* Cambridge, MA: Harvard University Press.

Friederich, Michael. 2007. "Uyghur Literary Representations of Xinjiang Realities." In *Situating the Uyghurs Between China and Central Asia.* Ed. Ildikó Bellér-Hann et al., 89–107. Aldershot, UK: Ashgate.

Thum, Rian. 2014. *The Sacred Routes of Uyghur History.* Cambridge, MA: Harvard University Press.

MAHJOOR (GHULAM AHMED MEHJOOR)

The northern Indian state of Jammu and Kashmir is the site of conflicting political claims between India, Pakistan, and China. The nation-states of India and Pakistan have employed aggressive strategies and rhetoric of territorial nationalism in the former princely state of Jammu and Kashmir since independence in 1947. The partition of India and Pakistan legitimized these forces of aggressive nationalism and enabled virile hatred for the "other" to irreparably mutilate a shared anti-colonial legacy and cultural heritage. Even today the wounds inflicted by the partition are yet to heal. It was in the wake of this polarization, virulence, and fragmentation on the Indian subcontinent in 1947 that Ghulam Ahmed Mehjoor (1885–1952), also known by the pen name Mahjoor, flourished as a poet and esteemed Kashmiri nationalist. In his writing, Mahjoor evoked a political and nationalist consciousness that challenged the creation of polarized religious identities and communalized politics. Mahjoor introduced both a new style and a new voice in Kashmiri poetry.

While the political conflict throughout the region tore his homeland apart, Mahjoor used the beauty of his homeland to give hope and inspiration to his readers. Springing from the religious, cultural, and linguistic crossroads of his home region, with Kashmiri Muslims, Kashmiri Pandits, merchants, nomads, and pilgrims, Mahjoor's poetry reflected that religious and cultural pluralism. In his poetry, many religious and cultural ideologies blended together in evocative harmony. He wrote poetry in Persian and Urdu, and of course in his native Kashmiri. It was in his Kashmiri poetry that Mahjoor introduced an earthy style that was new to the more formal structure and vocabulary of classical poetry in that language. With a classical training in the poetry of Persia, Urdu, and Kashmir, Mahjoor brought a clear and simple style to his Kashmiri poems. Many of these poems are still popular in Jammu and Kashmir today, not only as written poems but also as songs to be sung in celebration of Kashmiri culture.

The inspirations for Mahjoor's poetry came from many sources but often from the natural world of Jammu and Kashmir that surrounded him. In his poetry, the many themes and subjects evoke the beautiful music of life and the natural world; verdant, rolling hills; sparkling snow-topped mountains; gushing streams; dew-sprinkled meadows in summer and snowflake-blanketed meadows in winter;

the aroma of pines, firs, and conifers; a fertile landscape inundated with the alluring ripeness of loquat, cherry, apple, and pomegranate trees; an unmistakable vitality and zeal for life in the air; the rustling of autumn leaves that calms the harried soul; the lustrous snows of winter; a palpable rapture that beckons the observer to plunge into the tempestuous waters of existence; the tenuous throes of infancy in the vibrant atmosphere of spring, with tenderly sprouting flower buds feeling their way into existence; the unflinching faith of the mystic in communion with the divine; a mysticism that cannot be reduced to history.

In Mahjoor's poetry, we can glimpse a halcyon world of beautiful Kashmiri nature in which he attempts to counter political repression, conscripted democratic spaces, jeopardized cultural emancipation, bigotry breeding intolerance, and militarization stunting growth. But Mahjoor never turned away from the turmoil and anguish of his homeland, and the problems that afflicted the region during his lifetime still confront its inhabitants today. Recent years have seen more cultural oppression and political violence. Armed insurgency, counterinsurgency, militarization, dispossession, and depoliticization in Jammu and Kashmir began anew in 1989. The history of Kashmir is similar to that of other conflict zones. Also, although a class/caste hierarchy does not enjoy religious legitimacy in predominantly Muslim Kashmir, socioeconomic class and caste divisions in Kashmir are as well entrenched as they are in other South Asian societies. There is also a rigid gender hierarchy in Kashmir. These issues can no longer be ignored, from the role of women in a conflict zone; the reconceptualization of a woman's identity in a politically militarized zone; intersections of class, education, ethnicity, religious identity in theorizing a woman's identity; and women's agency or lack thereof are only a few of the problems that have developed out of Jammu and Kashmir in recent years.

Mahjoor wrote about the problems of his own time and did not shy away from controversy.

In one poem, he wrote the following:

Shun the dispute, open the discourse among yourselves,
Share true love among yourselves . . .

(Translation by Mohammad Ali Matto from the original in *Kulyati Mehjoor* 1983, 279.)

Coexistence in peace is the main lesson taught by Mahjoor. Voices like Mahjoor's constantly engage with multilayered understandings of the Kashmir imbroglio and move beyond the contours of conflict to reconciliation and healing. His poetry is as relevant today as it was in 1947. It reflects upon the difficult task of rebuilding a nation based on pluralism and respect for religious, ethnic, linguistic, and cultural identities. This is evident in the continued veneration of Mahjoor by the Hindus as well as the Muslims of Kashmir. Reading Mahjoor revitalizes the reality that plurality and heterogeneity adorn the architecture of Kashmir, with an emphasis on local political projects, regionalism, peripheral social communities, traditions that survive the ravages of time, and marginalized forms of knowledge.

Mahjoor's poetry has been an important window into Kashmiri nationalism and pluralism.

Nyla Ali Khan

See also: Literature, Dalit; Tharoor, Shashi; Women Writers, India

Further Reading

Khan, Nyla Ali, ed. 2012. *The Parchment of Kashmir: History, Society, and Polity.* New York: Palgrave Macmillan.

Khan, Nyla Ali. 2014. *The Life of a Kashmiri Woman: Dialectic of Resistance and Accommodation.* New York: Palgrave Macmillan.

Mehjoor, Ghulam Ahmed. 1983. *Kulyati Mehjoor.* Trans. Mohammad Ali Matto. Srinagar, IN: Jammu and Kashmir Cultural Academy of Art, Culture, and Languages.

MANGA

Manga, the genre of print comics produced in Japan, ranks alongside North American comics and the Franco-Belgian *bande dessinée* as one of three major contributors to the world's sequential art. As an art form, manga's lineage traces back to illustrated scrolls from the 11th century. However, the manga read today began to take shape in the late 19th century, as Japanese artists reinvented Western comics traditions. Manga's engaging, serial storytelling gained a mass audience as inexpensive entertainment after World War II. The rapidly expanding market boasted stories aimed at boys, girls, adult men, and adult women, and subjects ranged from heroic fantasies to hard-boiled crime drama to government instruction manuals. By the early 1960s, manga found new life in animation on television, called anime, and both mediums became keystones of modern Japanese pop culture. Throughout Asia, the Japanese industry grew alongside related industries in Korea, China, and beyond, each with its own point of view and artistic stamp. With a global audience and a multibillion dollar industry today, the influence of Japanese manga is felt globally.

"Manga," when the term was popularized in the modern sense by artist Katsuhika Hokusai (1760–1849) around 1815, meant "whimsical or irresponsible pictures." Hokusai's manga were quick, eloquent sketches of daily life, folktales, and ghost stories. In Japan, woodblock printing, exemplified by Hokusai's own famous print *The Great Wave Off Kanagawa*, turned art from a rarefied luxury to an easily distributed mass medium. Printers produced crowd-pleasing comics collections and humor books, called *toba-e* and *kibyoshi*, or yellow books, respectively. These precursors to manga amused thousands of readers. The delight in caricature, surety of line, and meticulous detail in costume and setting prevalent in manga today harkens back to the prints and collections of this period.

When Japan's borders opened in 1854, not only did an isolated society experience a rapid, brutal mission to become a military and technological force

Japanese Manga

The oldest known examples of Japanese comedic art are caricatures drawn on the beams of the roof of a Buddhist temple in the ancient capital of Nara that date back to the eighth century CE. The Tokugawa period (1603–1867) saw these comic arts become widely available to the masses, and the first inklings of the modern form of the style developed from children's picture books. At this point, the subject matter was often comedic and exaggerated depictions of everyday life, which is a theme that survives currently. It was in this period that the term "manga" was first popularized in the modern sense by Hokusai Katsushika, whose 15-volume Hokusai Manga saw the introduction of manga into the everyday lives of Japanese people.

The Meiji period (1868–1912) saw the introduction of manga as a viable political tool when its long history of satire was used by the Freedom and People's Rights Movement to satirize the government in addition to providing a platform that was relatively free from government censure. American influences in the 1920s and 1930s saw Japanese comic strips appearing in newspapers of the time, and when Japan entered WWII, manga became just as important a vehicle of propaganda as comics did in America. Manga during WWII were designed to demoralize the enemy, boost morale at home, and convince the subject communities that their lives would be much better under Japanese rule.

The end of the war saw a marked increase in demand for manga, mainly as a way to raise the spirits of the Japanese people in a period when the country as a whole was devastated. At this point, magazines devoted to manga were marketed at young children. Over the years, manga began depicting an increasing variety of topics, including the introduction of homosexuality in the 1970s. By the 1990s, manga had become an international hit, not only in Asian countries but worldwide, to the point that its style has been adopted by artists around the world, and conventions celebrate the medium in many countries.

Deanna Bibler

to be reckoned with, its artists and writers were also suddenly exposed to all of Western art and literature. The political cartoons of London's *Punch* magazine and German, English, and American newspaper comic strips intrigued Japanese artists. Cartooning was originally launched in Japan by a British man, Charles Wirgman, editor of Japan's *Punch* magazine, in 1862. But the publication's Japanese artists soon transformed the cartoon format to suit their own stories, symbols, and visual languages.

In the decades following, Japan's newspapers and magazines were filled with comic strips. The rise of nationalism in Japan and the outbreak of World War II obliterated many of these as the government insisted comic-strip creators produce propaganda for the war effort. Many creators left the country or ceased publication, while others accepted government positions, but the flood of

Shown here are a batch of manga titles, or Japanese comic books, that have developed as part of a long tradition of visual art and storytelling in Japan. (David Lichtneker/Alamy Stock Photo)

innovation in the format was effectively halted. Once the war ended, the postwar economic depression led people to seek out cheap entertainment. Movies were prohibitively expensive and very few people had access to televisions, so the public turned to print.

One man, Osamu Tezuka (1928–1989), known as the God of Manga, originated how we see manga today and influenced creators for decades. As an aspiring artist and storyteller, he saw an opportunity in the publishing industry to create engaging serial comics that would unfold slowly over time. He began serializing his work in cheaply produced volumes that encouraged readers to follow stories month to month. Tezuka drew his influences from many sources, but he was especially enamored of animation and film. He admired the feats from Walt Disney's animation empire and loved the sound, pacing, and editing that was fundamental to feature films. He saw no reason to limit the length of stories told or the need to keep characters static, as is typical in comic strips and superhero comics. As he gathered together like-minded artists, manga embraced the elements that mark the industry today: long-form stories, extended character development, cinematic storytelling, and the production of content with attention to appeal to readers of different ages and genres. Tezuka is also responsible for making the leap from comics to animation as, by 1963, his landmark manga *The Mighty Atom*, also known as *Astro Boy*, debuted on network television, directed by Tezuka. From that point forward, manga and anime became intertwined, and their stories continue to inspire and boost each other's successes.

Manga and Anime

Japanese animated series and feature movies have been circulated overseas since the early 1960s. Although the U.S. market was the first in the Western world to air anime series (e.g., *Astro Boy*, *Speed Racer*, *Kimba the White Lion*), it was European countries that became the most profitable markets for anime and later for manga: Italy, France, Spain, Germany. There, the popularity of these two media is mainstream and not only limited to fan niches. Televised anime gained popularity there among young watchers from 1978 and smoothed the way for the release of many Japanese animated movies at the theaters. This combined success was the access gate for manga, the publication of which informally started in Western countries between the late 1970s (in Italy and France, in kids' magazines) and early 1980s (in the United States) and then exploded as a huge market in the 1990s, with many new manga works, but also, and in the first phase especially, old manga titles that had already gained vast popular success through their anime versions.

The impact of manga and anime in the world also entails problematic sides, including the alleged violence of the action-centered titles, the extreme contents and scenes in many erotic and pornographic works (especially in Europe and North America), and the representations of ethnicities perceived as racist (especially in Asian nations). Nonetheless, the expansion of manga and anime's popularity has grown and adapted to the new media, worldwide: from a TV-centered consumption model to an Internet- and mobile-media-centered one, ample fan communities have formed around the world. Moreover, the cultural penetration of manga and anime languages and aesthetics has encouraged a wide production of "manga-like" comics by non-Japanese creators and has influenced the aesthetics and narratives of serial animation and live-action cinema produced in America, Asia, and Europe.

Marco Pellitteri

From the 1960s onward, a devoted manga-reading public fueled expansion after expansion. As creators entered middle age, they started penning stories for themselves as well as those aimed at children and teenagers. Thus a mature, morally ambiguous tradition of manga geared toward adult men was born. When, in the 1970s, editors decided to aggressively pursue the female half of the population, women were invited to take the lead as creators, initially creating stories for young girls and then for adult women.

With no one genre dominating output, every kind of story made its way to manga's pages, from romance to historical epic to sports to family dramas. To this day, creators and publishers usually co-own each work, meaning the creators decide when their stories end and when they want to try a new character or write for a different audience. Readers will follow creators from project to project, and, while there are occasional spin-offs or the continuation of a series, each story is finite. Manga narratives typically emphasize the journey over the destination, eschewing any definitive wrap-up, and given the longer page count, they have significant space for silence, expression, and gesture in telling their stories.

Unlike most other comics industries, Japanese manga dominates the print industry in Japan. Most people, from schoolchildren to businesspeople to grandparents, read manga. Manga is read in weekly and monthly magazines and now on mobile devices. There were over 270 magazines, ranging anywhere from 50 to 300 pages each issue, published in 2013. In 2014 manga accounted for almost 80 percent of digital book sales in Japan. Many indulge in reading manga while on their daily commute or as a break from a grueling study schedule. Artists are expected to create anywhere from 20 to 120 pages per week, and the industry hierarchy of art assistants, editors, and magazine publication is built to push out content weekly and monthly. Readers interact with the creators through letter columns and now social media, and manga stories may shift according to fan input.

While in the middle of the 20th century, the comics industry in the United States suffered through critical Senate hearings and a nationwide condemnation of the medium, the Japanese industry never had such a sustained negative campaign affect its popularity or reputation. The Japanese public continues to consider the medium as a varied popular art that is as prolific, exciting, and wide-ranging as television or film. Manga today is marketed by age range and gender, from children's manga (*kodomo*), boys' manga (*shonen*), girls' manga (*shojo*), women's manga (*josei*), men's manga (*seinen*), and adult pornographic manga (*hentai*). Everyone understands that readers will cross the gender and age-range lines, and publishers include elements to appeal to multiple audiences.

Robin E. Brenner

See also: Yaoi Comic Books, Japan

Further Reading

Anime News Network. 2015. "Manga Was Almost 80% of Japan's Digital Book Market." January 12. www.animenewsnetwork.com/news/2015-01-12/manga-was-almost-80 -percent-of-japan-digital-book-market/.83186. Accessed May 29, 2015.
Brenner, Robin E. 2007. *Understanding Manga and Anime.* Westport, CT: Libraries Unlimited.
Gravett, Paul. 2004. *Manga: Sixty Years of Japanese Comics.* London: Laurence King.
Koyama-Richard, Brigitte. 2007. *One Thousand Years of Manga.* Paris: Flammarion.
Nagata, Kazuaki. 2014. "Manga Seek Digital Ground as Print Magazines Languish." *Japan Times.* June 27. www.japantimes.co.jp/news/2014/06/27/business/corporate-business /manga-seek-digital-ground-as-print-magazines-languish/#.VWEKJFnpeNU. Accessed May 29, 2015.

MURAKAMI HARUKI (JAPANESE LITERATURE TODAY)

Despite Japanese society's reputation for homogeneity, recent and contemporary Japanese literature is as diverse as anywhere else in the world and probably more than most. Ranging from what is sometimes called "serious" literature (which the Japanese term *junbungaku*, or "pure literature") to "fan" fiction, from penetrating, introspective works to *shōjo manga* (young girls' comics), the range of Japanese writing is truly remarkable.

Perhaps one of the most distinguishing aspects of recent Japanese writing— writing produced from the early 1990s to the present—is that the question of what constitutes "Japanese writing" is coming increasingly into question. This is not merely a question of whether to include so-called "cosmopolitan" writers like Murakami Haruki, who writes in Japanese but is really a *global* writer; in fact, "Japanese literature" may no longer be bound to questions of nationality, ethnicity, or even language. It includes the works of Japanese-born writers of Korean ethnicity like Yang Seok-il (1936–), who considers himself Japanese, and those of Yu Miri (1968–), who does not. It *may* include Ian "Hideo" Levy (1950–), a California-born American scholar without a drop of Japanese blood in him yet who has written novels in Japanese since 1992; and possibly also Kazuo Ishiguro, an ethnic Japanese raised in the U.K. who sometimes writes *about* Japanese settings and characters but does so in English, as an outsider looking in.

If the Japanese literary world has indeed grown so inclusive, this is a rather novel development for a community that was, not so long ago, considerably more insular, whose literary productions were, ideally, expressions of the "national character," of "Japanese-ness" itself. Seen from another angle, however, it is precisely this inclusiveness—a kind of diversity—that has become a part of the national character, and this is clearly reflected in the kinds of writing we see today. Often this diversity is expressed through some of the younger writers of today, though not always.

Consider, for instance, Nakayama Kaho (1960–), whose work consistently, openly, and unapologetically expresses and aestheticizes her position as a lesbian. Her work connects in some ways with more traditional writings, as in *Marakeshu shinjū* (*Love Suicide at Marrakesh*, 2002), whose title, if not actual plot, calls to mind the famous "love suicide" (*shinjū*) tales of 17th-century Japan. At the same time, Nakayama's writing is undoubtedly linked to the ultracontemporary expressions of same-sex love and eroticism found in manga (narrative comic books) and Japanese animation.

Another writer, a generation younger, whose work resonates with the latest fashions and trends in Japanese entertainment, is Nishio Ishin (1981–), widely known in the world of *seishun entā* (adolescent entertainment). In some ways Nishio might be seen as one of many inheritors of the Murakami Haruki approach to literature, which determinedly rejected the idea of literary art (*bungei*) in favor of narrative, of storytelling (*monogatari, mono o kataru*). Whereas Murakami has been defensive on this point all along, however, writers like Nishio seem almost unaware that "literature" was *ever* anything other than simply entertainment. This is probably why Nishio experiences no apparent anxiety in combining elements of fiction, manga, and even games in his writing.

Not all contemporary writers in Japan are so fixated on the entertainment value of their work. A good many draw on personal background and individual experience to express their unique perspective on their world. Medoruma Shun (1960–) has been consistently critical of both Japanese and American attitudes toward his native Okinawa, and his major works tend to deal either with wartime experiences of Okinawans or the dangers they face even today from the continued presence of American military bases. His *Niji tori* (*Rainbow Bird*, 2006), for instance, develops its narrative through a disturbing intersection of images, from prostitution to drug abuse, from organized crime to the spontaneous criminal acts of American servicemen stationed in Okinawa; *Niji tori* culminates in the gang-rape of an Okinawan girl that is based on an actual incident from 1995. With a similarly critical eye toward recent history, though in a wholly different direction, the aforementioned Yu Miri, who writes in Japanese but is a Korean citizen, has concentrated much of her creative energy on reviving the personal narratives of her grandparents' generation, particularly their treatment as colonial subjects by the Japanese prior to the end of the Second World War in 1945.

Not all critics of Japan's recent historical past are descended from victims of that past. Murakami Haruki (1949–), in the course of his explorations of memory and the human capacity to revise or forget history, plays on the theme of Japanese war atrocities in such works as *Hitsuji o meguru bōken* (*A Wild Sheep Chase*, 1982) and *Nejimakidori kuronikuru* (*The Wind-up Bird Chronicle*, 1994–1996), though his own depictions, couched in fantastic settings and taking place in a sort of virtual reality, could be called "revisions" themselves. Murakami Ryū(1952–) also explores Japan's wartime past in works such as *Koin rokkā beibiizu* (*Coin-Locker Babies*, 1980) and *Kyōseichū* (*Symbiotic Worm*, 2000), both of which conclude with chemical weapons attacks, the latter utilizing long-forgotten stockpiles of such weapons discarded by the Imperial Japanese Army.

Much of the fiction produced by Japan's younger writers in recent years, not surprisingly, deals not with the distant past but with the challenges of growing up in Japan today. Between 2003 and 2004, three young writers of this type burst onto the scene more or less at the same time. Two of them, Kanehara Hitomi (1983–) and Wataya Risa (1984–), shocked the writing community by winning the coveted Akutagawa Prize while still teenagers for *Hebi ni piasu* (*Snakes and Earrings*, 2004) and *Keritai senaka* (*A Back I'd Like to Kick*, 2003), respectively, both about disaffected, nonconformist teenagers trying to find their place in Japan's rigidly homogenizing society. Shiraiwa Gen (1983–), at the same age, won the Bungei Prize for *Nobuta. o purodyūsu* (*Nobuta. Producing*, 2004), a novel about bullying and image in high school that became a wildly popular television drama.

One interesting new development in Japanese writing that seems to have gained ground from around the beginning of the new millennium is the setting of works outside of Japan, no doubt reflecting a more cosmopolitan, or at least more experienced, population. Whereas in prewar Japan, stories set in Shanghai by the likes of Akutagawa Ryūnosuke and Tanizaki Jun'ichirō had a certain exotic feel about them, many of today's novelists seem to bring with them considerably more complex experiences. Nishi Kanako (1977–), who was born in Tehran and spent several years of her childhood in Cairo, won the 2015 Naoki Prize for Popular Fiction with

"Saraba" ("Farewell"), a fictionalized account of her experiences growing up abroad. Another recent debut, Iwaki Kei (1971–) grounds her Dazai Osamu Prize-winning maiden work *Sayōnara, orenji* (*Farewell, Orange*, 2013) in her more than 20 years of living in Australia. And, of course, one of the most widely acclaimed works by the aforementioned Hideo Levy is his 2005 *Chiji ni kudakete* (*Broken, Broken into Thousands of Pieces*), based on his experiences in the aftermath of the September 11, 2001, World Trade Center attacks.

While Murakami Haruki is very likely the most widely recognized name in Japanese literature today, ironically he is one of the least "Japanese" among them, for he has himself gone beyond his cultural boundaries, extending both his readership and his themes out into the realm of the universal to become one of Japan's first truly global writers. How this has influenced other writers, or will do so in the future, remains a matter for debate. That vexing question aside, the discussion above would seem to suggest that Murakami is not alone in his jettisoning of traditional models of Japanese writing, but it might also suggest that those models are not entirely gone. We might note, for instance, that while the most recent winners of literary prizes in Japan are indeed considerably more cosmopolitan than winners might have been, say, half a century ago, the literary prize—a remnant itself of modern Japanese literary tradition—is still an important means of identifying, judging, and above all *classifying* new writers.

Matthew C. Strecher

See also: Kurosawa Akira (Chapter 3: Film)

Further Reading

Murakami, Haruki. 1997. *The Wind-Up Bird Chronicle*. Trans. Jay Rubin. New York: Knopf.
Rubin, Jay, 2002. *Murakami Haruki and the Music of Words*. London: Harvill Press.
Strecher, Matthew. 2002. *Dances with Sheep: The Quest for Identity in the Fiction of Murakami Haruki*. Ann Arbor: University of Michigan Press.
Strecher, Matthew. 2014. *The Forbidden Worlds of Haruki Murakami*. Minneapolis: University of Minnesota Press.

POPULAR LITERATURE, INDONESIA

Metropop, chick lit, fantasy pop, even religious pop, are some of the labels by which popular literature (*sastra pop*) is known in Indonesia today. Many of these genres are not exclusive to Indonesia and serve to signal that these works and their readers share in the global networks of young, hypermodern, and cosmopolitan culture.

Popular literature has been a shifting, often fiercely contested concept with roots in the tensions between official government institutions and burgeoning private presses. Its beginnings may be traced to early 20th-century cultural politics with the establishment in 1908 of the colonial government agency called the Balai

Pustaka (or Commission for People's Literature) to produce and distribute appropriate popular reading material for the native population, particularly those educated in the Western school system. The native readership thus shaped was literate in the High Malay language printed in the roman instead of Arabic or Javanese scripts. The cultural and linguistic identity that the Balai Pustaka sought to shape for its "people" ("*volk*") reproduced the racial segregation by which the colonizing Dutch protected their power in the East Indies: in the colonies, "popular" meant native. The year 1922 saw the publication of *Sitti Nurbaya*, written by the Sumatran veterinarian Marah Rusli and generally regarded as the first modern novel in the literary canon.

In its efforts to govern the intellectual and emotional development of its native subjects, the colonial government branded as "wild literature" ("*batjaan liar*") much of the reading material that did not bear its imprimatur. However, these attempts at ideological and cultural control came at a time of rapid intellectual and creative expansion among the non-European population of the archipelago and the rise of the Malay-language press. The language of the new works produced by these presses was not the highly edited language of Balai Pustaka but rather lingua franca Malay, scorned as "bazaar" or "babbling" Malay, the language of commerce and interethnic communications that suited the demands of a new print-based economy for flexibility and speed in a multicultural and swiftly changing urban society. Much of this popular fiction was written by authors of Chinese descent—often also employed as reporters by Malay-language newspapers—and many of their stories were based on cases of murder, sex, and scandal, especially in European and Eurasian communities. The tag "A story that really happened" ("*Jang betoel soedah kedjadian*") became a marker of popular works that straddled the line separating fact from fiction.

One prolific writer was Tan Boen Kim. He is known now especially for his 1915 *Nona Fientje de Feniks* (*Miss Fientje de Feniks*), based on a case involving the murder of a Eurasian prostitute. However, in addition to a string of fictionalized narratives around the mysterious deaths of indigenous women kept as housekeeper-concubines (*nyai*) he also published a compilation of defense pleas written by Dutch, Eurasian, Javanese, and Chinese lawyers and legal defenders, several of which were responses to charges of press offense (*persdelict*), "sowing hatred" (the infamous "*haatzaai artikelen*" that were used in colonial days and survive in postcolonial Indonesia as a form of censorship), and defamation brought against the popular newspapers and publications, as well as an account of his own experience in prison.

This popular literature was deemed "wild" for its unruly hybridization of language and cultural identity, its not-so-subtle suggestion of widespread miscegenation among Europeans in racially segregated colonial society, and its focus on sexuality and crime as topics for entertainment. But it was "wild" especially because it gave voice to a growing subaltern, often radical, political imagination. Notable among the writers of this genre is the Javanese journalist and labor activist Marco Kartodikromo, whose many works include the drama-novel *Matahariah*

(1919), in which the sexually charged intrigue surrounding the figure of the real-life spy Mata Hari (1876–1917) serves as a popularizing frame for a bold critique of the political and economic violence perpetrated by the colonial government as a tool of exploitative private capital. In the story, Marco calls for the formation of trade unions among Javanese peasants and workers, and it was one of the works for which he was accused of criminal press offense. He was to die in exile in the malaria-infested prison camp of Boven Digoel in 1932.

Tensions between Balai Pustaka literature and popular fiction, often called "roman pitjisan" ("penny romances"), continued into postcolonial Indonesia. The canon formed during colonial times changed little as the obligatory reading lists for school courses and exams in Indonesian literature were made up of literary works sanctioned by the Balai Pustaka. Common wisdom has it that reading is not a popular pastime in Indonesia, but even a brief look at popular literature quickly dispels this notion.

Perhaps the most popular form of non-Balai Pustaka fiction was the martial arts serial cerita silat and especially the works of the prolific writers Kho Ping Hoo and S. H. Mintardja. Set in precolonial times in China or Java, these stories follow the adventures of warrior heroes (sometimes heroines) through episodic multi-volume serials. Some of the longest are Kho Ping Hoo's Bukek Siansu (more than 700 titles) and Mintardja's Api Dibukit Menoreh (Fire in the Menoreh Mountains, nearly 400 volumes). Also extremely popular were graphic novels (cerita bergambar), of which the most well-known writer-artist was R. A. Kosasih, known as the "Father of Indonesian Comics," who repopularized stories from the traditional epics of India and Indonesia, the Mahabarata, Ramayana, and Panji. These comics are noteworthy not only for the quality of the art but also for the author's mastery of narrative skills reminiscent of the best shadow plays. So popular were silat and graphic stories that young readers would read them on the sly, fearing confiscation by parents and teachers suspicious of their "addictive" quality. (The Indonesian word used is kecanduan, from the word for opium.) These cheaply produced books were not collected by public and university libraries; instead, small privately run libraries (taman bacaan) rented them out at affordable rates. The 1970s and 1980s also saw the rise of the horror mystery. Especially popular was fiction by the journalist Abdullah Harahap, whose stories, with titles like Mystery of the Virgin from the Grave and Worshipper of Satan, offered a familiar tangle of sex, crime, and the supernatural. By this time, after the 1965–1969 purges of communism under the military regime of General Suharto (1921–2008), the political content and critical charge of colonial-era popular fiction had largely dissipated.

Martial arts and horror-mystery novels appealed to a young, male audience, but the early 1970s also saw the rise in popularity of fiction written by and for young women. Karmila, by Marga T., appeared as a serialized novel in the newspaper Kompas and was followed in 1973 by Pada sebuah kapal (On a Boat) by N. H. Dini. Both quickly became best sellers. These novels did not depend on the small book rentals and sidewalk hawkers, however, but were issued by major publishing houses, sometimes serialized in women's magazines as, for example, the romance

Dokter Nona Friska (*Miss Friska The Doctor*) by Mira W. Women's literature began to blur the line separating popular "pulp" fiction from "serious" literature. But women writers had to be careful with the way they handled the combination of sex, crime, and politics. Ayu Utami's novel *Saman* became a flashpoint of controversy for its exploration of alternative sexualities against the background of politics and resistance in New Order Indonesia. Labeled "perfumed literature" ("*sastra wangi*") by detractors, the novel sold well and led the way for other women writers, who have now come to dominate popular literature.

Indonesian genres of metropop and chick lit appeal to an audience of young women, best described in the 2004 self-ascribed "chick lit Indonesia" novel *Cintapuccino* by Icha Rahmanti as "we're-earning-our-own-money-from-internships-and-we're-a-bridging-generation" ("*Kami-sudah-bisa-cari-duit-sendiri-dengan-kerja-magang-dan-kami-cuma-generasi-penerus*"). Written in the urban slang known as *bahasa gaul*, many of these novels sport English-language titles (e.g., Clara Ng's *Indiana Chronicles* trilogy, Ilana Tan's *In a Blue Moon*). Widely criticized for encouraging consumerist values through their representation of Jakarta's urban elite and the ubiquitous lists of high-fashion brands beyond the average Indonesian reader's means, these romances often also explore issues such as domestic violence and date rape, which are of concern to young women.

The fall of Suharto in 1998 has seen a renaissance of popular literature with a pronounced Muslim character and a geographic shift of the imagination to the Middle East. This is not a nostalgic reconstruction of the past but rather a rendering of Muslims living in a thriving and strongly globalizing environment in Indonesia and beyond. Although there is some tension between Islamic popular literature, which is sometimes self-labeled "polite literature" ("*sastra santun*") because it eschews the soft eroticism and urban slang of metropop and chick lit, there are points of similarity as well. Much of this fiction is romance, and the style of the international travelogue, a staple of young women's literature, is also an important narrative technique here; but instead of London, New York, or Melbourne, the plots take the reader through carefully mapped-out sites in the Middle East. The landmarks are religious: mosques, tombs, universities, but they are enmeshed in the global culture of international hotel chains, shopping malls, and airports. A best-selling example is the novel *Ayat-ayat cinta* (*Verses of Love*, 2004) by Habiburrahman El Shirazy.

Inspirational popular literature, in the form of coming-of-age novels represented by the multivolume novels *The Rainbow Troops* (*Laskar pelangi*, 2005) and *Land of 5 Towers* (*Negeri 5 menara*, 2009) have recently broken sales records in Indonesia. Set in small towns and semirural areas, they turn away from the fast-paced cosmopolitanism and street slang of metropop and convey a strong educational message.

Sylvia Tiwon

See also: Pramoedya Ananta Toer

Further Reading

Hellwig, Tineke. 2012. *Women and Malay Voices: Undercurrent Murmurings in Indonesia's Colonial Past.* New York: Peter Lang.

Hirata, Andrea. 2014. *The Rainbow Troops: A Novel.* Trans. Angie Kilbane. Reprint, New York: Sarah Crichton Books.

Utami, Ayu. 2005. *Saman: A Novel.* Trans. Pamela Allen. Jakarta, ID: Equinox.

POPULAR LITERATURE, PHILIPPINES

Philippine popular culture can refer to *komiks* (comics), serialized novels and stories in Tagalog magazines, as well as romantic novelettes for literature; it can also include formula films, street art, soap operas, and variety shows on television. Influenced largely by both Spanish (1560–1898) and American colonial rule (1898–1946), these texts are informed by the conventions of romance, horror, fantasy, and comedy. While popular culture may have been described as formulaic, predictable, escapist, and devoid of realism, the scholarship of Bienvenido Lumbera, Nicanor Tiongson, Soledad Reyes, and Rolando Tolentino have looked into the dynamics of cultural production, the appropriation/transformation of forms, gender and class politics, and audience reception (see below for suggested further readings).

One of the earliest forms of popular literary texts were the metrical romances, the *awit* and the *korido*, narrative verses on princes and princesses in Europe and battles between Christians and Moors during the Middle Ages. Introduced during Spanish colonial rule, these sung or chanted texts attracted readers and listeners because of their adherence to the conventions of romance in literature: forbidden love, secret love, unspoken love, love triangles, reversal of fortunes, and secrets revealed in the end. These conventions continued to influence Philippine fiction and film well into the 20th and 21st centuries. The most beloved of these *awits*, *Pinagdaanang buhay ni Florante at ni Laura sa Cahariang Albania* (*The Lives Experienced by Florante and Laura in the Kingdom of Albany*, ca. 1838) by poet Francisco Baltazar (aka Balagtas, 1788–1862), however, deviated from most metrical romances because the suffering experienced by its main characters can be read as an allegory of colonial oppression.

Several decades later, in the 1920s, a new popular form named after Balagtas would gain popularity—the *balagtasan*. A poetic joust based on the traditional *duplo*, the *balagtasan* featured the country's top poets, among them, Jose Corazon de Jesus, Florentino Collantes, and Benigno Ramos. They were held in large venues such as the Teatro Zorilla and the Olympic Stadium and were attended by audiences numbering from 8,000 to 15,000. Among the topics were "Ang dalagang pilipina: noon at ngayon" ("The Filipina Maiden: Then and Now," 1925), "Panulat at sandata" ("Writings and Weapons," 1927), and "Alin ang mas mahalaga: bakal o ginto?" ("Which Is More Important: Iron or Gold?," 1928). Testament to the popularity of the poets and the *balagtasan* were the debates that spilled into the newspapers and outside the performance venues among other writers and fans.

At the time that spoken poetry continued to flourish during the American colonial period, the *komiks* (comics), *maikling kuwento* (short stories), and *nobelang itutuloy* (serialized novels) started to grow in number with new magazines such as *Liwayway* (*Dawn*, 1922 [this and the dates provided below are initial publication dates for journals]) in Tagalog and *Bisaya* (*Visayan*, 1930) and *Bannawag* (*Dawn*, 1934) in Ilocano. Comic strips had been introduced earlier with Jose Rizal's first comic strip of the folktale "The Monkey and the Turtle," published in *La Solidaridad* in early strips during the turn of the century. Later came the first colored strip, *Kulafu* (1933) by Francisco Reyes and Pedrito Reyes. However, the *komiks* reached greater popularity in the late 1920s and early 1930s through popular characters such as Tony Velasquez's Kenkoy (featured in *Album ng mga kabalbalan ni Kenkoy* [Album of the Mishaps of Kenkoy], 1929), Ponyang Halobaybay (1932), Nanong Pandak (early 1930s), Totong Barungkol (1936), and Sariling Bulilit (1932); Romeo-Borromeo's si Goryo't si Kikay (1930s); J. Z. Santos's Popoy and Bokyong Upos (1930s); and Francisco Coching's Marabini (1935).

In the 1940s, all-comics magazines became popular with the publication of *Halakhak komiks* (1946), *Pilipino komiks* (1947), *Tagalog klasiks* (1949), *Hiwaga komiks* (1950), and *Espesyal komiks* (1952). These comic books contained both short stories and serialized novels, with some comics dedicated to a particular genre, such as fantasy or horror. Among the most popular comic artists were Mars Ravelo, for his characters including the superhero Darna and the mermaid Dyesebel; Francisco Coching, famous for his folk heroes Pedro Penduko and Hagibis; Larry Alcala, for Kalabog and Bosyo; and Asiong Aksaya, for pioneering the use of Taglish or Tagalog-English for his characters.

Influenced by *pusong* or jester characters in Philippine folktales and American popular culture epitomized by stock characters in vaudeville theater, cartoonists created characters identified by physical traits (i.e., body size and shape) as well as professions (i.e., police officer, mechanic, street sweeper). On one hand, plots seemed to be predictable, focusing on mishaps brought about by either stupidity or the desire to take advantage of another person, the cleverness of children, and moral lessons. However, with the broken-English-speaking Kenkoy wearing a three-piece suit and two-toned shoes in a tropical country usually hit by storms and floods, one can read an indictment of the colonial way of thinking of many Filipinos. Moreover, the modern Ponyang Halobaybay with her modern dress and numerous suitors can be seen as the binary opposite of Kenkoy's faithful wife, Rosing, usually in a traditional Filipino costume, the *baro't saya*, thus reflecting the tension between modernity and tradition.

The contradictions of Filipino women are similarly portrayed in the female characters of the Tagalog short stories and novels found in the pages of popular newspapers and magazines such as *Liwayway* and *Taliba*. While simplicity and chastity were considered virtues characteristic of the *dalagang Pilipina* or Filipina maiden, the women fictionists created characters whose lives went beyond the home: Rita in Carmen Batacan's *Mga puso sa himpapawid* (*Hearts in the Air*, 1937) was an aviatrix; Leonor in Hilaria Labog's *Ang mahiwagang mang-aawit* (*The Mystery*

Singer, 1936) was a singer; Tinay in Susana de Guzman's *Dalawang kuwentista* (*Two Writers*, 1936) was a fictionist; Paz in Epifania Alvarez's *Ang guro sa nayon* (*The Teacher in the Village*) was a teacher; and Marcela in Labog's *Pagkatapos mangumpisal* (*After a Confession*, 1937) was a *bordadora* or embroiderer. Four strategies were employed by these fictionists: romantic conventions such as the separation of lovers, the better to focus the plot on the woman's narrative and relationships among women; ruptures and dissonance in otherwise conventional love stories; humor, to give commentaries on the powerful, such as aspiring politicians; and language code-switching and signifiers of modernity (radios, airplanes, trains) to articulate the influence of colonial rule.

Interestingly, and in spite of their popularity, very few of these women fictionists published their serialized novels or collections of short stories, resulting in a male-dominated canon of Philippine popular literature. For scholars and literary historians, and textbook writers, among the most significant novelists of the first half of the 20th century were Gabriel Beato Francisco, for his trilogy Fulgencio Galbillo (1907), *Capitan Bensio* (1907), and *Alfaro* (1909); Iñigo Ed. Regalado, for his anticolonial novel *Lalaking uliran o tulisan* (*A Model Man or a Bandit*, 1914) and his romantic novels exemplified by *May pagsinta'y walang puso* (*Love without a Heart*, 1911), and *Sampaguitang walang bango* (*A Jasmine Flower without Fragrance*, 1918); Faustino Aguilar, for *Pinaglahuan* (*Eclipsed*, 1907), and *Lihim ng isang pulo* (*The Secret of an Island*, 1926), which brought into focus class struggles between capitalists and workers; and Lope K. Santos, for *Banaag at sikat* (*From Early Dawn to Full Light*, 1906), which similarly used the "rich girl–poor boy" plot to articulate workers' struggles. For some novelists of this period, works were first serialized in magazines and later published as a book.

In contrast, the modern short story in the Philippines, introduced by the colonial educational system, had its beginnings in English. The form became popular only when written in Tagalog and other Philippine languages and published in magazines and newspapers starting in the 1920s. The forerunner of this form at the turn of the 20th century was the *dagli*, which had components of fiction, essay, and dialogue but was characterized by its short length. Published in newspapers such as *Muling Pagsilang* and *Lipang Kalabaw*, the *dagli* tackled themes of romance, modernity, social problems, colonial rule, and the desire for independence. Writers, many of them using pseudonyms, continued to write the *dagli* until the 1930s, but by then, the short story, influenced both by the romantic conventions of metrical romances and elements introduced by American short stories, had become more popularly written in magazines. Among the most noted short-story writers were Deogracias del Rosario, considered to be the "father" of the short story; Brigido Batungbakal in the Tagalog language; Magdalena Jalandoni in Ilongo; and Marcel Navarra in Cebuano.

Romance pocket books started to be popular in the late 1980s, with former comics writers such as Elena Patron, Helen Meriz, and Gilda Olvidad among the most popular authors. Influenced by both the conventions of romance passed from the *awit* and *corrido* to *nobelang itutuloy* (serialized novels), the *komiks*, and English pocket books such as Mills & Boon pulp romances, many writers stuck to the following formula: rich and attractive but sometimes distant male whose wealth is signified by a large house with a bathtub/swimming pool (in a country where water supply can sometimes be a problem); a villain/competitor for the man's heart; picturesque locales; unspoken/secret love; chance meetings; reversal of fortune; secret revealed at the end through a letter, diary, or locket; and finally happy endings. With a continually growing industry, among the publishers today are not only pioneers such as Precious Hearts and Valentine Romances but also Purple Shadow, Books for Pleasure, Kwento ng Puso, Heart-to-Heart, and Harrel Publishing. With the success of these romance novels, publishers have ventured into horror and suspense as well.

Realizing the potential of growing audiences, Anvil Publishing sponsored a popular novel-writing workshop in 1991, conducted by acclaimed novelist Lualhati Bautista. The purpose was to teach potential young fictionists to write more realistic novels and explore the genre to articulate social, economic, and political issues. Among the writers who wrote for Rosas were Bautista, Crisostomo Papa, Nanette Matilac, Roland Tolentino, Joi Barrios, Levy Balgos de la Cruz, and Suzette Doctolero, producing novelettes about the complexities of relationships, mail-order brides, censorship, violence against women, and poverty and inequality. Unfortunately, the line lasted only a few years.

With the advent of a new millennium, the first chick-lit novel, *Getting Better* (2000) by Tara Sering, was published and distributed by Summit Publishing, also the publisher of *Cosmopolitan Manila*. This was followed by other novels, such as Abi Aquino's *Drama Queen* (2003), Maya Calica's *The Break-up Diaries* (2003), and M. D. Balangue's *Mr. Write* (2004), among others. In these novels, the authors write using the contemporary English of Metro Manila, peppered with Filipino words and occasionally gay language, and feature characters that would appeal to a target market of educated, English-speaking, tech-savvy professional women from the middle to upper classes. While seemingly subscribing merely to the "fun and fearless female" reader of *Cosmopolitan*, critics such as Cristina Pantajo Hidalgo and Katrina Stuart Santiago have credited these chick-lit books for their realistic dialogue and situations and have looked into how these works interrogated stereotypes of the feminine and the feminist.

An unusual phenomenon in contemporary popular literature is the success of the Bob Ong books. With his first novel, *ABNKKBSPLAko?* (read phonetically as *Aba, Nakakabasa Pala Ako* or *So, I Can Read?*, 2001) by Visprint Inc., the author, using the pseudonym Bob Ong, reached unprecedented success, selling more than 250,000 copies. He then published several more books, such as *Ang paboritong libro ni hudas* (2003), *Stainless longganisa* (2005), and *Si* (2014). *ABNKKBSPLAko?* was made into a film in 2014. The success of these novels can perhaps be attributed to their wit and humor, quotable quotes, versatility in genre and topics, and interesting book trailers.

Popular literature remains popular because of three things: accessibility, sensitivity to markets and readership, and old and new formulas. A few decades ago, comics and romance pocket books could be rented from the neighborhood variety store; today most publications offer e-books. Writers and publishers have expanded their markets to include those who prefer English or Tagalog-English while continuing to recognize the double exposure provided by film adaptations. Finally, conventions have remained, and while they are less obvious than the "rich girl–poor boy" plot, what "works" is what is continually written and published.

Joi Barrios

See also: Comic-Book Heroines, Philippines

Further Reading

Barrios, Joi. 2000. *Ang Aking Prince Charming at Iba Pang Noveleta ng Pag-ibig* [My Prince Charming and Other Romance Novelettes]. Quezon City: University of the Philippines Press.

Cruz, Isagani. 2009. "Bob Ong as National Artist." *PhilStar*. August 27. www.philstar.com /education-and-home/499361/bob-ong-national-artist. Accessed November 27, 2015.

Lumbera, Bienvenido, and Cynthia Nograles Lumbera, eds. 1997. *Philippine Literature: A History and Anthology*. Pasig, PH: Anvil Publishing.

Reyes, Soledad. 2000. *Aliw: Selected Essays on Popular Culture*. Manila, PH: De La Salle University Press.

Santiago, Katrina Stuart. 2009. "The Pinay as Fun, Fearless Female: Philippine Chicklit Literature in the Age of the Transnation." *Humanities Diliman* 6, no. 1 & 2.

Tolentino, Rolando, and Aristotle Atienza, eds. 2007. *Ang Dagling Tagalog 1903–1936*. Quezon City: University of the Philippines Press.

Zafra, Galileo. 1999. *Balagtasan: Kasaysayan at Antolohiya*. Quezon City, PH: Ateneo de Manila University Press.

POPULAR NOVELS, AUSTRALIA

Best-selling popular fiction authors in Australia include Colleen McCullough (1937–2015) with her novel *The Thorn Birds* (1977) selling over 30 million copies worldwide and adapted as a popular television miniseries in 1983; Bryce Courtenay (1933–2012) with *The Power of One* (1989) selling over 7 million copies and adapted as a movie in 1992; and other popular authors including Matthew Reilly (*Scarecrow Returns*, 2012), Markus Zusak (*The Book Thief*, 2005), Di Morrissey (*The Road Back*, 2014), and Peter Corris (the Cliff Hardy detective series, 1980–2014) (Johnson-Woods 2012).

In the 2015 Dymock's Booklovers 101 survey, in which over 15,000 Australian readers voted for their favorite fiction books, 17 Australian-authored novels made the top 101 list, including Zusak's *The Book Thief* at No. 1 and Bryce Courtenay's *The Power of One* and Tim Winton's *Cloudstreet* (1992). The top-10 favorite novels overall were Zusak's *The Book Thief*, Jane Austen's *Pride and Prejudice*, Harper Lee's *To Kill a Mockingbird*, Raymond Feist's *Magician*, J. R. R. Tolkien's The Lord of the Rings series (books 1–3), John Green's *The Fault in Our Stars*, J. R. R. Tolkien's *The*

Hobbit, Charlotte Brontë's *Jane Eyre*, Lewis Carroll's *Alice's Adventures in Wonderland*, and at No. 10 on the list, J. K. Rowling's Harry Potter series.

By comparison, when tens of thousands of Australian readers voted for their favorite Australian novelists in 2014, the top-10 national authors included Matthew Reilly at No. 1, followed by Tim Winton (1960–), Kate Morton (1976–), Markus Zusak (1975–), Monica McInerney (1966–), Tony Park (1964–), Kerry Greenwood (1954–), Craig Silvey (1982–), Di Morrissey (1943–), and John Marsden (1950–) at No. 10.

Author Matthew Reilly (1974–) was inspired by reading *Lord of the Flies* in school and wrote his first novel, the action-thriller *Contest*, at age 19 while studying law, later self-publishing the novel in 1996. Since securing a major publishing deal, Reilly's subsequent action-thriller novels have included *Ice Station*, *Temple*, *Area 7*, *Scarecrow*, *Hover-Car Racer*, *Hell Island*, *Seven Ancient Wonders*, *The Six Sacred Stones*, *The Five Greatest Warriors*, *Scarecrow and the Army of Thieves* (published as *Scarecrow Returns* in the United States), and *The Tournament*, which combined have sold over 7 million copies worldwide (Reilly 2015).

Tim Winton (1960–) is a multi-award-winning Australian novelist, playwright, and short-story author. One of his best-loved works is the novel *Cloudstreet*, a story of two neighboring working-class families, the Lambs and the Pickles, rebuilding their lives after personal tragedies, also later adapted as a stage play (2001) and television miniseries (2011). Winton is also one of the few Australian writers to combine widespread literary acclaim with commercial appeal; his Lockie Leonard children's book series about a young surfer was also adapted to two successful children's television series, screening in 2007 and 2010.

Kate Morton's internationally best-selling gothic romance-mystery period novels, all based around the U.K., include *The House at Riverton* (aka *The Shifting Fog*, 2006), *The Forgotten Garden* (2008), *The Distant Hours* (2010), and *The Secret Keeper* (2012). Morton's literary influences include Enid Blyton and Emily Brontë.

Markus Zusak's best-selling *The Book Thief* (2005), the story of a nine-year-old girl in Nazi Germany during World War II, was adapted as a movie in 2013. Zusak's other successful and award-winning young-adult fiction books include *The Underdog* (1999), *Fighting Ruben Wolfe* (2000), *When Dogs Cry* (2001), and *I Am the Messenger* (2002).

Dublin-based Australian author Monica McInerney's romance/family relationships novels include *Alphabet Sisters* (2004), *Those Faraday Girls* (2007), and *Hello from the Gillespies* (2014). A collection of short stories, *All Together Now* (2008), was also short-listed for the 2009 Australian Book Industry Awards General Fiction Book of the Year prize, with *Those Faraday Girls* winning the award in 2008.

Former newspaper journalist Tony Park, also a major in the Australian Army Reserve who served in the Afghanistan conflict in 2002, is the author of 11 African-based thriller novels, including *Far Horizon* (1998), *Silent Predator* (2008), and *The Hunter* (2014). Park is also the coauthor of several nonfiction books, including *The Lost Battlefield of Kokoda* (2012) and *Bush Vet* (2013).

Kerry Greenwood is the author of the Miss Phryne Fisher series of detective novels set in 1920s Melbourne, Australia, beginning with *Cocaine Blues* (aka *Death by Misadventure*, 1989), adapted as the visually stylish and successful television series *Miss Fisher's Murder Mysteries*, airing from 2013. Her other novels range in genre across historical to science fiction, including the six installments of the Corinna Chapman detective-mystery series, from *Earthly Delights* (2004) through to *Cooking the Books* (2011).

Musician, songwriter, and acclaimed author Craig Silvey's two novels are *Rhubarb* (2004) and also the teenage coming-of-age novel set in an isolated Australian mining town, *Jasper Jones* (2009). Silvey also authored two popular children's books, *The World According to Warren* (2007) and *The Amber Amulet* (2012). His writing influences include Harper Lee, Mark Twain, and Truman Capote.

Environmental activist and also former journalist and television host Di Morrissey is the author of 23 best-selling novels with over 2 million copies sold worldwide, beginning with *Heart of the Dreaming* (1991) to the most recent, *The Road Back* (2014). Morrissey's popular novels often involve family sagas, exotic landscapes, and characters resolving personal dilemmas to find inner peace and a sense of belonging.

Australian schoolteacher John Marsden (1950–) is the author of the best-selling young-adult Tomorrow series (1993–1999) and the related Ellie Chronicles series (2003–2006) of novels, written in an attempt to create stories his own teenaged students might enjoy. The movie adaptation of the first book in the action-adventure series *Tomorrow, When the War Began* (2010) follows small-town Australian teenager Ellie Linton and her school friends as they cope with a sudden and unexpected hostile military invasion of Australia by an unnamed foreign power. In 1996, *Tomorrow, When the War Began* was voted one of the top 100 best books for young adults by the Young Adult Library Services Association. Marsden is currently Australia's best-selling young-adult fiction author.

Other popular and well-loved Australian authors with a more literary style include Peter Carey (1943–), author of *Bliss* (1981), *Illywhacker* (1985), and *The True History of the Kelly Gang* (2000); and Christos Tsiolkas (1965–) whose award-winning novel *The Slap* (2009) was also adapted as an Australian (2011), and later as an American (2015–), television miniseries.

J. T. Velikovsky

See also: Popular Movies, Australia (Chapter 3: Film)

Further Reading

Australian Government. "Australian Novels." www.australia.gov.au/about-australia/australian-story/austn-novels. Accessed March 24, 2016.

Cattanach, Andrew. "Australia's Favourite Novelist 2014—The Full List." *Booktopia.* http://blog.booktopia.com.au/2014/01/28/australias-favourite-novelist-2014-the-full-list. Accessed March 24, 2016.

Charrison, Emily. 2015. "Australia's 101 Favourite Books of All Time." *The New Daily.* March 30. http://thenewdaily.com.au/entertainment/2015/03/30/australias-101-favourite-bo oks-time. Accessed March 24, 2016.

Johnson-Woods, T. 2012. "Introduction: Two Centuries of Popular Australian Fiction." In *Sold by the Millions: Australia's Bestsellers.* Ed. T. Johnson-Woods and A. Sarwal, 1–21. Newcastle upon Tyne, UK: Cambridge Scholars Publishers.

PRAMOEDYA ANANTA TOER

"Someone may be very smart, but without writing he will vanish from the society and from the history. Writing is (working) (for your) eternity."

—Pramoedya Ananta Toer

Pramoedya Ananta Toer (1925–2006), affectionately referred to locally as Pram, born Javanese in Blora on February 6, 1925, was—and still is—a well-known Indonesian writer. Pram wrote novels, essays, and short stories. His work spanned from the colonial time to the Soeharto era. He wrote more than 50 literary pieces that have been translated into 41 languages. Pram was imprisoned several times during the colonialism of the Dutch, Soekarno's era, and Soeharto's era.

Many of Pramoedya Ananta Toer's writings have been banned in the past by the Indonesian government. His critiques of the government were revealed in a subtle way. However, he made very clear and harsh critiques involving colonialism, racism, and corruption.

When Indonesia proclaimed its independence in 1945, the Dutch wanted to come back to Indonesia. At that time, Pram joined an anticolonial movement for national liberation in Karawang. During this time he did not stop writing. He wrote short stories and books and also propaganda for nationalism in Indonesia. Therefore, the Dutch sent him to prison from 1947 to 1949. During his imprisonment, Pram kept writing. *The Fugitive* was one of his well-known novels written during this time.

Pram's writing not only included the setting of circumstances he experienced—such as war, colonialism, and independence—but was also a semiautobiography of his life, based on what he felt and thought during those eras. Eventually, Pram's writing took on more and more of a political nuance, especially when he was writing about corruption. During Soekarno's era, one of his fictions, titled "Korupsi," a fictional story of a corrupt civil servant, raised the conservative government's ire at that time.

Pram wrote in various media, such as journals and newspapers. He gained a widespread reputation as a social critic. Pram moved politically in the direction of the so-called left wing and, later, joined the Lekra Group of Writers, which was made up of artists and writers following a school of thought known as socialist realism. Lekra, initially popular under President Soekarno's administration, fell out of favor and was banned when his replacement, Soeharto, ushered in a New Order government.

In the early 1950s, Pram had an opportunity to live in the Netherlands by participating in a cultural exchange program. Then he went to China and Russia. His positive experience living in China led to his sympathetic concern for the Chinese descendants living in Indonesia, who were not being given equal opportunities of citizenship, such as being allowed to hold and excel in governmental posts, at that time.

Later, in the late 1950s, Pram became a lecturer in Universitas Res Publica. During his lectures, he often delivered powerful addresses on the history of Indonesia from the point of view of the colonized that had been silenced under the Dutch colonial administration and later by the government of Indonesia after independence.

Pram felt considerable sympathy for Chinese Indonesians. He often wrote stories related to this theme. One of his well-known writings was his correspondence with a fictional Chinese friend, as if he was writing to that friend discussing Indonesian governmental policy related to the existence of Chinese Indonesians and the history of Chinese Indonesians. In his writing, Pram often criticized the government for ignoring the needs of non-Javanese civilians and civilians living on islands other than Java Islands.

In 1965, when Soeharto replaced Soekarno, the government was called the New Order. During the process of replacement, several generals were killed. The Indonesian Communist Party was accused, by Soeharto's regime, of being the mastermind behind the killing, so that automatically the local Communist Party and its allies became the enemy of the government. Pram, being a left-leaning activist scholar, soon became a political prisoner. He was sent to prison without trial. His books were banned in all areas in Indonesia. All of his personal library collections were burned upon his arrest.

The longest imprisonment he experienced, during Soeharto's era, was on Buru Island, one of the Maluku isles. Buru Island is a remote prison for political prisoners and others imprisoned for serious offenses.

Pram was not only sent to prison but also labeled as a communist. Being labeled as a communist was very serious in Indonesia during the Soeharto era. It meant that he and his children were restricted from most jobs and other civil rights. Even applying for a passport required applicants to be certified as having no prior or current affiliation with the communist movement. Not only individual citizens who had been labeled as being too close with the formerly aboveground communist movement but also all of their family members were prohibited for four generations from traveling abroad or holding civil-service positions. Freedom of expression was uncommon during the Soeharto era.

During Pramoedya Ananta Toer's imprisonment on Buru Island, he remained a very active writer. Although he did not have access to pencils, pens, and paper, he continued writing during his imprisonment. He sometimes told his stories orally to his outlaw fellows. Some of his masterpieces were written in prison, such as the well-known Tetralogi Buru series (Buru Quartet). Buru Quartet consists of four novels that have a story line set around the time when Indonesia was forming itself as an independent and sovereign nation. Some of the stories written in these books were based on Pram's own life experience.

The titles of the Buru Quartet are *Bumi manusia*" (*The Earth of Mankind*), *Anak segala bangsa* (*Child of All Nations*), *Jejak langkah* (*Footsteps*), and *Rumah kaca* (*House of Glass*). The main character of this story is a journalist named Raden Mas Minke. The story of Minke actually is based on the life of Raden Tirto Adhi Surjo. He was a journalist who was active in the nationalist movement. Another character in these stories was Chinese.

Pram did his research for his stories long before he was sent to prison in Buru Island. His process for writing these stories from prison was rather unusual. Although he was not allowed to write, he had access to a typewriter because he helped the guards in writing reports. His fellow outlaws helped him by taking up some of his duties so that he could finish his story.

During his imprisonment in Buru Island, he also made the acquaintance of some women who were forced to be "comfort women" during the Japanese occupation. These women were forcibly brought to Buru to be sexually abused by the Japanese soldiers and, later, after World War II, never returned again to their hometowns because they were too ashamed of their experiences. Their stories were captured by Pram and became a book entitled *Perawan remaja dalam cengkraman militer* (*Young Virgins in the Military's Grip*).

Pram's books were translated into English by Max Lane and published internationally. Ironically, his books were banned from circulation in Indonesia. Most of his books were censored and taken off the shelves not long after they were published. The reason was because the government thought that the stories transmitted communist ideas. Although some of his stories demonstrated the importance of Islam in the movement to remove the Dutch from Indonesia, his stories were never religious.

Pram was released from prison in 1979, but he was still placed under house arrest until 1992. During this time he wrote several stories, such as *The Girl from the Coast*. This was a semifictional story based on his grandmother's experience. Unfortunately, part of these stories—the second and third volumes—were discovered and burned by the government censors. Another story he wrote during house arrest was *Arus balik* (*Reverse Current*).

Pram published *Nyanyi sunyi seorang bisu* (*A Mute's Soliloquy*) in 1995. This story was based on letters he wrote to his daughter, which couldn't be sent during his time of imprisonment on Buru.

Pram certainly was a good writer and was several times nominated as Southeast Asia's best writing candidate for the Noble Prize. His knowledge of international and regional affairs caused by political events in history make his writings very tantalizing. He combined his knowledge of history with his own personal life story to make his novels more interesting. Up until the late 1990s, Indonesians lived under the rule of strict censorship, and freedom of press was severely curtailed. Despite being censored in his own country, Pramoedya Ananta Toer has earned many accolades and awards from other countries, such as Philippines, Netherlands, France, Japan, Chile, Norway, and the United States, as well as UNESCO.

Pram experienced many difficult and challenging years of imprisonment, even mental and physical torture at the hands of prison guards. In later life, he suffered from complications of diabetes and heart disease and had to be hospitalized in 2006. Part of the medical explanation given for his critical diagnosis was attributed to his addiction to *kretek* (clove cigarettes). Pram died in 2006, when he was 81 years old.

Myrtati Dyah Artaria

See also: Indonesian Protest Music (Chapter 1: Popular Music)

Further Reading

Gogwilt, Chris. 1998. "Pramoedya Ananta Toer 1925 (Indonesian)." In *Encyclopedia of the Novel.* Ed. Paul Schellinger. Chicago, IL: Fitzroy Dearborn.

Kurniawan, Eka. 2006. *Pramoedya Ananta Toer dan Sastra Realisme Sosialis.* Jakarta, ID: Gramedia Pustaka Utama.

Teeuw, A. 1997. *Citra Manusia Indonesia dalam Karya Pramoedya Ananta Toer.* Jakarta, ID: Pustaka Jaya.

Vickers, Adrian. 2005. *A History of Modern Indonesia.* New York: Cambridge University Press.

Vltchek, Andre, Rossie Indira, and Nagesh Rao. 2006. *Exile: Pramoedya Ananta Toer in Conversation with Andre Vltchek and Rossie Indira.* Chicago: Haymarket Books.

THAROOR, SHASHI

The writings of Shashi Tharoor (1956–) span Indian colonial history, ancient Indian mythology, and the progress that India has made in the last 55 years as a democracy. Nothing about his writing is complete without his first, and by all accounts his most famous, work *The Great Indian Novel*, hereafter referred to as *The Novel*.

In a BBC interview on the 25th anniversary of the book, Tharoor described it as a book that still appeals to readers and is widely sold. In his interview, the author, a 27-year veteran of the United Nations and now Member of Parliament representing Kerala, a South Indian state, exclaimed that if the book were written today it would likely be banned in India.

Imagine a famous mythological story, widely read, deeply revered, and containing religious underpinnings. Now take one or a series of significant historical occurrences, for instance the period in American history from 1776 to 1787 (from the Declaration of Independence to the year the U.S. Constitution was signed). Finally, pick your favorite prominent historical figures during this time period and recall not just their glorious moments but also their controversial actions.

The Novel uses the mythological backdrop of *The Mahabharata*, an ancient Indian epic describing the famous battle of Kurukshetra between rival cousins, the Kauravas and the Pandavas. This battle is said to have lasted 18 days; *The Novel* has

18 chapters. *The Novel* weaves the ancient epic into modern times, using the historical developments of India's struggle to be free from British rule in the early 20th century. The characters in the novel are cleverly created, replacing those from the epic with fictional characters bearing a resemblance to famous Indian freedom fighters entrenched in the struggle that finally freed India from decades of British rule.

Of significance is the fact that the story of India's independence as taught in classrooms all over India has no resemblance or comparison to the epic that Tharoor uses as his backdrop, and therein lies the unique creativity and sheer genius of *The Novel*. Tharoor, a seasoned diplomat, is said to have woven the tale to include controversial events, according to some accounts, but for the most part, *The Novel* is a work of fiction that marries mythology and history to produce a timeless fictional work.

Tharoor used his success with *The Novel* to write 13 more books (at the time of writing and according to his official website, www.shashitharoor.in) in which he has used his personal, professional, and political knowledge to create funny, irreverent, and memorable works that provide a glimpse into Indian culture, languages, customs, religions, politics, and social practices. He is a cultural ambassador in the true sense of the word, introducing India to readers around the world in a manner that is informative (his works include nonfiction essays and compilations), intelligent, and inspiring.

In his 2007 work *The Elephant, the Tiger and the Cellphone*, his informative style of writing is illustrated by an entire glossary under the chapter title "The A to Z of Being Indian."

Here is a sample entry:

> Dowry: is the classic Indian social evil: the cause of much rural indebtedness, a great deal of human misery and sometimes the death of an unwanted bride, usually in a 'kitchen accident.' There are still those who justify dowry as recompense for the parents of the son, and many who, more 'progressively' argue that it is really intended for the bridal couple to make their start in life. Whatever the arguments, nothing can justify the misery caused by dowry; yet, despite years of campaigning for its abolition, and four decades during which the giving or receiving of dowry has been formally illegal, the iniquitous practice continues. In our country, social pressures are more powerful than legal or moral ones—even when the pressure is to do the wrong thing. (452)

The fact that Tharoor belongs to the breed of writers who are of Indian origin and reside primarily outside India, like Vikram Seth, V. S. Naipaul, and Salman Rushdie, does not in any way hamper his grasp of the nuances of Indian life, and he weaves them into his narrative. In one instance, he compares a snow-clad street displaying grime intermittently with pure snow to *laddoo*, a popular Indian sweet that is decorated with edible silver foil to mask uneven food coloring. This detail from an author living outside of India is a testament to not just his research but his attention to the mundane—the foil on *laddoo* is so common, most of us who grew up in India do not even pay attention to it. Tharoor, on the other hand, uses it in

The Novel most aptly and conjures for us a precise image: a dusty and slushy street, displaying specks of pure-white snow.

Most writing in India is done in English, a natural first language for a small subset of the total population but a default choice if you grow up in a cosmopolitan city. So Tharoor did not have to pick a language that would make his words accessible. However, it is not easy to use the backdrop of an ancient mythological story, written originally in Sanskrit, an ancient Indian language, to create an entire story with concepts such as *dharma* loosely translated as duty and *karma* loosely translated as destiny based on your deeds. Perhaps we have used one or more of these words, but their origins are best understood in epics like *Mahabharata*, which Tharoor has used to create a work that is modern and yet somehow timeless. Reading *The Novel* today, considering the change in the Indian political climate, the emergence of the Aam Admi Party (loosely translated as the "Common Man's Party"), and following the recent election of a prime minister (Narendra Modi) who has more than 12.7 million Twitter followers, one is surprised at the comparisons and lessons in *The Novel* that relate to contemporary India.

Of note about Tharoor's work is that he is perhaps one of only a handful of writers who has educated readers about India through his understanding of politics, government, and civic engagement. After *The Novel*, Tharoor's writings continued the common thread of civic life in India, and he fittingly devoted two books to Bollywood (the Indian equivalent of Hollywood) and cricket, perhaps the two most popular obsessions among Indians. Tharoor is a gifted satirist, which results in his books having chapters with titles like "India, Jones and the Template of Dhoom," editorials with titles like "The 'Claahs Struggle' with 'Tom-ah-tos,'" and quotes like "They say every dog has its day, Ganapathi, but for this terrier twilight came before tea-time" (from *The Novel*, 244).

His work is relevant since he has single-handedly managed to create a body of work that uses life in India as a backdrop for social commentary, political criticism, and global perspective. From praising the growth of the technology sector in India to critiquing the ever-increasing income inequality, Tharoor is a master at educating and advocating at the same time. He is perhaps one of the best-known nonresident Indians who moved back to India and is flourishing not as a doctor or an engineer (the claim to fame for many returned nonresident Indians) but as an elected representative to the Indian Parliament from the state that his parents called home. He was a close second to being appointed as the head of the UN when Ban Ki-Moon was selected, and he has played a prominent role in international diplomacy. As an author, he has taken these experiences and created works that will appeal to all readers who like writings that evoke vivid imagery, to all readers who read to travel to other parts of the world through words, and to all readers who are looking for mastery of the subject of Indian culture—reflected very obviously in *The Novel*, where he takes a complicated, multifamily epic, picks up a decade of political struggle, and creates an allegory of unmatched proportions in the world of storytelling.

While Tharoor has always maintained that *The Novel* is not historically accurate but fictionally appropriate in its account, it contains all the key players, events, and occurrences from India's freedom struggle, and for the most part sets it in the context of the characters from the *Mahabharata*. To that extent, it is educational and aptly belongs in a collection such as this encyclopedia, since the word *Mahabharata* translates as "great India!"

Protima Pandey

See also: Women Writers, India

Further Reading

Forester, E. M. 1924. *A Passage to India*. New York: Penguin.
Naipaul, V. S. 1961. *A House for Mr. Biswas*. London: Andre Deutsch.
Rushdie, Salman. 1981. *Midnight's Children*. New York: Random House.
Tharoor, Shashi. 2007. *The Elephant, the Tiger, and the Cell Phone: Reflections on India—The Emerging 21st-Century Power*. New Delhi: Penguin.

WOMEN WRITERS, INDIA

Historically, women's writing has survived under the constant threat of being erased or devalued in the context of the patriarchal society of India. For many women, existing traditions of devotion and romance often provided the stage to express their personal sentiments and experiences that would otherwise find little room to grow. Mirabai, a poet of the *bhakti* (devotional) tradition from North India, was born a princess and immersed herself in composing and performing songs of adoration for Krishna, an Indian god enshrined in her poetry of ecstatic lament. Mirabai's work resonates with a South Indian poet, Mahadeviyakka. Known familiarly as Akka (meaning "elder sister"), she is a Kannada female poet who joined the Virasaivite (Heroic Worship of Siva) sect and sang aloud of her love for Siva, whom she renames and addresses as Mallikarjuna (Lord, White as Jasmine). Akka's poetry points to a long-existing tradition of mystical ecstasy that borders on the erotic. The female voice also is preserved in more organic forms of literariness, such as folklore, musical and theatrical forms, as well as *akam/puram* (inner/outer) poetry from Tamil antiquity, where the *akam* poems, in particular, address quotidian themes of domesticity, familial relationships, and the internal order of things. Many such cultural forms inform the women writers from the modern nation of India because women have been predominant as always already present in the act of reckoning, speaking from the margins in poignant, honest, visceral, radical, and urgent ways.

Alongside literary poetic forms where women's voices deliberate on the injustices of war and the tribulations of domestic relationships, the folktale, often valorizing the female subject, retains the place of the woman as author and artist. In one such story, collected and retold by scholar A. K. Ramanujan, a woman who refuses to tell her story and song to anyone, including her husband, finds that it takes form as a pair of shoes and coat left at her doorstep. Her husband, suspicious, leaves after quarreling and learns later that the shoes and coat are nothing other than a song and a story hidden within his wife. When he asks her to relate them, she has no memory of her secret gifts. For the woman writer, then, turning her gift into the material of a story, tale, or song is an act of articulation and performance of meaning in a way that resists appropriation. The "woman-writer" revels in the inappropriate.

Modern Indian women writers forged their literary selves in the crucible of nationalist struggles against colonial rule. They were influenced by ascendant nationalist aspirations of the early 20th century and concomitant ideological forces behind British and Victorian institutional sensibilities, Christian missionary discourse, and imperial educational regimes. As the nations of South Asia emerged in the 1940s, women wrote while balancing emergent public practices of nationalism, socialism, citizenship, democratic politics, and, most crucially, with postcolonial navigations of a historical legacy of limitations set on self-representation. Women wrote on the lessons of colonial conquest and national becoming. Poets like Mahadevi Varma, Sarojini Naidu, and Subhadra Kumari Chauhan carved out gendered spaces of resistance and liberation, and many of them were affiliated with progressive writers' movements in regional, national, and global contexts. Modernity brought new complexities to the roles women played in social and domestic spheres. With the added pressures on labor productivity, the literary forms most suited and practical are the shorter forms, such as free-verse poems and short stories. Thus, while the number of women writers is in the hundreds, a few key names are mentioned here.

These 20th-century authors emerge from a polyphonous national literary tradition that has literary print publications in dozens of regional languages along with major ones in the national languages of Hindi and English. Ismat Chugtai (Urdu, 1915–1992) wrote stories that address themes of sexual desire, transgression, harassment, domestic habits, and many issues plaguing middle-class women. In her famous story, "Lihaf" ("The Quilt"), she suggests the story of romantic and sexual love between two women, a mistress and her servant, through the eyes of a child. Later, writers in Hindi and Urdu, like Mrinal Pande, Meherunnisa Parvez, Mridula Garg, and Hazira Shakoor continue to question the ways in which dogma, tradition, and patriarchy continue their chokehold in the lives of women, as in Shakoor's famous story, "Umr qaid" ("Life Sentence"), narrated in the voice of a guilt-stricken husband who realizes that his reform-minded zeal that had him accept a wife rejected at the wedding threshold meant that she was forced to live the life of an outsider in his family for the duration of their married years until her death. Amrita Pritam (Punjabi, 1919–2005) produces poetry, stories, and novels popularized through film adaptations, contending with issues of alienation, disempowerment, and melancholy. Pritam's work is emblematic of the pain and suffering endured by the exodus generated during the partition of Pakistan and India. Abburi Chaya Devi (Telugu, 1933–) expresses the differences between an academic feminist vision and the material reality for modern women in her famous short story "Srimathi-udyogini" ("Wife-Working Woman," 1975).

Feminist voices proliferated in the latter half of the 20th century with questions engendered by postcolonial approaches to thematic disparities like class, educational background, caste, and other privileges. These questions inform and are illuminated by writers like Triveni, Vaidehi, and Anupuma Niranjana in Kannada; Ambai in Tamil; Dhiruben Patel and Saroj Pathak in Gujarati; Mahasweta Devi in Bengali; and Saraswati Amma, Rajalekshmy, P. Vatsala, Sarah Joseph, and Kamala Das in Malayalam. Narrations often delineate the trajectory of victimhood and self-liberation as in Anupama Niranjana's story "The Incident and After," wherein the wife leaves the husband after he abandons her to her plight when they are attacked by a band of thugs on a deserted street while returning home from an evening out. Kamala Das (1934–2009), whose mother, Balamani Amma (1909–2004), is the celebrated poet of motherhood and traditional values associated with femininity, gains iconicity as the voice of female desire, agency, and pleasure in her short stories and poetry most aptly narrated in her memoir, "My Story." One of the best-known critics of the violence of state-building is Mahasweta Devi, author of over 100 books, whose stories and commentaries were translated by the feminist deconstructionist scholar Gayatri Chakraborty Spivak. Mahasweta Devi writes of the condition of the indigenous and the figure of the tribal, people who have often been "disappeared" in "encounters," people systematically disenfranchised in the so-called interest of the greater common good.

Parallel to nation-building and women writing within the national boundary, Indian women have migrated to Western metropolitan centers and written extensively, establishing a global reputation as Indian women writers of the diaspora. They reflect extensively on issues of belonging, identity, nostalgia, and concomitant themes of assimilation and agency. Such work is exemplified in the literary efforts of Kamala Markandaya, Bharati Mukherjee, and Anita Desai. In the 1980s to 1990s, a new generation of voices continued to wrestle with issues of making home in new places, gendered conflicts within domestic and public sphere, and the invisibility of being an Indian woman abroad. Meena Alexander crossed genres and penned these conflicts in her memoir, *Fault Lines*, while many other writers establish their literary reputations through the short-story form, as evident in Anjana Appachana's "Incantations," Chitra Bannerjee Divakaruni's "Arranged Marriage," and Jhumpa Lahiri's "The Interpreter of Maladies." Appachana's "Incantations" recounts the dramatic story of familial rape followed by a murder-suicide retold in the precocious and troubled witness born by the younger sister. These stories, imagined by an author living far from home, sensitively retell the lives of middle-class Indians living in the capital, Delhi—lives that are spliced with humor, diversity, and difference, dwelling on themes of intranational migration, one of the less-covered subjects of Indian women's literature. While Lahiri and Divakaruni continue to work through the novel form as well, their novels have also found new life and audiences in film adaptations.

Such literary voices grow in prolificity with authors that explore a variety of domestic and public matters that range from the sexual to the political. Ginu Kamani, Shauna Singh Baldwin, Thrity Umrigar, and Indira Ganesan, among others, have brought an urgency to questions of history as they impinge on contemporary culture. Kiran Desai, the daughter of literary luminary Anita Desai, grapples with her own mythic, literary connections to India in well-received novels *Hullabulloo in the Guava Orchard* and *The Inheritance of Loss*, both contending with life set in India, often centered on men of humble origins, such as the postal worker in the first novel, and men of authority, such as the judge in the latter novel. In 2007 Desai won the Booker for her second novel. For the contemporary woman writer, the world is the palate and the subject no longer remains confined to themes of gender, identity, and migration.

Arundhati Roy also burst onto the global literary scene with a Booker Prize for her first and only work of fiction, *The God of Small Things*. Set in a small town in Kerala that is also the actual place of her upbringing, Ayemenem, the novel fictionalizes and brings to life a host of issues that have heretofore remained at the margins of the Indian popular imaginary, love and desire across class, caste, and religious boundaries. Ever since the literary laurels granted Roy high literary status, every talk she gives in any city of the world is a rock-star event booked generally beyond capacity, and portions of her lectures were included in a film released for free on the Internet, *We*. Roy reserves all her authorial energies for writing that speaks about resistance of the disenfranchised populations within India, and her writing constantly takes aim at power iniquities of a global marketplace dominated by big corporate interests, power that replicates old-world imperialisms in the guise of new-world multinational monopolies.

Roy has gained a powerful following and global recognition as a woman writing in India. She has written on a range of subjects and expressed her ire against the nuclear tests conducted by India and Pakistan in 1998, big dam projects across the Indian nation in the name of development, and U.S. aggression and war in the Middle East. To write *Walking with the Comrades*—about the condition of decades-long resistance, displacement, and disenfranchisement of India's indigenous people—she traveled

Arundhati Roy, author and political activist, is seen here in 2013 at a protest against the decision by the Indian Supreme Court to reinstate the criminalization of homosexuality. Roy is one of the most prominent voices in Indian culture and politics, and also inspires readers and activists around the world with her fiction and nonfiction writing. (Jiti Chadha/Alamy Stock Photo)

with the Naxalite, Maoist-inspired groups that had roots in the Naxal region in the heart of the newly formed Indian states of Chhattisgarh and Jharkhand. Her books, often compilations of essays published in the active public sphere of Indian debate, newspapers, and magazines, such as *An Ordinary Person's Guide to Empire*, *Listening to Grasshoppers: Field Notes on Democracy*, and *Capitalism: A Ghost Story*, have provoked the ire of conservatives, liberals, scholars, and vested corporate, religious, and other fundamentalist groups that feel she's maligned them all with the acerbic bite of her words. Roy's voice, singular in its strident call against corporate greed, media monopolies, and national and global lobbying groups cloaked as foundations and philanthropies, resounds all the more loudly in a world homogenized through late capitalism and new imperialisms of the 21st century.

Shreerekha Subramanian

See also: Literature, Dalit

Further Reading

Tharu, Susie, and K. Lalita, eds. 1991. *Women Writing in India: 600 BC to the Present, Vol. I.* New York: Pandora.

Tharu, Susie, and K. Lalita, eds. 1993. *Women Writing in India: Vol. II: The 20th Century*. New York: The Feminist Press at the City University of New York.

YAOI COMIC BOOKS, JAPAN

The *yaoi*, or *fujoshi*, subculture in Japan has generated a lot of popularity domestically and internationally since it emerged in the 1970s. *Yaoi* refers to male homosexual-themed manga or animation products. It originated in Japan and is consumed in many other Asian countries, including China and Korea, and even in America, mainly by young female populations. It is a fascinating phenomenon in Japan because despite still being officially identified as a subculture, *yaoi* has obviously penetrated into the mainstream manga market and possesses its own subgenres. It is not rare for tourists and readers to walk into one of the anime buildings in Ikebuguro in Tokyo and find entire floors dedicated to *yaoi* products, mainly comic books. Importantly, *yaoi* comic books have feminist potentials and significance for the LGBT community in Japan and Asia.

Yaoi comic books' market presence shows that a large number of females in Japan are consuming fictional materials built on male homosexual romance. This indicates that there are disruptions and mismatches of gender relations in Japanese society. Generally speaking, Japanese society is much more masculinist and patriarchal than most Western societies. This means that in Japan women are assumed to be more domestic and submissive in their relations with men. In addition to this domesticity and submissiveness, Japanese women are also expected to conform to a definition of "appropriate" femininity based on passivity and less-expressive sexuality (Shigematsu 2012). This social reality of the gender inequality between Japanese men and women has subsequently determined the unequal distribution of entertainment resources in Japan, either romantic or pornographic. For example, corresponding to the idea of the "male gaze" in visual culture, it is not difficult to discover the frequent and constant focus on the female body in heterosexual manga or pornography in Japan. The consumption of *yaoi* comic books by Japanese women can thus be seen as their way to counter their disadvantaged position in the entertainment industry. In their enjoyment of *yaoi* comic books, Japanese women can gain romantic/sexual pleasure because these books cater to the female gaze by having two male characters expressing not only their sexual desires but also emotions and sensitivities. Just as Thorn (2004) has noted, the so-called "gay" characters in *yaoi* are actually the idealized version of heterosexual men for its female audiences.

The increasing economic power women have gained in postwar Japan has guaranteed a bustling market for *yaoi*. There have been criticisms about the distance between their economic power over cultural consumption and women's actual engagement with Japanese politics. But Japanese women's influence is still notable by the sheer increased visibility of men as objects of desire and consumption in the *yaoi* subculture. Moreover, the content of *yaoi* caters to the emotional and sexual needs of Japanese women in different ways. For example, usually there is no prominent female figures in *yaoi* comic books, and this may help female readers escape from the male-centered depiction of women in mainstream cultural products. At the same time, this can eliminate the sense of threat and competition potentially created by female characters. What is more, the central male characters usually have the personal characteristics deemed desirable by heterosexual women, such as sensitivity, gentility, emotionality. These male characteristics tend to be less stressed in heterosexual entertainment materials. However, it is noteworthy that these characteristics that are associated with homosexuality in *yaoi* are not particularly attractive to the majority of Japanese gay men. Japanese gay men prefer their own subgenre homosexual materials, *bara*. In contrast to mainstream *yaoi*, the homosexual men depicted in *bara* are hypermasculine, and the story line also tends to be more sexual and contains less romance and background building than even the most graphic *yaoi*. Therefore, it seems that while Japanese female readers of *yaoi* comic books and Japanese gay readers of *bara* comic books are all consuming representations of homosexuality, their needs tend to differ. So does the feminism of *yaoi* help the LGBT community or not?

The answer seems to be ambiguous as it depends on people's interactions in reality. At least in the fictional space, *yaoi* seems to have not broken down the social boundaries between brotherhood and homosexuality in reality. In a masculinist society like Japan, the strong homosocial culture between men means that they are allowed to share more intimacy within the boundaries of brotherhood. A lot of *yaoi* manga play on this boundary: the male "lovers" would engage in very romantic and erotic relationships with each other but in most cases still refuse to admit they are homosexual. They either insist on their intimacy being a form of brotherhood or on the particular personality of the man they fall in love with without association with gender. Therefore, even though the content itself seems to be explicitly homoerotic, the manga manages to conform to the homosocial normality of brotherhood. This contrast caters to heterosexual women's fantasy needs rather than to the political rights of gay men. Furthermore, as Thorn (2004) has noted, *yaoi* manga actually reinforces the divide of masculinity and femininity, of dominance and submission. This reinforcement is especially evident in the gender roles presented in the comic books, namely the *seme* and the *uke*, the "attacker" and the "attacked." In contrast, *bara* comic books present gay characters who are equally masculine, and this clearly indicates the different needs of gay men themselves.

Therefore, in its conformity to the homosocial boundary and rigid gender roles, the *yaoi* subculture seems to be more about Japanese women's own seeking of alternative entertainment than Japanese gay men's social recognition and movements. However, it is certain that some gay men also consume *yaoi* as it does increase their visibility, and female *yaoi* fans would very likely develop curiosity and desires to get to know more about LGBT communities. *Yaoi* still has the potential to bring together Japanese female fans with LGBT groups, despite their discrepant interests, because ultimately it is about their rebellious attitudes against unequal gender positions in reality.

Flair Donglai Shi

See also: Manga

Further Reading

McLelland, Mark. 2000. *Male Homosexuality in Modern Japan: Cultural Myths and Social Realities*. Surrey, UK: Curzon Press.

Shigematsu, Setsu. 2012. *Scream from the Shadows: The Women's Liberation Movement in Japan*. Minneapolis: University of Minnesota Press.

Sturken, Marita, and Lisa Cartwright. 2009. *Practices of Looking: An Introduction to Visual Culture*. Oxford, UK: Oxford University Press.

Thorn, Matthew. 2004. "Girls and Women Getting Out of Hand: The Pleasure and Politics of Japan's Amateur Comics Community." In *Fanning the Flames: Fans and Consumer Culture in Contemporary Japan*. Ed. William W. Kelly, 169–186. New York: State University of New York Press.

YU HUA, CHINA

The Chinese writer Yu Hua (余華) was born on April 3, 1960, in Hangzhou, Zhejiang Province. He was raised by doctor parents and worked as a dentist for five years before beginning to write professionally in 1983. His childhood memories and experiences from growing up during the Cultural Revolution (1966–1976) inform much of his writing. After the 1987 publication of his short story "On the Road at 18" (*Shiba sui chumen yuanxing* 十八歲出門遠行), Yu Hua moved to Beijing. The first Chinese author to win the James Joyce Foundation Award, in 2002, his literary work has been translated into over 15 languages.

Yu Hua belongs to the first generation of writers who grew up in the post-Mao period, and in the late 1980s, he was a key contributor to the literary avant-garde movement in China that included authors like Su Tong (蘇童, 1963–) and Ge Fei (格非, 1964–). Exposed to Western postmodernism in the form of translated works, he has cited the influence of foreign authors such as Franz Kafka and Kawabata Yasunari on his writing. Early in his career, he established his reputation with a series of provocative short stories that were characterized by their shocking depiction of brutal violence. In "1986" ("1986 nian" 1986 年, 1987), a wife and daughter in a small town come to terms with the ghostly reappearance of their husband and father, a former schoolteacher who was taken away during the Cultural Revolution. Borrowing the theme of madness from Lu Xun's seminal 1918 short story "Diary of a Madman," the story follows the madman as he fantasizes about and eventually self-inflicts the five traditional-style punishments. Another story, "The Past and the Punishments" ("Wangshi yu xingfa" 往事與刑罰, 1989), which was inspired by Kafka's "In the Penal Colony," follows an unnamed stranger's encounter with a punishment expert through a labyrinthine series of mysterious dates and memories. These early stories stood out from mainstream literature by challenging the concepts of historical reflection and time.

His first full-length novel, *Cries in the Drizzle* (*Zai xiyu zhong huhan* 在細雨中呼喊, formerly titled *Huhan yu xiyu*), was first published in the Shanghai literary journal *Harvest* (*Shouhuo* 收獲) in 1991 and reveals the transition from his early experimental style to his later signature "plain-realist" style. Set in a rural village in Zhejiang in the 1960s and 1970s, the bildungsroman, or spiritual and educational coming-of-age narrative, tells the story of the outcast Sun Guanglin, the middle of three brothers, and consists of a series of childhood memories about Sun Guanglin's tenuous relationships with his family members, neighbors, and classmates.

In the mid-1990s, his two most successful novels were *To Live* (*Huozhe* 活著, 1993), which was subsequently made into an award-winning film in 1994 by director Zhang Yimou, and *Chronicle of a Blood Merchant* (*Xu Sanguan mai xue ji* 許三觀賣血記, 1995), which was made into a South Korean film directed by Ha Jung Woo in 2015. These two novels were listed among the 10 most influential books of the decade by Shanghai's daily newspaper *Wenhui bao*. *To Live*, winner of Italy's Premio Grinzane Cavour literary prize, tells the serendipitous story of Fugui and his family as they try to survive the political tumult from the 1940s to the early 1980s. The main narrative is told from the perspective of Fugui, who gradually transforms from a good-for-nothing gambler that loses his family's fortune to an optimistic husband and protective father. *Chronicle of a Blood Merchant* takes place during roughly the same time and tells the story of Xu Sanguan, who works in a silk factory but must sell his blood on the side to support his family during difficult times. Both novels eloquently depict the devastating effects of modern Chinese history on families and the individual's spirit of endurance that arises out of desperation.

In 2005 and 2006, Yu Hua published *Brothers* (*Xiong di* 兄弟), a two-volume historical saga about two brothers, Baldy Li and Song Gang, spanning four decades of drastic social and political transformations in China. The first part of the satirical novel depicts the boys' childhood and is set against the backdrop of the Cultural Revolution in the fictional Liu town. Part two begins in the post-Mao period and ends with a scathing commentary on the crass materialism of New China during the Reform Era of the 1980s. Critics, on the one hand, attacked *Brothers* for its vulgar misogyny, comic exaggeration, and physical humor; on the other hand, the novel was a best seller in China, was short-listed for the Man Asian Literary Prize, and won the Prix Courrier International.

In an op-ed for the *New York Times* entitled "The Spirit of May 35th," Yu Hua explained the difference between the implicit critique in *Brothers* and the direct commentary in his next publication, a collection of essays entitled *China in Ten Words* (*Shi ge cihui li de zhongguo* 十個詞彙裡的中國, 2012). In the latter work, he defines 10 words pertinent to Chinese culture, such as "revolution," "Lu Xun," and "writing," using his autobiographical experiences as well as observations and anecdotes about contemporary society.

Most recently, Yu Hua published the novel *The Seventh Day* (*Diqi tian* 第七天, 2013), a fantastical tale about the wandering afterlife of a poor everyman, Yang Fei, which is based on actual news events, and a volume of collected essays written in the last decade entitled *We Live in a Huge Gap* (*Women shenhuo zai juda de chaju li* 我們生活在巨大的差距裡, 2015), which address his concern about the social disparities that have resulted from China's rapid economic development.

Yu Hua's narrative style is renowned for being direct and accessible to readers, and in his essay "Writing" from *China in Ten Words*, he recounts joking to critics about how his plain style was the result of a limited vocabulary resulting from the inferior education he received during the Cultural Revolution. In the same essay, he identifies the big-character posters or *dazi bao* (handwritten posters used to denounce counterrevolutionaries during the Maoist period) he authored in elementary school as the first literary works of his to be shared with the rest of the world. He has also explained his philosophy of blending the imaginary with the real: "All I can say now is that all of my efforts are directed toward bringing this tradition closer to the contemporary era, in other words, bringing the outdated form of fiction closer to the present day" ("Hypocritical Works" "Xuwei de zuopin" 虛偽的作品, 1994, 44). Yu Hua's belief in literature's ability to convey the universal human condition has ultimately attracted an international readership: "Human experience, combined with the power of the imagination and understanding, can break down all barriers, enabling a person truly to understand that thing called fate at work in his life—not unlike the experience of simultaneously seeing one's reflection in two different mirrors. Perhaps that is what makes literature magical" ("Author's Postscript" in Yu Hua's *To Live*, 249–250).

Angie C. Chau

See also: Literature, Post-1990, China

Further Reading

Li, Hua. 2011. *Contemporary Chinese Fiction by Su Tong and Yu Hua: Coming of Age in Troubled Times*. Leiden, NL: Brill.

Yu, Hua. 1989. "Hypocritical Works" "Xuwei de zuopin" 虛僞的作品, 1994, in *Shanghai wenlun* 5: 44–74.

Yu, Hua. 1996. *The Past and the Punishments*. Trans. Andrew Jones. Honolulu: University of Hawai'i Press.

Yu, Hua. 2003a. *Chronicle of a Blood Merchant*. Trans. Andrew F. Jones. New York: Anchor Books.

Yu, Hua. 2003b. *To Live*. Trans. Michael Berry. New York: Random House.

Yu, Hua. 2010. *Brothers*. Trans. Eileen Cheng-yin Chow and Carlos Rojas. New York: Anchor Books.

Yu, Hua. 2011. "The Spirit of May 35th." *New York Times*. June 23. http://www.nytimes.com/2011/06/24/opinion/global/24iht-june24-ihtmag-hua-28.html?_r=0. Accessed March 24, 2016.

Yu, Hua. 2012. *China in Ten Words*. Trans. Allan H. Barr. New York: Anchor Books.

Liu, Kang. 2002. "The Short-Lived Avant-Garde: The Transformation of Yu Hua." *MLQ: Modern Language Quarterly* 63, no. 1 (March): 89–117.

Chapter 3: Film

Introduction

National film industries in Asia and Oceania emerged and grew rapidly after World War II and the withdrawal of the European colonial powers. The popularity of local movies in various languages representing different societies and communities highlighted national cultures in the region that were culturally, religiously, and philosophically diverse and changing in a globalizing world. American, European, Asian, and, cross-regionally, indigenous movies were showcased, offering a popular mix of films for viewers in countries ranging from Australia and New Zealand to Indonesia and the Philippines, India, and China.

Bruce Lee (Little Dragon)

Bruce Lee (1940–1973), also known as Lee Jun-fan, was a martial arts teacher, actor, and filmmaker who had a profound effect on the global popularity of the Chinese martial arts. Born to Lee Hoi-chuen (a Cantonese opera star) and Grace Ho in San Francisco, he grew up in Hong Kong. Lee followed his father into the entertainment industry, where he appeared in approximately 20 films as a child actor. As a teenager, he studied Wing Chun kung fu with Ip Man. While Lee would go on to articulate his own fighting philosophy (Jeet Kune Do), it is clear that his early introduction to Wing Chun had a profound effect on his thinking about the martial arts.

Lee was involved in a number of fights as a teenager and did not excel in school. His mother convinced him to make a fresh start in the United States. After arriving in Washington State, Lee completed his GED and enrolled at the University of Washington. During this time, he taught martial arts and married Linda Emery.

Bruce and Linda eventually moved to California, where Lee continued to teach and pursued an acting career. He gained national exposure after being cast as Kato in the short-lived *Green Hornet* series (1966–1967) and made guest appearances on a number of television shows. Unhappy with his inability to win larger roles, Lee returned to Hong Kong and starred in three popular martial arts films. Yet his greatest success came with *Enter the Dragon* (1973), coproduced by Warner Bros. and Golden Harvest.

Unfortunately, Lee died of a cerebral edema just prior to the film's release. The wild popularity of *Enter the Dragon* ignited a global wave of interest in the Asian fighting systems, and his posthumous fame helped to promote public acceptance of the Chinese martial arts.

Benjamin N. Judkins

Today, national film industries in these magnificent and diverse parts of the world are transforming as movies are being made with computers, edited by third parties online, and downloaded or streamed onto large and small screens in the comfort of private homes, community gathering places, and public theaters. New Zealand Maori and Australia Aborigine feature films like *The Whale Rider* (2002) and *Rabbit-Proof Fence* (2002) have attained world-class stature. Bollywood musicals, Philippine *bomba* films, Vietnamese historical dramas, Chinese martial art films, and Korean romance movies are extremely popular, transregionally and internationally, often rivaling Hollywood productions.

With one of the oldest film industries, India's films have been remarkably influential, not only on the subcontinent but also in mainland and island Southeast Asia and around the world. Around the 1990s, the Hindi film industry based in Mumbai (Bombay) came to be internationally referred to as Bollywood, signaling its increasingly widespread popularity. In some areas of the world, like parts of Africa, Bollywood even transcends Hollywood in popularity. Bollywood films are usually characterized by a combination of light entertainment, colorful and joyful forms of dance and song, young love, and traditional family values in a sensibly cosmopolitan and teasingly erotic show of spectacular bodily movements. Current-day Bollywood films often incorporate some of the contradictions of traditional and modern capitalist values in ways that are distinct from the older popular genre of Indian cinema that focused more on local conflict and historical matters.

Similarly, the films of China, Japan, and South Korea have attracted a huge transnational following. In recent decades, films such as *Crouching Tiger, Hidden Dragon* (2000, China), *Farewell My Concubine* (1993, China), and *Chunhyang* (2000, South Korea) have proved to be huge international commercial successes. The newer "d generation" of East Asian digital filmmakers continue this tradition of producing highly popular films, locally, transregionally, and internationally. Like many of their counterparts around the region and beyond, they produce a wide variety of film styles and genres, including martial arts, comedy, Samurai, horror, anime, historical drama, action, and science fiction. An interesting and innovative feature of East Asian films is that they often draw audiences into the plot in an interactive way that provides a sense of psychological relief to the viewers. This is particularly the case in Japanese and Korean horror films, which often cover themes pertaining to local individual and collective self-perceived wrongs that have not been redressed by concerned states or cannot be spoken about safely in the context of the extended family.

Southeast Asian movies, like Tran Anh Hung's *The Scent of Green Papaya* (1993) and *Cyclo* (1995), or Apichatpong Weerasethakul's *Tropical Malady* (2004) and *Uncle Boonmee Who Can Recall His Past Lives* (2010), are also winning recognition and prestigious awards at international film festivals. Local film cultures are vitally connected to their respective popular culture. The filmmaking industry in the Philippines has been partly influenced by Hollywood and Spanish colonial influences. Films across the Southeast Asian region offer viewers a wide array of selections, from lighthearted comedies to serious dramas. Like popular Indonesian

Golf War

The Golf War is a powerful documentary on the widespread development of golf courses for the pleasure of the rich and the detriment of farmers in the Philippines. Film directors Jen Schradie and Matt DeVries investigate the controversial construction of a golf complex in the agricultural province of Batangas. This string of golf courses and marina has displaced small farmers who have lived there for generations. The directors allowed the town mayor, high government officials, land developers, golf boosters (including Tiger Woods), farmers, and recent college graduates who were now members of the New People's Army to speak for themselves, revealing a larger picture of local political unrest over the issue of land reform.

This film offers a way for viewers to see and discuss the complex interrelationship of international development policies and local social and economic structures. It also presents provocative material on human development. For example, while sports may provide a way for fathers in the United States to teach their sons about the meaning of life, in the Philippines, this type of bonding is not prevalent. Local Filipino fathers typically bond with their sons by working together on the farm or in another occupation.

Kathleen M. Nadeau

films, Filipino movies often explore issues of heroism and self-sacrifice for love of family and country. Philippine films, like the notorious *Imelda: macht, mythe, illusie* (*Imelda: Power, Myth, Illusion*, 2003) have exposed some of the outrageous extravagance and human rights abuses committed under the Marcos dictatorship (1965–1986). Recent Indonesian films, similarly, have denounced some of the atrocities of the Soeharto (Suharto) authoritarian regime (1967–1998). Recent Southeast Asian films, like the critically acclaimed Philippine film *Anak* (2000), also continue to wrestle with many of the problems of poverty and migration that cut across the region.

More broadly, Asian films in all their rich and colorful appreciation for cultural and historical differences, deal with the many moral ambiguities of individual and community life in an age of capitalist globalization. They offer fresh insights into a world that is, at once, global and local, marked by many of the contradictions of modernity and traditional patriarchal structures and subaltern experiences.

Australian and New Zealand film industries tend to focus on local histories, including the settlement and indigenous histories and cultures. Beginning in the 1970s, the Australian government set up a media school and foundation to fund upcoming young filmmakers. A popular Australian genre that evolved out of this context is the "Ocker" comedy. This type of comedy, lampooning white Australian culture, usually stars a male who experiences emotional and sexual tensions throughout the film. Typically, characters are down-to-earth, good-natured, and naïve. Peter Faiman's *Crocodile Dundee* (1986) is a good example of this genre. Another popular local film type looks at the struggles of ranch workers and others settling in the Australian outback. The recent productions of Australian filmmaker Baz Luhrman, like *Moulin Rouge* (2001), *Australia* (2008), and *The Great Gatsby* (2013), have achieved international fame for their flamboyance, dazzling cinematography, and postmodern style.

The New Zealand government, like that of Australia, established the New Zealand Film Commission to fund the projects of promising young filmmakers. Films like Peter Jackson's The Lord of the Rings series (2001, 2002, 2003) and his three Hobbit films (2012, 2013, 2014), Lee Tamahori's *Once Were Warriors* (1994), and Jane Campion's *The Piano* (1993) remain among the world's best and most popular films.

This chapter includes a sampling of the different cinemas and films of Asia and Oceania. Each of the entries is written by a specialist steeped in the local nuances and transmigrations of popular film genres and styles in his or her area of expertise. Some of the entries deal with cinemas in parts of the world that have scant literature available to English readers, such as North Korea, Xinjiang, and Tibet, while others take us on a journey through some of the best films of the ages, lauded internationally, from an inside perspective that opens new space for further reflection.

Kathleen M. Nadeau and Jeremy A. Murray

Further Reading

Dissanayake, Wimal. 2007. "Film in South and Southeast Asia." In *The Greenwood Encyclopedia of World Popular Culture, Volume 6: Asia and Pacific Oceania.* Ed. Gary Xu and Vinay Dharwadker, 105–126. Westport, CT: Greenwood Press.

Larkin, Brian. 2008. "Itineraries of Indian Cinema: African Videos, Bollywood, and Global Media." In *The Anthropology of Globalization, A Reader.* Ed. Jonathan Xavier Inda and Renato Rosaldo, 334–351. Malden, MA: Blackwell Publishing.

Tan, E. K. 2007. "Film in East Asia and Oceana." In *The Greenwood Encyclopedia of World Popular Culture, Volume 6: Asia and Pacific Oceania.* Ed. Gary Xu and Vinay Dharwadker, 91–104. Westport, CT: Greenwood Press.

AUSTRALIANS IN HOLLYWOOD

Success in Hollywood—the Los Angeles–based American film juggernaut—is for many in the industry the pinnacle of success. Australians, in recent years, have come to play an important role in Hollywood, both in front of and behind the camera. This special relationship between Australia and Hollywood has a long history, launched in part by Errol Flynn (1909–1959), who arrived from Australia to embody the romantic and swashbuckling leading man, starting with *Captain Blood* in 1935. Another now-historic example of an Australian taking Hollywood by storm is Paul Hogan's beloved *Crocodile Dundee* (1986).

While the film industry is highly globalized, and a blockbuster can potentially come from anywhere, it seems that many Australian filmmakers and actors find their way to Hollywood after honing their craft on smaller-budget productions in Australia. Baz Luhrman (1962–) has led the charge of Australian directors in recent years. Luhrman's first major film, *Strictly Ballroom* (1992), was a critical and art-house success, but with *Romeo + Juliet* (1996, starring Leonardo DiCaprio and Claire Danes), Luhrman had a megahit, which he followed with *Moulin Rouge* (2001), casting the Australian Nicole Kidman in the lead. Luhrman worked again with Kidman in *Australia* (2008), in which he also cast the Australian Hugh Jackman. In 2013 Luhrman returned with another blockbuster in *The Great Gatsby*, a kinetic reinvention of the classic American novel.

Also behind the camera, the Malaysian-born Australian James Wan (1977–) has had an enormous impact in Hollywood in the early 21st century. Beginning with the sleeper-hit horror films *Saw* (2004, and its many sequels) and *Insidious* (2010, and also a burgeoning franchise), Wan has gone on to direct one of the highest-grossing films in history: *Furious 7* (2015), the latest in the Fast and Furious franchise, has filled cinemas around the world, notably in China, where it has become one of the highest-grossing films in Chinese domestic box-office history. At the time of writing, Wan's success promises to continue, and he is scheduled to direct the first film in what will doubtless be another franchise, *Aquaman*, scheduled for 2018.

Australian actors, male and female, have also had a profound impact on global cinema, mostly via Hollywood. Nicole Kidman (1967–), Cate Blanchett (1969–), Hugh Jackman (1968–), and Russell Crowe (1964–) have perhaps been the most prominent Australian actors in recent years, dominating both the box office and the awards shows. Kidman arrived on the international scene with her roles alongside her former husband, Tom Cruise, in the blockbusters *Days of Thunder* (1990) and *Far and Away* (1992) before going on to win the Academy Award for her portrayal of Virginia Woolf in *The Hours* (2002). Blanchett first earned major international recognition for her role as Elizabeth I in *Elizabeth* (1998) and went on to win two Academy Awards, both for Best Supporting Actress for her roles as Katharine Hepburn in *The Aviator* (2004) and the title role of Woody Allen's *Blue Jasmine*

In recent years, Hollywood has seen a wave of Australian actors become some of the most reliable box office heavyweights in the film industry. From Russell Crowe and Nicole Kidman, to Margot Robbie and Chris Hemsworth (seen here in Los Angeles in 2015), Australians have become a mainstay of Hollywood's blockbusters and red carpets. (Featureflash/Dreamstime.com)

(2013). Jackman has not won an Academy Award at the time of writing, but he has been nominated (*Les Misérables*, 2012) and has won both a Golden Globe for Best Actor (*Les Misérables*, 2012) and a Tony Award for Outstanding Actor (*The Boy from Oz*, 2004). As a versatile showman, Jackman has also won accolades for hosting the Tony Awards and the Oscars. Crowe (born in New Zealand but a self-proclaimed Australian) won the Oscar for Best Actor for his leading role in *Gladiator* (2000), with nominations in the year before (*The Insider*, 1999) and the year after (*A Beautiful Mind*, 2001). Mel Gibson (1956–) was born in the United States but spent much of his childhood in Australia. Winner of the Academy Award for Best Director and Best Picture for his 1995 film *Braveheart*, Gibson has found controversy both on and off screen in recent years. Many others in the field of Australian actors who have had a major impact in Hollywood also stand out, like Geoffrey Rush (1951–, Academy Award for Best Actor, 1996), Guy Pearce (1967–), Toni Collette (1972–, Emmy and Golden Globe winner for *United States of Tara*), Naomi Watts (1968–), Chris and Liam Hemsworth (1983– and 1990–), Mia Wasikowska (1989–), Margot Robbie (1990–), and Heath Ledger (1979–2008, Academy Award for Best Supporting Actor, 2008).

To explain this phenomenon, some observers of the industry, like entertainment journalist Nancy Tartaglione, note that Hollywood producers are turning more and more to Australian casting agencies. The cost of auditioning online through video-chat calls has made it much easier for Australian hopefuls to demonstrate their talents to agencies in the United States than it would be to take a 15-hour flight across the Pacific Ocean. The American actor Michael Douglas (1944–), perhaps more controversially, cited the feminization of the American male as a reason that Australian men are taking some of the best roles. He referred to the ideal of rugged masculinity of men in Australia as the reason for their recent spike in popularity, in contrast to what he considered the more feminine male aesthetic in the United States. While certainly many would take issue with Douglas's generalization, it is interesting to note this remark from a Hollywood veteran and scion of his stature, lamenting this perceived growing distinction in the popular culture of America and Australia. (Douglas offered no parallel explanation for Australian women also rising in prominence in the Hollywood scene.)

As happens with any flight of human capital (colloquially referred to as "brain drain"), some in Australia are also concerned about the loss of so many talented filmmakers and actors to the bright lights of Hollywood. The Australian film industry is lively and full of talent, but its productions add up to only a fraction of the films that play in Australian cinemas and a still smaller fraction of movie houses around the world. Fleeing to the relatively high number of well-paying jobs in Los Angeles seems to make sense, though of course this is also an urge felt by millions of others around the world. Still, with a national population that is only slightly larger than the metropolitan region of Los Angeles, Australia continues to send a disproportionately large number of filmmakers and actors to Hollywood, to generate huge box-office revenue, and to collect many of the highest industry accolades.

Jeremy A. Murray

See also: Hollywood Films in China; Popular Movies, Australia

Further Reading

Buckmaster, Luke. 2015. "Hollywood's Australian Invasion." *BBC Culture.* July 13. www .bbc.com/culture/story/20150713-hollywoods-australian-invasion. Accessed September 26, 2015.

Jackson, Kym. 2012. *The Hollywood Survival Guide: For Aussie Actors.* Sydney, AU: Perfect Books.

Tartaglione, Nancy. 2013. "Wizards of Oz: What's Up with Aussie Actors' Proliferation of Pilot Season?" *Deadline.* April 10. http://deadline.com/2013/04/australian-actors -2013-tv-pilot-season-dominate-472067. Accessed September 26, 2015.

Zachariah, Lee. 2015. "Michael Douglas Is Worried about an Aussie Invasion of Holly-wood." *Vice.* July 20. www.vice.com/read/michael-douglas-is-worried-about-an-aussie -invasion-of-hollywood. Accessed September 26, 2015.

BOLLYWOOD GENDER STEREOTYPES

Popular Hindi cinema, better known as Bollywood, is one of the biggest film industries, producing more films annually than any other country in the world today. In India, Bollywood fulfills not only its primary function to entertain but tends to mold and influence opinion, construct images, and reinforce dominant cultural values. Consequently, it has taken on the role of custodian of national sentiments and cultural values. This, in turn, has perpetuated the enforcement of strict gender roles and gender stereotypes.

Bollywood has evolved over the years since independence, both in terms of content and technique. However, what remains a constant even today is that popular Hindi cinema is male oriented and furbished by and for male fantasies. The role of women characters in the films is relational and supportive to the male lead. They have less screen space and time as compared to their male counterparts.

Before independence, Hindi cinema focused on mythological stories and great epics. *Raja harishchandra* (1913) by Dhundiraj Govind Phalke, *Indrasabha* (1932) by V. Shantaram and J. J Madan, *Sant tukaram* (1936) by Vishnupant Govind Damle and Sheikh Fattelal were some of the films that were made during this era. Women depicted in these films were based on the parallels drawn from their mythological counterparts. Even the screen names assigned to them were those from mythology, such as Devi, Sita, Radha, and so on, and consequently they were depicted as the epitome of virtue and values, those who could do no wrong. The mythological figure of Sita from the epic *Ramayana* was frequently and commonly depicted. Sita is considered the ideal woman and wife who sees her husband as an idol. This kind of a depiction has had a lasting impact on the portrayal of Indian women in Bollywood, a construct from which even modern-day directors have had difficulty in breaking away.

In the decade after independence, from the 1950s, cinema was used to address social problems and issues that posed a challenge to nation-building. Within this larger framework of nation-building, movies like *Parineeta* (1950) and *Do bigha zamin* (1953), both by Bimal Roy, continued to portray women playing the role of traditional wife who works hard in the fields alongside her husband. This created the image of the *pativrata*, unconditional devotion to the husband. She was docile, submissive, sacrificing, sentimental, superstitious, and incapable of rational action. Such films created the notion that it was these traditional, devoted, and supporting women who were representative of true Indian women. Mention must be made here of the film *Mother India* (1957) by Mehboob Khan, which went on to attain iconic status in the history of Hindi films. Not only did the film depict the leading lady as a loyal and dutiful wife, but it had an abundance of allusions to Hindu mythology reflected in the image of a virtuous, sacrificing, and righteous mother. She became the embodiment of the mother goddess Shakti, one who represents great strength and also what it means to be a mother to society through self-sacrifice. Thus, this was another stereotype that was created in the early decades of independence.

The decades of the 1960s and 1970s were a transitional phase, moving from an essentially agrarian to an urban society, which, in turn, was considered to automatically usher in modernity. In Hindi cinema, this transitional phase has been depicted by portraying male and female protagonists as educated and wearing Western attire. This led to the women attaining glamorized screen personas while the plot and action remained essentially Indian in content. Movies such as *Love in Simla* (1960) by R. K. Nayyar, *Junglee* (1961) by Subodh Mukherjee, *An Evening in Paris* (1967) by Shakti Samanta, *Bobby* (1970) by Raj Kapoor, and *Bhala Manus* (1976) by Vishwamitra Gokel led not only to the Westernizing of the Indian woman but simultaneously made her presence almost inconsequential. It is during these decades that women on screen began to be perceived as sexual objects. This, in turn, resulted in the creation of another common stereotype, that of reducing the woman to merely the glamorous ladylove of the male hero. She had little to do in the film except to please the hero with her beauty and engage him in romancing her. A fallout of this type of stereotyping was that Bollywood tended to portray women as one-dimensional characters who were good or bad, virtuous or vampish, wife or mistress. These boundaries could never overlap, and it remains so even to this day.

The 1980s in Hindi cinema was considered the action era. This brought out a change in the content of the films, but the focus remained on the hero. It was he who was involved in all the action and drama. The heroine continued to remain only a glamorous component of the films. *Qurbani* (1980) by Feroz Khan, *Arjun* (1985) by Rahul Rawail, and *Tridev* (1989) by Rajiv Rai were male-centric films where the heroine served as a mere distraction; her role was no more than playing the hero's love interest and supporting all his endeavors. Sometimes she would be the reason for all the action entailed by the hero, and for this she had to be an elevated human being, or archetype, upholding all the values instilled in her.

The 1990s saw films that were a mix of both action and romance. While women were very much an important part of such films, there was no substance to their characters. *Jo jeeta wohi sikander* (1992) by Mansoor Khan, *Hum apke hain kaun* (1994) by Sooraj Barjatya, *Dilwale dulhaniya le jayenge* (1995) by Aditya Chopra, and *Dil to pagal hai* (1997) and *Kuch kuch hota hai* (1998) by Karan Johar were some of the films released during this decade that depicted women as modern, confident, and educated but who ultimately found themselves in matrimony and became completely domesticated and family oriented. The films highlighted the conditions for ideal womanhood at the cost of a woman's individual aspirations and choices. She was shown as the self-sacrificing family woman who put family first before her own self. The women portrayed in the films were passive, submissive wives who became perfect martyrs for their own families.

The 21st-century Hindi films continue to present and portray women in stereotypical roles as either damsels in distress who need to be rescued by knights in shining armor or the ideal devoted wives, self-sacrificing mothers, loyal sisters, or dutiful daughters-in-law. Films such as *Kabhi khushi kabhie gham* (2001) by Karan Johar, *Dil chahta hai* (2001) by Farhan Akhtar, *No Entry* (2005) by Anees Bazmee, *Wanted* (2009) by Prabhu Deva, and *Chennai Express* (2013) by Rohit Shetty tend to reveal that women exist only for the amorous pleasure of the heroes, and they are totally dependent on the men to protect them. The films portray man as the woman's savior; she is merely a decorative object in the film. While a man can be wayward, the woman is expected to maintain high ideals, values, and morals. Even if she was physically and emotionally abused, she was shown as refusing to leave her husband's side because instead of being depicted as a normal human being, she was elevated to a higher position of being ideal. The huge blockbuster films of Bollywood keep reinforcing stereotypes of women as young, beautiful, obedient, and always placing their families before themselves, and only marriage and motherhood gives them substance and makes them worthy of respect. The changes relating to women as depicted in Hindi films are merely cosmetic and continue to wield their image as largely decorative and secondary.

Sindhu Sara Thomas

See also: Lavani Dance and Film, India

Further Reading

Gehlawat, Ajay. 2010. *Reframing Bollywood: Theories of Popular Hindi Cinema.* New Delhi: Sage Publications, India.

Lal, Vinay, and Ashis Nandy. 2007. *Fingerprinting Popular Culture: The Mythic and the Iconic in Indian Cinema.* New Delhi: Oxford University Press India.

Saari, Anil. 2011. *Indian Cinema: The Faces Behind the Masks.* Oxford, UK: Oxford University Press.

Somaaya, Bhawana. 2012. *Mother Maiden Mistress: Women in Hindi Cinema, 1950–2010.* New York: HarperCollins.

CINEMA, CHINA

The rapid rise of Chinese cinema on the world stage in recent decades has attracted a great deal of attention. Thanks to the process of globalization and industrial restructuring initiated by the Chinese government in 2001, China's film industry has witnessed fundamental transformation and impressive development in the 21st century. Viewed from a global perspective, the Chinese film industry has undoubtedly become a force to be reckoned with in the international film market. Statistics from 2006 suggest that China had become the world's second-largest film market, which was supported by the significant number of domestic productions and remarkable box-office gross. Next only to the United States, China has surpassed other countries, such as the United Kingdom, France, Germany, Japan, Korea, India, and Australia, which traditionally represented important film markets.

As far as film production is concerned, not only blockbusters have thrived but also the humanistic concern and art-house aesthetics, credited to leading filmmakers of the Chinese "Fifth Generation" of filmmakers whose films have been popular both domestically and internationally in the past two decades, have continued in the new generations of filmmakers. For instance, Jia Zhangke's *A Touch of Sin* (2013) and Diao Yinan's *Black Coal, Thin Ice* (2014) have both won top honors at international film festivals such as in Cannes and Berlin. Although facing huge challenges down the road, the Chinese film industry has certainly played an important role in the economic and cultural lives of people not only in China but also the whole world.

One way to gauge the spectacular growth of the Chinese film industry is to look at the data before turning to further discussion. As the second-largest film market in the world, China's box-office receipts in 2014 reached 29.6 billion Chinese yuan (or about US$4.76 billion), up 36.15 percent from the previous year, and they made up 13 percent of the global box-office gross total. In that same year, a total of 388 films were released, with 66 of them earning over 10 million Chinese yuan (US$1.61 million) at the box office. Overall, the box-office receipts of domestic films accounted for more than 54 percent of the total gross, which stands at around 16.1 billion Chinese yuan (US$2.59 billion). The box-office record of 1.98 billion yuan (US$31 million) by a single film was established by *Transformers 4* in 2014 and was then broken by *Fast and Furious 7*, which has earned over 2 billion yuan (US$32 million) at the box office in 2015. These numbers will be more illuminative of the rapid growth of the Chinese film industry in the last 10 years when compared with data collected a decade ago. In 2002 the total box-office gross in China was 90 million yuan (US$14 million), which made up only 2 percent of the global box-office total. Back then, the average box-office take was only 2.5 million yuan (US$40,000). Indeed, the contrast could not be more dramatic.

The transformative change in the Chinese film industry must be understood in the context of globalization and changes in government policy. After joining the World Trade Organization (WTO) in 2001, China accelerated its integration into the international economic system. Recognizing the importance of film to both cultural and economic lives, the Chinese government issued a series of new policies in 2001 that were specifically aimed at promoting the domestic film industry. The change in policy freed Chinese film from its previous function as a propaganda tool for the government and allowed filmmakers to focus on churning out entertaining and commercial products.

With the reorientation in official policy, the Chinese film industry's transformation began in earnest in 2002. The market-oriented economy stimulated film production with its consumer-driven demand and competitive mechanisms. At the same time, the introduction of global cinema, especially Hollywood films, also

Wong Kar-Wai

Hong Kong's "poet of time," film director Wong Kar-Wai (1958–), first worked in TV and then as a screenwriter. He regularly collaborates with cinematographer Christopher Doyle and designer William Chang and is known for his improvisatory approach. His films often display a highly stylized use of set design and color and a distinct elliptical approach to editing. They frequently explore themes of loneliness, loss, memory, and displacement; critics have repeatedly traced these concerns back to anxieties over Hong Kong's identity prior to the British colony's 1997 handover to China. The pop culture–infused *Chungking Express* (1994) and *Fallen Angels* (1995) were Wong's first cult-classic hits overseas, but (anti) love stories *Happy Together* (1997) and *In the Mood for Love* (2000) cemented his reputation on the global art-film circuit, winning accolades at Cannes. Most recently, he returned to the *wuxia* (martial arts) genre with *The Grandmaster* (2013).

Luke Robinson

helped facilitate the transformation of Chinese commercial films, which has also led to both diversification and sophistication in audiences' taste. Having benefited from the recent industrial restructuring, Chinese cinema has entered the era of the "megamovie."

One of the milestone films that ushered in the megamovie era was *Hero* (dir. Zhang Yimou, 2002). With a gross revenue of 25 million yuan (US$4 million), this film was a huge box-office success both domestically and internationally. As one of the earliest megamovies in China, *Hero* introduced several revolutionary elements in filmmaking that ranged from its refreshing genre to its big budget to its international cast. The film adopted a complex narrative structure reminiscent of Akira Kurosawa's masterpiece *Rashomon* (1951). By combining the traditional martial arts genre with modern cinematic language, *Hero* tells a love story by fully utilizing the audiovisual effects and by grounding its cinematic aesthetic in the indigenous cultural tradition. With a budget of over US$30 million and a cast that included stars such as Jet Li, Tony Leung, Ziyi Zhang, and Maggie Cheung, the film's production quality was very high. For the first time since the death of Bruce Lee, a Chinese martial arts film once again mesmerized moviegoers around the world with its exotic cultural trappings and spectacular audiovisual effects.

Hero was also a harbinger for another trend, in which filmmakers increasingly turned to making commercial, big-budget films, such as *House of Flying Daggers* (dir. Yimou Zhang, 2004), *The Promise* (dir. Kaige Chen, 2005), and *Assembly* (dir. Xiaogang Feng, 2008). Although production quality varied, these commercial films tended to be well funded. Even so, it was still hard to compete with Hollywood films, especially when the government increased the number of imported movies per year. Criticized by both audiences and critics, it was harder and harder for these commercial films to survive under the shadow of Hollywood. Therefore, this era of megamovies lasted for almost 10 years and then transformed again due to market pressures.

Lower-budget comedies thus came into being. In more recent years, a new generation of filmmakers has burst onto the scene. Helped by robust economic growth and the rise of cyber culture in China, members of this generation are responsible for a number of blockbusters that did not conform to the established pattern of success. In 2012 the comedy *Lost in Thailand* (dir. Zheng Xu) earned a box-office take of over 1 billion yuan (US$16 million), which was unprecedented in Chinese film history. The popularity of *Lost in Thailand* signaled the end of the era of megamovies and reflected the Chinese filmmakers' continuous search for diversity in genres, subject matter, and artistic styles in filmmaking. Also at this point, the Chinese film market was blooming into one of the most energetic and rich potential markets with huge opportunities and benefits.

Although the Chinese film industry has experienced rapid development in the last two decades, it faces many challenges in the 21st century. As some critics have noted, the official policy concerning film production and distribution is too restrictive, the business model is outdated, and the entire industry badly needs restructuring. How the Chinese film industry will address these issues remains to be seen.

Yiyi Yin

See also: Hollywood Films in China; Movie Stars, China

Further Reading

Yin, Hong尹鸿, and Feng Feixue冯飞雪. 2015. "2014年中国电影产业备忘 [Chinese Film Report in 2014]." 电影艺术 [Film Art]: 13–26.

Yin, Hong尹鸿, and Yin Yiyi尹一伊. 2014. 中国电影产业年度报告 [Annual Report on Chinese Film Industry]. In 世界电影发展报告 [World Film Development Report]. Ed. Yin Hong, 31–59. Beijing: Chinese Film Press中国电影出版社.

Zhu, Ying, and Stanley Rosen, eds. 2010. *Art, Politics, and Commerce in Chinese Cinema.* Hong Kong: Hong Kong University Press.

CINEMA, MAORI

Maori cinema refers to the body of films made by Maori, the indigenous population of New Zealand, located to the southeast of Australia. Over the past 30 years, they have produced a growing number of films set in Maori communities. Expressing themselves through the medium of film, they have used the silver screen to share their political struggles and cultural stories as secondary people in their own country. Over the years, Maori cinema has gradually gained both national and international recognition, to the point that it is nowadays celebrated as one of the, if not the, most thriving indigenous cinemas in the world. However, Maori filmmaking has come a long way, and its popularity brings not only exciting opportunities but also new constraints for its future development.

The islands that make up New Zealand were inhabited by the Maori people long before the British settlers arrived on their shores in the early 19th century. From this period onward, the Maori people have been alienated from their ancestral land—which they call Aotearoa, "Land of the Long White Cloud"—and otherwise marginalized in New Zealand's bicultural society. Ever since the Treaty of Waitangi, a peace treaty signed by representatives of the British Crown and various Maori

Peter Jackson's New Zealand as Middle Earth

Among the most popular films of recent years are the six productions inspired by J. R. R. Tolkien's fantasy masterpieces: The Hobbit series (*An Unexpected Journey, The Battle of the Five Armies,* and *The Desolation of Smaug*) and The Lord of the Rings series (*The Fellowship of the Ring, The Two Towers,* and *The Return of the King*), with release dates ranging from 2001 to 2013. New Zealand filmmaker Peter Jackson chose his island nation's breathtaking landscape as the setting for Tolkien's Middle Earth. With his blockbuster movies, Jackson not only brought to life the classic novels for a new audience in a visually spectacular way, he also introduced the diverse and dramatic natural splendor of New Zealand to the world. Today, the tourist board of New Zealand welcomes droves of visitors from around the world who wish to discover Middle Earth for themselves as they saw it on the big screen.

Aaron R. Murray

chiefs in 1840, the Maori have been struggling for self-determination (*tino ran-gatiratanga*), that is, the right to decide for their own people—a struggle that is shared by many indigenous people around the world. While this struggle has most often been played out in the political sphere, it also has significant relevance in the cultural sphere. Especially since the so-called "Maori Renaissance" from the late 1960s, the right to freely practice Maori language and culture has been increasingly identified and acknowledged as an important right of the Maori people.

Radio and television initially offered the best opportunities for Maori people to have their voices heard and be seen in New Zealand's mainstream media. Although the tradition of Maori broadcasting stems from the early 1920s, when radio was introduced in New Zealand, it was in the 1970s that it became a key demand in the Maori struggle for cultural survival. During this period, initial strides toward Maori filmmaking were largely made in the field of television. The most important antecedent of Maori cinema was *Tangata whenua* (1974), a documentary series about the Maori people that aired on national television. The groundbreaking series was directed by Maori filmmaker Barry Barclay (1944–2008) and, for the first time on mainstream New Zealand TV, captured the language and culture of the Maori people on their own terms. Some years later, Merata Mita (1942–2010), another pioneering Maori filmmaker, came to represent the rise of Maori cinema outside—and against—the mainstream. She made a range of activist documentaries, including *Bastion Point: Day 507* (1980) and *Patu!* (1983), with which she began a rich tradition of independent documentaries representing Maori perspectives.

Barclay and Mita were among the first within the international indigenous movement to start exploring the field of narrative cinema, that is, the production of feature-length fiction films. In fact, the two Maori filmmakers were instrumental to the origins of indigenous narrative cinema worldwide. In the late 1980s, after a long and persistent lobby at the New Zealand Film Commission (NZFC), the government agency that was established in 1987 to support New Zealand film production, Barclay and Mita were successful in securing funding for their first feature film. Upon release, Barclay's *Ngati* (1987) received widespread recognition as the first indigenous feature-length fiction film ever made, while Mita's *Mauri* (1988) became known as the world's first narrative film by a female indigenous filmmaker.

Both Barclay and Mita took on an alternative mode of filmmaking, one that was founded on a commitment to community participation and empowerment. The Maori communities to be filmed were recognized as equal partners in the decision-making process of the production. When the films were completed, they were the first to appreciate them for their teaching potential, as there is always, to use Barclay's words, "a point of instruction" in indigenous films. By conveying stories that stressed the need to protect Maori rural lifestyles and cultural traditions, *Ngati* and *Mauri* broke away from the exotic "Maoriland" presented in most of the films made by non-Maori. Instead of a fast-paced and linear story line, a characteristic of mainstream cinema, both Maori films offered a slow-paced and multilayered narrative inspired by the oral storytelling traditions of the Maori people. They were not so much action driven and individual focused, another characteristic of mainstream cinema, but merely flow driven and community focused. Both films immediately received critical acclaim throughout the Maori and wider indigenous community for their portrayal of rural Maori life in post-war New Zealand society. However, operating outside the mainstream, they did not really participate in the wider world of film distribution and hence remained largely confined to select audiences.

In the early 1990s, *Once Were Warriors* (1994), the first Maori feature film to be set in the city, experienced a different fate. This Maori production marked the new direction of the NZFC to commit funding to Maori films with more commercial appeal. To engage wider audiences, Lee Tamahori, the film's director, largely returned to the characteristics of mainstream cinema—and with success. *Once Were Warriors* became New Zealand's highest-grossing movie of all time, breaking records at the domestic box office and reaching a large international audience. The film revolved around a Maori family trapped in a cycle of domestic violence and other social problems. Exploring the alienating experience of contemporary Maori in Auckland, the New Zealand city where nowadays the great majority of the Maori people dwell, *Once Were Warriors* painted a grim picture of urban Maori life. When the film came out, it came to occupy an ambivalent position in the annals of Maori cinema. On the one hand, *Once Were Warriors* received severe criticism for its mainstream characteristics, particularly its portrayal of Maori as failures isolated from the context of British colonization. On the other hand, the film received much praise for representing urban Maori identities, bringing the issue of domestic violence to the fore, and raising the profile of Maori culture in New Zealand and abroad.

Following the commercial success of *Once Were Warriors*, the expectation was raised that more Maori feature films would come out. However, it was another eight years before another feature film directed by a Maori made it to the theaters. This was not the internationally acclaimed *Whale Rider* (2002), which was directed by Niki Caro, a non-Maori New Zealand filmmaker, but Don Selwyn's little-known *The Maori Merchant of Venice* (2002), the first Maori feature film entirely spoken in the Maori language. However, from the 2000s, the NZFC increasingly sought to enhance Maori participation in New Zealand feature filmmaking. The NZFC provided funding to various projects with a Maori director, writer, and/or producer. To ensure their cultural integrity, all these projects were assessed and mentored by experienced Maori practitioners, while production teams wanting to make a film with Maori content were advised to seek support from the Maori community. These initiatives have resulted in the development of an indigenous cinema that is unique throughout the world. After decades of struggle, the new generation of Maori filmmakers now encounters a supportive institutional environment that facilitates the expression of their voices.

However, while Maori cinema continues to grow in popularity, its current course also poses several challenges. Most importantly is the question of to what extent integration into the mainstream enables Maori filmmaking to achieve its original ambitions. Inclusion in a state system that is still largely dominated by non-Maori practices and perspectives almost inevitably diminishes the political and cultural concerns of Maori filmmaking—concerns that remain highly relevant today despite the advances made in indigenous rights. The initial vision of Maori cinema also seems to be tempered by the commercial focus of the NZFC, as their business remains first and foremost to achieve successful New Zealand feature films in the global marketplace. Within this marketplace, Maori stories are increasingly being turned into easily consumable entertainment films to satisfy the desires of mainstream audiences who are looking for delightful and comfortable images of cultural difference. At the beginning of the 21st century, Maori cinema has become an established presence in the world of international filmmaking, with both pros and cons. Undoubtedly, its development will remain a key site in the indigenous struggle for self-determination and survival in the decades to come.

Emiel Martens

See also: Popular Movies, Australia

Further Reading

Blythe, Martin. 1994. *Naming the Other: Images of the Maori in New Zealand Film and Television*. Metuchen, NZ: The Scarecrow Press.

Martens, Emiel. 2012. "Maori on the Silver Screen: The Evolution of Indigenous Feature Filmmaking in Aotearoa/New Zealand." *International Journal of Critical Indigenous Studies* 5, no. 1 (October): 1–30.

Mita, Merata. 1996. "The Soul and the Image." In *Film in Aotearoa New Zealand*. Ed. Jonathan Dennis and Jan Bieringa, 36–56. Wellington, NZ: Victoria University Press.

Murray, Stuart. 2008. *Images of Dignity: Barry Barclay and Fourth Cinema*. Wellington, NZ: Huia Publishers.

CINEMA, TAIWAN

Taiwan cinema boasted one of the most vibrant industries in Southeast Asia during the 1960s; in fact, in 1968 Taiwan was the second-largest film-producing nation in the world. And Taiwan's premier director today, Hou Hsiao-Hsien (1947–), won the Best Director Award at the Cannes Film Festival in 2015, solidifying the prestige of a circle of elite directors from Taiwan that includes Ang Lee (1954–) and Tsai Mingliang (1957–). How is it that a small island off the coast of China possesses one of the most storied film traditions and such an impressive array of talent? The answer to this question reveals a vibrant Taiwanese film industry that has been shaped by history and has in turn reflected history for its audience, an industry that has envisioned the possibility of a brighter tomorrow.

Although the date of the first screening of a film in Taiwan is subject to debate, Taiwan cinema emerged during the Japanese colonial era, from 1895 to 1945. Films in Taiwan were primarily imported from Japan, China, and Hollywood. In addition to the filmic image, film exhibition in Taiwan included a *benshi*, a person who stood in front of the audience next to the screen and both narrated the silent films and provided a live commentary of the on-screen action.

When the Nationalists arrived in 1945 to govern the island at the end of the Second Sino-Japanese War, Japanese film centers in Taipei and around the island, including studios and distribution networks, were taken over by the KMT (Kuomintang, Guomindang, Nationalist Party). First, the KMT set up a Taiwan Film Studio in Taipei. Then, when the Nationalists' entire government fled to Taiwan after falling to the Communists in 1949, the government apparatus brought with it China Film Studio and Agricultural Education Film Studio. Following the KMT's assumption of control of the island after losing the civil war to the Communists on the mainland, the first film "made in Taiwan" was released in 1950: *Wind and Cloud on Ali Mountain* (dir. Zhang Ying [1919–1984] and Zhang Che [1923–2002]).

While early Mandarin films (*guoyu pian*) that were created by the state propagated political messages, local Taiwanese-dialect films (*taiyu pian*) of the late 1950s and early 1960s were both more diverse and produced at a higher volume. *Taiyu* films included hybrids of numerous genres: opera adaptations, action films, martial arts films, musicals, comedies, and romances. By the late 1960s the *taiyu* film industry was bankrupt, and by the early 1970s remaining *taiyu* film companies still in production made the full transition to creating *guoyu* films. A number of directors, actors, and actresses followed suit, continuing their careers in both *guoyu* film production and television. Overall, the influence of *taiyu pian* cannot be underestimated in the history of Taiwan cinema.

Taiwan's state filmmaking industry experienced a turning point in 1963. To take a look at that year's film production and importation for a moment: 70 Mandarin films were produced (including films from Hong Kong), and an impressive 96 Taiwanese films were made on the island; imported films included 9 Japanese films, 63 films from Europe, and a whopping 169 from the United States. Three factors that contributed to the paradigm shift in 1963 include, first, the widely popular exhibition of Hong Kong director Li Hanxiang's (1953–1996) film *The Love Eterne* on the island; second, the realization that homegrown talent, including Li Xing (1930–) and his film *Our Neighbor*, could be harnessed by the state film studios; and third, the emergence of Gong Hong's (1915–2004) managerial prowess at Zhongying Studio (Central Motion Picture Corporation, CMPC). The confluence of these three events arguably kick-started Taiwan's so-called "Golden Age," which extended from 1964 to 1969.

Gong Hong, a prolific and resourceful manager, produced films for the open domestic market alongside popular films from Hollywood and Hong Kong while also extending the international market of Taiwan films to Hong Kong, Singapore, and Malaysia by implementing a film movement known as "healthy realism," which represented positive aspects of KMT governance on the silver screen. Thanks to the growing influence of five key directors—Li Xing, Bai Jingrui (1931–1997), Song Cunshou (1930–2008), as well as Hong Kong transplants Li Hanxiang and King Hu (1932–1997)—Taiwan cinema was prominent throughout Southeast Asia and screened in more than 50 nations. In film circles, the healthy realist films evolved during the mid- to late 1960s into a mode of *wenyi*, or "literary art," films in the 1970s that often focused on romantic relationships and domestic affairs. Then, along with the decrease in Taiwan's international diplomatic prestige as the decade wore on, the *wenyi* film tradition transitioned to a new era of *kangri* (resist-Japanese) war films, which represented regional and global conflicts. Taiwan's film exhibition waned overseas during the 1970s and was unable to compete with Hong Kong cinema's regional appeal.

The famous Taiwan New Cinema Movement from approximately 1982 to 1988 was an aesthetic response to the filmmaking tradition that preceded it but also a political response to decades of governmental repression. Taiwan New Cinema, which made a splash on the international art-house circuit, might be characterized as "a step away from pedagogical orientation of Healthy Realism, the commercialism of studio genres, and the eclectic provincialism of *taiyu pian* (Taiwanese-language films)" (Yeh and Davis 2005, 56). Key figures in this movement included Hou Hsiao-Hsien, Edward Yang (1947–2007), Wu Nianzhen (1952–), Wang Tong (1942–), and Wan Ren (1950–).

Taiwan New Cinema films comprised only 14 percent of the total cinema production from 1982 to 1988, yet films such as *In Our Time* (dir. Tao, Yang, Ko, Chang, 1982) and *The Sandwich Man* (dir. Hou, Wan, Tseng, 1983) left an indelible impact on the film industry in Taiwan that in some ways is still felt to this day. In the 1990s, a second wave of directors came onto the scene, including Ang Lee, who made *Wedding Banquet* in 1993; and Tsai Ming-liang, who directed *Vive l'Amour* (1994); and works by Sylvia Chang (1953–). But categorizing this as a "second wave," just as citing "generations" when considering film on the mainland, is not absolute. For example, Hou Hsiao-Hsien and Edward Yang, who directed *The Terrorizers* in 1986 and *Yi yi* in 2000, made films spanning multiple decades.

While films from the Taiwan New Cinema and the Second Wave won film awards abroad, domestic feature production declined and audience interest in domestic productions decreased. For this reason, Taiwan New Cinema has also been blamed for the eventual decline of commercial cinema in Taiwan. Additional local factors, including the rise of cable television and unregulated video rental practices, also led to the general demise of film production on the island. By the year 2000, Hollywood controlled 93 percent of the Taiwan film market.

The re-emergence of Taiwan cinema may, however, be in the making today. Key indicators include the Wei Te-sheng's (1969–) box-office hit *Cape No. 7* (2008), which includes a catchy soundtrack and depicts the lives of young people in Taiwan today, and *Warriors of the Rainbow: Seediq Bale* (2011), which represents Taiwan's experience during Japanese colonialism. In addition, the success of films by women directors like Chen Ying Jung's (1980–) *Formula 17* (2004) and Zero Chou's (1969–) *Spider Lilies* (2007), and a future of cross-strait coproductions with Hong Kong and mainland China, indicates the potential for a bright new chapter for Taiwan's up-and-coming filmmakers.

James Wicks

See also: Cinema, China; Cinema, Tibet; Literature, Taiwan (Chapter 2: Books and Contemporary Literature)

Further Reading

Hong, Guo Juin. 2011. *Taiwan Cinema: A Contested Nation on Screen*. New York: Palgrave Macmillan.

Lee, Daw-ming. 2012. *Historical Dictionary of Taiwan Cinema*. Lanham, MD: Scarecrow Press.

Wicks, James. 2014. *Transnational Representations: The State of Taiwan Film in the 1960s and 1970s*. Hong Kong: Hong Kong University Press.

Yeh, Emilie Y, and Darrell W. Davis. 2005. *Taiwan Film Directors: A Treasure Island*. New York: Columbia University Press.

Zhang, Yingjin. 2004. *Chinese National Cinema*. New York: Routledge.

CINEMA, TIBET

Film, defined here by the nationality of its director, is a recent cultural development in Tibet. It can be divided into entertainment video films aimed at a local audience and art movies targeting international festivals, with little in between. In Tibet proper, the first feature film, *The Silent Holy Stones* (Lhing 'jags kyi ma ṇi rdo 'bum) by Pema Tseden (aka Wanma Caidan, 1969–), was released as late as 2005. In exile, Tenzing Sonam and his wife, Ritu Sarin, have dominated the documentary movie scene since the 1990s. On either side of the Himalayas, this late engaging with cinema can be explained by Tibet's relative remoteness from the Western world, low population density, relative poverty, and belated encounter with technology (wide TV coverage was only achieved in the early 2000s in Tibet). However, with the advent of new, cheap audiovisual technology, small-scale, locally distributed, low-budget videos are rapidly blooming both in Tibet and in exile.

Movies were not totally unheard of in Lhasa, the capital city of Tibet, before the Chinese takeover in the 1950s: Ladakhi Muslim merchants from northwest India would bring films and projectors along with their trade caravans in the 1930s. Also, British emissaries would entertain selected guests at the British Mission. Films like those of Charlie Chaplin and Rintintin were greatly appreciated—the 13th Dalai Lama (1875–1933) is said to have highly enjoyed the former. A few Tibetan aristocrats even bought small handheld cameras at that time and undertook filming everyday scenes for their own consumption. With the Chinese occupation, entertainment gave way to Marxist ideology: films from the People's Republic of China (PRC), Albania, or North Korea were shown in the remotest areas on makeshift screens, massively exposing Tibetans to radically new topics, like class struggle and the Sino-Japanese war in the 1930s. Moreover, films began being shot in Tibetan areas under the Chinese state's auspices, enriching the emerging "minority films" ("*shaoshu minzu dianying*") genre. They invariably celebrated the "peaceful liberation" of Tibet from "imperialists" and its "feudal" leaders (i.e., aristocrats and monasteries). The most famous such film, *Serfs* (*Nongnu*, 1963, by Li Jun), contributed greatly to the still widespread view among Han Chinese of Tibet as hell on earth, as it was repeatedly shown in the PRC—and still is today. After a 10-year interruption during the Cultural Revolution (1966–1976), minority films resumed, renewed in the 1990s, thanks to "main melody" films, in other words, state-funded, nationalist blockbusters such as *Red River Valley* (Feng Xiaoning, 1997) and *Songs of Tibet*

(Xie Fei, 2000), where the political content is made palatable by the inclusion of romance and rapturous backdrops. Those were and are still meant to support the official PRC narrative about Tibet and to counterbalance the Western cinemato- graphic and sympathetic representations of Tibet like *Seven Years in Tibet* (Jean- Jacques Annaud, 1997) or *Kundun* (Martin Scorsese, 1997) that were popular in the West at that time. In parallel, a few isolated independent Chinese filmmakers undertook to represent a Tibet different from that of the officially approved state discourse, but their films were equally estranged from a Tibetan vision of Tibet (i.e., Tian Zhuangzhuang's *Horse Thief*, 1985; Duan Jinchuan's *No. 16 Barkhor South Street*, 1996).

It was not until the mid-2000s that Tibetans in Tibet proper finally reappropri- ated their cinematographic narration. Between 2005 and 2015, seven independent feature films were made: Pema Tseden has so far directed *The Silent Holy Stones* (2005), *The Search* (2008), *Old Dog* (2010), *Sacred Arrow* (2014), and *Tharlo* (2015). He is supported by Tian Zhuangzhuang, turned producer and film mentor in the 1990s. Sonthar Gyal (1974–) has directed *The Sunbeaten Path* (2011) and *The River* (2015). Both are graduates from the prestigious Beijing Film Academy and mention Abbas Kiarostami, Ingmar Bergman, and Nuri Bilge Ceylan as sources of inspiration. Their films, belonging to global art cinema, have been selected in international fes- tivals (Pusan, Shanghai, Vancouver, Berlin, Deauville, Venice), occasionally reaping prizes. Among them, only *Sacred Arrow* (*G.yang mda'*) can be classified as "popular cinema." Contrary to Pema Tseden's first films, it was not financed by a cinema pro- ducer but commissioned by a local Tibetan tourism bureau to promote traditional local archery; its deliberately simple plot (a local archery competition doubled with love rivalry on a backdrop of tradition and modernity) and first-time hiring of pro- fessional Tibetan actors may indicate a shift toward a more mainstream cinema.

For popular cinema proper, one has to turn to films in DVD format, which never reach the cinema halls, and even less so an international arena, but are locally distributed: comedies, love and moral dramas, retellings of the Tibetan *Gesar* epic, now number in the tens. Often set in a nomadic environment, with a minimal scenario, they function on a low budget and with amateur actors, directed by aspiring filmmakers with no formal or professional training. Also, from 2012 onward, Tibetan students schooled in Chinese universities have presented their own films at student film festivals, where they have secured prizes. Buddhism, a strong iconic identity marker, often plays a role in these films. Another innovation to be noted is the inception of cartoons, led by Gentsu Gyatso (1978–), whose striking graphic style is inspired by Tibetan traditional religious art. *The Hunter and the Skeleton* (2011) is based on a Tibetan folktale, and *The Apple Tree* (2014) is an ecological variation on the classical Buddhist theme of benevolence and self- lessness incarnated by a tree destroyed by humans' unquenchable thirst for riches and power.

Due to the severely restricted political environment for Tibetans in China— an aspiring documentarian, Dhondup Wangchen, was jailed for six years in 2008 for interviewing Tibetans about the then-forthcoming 2008 Beijing

Olympics—documentary films all belong to the ethnographic and eschew political concerns, with the exception of *Kokonor* (2008) by the poet and filmmaker Chenaktsang Dorje Tsering (1963–), which portrays a local community of herders deprived of their ancestral grazing land by corrupt authorities.

In India and Nepal, where a small but visible Tibetan diaspora settled in the late 1950s, films started a little earlier. Documentarians Tenzing Sonam and Ritu Sarin began their international careers in the 1990s in India, treating topics beyond sole Tibetan concerns. Tsering Rithar Sherpa and Kalsang Tseten, both based in Nepal, make, respectively, fiction and documentary films set mainly in Nepalese society. Moreover, aspiring filmmakers have emerged since the mid-2000s in the Tibetan diaspora, directing mainly comedies (*New York ma-ray, mi york ray* by Namgyal Dorjee, 2004; *From Tsampa to Pizza* by Sonam Tsetan, 2007) or political works (*We Are No Monks* by Sonam Dondrup, 2004), which cater to a local exile audience. Aware of the limitations imposed by a sole exposition to Bollywood among exile Tibetans, Tenzing Sonam and Ritu Sarin have initiated an independent film festival in Dharamsala, where they live, bringing international art movies to a Tibetan audience with the aim of nurturing a film culture as well as grooming aspiring filmmakers in the Tibetan diaspora.

Françoise Robin

See also: TV and Radio, Tibet (Chapter 4: Television and Radio)

Further Reading

Chenaktsang, Dorje Tsering. T. 2008. "Reflections on Tibetan Film." In *Tibetan Modernities: Notes from the Field on Social and Cultural Change*. Ed. Ronald Schwartz and Robert Barnett, 267–281. Leiden, NL: Brill.

Dhondup, Yangdon. 2014. "Independent Tibetan Documentary Films: A Review of Dorje Tsering's Works." *High Peaks Pure Earth*. October 16. http://highpeakspureearth.com/2014/guest-post-by-yangdon-dhondup-independent-tibetan-documentary-films-a-review-of-dorje-tserings-works. Accessed November 1, 2014.

Donatti, Valeria, and Mara Matta, eds. 2009. *Tibetan Arts in Transition. Journey through Theatre, Cinema and Painting*. Rome: ASIA.

Frangville, Vanessa. 2013. "'Minority Film' and Tibet in the PRC: From 'Hell on Earth' to the 'Garden of Eden.'" *Latse Journal* 7: 8–27.

Norbu, Jamyang. 2010. "The Happy Light Bioscope Theatre & Other Stories." *Shadow Tibet*. February 10. www.jamyangnorbu.com/blog/2010/02/10/the-happy-light-bioscope-theatre-other-stories-part-i. Accessed May 30, 2015.

CINEMA, UYGHUR

The recent history of Uyghur popular film production in China's Xinjiang Uyghur Autonomous Region is divided into two periods. The early period began in the early 1980s with the arrival of for-profit film production and the circulation of VCR cassettes and ended around 2004 when VCD and DVD film sharing began to transform the economy of Xinjiang cinema and video. The earlier period was characterized by an influx of Indian, Western, and Islamic films, which were tightly controlled by government-funded Uyghur-language dubbing agencies. The second period, from 2005 to the present, has become an era of new forms of low-budget Uyghur cinema that are produced and circulated via new forms of digital film production as well as the establishment of numerous private dubbing companies.

In the early 1980s, the leading figure among Xinjiang-based filmmakers was a woman named Guang Chunlan—a member of the Shibe (*Xibo* 锡伯) ethnic group, which came to Xinjiang as part of the Manchu armies in the 18th century. For over a decade, she made a new film nearly every year. Made in close collaboration with Uyghur, Kazkah, and Han assistants, they focused on Uyghur-, Kazakh-, and Xinjiang-style humor and relationships. In these early films, there was little attention paid to political history and ethnic solidarity, instead they drew on the dramas that emerged from the new freedoms of city life and how political changes in the countryside were reflected in domestic life. Unlike later Xinjiang films, they did not place regional politics at the center of the film narratives but rather featured it as a comedic background.

By the late 1980s, when Guang Chunlan and other leading filmmakers attempted to introduce their work to a national audience, Xinjiang filmmaking began to change. Increasingly those attempting to reach a nationwide audience felt pressure to reduce the idiosyncratic regional characteristics that had been featured in the earlier films. As this happened, film distribution began to skew away from locally produced films. Instead, American action movies and Bollywood musical comedies overdubbed in Uyghur or Mandarin became increasingly influential among Xinjiang film watchers and circulated by both VCR cassette tapes and regional television broadcasts. By the end of the 1990s, movie stars such as Arnold Schwarzenegger and Bruce Lee had become cult figures among Uyghur audiences.

Although a dozen or so Uyghur-language films by Uyghur filmmakers such as Tahir Hamut and Shirzat Yaqüp were widely watched and praised by Uyghur viewers in the 1990s, by the early 2000s, when VCD and DVD technology reached the Xinjiang countryside, it had become increasingly less financially viable for local filmmakers to produce films. At the same time, following the protests in 1997 in Ghulja (Yinning 尹宁), locally produced film content became more and more closely controlled by official cultural agencies. By 2004 for-profit filmmaking by Xinjiang filmmakers was increasingly rare.

Over the following years, Uyghur filmmakers began to focus their attention on music videos for the rapidly expanding Uyghur-language popular-music market. As locally owned Xinjiang companies began to grow and expand, they also found new work creating highly lucrative television commercials and reality shows. The filmmakers who had found some success in the earlier era of for-profit filmmaking were also able to get some funding from government agencies. Tahir Hamut created a series of documentary films that follow the social production of Uyghur traditional arts such as carpet weaving, silk dyeing, and winemaking, and festivals such as the Islamic spring holiday Nawruz. Shirzat Yaqüp received funding to make several big-budget feature films, such as *The Turpan Love Song* (*Turpandiki muhebbet naxshisi*, 2011) and *Muhammad's 2008* (*Muhemmetning 2008—yili*, 2008), which highlighted official goals of national development and ethnic solidarity. Although the production of these films was quite professional, many Uyghur viewers saw these fiction films as state propaganda with little artistic value.

Beginning around 2013, the Uyghur stand-up comedian Abdukerim Abliz, who was often a featured actor in Yaqüp's films, began to act in and direct his own films and eventually his own situational comedy television show. Although state-mandated themes such as ethnic solidarity are often inserted into the narratives of his films, his 2014 blockbuster *Money on the Road* (*Pul digen shundak nerse*) was widely praised by Uyghur audiences (Byler 2014). Many viewers found Abliz's slapstick-style comportment and his quick-witted turns of phrase highly entertaining. Although film critics found a lack of character development in the film narrative, his ability to take stock figures from the Uyghur comic lexicon and turn them into a contemporary film about Uyghur rural-urban life marked what many people see as a new era in Uyghur cinema. More recently his episodic television show *Look at This Family* (*Bu a'ilige qarang*, 2014–2015) has also been widely praised for its comedic treatment of family relationships, Uyghur cultural mores, and urban living.

In many ways the filmmakers from the two early periods of Uyghur cinema are part of an older system of theatrical performance that emerged in the Maoist era (1949–1976). Emerging Uyghur filmmakers today are being educated in radically different ways (Byler 2015a). The emergence of affordable high-definition digital video and sound production has made the cost of professional-quality films much more affordable. Linkages between social media networks such as WeChat and video-hosting sites such as Youku has made video circulation wider and faster. Today it is not unusual for a short film by young filmmakers such as Memetjan Semet to be published on social media sites and receive more than 100,000 views within a few days (Byler 2015b).

Young Uyghur film students also use the same networks to view international films and communicate with filmmakers around the nation and the world. Unlike earlier filmmakers, who were trained using analogue film and sound production in the Chinese theater system, young filmmakers are learning from the national cinemas of Iran, Turkey, India, France, and the United States. They are watching foreign films with Chinese or Uyghur subtitles, or, increasingly, they are learning English by watching films. This new awareness of international cinema has produced shifts in the desires of Uyghur film watchers and, in turn, the content of new Uyghur films. Uyghur filmmakers are beginning to produce short films that focus on the voices of Uyghur women and on the dramas of everyday life in the city.

Of course, many young moviegoers like international movies because they are seen as happy and life affirming. Many of them primarily watch blockbuster action movies and romantic comedies in which true love prevails and good guys win—scenarios that many Uyghurs may see as a break from the bleakness they experience in their own lives. But when American films portray Muslims as malevolent protagonists, many young Uyghurs see themselves as being misrepresented. This, along with the rise of independent dubbing studios who focus on Arabic, Farsi, and Turkish translation into Uyghur, is perhaps a factor in the growing popularity of Palestinian, Iranian, and Turkish films.

Because of these changes in education and awareness, young filmmakers are seeing new value in translating the dialogues of their films and distributing them with Chinese and English subtitles. Many young filmmakers dream of a Uyghur cinema that may someday rival Iran's. They often believe that viewers from the Chinese-language market will not be interested in Uyghur films, but after watching the success of Iranian films in Western film festivals, they feel as though their work might someday receive recognition internationally.

Darren Byler

See also: Popular Music, Uyghur (Chapter 1: Popular Music)

Further Reading

Byler, Darren. 2014. "Review of the Uyghur Blockbuster 'Money on the Road.'" *Beijing Cream*. October 29. https://beigewind.wordpress.com/2014/10/29/review-of-the-uyghur-blockbuster-money-on-the-road. Accessed May 6, 2015.

Byler, Darren. 2015a. "'Lift' and the Future of Uyghur Film." *Beijing Cream*. February 15. https://beigewind.wordpress.com/2015/02/15/lift-and-the-future-of-uyghur-film. Accessed May 6, 2015.

Byler, Darren. 2015b. "Uyghur Women and Memetjan Semet's film 'Dad, I Love You.'" *Beijing Cream*. April 25. https://beigewind.wordpress.com/2015/04/25/uyghur-women-memetjan-semets-film-dad-i-love-you. Accessed May 6, 2015.

CINEMA, VIETNAM

The formations of a resilient Vietnamese film history, one that has survived times of war and extreme deprivation, can be mapped along the coordinates of the political and the popular. Since the founding of the Democratic Republic of Việt Nam in 1945, an independent Vietnamese cinema has been articulated by the state as a political endeavor, one expressed through a popular medium. The country's state-operated cinema began momentously with the establishment of sovereignty in the North. One of the first film clips produced was of Hồ Chí Minh's declaration at Ba Đình Square of the independence of the nation. After 1945 the Democratic Republic of Việt Nam began to pave the way for the making of state-sponsored films, ones premised on populist notions of the masses. In 1953 Hồ founded the Vietnamese State Enterprise for Photography and Motion Pictures and declared that Vietnamese cinema had two tasks: (1) to build socialism, and (2) to struggle for the liberation of the South for the reunification of the country.

Solidified by North Việt Nam's victory over the French one year later, the postcolonial state ensured through legislation that film would be an important industry in the years that followed. The year 1957 saw the opening of the first Vietnamese film journal, *Điện ảnh* (*Cinema*), and two years after, Việt Nam constructed its first film school, the Hà Nội Cinema School, and movie engineering plant. Soon after, the country's first independently produced feature film was released, in 1958. *Along the Same River* is widely considered to be a canonical film, the story of which features two lovers who are separated by a river at the 17th parallel. Known as the Demilitarized Zone (DMZ), this division of the country was enacted after the Geneva Conference in 1954 and enforced by the U.S. military thereafter. The DMZ also dictated the contrasting ways in which South Việt Nam would make films in the latter half of the century.

The South was marked more by its history of foreign occupation, and films made there were different in terms of ideology, means of production, and funding. During French colonialism and the American War, South Việt Nam was territorialized and controlled both by the French (who ruled Indochina mainly from Cochin China, or what is today southern Việt Nam) and Americans (who based their occupation in the southern regions), respectively. Under French supervision, filmmaking in Cochin China was rigorously monitored at the level of importation, distribution, and exhibition. During the American War, the main financers of southern Vietnamese films were U.S. government and private donors. The Republic of Việt Nam's production companies included the Republic's Army Film Service, the USIS, the National Motion Picture Center, and Freedom Films. For these studios, the chief output was documentaries and newsreels, with feature films rarely being made because of high production costs. Some independent films did not, however, highlight the war but were instead imbued with the intent to entertain and even titillate. *Four Misfits in Sai Gon* (1965) was shot on location in Sài Gòn and became a star vehicle for actress Thẩm Thúy Hằng, who at the time was known for both her beauty and buxom figure.

As *Four Misfits* and others like it show, Vietnamese films did not always hew to a propagandistic impulse, but rather, they referenced a redolent commercial film culture and a star system that has transnational connections with the diaspora today. For example, Vietnamese (American) actor Kiều Chinh, who starred in melodramatic films like *Stormy Love* (1972), remains a popular screen actor in the United States. She has been in a number of Vietnamese American and Asian American films since she immigrated to the United States in 1975. In the past 10 years, DVDs featuring actresses of yesteryear, such as Thẩm Thúy Hằng and Kiều Chinh, have been repackaged for the Vietnamese diaspora and distributed through production companies like Thúy Nga and Asia. Such films are marketed very pointedly in declaring on their covers that the movies are "pre-1975" and "made in color," selling for $4.99 in Vietnamese American enclaves or streamed online for a small fee. These films were often screened in movie theaters in prewar Sài Gòn, and their recirculation attests to a certain diasporic longing for experiencing the past through film in the present tense.

Following the country's reunification, the period after the war (1975–1987) began a new era in Vietnamese national cinema. Although a small number of feature films were made annually, because of a sparsely funded industry, Vietnamese-owned studios, such as Giải Phóng Studios (in the South) and Việt Nam Film Studios (in the North), were able to finance only a handful of well-received films. Patriotic films about Hồ Chí Minh, as in *Ho Chi Minh: Portrait of a Man* (1976), were produced alongside films that portrayed the everyday struggles of peasants during the American war, such as in Hoàng Sến's important movie *Abandoned Fields* (1979). After having studied in Russia, director Đặng Nhật Minh began making his mark during this time, particularly with his critically acclaimed film *When the Tenth Month Comes* (1984).

With the introduction of economic reforms called Đổi Mới (or Renovation) in 1987, state officials promoted a revival of arts and culture, and there was a certain laxity about themes and aesthetics, if only for a short time. Notable films like Đặng Nhật Minh's *Woman on the Perfume River* (1987) and Nguyễn Khắc Lợi's *The General Retires* (1991) were distinguished because of their critical take on social problems, their high aesthetic values, and the cultural heritage upon which the latter film was based—Nguyễn Huy Thiệp's acclaimed short story "The General Retires." In 1993, recognizing the cultural significance of film as a seventh art, the government began to allocate more funding for film production and stressed the importance of aesthetic value in filmmaking. Consequently, state-owned studios made more films per year in comparison to earlier years. Furthermore, as an increasing number of Vietnamese films began participating in international film festival circuits each year, more recognition from an international audience was being accorded to Vietnamese films. Some of these films include the documentary *How to Behave* (1987), made by the country's leading documentary filmmaker, Trần Văn Thủy, and female director Việt Linh's *Traveling Circus* (1988), especially notable because Linh remains one of a handful of women directors working in a male-dominated industry.

At the start of the new century, however, films like *Bar Girls* (2003), its sequel, *Street Cinderella* (2004), and *Long-Legged Girls* (2004), began to dramatically change the landscape of the Vietnamese film industry. Because of this shift toward more commercial filmmaking, the state was forced to cancel some of its major film projects, which authorities deemed unappealing. As part of its reconstituted policies, the Ministry of Culture and Information (now merged with the Ministry of Culture, Sports, and Tourism) considers box-office appeal in the making of films as a result of blockbuster films like *Bar Girls*. Starting in 2002, the state authorized the establishment of private film companies within the country, thus bringing about two important developments. Funding for films is currently privatized and thus very often transnational. Authorities have also abolished prefilm script censorship; only the final cut of the film is now reviewed. Such developments have led the way for many coproductions between countries like Korea and Việt Nam to take place.

Most crucially, since the country's era of marketization, the state has allowed for more collaborations between Việt Nam and its diasporic community, a community the state once denounced as traitors to the nation in the aftermath of what is called the American War in Việt Nam. Many of these creative and filmic collaborations now take place in South Việt Nam, specifically Hồ Chí Minh City, which represents the film industry's center for investment possibilities with respect to production and exhibition. Recent laws have further facilitated these developments. In 2007 the state set a quota for how many Vietnamese films (20 percent of the total) would screen in theaters nationwide. Other laws pertaining to citizenship and visas affect the ways in which the film industry has been infused with transnational capital and talent. Overseas Vietnamese can now stay in the country for up to five years, provided they obtain a visa in order to live and work in the country. In 2007 Việt Nam joined the WTO. A year later, Việt Nam amended its citizenship laws to allow diasporans to hold dual citizenship.

As part of the influx of capital and talent pouring into the country today, many diasporic directors are making films in the country. Some of the most important overseas films shot on location are Trần Anh Hùng's film *Cyclo* (1995) and *Vertical Ray of the Sun* (2000) as well as Tony Bùi's *Three Seasons* (1999). Even more recently, Vietnamese American Charlie Nguyễn's *The Rebel* (2007) was a landmark film for being a hybrid of both diasporic and local talent and money. The film also demonstrated that diasporic filmmaking can be popular both at home and abroad. As a result of *The Rebel*'s success, Vietnamese American–made films are regarded as being highly commercial (*phim thị trường*) but often eclipse the country's own artistic films (*phim nghệ thuật*), particularly those films that deal mostly with war and history. Box-office receipts for commercial films by Vietnamese American directors show the extraordinary rise of what Vietnamese cinema scholars label as the work of "Viet Kiều" (literally "Vietnamese sojourner" but generally meaning "overseas Vietnamese") directors. Integral to the development of an emergent film industry, Vietnamese American filmmakers, some of whom have grown up in Los Angeles and Orange County, now travel back and forth to Saigon to make movies in and about Việt Nam.

While finding success in Việt Nam, however, Vietnamese American directors are also confronted with the state's censoring of their films. Charlie Nguyễn's *Chinatown* (2013), for instance, a film about gangsters who live in a historically predominantly ethnic Chinese neighborhood, was censored for its graphic violence and then banned from being screened or distributed in the country. Eventually the film was leaked online, and the director has since decided to make lighthearted comedies instead. Nonetheless, the controversies surrounding *Chinatown*, involving a Vietnamese American director and his battles with the censorship board, exemplify the tensions inherent in making films that straddle the line between the political and the popular.

Nonetheless, as Vietnamese American director Nguyễn-Võ Minh-Nghiêm shows, artistic films like *Buffalo Boy* (2004) and *2030* (*Nuoc*, 2014) have found some national and international success in terms of reception. Many of these contemporary art-house films have been funded by transnational investors (in Korea, Japan, and France) and perform well in markets outside of the country. Funded with European monies, for instance, Bùi Thạc Chuyên's *Adrift* (2009) was highly acclaimed and traveled widely on the international film festival circuit. A film that has followed a similar path is Phan Đăng Di's *Bi, Don't Be Afraid* (2010), which won the Cannes Film Festival Award for Best Screenplay in 2010. That same year, the Academy of Motion Picture Arts and Sciences in Los Angeles held a two-week film series entitled "New Voices from Việt Nam," featuring this film and several others. More recently female director Nguyễn Hoàng Điệp's debut film *Flapping in the Middle of Nowhere* (2013), which deals with the hardships of Vietnamese youth in contemporary Hà Nội, has also been a critical hit at film festivals abroad.

Written from a statist perspective, official Vietnamese film history begins with the establishment of a sovereign nation in northern Việt Nam. But this kind of historiography tends to canonize those films that are overtly political and that have emerged from the North. What does not get highlighted in this history are the following: southern Vietnamese films produced during the Second Indochinese War; diasporic Vietnamese films about the refugee or reeducation experience of the 4 million overseas Vietnamese, many of whom fled the revolutionary regime; and the large number of colonial films produced before the founding of the Democratic Republic of Việt Nam in 1945; these films are missing or not included in its collection. Some of these films instead circulate on the Internet, are sold in DVD stores in Vietnamese community enclaves, and/or are screened at local film festivals in the United States. Vietnamese cinema, in all of its national and transnational circulations, thus constitutes a rich site of inquiry for scholars interested in tracing its political and historical lineage as well as its intersection with popular culture.

Lan Duong

See also: Cinema, China

Further Reading

"Business Opportunities: The New Vietnam Film Industry." 2010. *Việt Nam a Go Go*. January 15. www.bigbloggle.com/vietnam_agogo. Accessed August 15, 2010.

Dương, Lan. 2007. "*Long-Legged Girls* and the Transnational Circuits of Vietnamese Popular Culture." In *Transnational Feminism in Media and Cinema*. Ed. Katarzyna Marciniak, Áine O'Healy, and Anikó Imre, 163–184. New York: Palgrave Macmillan Press.

Rouse, Sarah. 1986. "South Vietnam's Film Legacy." *Historical Journal of Film, Radio and Television* 6, no. 2: 211–222.

"TV, Cinema Show More Vietnam Flicks." 2007. *Vietnam Net Bridge*. July 8. http://english.vietnamnet.vn/lifestyle/2007/07/715505. Accessed August 16, 2010.

Wilson, Dean. 2007. "Film Controls in Colonial Vietnam: 1896–1926." In *Vietnamese Cinema: Le Cinéma Vietnamien*. Ed. Philippe Dumont and Kirstie Gormley, 75–83. Lyon, FR: Asiexpo Edition.

DOCUMENTARIES, CHINA

On February 28, 2015, Chai Jing, a former investigative journalist at China Central Television (CCTV), posted her self-financed documentary *Under the Dome* online and through social media. Within days, this TED-like 104-minute film about air pollution in China had received over 200 million views; it was taken down a week later. Looking through the history of independent documentary films in China since their emergence in the late 1980s, it is not surprising to see the use of documentary as a medium to address social issues with a critical view of the government and another filmmaker who used to work for state media. What distinguishes Chai's documentary from the others is that almost no other independent documentaries were able to attract the same amount of audience and impact, except among film critics, scholars, and international film festivals. This article traces the major developments of Chinese documentary films, contributed by both official and nonofficial actors, over the past two decades.

In 1953 the Chinese Communist Party established the Central Newsreel and Documentary Film Studio, which had originated as the Yan'an Film Regiment founded in 1938. In the 1980s the Chinese audience watched "special theme" television series, such as *Yangtze River* (1983) and *River Elegy* (1988) on CCTV. Despite contrary views on the Yangtze River and the Yellow River, both series were prescripted with political commentary in search of cultural roots. The latter especially stirred controversy because it took a negative approach to Chinese culture, and some believed that it was one of the triggers of the 1989 protests.

At the same time as the broadcast of *River Elegy*, Wu Wenguang started shooting *Bumming in Beijing: The Last Dreamers* (1990). Wu was a television cameraman and producer for state media before becoming one of the founding figures of Chinese independent documentary filmmaking. At the time, he did not realize that he was making a documentary, but he wanted to replace the "official voice" with unscripted interviews. In *Bumming in Beijing*, Wu interviewed five "drifter" artist friends living in Beijing in pursuit of their art, yet without a residential permit (*hukou*) or stable income. Taking his friends as subjects, Wu acted as an onlooker, and he did not add any narration or music throughout the film. The documentary was considered groundbreaking for its contrast with contemporary mainstream media, and it was a significant beginning for Chinese independent documentary filmmaking. It attracted more audiences and funding from international film festivals outside mainland China, a path that many other independent filmmakers would follow.

Shot between 1988 and 1990, *Bumming in Beijing* does not directly address the 1989 protests, though one can see its influence: four out of five artists went abroad, and the last suffered a mental breakdown. Two other documentaries, however, chose Tiananmen as the subject. One was *Tiananmen* (1991) by Shi Jian, a CCTV producer and colleague of Wu Wenguang. Written and produced for CCTV, the documentary production started in 1988, but it was aborted by the summer of 1989. Originally proposed to celebrate the 40th anniversary of the People's Republic of China's (PRC) founding, the film failed to pass censorship for its "passive" portrayal of ordinary Beijing residents' daily lives. The other documentary was *The Square* (1994), codirected by Duan Jinchuan, who worked for state-run Tibetan television, and Zhang Yuan, a director of both features and documentaries. Filmed in black and white, the documentary captures one day in the life of Tiananmen

Square in 1994. Accompanied by a CCTV crew, Duan and Zhang were able to look closely at the tourists, children, and flag-raising and -lowering ceremonies. One can see the level of control through not only the omnipresent police but also the staged interviews with politically correct answers.

Unlike Wu Wenguang, who moved on to a career as an independent documentary filmmaker, Shi Jian stayed at CCTV and attempted to reform from within the system. In 1993 he helped launch *Oriental Horizon*, an investigative journalism program, and *Tell It Like It Is*, the first Chinese talk show, in 1996. The slogan for *Living Space*, a subprogram of *Oriental Horizon*, was "Let ordinary people tell their own stories." These programs became popular among the domestic audience, as they signified a shift away from propaganda and toward the audience's everyday concerns. Episodes in these programs might not qualify strictly as documentary films, but the focus on ordinary people became a common trend in both official and unofficial Chinese documentaries in the 1990s, influenced by these shows.

The boundary between "official" and "independent" documentaries might be porous, but they are by no means the same. While the mainstream media glorify China's economic boom since the late 1990s, independent documentary filmmakers trace marginalized people and the growing pains of rapid development. One example is Wang Bing's *West of the Tracks* (2003), which records the decline and death of a state-run factory complex in Northeast China. Once a pillar of Chinese socialist economy and industrialization in the Mao era, the district had to lay off its workers and shut down factories by the late 1990s. A graduate of Beijing Film Academy, this was Wang's debut. Using a digital video (DV) camera, he wandered around Shenyang's industrial Tiexi district, collected over 300 hours of footage between 1999 and 2001, and ended up with a nine-hour saga.

Wang continued to chase the disappearing socialist past in his second documentary, *Fengming: A Chinese Memoir* (2007). The three-hour film consists almost entirely of monologues by He Fengming, a woman in her seventies. She talked about her family's tragic experiences in the Mao years, especially during the Anti-Rightist Campaign of 1957; the Great Leap Forward Famine (1959–1961), when her husband starved to death in a labor camp; and the Cultural Revolution (1966–1976), when He Fengming was briefly imprisoned. This was not the first documentary, however, that focused on individuals who suffered through post-1949 political campaigns. Earlier in 2004, Hu Jie, a former Xinhua News Agency employee who had previously served in the army, directed *Searching for Lin Zhao's Soul*. The protagonist, Lin Zhao, was a female student at Beijing University before the Anti-Rightist Campaign. She became more critical of the Chinese Communist Party after being condemned as a "rightist," and she was executed in 1968 during the Cultural Revolution, leaving thousands of her letters behind, written in her own blood while in prison. Afterward Hu Jie made *Though I Am Gone* (2007) about a high school's vice principal who was beaten to death by female Red Guards in 1966. Most recently, he produced *Spark* (2013) about an underground journal, organized by a group of "rightist" students and teachers from Lanzhou University, covering the hunger and poverty during the Great Leap Forward Famine.

If Hu Jie's trilogies represent a kind of activism in uncovering the past, Ai Xiaoming's documentaries explore the truth of the present. Now retired, Ai was a comparative literature professor at Sun Yat-sen University. A feminist academic, she translated Eve Ensler's *Vagina Monologues* and brought it to the stage of her school. A human rights activist, she investigated the HIV/AIDS crisis in rural China through *Epic of the Central Plain* (2006). After the 2008 Sichuan earthquake, she brought her camera to hear from parents who had lost children in the earthquake due to substandard school buildings, as shown in *Our Children* (2009) and *Citizens' Investigation* (2009).

With the availability of digital video since the late 1990s, it has become impossible to count the number of independent documentary filmmakers in China. While earlier filmmakers generally had working relations with state-run media, more amateurs have now joined the field. Wu Wenguang, now an established documentary filmmaker, founded the Caochangdi Workstation in 2005, a studio that provides training in digital video filmmaking. So far, it has initiated the China Village Self-Governance Film Project (2005–2008), which recruited 10 villagers from across China to document their lives through camera, and Folk Memory Documentary History Project (2010–), which has produced hundreds of oral history interviews, mostly with senior villagers on the Great Leap Forward Famine.

Founded by art critic Li Xianting in 2008, the Li Xianting Film School serves a similar purpose as Wu's Workstation, except students come from a wider range of backgrounds. The school is located in Songzhuang, an artist community on the eastern outskirts of Beijing. The same place has hosted grassroots film festivals, including the China Documentary Film Festival since 2003 and the Beijing Independent Film Festival since 2006, though these often experience interference, if not cancelation, by local security forces. Other cities, like Nanjing, Chongqing, and Kunming, also hold similar events with increasing popularity and also encounter censorship. These festivals provide a platform for screenings and discussions of independent films.

Despite easier access to filmmaking with inexpensive and compact digital technology, and a wider circulation thanks to the Internet, making independent films in China is still a risky, and certainly not a profitable, business. The influence of independent documentaries remains limited as long as the restrictions stay tight. On the other hand, documentaries produced by official media have become more market and audience oriented. One example is the CCTV documentary series *A Bite of China* (2012), which introduces the history and story behind various Chinese foods. Now scheduled for a third season to air in 2016, this documentary series has received widespread popularity. The director has acknowledged that he borrows filming techniques from BBC documentary productions. In comparison to other edgy topics, food is a relatively safe and easy way to generate national and cultural identity among a Chinese audience.

State media productions do not enjoy the same kind of freedom as independent filmmakers do, but the latter can hardly catch up with the former in terms of budget and circulation. Chai Jing is one of the rare people who combine the benefits of both, but she is not the only one who left CCTV and started making independent documentaries. Cui Yongyuan, who made his name hosting the talk show *Tell It Like It Is* from 1996 to 2002, self-financed a trip to the United States and made a documentary, *Report on GMO* (2014), investigating the safety of genetically modified food. Now a professor at his alma mater, the Communication University of China, Cui has since started his own film studio devoted to oral history and documentary filmmaking. People like Cui and Chai, who walk between the worlds of official and independent documentary filmmaking, remind us again that the boundary between the two is often crossed.

Yidi Wu

See also: Cinema, China; Historical Dramas, China (Chapter 4: Television and Radio)

Further Reading

Berry, Chris, Lu Xinyu, and Lisa Rofel, eds. 2010. *The New Chinese Documentary Film Movement: For the Public Record.* Hong Kong: Hong Kong University Press.

Johnson, Ian. 2015. "China's Invisible History: An Interview with Filmmaker and Artist Hu Jie." *The New York Review of Books.* www.nybooks.com/blogs/nyrblog/2015/may/27/chinas-invisible-history-hu-jie/. Accessed March 26, 2016.

Pickowicz, Paul G., and Yingjin Zhang, eds. 2006. *From Underground to Independent: Alternative Film Culture in Contemporary China.* Lanham, MD: Rowman & Littlefield.

Qian, Ying. 2012. "Power in the Frame: China's Independent Documentary Movement." *New Left Review* 74: 105–123.

Robinson, Luke. 2013. *Independent Chinese Documentary: From the Studio to the Street.* New York: Palgrave Macmillan.

Wu, Wenguang. "Caochangdi Workstation." http://blog.sina.com.cn/ccdworkstation (in Chinese). Accessed March 26, 2016.

Zhang, Yingjin. 2010. *Cinema, Space, and Polylocality in a Globalizing China.* Honolulu: University of Hawai'i Press.

FENG XIAOGANG (CHINESE NEW YEAR CINEMA)

New Year Cinema (*Hesui pian* 贺岁片) is an indigenous popular commercial genre in contemporary Chinese cinema. Targeting specifically the film market of the New Year season in China (from Christmas and New Year to the Spring Festival, or the Lunar New Year), New Year Cinema usually celebrates the festive, seasonal atmosphere and is thus characterized by comic story lines, lighthearted ambience, and happy endings. But as the genre has developed, it has become, naturally enough, more diverse.

New Year Cinema has developed under the condition of the all-encompassing commercialization and marketization in Chinese society since the 1990s. In the face of increasing competition from other forms of popular entertainment, such as TV, and from imported and pirated Hollywood blockbusters, locally produced

Chinese cinema had to seek a means to survive by turning decisively to a reliance on market forces. The entire system, as a result, gradually shifted from a state-controlled structure to a more market-oriented one. It was in the process of this systemic change that this new genre called New Year Cinema came into being.

New Year Cinema in China was also influenced by its predecessor in Hong Kong, which started producing New Year films in the 1970s. Chinese filmmakers arguably replicated New Year Cinema almost directly from their Hong Kong counterparts; yet, the former also developed their own styles of New Year filmmaking, catering specifically to the local audience. The first New Year film imported to China was Jackie Chan's *Rumble in the Bronx* in 1995, which became one of the top-grossing films of that year. Two years later, Feng Xiaogang made the first New Year comedy in China, *Party A, Party B* (aka *Dream Factory*), which also became an immediate box-office hit. With the success of Feng's and some other directors' New Year productions in the years that followed, New Year Cinema soon developed into a unique cinematic genre. It became so popular over the years that even some "art-house" film-makers, such as Zhang Yimou and Chen Kaige, joined the bandwagon in order to gain their own share of this rapidly growing market. However, though some of these directors saw a moderate degree of success, many were not so successful.

Feng Xiaogang (冯小刚), quite incontrovertibly, is the most successful New Year Cinema director. Born in Beijing in 1958, Feng was trained in art design and had worked as a stage and cinema designer and a screenwriter before he directed his first film. His early New Year films made in the late 1990s, including *Party A, Party B* (1997), *Be There or Be Square* (1998), and *Sorry Baby* (1999), were all romantic comedies featuring quotable repartee and warmhearted stories. What made these films better known was his use of a unique style of humor, which was marked by the witty lines of urban youth,

The Chinese filmmaker, Feng Xiaogang, is seen here at the Rome International Film Festival in 2012, to present his film, *Back to 1942*. Feng is one of the most commercially successful directors in China today, where he started with lighthearted holiday films, and has recently begun to make dramatic and historical films as well. (AP Photo/Gregorio Borgia)

Zhang Yimou

Zhang Yimou (1951–) was a member of the first class to graduate from the Beijing Film Academy after the Cultural Revolution (1966–1976). He was the cinematographer on *Yellow Earth* (1984), the film that brought his "Fifth Generation" of Chinese filmmakers to worldwide attention. Zhang became noted internationally for directing lush period dramas, such as *Raise the Red Lantern* (1991), and for collaborating with actress Gong Li. Early clashes with the Chinese authorities over censorship issues earned him a reputation overseas as a "political" filmmaker. However, his transition back to respectability was sealed by the release of three *wuxia* (martial arts) blockbusters in the 2000s: *Hero* (2002), *House of Flying Daggers* (2004), and *Curse of the Golden Flower* (2006). *Hero* premiered in the Great Hall of the People on Tiananmen Square. Zhang is also famous for choreographing live events, like the Opening Ceremony of the 2008 Beijing Olympics.

Luke Robinson

cynical and sometimes satirical of their quotidian, sometimes marginalized, lives. This so-called "Feng-style humor," which was influenced by the writer Wang Shuo (also born in 1958), with whom Feng had worked closely since the years when he was a screenwriter, almost became a brand name and shaped his productions in the years to come. Yet, since his humor was largely based on northern dialects, these early films were more welcomed in North China than in the south. However, Feng addressed this issue by including in his cast stars from across the region of East Asia and even from Hollywood.

This effort to globalize his films took a first step in the making of *Sorry Baby*, starring the popular local comedian Ge You, who would appear in most of Feng's New Year comedies, and the Hong Kong–based Taiwanese actress Wu Chien-lien. In *Big Shot's Funeral* (2001), Feng went even further by including Donald Sutherland, along with Ge You and Rosamund Kwan (Hong Kong), on his shining list of stars. This strategy proved to be effective as these later films broke into broader markets and were well received among audiences of widely disparate cultural backgrounds. *Big Shot's Funeral*, for example, hit No. 1 at the box office in 2002, breaking the record set by Feng's earlier New Year film, *Be There or Be Square*, in 1998.

Lurking behind this astounding success in the market was increasing involvement of international capital in the production and distribution of these films. These investors offered financial sponsorship, international distribution channels, technological support, and so on, and also took their shares in the rapidly growing market for Chinese cinema. For instance, Columbia Film Production Asia distributed *Big Shot's Funeral* to the global market and cooperated with Feng in his film *Cell Phone* in 2003.

But the real game-changer was the domestic media corporations that thrived as the state monopoly of the Chinese film system collapsed in the 1990s. In Feng's case, four such major corporations—Beijing Forbidden City Film Corporation and China Film Corporation, both formerly state-controlled conglomerates restructured from former state institutions into shareholder enterprises, and Huayi Brothers Advertising Co. and its subsidiary Huayi Brothers Taihe Film Investment and Production Co., both private domestic enterprises—invested in his films. Yet, it was the latter that decisively reshaped Feng's New Year films into highly consumer-oriented products. Relying on such strategies as big budget, transnational casts, sleek audiovisual style, professional promotions, and heavy product placements, Feng's filmmaking marked a decidedly different model of production than that of the state-controlled studios.

However, at the same time, one should not minimize the role that state-controlled corporations have played, since in exchange for their share of market return they provided the necessary political and institutional endorsements thanks to their connections with the authorities. As such, in collaboration with state-controlled and international corporations, domestic private investors and producers, who had already integrated film, TV, and advertising into their multifield businesses, were able to maximize profits in the expanding market.

But although consumer oriented, Feng's New Year films were not simply mindless entertainment. Many, in fact, address important topics of contemporary social concern and, in his own words, "concerns in ordinary people's ordinary life," such as living abroad and extramarital affairs. Moreover, his streetwise humor served as a means through which ordinary people could satirize the establishment and express their discontent. Most intriguingly, some of his films exhibit a self-reflective quality. For instance, *Big Shot's Funeral* mocks the phenomenon of product placement, yet the products in the film are, ironically, advertised through placement; in other words, the film parodies the rampant commercialization of which his filmmaking is a product.

Apart from comedies, Feng also made films for the New Year market whose narratives are not so lighthearted, such as *A Sigh* (2000) and *A World without Thieves* (2004). He even made films that depict serious historical tragedies, including *Assembly* (2007), which deals with the 1946–1949 civil war, *Aftershock* (2010), which focuses on the 1976 Tangshan earthquake, and *Back to 1942* (2012), which looks at the famine of that year. But all of these films were produced on a model similar to that of his earlier comedies, a model that Feng has continued to employ in his recent comedies—two installments of *If You Are the One* (2008 and 2010) and *Personal Tailor* (2013). All of them contribute both to the formation as well as the diversification of New Year Cinema as a unique genre.

Haomin Gong

See also: Cinema, China; Spring Festival TV Gala, China (Chapter 4: Television and Radio)

Further Reading

Gong, Haomin. 2009. "Commerce and the Critical Edge: Negotiating the Politics of Postsocialist Film, the Case of Feng Xiaogang." *Journal of Chinese Cinemas* 3, no. 3: 193–214.

Kong, Shuyu. 2007. "Genre Film, Media Corporations, and the Commercialisation of the Chinese Film Industry: The Case of 'New Year Comedies'." *Asian Studies Review* 31, no. 3: 227–242.

McGrath, Jason. 2005. "Metacinema for the Masses: Three Films by Feng Xiaogang." *Modern Chinese Literature and Culture* 17, no. 2: 90–132.

Zhang, Rui. 2008. *The Cinema of Feng Xiaogang: Commercialization and Censorship in Chinese Cinema after 1989.* Hong Kong: Hong Kong University Press.

HOLLYWOOD FILMS IN CHINA

Hollywood has a long history in China. Lured by the enormous market potential there, major U.S. film studios have been actively involved in marketing and distributing their films in the country since the early 20th century. Although banned in China during the Cold War years, American films have made a significant comeback in the last few decades. However, the reception of Hollywood films in China has always been affected by cultural barriers, political circumstances, and the larger process of globalization.

In the early decades of the 20th century, Hollywood films completely dominated the Chinese film market. At its peak, Hollywood's share of the box-office revenue in China exceeded 75 percent. Among those popular Hollywood movies, the most successful genres were comedy, melodrama, and Disney animation. To Chinese audience and filmmakers, Hollywood's engaging narrative patterns, humanistic concerns, and spectacular visual effects were extremely attractive. One indication of Hollywood's popularity in China and its impact on Chinese filmmaking is that there was a wave of Chinese remakes of Hollywood films during the Republican period (1912–1949). For instance, shortly after *Gone with the Wind* (dir. Victor Fleming, 1939) premiered in China, a Chinese remake version of the film appeared in Shanghai. The remake version starred the famous Chinese actress Yunshang Chen and incorporated the original story into a localized Chinese context. Instead of copying the Hollywood version entirely, the director Shankun Zhang located the story in the Chinese countryside during ancient times. Many Chinese filmmakers also tried to imitate Hollywood style in their own works. To a large extent, Chinese cinema of this period was profoundly influenced by Hollywood because Chinese moviegoers increasingly expected Hollywood-style entertainment that would allow them to escape their reality and find refuge in the dream world of cinematic fantasy.

The Communist victory in 1949 and the subsequent Cold War brought an end to the Hollywood Empire in China. For both political and economic reasons, Hollywood was expelled from China for the next 30 years until China reopened to the outside world and embarked on the path of modernization in the early 1980s. Against this backdrop, Hollywood reemerged in China. However, in contrast to the situation in the Republican period before 1949, Hollywood's expansion in China in the past few decades has been subject to a number of official restrictions. Chief among them is the limit on the number of American films to be released in China each year. Yet, despite the obstacles, Hollywood is determined to strengthen its position in the Chinese film market. Studios have tried to produce films that are unlikely to have troubles with the Chinese censors, and American studios have set up branch offices in China to better engage with both government officials and leaders in the native film industry. Although China's film market has been dominated by domestic films, thanks to the government's protectionist policy, Hollywood since the 1990s has firmly reestablished itself in China as a cultural force to be reckoned with.

The process of globalization of the last few decades has undoubtedly assisted Hollywood's reemergence in China. China's entry in the World Trade Organization (WTO) in 2001 obliged the government to open the door of the Chinese film market to foreign competition. In November 1999, the Chinese government agreed to allow film business with inward investment and to increase the number of foreign films to be released in China from 10 to 20 per year. In 2012 the number was increased from 20 to 34 Hollywood films each year. Statistically, Hollywood's market share in China in the early 2000s was slightly under 20 percent; today it accounts for half.

It should be noted that there is a clear pattern in the type of films that the Chinese pick for import and distribution. Big-budget studio films, especially action-packed movies, fantasy movies, and animation films have been the favorites of the Chinese audience. Basically, when China relaxed the restriction on foreign films, domestic Chinese cinema started reforming under the economic-oriented market. Therefore, protecting cultural and market territory became a significant issue for the Chinese government while dealing with imported foreign movies. For both economic and political reasons, the Chinese government carefully censors all imported foreign films and makes sure the themes, ideological orientations, genres, and casts are acceptable to the regime. Subsequently, many Hollywood films that deal with sensitive subjects do not have a chance to reach audiences in China, especially art cinema with significant cultural specificity.

With high production quality and a sophisticated marketing strategy, Hollywood has seduced Chinese audiences as it has done to audiences all over the world. As one of the most powerful cultural institutions and revenue generators in the world, Hollywood has profited enormously from its business operations in China. In 2014 the box-office revenue generated by 34 Hollywood films was almost equal to the box office of 300 domestic Chinese films combined. The average box-office receipt of each imported film was also much higher than the average box-office receipt of domestic films. The blockbuster in 2014 was the latest in the Transformers series (dir. Michael Bay), which brought in 1.98 billion Chinese yuan (or about US$31.97 million) gross income in China, a number even higher than the film's box office in the United States. One year later, *Fast and Furious 7* (dir. James Wan) broke *Transformer 4*'s record by raking in a box-office revenue of over 2 billion Chinese yuan (about US$32 million).

There are several reasons behind Hollywood's popularity in China. First, China's domestic film industry and film market are still undergoing a transitional phase. Not surprisingly, the average quality of domestic films remains low and is not on par with foreign competition. In contrast, Hollywood is a mature industry, with more than a century of experience in product development and marketing strategy. It not only dwarfs China's film industry but also the film industry of every other nation in the world when it comes to creative energy, production quality, and market appeal. Second, Hollywood has made specific efforts to study and accommodate the Chinese film market. By deliberately incorporating Chinese elements that include Chinese characters, Chinese locales, Chinese performers, and references to Chinese traditional culture into its films, Hollywood tries hard to appeal to Chinese sentiments and aesthetic tastes. In the past few years, Chinese motifs are conspicuously visible in many of the American blockbusters released in China. Films such as *Looper* (dir. Rian Johnson, 2012), *Transformer 4*, and *X-men: Days of Future Past* (dir. Bryan Singer, 2014) all feature at least one lead Chinese character or an important Chinese location. Some films, such as *Iron Man 3* (dir. Shane Black, 2013), even provide a Chinese version that stars Chinese performers for the Chinese film market. These efforts have helped bridge the cultural barrier and made Hollywood films more accessible to the Chinese audience.

The dual role Hollywood films have played in China, both as a competitor and an existential threat to the native film industry on the one hand, and as a source of inspiration and a model for business success on the other, is a key to understanding Hollywood's reception in China. However, as China's own film industry matures and becomes more competitive in the coming years, Hollywood will face increasing challenges. How Chinese moviegoers will react to American films in the future remains to be seen.

Yiyi Yin

See also: Cinema, China

Further Reading

Xiao, Zhiwei. 1990. "American Films in China prior to 1950." In *Art, Politics, and Commerce in Chinese Cinema.* Ed. Ying Zhu and Stanley Rosen, 55–70. Hong Kong: Hong Kong University Press.

Xiao, Zhiwei. 2004. "The Expulsion of American Films from China, 1949–1950." *Twenty Century China,* 64–81.

KUROSAWA AKIRA (1910–1998)

Akira Kurosawa remains the best-known Japanese filmmaker in the world. Within Japan, during his lifetime, he was a towering figure in cinema, and he was the first Japanese director whose film was invited to screen at the prestigious Venice Film Festival. The year was 1951, and the film was *Rashomon*. Its reception at Venice was ecstatic, and thereafter Kurosawa films were regular prizewinners overseas.

At home in Japan, his work consistently ranked in the top 10 films each year as selected by the important journal of film criticism *Kinema jumpo*. Kurosawa worked in many film genres—crime and mystery, medical dramas, adaptations of literary classics—but it was his samurai films, especially *Seven Samurai* and *Yojimbo*, that became his greatest popular hits and were, along with *Godzilla*, Japan's most famous cultural exports.

Kurosawa was born in 1910, and though he wanted to be a painter, he elected to take a more practical and remunerative path by joining the Photo Chemical Laboratory (PCL) film studio in 1936 (subsequently renamed Toho Studios) as an apprentice director in training. New recruits were apprenticed to an established director under whom they trained in all phases of production. Kurosawa's mentor was Kajiro Yamamoto (1902–1974), who directed some of Japan's most famous propaganda films during the war. World War II was underway when Kurosawa was promoted to director in 1943 and allowed to make his first film. His first four films—*Sanshiro Sugata* (1943), *The Most Beautiful* (1944), *Sanshiro Sugata Part II* (1944), and *The Men Who Tread on the Tiger's Tail* (1945)—were made during the war, when Japan's film industry, like the country at large, functioned with severely constrained resources. Of these, only one—*The Most Beautiful*—is a straight-ahead propaganda film made on behalf of the military. Each of these early films shows Kurosawa's mastery of film style and narrative and his superior gifts in fashioning a unique stylistic profile in a medium that is otherwise fairly standard and homogenous.

While Kurosawa's filmmaking talents are on clear display in these early films, it was the end of the war, the devastation of Japan, and the new freedoms undertaken during the Allied occupation of Japan that furnished the grounds on which Kurosawa was able to become a great filmmaker. He responded earnestly to the new political and social freedoms of the postwar period, especially the ethic and ideal of individualism as promoted by occupation authorities. Kurosawa undertook a series of films set amid the wreckage of a nation ruined by war, and he placed strong, rebellious, individual heroes at the center of stories that functioned as symbolic parables of national recovery. Masterworks among these films include *Drunken Angel* (1948), *Stray Dog* (1949), and *Ikiru* (1952). *Drunken Angel* represented Kurosawa's first collaboration with actor Toshiro Mifune, with whom he worked closely on most of his subsequent films. Mifune joined an extensive Kurosawa entourage and repertory company, first-rate collaborators on whom Kurosawa deeply depended. These included screenwriters Ryuzo Kikushima (1914–1989) and Shinobu Hashimoto (1918–), composer Fumio Hayasaka (1914–1955), cinematographer Asakazu Nakai (1901–1988), production designer Yoshiro Muraki (1924–2009), and production supervisor Teruyo Nogami. This group became known as the Kurosawa Company, and with these collaborators Kurosawa embarked on the string of masterpieces for which he is known today.

The zenith of Kurosawa's career lasted from 1950 to 1965, from *Rashomon* to *Red Beard*. *Rashomon* (1950) pioneered the now-familiar cinematic device of flashbacks told from the point of view of unreliable narrators. A crime occurs in the woods—a samurai dies, his wife is disgraced, a thief is arrested nearby. The thief, the wife, and the samurai's spirit (channeled by a medium) relate different accounts of the events. A fourth account is provided by a witness. Each recounted history is most flattering to the one narrating it. Kurosawa constructs a parable of the darkness in the human heart. The propensity for people to lie that he dramatizes had a topical salience that related to questions about war guilt and war crimes, as these had been raised in the trials conducted by the Allied powers in Tokyo and throughout Southeast Asia. *Rashomon* was a period film set in the Heian era and also spoke about the Japan of today.

Flush with the success of the Grand Prize at Venice for *Rashomon*, Kurosawa made a series of now-classic films, alternating contemporary life pictures with period pieces. *Ikiru* portrayed a lowly clerk in a vast government bureaucracy who, upon learning he is dying of cancer, transforms his life and performs one meaningful act before he dies. It was Kurosawa's supreme statement of his existential belief that each person must struggle against a hostile world to discover truth and meaning and that attaining such enlightenment is a difficult and arduous process. His next film, *Seven Samurai* (1954), is sometimes regarded as the greatest Japanese film ever made, and it is probably true to say that this is also the most influential film ever made, if influence is measured by the impact of its film style and by the numerous official and unofficial remakes that it has inspired. Seven samurai defend a village of farmers against bandits—from this elegant premise, Kurosawa builds an epic vision of history, adventure, and heroism. It was the first of his films set during the 16th-century samurai wars, a period that he made his own in numerous subsequent films.

Kurosawa explored the problems of contemporary Japan in several key films. *Record of a Living Being* (1955) depicts Japanese anxieties about living under the United States' nuclear umbrella

Few directors have had a greater impact on film in their own country and around the world than Japan's Akira Kurosawa (1910–1988). George Lucas, Clint Eastwood, and countless others cite Kurosawa as a formative influence in their careers. This is a poster for Kurosawa's spectacular *Seven Samurai* (1954). (Toho Company/Photofest)

during the Cold War. *The Bad Sleep Well* (1960) dramatizes the antidemocratic collusion of corrupt corporate powers with government officials whom they bribe for support. *High and Low* (1963) shows the inequalities of wealth and power that Japan's postwar economic recovery had helped to deepen. Kurosawa's love for literature resulted in adaptations of Dostoevsky (*The Idiot*, 1951), Shakespeare (*Throne of Blood*, 1957), and Gorky (*The Lower Depths*, 1957). And he returned to the samurai genre in three of his most popular films, using the period setting as commentary on contemporary Japan—*The Hidden Fortress* (1958), *Yojimbo* (1961), and *Sanjuro* (1962). *The Hidden Fortress* inspired George Lucas in making *Star Wars* (1977), and *Yojimbo* gave Toshiro Mifune his most iconographic role as a cynical, wandering *ronin* (an unemployed samurai).

Red Beard was the last film in Kurosawa's greatest period of production. Its story of doctors working in a slum medical clinic in the 19th century was Kurosawa's final epic statement of the existential individualism that underlay his conception of heroism. Although the film was a great popular success, television was eroding the basis of the film industry, and Kurosawa thereafter found it very difficult to raise funds for movies. During the next 28 years, he worked when he could and made only a few films compared with his past prolific output. Three films stand out from this group, comparable in stature to his earlier work: *Dersu uzala* (1975), funded by the Soviet Union and filmed there, is a splendid meditation on the vastness and beauty of nature; *Kagemusha* (1980), made with the support of American directors George Lucas and Francis Coppola; and *Ran* (1985) were his final epic portraits of the samurai world that he deeply loved.

Kurosawa died in 1998 after years of declining health and inactivity. He left behind a body of work that virtually defined Japan and its history for popular audiences throughout the world, even though Kurosawa had always insisted that he made movies primarily for the Japanese audience. The history of cinema has seen many great filmmakers, but there have only been a few giant figures whose work is essential for an understanding of the medium. Kurosawa was one of these.

Stephen Prince

See also: Murakami, Haruki (Chapter 2: Books and Contemporary Literature)

Further Reading

Kurosawa, Akira. 1983. *Something Like an Autobiography*. New York: Vintage Books.
Prince, Stephen. 1999. *The Warrior's Camera: The Cinema of Akira Kurosawa*. New Jersey: Princeton University Press.
Richie, Donald. 1999. *The Films of Akira Kurosawa*. Berkeley: University of California Press.

LAVANI DANCE AND FILM, INDIA

The word *lavani* is derived from the Maharashtrian word *lavanya*, which means "beauty." *Lavani* is a combination of dance and music that depicts the various aspects of society, such as religion, politics, and romance. *Lavani* dance is performed on the beats of a *dholki*, a percussion instrument, at a fast tempo. The costume of the *lavani* dancers is a nine-yard-long sari (traditional Maharashtrian Indian women's attire) in a bright color, locally known as *navvari*. The female artists are adorned with heavy golden jewelry, including necklaces, earrings, *payal* (anklets), *kamarpatta* (jeweled waistband), and bangles. They wear a bright red *bindi* (vermillion) on their forehead, which adds to the brightness of their attire. The *lavani* dancers, who are mostly women, synchronize sensually to catchy, rhythmic beats and teasing lyrics.

The state of Maharashtra in India was once torn by battle, and the *lavani* dance served as a mode of entertainment and a morale booster for tired soldiers during the 18th and 19th centuries. The dance peaked in popularity during the Peshwai (a dynasty seated in Pune City in the state of Maharashtra, India) rule, when it was given royal support by the ruling elite. Marathi poets like Honaji Bala, Ramjoshi, and Prabhakar took *lavani* to new heights of fame and popularity.

Some of the most popular films in the Marathi language, like *Pinjara* (*Cage*) and *Natarang* (*Theatre Artist*) have portrayed the *lavani* dance in a beautiful manner. There are two types of *lavani* dance: *nirguni lavani*, which is philosophical in nature, and *shringari lavani*, which is sensual and erotic in nature. *Shringari lavani* talks about a married woman's longing for her husband/lover and wives bidding farewell to their husbands leaving for war. It can be traced back to as early as the 17th century. *Shringari lavani* is performed by only women, whereas the script is written by men. This type of *lavani* is very popular in the state of Madhya Pradesh (Central India). On the basis of how the *lavani* is performed, it can be further categorized as *phadachi lavani* or *baithakichi lavani*. The *phadachi lavani* is performed in a theatrical gathering before a large audience (mostly in the open). The *baithakichi lavani* is presented in a closed chamber before a selected audience.

A woman's sexuality and her innermost thoughts, feelings, and desires were expressed in the form of *lavani*. However, this expression also became the basis of women's marginalization in Indian society. The sexuality of the lower-caste women came to be controlled through *lavani* as it created a vicious circle for the performers. For example, women from the Kolhati community had to continue to perform the Lavani, as this was the only skill they knew, and they had to perform to sustain themselves.

By the turn of the 20th century, *lavani* came under the influence of commercial Hindi and Marathi cinema, where the dancers were now earning their livelihood by performing raunchier versions of this art form. *Lavani* dancers were compelled to satisfy the tastes of a modernizing audience who understood folk art less and demanded crude, vulgar versions of the art form, thereby further denigrating the status of the lower-caste *lavani* performer.

Sangeet bari theaters are prevalent in the state of Maharashtra, with 45 such theaters across Pune, Solapur, Satara, Sangli, Kolhapur, Ahmednagar, and Marathwada. Although they have maintained the tradition of performing *lavani*, the quality is deteriorating.

There are 8 to 10 dance troupes attached to each theater. Each troupe, known as a *sangeet* (song) party, has one or two *malkins* (lady owners) by whose name it is known.

The *sangeet bari* is an intimate setting where the dancers are allowed to communicate with the audience through their performance. This is how *baithakichi lavani* (where the audience is seated in an enclosed space) emerged. This type of *lavani* emphasizes facial expression, singing, interacting, and creating a personalized experience. Traditional *lavani* requires a patient audience that is interested in fine work, smart words, subtle gestures, and a play of emotions.

An initiation ceremony marks a girl's entry into the profession of a *lavani* dancer. This occurs between the ages of 12 and 15 years. The initiation ceremony entails the wearing of the *ghungroo* (heavy anklets with bells). Once a girl has been introduced to the profession after the ceremonious initiation, she is not allowed to marry. Most of the women who start dancing in *sangeet baris* as *lavani* dancers belong to nomadic tribes, such as Bhatu Kolhati, Dombari, and Kalwaat. Women from these communities have been performing *lavani* for centuries. They are expected to be under the patronage of a man whom they call *malak* (male owner).

As cinema became popular, the *lavani* dance was also introduced in films. With growing acceptance, *lavani* dancers revived the dance and brought it out in a positive light. The introduction of traditional music and social messages, state-level competitions, special performances for women audiences, urban music theater productions and international success helped redeem the folk art. *Lavani* in its most recent "modern" form has found a place in Bollywood films with stars like Vidya Balan and Rani Mukherjee giving their own spin to the centuries-old dance.

Marathi film music is increasingly experimenting with raunchy and tongue-in-cheek lyrics. Double meaning or no double meaning, this musical genre has recently gained increasing popularity. Bollywood has popularized *lavani* with well-known numbers such as Katrina Kaif's "Chikni chamel" ("Smooth Jasmine Flower") from the 2012 Hindi blockbuster film *Agneepath* (*The Path of Fire*); Vidya Balan performing a *lavani* dance to the song "Mala jau de" ("Let Me Go") in the Bollywood film *Ferrari ki sawaari* (*Ride in a Ferrari*) and Helen's "Mungda mungda" ("Ant, Ant") in the hit film *Inkaar* (*Rejection*) in 1978. Although the songs are not from the *lavani* tradition, their dance style is associated with it.

Apart from Bollywood beauties, an American dancer has achieved notoriety for doing the Maharashtrian folk dance. The winner of the third season of the American TV show *So You Think You Can Dance*, Lauren Gottlieb, performed a *lavani* number in Remo D'Souza's 3D dance film *Any Body Can Dance* (*ABCD*).

Susannah Malkan

See also: Bollywood Gender Stereotypes

Further Reading

Das, Soma. 2015. "Tune into the World of Traditional Lavani." *MiD DAY*. April 28. www.mid-day.com/articles/tune-into-the-world-of-traditional-lavani/16170180. Accessed April 18, 2015.

PTI, Mumbai. "Bollywood Going Gaga over 'Lavani' Numbers." *Hindustan Times.* July 22. www.hindustantimes.com/bollywood/bollywood-going-gaga-over-lavani-numbers/article1-893039.aspx. Accessed May 15, 2015.

Shetty, Akshata. 2013. "Marathi Film Songs Get Raunchy with Lavani Item Numbers." *Times of India.* September 3. http://timesofindia.indiatimes.com/entertainment/marathi/movies/news/Marathi-film-songs-get-raunchy-with-lavani-item-numbers/articleshow/22226146.cms. Accessed May 15, 2015.

MOVIE STARS, CHINA

China is a big cultural space that accommodates different types of movie stars. On the one hand, China's movie and celebrity culture are not much different from those in the rest of the world. On the other hand, China has its own cultural specificity that makes its movie and star culture different from those of many other countries.

This cultural specificity is mainly a political one. The Chinese government has a tight control over ideology and culture, including different movies and their stars. There are many cases in which foreign stars are, because of their political stances, banned by the government and prohibited to enter China. One famous example is the American movie star Brad Pitt (1963–), who was not allowed to enter China after he had appeared in the 1997 movie *Seven Years in Tibet.* However, besides seeing this ideological control as an illiberal wrongdoing, we may also put China's ideological control in a deeper historical context, which can be roughly divided into different periods.

In the late 1920s, when Shanghai's entertainment industry and movie-star culture began to develop, they were already entangled with different kinds of politics. In that period, with the arrival of Western culture (in terms of its impact

Tony Leung Chiu-wai (1962–)

Born in Hong Kong, Leung was one of the brightest young TV stars in the 1980s, fronting popular drama series like *Police Cadet* and *The Duke of Mount Deer* (both 1984). He left TV for cinema and since 1989 has demonstrated his immense talent and range in numerous lighthearted movies, such as *Tokyo Raiders* (2000), the contemporary police-gangster classic *Infernal Affairs* (2002, the basis of Scorsese's *The Departed* [2006]), and many others that have garnered international acclaim. He has worked with leading Asian directors including Hou Hsiao-hsien (*A City of Sadness*, 1989; *Flowers of Shanghai*, 1998), John Woo (*Hard Boiled*, 1992; *Red Cliff*, 2008[I], 2009[II]), Zhang Yimou (*Hero*, 2002), and Ang Lee (*Lust, Caution*, 2007). His long-running collaboration with Wong Kar-wai has included seven films, with award-winning roles in *Chungking Express* (1994), *In the Mood for Love* (2000), *2046* (2004), and *Happy Together* (2007).

Desmond Cheung

on economy, technology, violence, philosophy, etc.) and the rise of different local forces, China's old political system was disintegrating and transforming. Different political forces, including the warlords, the Nationalist Party, the Communist Party, and different foreign forces such as Russia and Japan, did much propaganda work to attract and mobilize people. Movie stars were also used in propaganda. For example, the famous female movie star Li Xianglan (李香蘭 1920–2014, also named Yoshiko Yamaguchi / やまぐちよしこ / 山口淑子) was well known for her promotion of Japanese imperialism in Asia.

Propaganda requires people to pay attention to morality based on rigid principles, while entertainment offers people pleasure and relaxation. Pure entertainment, including movies and celebrity culture, which were deemed useless to propagate ideology (e.g., anti-imperialism, communism, nationalism), was often condemned as "yellow" (a term in Chinese suggesting pornography or moral deviance) and unhealthy culture. For instance, many movie stars nurtured in the dance school and troupes of Li Jinhui (黎錦暉 1891–1967) were criticized. The authoritative or illiberal way of interpreting and using movie stars was not only practiced and shaped by the Communist Party but also by the Nationalist Party and Japanese government, which coexisted in the same chaotic China.

The ideological control and propaganda tendency were strengthened after the establishment of the socialist state, when the Chinese Communist Party (CCP) had won the Chinese Civil War (1946–1950) and founded the People's Republic of China (PRC) in 1949. The CCP nationalized Shanghai's entertainment industry. The stardom of many Chinese movie stars was also very different from those of 1930s Shanghai. After 1949, "star" (*mingxing* 明星) became a negative word, because the word expressed the individual's extraordinary and individualistic charisma, which was unfavorable to the promotion of socialist collectivism. In many movie magazines, the term "star" was soon replaced by the term "art and cultural workers" (*wenyi gongzuozhe* 文藝工作者), which played down individualism and emphasized collectivism.

From 1949 to the early 1980s, the Chinese government often used prominent movie actors to propagate the socialist revolution. Zhao Dan (趙丹 1915–1980) and Zhang Ruifang (張瑞芳 1918–2012) were two famous movie stars who promoted socialism in official films, glorifying the good sides of the "new society" and condemning the bad sides of the "old society." Besides local stars, there were also foreign stars that support China's socialist revolution. Although capitalist countries' stars, such as those from America, Japan, and British Hong Kong, were banned, people in China's urban area could see the Soviet Union's movie stars, including Marina Ladynina (1908–2003) and Vera Maretskaya (1906–1978). After the Sino-Soviet split in 1960, the socialist Albania replaced the Soviet Union as the most influential country that offered China foreign movies and stars.

Since the early 1980s, the government has used fewer and fewer movies and movie stars as a tool of propaganda. Not only were Chinese films and movie stars allowed to be market oriented, but more foreign movie stars were also allowed to enter China and perform for their fans. Besides Western movie stars, stars from

Chow Yun-fat (1955–)

An actor from Hong Kong, Chow's filmography of nearly 100 titles has made him one of the few Asian superstars recognized internationally. His work, spanning five decades, illustrates the history of Hong Kong cinema itself. He captivated local and Asian audiences in the TV drama *The Bund* (1980), set in 1920s gangster-ridden Shanghai, which presaged his lead roles in John Woo's movies, *A Better Tomorrow* (1986), *The Killer* (1989), *Hard Boiled* (1992), and Chow's American debut, *The Replacement Killers* (1998), as well as a lighter subgenre beginning with *God of Gamblers* (1989). These spawned countless gangster movies set in a world centered on brotherhood and honor. Chow has played a different kind of hero in martial arts films, famously Ang Lee's Academy Award-winning *Crouching Tiger, Hidden Dragon* (2000). Chow has also appeared in Hollywood productions including *Anna and the King* (1999) and *Pirates of the Caribbean: At World's End* (2007).

Desmond Cheung

Taiwan, Hong Kong, Japan, and Korea have been very popular since the early 1980s, including Taiwan's Jay Chou (Zhou Jielun 周杰倫, 1979–), Japan and Taiwan's Takeshi Kaneshiro (かねしろたけし, aka Jin Chengwu 金城武, 1973–), Hong Kong's Chow Yun Fat (Zhou Runfa 周潤發, 1955–), Korea's Jeon Ji Hyeon (전지현 全智賢, 1981–), and China's Zhang Ziyi (章子怡, 1979–). These are the big stars that are often used in Chinese and Asian big-budget movies. While movie stars were used as political propaganda instead of profitable commodity in the previous socialist period, in the postsocialist period the industry has transformed and opened significantly.

This does not mean, however, that China's government has completely given up using movie stars for political propaganda. China's government still often uses culture for political purpose, compared with many other countries in the world. For example, in recent years many movie stars, including Jackie Chan (Cheng Long 成龍, 1954–), Stephen Chow (Zhou Xingchi 周星馳, 1962–), Zhang Guoli (張國立, 1955–), and Peng Dan (彭丹, 1972–), have been selected as special members of China's People's Political Consultative Conference (CPPCC), an official institution that is famous for absorbing different social elites as political consultants. In the official films *The Founding of a Republic* (*Jianguo daye* 建國大業, 2009) and *Beginning of the Great Revival* (*Jiandang weiye* 建黨偉業, 2011), many movie stars were mobilized to celebrate the anniversary of the founding of the PRC (1949) and CCP (1921) respectively. As a cultural space for local and foreign movie stars, China, because of its specific political structure, is still different from many other cultural spaces.

Li Cho Kiu

See also: Cinema, China

Further Reading

Edwards, Louise, and Elaine Jeffreys. 2010. *Celebrity in China*. Hong Kong: Hong Kong University Press.

Farquhar, Mary, and Zhang Yingjin. 2010. *Chinese Film Stars*. London: Routledge.

MOVIES, NORTH KOREA

Movies are a major state venture in North Korea, a country officially called the Democratic People's Republic of Korea (DPRK). With no private film companies, movies are almost entirely funded, produced, and distributed within the public sector, although there have been (and will be) movies made jointly with foreign governments and foreign private companies. On average, a handful of movies are produced in North Korea each year, and they are enjoyed by an eager moviegoing population throughout the country. Approved foreign movies are also shown, especially those from China, Russia, and Eastern Europe. Outside the official world, however, North Korea has a thriving bootleg movie scene, where South Korean and American blockbusters are bought and distributed on DVDs and memory sticks. So while movies in North Korea are officially state-controlled projects with the aim of propaganda, the people themselves have more choices than the outside world commonly believes, with some access to unapproved movies from other regions, which the people enjoy privately.

Soon after the DPRK was established in 1948, the North Korean government set up a film studio northwest of central Pyongyang, the capital city. The first feature movie, released in 1949, was *Nae kohyang* (*My Hometown*), which tells the story of DPRK's founding not at the hands of the Soviet Union but by the sweat and blood of ordinary Korean people. With *Nae kohyang*, movies became an important instrument of propaganda and education in North Korea. This also entailed supporting filmmakers and actors with food, housing, and training, some even going to the Soviet Union to receive more education. Movies were more than entertainment: the mass appeal of the movie format was the perfect grounds for political education. The spectacular interaction the movies had with the audience was one crucial way of experiencing and imagining socialism. Many screenwriters, actors, and directors who had their start during the colonial period (1910–1945), when Korea was a colony of the Japanese Empire, agreed with North Korea's cinematic mission. Socialism as a radical and modern idea was attractive to many Korean artists because they, too, sought something radical and modern in art.

An early movie that exemplified North Korea's cinematic mission is *Sinhonbubu* (*Newlyweds*), released in 1955. The movie was directed by Yun Ryonggyu (Yun is the family name, which is written first in East Asia). Yun began his filmmaking career in Japan and, after moving to North Korea, directed acclaimed movies such as *Ppalch'isan ch'ŏnyŏ* (*Partisan Girl*, 1954) and *Ch'unhyangjŏn* (*Tale of Ch'unhyang*, 1959). A supporting actress in *Sinhonbubu* is Mun Yebong (1917–1999). Mun is a seminal figure in the history of Korean cinema. She was in the first sound movie in Korea, also *Ch'unhyangjŏn*, released in 1935, and starred in *Nae kohyang*, the first movie in North Korea. Mun had a long career and earned the title of People's Actress in 1982. *Sinhonbubu* tells the story of a couple who are facing the issue of advancing one's career and starting a family. The husband, Yŏngch'ŏl, wants to be the best train engineer and help build socialism, but he also wants a traditional Korean family with the wife as a homemaker. Ŭnsil wants to be a devoted wife, but she knows the importance of building a new country. She is motivated by her friends still working alongside men, and she vows to return to work. The couple gets into a long and bitter fight, which damages Yŏnch'ŏl's career and makes Ŭnsil doubt the institution of marriage. In the end, however, the couple realizes that building socialism starts with revolution within the household. Ŭnsil becomes a dutiful wife as well as a factory worker, and Yŏnch'ŏl carries out a public self-criticism and promises to change his ways. For the audience, *Sinhonbubu* offers a simple message: the grand vision of socialism starts with the individual and inside the home.

The screen was one effective and entertaining way to constantly educate the public. This cinematic mission became more concretized in the 1970s with the publication of Kim Jong Il's (Kim Chŏngil, 1942–2011) *The Theory of Cinematic Art* in 1973. Kim Jong Il had started his political career in the party propaganda department and was keenly interested in using various art forms as political instruments. *The Theory of Cinematic Art* became the ultimate guide to North Korean filmmakers, and the practice continues today. The foundation of this book is not Soviet film theory but the ideological philosophy of Juche (*Chuch'e*). The creation of Juche is credited to North Korea's founding leader Kim Il Sung (Kim Ilsŏng, 1912–1994). The main idea of Juche is that all human beings are capable of changing the world through self-reliance, and this capacity is applied to society and government. For Kim Jong Il, movies based on Juche had to properly represent the self-reliant spirit of ordinary people and simultaneously offer a utopian vision of a better world. This formula is strictly followed even today. From outside of North Korea, having such a theory amounts to censorship and curtailment of artistic freedom, unavoidably leading to bad movie making. While the lack of artistic freedom in North Korea is a major impediment for its movie industry, what makes a good movie is an extremely difficult question. Money and artistic freedom do not necessarily make for good movies, and even American production companies follow certain rules in the plot or in the overall message.

North Korea's strict codes in movie making do not mean that only a certain type of movie is made. The genres in North Korean cinema range from comedy and war movies to sports and fantasy movies. An interesting fantasy movie is *Pulgasari*, released in 1985. The title refers to an iron-eating monster that grows up to destroy the village that raised it. The movie was a joint production with Japan's Toho Production Company, the company that created Godzilla. (Kim Jong Il was a fan of Godzilla movies.) The director is Shin Sang Ok (Sin Sangok, 1926–2006), a prolific director who started making movies in South Korea. In 1978 he went to North Korea and began a second career in the socialist country, making seven movies with Kim Jong Il as producer. When Shin and Choi Eun Hee (Ch'oe Ŭnhŭi, 1926–), a famous actress and his former wife, were forced to stay in North Korea in

1986, they sought asylum in the United States while visiting Vienna for a film festival. *Pulgasari* is his most famous work in North Korea and has since gained fans throughout the world, mostly for its campiness and as kitsch. Along with *Pulgasari*, many North Korean movies can be easily found on the Internet.

The North Korean movie with the most international screenings in history is the 2012 movie *Comrade Kim Goes Flying*. It is about a rural mining worker who follows her dream to become a famous acrobat. One reason for the attention is that the movie is made by production companies from North Korea, the United Kingdom, and Belgium. Perhaps the day will come when the world's moviegoers will have the choice of a North Korean movie for a matinee.

Cheehyung Harrison Kim

See also: Popular Music, North Korea (Chapter 1: Popular Music)

Further Reading

Armstrong, Charles K. 2003. "The Cultural Cold War in Korea, 1945–1950." *The Journal of Korean Studies* 62, no. 1: 71–99.

Chung, Steven. 2014. *Split Screen Korea: Shin Sang-ok and Postwar Cinema*. Minneapolis: University of Minnesota Press.

Kim, Cheehyung. 2012. "Total, Thus Broken: *Chuch'e Sasang* and North Korea's Terrain of Subjectivity." *The Journal of Korean Studies* 17, no. 1: 69–96.

Kim, Kyung Hyun, and Youngmin Choe, eds. 2014. *The Korean Popular Culture Reader*. Durham, NC: Duke University Press.

POPULAR MOVIES, AUSTRALIA

Popular Australian movies at the Australian cinema box office include comedies, musicals, and adventure films, all with strong creative influences from classical Hollywood and international cinema. The horror genre also has a history of popularity in Australia, with the Mad Max, Wolf Creek, and SAW series originating in Australia.

The 10 most popular Australian-made movies at the Australian theatrical cinema box office are *Crocodile Dundee* (1986), *Australia* (2008), *Babe* (1995), *Happy Feet* (2006), *Moulin Rouge!* (2001), *The Great Gatsby* (2013), *Crocodile Dundee II* (1988), *Strictly Ballroom* (1992), *Red Dog* (2011), and *The Dish* (2000).

Comedian Paul Hogan stars in, and cowrote, two of the top-10 Australian movies. The No. 1 movie, *Crocodile Dundee* (1986) is a classic "fish out of water" romantic-comedy-adventure story of an American reporter, Sue Charlton (played by Linda Kozlowski), who travels to outback Australia to meet a famed crocodile poacher, Mick "Crocodile" Dundee (played by Paul Hogan). Sue invites Mick back to New York City, where they fall in love and his "bushman" skills allow him to solve their problems in unexpected and humorous ways. The film was nominated for an Oscar for Best Writing and also won various major awards. The film's story bears a resemblance to Frank Capra's classic *Mr. Deeds Goes to Town* (1936) and the real-life survival story of Australian outback bushman Rodney Ansell. Cowriter and star of the movie Paul Hogan had previously enjoyed a successful career as a television comedian, playing lovable laconic larrikin Aussie characters similar to Mick "Crocodile" Dundee, in *The Paul Hogan Show* in the 1970s. The successful sequel to *Crocodile Dundee* (1986), and seventh most popular Australian movie, *Crocodile Dundee II* followed in 1988, with a story line picking up one year later: Sue is pursued by Colombian drug barons in New York for incriminating photographic evidence; Mick takes her to his ranch in Australia and uses his outback survival skills to defeat the gangsters. A third film in the franchise, *Crocodile Dundee in Los Angeles* (2001) was not as successful either critically or commercially yet still makes the Australian top-100 list at No. 34.

Director-writer Baz Luhrmann is creatively involved in four of the top-10 movies. His first feature film, *Strictly Ballroom* (1992), is a musical romantic comedy about competitive ballroom dancing told in classic Hollywood cinema style reminiscent of Busby Berkeley and Fred Astaire–Ginger Rogers movies and intercut with *cinéma vérité* mockumentary footage of interviews with key characters. Luhrmann's *Moulin Rouge!* (2001) is a visually spectacular opera, Bollywood, and Greek tragedy–inspired "jukebox musical" dance romance, starring Australian actress Nicole Kidman and Scottish actor Ewan McGregor. It tells the tragic love story of a poet, a courtesan, and a jealous duke at the Paris Moulin Rouge cabaret in 1899. The movie won Oscars for Best Art Direction and Best Costume Design. Previously, American filmmaker John Huston cowrote and directed a similar musical dance dramedy, *Moulin Rouge* (1952), based on the novel by Pierre La Mure, about the life of French artist Henri de Toulouse-Lautrec (1864–1901).

The second most popular movie, *Australia* (2008), also cowritten and directed by Luhrmann, is an epic historical romance set during World War II in the style of classic Hollywood epics such as *Gone with the Wind* (1939) and Howard Hawks's *Red River* (1948). The film tells the story of an English aristocrat (Nicole Kidman) who inherits a property in Australia and with the help of a cattle drover (Hugh Jackman) must drive her cattle herd overland in outback Australia, ultimately experiencing the WWII Japanese aerial bombing of the coastal Australian town of Darwin. Luhrmann's fourth film in the top-10 list, *The Great Gatsby* (2013), is an adaptation of F. Scott Fitzgerald's classic 1925 novel and stars Leonardo DiCaprio, Carey Mulligan, and Australian actor Joel Edgerton. Four previous film adaptations had been produced of *The Great Gatsby*, in 1926, 1949, 1974, and 2000.

Two films in the top-10 list involve George Miller, also the writer-director of the iconic postapocalyptic Mad Max films (1979, 1981, 1985, 2015). *Babe* (1995), produced and cowritten by Miller, is an adaptation of a 1983 children's novel, *The Sheep-Pig* by Dick King-Smith. Set in rural England, the film tells the story of a pig raised by sheepdogs who learns to herd sheep. Miller also cowrote and directed the computer-animated family musical *Happy Feet* (2006), a Pixar-style movie featuring the voice of comedian Robin Williams (1951–2014). It tells the story of an emperor penguin in Antarctica who, unlike the others, cannot sing but is an excellent tap dancer. The film won the Best Animated Feature Oscar in 2007. It should be noted that there are two famous Australian film directors named George Miller: one, born in 1945, directed the Mad Max movie series and was also involved in creating the Oscar-winning *Babe* and *Happy Feet* movies. The other, George T. Miller, born in 1943, directed *The Man from Snowy River* (1982), another top-100 Australian movie, costarring Kirk Douglas in dual roles and based on the famous Australian poem by A. B. "Banjo" Paterson. As an adaptation of a famous poem to a movie, the latter movie also bears some similarities to D. W. Griffith's *Enoch Arden* (1911).

The ninth most popular movie is the adventure comedy *Red Dog* (2011), directed by Kriv Stenders, an adaptation of the novel *Red Dog* (2002) by Louis de Bernières. The novel, in turn, is loosely based on the true story of a Kelpie/cattle dog mix nicknamed Red Dog, who hitched rides around outback mining regions of Western Australia in the 1970s in search of his long-lost master. Similar American movies include *Homeward Bound* and *The Incredible Journey* (1963, 1993).

The tenth most popular Australian movie is *The Dish* (2000), a historical dramedy loosely based on the true story of how the radio telescope at Parkes Observatory in rural Australia was used to relay NASA radio signals and live television footage during the 1969 *Apollo 11* moon landing. The film was cocreated by Working Dog Productions, an experienced team of successful Australian television comedy writers and performers, as indeed were the creators behind the Crocodile Dundee series. Critics viewed *The Dish* (2000) as a typically charming, heartwarming, and laconically witty Australian comedy drama, with a story line somewhat similar to the movie *Apollo 13* (1995).

Other popular Australian movies at the Australian box office vary widely in genre, from quirky comedies: *The Adventures of Priscilla, Queen of the Desert* (1994), *Muriel's Wedding* (1994), *The Castle* (1997), and *Kenny* (2006); to historical epics *Picnic at Hanging Rock* (1975), *The Man from Snowy River* (1982), *Phar Lap* (1983), *Ned Kelly* (2003), and *Ten Canoes* (2006); to war movies *Gallipoli* (1981), *Breaker Morant* (1980), *Kokoda* (2006), *Beneath Hill 60* (2010), and *Tomorrow, When the War Began* (2010).

Various Australian movie directors have also made the transition to directing popular movies in the United States, including Peter Weir, Bruce Beresford, Jane Campion, Mel Gibson, Gillian Armstrong, Phillip Noyce, and Stuart Beattie. Some have dubbed these transcultural movie directors "Americauteurs," a *portmanteau* term combining the words "America" and "auteurs."

Top-Grossing Movies Overall in Australia

Top-grossing movies historically in Australia include *Gone with the Wind* (1940), *The Sound of Music* (1965), *Star Wars* (1977), *Grease* (1978), *E.T., The Extra-Terrestrial* (1982), *Titanic* (1997), *Harry Potter and the Sorcerer's Stone* (2001), the Lord of the Rings trilogy (2001, 2002, 2003), and *Avatar* (2009). *Crocodile Dundee* (1986) is the eighth most popular movie at the Australian box office overall, with *Avatar* (2009) in the No. 1 position. *Crocodile Dundee* is also the 23rd highest return-on-investment (RoI) movie to date internationally, with *Mad Max* (1980) as the second-highest RoI movie.

Historically, the world's first feature-length movie (a film one hour or longer in duration) is the Australian film *The Story of the Kelly Gang* (1906, 60 minutes, also remade in 1910, 70 minutes), a film that portrays the true story of the Australian bushranger (or "outlaw") Edward "Ned" Kelly (Jackson and Shirley 2006). The Kelly Gang was roughly the Australian equivalent of the Hole in the Wall Gang, portrayed in the American movie *Butch Cassidy and the Sundance Kid* (1969). Australia was a pioneer in creating feature-length movies, having already produced 20 of them by 1911, when America's first feature film, *Enoch Arden*, directed by D. W. Griffith, was produced (Adams in Hocking 2006, 200).

J. T. Velikovsky

See also: Popular Novels, Australia (Chapter 2: Books and Contemporary Literature)

Further Reading

Given, J., R. Curtis, and M. McCutcheon. 2013. "Cinema in Australia: An Industry Profile." Hawthorn, AU: Swinburne University of Technology. http://researchbank.swinburne.edu.au/vital/access/manager/Repository/swin:32121. Accessed March 26, 2016.

Hocking, Scott, and Bill Collins, eds. 2006. *100 Greatest Films of Australian Cinema*. Richmond, AU: Scribal Publishing.

Jackson, Sally and Graham Shirley. 2006. *The Story of the Kelly Gang*. National Film and Sound Archive, Australia.

Murray, S., Raffaele Caputo, and Australian Film Commission. 1993. *Australian Film 1978–1992: A Survey of Theatrical Features*. Melbourne, AU: Oxford University Press, in association with the Australian Film Commission and *Cinema Papers*.

Sabine, James, and Australian Film Institute, eds. 1995. *A Century of Australian Cinema*. Port Melbourne, AU: Mandarin.

SHAKESPEARE IN BOLLYWOOD

William Shakespeare is such a popular playwright that he has accumulated more than 410 adaptations of his plays for cinema and television worldwide. There are two main reasons behind the popularity of Shakespeare in Bollywood, the Indian movie industry based in Mumbai (formerly Bombay). Primarily, it is due to the long span of British rule in India, resulting in the popularity of the English language, and English becoming almost an Indian language in the Indian subcontinent. From the time of early schooling, Shakespeare is prescribed in textbooks, and so the metaplots of Shakespeare stand rooted in the psyche of Indian audiences. Indianization of Shakespearean plots thus becomes a matter of interest among the audience of Bollywood cinema. Giving Shakespeare an Indian touch also negotiates the postcolonial identity of the Indian masses. Secondly, the universal appeal of Shakespearean plots and his artistic brilliance give him seminal importance in the Indian entertainment industry. Shakespearean plots touch almost every aspect of human emotion and present harsh realities of life emerging out of emotional imbalances and misunderstandings in the lives of their characters. In other words, the universality of Shakespearean themes—for example, the indecision of King Lear, the madness of Hamlet, the jealousy of Othello, the ambition of Macbeth—are eternal problems of humanity, and with their manifestation and theatrical presentation a person from any culture can easily relate to the work.

In Bollywood, Shakespearean tragedies have received major attention and positive reception, notably in the recent work of director Vishal Bhardwaj. *Macbeth* has been made into *Maqbool* (2003), directed by Bhardwaj. The medieval setting of *Macbeth* has been cast into the world of current organized crime. Although this is a great departure from the original story line, still the actors, like Pankaj Kapoor, Irfan Khan, Tabu, and Masumeh Makhija, make the film worthwhile. *Othello* inspired Bhardwaj to make *Omkara* (2006), casting Ajay Devgn, Kareena Kapoor, Konkona Sen Sharma, Saif Ali Khan, Vivek Oberoi, Naseeruddin Shah, and Bipasha Basu. *Hamlet* has been adapted into Bhardwaj's *Haider* (2014), a political drama. The film is set in Kashmir, and the young actor, Shahid Kapoor, delivers forceful soliloquies in the title role. Tabu and Kay Kay Menon also star, and the film has received major accolades. Another tragedy, *Romeo and Juliet*, has several Bollywood remakes, including *Bobby* (1973), *Ek duuje ke liye* (1981), *Sanam teri kasam* (1982), *Qayamat se qayamat tak* (1988), *Saudagar* (1991), *Ishaqzaade* (2012), *Issaq* (2013), and *Goliyon ki raasleela: ram-leela* (2013).

Bobby is a trendsetting film that introduced the concept of teenage romance in Bollywood. It is also important for its use of the rich–poor gap in the emotional and dramatic realm, and it is set in Mumbai. *Ek duuje ke liye* (*Made for Each Other*, 1981) is directed by K. Balachander and came to Bollywood via the Telugu, or southeast Indian, film *Maro charitra* (1978). This work also shows the clash of cultures in the context of a love story. Vasu, the protagonist, has Tamil (southern Indian or Sri Lankan) origins and loves Sapna, a woman from North India. Cultural clashes create obstacles to their love and run through the plot in this imagining of *Romeo and Juliet*. Narendra Bedi directed and Barkha Roy–produced *Sanam teri kasam* (1982), starring Kamal Haasan, Reena Roy, Kader Khan, and Ranjeet. It is the story of protagonist Sunil, who is in search of his missing father. *Sanam teri kasam* is widely known in Bollywood for its musical numbers like "Nisha, nisha, nisha," "Sheeshe ke gharon mein," "Kitne bhi tu kar le sitam," and others. Mansoor Khan directed *Qayamat se qayamat tak* (1988), which is also a musical and romantic blockbuster. Directed by Subhash Ghai, *Saudagar* (1991) stars the two veteran actors Dilip Kumar and Raaj Kumar in the lead roles. The influence of Shakespeare's characters of Romeo and Juliet is evident in the actor Mandhaari's role, which is a parallel to Shakespeare's Friar Laurence. A romantic thriller, *Ishaqzaade* (2012), also known as *Born to Hate . . . Destined to Love*, received critical acclaim and box-office success. It is the fervent story of two lovers from different communities, and thus it can easily be compared to *Romeo and Juliet*. A 2013 Manish Tiwary–directed romantic film, *Issaq*, also runs parallel to *Romeo and Juliet*. Also in 2013, Sanjay Leela Bhansali directed *Goliyon ki raasleela* in yet another interpretation of the classic love story.

Shakespeare's *The Comedy of Errors* came to Bollywood as the musical *Do dooni char* (1968), which was an interpretation of the Bengali film *Bhrantibilas* (1963). It is a story of a banker and his associate who travel to a small city on business, where they become involved in a case of mistaken identity. Another Bollywood film based on *The Comedy of Errors* is *Angoor* (1982), written and directed by Gulzar. It is a story of two sets of identical twins, which leads to confusion, melodrama, and comedy. Neil Bhoopalam, Tara Sharma, Koel Puri, and Purab Kohli star in director Sharat Katariya's interpretation of *A Midsummer Night's Dream*, *10ml Love* (2010). It is a romantic comedy with a love quadrangle, which includes magic and madness cast with medieval effects, though it was ultimately not a hugely successful film.

Most adaptations of Shakespeare have been made in the postindependence and the postcolonial (after 1947) phase of Indian cinema, although his plays were well received in theaters before independence. Shakespeare's introduction to India was part of the 19th-century English education mission of Thomas Babington Macaulay (1800–1859). Macaulayism was a significant part of the British civilizing mission. The popularity of Shakespeare in Indian cinema before independence was relatively low. There are two major reasons for this. First, before independence, the cinematic techniques of Indian cinema were not very advanced. It was the beginning of Indian cinema, and at that time more artistic and cinematic emphasis was placed on Indian issues and mythology. Second, adaptation is a precise and crucial act. Here the director has to become "glocal," combining aspects of the global and the local; on the one hand, the director has to negotiate global expectations, and on the other hand, she or he has to address the expectations of the local masses.

The postmodern phase of artistic production and cultural studies opened new vistas of experimentation for filmmakers and other artists. In this phase, adaptations became much more popular. The trend of adapting world literature in Indian cinema has been influenced by the advancement of techniques and the enthusiasm of the directors to play with the original texts; the open windows of creativity in the phase of liberalization, privatization, and globalization; and the concept of the free market. Shakespeare has received a favorable reception in the cultural expressions of almost every language of India.

Alka Singh

See also: Bollywood Gender Stereotypes

Further Reading

Chakravarti, Paromita. 2003. "Modernity, Postcoloniality, and Othello: The Case of Saptapadi." In *Remaking Shakespeare: Performance across Media, Genres, and Cultures.* Ed. Pascale Aebischer, Edward J. Easche, and Nigel Wheale, 39–55. New York: Palgrave Macmillan.

Kendal, Geoffrey. 1986. *The Shakespearewallah.* London: Sidgwick & Jackson.

Trivedi, Poonam. 2005. "'It Is the Bloody Business Which Informs Thus . . .': Local Politics and Performative Praxis, *Macbeth* in India." In *World-wide Shakespeares: Local Appropriations in Film and Performance.* Ed. Sonia Massai, 47–56. New York: Routledge.

Trivedi, Poonam. 2007. "Filmi; Shakespeare." *Literature/Film Quarterly* 35, no. 2: 148–158.

Trivedi, Poonam, and Dennis Bartholomeusz. 2005. *India's Shakespeare: Translation, Interpretation, and Performance.* Delhi: Pearson Education India.

Yadava, Mukesh. 2014. "Domesticating Shakespeare: A Study of Indian Adaptation of Shakespeare in Popular Culture." *European Journal of English Language and Literature Studies* 2, no. 3 (September): 48–58.

Chapter 4: Television and Radio

Introduction

While some, having come of age in an era of the global Internet, may think that television and radio are fading as traditional media, they both continue to be hugely important around the world, and especially in Asia and Oceania. As with other aspects of popular culture, both television and radio vary widely across these regions. Some governments exercise strict control of the airwaves and the networks, while other countries experience television and radio in an environment of relative freedom and diversity. In some countries of the region, a huge spectrum of news and entertainment can be found on offer on television and radio, while in others, poverty or unstable political conditions prevent the production of, and access to, as broad an array of television and radio programming.

Though relatively recent as media, with just under a century of history, public television and radio have flourished as modes of communication, propaganda, and entertainment. The advent of new media, from cell phones to the Internet and its many platforms, has limited the centrality of television and radio as modes of effective transmission of news and political messages, just as the newspaper was challenged but not completely eclipsed by television and radio. Still, for many, television and radio, and their programming as carried through new media, continue to shape public opinion and in many ways define and reflect popular and political culture.

Like the country that produces it, television and radio in India are hugely diverse and rich in different cultural traditions. The many languages spoken in India are reflected in television and radio broadcasting. Soap operas and situation comedies (sitcoms) delight Indian audiences, though they also draw criticism for their conservative depiction of gender roles, much like some Bollywood films. Historical epics are also popular in India, including the biographies of famous figures like Ashoka the Great (304–232 BCE), the Mauryan dynasty ruler who converted to Buddhism during his reign and propagated the religion throughout his realm. The great Hindu texts, the *Ramayana* and the *Mahabharata* (from which the *Bhagavad Gita* is a selection), are also the subjects of much-loved and even revered historical serial dramas.

In China, the soap opera and the historical drama are blended into one, with melodramatic tales of the dynastic past as common subjects for some of the most popular Chinese television programming. Dramas depicting the Qing era (1644–1911) feature the famous queue hairstyle for men, who sport a long braided pigtail and a shaven forelock. Ming-era dramas (1368–1644) feature leading men with long, flowing locks, in the style of that time. In both dynasties, television producers portray women in the lavish splendor of the palace, sometimes selecting the imperial harem as the setting for the most salacious drama. These historical dramas, produced either in Hong Kong, Taiwan, or the mainland People's Republic of China (PRC), are wildly popular in Chinese diaspora communities around the world, and a visitor to a Chinese enclave in any country is very likely to witness them playing in teahouses, restaurants, or shops.

Soap operas produced in South Korea have become something of a global phenomenon as well in recent years, but they have also reached beyond their own cultural boundaries, becoming popular among diverse communities in neighboring and distant countries. As a major driver of the massive Korean Wave, or K-Wave, beginning in the late 1990s, Korean soap operas have led the way for Korean popular culture to spread not only beyond its borders but also beyond Korean consumers. Japanese television is also popular beyond its borders and its cultural categories.

Of course the juggernaut of American popular culture plays an important role in the television and radio of many regions of Asia and Oceania. Some countries, like China, Vietnam, and others, have television and radio infrastructures that continue to have relatively strong control of the airwaves. For many countries, and not only authoritarian ones, governments have historically limited the amount of foreign programming on their airwaves, and this often targeted American shows that might otherwise dominate ratings. (This would be due in part to the American shows' popularity and relatively high production value but also to the ability of powerful U.S. producers to effectively export their shows and infiltrate foreign markets.) It is also important to note that U.S. culture is often filtered through television adaptations and re-creations. Singing competitions, for example, received their impetus from similar British and American programs, but in the past decade they have taken on local characteristics and local relevance. American programs like *Friends* or *Two and a Half Men*, for example, have been hugely popular in many countries of Asia and Oceania.

Radio and television have also historically been means for political expression of all kinds. Of course, powerful political parties and governments realized early in the history of radio and television how important these media could be in shaping public opinion, defining political questions, inciting fear or outrage, and organizing the loyal among their audiences. The label of "propaganda" for this type of broadcasting has a negative connotation in the English language, but "political advocacy" may be a softer term for a similar practice. If politically driven media are too heavy-handed, as is sometimes the case in the PRC, audiences will learn to decode the biased messages and seek accurate reporting elsewhere. News outlets in all parts of the world, including and perhaps most effectively in the United States, use their platforms to spread ideas that are compatible with the worldviews of those who control the platforms. If an advertiser, for example, sees its product criticized on a program that it sponsors, surely it will withdraw funding. In some but not all political environments, it is rare for a government or political party to be ridiculed on a media platform that it controls. There are exceptions to this general statement, but in India, China, Australia, the United States, and other countries, many radio and television outlets are explicitly biased in the news and entertainment that they permit to be aired on their platforms. Political parties and aspiring politicians in India use both news and dramatic television to promote their causes and careers. In Australia (and globally) media mogul Rupert Murdoch (1931–) controls vast amounts of media platforms, from print to television, and often with his subordinate programmers uses this media to promote his political agenda. In China, China Central Television (CCTV) tightly controls the news and entertainment broadcast on its many channels.

With the advent of various new media, like podcasting, news-aggregating websites, and streaming content, the consumer can choose with more precision her or his preferred sources of information and entertainment. This may put more power in the hands of the consumer, who can perhaps avoid the media saturation of conventional broadcasting on the airwaves of television and radio. In reality, after an initial lag, conventional news outlets have learned to make the most of these new media platforms as well. In fact, new media avenues have allowed the more targeted delivery of television and radio programming to its intended audiences. This development has moved viewers and listeners, as well as news outlets, away from news reporting and toward opinion-driven "infotainment," which, instead of truly edifying its audience, has the potential to simply reinforce the views of the audience it targets.

Jeremy A. Murray and Kathleen M. Nadeau

Further Reading

Keane, Michael, and Albert Moran. 2009. *Television across Asia: TV Industries, Programme Formats and Globalisation.* London: Routledge.

Mehta, Nalin. 2015. *Behind a Billion Screens: What Television Tells Us about Modern India.* Noida, IN: HarperCollins India.

Moran, Albert, and Chris Keating. 2009. *The A to Z of Australian Radio and Television.* Lanham, MD: Scarecrow Press (Rowman & Littlefield).

Zhu, Ying. 2012. *Two Billion Eyes: The Story of China Central Television.* New York: The New Press.

DATING SHOWS, CHINA

In recent years, with rising concern for the unmarried women and men in big cities in China, an entire industry providing various products and services to help people solve dating and marital problems has emerged. Against this background, several dating shows appeared on Chinese television screens in 2010 and became a primetime programming staple.

In this wave of Chinese dating shows, the most popular and influential one is *If You Are the One* (*Feichengwurao* 非诚勿扰), which airs on the Jiangsu Provincial TV Station. Literally translated into "if you are not sincere, please do not bother to come" with an interesting tongue-in-cheek effect, the show's name, *Feichengwurao*, is borrowed from a popular 2008 romantic comedy directed by Feng Xiaogang in which an unlikely couple comes together through a tortuous yet hilarious path of blind dates. Inspired by the Australian show *Taken Out*, *If You Are the One* adapts the former's basic format: five times each episode, a new guy presents himself to a lineup of 24 women through a few previously prepared video clips and then takes questions from them. The women decide whether they should dismiss him by switching the podium light off. After three rounds of interaction, if there are still lights kept on for the male, he survives the trial and has a chance to pick a woman for a date.

Produced by Jiangsu TV Station, the first episode of *If You Are the One* was aired on January 15, 2010, and the show only took a couple of weeks to earn one of the highest ratings nationwide. In the first half of 2010, *If You Are the One* broke ratings records with around 50 million people watching every episode, an audience second only to the China Central Television Evening News Broadcast. The popularity of *If You Are the One* helped to create quite a few copycats. In the first half of 2010, 12 new dating shows were launched by Chinese provincial satellite TV stations, with similar, though not identical, formats. For instance, in *Love to Love* (*Aiqing lianliankan* 爱情连连看) on the Zhejiang Provincial TV Station, female contestants were selected on the spot by computer screening; in *Marriage Battle* (*Hunyin baoweizhan* 婚姻保卫战), another dating show produced by the Zhejiang Provincial TV Station, all the female participants recruited were divorcees; in *Bed of Roses* (*Chenxinruyi* 称心如意) on the Hunan Provincial TV Station, contestants' mothers were invited to join the show to help their sons or daughters pick their dates.

The runaway success of *If You Are the One* also generated its own publicity. There were behind-the-scenes shows about its production, special columns in newspapers offering updates, and online fan clubs following every word, whisper, and clue therein. Having achieved fame due to the high exposure of the show, several contestants were categorized as "celebrities" by the Baidu Encyclopedia, a web-based encyclopedia provided by the largest Chinese search engine, Baidu.

If You Are the One was at the same time the center of controversy. It was reported that some participants are actors and actresses hired by the show, hence diminishing its claim to authenticity. It was also revealed that some successful dates were just for show and that a few newly made couples split up right after they came off the stage. Furthermore, some of the Chinese media's opinion makers and moral guardians, including famous columnists, educationists, media commentators, and government officials, raised their voice against the prevailing materialism exhibited in this show. For example, Ma Nuo, a female participant, rejected the offer of a bicycle ride from an unemployed suitor by overtly claiming: "I would rather cry in a BMW than laugh on a bicycle." Another contestant by the name of Zhu Zhenfang refused to shake hands with a male contestant, explaining that her basic criteria for a future boyfriend was that he must earn at least 200,000 Chinese yuan (approximately US$32,700) per month and own a mansion, which the man apparently did not measure up to. Millions of enraged Chinese netizens not only nicknamed Ma and Zhu "BMW Lady" and "Mansion Lady" but also conducted mass Internet searches for their private information. Succumbing to tremendous public pressure, both Ma and Zhu ended up ignominiously quitting the show. Such examples of blatant materialism exhibited in the show aroused heated debates in online forums, newspapers, and TV reports, culminating in a tightening of censorship on Chinese dating shows in general.

Consequently, in July 2010 the "Notice on Further Regulating TV Programs about Marriage, Love and Friendship" and the "Notice on Enhancing the Management of TV Programs on Intimacy and Romance" were released by the State Administration of Radio, Film and Television, criticizing *If You Are the One* for "deviating from the socialist core value system and damaging the image of broadcast media." According to the regulations, the following aspects should now be incorporated when producing and broadcasting dating shows:

1. The identity of the participants should be carefully checked, and identity fraud is strictly prohibited.
2. Instead of focusing on "the second generation of the rich," or actors/actresses and models, participants should be selected from a wider range of the population, and morally provocative participants should not be invited.
3. Dating shows should be strictly censored before broadcasting and rebroadcasting, and live broadcasting is not allowed.
4. Vulgar topics involving sex, materialism, and other unhealthy, incorrect viewpoints on marriage should be avoided.
5. Moral guidance should be provided to the participants, and discretion should be shown in choosing the host/hostess.

Obliged to meet the censorship and propaganda demands of the government, the Jiangsu Provincial TV Station promptly responded through the official website of *The People's Daily* on June 10, pronouncing its strong support for the guideline made by the media authority and expressing its resolution to elevate the quality of *If You Are the One* according to these guidelines. Since then, tremendous changes have gradually taken place both in terms of the format and content in order to downplay the materialistic overtones of the show. With decreasing societal debates, the fad of Chinese dating shows has gradually faded away. Programs such as *Marriage Battle*, *Bed of Roses*, and others have been canceled due to unsatisfactory ratings. Since 2012, ratings of *If You Are the One* have been trounced by new reality shows such as *The Voice of China* (*Zhongguo haoshengyin* 中国好声音), *I Am a Singer* (*Wo shi geshou* 我是歌手), *Where Are We Going, Dad?* (*Baba qunaer* 爸爸去哪儿), and others.

Siyu Chen

See also: TV Singing Competitions, China

Further Reading

Chen, Siyu 陈思宇. Forthcoming. "Disciplining Desiring Subjects through the Remodeling of Masculinity—A Case Study of a Chinese Reality Dating Show." *Modern China*.

Kong, Shuyu. 2013. "Are You the One? The Competing Public Voices of China's Post-1980s Generation." In *Restless China*. Ed. Perry Link, Richard P. Madsen, and Paul G. Pickowicz, 127–148. Lanham, MD: Rowman & Littlefield Publishers.

Luo, Wei and Zhen Sun. 2014. "Are You the One? China's TV Dating Shows and the Sheng Nü's Predicament." *Feminist Media Studies*, ahead-of-print: 1–18.

Wu, Jing. 2012. "Post-socialist Articulationof Gender Positions: Contested Public Sphere of Reality Dating Shows." In *Women and the Media in Asia: The Precarious Self*. Ed. Youna Kim, 220–236. Hampshire, UK: Palgrave Macmillan.

HAKKA SISTERS, HONG KONG

Hakka Sisters, also known as *Hakka Women* (客家女人), is a popular Hong Kong TV series that was first aired on the Internet by the TV station HKTV in early 2015. The original name of the series is *Never to Be a Hongkonger Again*, which seems to echo the sensational but also highly sensitive book entitled *Never to Be a Chinese Again* by the writer Zukang Zhong. As the book heavily criticizes the authoritarian regime in mainland China and also the many flaws of Chinese culture the writer perceives, the TV series tells an equally poignant story about Hong Kong–mainland relations.

The series is a family-oriented drama that features the sibling rivalry between two sisters of the Hakka ethnicity from a southern Chinese village near Dongguan. Leung Mei Hang (the younger sister, played by Maggie Cheung) and Leung Mei Tin (the older sister, played by Prudence Liew) are living a hard life with their mother in a small rural village in China in the 1970s and 1980s. One day they are given an opportunity to live with their uncle, who illegally escaped to Hong Kong under the Mao regime, but only one of them can be sent to Hong Kong and potentially become a Hong Kong citizen. In the late 1970s, mainland China was just starting to implement Deng Xiaoping's economic reform, and mainland Chinese people were just starting to see the tremendous gap between Hong Kong and the mainland in terms of living standards. Therefore, the opportunity to become a Hong Kong citizen has life-changing significance for the two sisters. Even though they promise each other that their sororal love will remain as strong as ever, this opportunity for only one of them has nonetheless put a wedge between the sisters. Mei Tin is first selected by their mother as she considers her to be more mature for handling the competitive life in Hong Kong, but after this decision is announced Mei Hang tells a lie about being sexually assaulted by a pervert in the village and this changes their mother's mind and she sends Mei Hang to Hong Kong instead without even telling Mei Tin.

Both sisters go through a difficult time growing up in their respective environments after separation, but both manage to become successful women. As the series moves back to its contemporary times, Mei Hang is now a very able office lady working in an influential PR consultant firm while Mei Tin has become a rich businesswoman in Dongguan and also the representative of her village. However, the long separation and the drastically different nurturing environments of the two sisters have resulted in their very different personalities. Highly educated, arrogant, and fussy, Mei Hang seems to embody all the stereotypical traits associated with "Kong Girl" (港女). She is very particular about professionalism as she scolds her underlings for their "horrendous English," and she also despises almost everything associated with the mainland. For example, in one scene that is often singled out and shared by many Hongkongers on the Internet, Mei Hang dines at a local café but soon becomes very angry as she sees all the simplified Chinese characters on the menu instead of the traditional characters that are used in Hong Kong. Interestingly, while she scolds the waiter for the café's use of mainland Chinese vocabularies instead of Hong Kong Chinese vocabularies, a lot of the examples she cites are actually loanwords from English in the first place, such as "salad" (Hong Kong Chinese: 沙律, mainland Chinese: 色拉). This sociolinguistic attitude represented in the drama is thus very indicative of the association between Westernization and modernization in East Asia. As mainland China joined the West-dominated neoliberal world order much later than the former British colony Hong Kong, their different degrees of economic development and cultural hybridity have produced a hierarchy of modernity, with Hong Kong perceived as more advanced than China. But as Mei Hang's resentment against the simplified characters shows, Hong Kong's position within this hierarchy is also becoming increasingly unstable, with a fast-developing mainland China. In contrast to Mei Hang, Mei Tin embodies many of the positive and negative traits stereotypically associated with mainland Chinese women of her generation. She is uneducated but tough, strict but also well respected by fellow villagers. She works very hard as a boss for her restaurant and factory but is also very shrewd in her reliance upon "*guanxi*" to solve problems. Since *guanxi* is a problematic form of instrumental social networking that is often attributed to mainland China's loose enforcement of laws and regulations and is also associated with corruption, Mei Hang despises her sister's approach even though sometimes Mei Tin's connections do help Mei Hang secure the projects she wants to do.

Apart from the prominent cultural conflicts between the Hakka sisters, the drama also portrays various other poignant social issues that people of different generations are concerned about in Hong Kong and mainland China. It tells the story of a Hong Kong young man who struggles between his inner desire for social justice and his family's desire for stability and money. It tells Mei Hang's uncle's story, who struggles to pay a hospital placement for his child so he can be a Hong Kong citizen. It also tells of the difficulties Mei Hang has when she has to persuade a Dongguan villager to move out so she can secure a real-estate project in the mainland for her company. Most importantly, while Hong Kong cultural products in the past often portrayed an image of the mainlander as someone who is poor, crass, rude, and unfashionable but innocent, *Hakka Sisters* presents the tremendous changes that have taken place in mainland China in the last 20 years by portraying many of the mainland characters as rich, smart, and still rude but fearfully so. As Mei Tin often comes to Hong Kong to buy luxury goods, and Mei Hang often has to accept projects from mainland China, the increasing level of economic symbiosis is represented in the series. In the 21st century, as the TV series reflects, Hong Kong no longer enjoys a one-way "northbound colonialism" of mainland China through economic investment and cultural dominance but has to rely on money from mainland China to support many of its local industries (Law 2000). Perhaps to recognize the mutual dependence that underlies the conflicts, the ending of the story contains a scene where Mei Hang, now taking over her sister's restaurant, kindly tells a customer who just moved to Dongguan from another province that she should be proud to be a "new Dongguaner." After all, the featuring of the Hakka ethnicity in the series is not without reason: "Hakka" means "guest home" (客家) in Chinese, and the Hakka people embody the identity of the immigrant as historically they moved around many parts of China. No matter whether one moves to Dongguan or Hong Kong, the drama seems to suggest, one should be able to feel at home without compromising one's identity as a guest.

In addition to its moving story line and poignant reflections of Hong Kong society, the success of the series can also be attributed to its timing. The filming of the series started in 2013 when Hong Kong–mainland relations were deteriorating and the Occupy Central Movement was in the making. In late 2014, triggered by the Chinese government's refusal to grant Hong Kong people the democratic right to choose election candidates, Occupy Central broke out and culminated in the famous Umbrella Movement, which has seen the participation of a large number of university students and young workers. As political and cultural conflicts between Hong Kong and the mainland are often intertwined with each other, the many cultural differences between its central characters presented by *Hakka Sisters* resonate well with Hong Kong viewers. The reconciliatory aspects of the series also offer some hope for solution at the interpersonal level. The success of the series has also raised hope for a diversifying force against the enduring dominance of the TV station TVB in the popular TV drama market in Hong Kong.

Flair Donglai Shi

See also: Historical Dramas, China; Television Dramas, Korea

Further Reading

Constable, Nicole. 2005. *Guest People: Hakka Identity in China and Abroad*. Seattle: University of Washington Press.

Law, Wing-Sang. 2000. "Northbound Colonialism: A Politics of Post-PC Hong Kong." *East Asia Cultures Critique* 8, no. 1: 201–233.

Lo, Sonny. 2015. *Hong Kong's Indigenous Democracy: Origins, Evolution and Contentions*. New York: Palgrave Macmillan.

Ma, Jiewei 馬傑偉, and Zhongjian Zeng 曾仲堅. 2010. 影視香港:身份認同的時代變奏 [Hong Kong on Screen: The Changing Times of Identity]. Hong Kong: Chinese University of Hong Kong Press.

Wong, S. C. H., and W. H. Wong. 2015. *TV Dramas in Hong Kong: A History and Industry Analysis*. Los Angeles, CA: Bridge21 Publications.

Zheng, Yongnian. 1999. *Discovering Chinese Nationalism in China: Modernization, Identity, and International Relations*. Cambridge, UK: Cambridge University Press.

HISTORICAL DRAMAS, CHINA

Similar to Western television dramas such as *Game of Thrones* or *True Detective*, Chinese serial television dramas involve multiple characters, have complicated plots, and vary in length. Some are as short as 10 episodes, while others run over 200 episodes. These serial dramas come in a variety of genres, such as comedy, historical, or crime. Historical dramas can be further subdivided into historical reenactment, historical fiction, legends and myths, and martial arts. Since their inception in the 1980s, historical dramas have enjoyed great popularity among both audiences and television producers in China. The richness of China's long history gives screenwriters a large pool of source material to work from as well as greater freedom to explore subjects and themes (such as government corruption or public unrest) that would otherwise invite censorship if depicted in contemporary settin.gs.

The first historical dramas to air in mainland China, following the popularization of television sets in the 1980s, were martial arts serial dramas imported from Hong Kong. Among them were *Huo Yuanjia* (1983), *The Legend of the Condor Heroes* (1983), and *The Return of the Condor Heroes* (1983). These shows enjoyed extremely high reception rates across the mainland, and their theme songs also became instant hits. Some audiences even started learning Cantonese, the regional dialect previously spoken in only Hong Kong and China's Canton Province. China was finally opening its doors to the outside world after a long halt in art production during the 1966–1976 Cultural Revolution. The success of these imported martial arts dramas inspired local directors to turn to historical topics as a source of narrative material for television.

The earliest serial dramas in mainland China were adaptations of China's four greatest classical novels, including *The Dream of the Red Chamber* (1986) and *The Journey to the West* (1988). *The Dream of the Red Chamber* is a 36-episode drama that illustrates the rise and decay of a large feudal family in the mid-18th century during China's Qing dynasty (1644–1912), while *The Journey to the West* is an entertaining fantasy tale of a Buddhist monk who goes on an arduous pilgrimage to India with his three disciples during China's Tang dynasty (618–916 CE) in order to receive Buddhist scriptures to bring back to China. Television producers from this early era were extremely devoted and serious about their work. For example, to ensure accuracy to the original literature, the director of *The Dream of the Red Chamber* recruited some of China's renowned literary scholars to teach the novel to the cast for more than six months prior to filming. Some of the show's leading actors and actresses, who were in their late teens when production began, refer to their three-year filming experience as having attended the "Red Chamber University." Moreover, the 25-episode *Journey to the West* was six years in the making. Upon airing, both dramas enjoyed high viewing rates of over 80 percent across China (Zhong 2010, 48). During the 1990s, two more classical novels, *The Romance of the Three Kingdoms* (1994) and *The Water Margin* (1998), were subsequently produced. Both shows enjoyed immense critical and commercial success. These adaptations of Chinese literature proved that television is a powerful medium to popularize traditional classics.

Following the successful adaptation of the four great literary classics, there was emerging interest in historical reenactment dramas and imperial court dramas in particular. *Wu Zetian* (1995) is a 30-episode drama based on the life of Wu Zetian (624–705 CE), the first and only female emperor in Chinese history. Xiaoqing Liu (1951–), one of China's most highly regarded actresses, played Wu Zetian. Despite being in her forties, Liu successfully played a role that spanned 68 years, from age 14 to 82. This drama was praised for not only its complex story line and Liu's outstanding performance but also its makeup, costumes, and soundtrack. It became a big hit in not only mainland China but also Taiwan and Hong Kong, thereby marking the first time that a mainland Chinese television drama and television star gained mainstream popularity and stardom in Hong Kong and Taiwan.

Various other highly regarded imperial court dramas of the 1990s include *Tang ming huang* (1992), *Yong Zheng Dynasty* (1999), and *Kangxi Dynasty* (2001). Many such imperial enactment dramas explored the theme of anticorruption, thereby allegorizing the contemporary Chinese political system while also promoting nationalism and heroism. These historical enactment dramas became popular among Hong Kong and Taiwanese audiences as well, who praised mainland Chinese producers for their meticulous attention to detail and devotion to historical accuracy.

In 1998 *Huanzhu gege*, a historical fiction drama coproduced by both mainland China and Taiwan, became a massive hit that swept through China, Taiwan, Hong Kong, and other parts of Asia. Based on a novel written by renowned Taiwanese romance writer Qiong Yao (1938–), *Huanzhu gege* is a coming-of-age tale that tells the story of an orphaned girl who becomes a princess by accident after befriending the illegitimate daughter of Qing dynasty emperor Qianlong (1711–1799). Praised for its comedic style and touching romance, the show enjoyed great commercial success. Moreover, its three leading cast members, Vicki Zhao (1976–), Ruby Lin

(1976–), and Bingbing Fan (1981–) became teen idols overnight. Even today, these three actresses are still among China's biggest stars.

Huanzhu gege marked the beginning of an era of Chinese mainlander television megastars and historical dramas that incorporated elements from popular culture. During the previous decade, historical television dramas either stuck close to actual historical figures and events or adapted pieces of classical literature. Starting from the late 1990s, historical fiction became increasingly popular, as there has been a shift in emphasis on the entertainment and commercial value of television shows in China. Many historical dramas adopted a playful style, and they became anachronistic in the sense that characters set in historical times speak and think in a contemporary manner. Such dramas include *Hunchback Liu the Prime Minister* (1994), *Emperor Kangxi Traveling Undercover* (1999), and *The Bronze Teeth/The Eloquent Ji Xiaolan* (2009), all of which starred Guoli Zhang (1955–). Zhang is a film director, actor, and comedian who became renowned for playing Chinese emperors in various Qing dynasty imperial comedies.

In the 2000s, anachronistic historical fiction dramas became even more popular. For example, *Scarlet Heart* (2011) is a television drama based on contemporary Chinese writer Tong Hua's (1982–) novel, which tells the tale of a woman from the 21st century who becomes trapped inside the body of her previous incarnation and gets sent back in time to the Qing dynasty. Today, Chinese historical television dramas have spread across not only Asia but also Western countries. For example, in 2015 *Empress in the Palace* (2011) was introduced to Netflix.

Monica Liu

See also: Documentaries, China (Chapter 3: Film); Television Dramas, Korea

Further Reading

Si, Hongyue 司洪岳. 2012. 关于历史题材电视剧今年持续"升温"现象的原因探析 [An Analysis Regarding Why Historical Chinese Television Dramas Are Persistently Becoming More Popular This Year]. *Dongnan Chuanbo* 东南传播 8: 113–114.

Zhong, Xueping. 2010. *Mainstream Culture Refocused: Television Drama, Society, and the Production of Meaning in Reform-Era China*. Honolulu: University of Hawai'i Press.

Zhu, Ying. 2008. *Television in Post-Reform China: Serial Dramas, Confucian Leadership and the Global Television Market*. New York: Routledge.

LOTTERY SHOW, PHILIPPINES

The Philippine government has a monopoly on lottery operations and runs this through a national agency, the Philippine Charity Sweepstakes Office (PCSO), created by law on October 30, 1934. Thirty percent of the net retail receipts from PCSO's lottery operations go to the agency's charity fund, from which funds are allotted to agency programs related to health and medical care assistance, including hospitalizations, treatments like chemotherapy and dialysis, ambulance donation, medical equipment donation, hospital facility upgrading, and other such programs.

The Philippine Charity Sweepstakes Office's mandate is to raise and provide funds for these charitable programs, which it does at present by running lottery games, among them the variants of online Philippine Lottery, more commonly known as the PCSO Lotto. For transparency, draws for the lotto and PCSO's other number games are televised: the evening draw (9:00 p.m.) is aired live, while the morning (11:00 a.m.) and afternoon (4:00 p.m.) draws are filmed live and the results shown as edited video material on the evening program.

Background of the Philippine Lottery Draw TV Show

The first online lottery draw was held on March 8, 1995, and broadcast over the state channel, People's Television Network Inc. (PTNI or PTV). There was only one game at the time—the Lotto 6/42 for Luzon (one of the three main clusters of islands of the Philippines—the others are the Visayas and Mindanao), and the lotto draw was held every Tuesday. After a year, draws were expanded to include the Visayas and Mindanao.

The first show host was veteran TV presenter Tina Revilla, later alternating with Cathy Villar in the late 1990s. In 2000, when the Superlotto 6/49 was introduced, actress Timmy Cruz was hired to host the Sunday draw TV program.

In 2003, then-president Gloria Macapagal-Arroyo called for austerity measures for all government agencies. PCSO responded by using in-house talent—PCSO employees—who were trained by the PCSO Lotto production team. Among the first batch of in-house hosts were Erik Imson and Dindo de Viterbo, later including other employees, both male and female. This practice continues to this day, with the in-house talent receiving a modest additional allowance for their work.

During the first three years of the Philippine Charity Sweepstakes Office Lotto, the draw show was aired live from the PTV studio in Quezon City. To save on costs, a draw court was built in one of the halls of the Quezon Institute, a former hospital rented at the time by PCSO as its offices. The lotto show began broadcasting from there in 1998.

The Show Today

The show is produced by Philippine Charity Sweepstakes Office through its Creative Division of the Gaming Technology Department. It airs at 9:00 p.m. over Philippine TV and lasts for 15 minutes. The evening draw is aired live. The morning (11:00 a.m.) and afternoon (4:00 p.m.) draws for the number games Suertres Lotto and EZ 2 Lotto are taped live and the results are aired as a pretaped segment before the end of the show.

The present schedule of the lotto draws is as follows:
Sunday: Ultra Lotto 6/58, Superlotto 6/49, Suertres Lotto (three numbers), and EZ 2 Lotto (two numbers)
Monday and Wednesday: Grandlotto 6/55, Megalotto 6/45, 4Digit (four numbers), Suertres Lotto, and EZ 2 Lotto

Tuesday and Thursday: Superlotto 6/49, Lotto 6/42, 6Digit (six numbers), Suertres Lotto, and EZ 2 Lotto
Friday: Ultralotto 6/58, Megalotto 6/45, 4Digit, Suertres Lotto, and EZ 2 Lotto
Saturday: Grandlotto 6/55, Lotto 6/42, 6Digit, Suertres Lotto, and EZ 2 Lotto

The minimum prizes for the various lotto games are as follows:

- Lotto 6/42: Php 6 million (about US$128,000)
- Megalotto 6/45: Php 9 million (US$192,000)
- Superlotto 6/49: Php 16 million (US$341,000)
- Grandlotto 6/55: Php 30 million (US$640,000)
- Ultralotto 6/58: Php 50 million (US$1.06 million)

The highest jackpot ever won was Php 741 million (about US$15.8 million), won by a Filipino American visiting the Philippines at the time. Lotto prizes are tax-paid by PCSO, thus the winners receive the entire jackpot amount.

Aired over the nightly program are excerpts of the draw procedures, including the weighing of the balls for the draw machines, the loading by the draw chairman (chosen from applicants from the public) of the draw balls into the draw machines, the actual draw itself, and the official results. Present at all draws to observe the proceedings are draw judges (members of the public), employees of PCSO and the government's Commission on Audit, and other spectators who may care to watch the draws live.

In addition to the draws, the Philippine Charity Sweepstakes Office Lotto TV show also airs commercials about the agency's other gaming products, such as scratch tickets and mini-sweepstakes; brief institutional segments about the agency's latest programs and endeavors, some with testimonials from patients and other beneficiaries; and public service announcements related to PCSO. The show also airs regular reports on the PCSO's flagship social welfare program, the Individual Medical Assistance Program; the Ambulance Donation Program; medical and dental missions; and the agency's other programs and accomplishments.

Jenny Ortuoste

See also: Horse Racing, Philippines (Chapter 6: Sports)

Further Reading

Casas, Arnel N. Manager, Gaming Technology Department, Philippine Charity Sweepstakes Office. Personal interview, August 2015.
Philippine Charity Sweepstakes Office. www.pcso.gov.ph. Accessed March 10, 2016.

MAHABHARATA AND RAMAYANA
The two ancient and mythological epics, *Mahabharata* and *Ramayana*, continue to be exceedingly popular sacred adventure stories in India, Indonesia, and around

the world. They are featured in comics, children's books, movie houses, theatrical and dance performances, and television series. Almost every Hindu household has a copy of these ancient epics of valor and heroism. Hindu parents, elders, and teachers use them to illustrate the meaning of right and wrong and other cultural values for children, and televised serials of them have been enormously popular.

The *Mahabharata* is one of India's great epic adventure stories featured in numerous television and film dramatizations. It concerns a tug-of-war between good and evil. Once upon a time, there were five Pandava brothers, fatherless in childhood, who grew up together with 100 rambunctious cousins. Of royal parentage, the Panadavas' fathers were gods, while their 100 cousins emerged out of earthen jars made of clay and earth, which symbolized their human beginnings. As a young man, the eldest Kaurava, succumbing to feelings of jealousy and greed, and at the behest of his mother, wanted to be crowned king, instead of Yudisthira, the rightful heir and eldest Pandava brother. The cousin raised an army to challenge the Pandavas for the throne. One of the Pandava brothers, Arjuna, the perfect and righteous warrior, tried all peaceful means to compromise with this cousin but for naught. Without recourse, Arjuna, after entering into a long discussion with the divine philosopher Krishna, dejectedly went into battle with his army against his own relatives. There are many symbolic meanings in this great ancient epic story of humankind. The great exchange between the warrior prince, Arjuna, and God, Krishna, comes to us through the high religious and philosophical text of Hinduism, *Bhagavad Gita* (Song of the Lord), which is a part of the *Mahabharata*. The epic's resolution ultimately balances good over evil, restores life, meditates on non-violence, and culminates on the path to moksha (salvation).

In 1987 and 1988 a television series, on another great epic adventure story, the *Ramayana*, produced by B. R. Chopra, aired every Sunday morning and, literally, brought the nation to a standstill. Local businesses and shops everywhere closed down as thousands of people made their way home or gathered around available televisions installed in store windows and various local community centers. This series was a huge success that took the nation by storm. The more recent 2014 version that aired on Star Plus, during primetime, was just as spellbinding for the nation. Age-old epic narratives of Hinduism are continually given new life with new technologies and Internet speeds that perpetuate the inspirational and cultural appeal of ancient Hindu mythology for the wider community via satellite, locally and globally, into the 21st century.

The *Ramayana* is a story of God Vishnu's incarnation as man, Prince Rama. Rama was exiled from his father's kingdom for 14 years, before he could assume his rightful place on the throne. Rama was accompanied by his faithful wife, Sita, and loyal brother, Lakshmana. While hidden deep in the forest, the evil king of Lanka heard of Sita's beauty and longed to have her for himself. However, Sita was well-protected by the warrior Prince Rama, and not to be had. Then, one day, a golden deer crossed their path, Rama went off after it, leaving his brother to guard Sita in his stead. Sita, worrying about her husband, sent him off to find Rama. Shortly after, a beggar appeared at the campsite. Sita, being a compassionate and goodhearted woman, offered him a meal, and in a flash, the beggar transformed into the ten-headed King Ravana and whisked her away.

Rama, with his brother, upon returning to the campsite, and finding his wife gone, let out a deep groaning sigh of great lament and began to look for her, far and wide. He asked the help of the Monkey King Sugriva, who rallied all the monkeys, especially Hanuman, and animals of the forests to join in the search. They built a bridge across the ocean channel to reach Lanka, where they battled the evil forces of Ravana and rescued Sita. Sita, who remained faithful, even in captivity, was overjoyed to see Rama, but then it came to be that he sent her away saying, "I cannot stay with a woman who has been in another man's house." Sita, weeping a river of tears in an effort to prove her purity, jumped into a pyre, but, Agni, the great god of fire, saved and carried her out of the fire. Modern Indian feminists have repeatedly put forth the question how many fire tests does Goddess Sita have to undergo to prove her purity? Sita remains a valorized ideal of femininity for modern Hindu Indian women who also have made progress in rescuing Sita's voice within the epic. In many ways, Sita haunts the popular present both in her presence and absence within the epic text.

Ancient Hindu scripture indicates that all goddesses are ultimately the same goddess, or *devi*, and it is interesting to note that, unlike the Christian version of a solely male god who is untouched by sin, Hindu gods and goddesses contain within themselves emanations of both good and evil. It is perhaps this deep understanding of human nature and our struggles within individual selves, for righteousness and the commonweal, not only for ourselves and our own families but all of humanity that makes these ancient epics of India timeless and popular through multiple media.

Following this serial, during the 1989 elections, the Hindu nationalist Bharatiya Janata Party (BJP) grew in stature to become the single largest opposing party against the India National Congress. Local Hindu processions, especially in northern India, were no longer being viewed as devotional parades but rather as a flaunting and arrogant show of a new strain of muscular Hinduism. These aggressive processions, sometimes, broke out into riots, especially between Hindus and Muslims. Many scholars have addressed the ideological work these televised serials did in dimming the place of minorities, especially Muslims in India, and sweeping aside the diversity of India under the banner of "Hinduism." The serial showing of the Ramayana is a telling example of how public media and art, sometimes, can unexpectedly work in tandem with many political events such as the rise of the Hindu right and communal conflicts marking late 20th- and early 21st-century India.

Kathleen M. Nadeau

The great historical epics of India, the *Mahabharata* and the *Ramayana*, have been staged, televised, and produced as films in many versions. This is a still from a recent television serial version of the *Ramayana*. (Joerg Boethling/Alamy Stock Photo)

See also: Comic Books, India (Chapter 2: Books and Contemporary Literature); Tharoor, Shashi (Chapter 2: Books and Contemporary Literature)

Further Reading

Dutt, Romesh C. 2002. *The Ramayana and Mahabharata, Condensed into English Verse.* New York: Dover Publications.

Rajagopal, Arvind. 2001. *Politics after Television: Religious Nationalism and the Reshaping of the Indian Public.* Cambridge: Cambridge University Press.

Tharoor, Shashi. 1993. *The Great Indian Novel.* New York: Arcade Publications.

RADIO AND TELEVISION, TIBET

Tibetan radio and television share two key features. First is their obvious political agenda. Radio, then terrestrial television, and finally satellite television have been powerful instruments of state propaganda since the takeover of Tibetan areas by the People's Republic of China (PRC); and they have conversely been used as counterpropaganda by Tibetan exiles. The role of these media has been crucial in reaching a far wider audience than the print medium in areas where literacy was and remains low. Second, both television and radio are broadcasted and received transnationally. Especially in China, where information is curtailed, these transnational media have been a major challenge to official discourse. To a much lesser extent, the fact that Tibetans in India and Nepal are able to watch programs in their own language (as well as in Chinese) produced in the PRC has also stirred issues of cultural loyalty. Since their inception, Tibetan media have been transnational, fostering debates about foreign involvement in Chinese affairs and about Chinese authorities jamming or blocking critical reporting from abroad.

There are thus two sets of polarized "Tibetan media" crossing over the Himalayas. On one hand are those produced in several locations and Tibetan dialects by a powerful state, the PRC, broadcasting lavish programs nearly 24 hours a day. On the other hand are those produced by a marginal diaspora, animated with an equally strong yet opposing nationalistic agenda. These exile stations barely manage to air cheaply produced programs for just over an hour per day (or even one hour per week for television) and with far fewer financial and technological resources. Whereas transnational reception of PRC programs in India and Nepal has never been blocked, nor even questioned, the transnational reception of foreign programs in the PRC is met with strong reactions from the Chinese authorities: jamming, blocking, dismantling of satellite dishes, official bans, and even arrests. On the whole, Tibetans in the PRC enjoy and trust these programs produced in their own language in the United States, Europe, or India, whereas they scorn most PRC programs as propagandist or culturally insensitive.

Radio broadcasting was started by the British in the Tibetan capital of Lhasa in 1948. At the end of World War II, as a token of gratitude for allowing two American officers to cross Tibet to reach China, the president of the United States sent the Tibetan government three full radio stations and a few transmitters. Two British agents trained Tibetans to operate stations that served a double purpose. They were mainly used for commercial transactions, especially between the capital, Lhasa, and the eastern province of Kham. But broadcasting to the outside world also started in January 1950, featuring half an hour of daily news read in Tibetan, Chinese, and English, countering Chinese propaganda and refuting that Tibet was a part of China. In 1950, as the Tibetan army surrendered in Kham and started the political integration of Tibetan populations into the PRC, Tibetans were no longer allowed a communication network of their own.

The expansion of media infrastructures in the Tibetan parts of the PRC was very slow for the next three decades, being limited to a handful of central radio channels mostly in Chinese from Beijing and the province capitals. In the 1980s, broadcasting in the Tibetan language increased in time, in number of channels (local channels were created), and in diversity of programs. Television picked up a few years later. "Xizang" (the word for "Tibet" in Chinese) TV (XZTV) started as a terrestrial channel in 1985, with just a few hours a day in Tibetan interspersed within Chinese-language programs. A few years later, similar insertions of the Amdo dialect were made within the Chinese programs of Qinghai TV (QTV). In 1999 XZTV launched a satellite channel with programs in Tibetan for several hours a day, gradually expanding to 24 hours in 2007. The Chinese authorities explicitly stated their aim to intensify viewership not only among the furthest reaches of Tibetan society (by implementing compulsory television connections in rural households and monasteries) but also among the Tibetan refugees in South Asia. As for the other main dialects, QTV launched a satellite version in the Amdo language in 2006, renamed Amdo TV in 2015, airing now for six hours per day (repeated once). A Kham-dialect satellite television station was created in Sichuan in 2009, offering 18 hours of programming per day.

The most significant shows on these official stations include news (comprising a dubbed version of Beijing's central television news in Chinese and local news in Tibetan), cultural programs about Tibet or famed Tibetans, and dubbed Chinese series (mostly historical and social drama on XZTV, kung fu and urban shows on Amdo TV, and soap operas on Kham TV). XZTV clearly contains the most propaganda and political restrictions. Amdo TV holds more self-produced shows about customs and culture and frequently uses Tibetan subtitles, which are important tools of minority language preservation in a context of rapid sinicization (adaptation or implementation of Chinese cultural and political characteristics).

Most significant to Tibetans' hearts are the programs broadcasted in Tibetan from outside China. All India Radio opened in 1961 a daily 75-minute service in Tibetan, featuring mostly speeches of the Dalai Lama, prayers, and music. It played a vital role in transnational Tibetan politics up until the 1990s. It is still running, but its reach within Tibet is geographically limited to the parts closest to India. Three other main radio stations have since taken the lead but face unremitting jamming by the Chinese authorities (loud drums, Chinese opera, or screeching noises).

The first two are overseen by the U.S. Broadcasting Board of Governors, so the U.S. government, which prompts the PRC to denounce this as a form of American "soft power": Voice of America (VoA, launched in Tibetan in 1991) and Radio Free Asia (RFA, 1996). While the first is considered by the United States as "general broadcasting," that is, a way to provide reliable international and American news to regions where the free flow of information is impeded, the second is considered as "surrogate broadcasting," in that it emphasizes news pertaining to the targeted country, bypassing the local (in this case PRC state) information. Their shortwave programs are about one to two hours long, transmitted through "skywave" or "skip" broadcasting (radio signals refracted through the ionosphere in the upper atmosphere) and the Internet, repeated throughout the day without overlap, so that the combined broadcasts amount to 14 hours daily.

VoA launched a one-hour-per-week television format in 2005, simultaneously broadcasted live from Washington on satellite television, radio, and the Internet. It contains a news bulletin, often featuring the Dalai Lama's whereabouts, followed by what is perhaps the most famous Tibetan media program overall: *Kun-gleng* (literally, "discuss about everything," known in English as "Talk to VoA"), featuring guest speakers and public phone-in participation. RFA launched its own short video webcasts (less than 10 minutes) in 2008.

There have been several other clandestine or independent radio programs, but Voice of Tibet (VoT), started by Norwegian nongovernmental organizations (NGOs) in 1997, is the most long-standing one. It is also the only media service in Tibetan with a Tibetan editorial board in charge, involving trained journalists. As for RFA, its 45-minute daily program focuses on Tibetan issues only, in the three dialects and in Chinese (aiming to reach Chinese audiences).

Finally, the Department of Information and International Relations of the Tibetan government in exile created a web-only television station in 2005. It started as a project to provide online access to documentaries (in Tibetan, English, and Hindi, of all historical periods) to Tibetan communities in Asia and the West. In 2009 it launched a half-hour news program in Tibetan, available to podcast, recorded only once a month and in standard Tibetan only.

Isabelle Henrion-Dourcy

See also: Spring Festival Television Gala, China

Further Reading

Barnett, Robert. 2009. "Television Drama Series in Tibet." In *Tibetan Arts in Transition: A Journey through Theatre, Cinema and Painting*, 51–70. Seminar Proceedings, Rome and Naples 2008–2009.
Biener, Hansjörg. 2002. "Broadcasting to Tibet." *Central Asian Survey* 21, no. 4: 417–422.
Radio Free Asia. www.rfa.org/english/news/tibet. Accessed March 26, 2016.
Voice of Tibet. www.vot.org. Accessed March 26, 2016.
Voice of Tibetan English. www.voatibetanenglish.com. Accessed March 26, 2016.

SPRING FESTIVAL TELEVISION GALA, CHINA

Spring Festival Television Gala (SFTG) is a variety show produced and broadcasted by China Central Television (CCTV) every Chinese New Year's Eve. It has been claimed as one of the most watched television programs in the world. In 2014 SFTG was even promoted by China's government to the status of "national project" (*guojia xiangmu* 國家項目), making its scale on par with that of the Beijing Olympic Games in 2008.

The historical origin of SFTG dates back to 1956. In that year, China's government produced a film called *The Spring Festival Celebration* (*Chunjie dalianhuan* 春節大聯歡), in which many national elites, including outstanding workers, farmers, scientists, and intellectuals, were gathered to celebrate the Chinese New Year (also called Spring Festival). The film, however, has little direct connection with the current SFTG, which is a variety TV show featuring singing, dancing, comedy, and *xiangsheng* (相聲, Chinese comic dialogues). Since 1983 SFTG has become a yearly live TV show broadcasted to the Chinese-speaking audience in China and abroad. On Chinese New Year's Eve (which comes around late January or early February and follows the lunar calendar), SFTG begins at 8:00 p.m. on the last day of the year and ends at around 12:30 a.m. on the first day of the new year. During the show, many Chinese families gather at home, dine, and watch the show together. It has been said that watching SFTG with family members is a Chinese New Year ritual for many mainland Chinese people.

While SFTG brings feelings of harmony and peacefulness to many Chinese families, it also has its political and economic values. China's government always aims to present the best face of the Chinese nation via broadcasting SFTG to TV screens nationwide. The selection of the performances and performers of SFTG often involves politics. For example, singers from China's army, including the renowned Song Zuying (宋祖英, 1966–) and Peng Liyuan (彭麗媛 1962–, the wife of current People's Republic of China leader, Xi Jinping), are always featured in SFTG. Because of the need to promote national unification, some Taiwan, Hong Kong, and Macau singers and movie stars are paired up to perform as brothers, sisters, and couples, hiding their local characters and languages.

In the 1990s, SFTG even had one session featuring a video glorifying the political leaders, including Mao Zedong, Deng Xiaoping, and Jiang Zemin. The official "national picture" not only tries to include as many national elites as possible, proportionally, it also marginalizes and excludes the elements that are disliked by the government. For instance, ethnic minority performers are rarely found, and gender minorities, such as the LGBT groups, are even more marginalized. Any national contradictions and dissatisfactions are not found in the show. Besides political values, SFTG also generates huge economic value. The cost of advertising during the show is extremely high. SFTG also once used product placement, but it was soon protested by the audiences. Moreover, the performers usually derive a lot of business opportunities after the show, since performing on it is an honorable achievement for the performer and can make the performer truly famous nationwide.

While SFTG is still a very influential TV show, it is questionable whether its power can be further sustained and expanded with the arrival of new media. SFTG's media impact mainly comes from the fact that many families gather and watch TV together on Chinese New Year's Eve. With new media—such as digital broadcasting, the Internet, smartphones, and tablets—having become widely available to new generations, SFTG's appeal has decreased.

For example, many audiences have turned to watching satellite TV. In recent years, Hunan TV, Zhejiang TV, and Shanghai Dragon (dongfang) TV have organized their own Spring Festival television galas, which seem to be less constrained by the government. Those satellite TV stations can make their own shows according to the audience's preference: local stars who speak local languages are chosen, and foreign international stars are paid a very high price to perform. Other less competitive satellite TV stations also develop new forms of Spring Festival show. In 2007, Hainan satellite TV and Xinjiang satellite TV, one located in southern China and another in the northwest, collaborated to organize a translocal Spring Festival show. Unlike the CCTV's SFTG, the satellite TV stations present a more local or provincial Spring Festival show with their own global connections. Without the burden of balancing different localities and constructing a harmonious nation, the satellite TV stations' shows can better connect to local feelings and tastes (jie di qi 接地氣).

The Internet's arrival also challenges CCTV's SFTG. Although it is also broadcasted online, the Internet distracts people from the TV screen to their own computer and mobile screens. People can easily toggle to other pages and can even create their own Spring Festival galas. Since 2008 netizens have begun to organize an online *shanzhai* Spring Festival show (山寨春晚). The word *shanzhai* (山寨) literally means "mountain stronghold" or "mountain village." In China, *shanzhai* culture refers to a local band doing cover versions of famous songs, which are usually seen as fake or parody. The show is performed by unknown *shanzhai* stars (山寨明星), whose performances imitate the real big stars in CCTV's SFTG.

This does not mean that the alternative Spring Festival shows are challengers to the CCTV SFTG. CCTV's SFTG is still extremely powerful. Both satellite shows and *shanzhai* shows are allowed by the government. However, alternative shows' content and structure are relatively different from the CCTV's SFTG in many aspects, including the production mechanisms and ideology. Therefore, we can say that in recent years there has been a decentralization and diversification of Spring Festival gala shows in China.

Li Cho Kiu

See also: Xiangsheng: Chinese Comic Dialogues

Further Reading

Lu, Xinyu. 2008. "Ritual, Television, and State Ideology: Rereading CCTV's 2006 Spring Festival Gala." In *TV China: A Reader on New Media*. Ed. Ying Zhu and Chris Berry, 111–128. Bloomington: Indiana University Press.

TELEVISION DRAMAS, KOREA

The Korean Wave, the spread of popular South Korean culture in the late 1990s, challenges a conventional notion of the globalization process: that cultural flows go from the West to the rest. Korean dramas, as the main part of the Korean Wave, have penetrated many Asian countries and changed local popular cultural practices since the late 1990s. During the earlier period, Japanese pop music, films, and TV soap operas were in high demand in the majority of Asian countries. The Asian economic crisis in the late 1990s, however, prompted the Korean government to focus on the export of Korean cultural products to make up for the loss of investment savings and faltering prices of manufactured goods. The rest of the East and Southeast Asian countries welcomed the cheaper prices of Korean programs, which fit nicely into their economies, already weakened by the crisis. Korean dramas helped local viewers take a break from the harsh reality caused by the economic downturn by connecting Korean stories to their own life issues and even becoming agents of change by making sense of Asian values of love, family, and gender.

Korean dramas initially were popular in ethnic Chinese countries such as Taiwan, Hong Kong, and Singapore. Particularly, carefully crafted dubbing and subtitling of Korean dramas allowed Chinese viewers to feel connected to the foreign contents. For example, *Daejanggeum* (*Jewel in the Palace*), a historical drama of the first woman royal physician, was extremely popular despite foreign historical features because a Hong Kong TV station put great effort into localizing Korean content by adding Chinese recipes and medical practices.

Mainland China is not immune to the craze of Korean dramas. The 2014 drama *My Love from the Star* (*Byeoreseo on geudae*), a love story between an alien who lived in Korea for 400 years and an arrogant movie star, was a huge hit in China and had 2.5 billion views. *Winter Sonata* (*Gyeoul yeonga*), starring Bae Yong Joon, became the first major hit in Japan when NHK, the Japan Broadcasting Corporation, showed the Korean drama in 2003 to boost its declining ratings. Because of its popularity, the series were aired multiple times afterward with record viewer ratings. Bae's gentle and caring image in the drama attracted middle-aged Japanese women who were tired of Japanese tough masculinity as perceived and depicted by some in the media and real life.

Competing against Western movies and films, Korean dramas have become popularly consumed throughout Asia due to several factors. First, Korean dramas express East Asian sentiments originating from Confucianism, a common philosophy that originated in China and is now shared by many countries in the region. While Western dramas attract viewers with ostentatious sexuality and violence, Korean dramas emphasize Confucian family values and group harmony that help East Asian viewers to be easily connected to their life stories.

Because Korean dramas strongly emphasize traditional family values, their story lines often describe how parents or other family members decide their children's marriage partner of the same social class. *The Secret Garden* (*Sikeurit gadeun*, 2010) and *Boys over Flowers* (*Kkotboda namja*, 2009), for example, involve status and class differences between two families as the major backdrop, showing a typical love story between a rich man and a poor woman. The rich man's parents pressure him to marry a woman of the same social status, while threatening and bribing the poor woman's family to give up her rich lover. Marriage, in this sense, is a matter between two families, creating a political and economic alliance rather than uniting two individuals in love. Due to a long tradition of arranged marriage and status endogamy (or marriage within one's community), East Asian viewers feel attracted to this modern-day marriage conflict.

Korean dramas also offer viewers an Asian version of fantasy or an escape from their reality. Many viewers feel nostalgia "in the intentional misrecognition of the past as an 'ideal'" (Chua 2012, 96). Some scholars explain that many married males in Hong Kong watch Korean dramas because the image of soft, sacrificial, and more feminine women evoke those men's sense of a nostalgia for more traditional gender roles. As educated, middle-class men married to women with careers, some of these Hong Kong men are expected to share household chores and childcare, yet they are also highly pressured to be the major breadwinner in the family. Caught between tradition and modernity, these men find Korean women in the dramas to be ideal women of the past (specifically, beautiful, wise, and submissive), and this gives them the experience of a temporary emotional break from their reality.

Despite their fictitious nature, Korean dramas often involve a strong sense of human agency. They offer Korean women an opportunity to think more critically about their own lives in relation to the constricted lives of women in ancient Korea. Many Korean dramas, usually written by women, critically portray male chauvinistic practices in Korean families, echoing many women's personal experience. For instance, A Son and a Daughter (Adeulgwa ddal), a popular soap opera in the early 1990s of boy-and-girl twins, dramatized sexist practices in a traditional family that provides all the support for the boy while ignoring the girl's needs and desires. This soap opera encouraged some Korean women to reflect upon their own upbringing and construct their ideas of gender, family, and work by watching and commenting upon the Korean drama.

Japanese middle-aged women, the ardent fan base of Korean dramas, also become active agents. They construct new subjectivities through Korean dramas by reflecting upon the historical relationship between the two countries as well as their individual life. They actively organize fan-club meetings and drama site tours, learn Korean language and culture (once devalued as the culture of a colony), and do not hesitate to express their changing opinions of Korea.

Korean dramas sometimes play an important role in social movements. Lisa Yuk Ming Leung's research (2009) suggests that social movements can utilize popular culture as a source of protest strategies. During the 2005 World Trade Organization Ministerial Conference at Hong Kong, Korean farmers, seriously disadvantaged by the Korean government's free-trade agreements, protested against cutting trade barriers of agricultural products. Initially demonized as violent protesters, Korean farmers acquired "affect mobilization" of Hong Kong residents after using the Daejanggeum theme song because many Hong Kong residents were great fans of the drama series. Hong Kong newspapers expressed Hong Kong people's sympathy for arrested farmers particularly because Yi Young Ae, the main actress of the drama, wrote a letter to the Hong Kong government asking for leniency. Thus, Korean dramas, as a cultural flow from Asia to Asia, have seized the hearts of many Asian people and given them opportunities to think, express, and sometimes act in their lives.

Kyejung R. Yang

See also: The "Gangnam Style" Fad (Chapter 5: Internet and Social Media); Historical Dramas, China

Further Reading

Abelmann, Nancy. 2003. *The Melodrama of Mobility: Women, Talk, and Class in Contemporary South Korea*. Hawaii: University of Hawai'i Press.

Chua, Beng Huat. 2006. *Structure, Audience, and Soft Power in East Asian Pop Culture.* Hong Kong: Hong Kong University Press.

Cho, Hae-joang. 2005. "Reading the Korean Wave: A Sign of Global Shift." *Korea Journal* 45, no. 4 (Winter): 147–166.

Iwabuchi, Koichi, and Beng Huat Chua. 2008. *East Asian Pop Culture: Analyzing the Korean Wave.* Hong Kong: Hong Kong University Press.

Leung, Lisa Yuk Ming. 2009. "Daejanggeum as 'Affective Mobilization': Lessons for (Transnational) Popular Culture and Civil Society." *Inter-Asia Cultural Studies* 10, no. 1: 51–66.

Lin, Angel M. Y., and Avin Tong. 2007. "Crossing Boundaries: Male Consumption of Korean TV Dramas and Negotiation of Gender Relations in Modern Day Hong Kong." *Journal of Gender Studies* 16, no. 3: 217–232.

TELEVISION, INDIA

For 1.3 billion Indians, television is a major source of entertainment and information. From urban drawing rooms to rural dwellings, the television has become omnipresent in India. This electronic medium had a modest beginning in India as part of All India Radio (AIR) on September 15, 1959. Indian television was broadcasted twice a week only from New Delhi! By 1976, 45 million people had access to eight television stations. In the same year, television became an independent entity after it separated from AIR and took on a new name, Doordarshan. The next landmark was the introduction of color television sets in 1982. Millions of viewers appreciated programs such as the soap opera *Hum log* (1984) and stories from Indian classics such as the *Ramayana* (1987–1988) and *Mahabharata* (1988–1989). Running into 94 episodes, the *Mahabharata*, produced by B. R. Chopra, enthralled audiences. Television broadcasting in India witnessed its next leap forward from the late 1980s into the early 1990s with the introduction of independent satellite channels and cable TV. The Indian government's liberalization program of the early 1990s encouraged the exponential growth of Indian television, which accelerated after broadcasting Hong Kong–based Satellite Television Asian Region (STAR). Another satellite channel, Indian-owned Zee TV, was founded in 1992. By 1995 there were 48 terrestrial and satellite channels all together. By 2007 there were more than 300 satellite networks, giving viewers a wide range of choices. The Indian TV industry surged ahead with considerable pace, serving 277 million viewers.

Another milestone in India's booming TV industry was the establishment of New Delhi Television Limited (NDTV, 1988) by husband-and-wife team Prannoy and Radhika Roy. The growth of NDTV was phenomenal, and by 2014 it was generating revenue of US$80 million with a workforce of 1,491 people. The crowning glory of the network is the English news channel, NDTV 24x7, beaming to a large Indian as well as overseas audience. NDTV 24x7 has the highest number of viewers among news channels in English, according to nationwide surveys. The channel can be accessed in the United States through Time Warner Cable and DirecTV. In Australia, Singapore, and Canada, NDTV 24x7 can be viewed through different TV platforms.

The talk shows and public shows broadcast by NDTV relate to political affairs. Anchored by senior journalists, the talk and public shows are studio based. It has also introduced programs in Hindi. Some of the popular Hindi programs are *Mukabla* (*Tussle*), *Hum log* (*We People*), and *Badi khabr* (*Big News*). One of NDTV's innovations is the launching of a two-in-one channel: NDTV Profit and NDTV Prime. The one-hour program *Property Show* advises viewers about real-estate matters, whereas *Car and Bike Show* offers information about trends in the automobile industry abroad and the launching of new cars. NDTV's international channels are ATN NDTV 24x7, NDTV Worldwide, NDTV Convergence, and Indiaroots. NDTV has engaged in social activities such as the Greenathon campaign, Support My School, Save Our Tigers, Marks for Sports, Fit India Movement, and Save India's Coasts. The flagship channel of Zee Entertainment Enterprises Limited, Zee TV, has carved out a niche in the Indian television industry. It dishes out news in Hindi, soap operas, movies, dance programs, and special award shows. It is much appreciated by the Indian diaspora and launches various programs abroad as well.

Star TV has transformed the landscape of TV broadcasting in India. The headquarters of Star India Private Limited is located in STAR House, Mumbai, with reporters based in 20 branches across the country for dissemination of news. In its earlier incarnation, Star TV included an English-language entertainment channel (Star Plus), Prime Sports (later designated as Star Sports), Star Movies, and BBC. Star Plus in its new incarnation as Star World began to broadcast English-language programs. The Indian diaspora also enjoys the various programs of Star TV, such as ESPN, Channel V, Star One, Star News, and Star Gold. In terms of growth, profitability, and mass appeal, it became a major player in Indian TV broadcasting. STAR Cricket, renamed as Star Sports 3, is a popular channel, and Star TV is going for national sports network broadcasting in major Indian languages. Star Movies in English and Star Gold in Hindi are two channels dishing out blockbusters. Star TV began broadcasting in high definition (HD) with the launch of HD versions of its major channels in 2011. The launch of *Kaun banega crorepati*, the Indian version of *Who Wants to Be a Millionaire?*, in 2000 was a runway success. Some of the popular serials of Star TV include *Diya aur baati hum* (*We Are Light and Candle*), *Pyaar ka dard hai* (*Pathos of Love*), *Saath nibhaana saathiya* (*Friends, Get United*), *Iss pyaar ko kya naam doon* (*What Name I Give for This Love*), and the *Mahabharata* (since September 2013).

The TV industry in India was estimated to be worth 475 billion rupees by 2014. The industry had also introduced major innovations. The direct-to-home (DTH) technology has become a common feature by which the subscriber receives signals directly in home. The induction of HD into existing channels provides good-quality sound and excellent picture quality. With the advent of terrestrial, cable, and satellite television into rural areas, the regional sector is also growing considerably. Sun TV (Tamil), Udaya TV (Kannada), OTV (Oriya), Asianet (Malayalam), and other channels broadcast in various regional languages. The channels dedicated to music are MTV and Sony Mix Channel V. The influence of movies, particularly of the Bollywood genre, is an important part of Indian popular media. Star Movies, Star

Gold, Zee Classic, Zee Cinema, Sony Pix, and others offer popular movies. *Colors Comedy Night with Kapil* is a popular sketch-comedy and celebrity talk show. The TV channels have also exploited Indians' cricket mania. For religiously minded people, there are channels such as Aastha, Sadhna, Jagran, Sanskar, Quran TV, GOD, and others. The booming TV industry also caters to children, who very much appreciate Hungama, Cartoon Network, Animax, Disney, Splash, and others. After the United States and China, India has become the third-largest market for cable subscribers in the world. Indian television has a seminal role in the age of globalization.

Patit Paban Mishra and Sangita Babu

See also: Bollywood Gender Stereotypes (Chapter 3: Film)

Further Reading

Butcher, Melissa. 2003. *Transnational Television, Cultural Identity and Change: When STAR Came to India.* Thousand Oaks, CA: Sage Publications.
Gupta, Nilanjana. 1998. *Switching Channels: Ideologies of Television in India.* New Delhi: Oxford University Press.
Mankekar, Purnima. 1999. *Screening Culture, Viewing Politics: An Ethnography of Television, Womanhood, and Nation in Postcolonial India.* Durham, NC: Duke University Press.
Mehta, Nalin. 2008. *Television in India: Satellites, Politics and Cultural Change.* New York: Routledge.
Ninan, Sevanti. 1995. *Through the Magic Window: Television and Change in India.* New York: Penguin Books.

TELEVISION, INDONESIA

On August 24, 1962, residents of Jakarta, the capital of Indonesia, watched their first public television broadcast of the opening ceremonies of the Fourth Asia Games at Gelora Bung Karno Stadium in Jakarta. This television spectacle both entertained and united Indonesian viewers on a scale never seen before. The television studios, broadcast towers, and the 120,000-capacity stadium were each designed and built specifically to promote this pan-Asia sporting event. Over the following decades, television grew to be one of the most far-reaching media outlets in Indonesia, today reaching over 90 percent of the population (Rakhmani 2014). This section will provide a brief survey of the growth and development of television in Indonesia to the present day by focusing on three key phases: the early history of television as a state monopoly and cultural tool for supporting state authority, the privatization of television in the late 1980s and early 1990s as a medium of growing commercialization, and the current proliferation of a massive television industry. We will also explore a few examples of television shows that shaped popular television history, namely the children's television series *Si unyil* and Indonesia's most popular television genre, *sinetron*. Overall we will see how television is at once a spectacle and a serious point of consideration in the history of popular culture in Indonesia because of its use as a tool for political control, a medium for generating advertising revenue, and a popular form of daily entertainment for the majority of Indonesian citizens.

The first public television broadcast in 1962 was a display of new technological advancement that amazed Indonesian audiences in Jakarta. Television broadcasts in the early years of television in Indonesia were primarily restricted to the Jakarta metropolitan area, only aired programs for three to four hours per day, and were controlled by one state-owned television station. Televisi Republik Indonesia (Television of the Republic of Indonesia, TVRI) held a monopoly on television broadcasting from 1962 to 1989. In 1965 Indonesia experienced major changes in presidential leadership. The first president and revolutionary leader of Indonesia from Dutch colonial control, Sukarno (1901–1970), was removed from office in a dramatic military coup from 1965 to 1967. He was replaced by President Suharto (1921–2008), who would remain in office for the next 31 years until his resignation in 1998. During his time as president, Suharto controlled the state monopoly over TVRI in order to promote his vision of a unified Indonesian nation, called the "New Order" (*Orde Baru*). In the early years of his presidency, television broadcast technology was limited. It wasn't until Indonesia launched its first domestic broadcast satellite, *Palapa*, in 1976, that television was broadcast across the nation.

The new satellite gave President Suharto a national platform to communicate to the nation his message of a unified New Order for Indonesia. A seemingly innocuous children's television show, *Si unyil*, is one such example of how the New Order government used television to promote state authority. *Si unyil* (named after the main character) first aired in 1981 as a Sunday-morning puppet-based television show. Many areas in Indonesia have long traditions of puppetry, such as the *wayang* shadow plays of Java and Bali. *Si unyil* modernized puppetry for TV audiences to entertain children and convey lessons concerned with the unity of the Indonesian nation. It told the story of a typical Indonesian family living in a rural village and contained messages about patriotism, family planning, the Indonesian military, the environment, and public health. *Si unyil* was part of a centralized cultural project to promote national development projects, construct an ideal national citizen, and circulate ideas of official national culture (Kitley 2000, 115).

The privatization of the television industry in Indonesia occurred in the late 1980s and early 1990s when the first privately owned television channels formed: Rajawali Citra Television Indonesia (RCTI) in 1988, Surya Citra Television (SCTV) in 1989, and Televisi Pendidikan Indonesia (Indonesian Education Television, TPI) in 1990. While these channels were no longer owned by the state nor centered exclusively in Jakarta—in some cases building offices in Surabaya, Yogyakarta, and Bali and extending their broadcasts nationally—television still remained closely linked with President Suharto's administration. For example, President Suharto's third son, Bamban Trihatmojo (1953–), owned RCTI; his cousin, Sudwikatmono

(1934–2011), owned 20 percent of the market shares for SCTV; and his eldest daughter, Siti Hardiyanti Rukmana (called Tutut, 1943–), owned a large portion of TPI, which was for a time the only station other than TVRI broadcasting on a national scale because they utilized TVRI facilities (Sen and Hill 2006, 111–112). Privatization was followed by deregulation—in 1993 a bill passed allowing private channels to broadcast nationally through the *Palapa* satellite—but this also did not lead to any great shift toward a more liberal or democratic television market (Kitley 2000, 331). The New Order government no longer held a monopoly on television, but they did control how licenses were issued to private operators, and the family ties mentioned above ensured that the newly privatized television market was still aligned with state interests.

After deregulation, Indonesian audiences started seeing more regionally generated content and international broadcasts on television. Many stations began producing more localized programming, in some cases giving stations more regional autonomy. In 1994 RCTI produced the series *Si doel anak sekolahan*, about a Betawi family, indigenous to the Jakarta area, dealing with changes taking place in the city from a local perspective. This was very different from the imagery of national harmony portrayed previously on television (Sen and Hill 2006, 225). Technological advancements, namely the use of parabola antennae introduced in 1983, made it possible to receive international broadcast signals (Sen and Hill 2006, 116). Stations also started broadcasting more imported material—series from the United States, *telenovela* from Latin America, and films from India, Hong Kong, and Taiwan.

As Indonesia saw greater numbers of private television channels, a growing number of audiences across the archipelago, and greater international television influence, a television genre emerged in Indonesia that is still the most popular today: *sinetron* (Indonesian soap operas). *Sinetron* is shorthand for *sinema elektronik* (electronic cinema), a term coined by Soemardjono (1927–1998), one of the founders of the Institute Kesenian Jakarta (Jakarta Art Institute). The very first television series, *Losmen* (*The Inn*), aired on TVRI in the early 1980s, but it wasn't until 1989 that the term *sinetron* was first applied to the television series *Jendela rumah kita* (*The Window into Our Home*). Over 15 years later, there are now hundreds of *sinetron*, some of them with episodes numbering in the thousands. There are many genres of *sinetron* (comedy, drama, or horror), for all ages (kids, teens, or adults). The plot of a typical *sinetron* tends to portray the day-to-day lives of characters through melodramatic story lines and complicated emotional relationships, not unlike soap operas globally. By far the most distinctive and popular genres of *sinetron* in Indonesia today are the *sinetron religi* or *Islami* (religious or Islamic soap operas). It is not surprising to find religious themes entering into popular culture in this way since Indonesia is the largest-majority Muslim nation in the world with 90 percent of the population actively practicing Islam. In order to gain high ratings, *sinetron* producers must appeal to the moral values of their audiences (Rakhmani 2014). *Sinetron* remain a major part of Indonesian popular cultural, and because they attract such large audiences of viewers, they are able to generate massive advertising revenue to support the television industry in Indonesia today.

Megan Robin Hewitt

See also: Social Media, Indonesia (Chapter 5: Internet and Social Media)

Further Reading

Kitley, Philip. 2000. *Television, Nation, and Culture in Indonesia.* Athens, OH: Ohio University Press.

Rakhmani, Inaya. 2014. "Fifteen Years of Sinetron Religi." *Inside Indonesia* 118. www.insideindonesia.org/fifteen-years-of-sinetron-religi. Accessed April 30, 2015.

Sen, Krishna, and David T. Hill. 2006. "Television: Transborder Transmissions, Local Images." In *Media, Culture and Politics in Indonesia.* Ed. Krishna Sen and David T. Hill, 108–136. Jakarta, ID: Equinox Publishing.

TELEVISION, JAPAN

As an advanced industrial country, Japan has a very lively and robust market for television. It would be fair to say that television is an important part of many people's everyday lives. In fact, Japanese companies were among the earliest to enable television reception through cellular phone. Using a technology called One Seg, the cellular phone was able to receive broadcasts that remained fairly clear and stable even as the cellular phone user moved around. First released in 2005, this system was incredibly popular. In fact, some thought that the iPhone would not succeed in Japan because it was initially incompatible with the One Seg system. While One Seg itself is now obsolete due to the popularity of smartphones and streaming video, its story suggests the importance of maintaining connections to televisual media throughout Japan. Relatedly, some automobile shops now sell conversion kits that allow people to watch television through their car's dashboard navigation system.

Although television is certainly a ubiquitous part of social life in contemporary Japan, this was not always the case. While prewar Japan had witnessed the expansion of radio broadcasting, the television industry developed in postwar Japan. Initially, U.S. occupation (1945–1952) authorities had not been enthusiastic regarding television, as they saw it as an unnecessary luxury. In the last few years of the occupation, however, some began to envision television as an effective means of spreading anticommunist sentiment in Asia. In the aftermath of the occupation, encouragement from the Ministry of International Trade and Industry (MITI) helped to bring foreign television technology into Japan. Japanese electronics firms used this knowledge to develop a domestic production system. As the Japanese economy recovered throughout the 1950s, a black-and-white television set became one of the "three sacred objects" that signified a comfortable middle-class lifestyle (the other two were a washing machine and a refrigerator). In spite of its symbolic importance, however, the number of television owners remained a small proportion of the populace until the 1960s. By the time of the Tokyo Olympics in 1964, approximately 85 percent of the populace owned a television.

In this same period, the *tarento* (talent) that continue to play such an important part of Japan's media landscape emerged. *Tarento* are not skilled actors as much as they are performers whose performances cross many platforms. These jack-of-all-trades figures thus might act, model, sing, perform in comedies, appear on cooking shows, and so on. Thus for the *tarento*, ironically, media saturation and repeated viewings across different genres carry more significance than actual talent. This situation is a result of the historical conditions in which the Japanese television industry emerged. When Japanese programs first aired in the 1950s, television productions had to subcontract film stars. As box-office returns began to ebb, however, film executives became less inclined to allow their stars to participate in the television industry, which they saw as cutting into their profit margins. With their access to established film stars cut off, television studios first turned to theater actors. Due to television's popularity, however, television studios needed an influx of even more actors and thus established agencies to train actors. However, these newer actors were not skilled in the craft of acting. As a result, the *tarento* are celebrities that demonstrate a strong personality with which viewers can identify a lifestyle or personality type.

Tarento frequently appear in variety shows and game shows. The Japanese variety show features discussion of current events, short games, musical performances, and other forms of light entertainment. Hosts of these shows often wear extravagant clothing, and the overall mood of the show is incredibly jocular. Some of the humor of the shows can at times verge on the childish, scatological, and prurient. These shows often produce popular catch phrases and offer an interesting window into Japanese popular culture. The *tarento* often also host game shows, which can include word games, puzzles, and physical challenges. One of the most popular is *Sasuke*, in which contestants compete to advance to the finals of an incredibly challenging obstacle course. As a testament to its great difficulty, all four levels have only been completed five times out of the 31 total seasons. Another popular competition is the annual Red and White Song Battle. In this competition, broadcast on New Year's Eve, the most popular female musical acts of the past year are placed on the red team and the most popular male acts on the white team. These singers then perform their hits for the nation watching at home. At the end of the event, the audience and a panel of judges chooses the winning team. Watching this event with family members has been a key part of the New Year's holiday for many Japanese people.

One of the most popular types of television show is the drama. Dramas are plot-driven shows that air one night a week. Dramas can focus on topics such as family, love, or even social problems like unemployment and alcoholism. Recent years have seen the rise of the trendy drama, which places a greater emphasis on affect or mood than it does on the plot itself. Using recognized *tarento*, in other words, the trendy drama tries to get the viewer to imagine and identify with a specific lifestyle or emotive impression. In recent years, dramas imported from Korea, dubbed the "Korean Wave," have also become popular. The actor Bae Yong Joon, for example, became one of the most sought-after celebrities in Japan due to the incredible success of the Korean drama *Winter Sonata*. Further highlighting the global reach of contemporary popular culture, fans across the world also trade and distribute Japanese dramas.

For many Japanese, television is also an important source of news. Japanese news programs tend to offer long explanations of current events. Instead of relying on flashy images, Japanese newscasters often employ charts and graphs to convey the outlines of a story. NHK is especially known for having a very facts-driven approach to news. Other stations, such as TV Asahi, might offer more commentary from news anchors. In the 1960s, NHK devoted approximately 25 percent of its airtime to news. News remains an important vehicle for transmitting information about important issues and thus for the function of democracy in Japan.

Japanese television channels broadcast live sporting events, which are often widely viewed. Japanese professional baseball retains a large audience. Given the recent success of Japanese baseball players in the United States' professional leagues, Japanese networks will also often air American baseball games that feature Japanese players. The success of J-League soccer has also seen its games broadcast more widely. The six Grand Sumo tournaments are also aired in their entirety. The January tournament, taking place just after the New Year holiday, is especially popular. Another sporting event with a large audience is the yearly high school baseball championships, where representatives from each prefecture compete to become the national champion. Viewers seem particularly enamored with the players' youthful enthusiasm and the purity of their competitive spirit. The competition takes place at the legendary Koshien Stadium, the home of the professional Hanshin Tigers. Many of the stars of Japanese professional baseball, such as Matsuzaka Daisuke, Matsui Hideki, and Darvish Yu, first came to prominence after impressive performances in the national high school tournament. The national high school baseball championships are a topic of discussion throughout the nation in the period in which they are broadcast.

Anime (animated shows and movies) are, of course, also an important part of the Japanese television landscape. Anime have been created for a variety of audiences, including boys, girls, men, and women. While the themes of anime vary, one common feature is the artistic style. Anime artists often focus on the quality of the created image and place less emphasis on movement. One common attribute of anime is the enlarged eyes of the characters. Anime have become incredibly popular and are one of Japan's signature global exports.

In contrast to the media environment in the United States, Japanese television is largely dominated by six main channels. While satellite and cable channels exist, most people watch the six main broadcast channels. NHK, which had broadcast radio programs and propaganda for the Imperial Japanese Army in the prewar and wartime period, was the first channel available and began broadcasting in 1953. NHK is an independent corporation supported by viewers. By law, anyone owning a television that is capable of receiving NHK is required to pay a reception fee.

Ryan Moran

See also: Manga; Social Media, Japan

Further Reading

Kraus, Ellis. 1998. "Changing Television News in Japan." *Journal of Asian Studies* 57, no. 3 (August): 663–692.

Lukács, Gabriella. 2010. *Scripted Affects, Branded Selves: Television, Subjectivity, and Capitalism in 1990s Japan.* Durham, NC: Duke University Press.

Morris-Suzuki, Tessa. 1994. *The Technological Transformation of Japan.* Cambridge, UK: Cambridge University Press.

Partner, Simon. 1999. *Assembled in Japan: Electrical Goods and the Making of the Japanese Consumer.* Berkeley: University of California Press.

TV SINGING COMPETITIONS, CHINA

Singing competitions on Chinese television have undergone significant changes from the early form of "expert-appraising" contests to the present more inclusive "mass-selecting" shows. The competitions emerged in the mid-1980s when the number of TV sets increased rapidly and television became an important means of popular entertainment and mass communication in China.

Early singing competitions, largely organized by state-subsidized television stations, took it as their mission to select talented singers for the nation and to entertain and educate the masses. The contestants' performances were assessed and commented on by a panel of professional musicians/judges on stage. The audience, on site or off, on the other hand, were passive viewers, supposed to be entertained and educated by the competition. The situation changed most significantly around the year 2000, with the spread of technology in communication, such as mobile phones and the importation of "foreign" concepts of reality shows. Meanwhile, television stations, cut off from state subsidies, began to emphasize the audience's participation in order to increase the popularity of the program, attract more advertisers, and generate more revenue. Modeling on European, American, and Korean reality shows, the new wave of TV singing competitions invite the audience's participation through text-message voting off site. Although off-site voting was banned by the SARFT (State Administration of Radio, Film, and Television) in 2007, organizers of singing competitions bring about on-site audience voting to create a more inviting environment.

The history of singing competitions on Chinese television can be traced back to the *Young Singers Competition* (Qingnian geshou dianshi dajiangsai 青年歌手电视大奖赛), a biennial national contest launched by CCTV (China Central Television) in 1984. The organizers of the program held very high standards when selecting contestants in terms of age, appearance, and social background. Candidates, selected from across the nation by local state-television stations, represent their own provinces to compete for winners in two categories: professional and amateur. Starting in 1986, the program further distinguished three different singing styles: bel canto (operatic style), folk, and popular. Largely unconcerned with the audience's participation, the competition organizers emphasized the judges' expertise and focused on the contestants' professional knowledge of music and singing skills. However, rules began to change in the early 2000s when CCTV's *Young Singers Competition* was challenged by popular reality shows run by local satellite TV stations. In 2006, the program stopped splitting the contestants into professionals and amateurs and began to pay more attention to interactions with the audience.

The strongest competitor of the *Young Singers Competition* was *Super Girl* (*Chaoji nüsheng* 超级女声), an all-female singing competition launched by Hunan TV in 2004. *Super Girl*, boasting a "zero threshold" for contestants, attracts an unprecedented number of participants. The competition is conducted on the regional level and the national level. In order to advance to the national level, contestants must go through three rounds of competition on the regional level: preliminary audition (*haixuan* 海选), second-round selection (*fuxuan* 复选), and a final elimination contest (*jinji sai* 晋级赛). Contestants who pass all three rounds on the regional level gather in Changsha, headquarters of Hunan TV, to compete to be the final winner. Professional judges, mainly veteran singers, celebrities, and television producers, select the top 50 candidates for each of the five participating regions in the preliminary audition, and the top 20 in the second-round selection. In the final elimination contests, a vote-in system is activated and television viewers can join in the selecting process and vote for their favorite contestants via text messaging (in 2005) and phone calls (in 2006). The audience's votes are counterbalanced by votes from popular judges—made up of a few dozen previously eliminated contestants (in 2005) and media workers (in 2006)—as well as the professional judges. The audience's votes determine the final winners of the competition.

Super Girl garnered massive attention and popularity, gained astounding commercial success, and catalyzed unprecedented audience participation. The second season in 2005, in particular, became a media and cultural spectacle. More than 150,000 people that year signed up for the preliminary auditions, and more than 400 million people watched the final episode. The show generated not only the highest advertising fee for the final episode but also other revenue venues such as sponsorship in text messages. The three winners selected by the audience, Li Yunchun (the champion), Zhang Liangyin (the runner-up), and Zhou Bichang (third place), have all become successful singers with large, devoted fan bases.

In 2007 *Super Girl* was canceled due to stricter regulations set by the SARFT for "healthier" entertainment. Although *Super Girl* was revived as *Happen Girl* in 2009 and 2011, the show lost its impressive media coverage and popularity enjoyed in the previous seasons, largely due to the cancelation of the audience vote-in system. However, the successful business model of *Super Girl* has inspired many singing talent shows on Chinese television since 2004. In the subsequent decade, more than 30 shows have been aired, such as CCTV's *Star Boulevard* (*Xingguang dadao* 星光大道, 2004–), Jiangxi TV's *Chinese Red Song Competition* (*Zhongguo hongge hui* 中国红歌会, 2006–2013), Jiangsu TV's *Absolute Resonance* (*Judui chang xiang* 绝对唱响, 2006–2010), Anhui TV's *Crazy about Singing* (*Wo wei ge kuang* 我为歌狂, 2013 and 2014), Shanghai Dragon TV's *Chinese Idol* (*Zhongguo meng zhi sheng* 中国梦之声, 2013–), and Beijing TV's *Chinese Duets* (*Zui mei hesheng* 最美合声, 2013–).

Despite increasingly harsh critiques from the central government and tighter regulations by the SARFT, singing competitions remain one of the most popular subgenres of reality show on Chinese television. As of 2015, the most watched singing competitions include Zhengjiang TV's *The Voice of China* (*Zhongguo hao shengyin* 中国好声音, 2012–), CCTV-3's *Sing My Song* (*Zhongguo hao gequ* 中国好歌曲, 2014–), and Hunan TV's *I Am a Singer* (*Wo shi geshou* 我是歌手, 2013–). These shows, various in details, all model on foreign television talent contests and continue to promote audience participation and/or grassroots success stories. *I Am a Singer*, for example, is modeled on the Korean reality show of the same name. It is aired on a weekly basis. Each week, contestants practice a song of their own choice and perform live for an audience of 500 in a studio. The audience's votes determine which one of the seven singers should be eliminated after the live performance. A new singer is brought in the next week for another round of competition. *I Am*

Singing competitions have been extremely popular on Chinese television in recent years, changing to incorporate more audience participation through voting for their favorite contestants. Here, the popular Chinese singer, Wang Feng (right) sings with a contestant on *The Voice of China* in 2013. (Imaginechina/Corbis)

a Singer has two unique selling points: first, all contestants are well-known and well-established singers; second, the votes of the audience alone determine the contestants' weekly rankings and the final winners.

The Voice of China and *Sing My Song* are both modeled on the Dutch program *The Voice of Holland*. The major difference of the two programs is that the contestants of *Sing My Song* must compose and perform their own songs. Both programs invite famous musicians and producers as judges/coaches who offer *mis en place* training for selected contestants and promise to help them make records in the near future. Both programs consist of three stages: the blind audition, the battle, and the live performance. Contestants compete to join the teams of judges/coaches in the blind audition, and then any two selected members of each team compete in the battle phase to advance into the first rounds of live performance. In various rounds of the live performance, public votes from the audience on site together with the professional coaches determine the final winners, who gain the opportunity of working with the coaches on their own careers as young musicians.

Jun Lei

See also: Dating Shows, China

Further Reading

Bai, Ruoyun. 2014. "'Clean Up the Screen,' Regulating Television Entertainment in the 2000s." In *Rethinking Chinese Television*. Ed. Bai Ruoyun and Geng Song, 69–86. New York: Routledge.

Yang, Ling. 2014. "Reality Talent Shows in China: Transnational Format, Affective Engagement, and the Chinese Dream." In *A Companion to Reality Television*. Ed. Laurie Ouellette, 517–540. Hoboken, NJ: Wiley-Blackwell.

Yin, Hong 尹鸿, Ran Ruxue 冉儒学，and Lu Hong 陆虹. 2006. *Yule xuanfeng: renshi dianshi zhenren xiu* 娱乐旋风：认识电视真人秀 [A Whirlwind of Entertainment: Understanding Reality TV]. Beijing: China Radio and TV Publishing House.

XIANGSHENG: CHINESE COMIC DIALOGUES

The Chinese comedic art called *xiangsheng* (相声), as it appears in the 21st century on stage, television, and the Internet, looks something like what Westerners call "stand-up comedy." It can involve one to five performers, but two performers is by far the most common form, so it is sometimes be called "comedians' dialogue" in English. It is also referred to as "crosstalk," but this translation is not ideal, because it appears to have sprung from a confusion of *xiāng* "each other" with *xiàng* "face." The original sense of the two characters 相声 is "face and voice." The actors use words, gestures, and facial expressions to help an audience to imagine, without props or scenery, droll scenes packed with puns, punch lines, put-downs, preposterous pretense, and other pieces of play. In recent times *xiangsheng*, here again resembling stand-up comedy, has lived on satire of contemporary society and politics—although performers working inside the People's Republic of China have to avoid naming names. Today, *xiangsheng* is a common part of China's annual Spring Festival Television Gala.

A hundred years ago the content was very different. *Xiangsheng* originally grew out of *xi* (戏), meaning "opera" or "drama," and, like *xi*, consisted of set scripts whose content was well known to audiences in advance. The reason for listening was not to hear witty new commentary but to enjoy and to evaluate the skill with which the performers could render well-established pieces, such as "Selling Cloth," in which a hawker spouts a fountain of words that leaves the performer, and in another sense the observing audience, quite breathless. Opera-style singing was important as well. Of the two performers, one was called the "joke setter" and the other the "joke cracker." The joke cracker was incorrigibly nutty—although what he said always had its weird logic, and this was part of the fun. The joke setter represented the audience's normal rationality on stage by providing short responses like "Really?," "Oh, come *on!*," and the like. In recent decades the distinction between these two traditional roles has largely dissolved, however.

Xiangsheng has always been viewed as a popular or even vulgar art form. Even among the subliterate popular Chinese arts, such as storytelling, drum singing, and clapper tales, *xiangsheng* has ranked especially low. It is probably the Chinese art most deeply soaked in the daily life of ordinary people.

Around the middle of the 20th century, two very large forces—one technological, the other political—impinged upon *xiangsheng* and changed its nature in a number of ways.

During the first half of the century, *xiangsheng* had been centered in northern towns and cities, notably Beijing, Tianjin, and Shenyang. Performers worked in entertainment districts or marketplaces. They wore gowns (*dagua* 大褂) and used folding fans to fan themselves or—more importantly—to slam shut and use as mini-clubs in mock attack on the other performer. They would begin by using a white powder to write on the ground a menu of their offerings. Then they used singing or a short comic piece (called a "cushion" *dianhua* 垫话) to try to attract a crowd, who, once captured, would be ethically obliged to address the question of how many coppers to put into a bowl after the performance. Later, largely under the influence of technology, most of these customs completely disappeared.

Radio was the first medium to bring changes. In the 1950s, *xiangsheng* began to be broadcast all across China on radio. This change greatly expanded the reach of *xiangsheng* but also affected the nature of the art itself: radio could deliver sound only, not sight. Of *xiangsheng*'s two traditional components, "face and voice," one now was gone. Performers had to be aware that, whatever they did, audiences now could hear only, not see.

In the 1980s, when television spread in China, expression and gesture were restored to *xiangsheng*, but the problem of the electronic wall between performer and audience remained. In early 20th-century performances, listeners had stood in an oval around two performers who faced each other at a distance of 20 feet or so. What the artists called *jiaoliu* (交流), or "communion with the audience," was considered essential to good performance. With radio and other electronic media, the separation of performers from audience has made *jiaoliu* much less intimate than it used to be, even during live performance. By the 1950s and 1960s, audiences were sitting in rows of seats inside auditoriums, while performers stood on stage, shoulder to shoulder, behind microphones. People bought tickets instead of dropping coins in bowls.

By the early 21st century, elderly aficionados of *xiangsheng*, pining for the 1940s and 1950s, despaired that "real" *xiangsheng* would ever return to the world. A return does, indeed, seem unlikely. To expect the various technological changes to reverse would be like waiting for an egg to unscramble. Meanwhile, the *xiangsheng* spirit has given rise to new artistic forms. Skits called *xiaopin* (小品), whose techniques of clever repartee owe a clear debt to *xiangsheng*, have emerged on television and the Internet.

The major political influence on *xiangsheng* arose from leaders of the Communist Party of China, who made a conscious decision in 1950 to use *xiangsheng* as a tool in spreading correct political and social attitudes (and, incidentally, standard Mandarin pronunciation) among "the masses." *Xiangsheng* had to be "improved," meaning cleansed of things like smut (which was known, in the jargon of the art, as "non-vegetarian *xiangsheng*") and backward social attitudes such as ridicule of the disabled. The authorities ordered that *xiangsheng* be recast as a tool for "praising" the new Communist society.

The puzzle of how to use an inherently satiric art as a tool in praising something gave rise, between 1950 and 1957, to a number of lively experiments in *xiangsheng*, but Mao Zedong's Anti-Rightist Campaign in 1957 abruptly ended all of these. The Maoist *xiangsheng* of ensuing years was obliged to convey "correct" political messages with super clarity. Problems remained, however, because audiences did not always laugh in prescribed ways, and this worried officials.

Authoritarian control of *xiangsheng* abated after Mao died in 1976, and from then until 1980 the *xiangsheng* world enjoyed an interlude that allowed satire of the kind that had been possible during the early 1950s—although now, after the "ten years of a rampaging Gang of Four," there was fresh material to work with. From the 1980s to the early 21st century, the scope that political authorities have allowed to *xiangsheng* has fluctuated, but on the whole it has grown larger. In contemporary times almost anything has been all right so long as one avoids incorrect comments on "sensitive" issues: Tibet, Xinjiang, Taiwan, Falun Gong, the June Fourth Massacre, the wealth of top leaders, the Nobel Peace Prize, and others.

Despite these two great tides of change in *xiangsheng*, however, its techniques have remained sufficiently continuous through the years that one can, and people do, use the same term, *xiangsheng*, to refer to the art in the 1910s as well as the 2010s.

Perry Link

See also: Spring Festival Television Gala, China

Further Reading

Kaikkonnen, Marja. 1990. *Modern Xiangsheng as Didactic Entertainment*. Stockholm, SE: Institute of Oriental Languages.

Link, Perry. 2007. "The Crocodile Bird: *Xiangsheng* in the Early 1950s." In *Dilemmas of Victory: The Early Years of the People's Republic of China*. Ed. Jeremy Brown and Paul G. Pickowicz, 207–231. Cambridge, MA: Harvard University Press.

Wang, Jue王决, Wang Jingshou 汪景寿, and Fujita Kaori 藤田香. 1995. 中国相声史 [A History of Chinese *Xiangsheng*]. Beijing: Yanshan chubanshe燕山出版社.

Chapter 5: Internet and Social Media

Introduction

The Internet is transforming rapidly, as are the social media that people use to share information and entertainment and to connect. As we see in the entries in this chapter, these platforms of communication and entertainment are also put to serious political use in Asia and Oceania. As in other parts of the world, Internet users in Asia and Oceania continue to reinvent and reimagine the Internet and its possibilities, redefining the media of the Internet and redefining themselves as members of society, consumers, and political participants.

While popular culture on the Internet may bring to mind the frivolities of "selfies," gossipy instant messaging, and celebrity updates, a generation is now coming of age with these new media, and they take it for granted that these multifaceted tools of the Internet are more than modes of diversion and light entertainment. Social media are tools of organization, modes of both lighthearted and serious self-expression, and means of self-identification and social participation. The power of the Internet and social media has been proven again and again in recent years, growing so fast, and expanding into so many realms of our daily lives, that it is no longer easy to categorize the modes of communication and connection. As in the rest of the world, people use these tools every day, and powerful cultural and political forces have also taken note and begun to curb, co-opt, and utilize the Internet and social media in their own ways.

Censorship of the Internet and its use is an important point to consider here. Not everyone has free and open access to the Internet, and some governments constrain or closely monitor their Internet users and their online behavior. As a point of reference for the reader, the freedom of Internet use in the United States, while perhaps seemingly unrestricted, is also not without controversy. The complex system of legal constraints, intellectual property protection, and government seizure of computers and domains in the United States leads some, like Reporters Without Borders and the OpenNet Initiative, to view the U.S. government as unfriendly to Internet freedom and especially aggressive in its monitoring of Internet use and communication.

The Internet is used and monitored differently by the people, corporations, and governments of Asia and Oceania. People under the different governments have widely ranging degrees of access and usage of the Internet and social media—for example, the contrasts are significant between Internet use in North and South Korea or between Taiwan, Hong Kong, and mainland China. In North Korea, for

Hunger Games Salute (Thailand)

Many in Thailand opposed the military coup that took place there in the spring of 2014. In the fall of that year, an unlikely symbol of protest spread around the country, as people held aloft their hands with the middle three fingers extended, in what has become known as the "Hunger Games Salute," named for the American Hunger Games film franchise. These films, released in four installments each year from 2012 through 2015, are based on the young-adult novels of Suzanne Collins and take place in an Orwellian future of oppression and brutality. In the stories, young people living in conquered districts are forced to fight to the death like gladiators, until they rise in rebellion against the authorities, led by the character Katniss Everdeen (played in the films by Oscar winner Jennifer Lawrence). The films were hugely popular in the United States and also around the world, bringing in billions of dollars at the box office.

Kathleen M. Nadeau and Jeremy A. Murray

example, general online access to the global Internet is largely restricted, and most users only have access to the domestic intranet, Kwangmyong, which includes e-mail, social media, and approved news and information pages. In the People's Republic of China (PRC), censorship and constraints on access are far less severe than in North Korea, but they are still significant and can be calibrated to suit the political climate. State censors can and do shut down websites, imprison dissident netizens, slow down access to certain websites to the point of inaccessibility, and limit sensitive search terms. State censors within the PRC block some websites, like Twitter, Facebook, and Google, sites that are hugely popular on the global Internet. Some savvy Internet users find their way around this blockage, and leaders of these and other websites try to negotiate permissions for the websites to operate in China, though this sometimes means self-censorship or submitting to Chinese censorship, and even more controversially, allowing Chinese law enforcement access to user data. Some, like the professional networking site LinkedIn and the ride-sharing company Uber, have found a way to do business with the Chinese government. But like all foreign companies, even Internet giants like these must now do business with an increasingly robust Chinese domestic economy. For example, the search engine Baidu and the online marketplace Alibaba dominate the Chinese landscape in a way that may preclude competition from Google and Amazon, even if the latter were given fuller access. Amazon does have access to Chinese consumers but is largely unable to compete effectively with Alibaba.

Other countries and regions, like Hong Kong, Taiwan, South Korea, Australia, New Zealand, Japan, and others, experience relatively unfettered access to the global Internet, but it should again be noted that these governments still monitor and curtail aspects of Internet use within their jurisdiction to varying degrees, starting, of course, with criminal activity. The government of South Korea, for example, has a complex monitoring system of the Internet, which can include censoring activity that is considered subversive or immoral. In Southeast Asia, Burma and Vietnam impose significant constraints and exercise powerful control over the Internet. Religion and its advocacy or denigration is controversial online in Asia and Oceania, as in the United States. Online visual representations of the prophet Muhammad, for example, or antihomosexual materials (expressed as Christian or other religious belief) gives rise to questions of free speech and how intrusive a state censor can or should be.

Beyond the constraints on Internet use, which affect all countries to varying degrees, the Internet has profoundly affected the way that people communicate. In some regions of Asia, for example, the arrival of cheap cell phones meant that sometimes the traditional landline telephone was leapfrogged in favor of the cell phone's affordability and convenience. The infrastructure cost of telephone wiring was bypassed, and for many people in this part of the world, as with many young people around the globe, the cell phone has been the first and main means of person-to-person telecommunication. Text messages, or SMS (short message service), are the preferred mode of convenient communication, and where prepaid cell phones are preferred over subscriber plans, texting is often much cheaper. Accessibility to the Internet, however, does not always come with cell-phone access. For most countries in Central Asia, Internet access is constrained by a lack of supporting infrastructure and relative per capita poverty, which precludes ownership of smartphones or personal computers. In these countries, like Kazakhstan, however, Internet use is also seeing its most rapid growth. Internet cafés are generally the most common locales for Internet use in Central Asia, and access can fluctuate with shifts in political leadership or conflict in the region.

As with communication, the Internet has also transformed entertainment, with online sensations being born overnight in viral videos and massively shared content. Microblog platforms like Twitter, or in China, Weibo, have become prevalent in both communication and entertainment. Facebook and YouTube have also taken root in most countries of Asia and Oceania. Original YouTube content in many countries has led to the kind of viral celebrity seen in the United States. Facebook and Twitter have allowed new modes for social connections to be made and maintained, sometimes with political implications, as they can potentially facilitate online organization of advocacy groups. While this can potentially be politically subversive, it can also mobilize aid organizations and fuel humanitarian fund-raising drives.

The entries in this section, while not exhaustive on Internet and social media use in Asia and Oceania, will provide some very useful and representative snapshots of the Internet landscape at the time of writing.

Jeremy A. Murray and Kathleen M. Nadeau

Further Reading

Cui, Litang, and Michael H. Prosser. 2014. *Social Media in Asia*. Doerzbach, Germany: Dignity Press.

DeNardis, Laura. 2014. *The Global War for Internet Governance*. New Haven, CT: Yale University Press.

Willnat, Lars, and Annette Aw. 2014. *Social Media, Culture and Politics in Asia*. Frankfurt, Germany: Peter Lang Publishing.

Yang, Guobin. 2015. *China's Contested Internet*. Copenhagen, DK: Nordic Institute of Asian Studies.

AMNESTY INTERNATIONAL AND POP CULTURE

Amnesty International (AI) uses pop culture in various forms to spur people to advocate for human rights around the globe. Through the use of musicians, actors, Facebook, and Twitter, AI has harnessed new ways to involve members in exciting and innovative ways. How one disseminates information has changed over the years, from gossip to letters, newspapers, TV personalities, and now through the Internet in various forms. The use of pop culture is reaching many potential activists and spurring change in various countries.

Amnesty International is a nongovernmental organization (NGO) that focuses on human rights around the globe. This Nobel Peace Prize recipient (1977) is independent of any government, political ideology, economic interest, or religion and is funded mainly by membership fees and public donations. Its vision is for every person to enjoy all the rights enshrined in the Universal Declaration of Human Rights and other international human rights standards, such as The Convention on the Elimination of All Forms of Discrimination against Women (CEDAW) and the Convention on the Rights of the Child (CRC) (Amnesty International 2015). One of AI's stated objectives is to conduct research and generate Actions to prevent and end grave abuses of human rights and to demand justice for those whose rights have been violated. Actions are ways in which people learn about a human rights issue and how to advocate for/against it, such as signing a petition, attending an event, donating, writing columns, visiting a representative, and so on.

Each country is allowed to start and run its own version of Amnesty International, in which dues-paying members get to vote on what issues or campaigns they find important, be it a local, international, or a foreign issue, as long as they follow guidelines set up by the main office in London, England. For example, India, Hong Kong, Mongolia, and Nepal all have their own version of Amnesty International within their borders. Nepal focuses on six campaigns: gender violence, Iraqi militias, torture, enforced disappearances in Syria, prisoners of conscience (POCs), and their My Body/My Rights campaign, which seeks to safeguard people's sexual and reproductive rights.

Amnesty International is a grassroots movement. A grassroots movement, in the sense of justice, is about a group of ordinary citizens who come together around an issue in order to influence people in powerful positions, whose power depends on cooperation from the people within their borders. This can also be achieved on a worldwide scale in which grassroots movements from various countries can exert their collective power on a single government, focusing on one issue, such as female genital mutilation. Amnesty International has over 2 million dues-paying members and over 5 million activists that help on various campaigns. One way in which AI attempts to get people to join the cause is by using pop icons to attract ordinary citizens to participate.

The use of pop icons draws people from various backgrounds that might not have known about the organization. For example, in Taiwan, not only does AI

Taiwan use pop-culture icons to draw citizens to participate, the president of the chapter is the lead singer of Chthonic, a well-known heavy-metal group in Taiwan, Freddy Lim (1976–). Lim has an active Facebook page, with 17,000 followers, in which he posts various human rights Actions, reaching people not associated with AI. Another example of a pop icon helping AI is the 14th Dalai Lama, Tenzin Gyatso (1935–). Along with his 20 million Tibetan Buddhist followers, millions of people admire the Dalai Lama for his wisdom and grace. The Dalai Lama has lent his voice and likeness to Amnesty International for various campaigns, such as the Make Your Mark for Human Rights (1998) event in Paris, France, and the Shine a Light (2011) event in Long Beach, California. Amnesty International stated that the Make Your Mark for Human Rights events garnered 3 million thumbprints collected from 34 countries, which led to 17 prisoners of conscience being released.

Another way in which AI tries to connect with people is through the use of popular social media outlets like Twitter and Facebook. Amnesty International has learned how to reach millions of people by teaching about human rights abuses and how to eliminate such abuses. The way that AI uses these various media outlets is by finding properly educated researchers (all volunteers) that focus on countries or themes and having them post journal articles, newsletters, and Actions on the abuses they are researching. Not only does AI post these items on its Twitter and Facebook accounts, each country specialist or thematic specialist has the option to create his or her own accounts and post these items there as well. For instance, the main AI account has 1,340,000 followers on Twitter, AI Thailand has 714 followers, and AI Women's Rights has about 7,000 followers. You see the same pattern with Facebook as well. The main AI account has 743,000 followers and AI Pakistan has 1,000 followers. This allows the person who follows the group more control over the information that he or she gets, making the experience more personalized.

The # symbol, called a hashtag, is used to demark keywords or topics in a post on Twitter or Facebook and link all these hashtagged tweets and posts together on the individual platforms. By adding a hashtag before a word or short phrase, without using a space, that word or phrase becomes an active link, which, with a single click, allows the user to view every other post that contains that same hashtag. Each hashtagged word or phrase becomes its own category, allowing users to see who is also addressing the same topic. This, in return, allows people with the same trending interests to virtually connect around the world, validating issues and topics among the community. Hashtags were created originally for Twitter as a way to categorize messages, so that if you clicked the hashtagged word or phrase, you would be able to see all the posts that have that same hashtag. For example, if AI was to post a picture with the word #Prageeth and you were to click that hashtagged word, either on Twitter or Facebook, it would take you to every tweet or post that had that same hashtag. This allows users to click the link and find others who are posting on the subject, which in turn allows others to see the post. The more people post or tweet that hashtag, the more popular it gets; if the post is very popular, it can be seen by millions of Twitter or Facebook users.

As an example of using Facebook or Twitter, the Sri Lankan country specialist created an Action in which he had people learn about journalists living in Sri Lanka. These journalists wrote articles about the atrocities committed by both the government and the rebel group in Sri Lanka during the civil war (1983–2009). A pro-opposition journalist, Eknaligoda Prageeth, disappeared in 2010, and the government has yet to start any formal investigation into his whereabouts. Amnesty International created an Action that asked all members who were part of the one-day educational program to take a picture of themselves holding a picture of Prageeth or a sign stating "Where is #Prageeth?" and post it on the AI Sri Lankan Twitter and Facebook accounts.

Brandon Fryman

See also: Protest Music, Indonesia (Chapter 1: Popular Music)

Further Reading

Amnesty International. www.amnesty.org. Accessed February 20, 2015.
Hopgood, Stephen. 2006. *Keepers of the Flame: Understanding Amnesty International.* Ithaca, NY: Cornell University Press.

EGAO AND ONLINE SATIRE, CHINA

In Mandarin Chinese, *egao* literally means "making bad" or "evil doing." Popularized along the developments of participatory online platforms in the country, *egao* indicates an online-specific genre of satirical humor and grotesque parody circulating in the form of user-generated content. From its beginnings as a form of vernacular creativity developed by humorous Internet users, *egao* has become a widely popular phenomenon generating fleeting celebrities, circulating across mass media, and crossing national and linguistic borders.

Since the early years of its adoption in China, the Internet has been understood as a space of interpersonal interaction, public opinion guidance, and national governance but also as a space of leisure, fun, and excitement. As one of the first Chinese media theorists puts it, "the Internet is a place of ecstasy" (Yan 1997, 72). As expected, with the popularization of Internet access and the participatory possibilities of Web 2.0 platforms and mobile devices, fun, humor, and leisure have become some of the main components of Chinese Internet users' engagement with the medium. In contrast to forms of humor distributed through traditional media, online platforms and services allow and encourage the creative contributions of users. User-generated content (UGC) is at the center of most contemporary Internet platforms' business model, and in light of its popularity, humorous content makes up a large part of what gets disseminated on a daily basis across Chinese social media. Online humor includes many forms and genres constantly in the making, from funny stories copy-pasted across discussion boards to animated GIFs, music videos, and funny photomontages. In China, the most prominent term indicating a locally specific genre of humorous content is *egao.*

The term *egao* (恶搞), in Mandarin Chinese literally meaning "evil doing," rose to wide popularity in China around the early 2000s. The curious composition of the word *egao* is due to its etymological derivation from the Japanese term *kuso*. In Japan, *kuso* is a slang term used in early online communities to indicate a form of aesthetic appreciation of badly made content—specifically, poorly designed video games. Through the mediation of Internet users in Taiwan and Hong Kong, the term *kuso* has been adopted across Greater China in its Mandarin translation *egao* with a much wider scope of meanings. As many other vernacular terms negotiated by users of online platforms, *egao* is quite fluid and vaguely defined and does not indicate a specific genre of humor or satire directed at precise topics. Rather, *egao* is a flexible descriptor for vernacular forms of humor that privilege certain grotesque aesthetics, politically incorrect in-jokes, or a playful harshness in making fun of someone or something.

Originally, *egao* had a strong overtone of amateur parody, camp, or satire created through simple technical means and disseminated through online platforms. Early pieces of *egao* relied on little more than basic editing tools such as Microsoft Paint, the QQ screen-capture and editing tool, or Adobe Photoshop. One of the earliest examples of *egao*, widely quoted across academic literature, is the series of photomontages of "Little Fatty," a chubby kid whose funny face from a photograph made available online was PSed ("Photoshopped") on a wide range of popular images to great comic effect. Little Fatty, later identified as Shanghai resident Qian Zhijun, rode the *egao* train and achieved relative celebrity by virtue of his online exposure, even participating in movies, advertisements, and television shows. The case of Little Fatty exemplifies how quickly *egao* can move from the vernacular creativity of Internet users into pop culture, mass media, and commercial settings.

Another widely documented *egao* case is the video "The Bloody Case that Started from a Steamed Bun" ("*Yige mantou yinfa de xue'an*" 一个馒头引发的血案), a parody of the blockbuster movie *The Promise* (2005) by director Chen Kaige. Hu Ge, the creator of the parody, was threatened with legal action by Chen Kaige and received several notices from the Chinese Communist Party Propaganda Department. Regardless, after being hailed by Internet users as a founding father of *egao*, he embraced his newfound celebrity status and moved on with his career, directing commercials and short movies. Similarly, other characters, symbols, words, and celebrities made popular by the circulation of *egao* are over time appropriated by popular culture and commodified across media, such as in the case of the "Grass Mud Horse," a fantastical animal invented as a homophone to a Mandarin profanity that has been widely depicted as an alpaca and marketed in countless forms.

Besides these well-known examples, *egao* encompasses a constantly growing repertoire, impossible to summarize or circumscribe, ranging from animated GIF photomontages of Barack Obama and Kim Jong-un to audiovisual mash-ups and remixes of television series and Japanese anime, from humorous texts copy-pasted across discussion boards to sexualized emoticons shared over instant-messaging platforms. At some point in 2015, Chinese Internet users unearthed an old TV spot featuring Hong Kong actor Jackie Chan making a strange noise to describe the effect of a shampoo on his own hair. The quirky vocalization, transcribed with the nonexistent pinyin (or Chinese Romanization) syllable *duang*, rapidly became a massively trending topic on Chinese online platforms, inspiring a cascade of photomontages, emoticons, animated GIFs, and video remixes parodying the shampoo TV spot, while *duang* was added to the ever-growing lexicon of Chinese online vernacular repertoires.

At the early stages of its popularity, *egao* generated knee-jerk reactions from the Chinese authorities and was targeted with attempts at engendering moral panic through editorials and opinion pieces on popular media as well as recurring calls for a crackdown on amateur parodies targeting sensitive topics, party members, public figures, or even private individuals. Gradually, with the realization that *egao* helped to channel grassroots creativity and to vent widely shared discontents, local discourses have portrayed it as a weapon of the masses employed by Chinese Internet users to participate in a burgeoning online civil society. As an opinion piece on *China Daily* explains, the two characters for *egao*, meaning "evil" and "work," combine to describe "a subculture that is characterized by humor, revelry, subversion, grass-root spontaneity, defiance of authority, mass participation and multi-media high-tech" (Huang 2006).

A similar understanding of *egao* is shared by Euro-American scholarship, often focused on the most prominent examples of parodies with political overtones or wide-ranging implications across media. In this sort of analyses, *egao* is construed as a site of a power struggle and cultural intervention providing emotional catharsis to a new generation of citizens. These arguments often interpret the flourishing of vernacular creativity in online spaces as a reaction to the tight control exercised by the Chinese authorities. Alternative understandings of *egao* seek to complicate the theorization of this profane form of humor beyond its immediate appearance as a malicious form of resistance: *egao* should be interpreted at different scales, as at the same time "a genre, a mode, a practice, an ethos and a culture" (Rea 2013, 151). Moreover, the multilingual and cross-cultural nature of much *egao*, founded on the practices of copy-pasting, editing, remixing, and mashing up, raises questions of cultural specificity, calling into question how "Chinese" this phenomenon might be in the larger ecologies of circulation of online humor.

Gabriele de Seta

See also: Sui, Mike

Further Reading

Gong, Haomin, and Xin Yang. 2010. "Digitized Parody: The Politics of *Egao* in Contemporary China." *China Information* 24, no. 1: 3–26. doi: 10.1177/0920203X09350249.

Huang, Qing. 2006. "Parody Can Help People Ease Work Pressure." *China Daily*. July 22. www.chinadaily.com.cn/cndy/2006-07/22/content_646887.htm. Accessed March 26, 2016.

Li, Henry Siling. 2009. "The Turn to the Self: From 'Big Character Posters' to YouTube Videos." *Chinese Journal of Communication* 2, no. 1: 50–60. doi: 10.1080/17544750802639077.

Rea, Christopher G. 2013. "Spoofing (e'gao) Culture on the Chinese Internet." In *Humour in Chinese Life and Culture: Resistance and Control in Modern Times*. Ed. Jessica Milner Davis and Jocelyn Chey, 149–172. Hong Kong: Hong Kong University Press.

Shifman, Limor. 2014. *Memes in Digital Culture*. The MIT Press Essential Knowledge Series. Cambridge, MA: MIT Press.

Wallis, Cara. 2011. "New Media Practices in China: Youth Patterns, Processes, and Politics." *International Journal of Communication* 5: 406–436.

Wang, Shaojung Sharon. 2012. "China's Internet Lexicon: Symbolic Meaning and Commoditization of Grass Mud Horse in the Harmonious Society." *First Monday* 17, no. 1. www.firstmonday.dk/ojs/index.php/fm/article/view/3758. Accessed March 26, 2016.

Yan, F. 1997. "Shenghuo zai wangluo zhong—Shangpian" [Living in the Internet—First part]. In *Shenghuo zai wangluo zhong* [Living in the Internet]. Ed. F. Yan and Wei Bu, 3–114. Beijing, China: Zhongguo Renmin Daxue Chubanshe.

THE "GANGNAM STYLE" FAD

In 2012 the world was hit with a cultural phenomenon inspired by the South Korean song "Gangnam Style" and its accompanying music video, cowritten by Yoo Gun-hyung (1979–) and Park Jae-sang (1977–). Park Jae-sang would also be the one to provide the vocals under his stage name, Psy, making this his 18th single release on his sixth studio album, *Psy 6 Part 1*.

Many have categorized Psy's "Gangnam Style" as K-pop and considered it to be part of the *Hallyu* (Korean Wave) because of its global reach and how it has achieved the *Hallyu* objective of spreading South Korean culture and entertainment abroad. There have even been episodes involving high-profile leaders who have bolstered this view, such as when U.S. president Barack Obama remarked to South Korean president Park Geun-hye that "around the world, people are being swept up by Korean culture—the Korean Wave. And as I mentioned to President Park, my daughters have taught me a pretty good Gangnam Style" (Eckert 2013). In another reference, UN Secretary General Ban Ki-moon, a South Korean native, expressed his pride in how Psy had brought K-pop and South Korea's sense of humor to a global audience.

On the other hand, there have been those who disagree, claiming that Psy does not promote the same physical characteristics as many of the acts involved in the K-pop genre, nor does he allow his songs to be manufactured for him, instead relying on his own talents for lyrical creation. Euny Hong, an American-born author raised in South Korea, commented on this during an interview with *Huffington Post*, asserting that Psy "is and isn't the harbinger of Korean Wave," citing the above reasons (Crum 2014).

"Gangnam Style" was released on July 15, 2012. Originally intended mainly for his local K-pop market, where it debuted at No. 1 on South Korea's *Gaon* chart, it burst onto the global scene when the full version of the music video was uploaded onto the video-sharing website YouTube. Its first day on the popular website it garnered more than 500,000 views, and by the end of December it had broken a YouTube record when it was the first video to receive more than 1 billion views, and then soon after, more than 2 billion views. The records broken did not stop there. "Gangnam Style" has managed to collect the following records: most-viewed K-pop video on YouTube, most-"liked" video on YouTube, first K-pop song to top the U.K. Singles Chart, and most-viewed video on YouTube overall. It was when the video broke the 2-billion-view mark that it hit news again, as "Gangnam Style" "broke" the original YouTube counter. As originally coded, YouTube kept track of views up to 32 integers, but after surpassing the 2-billion mark, Google, the owners of YouTube, had to go on record saying, "'Gangnam Style' has been viewed so many times we have to upgrade!"

"Gangnam Style" started out as a slow-rolling storm that turned into a hurricane. In its original market in South Korea, while the song was generally well received, it was criticized for failing to accurately portray South Korean culture and as being nothing more than a generically catchy beat with nonsensical lyrics. "Gangnam Style" initially did poorly in its Japanese markets, which led to the cancelation of a planned Japanese rerelease of "Gangnam Style" by Psy's Japanese record label, YGEX. Many factors have been attributed to the poor reception in Japan. One account is that Psy did not fit the polished K-pop image that was promoted in Japan, and others believe that negative reception could be due to the lack of coverage of the hit in Japan due to bilateral diplomatic tensions during this time.

Looking at the popularity and impact of "Gangnam Style" on Western culture, one might first look at its sales as an indicator. "Gangnam Style" was certified multiple times as platinum in over 13 European and North American countries as well as being certified gold in two of them. "Gangnam Style" inspired three of the five largest recorded flash mobs in France and Italy. Many Western news outlets reported on how "Gangnam Style" had transversed cultures, one example being when *Agence France-Presse* commented on how "Gangnam Style" opened countries up to the Korean Wave. While Korean television drama and popular music had already found avid audiences throughout East Asia, for many beyond this region, "Gangnam Style" was their introduction to the phenomenon of K-Wave and K-pop.

In the United States, after the release of the single, Psy made many appearances across different venues, allowing the United States to be exposed to "Gangnam Style" as much as possible. Such venues included baseball games, the MTV Music Awards, *The Ellen DeGeneres Show*, the American Music Awards, and *The Tonight Show with Jay Leno*, just to name a few. The popularity of "Gangnam Style" in the West has inspired many parodies, which were performed live or uploaded online. These homages to "Gangnam Style" have not just been tied to music but also politics, sports, and television. Even Google executive chairperson Eric Schmidt did the "Gangnam Style" dance when visiting the Seoul, Korea, offices.

"Gangnam Style" takes its name from the Gangnam District of Seoul, South Korea. Gangnam District is believed to be a hip, trend-setting district, and Psy draws a comparison between Gangnam and Rodeo Drive of Beverly Hills, using this as inspiration for the video's eclectic and humorous style of clothing and dance. Both Psy and Hong grew up in the Gangnam District during the 1980s. Hong has commented that the area was not as affluent when she lived there, giving some insight into the rapid changes that the district has seen and perhaps contributing to Psy's tongue-in-cheek portrayal of the district's lavish, nouveau-riche culture.

Daniel A. Stolp

See also: K-pop (Chapter 1: Popular Music)

Further Reading

Crum, Maddie. 2014. "'Korean Cool' Is More Than Just 'Gangnam Style.'" *Huffington Post.* August 6. www.huffingtonpost.com/2014/08/06/korean-cool-book_n_5655269.html. Accessed June 13, 2015.

Eckert, Paul. 2013. "North Korea Has Gained Nothing from Recent Threats, Obama Says." *Reuters.* May 7. www.reuters.com/article/2013/05/07/us-korea-north-us-obama-idUS BRE9460TK20130507. Accessed May 31, 2015.

Hong, Euny. 2014. *The Birth of Korean Cool: How One Nation Is Conquering the World through Pop Culture.* New York: Picador.

GREAT FIREWALL, CHINA

Chinese authorities have regulated the Internet since the early days of the country going online. The government's efforts to regulate and control the development of networked communications have been famously paralleled to the construction of a "Great Firewall," a play on words combining the Great Wall of China and the technical term for a network security system. The Great Firewall, also abbreviated as GFW, has become a shorthand term to indicate an ensemble of legal provisions, infrastructural projects, governmental intervention, and political campaigns targeting the dissemination of online content in China. While the term has entered popular culture and media discourse, it does not indicate a specific artifact or technology but broadly encapsulates the limitations, surveillance, and censorship, which, to debatable degrees, influence the way people use the Internet in China.

Over 20 years of Internet development in the country, the Chinese government has consistently stepped up its attempts at regulating the increasingly pervasive development of information and communication technologies (ICTs) within the national borders of the People's Republic of China (PRC). From an early approach at Internet governance mostly grounded in laws and guidelines, Chinese authorities have reinforced their grasp on online spaces by developing refined monitoring and filtering systems and augmenting them with task forces of state-employed censors. The interplay between these measures, significantly more flexible and refined than a simple firewall, allows authorities to monitor and prosecute local websites and Internet users for the dissemination of sensitive, illegal, and immoral content as well as effectively controlling the information that is accessible online from within the country at any time.

Curiously, the term "Great Firewall" was not invented by Chinese authorities but proposed by writers Geremie Barmé and Sang Ye in June 1997 as the title of a report on the development of the Internet in China published by *Wired* magazine. Barmé and Sang were quoting an unnamed Chinese engineer who explained to them how China was building a system to force Internet service providers (ISPs) to impede access to problematic websites from within the country, and especially the ones promoting separatist movements, religious sects, and pro-democracy activism.

Since 1997, the apparatus of control at the disposal of Chinese authorities has been substantially expanded and diversified. The Great Firewall now includes constantly updated regulations and party guidelines for media outlets, larger infrastructural projects, such as the Golden Shield Project (*Jindun Gongcheng* 金盾工程) or the Green Dam Youth Escort (*Lüba·Huaqi Huhang* 绿坝·花季护航), and nationwide campaigns such as the 2014 Sweeping Away Pornography and Striking Illegality—Clean Web campaign (*Saohuang Dafei·Jingwang* 扫黄打非·净网). Thanks to its evocative combination of national heritage and filtering technology, the metaphor of the Great Firewall has entered popular culture in both the English and Chinese languages, achieving currency in news coverage and media scholarship. While the English term "Great Firewall" is used as a shorthand for the ensemble of measures through which Chinese authorities control ICTs, in Chinese it is most often used by Internet users, in its acronym GFW, to refer to practical instances of censorship or blockage that have to be circumvented by "crossing the wall" (*fānqiáng* 翻墙) through virtual private networks (VPNs) or other technologies.

Chinese authorities' control over media did not begin with the arrival of the Internet. As scholars like Jack L. Qiu explain, there has historically been very little difference between "censorship" and "regulation" in Chinese political culture, and the demands of authorities have often had the upper hand over media rights and free speech. China got its first Internet connection in 1994, and relevant regulations closely followed the development of the medium, as the authorities worried about the potential dangers brought by a looming information revolution.

The legal instruments put in place since the early years of ICTs in China had the declared purpose of censoring content harmful to social stability and national security while at the same time protecting local Internet industries from foreign competition. Through subsequent iterations, this combination of censorship and protectionism has coalesced into a highly centralized and regulated national infrastructure: Internet traffic enters China from a few tightly monitored gateways. ISPs are required to obtain official licenses and are required to archive user data. Internet users are registered through increasingly comprehensive and detailed schemes of identification.

The Great Firewall is not programmed to monitor or censor specific kinds of websites or information. Rather, it is constantly updated and refined to block access to information, stifle discussions, or hinder dissemination of content according to the political climate and the current events in China and abroad. As evidenced by Jason Q. Ng, the span of topics falling under these different forms of media control is rather broad, often inconsistent, and its rationale sometimes unfathomable. Along with well-documented sensitive issues such as the Tiananmen Square protests of 1989, the Falun Gong and other religious cults, rumors about Chinese Communist Party members, and ethnic tensions in Tibet and Xinjiang, the Great Firewall flags or blocks terms that have no apparent connection with any sensitive issue or current political concern.

With the development of the Web 2.0 and the massive penetration of the Internet into everyday life, as these forms of filtering showed their infrastructural and organizational costs and limitations, Chinese authorities have increasingly delegated control to ISPs, social media platforms, and individual websites. In addition to techniques such as DNS (domain name system) poisoning, IP (Internet protocol) header filtering, deep-packet inspection, and proxy filtering, authorities resort to legal pressure on service providers, keyword blacklists enforced on companies and online platforms, as well as social pressure on individual users, in order to maintain a degree of control over information shared online.

The Great Firewall has been described as "the most extensive effort to selectively censor human expression ever implemented" (King, Pan, and Roberts 2013, 326), and its functioning has been perused and tested at different scales and in different times to try to get a sense of the political implications of what was considered sensitive and dangerous by Chinese authorities. Some theorizations have identified it as an authoritarian infrastructure limiting freedom of speech and hindering democratic change in China. Others have challenged this assumption by showing how the activities of Chinese Internet users are not more culturally or linguistically secluded than other national populations and how a large percentage of them approve of governmental control over the Internet. Ultimately, the metaphor of the Great Firewall evokes a convenient imagination of China's national sovereignty applied to communication technologies, but its actual composition and functioning is worth exploring in depth to understand how control, surveillance, and censorship work at different scales.

Gabriele de Seta

See also: Radio and Television, Tibet (Chapter 4: Television and Radio)

Further Reading

Du, Xueping. 1999. "Internet Diffusion and Usage in China." *Prometheus* 17, no. 4: 405–420. doi: 10.1080/08109029908632119.

Endeshaw, Assafa. 2004. "Internet Regulation in China: The Never-ending Cat and Mouse Game." *Information & Communications Technology Law* 13, no. 1: 41–57. doi: 10.1080/1360083042000190634.

Guo, Steve, and Guangchao Feng. 2012. "Understanding Support for Internet Censorship in China: An Elaboration of the Theory of Reasoned Action." *Journal of Chinese Political Science* 17, no. 1: 33–52. doi: 10.1007/s11366-011-9177-8.

King, Gary, Jennifer Pan, and Margaret E. Roberts. 2013. "How Censorship in China Allows Government Criticism but Silences Collective Expression." *American Political Science Review* 107, no. 2: 326–343. doi: 10.1017/S0003055413000014.

Ng, Jason Q. 2013. *Blocked on Weibo: What Gets Suppressed on China's Version of Twitter (and Why)*. New York: The New Press.

Taneja, Harsh, and Angela Xiao Wu. 2014. "Does the Great Firewall Really Isolate the Chinese? Integrating Access Blockage with Cultural Factors to Explain Web User Behavior." *The Information Society* 30, no. 5: 297–309. doi: 10.1080/01972243.2014.944728.

HAN HAN

If one asks Chinese youth, especially those born in the 1980s and 1990s, who are the most popular and influential people in their generation, definitely the name of Han Han must be near the top of the list. However, when we ask who Han Han is, the answer must be diverse and contradictory. Yes, these are precisely the characteristics of Han Han that make him who he is. He is talented in multiple areas and is a self-made figure, not the princeling or second generation of a wealthy or government-official family. In fact, Han Han did not even finish high school but still has a sharp mind and unique opinions on political and social affairs, making him a prominent public intellectual.

Many love Han Han, and even adulate him, calling him "the Lu Xun of Our Age." Lu Xun (1881–1936) was one of the most influential Chinese writers in the early 20th century. His work focused on criticism of society and humanity. Some refer to Han Han in this way, and others call him a spokesperson for the 1980s generation. Still others dislike Han, saying that his commentaries lack depth and merely hit hot topics in order to attract naive readers. Some even question the authenticity of his works and suggest that he has plagiarized his writings or that he uses a ghostwriter. Although there are many controversies about him, there is no doubt that his popularity is not only because of his writing talent and unique personality; his prominence also reflects the values of a young generation in contemporary China. Compared to older Chinese, the young generation is more realistic, self-centered, and

The Chinese cultural sensation, Han Han, seen here in 2015, defies categorization. A racecar driver, filmmaker, author, actor, singer, and more, he became extremely popular as an essayist and blogger, with savvy cultural criticism that many consider to be the voice of a generation. (Imaginechina/Corbis)

materialistic. They pursue a better life and good governance but do not seem to really care about whether the country is governed by a one-party or multiparty system.

Born in 1982, and living in Shanghai, Han Han is most famously a prominent Chinese writer. He has published over 20 books since 2000, and most of the books are ranked on the annual best-seller list. His first novel, *San chong men* (*Triple Doorway*), as of 2012, had sold more than 2 million copies. He is also a commenter on current affairs in China; as of May 13, 2015, his blog on Sina.com had attracted over 601 million visitors, a national record, and since the end of 2009 his postings have averaged more than a million readers. He directed a film, *Houhui wu qi* (*The Continent*), in 2014, which has earned over 600 million yuan in box-office revenues. Beyond his literary talent, he is also a professional racecar driver. His literary talents, good looks, and wealth—as one of the best-paid writers in China today—put him frequently on the covers of fashion magazines.

Han Han became famous in the late 1990s. His public image has gone through a number of stages. He has been controversial ever since his rise to fame. In 1999, during his first year of senior high school, Han Han won first prize in the New Concept Essay Competition, an annual event organized by several Chinese universities and the prestigious Mengya Literature Press. That same year, however, Han failed his school examinations in seven different subjects and did not advance to the second year of high school. The next year, 2000, his first novel was published and became a hit. This book suggested that the Chinese education system has a negative impact on students' personality development. After writing this novel, Han Han again failed his exams and dropped out of school.

The sharply contrasting images that Han Han presented—as China's youngest best-selling writer as well as a spectacular academic underachiever—attracted wide attention in the media. As news of the Han Han phenomenon spread, a heated debate arose over what was meant by "quality education" and the ways in which schools should account for both conventional talent and deviant genius like his. During these years, Han was attracting a huge legion of followers among high school students, especially those who were disaffected with the educational systems they found themselves in. It was they who found the greatest resonance with Han's maverick personality. Although he was a hero for some of the young high school students because he showed them a different path to success outside of the college entrance examination system, in the mainstream of society and media, the young Han appeared as a brilliant aberration but hardly a model for all students.

Han's grand entry onto the public stage came in 2006, when he was 24 years old, in what came to be known as "the great Han-Bai debate." That debate was also what marked the shift in his public image from "deviant genius" to "young rebel." On March 2, 2006, Han posted a blog entry called "Let's Be Frank: The Literary Arena Is Worthless" ("Wentan shi ge pi, shei ye bie zhuangbi"). This was in direct response to an article by literary critic Bai Ye entitled "The Current Status and Future of the 1980s Generation" ("80 hou xianzhuang yu weilai"). Han and Bai then locked horns on questions of who qualifies as a real writer, what authentic literature is, and the true nature of literary expression on the Internet. This debate involved many well-known intellectuals and celebrities. Han fought back against this daunting opposition and generated a glowing-hot spot on the Internet. When the dust had settled, netizens were left with deep impressions not only of Han's stunning rebelliousness but also of the amazing solidarity, belligerence, and feistiness of his fans. The Han-Bai debate fixed Han's image in the public mind as an uninhibited young rebel who could also write well. It also made Han known to a much wider circle, including opponents as well as supporters.

The year 2008 was particularly eventful in China. First came the Tibetan uprising in March, then the Sichun earthquake in May, then protests arising from Western media reports that were critical of the pre-Olympic torch relay, then the Olympics themselves, then the great fire at the CCTV Tower, and finally the scandal over the Sanlu company's tainted milk. The massive crowds that were mobilized to welcome the Olympics became Han Han's cue to begin his career of blogging on current events. His public image turned into one of "commentator" on public affairs and "public intellectual." These changes brought a sharp increase in his popularity and number of readers, who now included not only disaffected youth and the "1980s generation" but many older people as well and many other sectors of society. Increasing numbers of young people in the elite, including members of the Communist Party, joined in following him. The year 2008 was also the one in which Han Han's name began to appear with frequency in both the domestic and international media. He won a numbers of prizes, and *Time* magazine named him one of the 100 most influential people in the world.

Since 2008, Han's most critical commentary has focused on topics in society and public affairs as well as problems of radical nationalism on the world stage. He reiterated his preference for critiquing nationalism, money worship, lack of empathy, society, corruption, environment pollution, and flaws in government. His sharp and very unique view of public affairs, independence of thought, authenticity, and aloof attitude toward the rich and powerful caused Han Han's readership to soar into the millions and drew much more media attention, both domestic and foreign. During the same period, Han's blogs began to draw special attention from government censors of the Internet. His more outspoken pieces began to be deleted shortly after they appeared. His pace in posting blogs also declined sharply.

Toward the end of 2011, after nearly a half-year of silence, Han wrote three articles on his blog—"On Revolution," "On Democracy," and "On Freedom"—in which he discussed some of the most sensitive issues in China in a very direct way in phrases such as the following: "Revolution may not be the best option for China" ("On Revolution"); "A revolution makes no guarantee of democracy" ("On Revolution"); and "The quality of citizens will not prevent democracy from arriving, but it can determine its quality" ("On Democracy"). This was the first time Han had written directly on the sensitive topic of democracy after he had become famous in China. What he wrote sent shock waves through the Chinese Internet and sparked a lively debate on democracy and revolution among intellectuals and ordinary netizens alike. Does China need democracy? What kind of democracy does China want? Will a revolution bring democracy to China? And so on.

The debate led to a detailed examination of Han's personal position on democracy. Why had he changed from a prodemocracy position to one that questioned democracy? Did he possess an intellect that qualified him to say anything significant about democracy? This debate caused a great war between thinkers who call themselves China's "New Left" and the intellectuals who are known as the "liberals." The New Left, formerly Han's critics, now found that he had become somewhat intellectually mature. On the other hand, the liberal intellectuals—people who formerly had supported him—now saw him as betraying the cause. Han's new position seemed to break the old molds of "left" and "right." People who attacked his new views on democracy came from both sides; his defenders also came from both sides. With this great debate, which unfolded on the Internet, a blogger writing as Maitian (literally, "wheat field") and another prominent thinker and popular science writer, Fang Zhouzi, started to question whether Han had really written the works attributed to him. Fang suggested that Han's literary genius was a fraud and that he was not, in fact, the author of these works. The debate, originally about democracy, turned into a widely watched war of attrition between Han and Fang that lasted about two months. Each side had substantial fan support.

In the aftermath of the Han-Fang debate, Han Han has rarely written critical articles on political and social affairs, although he continues to publish books. He directed a film and even started to invest in the restaurant industry. Since he often posts images of his lovely daughter on the Internet, he has received a new playful nickname: "the Father-in-Law of the Countryman."

Lijun Yang

See also: Egao and Online Satire, China

Further Reading

Han, Han. 2012. *This Generation: Dispatches from China's Most Popular Literary Star (and Race Car Driver)*. Trans. Allan H. Barr. New York: Simon & Schuster.

Johnson, Ian. 2012. "Han Han: Why Aren't You Grateful?" *The New York Review of Books*. October 1. http://www.nybooks.com/daily/2012/10/01/han-han-why-arent-you-grateful/. Accessed March 26, 2016.

Osnos, Evan. 2010. "It's Not Beautiful." *The New Yorker* (May 24): 54–63.

Osnos, Evan. 2011a. "Han Han Finds a New Crowd to Irritate." *The New Yorker*. December 28. www.newyorker.com/online/blogs/evanosnos/2011/12/han-han-finds-a-newcrowd-to-irritate.html#ixzz2HpWGzQPD. Accessed March 26, 2016.

Osnos, Evan. 2011b. "The Han Dynasty." *The New Yorker* (July 4): 50–59.

Yang, Lijun. 2013. "Han Han and the Public." In *Restless China*. Ed. Perry Link, Richard Madsen, and Paul G. Pickowicz, 109–128. Lanham, MD: Rowman & Littlefield.

INDIGENOUS ORAL LORE AND DIGITAL MEDIA, THAILAND (KAREN)

Every indigenous village presents itself as a religio-cultural oasis of sacred wisdom. Among the Karen, known as Pgaz K'Nyau, the sacred wisdom is expressed through the knowledge of what they call *hta*. The knowledge of the *hta* within each community is gradated. The women and men elders, healers, and shamans show greater depth of wisdom and local knowledge than the young adults, the youth, and the children.

For the Karen leaders, who are adept with the use of the *hta* as an evocative medium, they are aware of the power latent in the *hta*. They actually exercise an influential agency over the community. The *hta* are "the cultural idioms that the Karen people used in the continuous process of change, adaptation, contestation and co-existence, depending on the situation and context" (Trakansuphakon 2007, 151). These leaders are able to keep the traditional poems alive on pivotal occasions when the *hta* is spoken, chanted, and sung to awaken the mind and heart of the audience.

From the early period of the Karen communities to the present, *hta* is always spoken for the listening pleasure of a crowd. The Karen leaders use *hta* to address the rapid changes affecting their upland communities. Due to the unequal power relations between the Karen communities, the government, and the multinational companies, the *hta* exhorts the community to rise up to the challenge with the saying, "In the past, when I was a child, you kicked me and I was afraid of you. Nowadays, my head is equal to you. If you kick me once, I will kick you back once." Furthermore, the *hta* "If you can walk on a rope, I can walk on the blade of a sword" affirms that the community has an edge over the adversaries in their struggle. In exhorting the communities to work concertedly within a web of networks to ensure the effectiveness of the struggle at the grassroots, the Karen leaders use the *hta* "You cannot cross a river with one bamboo rod; you cannot make rice wine with one rice grain." The following *hta* reinforces the preceding *hta*: "Our brothers and sisters join their fingers together; even if the sky falls down we will lift it up."

The prevalence of digital technology has occasioned the young-adult leaders to rise to the challenge of using creative ways of sustaining the sacred wisdom among the young. This new echelon of leaders comprises the composers and artists who are still rooted in their living traditions. Popular among them are the De Por Thu, Hs5dso2, Pongsiri Khaowvilad, Kwanfa Nadam, and Ploshar just to name a few.

Over time and place, the transmission of *hta* has morphed. The *hta* chanted in the festive celebrations of the upland village communities is now transmitted to the city-dwelling youth who are studying in tertiary institutions and working in industrial sites or corporate firms. By the process of assimilation, the dominant Thai culture is subtly eroding the ethnic identity of the young Karen. To firm up their ethnicity, the digital mass media of the young provides the emerging leaders with innovative ways of communicating the *hta*. The proliferation of melodious pop songs and informative dramas of diverse genres are readily accessible via DVDs, video clips, and YouTube posts that the young enjoy viewing through their smartphone, MP3, MP4, tablet, or laptop. At the same time, the young-adult leaders organize fora and concerts in the villages for the young Karen still living there to be instructed in the sacred wisdom of the *hta*. In addition, the radio stations located in the villages regularly broadcast these pop songs. These songs keep the sacred wisdom alive in the hearts of the villagers, especially among the upcoming generation of youth who have opted for the farm life.

The song entitled "Sek loso" is a case in point. It is a song accompanied by the traditional harp called *tei na*. The lyrics of the song are rich in *hta* that exhort the young Karen to be rooted in their indigenous identity. In the cities, the ethnic identity of the young Karen is eroded by the pervasive influence of modernity and secularism as a result of globalization.

The *hta* urges the young to be reenchanted with the Karen cosmology of their grandparents. This cosmology, as Nadarajah opines, promotes "a lifestyle guided by the principles of limit and balance and help us to live sustainably and spiritually" and fosters "an active spiritual self-awareness" that "put our spiritual selves in direct dialogue with the exterior world" (Nadarajah 2013, 79).

The deepest core of the indigenous cosmology is spirituality. In the opinion of Ananta Kumar Giri and Philip Qarles Von Ufford, spirituality comprises "practices of self-cultivation including spiritual mobilization of self and society." This spirituality enables the young Karen to situate themselves in "the larger purpose of the collective and natural cosmos" so that they learn to live "such values as sacredness, compassion, love, respect, balance, empathy, service, joy, wisdom and peacefulness." (Giri and Von Ufford 2004, 4)

Hence the *hta* of the song "Sek loso" calls on the young to cultivate a reverence for the land and the spirit world of the ancestors and the Creator, whose presence make nature spirited and sacred. At the same time, the *hta* urges the young to live with filial gratitude to the ancestors:

> *Our ancestors prepare all the basic resources that are considered as our valuable heritage. We have to protect and sustain our future generation. We live in the land of our grandmother. We live in the land of our grandfather. They planted oranges for us. They planted jackfruit for us. We eat and take care and there will be enough for us forever.*
> *Since we benefit from the forest, we have to take care of the forest. When we eat fish, we need to take care of the river.*

On the other hand, the current global environmental crisis with its climate change occasions the young-adult leaders to use the *hta* to query the eco-sensitivity of the state-condoned cash-crop plantations. These plantations facilitate the encroachment of the multinational agro-companies. The purpose of these profit-driven companies is to financialize farming and introduce the large-scale use of chemicals and GMO species. Moreover the *hta* raises further questions about the long-term attainability of food sovereignty in the nation-state, including the sustainability of the subsistent livelihood of the villages in terms of food security in the ancestral homeland.

In the modern world, the young Karen leaders see the *hta* as a very important source of rerooting and reenchanting the young in their religio-cultural heritage, a process Jeffery Carlson describes as "traditioning." In "traditioning," the young Karen in the cities, as Matthews Samson asserts, "find a place from which to act within the world, a need to blur (and perhaps cross) boundaries in the continuing struggle to renew a sense of self and community" (Samson 2012, 72). As the *hta* nurtures the sense of "traditioning" in the young Karen, they too have to discover "the past is not simply left behind, and space has to be made for the ancestors who may yet speak again in unimagined places," like the cities. The young Karen living in the confluence of many diverse traditions in the cities need to realize what Samson has insightfully asserted, that "pluralism itself becomes a resource for re-enchantment rather than a threat" (Samson 2012, 70).

As intercultural relations between the dominant and ethnic cultures become mutually enriched, the evocative medium of digitalized *hta* also alerts the young of the other ethnic communities, including the young Thai, to be aware of their own need for "traditioning" so that they too desire to be reenchanted with their ethnic cosmologies and spiritualities. The era of digitalized *hta* has reversed the adverse process of assimilation that erases the identity of the young Karen. At the same time, this emerging era has awakened the young and the public of mainstream society to the need to return to their roots and savor the richness of their religio-cultural traditions.

In this way, the digitalized *hta* has become an evocative medium for the marginal ethnic communities and mainstream society as well. Moreover, the digitalized *hta* is awakening the political, civil, and religious leaders of mainstream cultures, religions, and societies to the need to negotiate the ecological crisis with the sacred wisdom of the cosmologies and spiritualities of the diverse communities. In addition, the digitalized *hta* calls for an end to militaristic and militant violence, corruption at all levels of the government bureaucracy, including the need for accountability, transparency, and good governance.

What the Karen have done in northern Thailand is also an emerging phenomenon of the other indigenous communities in Asia, Australia, Africa, Latin America, Europe, United States, and Canada. Digitalizing the sacred wisdom inherent in the diverse indigenous cosmologies and spiritualities in terms of contemporary songs and dramas has become an evocative medium to deepen the eco-sensitivity of existing generations due to the proliferation of literature in cosmology, ecology, science, spirituality, development, and religious studies. The digital audiovisual images of the sacred wisdom of the indigenous communities have convinced a sizable population of humankind that we are living in a sacred web. In this web, human life is interrelated and interdependent with all other species and the earth's multiple ecosystems. Furthermore, the digital media is awakening more citizens in our global village to the idea that we are living in a mystical age. This age posits the relevance of indigenous wisdom and the need for more holistic cosmologies and spiritualities for humankind to attain a more sustainable livelihood of dignity and reverence in our relationship with Mother Earth and creation.

Jojo M. Fung, SJ

See also: Cinema, Maori (Chapter 3: Film)

Further Reading

Chareon and Tenagoo. 2015. "Sek loso." YouTube. www.youtube.com/watch?v=n5x18 _VzgCE. Accessed May 26, 2015.

Giri, Ananta Kumar, and Philip Qarles Van Ufford. 2004. "A Moral Critique of Development: Ethics, Aesthetics and Responsibility." Development Research Series Research Center on Development and International Relations (DIR), Working Paper No. 138. Aalborg East: DIR & Institute for History, International and Social Studies Aalborg University, 1–43.

Mathew, Babu Puthenkulam. 2015. "Digital Media and Christian Mission: Challenges and Opportunities." *Ishvani Documentation and Mission Digest* 23, no. 1: 36–55.

Nadarajah, Manikam. 2013. *Living Pathways: Meditations on Sustainable Cultures and Cosmologies in Asia.* Penang, MY: Areca Books.

Samson, Mathews C. 2012. "Conversion at the Boundaries of Religion, Identity, and Politics in Pluralicultural Guatemala." In *Beyond Conversion & Syncretism: Indigenous Encounters with Missionary Christianity, 1800–2000.* Ed. David Lindenfeld and Miles Richardson, 51–78. New York: Berghahn Books.

Trakansuphakon, Prasert. 2007. "Space of Resistance and Place of Local Knowledge in the Northern Thailand Ecological Movement." PhD dissertation, Chiangmai University, Thailand.

INTERNET ADDICTION, CHINA

Internet addiction, which is sometimes referred to as "Internet addiction disorder," "pathological Internet use," and "problematic Internet use," involves excessive usage of the Internet to the detriment of normal social relationships, emotional stability, and daily life function. Extreme Internet addiction can also result in physical impairment, and in certain cases has led to suicide and death. In China, as elsewhere, Internet addiction has generally taken the form of online gaming. The Chinese Ministry of Health estimates that in 95 percent of diagnosed cases, patients are addicted to online games. In recent years, the Chinese government has taken proactive measures to combat what it perceives as a growing epidemic of Internet addiction, particularly among youths.

As yet, there is no consensus on how to define Internet addiction. Some psychiatrists categorize Internet addiction as an impulse-control disorder. Impulse-control disorders, such as kleptomania, involve the failure to resist temptation, often leading to self-harm or injury to others. Others define Internet addiction as a behavioral addiction or nonsubstance addiction. Behavioral (nonsubstance) addictions, such as pathological gambling, produce neurological reactions similar to those triggered by drug use. As a result, addicts feel a compulsion to perform a particular behavior regardless of its adverse consequences.

There is some controversy as to whether or not Internet addiction should be considered a valid psychological disorder. In the United States, for example, Internet addiction is not included in the most recent edition of the *Diagnostic and Statistical Manual* (*DSM V*), a comprehensive guide to psychological disorders that is published by the American Psychiatric Association. Those who are in favor of listing Internet addiction as a psychological disorder argue that Internet usage can result in the same neurological responses as those triggered by substance abuse. They believe that the symptoms of Internet addiction, including an uncontrollable desire to be online, depressive or irritable moods when the Internet is not available, and a loss of normal professional and personal relationships, are similar to symptoms exhibited by drug addicts. Those who do not believe that Internet addiction is a psychological illness make the argument that addiction to being online is not a single disorder but several separate or interrelated disorders, including anxiety, depression, and attention deficit hyperactivity disorder (ADHD). Some argue that "socially problematic Internet use" is not an actual psychological condition but rather an alternative way of pursuing social interaction in a virtual setting or a means of relieving stress from the pressures of everyday life.

Although there is not yet a consensus on how to understand Internet addiction in the United States, there is far greater agreement in China. As early as 2008, the Chinese Ministry of Health declared that Internet addiction is a legitimate clinical disorder and has since then released specific procedures on how to diagnose and treat patients who are suspected of being Internet addicts. Mental health specialists in China believe that Internet addiction is a serious epidemic that has grown in tandem with increased Internet access in China. Over the past decade, Internet usage in China has dramatically increased. Between 2005 and 2014, it is estimated that the number of Internet users in China has grown from 103 million to 630 million, the vast majority of whom access the Internet through mobile devices. As a result of the increase in Internet access, the number of Internet addicts has also grown. Recent studies have suggested that as many as 11 percent of youths (between the ages of 13 and 18) are either moderately or severely addicted to the Internet, while the Chinese Ministry of Health estimates that at least 24 million Chinese could be considered Internet addicts, with an additional 28 million exhibiting addictive tendencies.

The Chinese government has taken a variety of measures to cope with this problem. In 2007 the first state-level legislation was adopted that aimed to regulate Internet usage among Chinese citizens. This legislation has specifically targeted Internet cafés and online gaming websites. Owners of Internet cafés are required to keep records of their customers' Internet use; those who fail to abide by these regulations can have their license revoked. Additionally, gaming websites are required to set curfews and time limits so as to reduce the amount of time that gamers can spend on a particular site. Finally, Internet users who are suspected of addictive behavior may be involuntarily sent to an addiction treatment center.

The first inpatient treatment center for Internet addiction in China opened in Beijing in 2004. Managed by the psychiatrist Tao Ran, who is also the director of the Addiction Studies Center at the Military General Hospital in Beijing, the Daxing Internet Addiction Treatment Center combines boot-camp-style military discipline along with more conventional treatments, such as talk therapy and drug therapy. Patients who are admitted to the treatment center are not allowed to use any electronic devices and are prohibited from having contact with the outside world for periods ranging from three months to a full year. Tao claims that his treatment method results in a 70 percent success rate, though this number is difficult to substantiate.

Since the establishment of the Daxing treatment center, over 300 other Internet addiction treatment centers have been established throughout China, many of which employ similar methods to the ones devised by Tao Ran. Some of these treatment centers, however, are unregulated and managed by entrepreneurs who lack legitimate psychiatric credentials. Lack of appropriate oversight at some of these facilities has resulted in the hospitalization and death of several patients. The prevalent use of electroshock therapy in unlicensed addiction treatment centers, for example, has led to several deaths; since 2009, however, the Chinese government has banned electroshock therapy as a treatment for Internet addiction.

Due to the amount of attention focused on Internet addiction in China, much of the current scientific and medical research on the disorder has been pioneered by Chinese psychiatrists. It is estimated that over half of all medical publications on Internet addiction have been authored by researchers in China, Taiwan, and Hong Kong.

Emily Baum

See also: Video Games, China (Chapter 7: Video Games)

Further Reading

Bax, Trent. 2014. *Youth and Internet Addiction in China.* New York: Routledge.

China Internet Network Information Center (CNNIC). 2014. "Statistical Report on Internet Development in China." www1.cnnic.cn/IDR/ReportDownloads/201404/U020140417607531610855.pdf. Accessed June 10, 2015.

Ko, C. H. et al. 2012. "The Association between Internet Addiction and Psychiatric Disorder: A Review of the Literature." *European Psychiatry* 27, no. 1: 1–8.

Lam, L. T. et al. 2009. "Factors Associated with Internet Addiction among Adolescents." *Cyberpsychology and Behavior* 12, no. 1: 551–555.

Manjikian, Mary. 2012. *Threat Talk: The Comparative Politics of Internet Addiction.* Burlington, VT: Ashgate Publishing.

Shlam, Shosh, and Hilla Medalia. 2014. "China's Web Junkies." *New York Times.* January 19. www.nytimes.com/2014/01/20/opinion/chinas-web-junkies.html?_r=0. Accessed June 10, 2015.

Yang, Yang. 2013. "Breaking the Web of Internet Addiction." *China Daily.* December 13. http://usa.chinadaily.com.cn/epaper/2013-12/13/content_17173126.htm. Accessed June 10, 2015.

INTERNET CENSORSHIP, CAMBODIA

Although much of the population lives in the rural countryside, young Cambodians have joined the global Internet community through the likes of social media sites. Since technology and Internet access have become increasingly affordable, more Cambodians have had the opportunity of navigating through the endless world that we know as the Internet. Whether it is used to communicate with friends, send virtual images of roses to sweethearts, or share new music, the Internet proves to be something more significant than a place for endless entertainment. In a country where a majority of the population lives in poverty and oppression under the stern rule of the small but powerful elite, the Internet has become a platform for political freedom and expression.

The risks and fears of public criticism pertaining to Hun Sen's government are all too real for the Cambodian people. By facilitating corrupt policies and enacting harsh punishments through intimidation, Prime Minister Hun Sen does not fall short of authoritarian characteristics. Unofficially dubbed a dictator, Hun Sen rose to power in the 1990s and has openly declared that he is going to continue to rule over Cambodia until he is 74 years old. Hun Sen's political party, the Cambodian People's Party (CPP), eventually became the ruling party and has dominated in national elections since. However, critics maintain that the results of these elections are ultimately fraud and the product of a false democracy under Hun Sen's authoritarian government.

By governing with an iron fist, Hun Sen has managed to dominate his political opponents and critics and appoint members who enable the facilitation of his unlawful policies. He has even appointed his own children to positions in the armed forces and parliament. Most notable is the CPP's control over the media. In one way or another, Cambodia's television networks have some connection to Hun Sen and the CPP. For instance, Hun Sen's daughter, Hun Mana, is the owner of Bayon Television. Other major television stations, such as CTN, MyTV, and Apsara TV, are owned by members of the CPP and are closely affiliated with Hun Sen.

Under the CPP, Cambodia's citizens have faced adversity and intimidation perpetrated by the government. The fear of publicly criticizing the government is widespread, and many choose not to discuss the matter with people outside of their trusted circles. In recent years, however, that has changed. Sam Rainsy has risen to popularity with those who call for democracy, as well as the poor, rural majority. Sam Rainsy is the leader of the opposition party, the Cambodia National Rescue Party (CNRP), which aims to deliver Cambodians' rights and liberties that the CPP refuses to deliver. The CNRP is viewed favorably among Hun Sen's critics, but even they cannot escape the restraints set about by the CPP. Due to their rise in popularity, visible in the general election of 2013, members of the CNRP have become a target for Hun Sen's CPP. In 2014 Hun Sen officially placed a ban on public gatherings and protests, especially that of opposition parties, in Freedom Park of Phnom Penh. The ban was ordered after multiple protests beginning in January and continuing throughout the summer of 2014. In the true fashion of the CPP, peaceful protesters were harassed, beaten, and detained by police officers and baton-wielding thugs.

These attacks explain why so many Cambodians are afraid to speak their minds. The predominantly CPP government is notorious for its sometimes fatal actions against those who publicly criticize its policies, thereby silencing the political opinion of much of the population. It has come to a point in which critics of the government must hide their identity or disguise themselves in some other form to be able to truly voice their opinions. Thanks to the introduction of media-sharing sites on the Internet, some Cambodians are able to do just that.

With the help of video-editing software, innovative individuals have flocked to websites such as YouTube to upload their carefully edited videos. Uploaders are able to hide their identity by distorting their voices or blurring out their faces. For example, the YouTube user YouLike Khmer is unique in that the user uploads videos of an animated cat named Tom, who voices criticisms against Hun Sen and the CPP in a high-pitched cartoon voice. Tom the cat embodies the voices and beliefs of the predominantly silent public. What most people are afraid to say in public is what Tom the cat expresses for them. There are different variants of these anonymous political videos. Some choose to upload videos that simply consist of an audio recording of their voice accompanied by a single image of the political figure they are discussing. Viewers leave comments either praising or challenging the uploader's concerns. Some videos garner up to hundreds of thousands of views, not only from Cambodia but worldwide.

Still, the government has cracked down on some Internet users and charged them on the premise of incitement. In August 2015, the government announced its plan to form a new cybercrime department that will be responsible for closely monitoring online activities. The government claims that this action is solely to prevent online "crime" in order to maintain national security. However, NGOs and members of the CNRP argue that it would suppress the people's right to Internet freedom. Ultimately the people will be denied the freedom of expression and information that has been guaranteed under the Cambodian Constitution, as well as the United Nation's Declaration of Universal Human Rights, which was ratified by the government itself.

This series of human rights abuses captured the attention of the national and international community after several arrests were carried out. Senator Hong Sok Hour of the CNRP was arrested in August 2015 for publicly sharing and criticizing a Vietnam–Cambodia border treaty from 1979 on Facebook. He was set to go on trial in October 2015 and will be tried for treason. Another notable arrest occurred in September 2015, only a month after Hong Sok Hour's arrest. University student Kong Ray simply posted a comment on Facebook calling for a "colour revolution" and was arrested soon after. These arrests were viewed as a strategy for Hun Sen's government to brandish its guns (quite literally) and instill fear into the population. Those who are still brave enough continue to post their political concerns through their anonymous identities.

NGOs in the country quickly responded to these arrests and took the liberty of issuing the Nine Principles of Internet Freedom, which aims to maintain people's rights to Internet liberty and calls for a lift on censorship. The chances of the government taking these principles into serious consideration are very slim. In an effort to raise awareness, American filmmaker Ellen Grant documented government brutality and oppression on the Cambodian people in her film *Cyber-Democracy: Cambodia, Kafka's Kingdom*. In the film, she highlights the government's strict control on the circulation of information.

Since an overwhelming majority of news sources are controlled by the CPP, some Cambodians turn to independent news sources, such as Radio Free Asia (RFA) and Voices of Asia (VOA). While CPP-controlled news networks are clearly biased and avoid broadcasting news that may portray the government in a negative light, independent news sources reveal the human rights abuses around the country. The CPP-controlled networks are filled with propaganda favoring the CPP and its alleged achievements while criticizing opposition parties and activists. Further, independent news sources are worthy of attention because of their accessibility to poor people in the countryside who are often the target of human rights abuses such as land-grabbing, In rural areas where the majority of the population is illiterate, RFA and VOA provide information in the form of radio podcasts. Even in the rural countryside, will you find an illiterate farmer listening to a podcast from the previous week. State-controlled media continue to try to limit the public's knowledge of human rights and political events. It is for this reason that independent news sources are so important. The formation of the cybercrime department threatens the accessibility of real news to the people as well as the circulation of information.

The future is uncertain for the people of Cambodia as far as their Internet freedom is concerned. The Internet has served as an arena for the circulation of ideas, opinions, and information. However, under the rule of an oppressive regime, this freedom is threatened through coercion, fear, and intimidation. There is still the question of whether or not simply blurring one's face or distorting one's voice is sufficient to avoid persecution from the government. Perhaps with enough pressure from the international, as well as the internal, community, Hun Sen and his government will have no choice but to yield to the rights of the people. In retrospect, history has shown that the frustration of the oppressed majority will be the driving force behind their call for justice. It is only then that Cambodians can truly be free.

Barbara Sum

See also: Amnesty International and Pop Culture; Great Firewall, China

Further Reading

Cain, Geoffrey. 2013. "Prising Open Free Speech in the 'Pearl of Asia'." *Index on Censorship* 42, no. 2: 114–117.

The Economist. 2014. "Released, but Hardly Free." June 4. http://www.economist.com/blogs /banyan/2014/06/labour-activism-cambodia. Accessed October 2, 2015.

FIDH. 2015. "The Human Rights Situation in Cambodia." https://www.fidh.org/en/region /asia/cambodia/The-human-rights-situation-in. Accessed September 30, 2015.

Heder, Steve. 2005. "Hun Sen's Consolidation: Death or Beginning of Reform?" *Southeast Asian Affairs*: 113–30.

Human Rights Watch. 2015. "Cambodia: Drop Case Against Opposition Senator." October 1. https://www.hrw.org/news/2015/10/01/cambodia-drop-case-against-opposition-senator. Accessed October 3, 2015.

Neou, Vannarin. 2015. "Following Arrests, Groups Issue Nine Principles of Internet Freedom." *VOA*. September 15. http://www.voacambodia.com/content/following-arrests-groups-issue-nine-principles-of-internet-freedom/2964547.html. Accessed September 26, 2015.

OHCHR. 2015. "Cambodia's NGO Bill Threatens a Free and Independent Civil Society—UN Expert Urges Senate to Reject It." *Nations Unies Droits de L'homme*. October 4. http://www.ohchr.org/en/NewsEvents/Pages/DisplayNews.aspx?NewsID=16240&LangID=E. Accessed March 26, 2016.

Peang-Meth, Gaffar. 2015. "Film Highlights Cambodian Cruelty." *Pacific Daily News*. September 25. http://www.guampdn.com/story/opinion/2015/09/25/film-highlights-cambodian-cruelty/72774524/. Accessed September 26, 2015.

So, Chivey. 2015. "Cambodian Government Plans Stricter Internet Controls." *Radio Free Asia*. September 10. http://www.rfa.org/english/news/cambodia/controls-09102015155636.html. Accessed September 26, 2015.

Strangio, Sebastian. 2014. *Hun Sen's Cambodia*. New Haven, CT: Yale University Press.

Taing, Vida. 2015. "Monitoring the Internet." *Phnom Penh Post*. September 8. http://www.phnompenhpost.com/national/monitoring-internet. Accessed September 26, 2015.

Ten, Soksreinith. 2015. "Filmmaker Documents Rise of Cambodian 'Cyber-Democracy'" *VOA*. August 22. http://www.voacambodia.com/content/filmmaker-documents-rise-of-cambodian-cyber-democracy/2927355.html. Accessed September 26, 2015.

UN. 2015. "The Universal Declaration of Human Rights." UN News Center. http://www.un.org/en/universal-declaration-human-rights/. Accessed September 30, 2015.

INTERNET AND SOCIAL MEDIA, UYGHUR

The Uyghur-language Internet in the Xinjiang Uyghur Autonomous Region makes up one of the largest Internet domains in China apart from Chinese- and English-language networks. Since the early 2000s, Uyghur programmers and software designers have introduced Arabic-script Turkic-language websites and social media to the Chinese public. Today a majority of the Uyghur population of approximately 10 million use Uyghur-language Internet and social media on a daily basis. The recent spread of smartphone usage has transformed Uyghur everyday life in complex ways. One result of the growing sense of interconnectedness and knowledge of e-commerce that comes from social media use has been the growth of Uyghur tech entrepreneurship.

Although the ability to design websites using the Arabic-based script used by Uyghurs has been available for more than two decades, it was not until 2007 that a critical mass of Internet-savvy programmers and computer users began to produce Uyghur-language social media discussion forums such as Misranim, Diyarim, Selkin, and Xebnem. Before this time, computers were seen primarily as gaming machines and secondly as word processors. Three years later, in 2010 (after the nine-month absence of Internet access following the riots of July 5, 2009, and the erasure of the majority of these pioneering Web forums), cheap 3G cellular phone and Web service reached Xinjiang.

Over the next four years, Internet usage exploded across Xinjiang. By 2015 a Uyghur-language news application called Nur had been downloaded and installed on 5 million smartphones across the Uyghur-speaking world. According to leading programmers in the industry, the app, which features Uyghur-language translations of Chinese-language news articles from state-owned media organizations such as Xinhua and Tianshan Wang, has an average of over 500,000 unique users per day.

Because most rural Uyghurs do not have cable or broadband access to the Internet in their homes, the arrival of smartphones over the past four years has been a transformational development in the way Uyghur use of the Internet has moved from the domain of specialized urban professionals to an element of daily communication of farmers and service workers in every small town and village. In addition, because a relatively large proportion of the Uyghur population is not proficient enough in Chinese to navigate Chinese-language websites, the further development of Uyghur-language digital platforms such as Nur and word-processing apps such as Xatirem has further solidified the importance of the Internet in Uyghur daily life.

Perhaps most importantly, the oral communication function of social media apps such as WeChat has connected Uyghurs across time and space in ways that were never possible before. Since apps such as WeChat do not depend on literacy, the threshold of technical ability is significantly lowered. Furthermore, since spoken language is much harder to track and censor, people feel freer to speak openly with friends and family about sensitive topics related to the politics of the region. It is perhaps for this reason that WeChat has become a major vehicle for Islamic moral and religious instruction. Beginning in 2014, difficulty in policing the spread of religious ideas via social media has resulted in periodic blockage of 3G and broadband Internet service in various cities, such as Yaken (Shache莎车) and Hotan (Hetian 和田).

Yet, despite these blockages, millions of Uyghurs living thousands of kilometers from their friends and relatives communicate daily using WeChat. Despite the threat of censorship, when acts of violence against Uyghurs occur, messages subtly pointing out the hypocrisies and injustices perpetuated by Chinese police forces and policy makers begin to circulate on WeChat. Social media users often transform song lyrics or popular poems to create a satirical commentary of the social life they are experiencing.

Of course, many users have also taken to using the social media application as an online marketing tool. It has become the vehicle by which many entrepreneurs sell clothes, purses, and perfume. It has also become the site of a number of English instruction, childhood education, and psychology podcasts in the Uyghur language. Filmmakers, writers, and musicians also communicate directly with their fans using this medium. Since it is a form of media open to government censorship, many WeChat entrepreneurs spend substantial amounts of time "cleaning up" their accounts every day: deleting questionable posts and banning problematic people from their WeChat circles.

Given the phenomenal success of Uyghur-language smartphone technology, it is a bit surprising that it has taken traditional Internet sites more time to develop a mainstream following. Although the most popular Uyghur-language Internet forum, Misranim, was developed in 2007, eight years later it still has only around 10,000 to 15,000 unique users per day. Despite the widespread use of social media apps via smartphones, many people are still quite suspicious of Uyghur-language e-commerce platforms that mimic the Amazon, eBay, Alibaba, and Taobao models. Although there are currently several Uyghur-language e-commerce Web platforms, many of them receive only around 5,000 unique visitors per day. In early 2015, a group of young entrepreneurs developed a new e-commerce platform called Dostum. After receiving the endorsement of a young pop star named Ablajan Awut Ayup and investing 150,000 yuan for a one-minute spot over the course of three months on the new reality TV show *Xinjiang's Got Talent*, Dostum received more than 20,000 unique visitors. The surge in visitors was enough to crash the website's server. The broadcast of the ad marked one of the first times a Uyghur-language website was advertised on Xinjiang provincial TV.

In the future it is likely that cell-phone technology and Internet connectedness will play a greater role in Uyghur life. Despite the immobility of most Uyghurs due

Internet in Tibet

The nascent Tibetan cyberspace can be traced back to the early 2000s, with the increased use of the Internet within the People's Republic of China (PRC).

Tibetan cyberspace can be divided into binaries of Tibetan language and Chinese language, with some users active in both languages. Tibetan-language Internet and social media use has taken longer to develop due to technical hindrances in the form of the correct rendering of Tibetan fonts and the lack of user-friendly input methods. Significant developments were the introduction of Microsoft's Himalaya Font in Windows Vista in 2007 and the inclusion of a Tibetan keyboard on Apple iOS 4.2 devices in 2010, thanks to the digital strides made by India-based monk Lobsang Monlam.

Noteworthy Chinese-language websites have been New Tibet (2003) and TibetCul (2003–present). Noteworthy Tibetan-language websites have been Rangdrol and Sangdhor (now defunct), Gendun Choephel, Korawa, Tsanpo, and Chodme (2005), dedicated to literature and poetry. These sites have blog-hosting capabilities for users, and some have BBS, news features, online shops, and their own social networks.

Increasingly, Tibetan cyberspace is going mobile through the widespread use of Chinese mobile apps such as WeChat. WeChat has a Chinese-language interface but supports Tibetan, hence the popularity of the iPhone over Android. Under heavy governmental censorship, the landscape of the Tibetan Internet changes quickly, and sites can be closed down without notice. Diaspora-based projects such as High Peaks Pure Earth and Tibet Web Digest translate the Tibetan Internet into English.

Dechen Pemba

to state policies that prevent them from traveling freely, the Internet provides them with a way of staying connected with the broader Uyghur world and staying up to date with national and international news. The diversity of news sources as well as the ability to communicate directly with friends in distant locations provides online social media users with a feeling of the richness and openness of human experience.

Of course, as in other social settings, Uyghur Internet and social media also provides a public space in which to build one's public persona. WeChat in particular has become a platform for expanding one's public persona. Many people use it as a forum to post things that show their religiosity, morality, progressiveness, ethnic spirit, or patriotism. People post selfies, participate in ice-bucket challenges, copy and paste life-affirming quotes, and advertise their locally sourced, halal products. Uyghur social media offers a way to build a new capitalistic economy of consumption, but it also offers a way for people to more fully experience what it means to be human. While it provides information about distant places in the outside world, the Internet also, at times, serves to strengthen users' preconceptions and biases because people often attempt to confirm their suspicions on the Internet by making connections with likeminded people and sharing similar ideas on their Web pages.

Darren Byler

See also: Cinema, Uyghur (Chapter 3: Film); Popular Music, Uyghur (Chapter 1: Popular Music)

Further Reading

Byler, Darren. 2014. "Traffic Lights and Uyghur Black Humor." *Beijing Cream*. https://bei gewind.wordpress.com/2014/04/26/traffic-lights-and-uyghur-black-humor. Accessed April 30, 2015.

Harris, Rachel, and Aziz Isa. 2011. "Perspectives on the Uyghur Internet." *Inner Asia* 13, no. 1: 27–49.

Olsen, Alexa. 2014. "Welcome to the Uighur Web." *Foreign Policy*. April 21. http://foreign policy.com/2014/04/21/welcome-to-the-uighur-web. Accessed April 30, 2015.

MOBILE PHONES, PHILIPPINES

In 2005 the Philippines earned the dubious reputation of being the world's "texting capital" because of Filipinos' penchant for owning and using mobile phones. They sent and/or received some 250 million text messages daily. Despite its status as a third-world country, the Philippines has kept pace with globalization and technological advances as exemplified by the mobile phone. By 2010 at least 80 percent of the country's more than 95 million Filipinos, including the poor, already owned and used mobile phones. However, while mobile-phone ownership cut across economic status, race, and age, the Filipinos culture, as reflected in the modes of mobile-phone acquisition and use, greatly differed in a number of ways.

Historically, the country's telecommunications industry started in the 1990s when the first, and monopolistic, company, known as Philippine Long Distance

Telephone Company (PLDT), established Piltel. The latter provided the country's first cellular mobile-phone service and operated under the Mobiline brand using analog technology. In 1994 another firm, Islacom, introduced the first digital mobile communication service in the Philippines using GSM (global system for mobile) communications, a world-standard digital technology. Also in 1994, Globe, a telecommunication company, introduced the prepaid and short messaging system (SMS) services. By 2001 it had acquired full ownership of Islacom. Still another telecommunication company, Smart, started commercial operations in 1994 with a novel marketing strategy. It offered cheap "package plans," making mobile-phone services affordable to a wide range of customers, including the poor sector. By 1997 Smart had succeeded in capturing a major market share, thus becoming the country's largest mobile-phone network.

The year 1999 witnessed the abovementioned telecom companies' introduction of both postpaid and prepaid GSM services to the country's mobile-phone owners/users. They soon expanded their services in major cities across the country. The iconic mobile phones had become more than just a device with SMS and voice-call features. With their numerous functions, the phones served as organizer or planner, watch, recorder, camera, music player, and more. Inevitably, society's affluent sector came to use the mobile phone as another social status symbol. Depending on their phones' model, brand, and design, proud owners would brag about their mobile phones, believing that these gadgets enhanced their social status.

The demand for mobile phones increased dramatically with the advent of the Android and smartphones. These new marvels of information and communication technology enabled users to surf the Internet, download movies and music, conduct business, play games, and book flights—in short, one could do practically anything and everything using the modern mobile phones. One could also attribute the significant increase in mobile-phone use to the high acquisition cost of landline phones in the Philippines. Moreover, despite its dominance in the telecommunication industry, the PLDT could not provide its clients with competitive rates for its services.

A number of research studies on mobile-phone use among selected sectors in Philippine society have invariably shown that there are no marked differences between the rich and the poor in terms of mobile-phone ownership and use. Both rich and poor mobile-phone users consider the mobile phone essential and necessary in their daily transactions and interaction. Nonetheless, research also shows that the rich and poor sectors exhibit dramatic differences in their choice of mobile-phone brands, models, and services, as well as in their modes of payment. On one hand, the poor generally buy the cheaper models and prefer prepaid plans or electronic loading. Some of them also buy the more affordable secondhand and reconditioned mobile phones, and they make payments for these products and/or services on an installment basis. Some even resort to trading in their mobile phones for better ones. A fair number receive new or old phones as gifts from their rich or well-off relatives.

Cases involving informal settlers and indigenous peoples in the Philippines provide us with some pertinent information. The informal settlers, for instance, seem to manifest their priorities by whimsically allocating a relatively large portion of their meager incomes to purchasing, loading, and operating mobile phones—even at the expense of their more basic needs, such as food, clothing, and housing. They do not seem to care about their arbitrary and capricious use of their household income as long as they keep enjoying the world's new technologies and are able to regularly connect with friends, parents, and relatives.

Similarly, members of the country's poor indigenous groups, who live almost outside of mainstream Philippine society, have now become regular mobile-phone users themselves. It's interesting to think that a decade ago, in 2006, only a relatively few indigenous peoples were aware of the strange gadget's existence. One could easily attribute this to the indigenous peoples' distant habitats in the mountains or the hinterlands. It eventually became a common practice among indigenous peoples to maintain and operate a so-called "community mobile phone." A community member could use the phone for a fee of some two Philippine pesos only (approximately US$0.04).

In the beginning, the *barangay* chairperson, among a rare few, would own the community mobile phone. Nowadays, the community mobile-phone system no longer exists. After all, many members of the indigenous groups can now purchase their own mobile phones, at least the inexpensive types. Naturally, these inexpensive types are the simple mobile-phone models (not "smart" or Android), which operate with minimal functions. Also, these are not Wi-Fi enabled and cannot be used for Internet purposes.

On the other hand, the rich, consisting of corporate executives and managers, either buy their top-of-the-line Android, iPhone, and Samsung Galaxy mobile phones in cash or obtain these on attractive terms through their companies. Their payment plans would almost certainly be postpaid.

Meanwhile, a comparative study of mobile-phone use between the adult and youth sectors of the population showed that adult users simply use their phones without any serious attempts at "improving" the gadgets' appearance. In contrast, youthful users apply significant embellishments to their own phones.

Furthermore, adult users often apply uppercase ("all caps") when texting, send straight text, and avoid abbreviating or using "text language." They use mainly the mobile phone's text and call functions. Seldom do they explore the use of their phone's many other features, such as games, organizer/planner, calculator, music player, or clock. In contrast, youthful users upgrade and decorate their phones. They spend time, effort, and money in sprucing up their phones with covers or cases, holders, hangings, and other artworks. They often change their ringtones and backlights and use abbreviations or text language. Adventurous and expressive, they use graphics, animation, embellished letters, and many characters and accents. They usually explore and experiment with the mobile phone's other features and uses, such as alarm, calendar, radio, organizer, and recorder.

In short, the mobile phone has become an expression or extension of the youth, particularly their fashion sense: color combinations of stickers on covers and cases, matching chains, bells, and other decorations—all representing their personality and identity. There are numerous benefits of the mobile phone, such as easy communication, access to information, and many other functions. In business, it has become a tool in negotiations, selling products, and determining the best prices of products or merchandise. Mobile-phone services have created new jobs and job opportunities, such as airtime load retailing or e-loading, mobile-phone repairs, software installation, sale of accessories, mobile money transfers, and more.

Lourdes M. Portus

See also: Social Media, Philippines

Further Reading

Pertierra, Raul. 2006. *Transforming Technologies: Altered Selves. Mobile Phone and Internet Use in the Philippines.* Manila, PH: De La Salle University Press.

Pertierra, Raul, and Eduardo Ugarte. 2002. *Txt-ing Selves: Cellphones and Philippine Modernity.* Manila, PH: De La Salle University Press.

Portus, Lourdes. 2008. "How the Urban Poor Acquire, Negotiate, Resist and Give Meanings to the Mobile Phone." In *Handbook of Mobile Communication Studies.* Ed. James E. Katz, 105–118. Cambridge, MA: MIT Press.

Portus, Lourdes. 2011. "M-Enabled Learning: Mobile Phone's Contribution to Education." In *Mobile Communication: Dimensions of Social Policy.* Ed. James E. Katz, 211–230. New Brunswick, NJ: Transaction Publishers.

POPULAR TRANSMEDIA, AUSTRALIA

Transmedia storytelling, also known as multiplatform or cross-media storytelling, refers to the creation of a unified story experience across more than one media, including television series, Internet webisodes, fictional online character blogs, social media (Facebook, Twitter), mobile apps, and also movies, novels, and games, including online participatory fan culture. Adaptations to another media, or sequels within the same media, are not considered transmedia storytelling but are instead considered franchising, a phenomenon that dates back to Homer, Shakespeare, the Bible, and even *The Epic of Gilgamesh* (ca. 2100 BCE). Examples of popular transmedia in Australia include *Fat Cow Motel* (2003–); *Summer Bay Interactive*, (2008) based on the long-running popular Australian television soap opera *Home and Away* (1988–); and also *Find 815* (2007–2008), an online alternate-reality game that extended the narrative of the popular American television series *Lost* (2004–2010).

The term "transmedia" is usually dated to Marsha Kinder's use of the term "transmedia intertextuality" in *Playing with Power in Movies, Television, and Video Games: From Muppet Babies to Teenage Mutant Ninja Turtles* (1993), in which she analyzed the Teenage Mutant Ninja Turtles franchise from the comics in 1984, to a television series in 1987, video games in 1989, and the first feature film in 1990. Some thought leaders in the field of transmedia have recently included Henry Jenkins, Jeff Gomez, and Christy Dena. Although many consider transmedia storytelling across *two or more* media, in 2010 the Producer's Guild of America added "transmedia producer" to their code of credits:

> A *Transmedia Narrative* project or franchise must consist of three (or more) narrative storylines existing within the same fictional universe on any of the following platforms: Film, Television, Short Film, Broadband, Publishing, Comics, Animation, Mobile, Special Venues, DVD/Blu-ray/CD-ROM, Narrative Commercial and Marketing rollouts, and other technologies that may or may not currently exist. These narrative extensions are NOT the same as repurposing material from one platform to be cut or repurposed to different platforms. (PGA 2010, online)

Popular early transmedia consumed online in Australia included *The Beast* (2001), an Internet alternate reality game (or ARG) promoting the Steven Spielberg/Stanley Kubrick movie *AI: Artificial Intelligence* (2001); however, one of the earliest Australian-produced transmedia experiences was the 13-part half-hour episode "whodunit" ABC-TV television mystery series *Fat Cow Motel* (2003), where viewers were invited to solve the weekly mystery using e-mail, voice mail, the Web, and SMS-text clues. Similarly the Australian/American/Canadian coproduced children's transmedia television series *dirtgirlworld* (2011–2013), which screened in 128 countries, allowed viewers to engage with the story online, via blogs, on Facebook, and through e-mail narrative extensions.

The narrative of the hit American TV series *Lost* also included the Australian-produced ARG *Find 815* (2008), allowing fans of the show to solve mysteries and discover additional backstory around the fictional Oceanic Flight 815 that crashed on the island at the beginning of the series using phone messages, online video blogs, and fictitious (or spoof) websites to solve the clues. Australian teen drama television series *Slide* (2011), which also screened in the United States on TeenNick in 2012, included YouTube webisodes as well as Facebook and Twitter content expanding the series narrative, with some commentators noting similarities to the British teen-drama television series *Skins* (2007–2013). *Summer Bay Interactive* (2008) included online content for fans of the popular Australian soap opera *Home and Away* when the 2008 Beijing Olympics interrupted the show's regular on-air schedule.

In the reality-TV, interactive talent show, and current affairs series genres, popular transmedia storytelling examples include *Australian Idol* (2003–2009), where participating fans could vote via SMS for their favorite contestants, and likewise with *Big Brother Interactive* (2001–2012), fans could vote via SMS and subscribers could view *Big Brother: Uncut, Unseen, Unreal* footage online as webisodes and as a DVD. The three-part reality TV series *Go Back to Where You Came From* (2011), exploring multicultural ethnic issues in Australia, involved nonfiction transmedia components including social media elements where viewers could comment online, an interactive game, and an educational materials package for schools. The ongoing ABC-TV current affairs commentary program *Q&A* (2008–) also includes interactive Twitter questions for the weekly invited celebrity guest panel and online forums for the ongoing discussion of related political and social issues, enabling what is also called "multimodal discourse."

The television series *Bikie Wars: Brothers in Arms* (2012) dramatized the real-life Australian biker-gang shoot-out known as the Milperra Massacre of 1984, based on the historical book *Brothers in Arms* (2001) written by Lindsay Simpson and Sandra Harvey; the show's website provided additional historical detail and photographic material.

The website of the popular fiction series *Miss Fisher's Murder Mysteries*, adapted for television from the novels written by Australian novelist Kerry Greenwood (1954–), also features online video content as well as story and character biographies. The website for the Australian mystery-thriller miniseries *Conspiracy 365* (2012–2014), based on the novel series of the same name (published 2010–2013) by Gabrielle Lord (1946–), includes games, additional character content, and story clues. The popular Australian family drama series *Packed to the Rafters* (2008–2013) also included transmedia story content online. The popular dramedy television series *Offspring* (2010) website also included an online spin-off webisode series, *Offspring: The Nurses* (2010). Microbudget web series *The Newtown Girls* (2012), set within Sydney's inner-city Newtown lesbian subculture, has been viewed in over 200 countries and included interactive components where viewers could vote on which characters got together romantically. The online dramedy soap *Forget the Rules* (2005–2007) for television, broadband, and mobile phones likewise included fan forums and an audience voting participatory fan-culture feature that allowed viewers to influence the ongoing story line of the series.

The popular Australian transmedia television drama series *Scorched* (2009) won the 2009 International Academy of Television Arts & Sciences' International Digital Emmy Award for Best (Fiction) Digital Program. The transmedia extended narrative of *Scorched* integrated a telemovie, an episodic online prequel and sequel drama, and also featured an online news network with extensive (fictional) weather reports and newscasts from the climate-change-ravaged future world in the year 2012.

J. T. Velikovsky

See also: Popular Albums, Australia (Chapter 1: Popular Music); Popular Movies, Australia (Chapter 3: Film); Popular Novels, Australia (Chapter 2: Books and Contemporary Literature)

Further Reading

Dena, C. 2009. *Transmedia Practice: Theorising the Practice of Expressing a Fictional World across Distinct Media and Environments.* PhD thesis, Department of Media and Communications, University of Sydney. www.christydena.com/phd. Accessed March 26, 2016.

Jenkins, H. 2008. *Convergence Culture: Where Old and New Media Collide*, revised ed. New York: New York University Press.

Kinder, Marsha. 1993. *Playing with Power in Movies, Television, and Video Games: From Muppet Babies to Teenage Mutant Ninja Turtles.* Berkeley: University of California Press.

PGA (Producers Guild of America). 2010. "PGA Board of Directors Approves Addition of Transmedia Producers to Guild's Producers Code of Credits." http://www.producersguild.

org/news/39637/General-PGA-Board-of-Directors-Approves-Addition-of-Transmedia
-Produce.htm. Accessed March 26, 2016.

Polson, D., A-M. Cook, J. T. Velikovsky, and A. Brackin, eds. 2014. *Transmedia Practice: A Collective Approach*. London: ID-Press.

SOCIAL MEDIA, AUSTRALIA

Australians have a long-standing reputation as early adopters of technology. Social media is no exception, with Australia consistently listed at or near the top of social media usage rankings. Although Australia is geographically located in the Asia Pacific region, it sits culturally within the Anglosphere, a group of English-speaking countries with common British colonial heritage. Although Australia has produced its own online media platforms, few have lasted. Instead, most social media platforms used by Australians originate from the United States, a country with close economic and political ties to Australia. Indeed, Australians' patterns of social media use have generally followed those of the United States, in contrast to other Asia Pacific countries, which, for a variety of reasons, have developed their own platforms or adopted existing platforms in unique ways.

Australians' keen adoption of American social media platforms continues to the present day. Its latest incarnation is the tendency toward hybrid media ecosystems, fueled by the increasing convergence and interoperability of social media platforms, most notably social television's fusing of digital television and video, mobile device use, instant messaging, and microblogging.

Social media use in Australia has its roots in 1989, when the Australian Academic and Research Network (AARNet) first offered permanent Internet access. Available only within universities, this network popularized bulletin board systems (BBS) and new models for information sharing via the campus-wide information systems (CWIS) movement. In 1992 the not-for-profit Australian Public Access Network Association (APANA) used this infrastructure to provide free BBS and newsgroups hosting.

In 1993 the U.S. Clinton administration reformed Internet regulatory structures, which allowed early commercial services to expand. This included U.S. companies expanding into Asia Pacific markets such as Apple's eWorld; CompuServe, which has been credited with popularizing e-mail; and America Online (AOL), which developed social media precursors such as member-created communities. The same year also saw the release of Mosaic, the first web browser.

In the period from 1993 to 1994, Australian Internet adoption rates were among the fastest in the world. However, the Australian industry was held back by the government's unwillingness to restructure the local telecommunications sector. Internet access became gradually more affordable as the 1990s progressed. United States–based social media platforms began to appear, with theGlobe.com, AuctionWeb (later eBay), Classmates.com, and Match.com launching in 1995 and Hotmail and ICQ in 1996. In Australia, 1995 saw the founding of the LookSmart Web directory and Sausage Software, which developed early authoring and micropayment systems.

The world's first "fully formed" social networking site, SixDegrees.com, was released in 1997. This site now receives 90 percent of its traffic from Asia, especially Indonesia, and was headquartered for some time in Australia from 2009. At the end of 1997, Australia had an estimated 1.6 million Internet users. This figure kept expanding rapidly. By 2000 Australian households with Internet access had increased ninefold from 1996.

By 2001 other platforms were setting the scene for today's social media era: Google (1998), Napster (1999), and Wikipedia and iTunes (2001). By then the U.S. "dot com boom" had crashed. Although many online businesses went under as a result, the huge investment in technology and infrastructure brought about by the boom laid the foundation for a second wave of Internet companies, including today's social media services.

A full 75 percent of Australians over 15 years old had Internet access by 2002, behind only Sweden and the United States. However, computers were still more common in urban and richer areas, and most people were still on dial-up. Skype, LinkedIn, and MySpace launched in 2003, later followed by YouTube in 2005, and Twitter and Facebook in 2006. The same period saw the first signs of the rise of mobile devices. By 2005 the use of short messaging service (SMS), or text messages, was widespread. The Cronulla riots in December 2005 saw SMS used to rally crowds and incite racist sentiment. This prompted the NSW Police assistant commissioner to state: "My message is this in regard to SMS messages and swarming crowds; this is ludicrous behaviour; it is unAustralian" (Kennedy, 2005).

By 2006 online social networking was becoming established in Australia via sites like Bebo. The young increasingly came online, with computers now in 90 percent of households with children (Australian Bureau of Statistics 2011). A 2007 Nielsen survey had 61 percent of online Australians reading wikis (up from 37 percent in 2006), 60 percent reading blogs (up from 48 percent), and 41 percent publishing their own content. By then YouTube and MySpace had become the most popular social media sites, followed by Flickr. A new microblogging site called Twitter was also beginning to attract a user base.

According to a 2008 Sensis report, 36 percent of all Australians had, by then, accessed a social networking site. The same report also notes increasing frequencies of use, with 91 percent of 14- to 17-year-olds accessing online social networking, as well as a trend toward online video and audio. A 2008–2009 survey by the Australian Bureau of Statistics notes an increase in mobile computing by young people. Notably, the first smartphone, the iPhone, had been released the previous year. However, older adults were also identified as turning to online social networking. The year 2008 also saw a major social-media-driven controversy: a party promoted on MySpace by Melbourne teenager Corey Worthington led to what the media described as a "rampage" by 500 young people through his family home and neighborhood.

By 2010 social media was becoming central to everyday Australian life. Pinterest and Instagram had launched, and Facebook was on the rise. Nielsen reported that Australians were increasingly using Twitter, and Australians, Brazilians, and

Filipinos were cited as the world's top social media users. This year also saw a federal election fought largely on broadband policy issues.

In Australia, 2011 could be called the year of Facebook, Twitter, and YouTube. Internationally, the tactics of the civil movements known as the Arab Spring catapulted social media into the political mainstream. YouTube use in Australia exploded, MySpace dropped in popularity, Blogspot became mainstream, Tumblr use tripled, and both LinkedIn's and Twitter's user bases doubled. Older Australians kept warming to social media, and Australia was at the top of the 10 developed countries included within Nielsen's social media reporting.

This pattern continued into 2012. Over half of Australia's population (11–12 million) now used Facebook, according to Adcorp, with YouTube close behind, services like Flickr and Reddit emerging, and 71 percent of Australians now using apps to access an increasing number of niche mobile services. The Australian Communications and Media Authority (ACMA) noted that children's mobile-phone and Internet access had continued to grow, especially among those from urban, English-speaking, and educated backgrounds. ACMA also noted that almost all young people (95–100 percent) were regular users of social media. A growing number of young people saw the Internet as important to their lives, with most rating their online experiences as positive. Awareness of online privacy and safety issues was generally high, especially among older children and girls. A general move with age from game playing to online socializing was reflected in young people's choice of platforms: younger children accessed YouTube, then Moshi Monsters, Club Penguin, and Facebook, whereas Facebook ruled supreme for older children, followed by YouTube.

By 2013 Google noted that 65 percent of Australians owned smartphones. Most households had broadband, mobile Facebook use was burgeoning, and Australians were still counted among the world's keenest social media users. Use of both Instagram and Tumblr rose dramatically, and use of location service Foursquare declined, potentially due to increasing consumer awareness about privacy. Local differences also emerged, such as the popularity of video-sharing service Vine in Melbourne.

For some in the media, 2014 was the year when social media transformed the way viewers engaged with television. Viewers increasingly used Facebook and Twitter to comment in real time on television shows, in turn driving audiences and creating stronger demand for online "catch-up" TV. One-off sporting events including the NRL Grand Final and car races generated much of the Twitter activity. But most activity was in response to recurring programs: reality shows (*The Block Glasshouse, The Bachelor Australia, X Factor*) current affairs (*Q&A*), news, and drama.

Australian social media activism came to the fore in 2014. An online campaign forced supermarket chain Aldi to withdraw a controversial Australia Day T-shirt from sale, and a Change.org petition distributed via Twitter and Facebook facilitated a boycott of an Australian visit by American "pickup artist" Julien Blanc. The subsequent media attention led to the Australian government revoking Blanc's visa and other campaigns leading to Singapore and the U.K. also blocking or rescinding visas. Video sharing took off in 2014, particularly by women; interestingly, some have seen this trend as being closer to countries like Russia than the United Kingdom or United States. The year 2014 also saw 17- to 25-year-old Australians taking to targeted social messaging service Snapchat, which combines sharing of video content and messaging to a select number of recipients, unlike the broader distribution provided by other social media. Some have seen this as a response by consumers to increasing concerns about privacy.

Stefan Schutt

See also: Popular Transmedia, Australia

Further Reading

Australian Bureau of Statistics. 2011. *Australian Social Trends, June 2011: Online @ home.* www.ausstats.abs.gov.au/ausstats/subscriber.nsf/LookupAttach/4102.0Publication 29.06.116/$File/41020_Online_Jun2011.pdf. Accessed March 26, 2016.

Australian Communications and Media Authority. 2013. *Like, Post, Share: Young Australians' Experience of Social Media.* www.cybersmart.gov.au/About%20Cybersmart/Research/~/media/Cybersmart/About%20Cybersmart/Documents/Newspoll%20Quantitative%20Like%20Post%20Share%20%20final%20PDF.pdf. Accessed March 26, 2016.

Boyd, Danah, and Nicole B. Ellison. 2007. "Social Network Sites: Definition, History, and Scholarship." *Journal of Computer-Mediated Communication* 3, no. 1: 210–230.

Clarke, Roger. 2004. "Origins and Nature of the Internet in Australia." www.rogerclarke.com/II/OzI04.html. Accessed March 26, 2016.

Kennedy, Les. 2005. "Police Act Swiftly to Curb Attacks." *Sydney Morning Herald.* December 13. http://www.smh.com.au/news/national/police-act-swiftly-to-curb-attacks/2005/12/12/1134236005953.html. Accessed March 26, 2016.

Social Media News. 2015. "Social Media Statistics." www.socialmedianews.com.au/social-media-statistics. Accessed March 26, 2016.

SOCIAL MEDIA, INDONESIA

The 2012 Indonesian film *#RepublikTwitter* (*#TheTwitterRepublic*) opens by panning over the clay tile rooftops of Jogja, Central Java. Merapi Mountain stands tall in the background as the camera tracks past a young man staring down at his smartphone before zooming into a college dormitory. Sukmo, the male lead, is browsing the Internet while talking to his roommate about moving to Jakarta to meet a girl he met on Twitter. The next scene cuts to Jakarta, where Dyah, the female lead, sits at her computer in her modern Jakarta home, laughing quietly to herself. Cut back to Jogja, where Sukmo and his roommate are embarking on a road trip to Jakarta, the montage of which is accompanied by the pop song, "I Want to Tweet, Tweet, Tweet Right Now." The rest of the movie proceeds in typical romantic-comedy fashion—small-town college boy meets big-city professional girl. The film revolves around the role of social media in daily life in Indonesia and shows us the pervasiveness of social media in Indonesian popular culture. The Internet and social media have changed the ways in which humans connect with one another across the globe. Indonesia is no exception and in fact boasts one of the most active social media hubs in the world. In this section we will explore some of the ways in which Indonesians engage with social media by looking at recent trends in a growing social media landscape, public spaces for online access, online gaming as a social medium, and the growing online start-up industry in Indonesia. Just as *#RepublikTwitter* explores the potential dangers and unforeseen prospects of finding romance online, so too must our understanding of social media in Indonesia take into account some of the problems associated with changes in communication, entertainment, and technology, as well as the potential for local communities to develop innovative ways of interacting with global phenomena. Indonesia does not merely follow the global trends in social media but absorbs and adapts to global trends in innovative ways. Local initiatives and public spaces that provide greater accessibility to Internet technologies have the potential to reshape the landscape of social media, perhaps even leading the way for new technologies and new conceptions of what social media means globally.

The social media landscape in Indonesia receives a great deal of international attention because of its rapid growth over the past five years, but the statistical data on social media usage in Indonesia contains contradictory trends. Despite huge growth in the number of Internet users—nearly doubling from 2013 to 2014 to a total of 72.7 million users—the rate of Internet penetration is still fairly low. It was estimated in 2015 that only 28 percent of the population of Indonesia is connected to the Internet, compared to the global average of 42 percent (Kemp 2015). Nevertheless, Indonesia frequently ranks in the top five countries with the greatest number of Facebook and Twitter users internationally. There is much speculation about the reasons for such rapid growth, but one notable reason for the strength of social media in Indonesia is the fact that it is primarily a mobile-phone phenomenon. Many Indonesians own more than one mobile device, and 50 percent of the total Web traffic comes from mobile-phone use (Kemp 2015). With a growing middle class and increased affordability of Internet technologies, the social media landscape in Indonesia continues to grow.

Many agree that statistical analyses only present a fraction of the full picture of social media use in Indonesia. Internet technologies tend to be more readily available to urban middle-to-upper-class communities in the biggest cities of Indonesia, most of which are located on the island of Java. The rapid expansion of Internet technologies in urban centers is also accompanied by local adaptations and innovations in rural communities. For example, in 2000 a local community by the name of Angkringan in Bantul, Central Java, teamed up with a number of university students in Malang, East Java, to develop a low-budget Wi-Fi receiver for low-income communities, called a *wajanbolic* antenna. Made from a frying pan (*wajan*) wrapped in aluminum foil attached to a tube and wired to a Wi-Fi USB stick, the *wajanbolic* is connected to a personal computer for members of their community to access a shared Internet connection, lowering the individual cost of Internet access (Jurriëns 2009). As a result of different patterns of Internet use and local innovation, individuals living in rural communities or among lower socioeconomic segments of society are not always represented in the global statistics. It is likely that the rate of Internet penetration in Indonesia is actually far greater than statistics report.

In addition to new do-it-yourself technologies, you also find public spaces that broaden rural access to the Internet, social media, and especially gaming. A *warnet* (shortened from *warung Internet*) is the Indonesian version of an Internet café. In the 1980s and early 1990s, it was common to find public telephone kiosks, called *wartel* (shortened from *warung telekomunikasi*). When Internet subscription services became available in the mid-1990s, these *wartel* provided the first public Internet access sites. By the late 1990s, many *wartel* were converted into *warnet*, where people could use public computers to access the Internet (Hill and Sen 1997). From big cities to small towns, you find *warnet* all across Indonesia today. They typically consist of a number of small booths with computers rented out by the hour. They have also become home to many online gaming communities. Walking into a *warnet*, you will often find a busy den of college students playing a variety of online games at all hours of the night. When not gaming, fellow gamers sit together outside the *warnet*, drinking coffee, smoking clove cigarettes, and chatting about the games they are playing inside. In some respects, these *warnet* redefine social media in the Indonesian context as a public space where gamers socialize and access the Internet, regardless of economic restrictions.

Indonesia has recently become a site for greater investment in social media start-ups and game development. From February 23 to 27, 2015, Jakarta hosted the international Social Media Week Conference around the theme "Upwardly Mobile: The Rise of the Connected Class." Thousands of corporate, small- and medium-sized business, media, and government representatives gathered for a week of seminars, keynote presentations, and start-up presentations. Events such as this show a shared global interest in the future of social media and the role of Indonesia in that development.

Megan Robin Hewitt

See also: Video Games, Indonesia (Chapter 7: Video Games)

Further Reading

Hill, David T., and Krishna Sen. 1997. "Wiring the Warung to Global Gateways: The Internet in Indonesia." *Indonesia*, no. 63: 67–89.

Jurriëns, Edwin. 2009. "Frying the Wires, Freeing the Waves: A Wajanbolic Antenna." *Inside Indonesia* 95. www.insideindonesia.org/frying-the-wires-freeing-the-waves. Accessed April 30, 2015.

Kemp, Simon. 2015. "Digital, Social & Mobile Worldwide in 2015." *We Are Social.* January 21. http://wearesocial.net/blog/2015/01/digital-social-mobile-worldwide-2015/. Accessed May 27, 2015.

Zulkarnain, Iskandar. 2014. "'Playable' Nationalism: 'Nusantara Online' and the 'Gamic' Reconstructions of National History." *Sojourn: Journal of Social Issues in Southeast Asia* 29, no. 1:31–62.

SOCIAL MEDIA, JAPAN

Japanese Internet culture has evolved from a number of different factors: early and now ubiquitous wireless Internet access, the creativity of large pop-culture fan communities, and prevailing cultural concerns about privacy and anonymity. In this environment, social media has become a major presence in Japanese culture. The earthquake, tsunami, and nuclear disaster in 2011 became a milestone for the growing popularity of social media, cementing its importance as a cultural phenomenon in Japan. Since then, social media technologies are increasingly hailed as a force of—rather than a mere tool for—social change. This entry examines the historical and cultural conditions for this understanding of social media.

Early and widespread access to mobile Internet connection has been an important factor in the development of Japanese Internet culture. NTT DoCoMo, Japan's largest wireless carrier, launched the I-mode mobile Internet service in 1999, after which it became very popular. I-mode used modified Internet protocols and formats to transmit and display content especially made or converted for mobile phones, and users could not access regular Internet addresses. A large part of the Japanese Web was once adapted for mobile consumption in this way. Now the majority of cell-phone subscribers instead have access to the regular Internet regardless of device.

In 1999, the same year that I-mode made mobile Internet connections widely available, 2channel launched its textboard service. With the slogan "From 'hacking' to 'tonight's side dishes,'" 2channel provides hundreds of separate forums divided by topic. 2channel's simple, text-based interface introduces an economy of attention: each forum has a maximum number of conversations, listed by popularity, and users "raise" (*age*) or "lower" (*sage*) threads, pushing unpopular threads down the list and eventually deleting them.

Most importantly, 2channel's textboards require no registration and are completely anonymous. Users can post using a protected "tripcode" to prove their identity across messages, but the vast majority of users do not. This is a major difference from the current conventions of social network services that (in order to monetize their preferences) require users to register an account via e-mail in order to participate. From the early 2000s, 2channel became a major cultural phenomenon, achieving a massive readership, and it continued to grow even as other social networking sites gained traction among Japanese Internet users: since 2007, about 2.5 million posts are made daily on the site.

Niconico is another important center for anonymous Internet culture. Launched in 2006, this video-streaming service allows users to add subtitles and text annotations to any video they are watching; these annotations then scroll or blink across the screen for other viewers, and popular videos often have so many accumulated annotations that the actual image can barely be seen at all. These platforms allow for a sense of collectively experiencing all kinds of events as they unfold. At the same time, the sheer amount of content makes it difficult for these sites to prevent illegal postings as required by law, and as a result, anonymous forums are famously abundant in chauvinism, hate speech, and slander.

Such aspects of anonymous Internet culture remain, with many of the derivatives that have become popular in other countries. At the same time, these environments have provided safer spaces for communities of fans and enthusiasts to discuss and develop their interests. Offline expressions of fan culture like cosplay and fan fiction have their online equivalents in *oekaki* picture-boards: versions of 2channel's anonymous boards where users contribute and discuss paintings made with simple in-browser software. Today, the most popular topics discussed on social media usually involve video games, anime, and graphic novels.

As cell phones continued to proliferate, online jargon was further popularized with the "cell-phone novel" phenomenon, where extremely short works of fiction suitable for reading and writing on a mobile phone started to outsell conventional printed books. In 2007 five out of 10 annual best sellers had been written on cell phones. The popularity of celebrity blogs also helped normalize Internet culture and jargon. However, a great sense of moral panic often surrounds Internet culture, often phrased as anxiety regarding deteriorating standards of privacy, language, and education.

Today, privacy remains an important concern to Japanese social media users who, especially compared to many Western social media populations, have long been relatively reluctant to show personal information and photos on the Internet. When Mixi launched in 2004 (the same year as Facebook), and became the first, and soon most popular, social networking service in Japan, most users elected not

As around the world, social media sites and the smart phones and tablets used to access them, have become ubiquitous in Japan, and most of Asia and Oceania. Here, commuters are engrossed in their devices on a Tokyo subway in 2015. (Mirko Vitali/Dreamstime.com)

to show their real names or photographs. For years, Mixi nevertheless remained the social network of choice for young Japanese—despite enforcing an 18-year age limit and requiring both an invitation and an e-mail address registered to a Japanese cell phone to create an account. In recent years, Mixi has struggled to keep up with competitors like Facebook, which more than doubled its active users in the country in 2012. Meanwhile, Japanese-Korean messaging and microblogging application Line has become popular across Asia, with more than half of its registered users outside the country.

On March 11, 2011, the world watched in real time as tsunami waves overshadowed, then engulfed, the northeastern coast of the Japanese mainland. Killing some 16,000 people and costing hundreds of billions in material destruction, the earthquake, tsunami, and nuclear accident known as the "3.11 disaster" also became the most mediated disaster event in history. While the tsunami swept away power and phone lines, survivors in stricken areas could often access the Internet through their cell phones. People turned to social media for help and information, and even public television used video-streaming platforms to reach users isolated without access to radio or television. Here, social media affected how disaster information reached audiences and how relief work could be better coordinated. But as the localized destruction of the earthquake and tsunami turned into the widespread uncertainty and fear around radiation leaking from the fractured Fukushima-1 reactors, social media became an important way to find alternative information sources, voice common concerns, and challenge government propaganda.

Attitudes toward social media changed in two ways after the 2011 disaster. First, newspaper and television news portrayed social media as representative of popular opinion in a way that Internet culture had never been before. In particular, Twitter became famous as the social media platform of ordinary people—a barometer of public opinion, knowledge, and anxieties. The increased popularity of the platform could be witnessed later that year, as Japanese New Year's celebrations set a new record at 16,000 tweets per second, ultimately crashing the Twitter platform. Secondly, social media itself also became a symbol of citizens' political participation. In fact, Twitter was itself widely credited as a force of social change in making information about radiation leaks and demonstrations against the government's handling of nuclear disaster widely available.

This idealized view presents social media as free, open, and uncensored, as opposed to traditional mass-media outlets. Certainly, mass media could not represent the unfolding complexity of the disaster situation. In most cases, however, the distinction between new and old media is not as clearly cut: in the immediate aftermath of the 2011 disaster, imagery first posted and circulated on social media platforms was picked up by television news, while television broadcasts were recorded and uploaded to video-streaming platforms like YouTube, Vimeo, and Niconico. Later, news websites, scans, and recordings remained important as archives for collaborative efforts to document the disaster experience. Both forms of media can contribute to panic and misinformation, but between old and new, critical readerships have emerged that attempt to harness both toward better understanding the world.

Love Kindstrand

See also: Egao and Online Satire, China; *Weishidai* (Micro-Era), China

Further Reading

Cheng, John William. 2014. "The Effects of the Use of Mass and Social Media on Post-Disaster Recovery: A Theoretical Framework." *Journal of the Graduate School of Asia-Pacific Studies* 28: 45–64.

Kindstrand, Love, David H. Slater, and Nishimura Keiko. 2012. "Mobilizing Discontent: Social Media and Networked Activism since the Great East Japan Earthquake." In *The Routledge Handbook of New Media in Asia*. Ed. Larissa Hjorth and Olivia Khoo, 53–65. New York: Routledge.

Liscutin, Nicola. 2011. "Indignez-Vous! 'Fukushima,' New Media and Anti-Nuclear Activism in Japan." *The Asia-Pacific Journal* 9, no. 47.

Slater, David H., Nishimura Keiko, and Love Kindstrand. 2012. "Social Media, Information, and Political Activism in Japan's 3.11 Crisis." *The Asia-Pacific Journal* 10, no. 24.

Takahashi, Toshie. 2014. "Youth, Social Media and Connectivity in Japan." In *The Language of Social Media: Community and Identity on the Internet*. Ed. P. Seargeant and C. Tagg, 186–207. New York: Palgrave Macmillan.

SOCIAL MEDIA, PHILIPPINES

The Philippines enjoys a colorful history of groundbreaking and occasionally insubordinate mobile and online media technology being utilized to meet political and social goals. Metro Manila, in particular, has been proclaimed as the texting capital of the world. The widespread use of the mobile phone for political deployment has been partly responsible for such distinction. Incidentally, this gadget has become both a symbol and a tool of democracy (Rafael 2003). More recently, the Philippines has been adjudged as the social networking capital of the world. This label stems from the extensive and creative utilization of online media channels for civic engagement and political involvement. The Filipinos' strong endorsement of Facebook and Twitter, not only for social interaction but also for building and mobilizing political networks, has further supported this claim.

Notable episodes that highlight the deployment of mobile and online media technology in the Philippines have been ubiquitous. In 2001 mobile phones were used by activists to spread information and mobilize a series of mass actions that culminated in the removal of President Joseph "Erap" Estrada amid allegations of massive corruption. This string of protests marked the second time since 1986 that a head of state was ousted from office, a phenomenon that was popularly known as the Second People Power Revolution. But unlike the first, which led to the demise of a 20-year-old dictatorship through relentless street demonstrations, the second heavily relied on technology to swiftly convey messages and coordinate action.

Short message service (SMS, or more colloquially, text messaging) was a helpful tool in bringing together Filipinos of different economic and social backgrounds at a time when a dissenting critical mass was needed. The years that followed saw the immense utilization of both SMS and social networking sites (SNS) as media of expression and communication. In 2009 collective grief over the death of former president Corazon Aquino was expressed through social media. Tributes, expressions of sympathy and loss, and news updates surrounding the demise of the former leader and icon of Philippine democracy flooded SNS, including Facebook (the dominant SNS), Multiply (popular before Facebook), Friendster (the precursor of Facebook), and Plurk (similar to Twitter). Typhoon Ketsana (called Typhoon Ondoy in the Philippines) hit and caused immense damage and loss of life in the same year. Once again, online social networking became one of the more effective platforms of information dissemination and emergency mobilization. The national elections of 2010 and 2013 and the subsequent public disclosure of corruption cases involving many members of the national legislature likewise showcased the creativity and savvy of Filipinos in maximizing online social networking resources. From satirical memes and insightful infographics to professionally crafted videos, feelings of displeasure, frustration, and anger were displayed online in no small measure. Euphoria surrounding Pope Francis's visit to the Philippines in January 2015 was likewise conveyed via social media. Akin to a detailed play-by-play account of a major sports event as it unfolds, running commentaries on social media about the pontiff's itinerary, speeches, and even mannerisms were provided. On the whole, these experiences demonstrate how social media in the Philippines ceases to exclusively serve as "spaces for socializing"; these online platforms are now treated as "emerging forms of civic engagement, participation, and politics" (Hjorth and Arnold 2011, 30).

It is widely assumed that Filipinos who are young professionals or those who enjoy a relative abundance of time and money dominate social networking. However, the events mentioned above indicate that the aforementioned are not the only significant category of users. Interest has, in fact, spread across generations. Parents and even grandparents from all social classes have started to use SNS to maintain contact with family and friends—particularly those who are overseas. Female "caregivers," who comprise a huge part of overseas Filipino workers (OFWs), have played a significant role in the accelerated use and reliance on information and communication technologies (ICTs).

Based on the study of Larissa Hjorth and Michael Arnold (2011), two key motivations for utilizing ICT and SNS have emerged in their conversations with Filipino users. Social media resources help maintain family relations in the context of global and national migration. For example, mobile phones, most notably smartphones, and other similar devices have been instrumental in helping the geographic and social mobility of Filipino caregivers in Hong Kong while at the same time affording them a way of keeping in contact with family and strengthening traditional family life despite the distance (McKay 2007). In other words, social media affords users an assortment of new and alternative ways of sustaining intimate ties with relatives and friends abroad or those left behind. The desire to engage in political activities or interrogate social issues in a personal capacity has likewise encouraged dependence on ICT and SNS. The disengagement of the youth from conventional political activity has been viewed in countries like the United States, Germany, Sweden, and the United Kingdom as a discouraging development that does not bode well for civic life (Bennett 2008). Social media serve as an antidote to this perceived weakness by providing users with channels and platforms to express their position on issues of national and global importance without having to be an actual member of a political party or cause-oriented group. Profile pictures and status messages in Facebook, for instance, may reveal a person's ideological persuasion and political inclination. Tweets, customarily shorter and thus more straightforward, can create a similar impact in terms of demonstrating the extent of one's advocacy or belief. Paraphrasing Hjorth and Arnold's (2011) words, institutional membership and overt involvement in political affairs are not the only indicators of constructive politicization; the construction (and reconstruction) of one's identity via SNS is to a certain extent a reflection and a product of political realities. Put alternatively, the immediate social context or environment influences the type of political culture one is socialized into.

Another factor that generates widespread support for ICT and SNS is their accessibility. Unlike the customarily top-down and noninteractive traditional media, ICT and SNS (collectively known in the vernacular as "new media") facilitate personal interaction and "the free flow of opinions," attributes that make these mechanisms more valuable to their users (Pertierra 2012, 16). Unlike the television, radio, and newspaper, mobile phones and SNS are bereft of strict censors or filters that dissuade and even stifle the dissemination of controversial and critical viewpoints. While traditional media can be generally regarded as controlled by the political elite, the emergence of ICT and SNS as alternative sources of information and platforms for political participation target a wider and more diverse audience and are more inclined to accommodate dissenting narratives and views. For example, online fora or threads pertaining to a particular topic or issue afford users and readers alike more freedom to exchange and challenge ideas outright.

Enrique Niño P. Leviste

See also: Mobile Phones, Philippines; Video Games, Philippines (Chapter 7: Video Games)

Further Reading

Bennett, W. Lance. 2008. "Changing Citizenship in the Digital Age." In *Civic Life Online: Learning How Digital Media Can Engage Youth.* Ed. W. Lance Bennett, 1–24. Cambridge, MA: MIT Press.

Hjorth, Larissa, and Michael Arnold. 2011. "The Personal and the Political: Social Networking in Manila." *International Journal of Learning and Media* 3, 29–39.

McKay, Deirdre. 2007. "'Sending Dollars Shows Feeling'—Emotions and Economies in Filipino Migration." *Mobilities* 2, 175–194.

Pertierra, Raul. 2012. *The New Media, Society and Politics in the Philippines*. Berlin: Friedrich-Ebert-Stiftung.

Rafael, Vicente. 2003. "The Cell Phone and the Crowd: Messianic Politics in the Contemporary Philippines." *Public Culture* 15, 399–425.

SUI, MIKE

Mike Sui, a Chinese American comedian who grew up in Beijing and Wisconsin, made his name as a star *laowai* (the popular Mandarin word for "foreigner") in China after he released his video "12 Beijingers" on the Chinese video site Youku in 2012. In this video, made up of numerous drifting conversations, he plays all 12 roles of different national/regional/racial/sexual identities, such as American, Russian, African American, Beijinger, gay, Taiwanese, and more. In addition to the frequent uses of Mandarin English code-switching, Sui employs a broad range of stereotypical mannerisms and accents to mark these identities. For example, his American speaks Mandarin with a loss of firm intonation that's regarded as typical for *laowais* in China, whereas his Beijinger, named Li Lei (the name of the Chinese student often cited in the standard English textbooks in China), loves to speak English but with a heavy Beijing accent. This video went viral in Chinese cyberspace not just because of his impeccable linguistic skills but also because Chinese netizens were surprised to find a "foreigner" (as he looks more Caucasian than Asian) to be so familiar with popular discourses in the Chinese public sphere. In Michel Foucault's notion of discourse as a linguistic term, the cultural knowledge embedded in discourse is what adds social value to language, especially in the context of second-language learning. Therefore, when Sui assumes the identity of a Taiwanese guy and enacts it with a "feminine" Taiwanese accent, he simultaneously displays his ability to do so and his knowledge of the sociolinguistic perceptions mainland Chinese people have about Taiwanese men.

Of course, Mike Sui is not the first "foreigner" to become a popular star in China. In the 1990s, an American named Da Shan became the first foreigner to appear constantly on China's official channel CCTV as a host and entertainer. Later in the 2000s, many foreigners, such as Hao Ge (Liberian) and Cao-Cao (American), achieved temporary fame by participating in popular reality TV shows and singing contests in China. As it has been more than 35 years since Deng Xiaoping's implementation of the Open Door policy, it has become increasingly difficult nowadays for a *laowai* to achieve fame solely based on his or her Mandarin skills. But since his surge to stardom in 2012, Mike Sui has firmly established himself within the entertainment circle in China: in 2013 he acted a major role as the French suitor of the female lead in the popular Internet TV series *Never Give Up, Dodo!*, and in 2014 he appeared in the movie *My Old Classmate*, again as a foreign antagonist of the male lead in his pursuit for the female protagonist. In 2015 he released a new video on Youku entitled "Mike Sui's 18 Imitation Show," which went viral again, and it is often circulated on the Chinese Internet with provocative titles like "An Amazing *Laowai*." This new video can be seen as a sequel to his 2012 "tour de force" as many characters, such as Li Lei and the Taiwanese guy, reappear, and its format and style do not differ greatly from the 2010 episode. It simply adds more international characters to the conversations: This time we have a migrant worker from Xinjiang (China's autonomous Uyghur province), a North Korean defector, a transvestite Japanese man, and a South Korean guy with an "iPhone face" (referring to plastic surgery). In his hyperbolic acting, Mike Sui again enacts Chinese people's stereotypes about these groups. For example, the Xinjiang man is represented as very rude, as he spits on the seat in the train, and hypermasculine, as he misrecognizes the fashionable Shanghainese man as a girl. More shockingly, in his embodiment of the North Korean defector, Sui bursts into tearful exclamations and kisses good-bye the tree bark he takes out of his bag upon receiving a biscuit from train staff. Surprisingly, such insensitive fun-making of the North Korean famine has received high praise from Chinese netizens.

To explain the reasons behind such a positive reception of Sui, it has to be noted that cultural pleasure often derives from a sense of defamiliarization. But in Sui's case, he generates this pleasure in his audience through his own racial displacement in a sinocentric representational practice. In spite of his playing with regional identities inside China, his perspective, against which the stereotypes are located, is essentially an assumed general Chinese perspective, because it is the different standards of political correctness within a homogeneous Chinese society that allow him to essentialize, mimic, and ultimately capitalize on imagined Others. For example, considering the critical public discourses on postcolonialism and multiculturalism in the West, Sui's mimicries of peoples of other cultures and ethnicities would be easily rendered as a distorted form of masking that is racist and offensive in the Western context. In contrast, the Chinese audience, in their equally essentialist confusion/conflation of race, geography, and modernity, may be able to gain a smug feeling of pleasure in viewing a supposedly superior Westerner actively opt for a Chinese worldview, whose own superiority was confirmed by marginal subalterns such as Xinjiang and North Korea. The importance of Sui's racial displacement, as a foil for a sinocentric psychology, is manifested in the marketing strategies he or his proxies employ to boost the Internet circulation of his works. Despite his mixed identity and childhood experience in Beijing, which actually pinpoint his native-speaker status vis-à-vis the Chinese language and culture, he is nevertheless constantly being sold as an amazing *laowai* who is able to penetrate the Chinese psyche. It would be safe to say that a "Chinese Chinese" comedian would not produce the same Internet sensation even if he or she followed the exact script. Moreover, this kind of "Chinese Chinese" comedian probably would not dare follow such a script, which contains such blatantly negative portraits of internal and external subalterns, in fear of inducing racial disharmony and conflicts. Sui's self-inflicted foreignness, then, also functions as a distancing mechanism that grants him a certain degree of immunity vis-à-vis Chinese politics.

Therefore, the phenomenon of Mike Sui, in his popularity, demonstrates an increasingly globalized and multiracial/cultural Chinese society on the one hand, and the problematics of its irreconcilability with a sinocentric essentialism on the other hand. If in the fast pace of globalization the Chinese society has leveled up its demands upon the popular foreign Other, from a command of Chinese phonetics and semantics to that of Chinese pragmatics and discourses, this expanded spectrum stretching from the syllable to the social still remains in a monolithic worldview short of breadth and plurality. In this context, Mike Sui has to capitalize on both his foreignness and the stereotypes in Chinese society in his representations of Others. His challenge to China's constructed homogeneity is thus only at the phenotextual level, as the defamiliarization produced by his skin color is eventually canceled out by his ideological conformism toward the assumed notion of Chineseness. If he does not break from such conformism, it is almost certain that he can only play the foreigner in the mainstream Chinese cultural industry, as he has done so far.

Flair Donglai Shi

See also: Egao and Online Satire, China

Further Reading

Dikötter, Frank. 2015. *The Discourse of Race in Modern China.* New York: C. Hurst & Co. Publishers Ltd.

Enkvist, Nils Erik. 1991. "From Phoneme to Discourse: A Half-Century of Linguistics." *The Modern Language Review* 86, no. 4: xxxi–xiii.

Foucault, Michel. 2002. *Archaeology of Knowledge,* 2nd ed. London: Routledge.

Spencer, Stephen. 2014. *Race and Ethnicity: Culture, Identity and Representation.* London: Routledge.

Spivak, Gayatri. 1999. *A Critique of Postcolonial Reason: Toward a History of the Vanishing Present.* Cambridge, MA: Harvard University Press.

Stacy, R. H. 1977. *Defamiliarization in Language and Literature.* Syracuse, NY: Syracuse University Press.

WEISHIDAI (MICRO-ERA), CHINA

The development of mobile media and social-networking platforms in China is going through a process of miniaturization, leading many to speculate about the inception of a new era in local communication technologies. In Chinese this has been referred to as a *weishidai,* a "micro-era" of ubiquitous, pervasive, and lightweight digital media. Inspired by the popularity of the prefix *wei* ("micro"), and entering common parlance through popular culture, *weishidai* is a useful shorthand to describe the contemporary configuration of digital media in China. In the micro-era of Chinese digital media, the ubiquity and pervasiveness of miniaturized communication technologies allow personalized articulations of micro-sociality and new forms of engagement with content and leisure.

When the microblogging platform Sina Weibo (Xinlang Weibo 新浪微博) was launched by the SINA Corporation in 2009, the character *wei* (微) was just a direct translation of the English-language prefix "micro." Microblogging platforms, such as Tumblr and Twitter, allow users to publish short textual or multimedia posts on personal profile pages and to follow and be followed by other users. Given its popularity—built on successful design decisions and undeniably helped by the blockage of Twitter within the People's Republic of China (PRC) national borders—Sina Weibo, often just generically referred to as Weibo, has become the gold standard for microblogging in China. A side effect of Chinese digital media users' enthusiastic uptake of Weibo platforms has been the increasing buzz around *wei*, the "micro" prefix. When, in 2011, Tencent, another prominent Chinese Internet company, released the instant-messaging mobile application WeChat (Weixin 微信), the app quickly topped the charts in terms of the number of monthly users. With the internationalization of WeChat, the *wei* prefix gained another layer of meaning: while literally meaning "micro-letter" in Mandarin Chinese, the English name of the app adds an intimate social-networking aspect to the miniaturization of online communications.

In the wake of these successes, the *wei* prefix has been incorporated into the branding of an increasing number of platforms, services, and cultural products. After *weibo* and *weixin*, everything Internet related seems to require miniaturization: from commercial transactions, with *weihuo* (micro-goods), *weiguanggao* (micro-advertisement), and *weizhifu* (micro-payments); through business, with *weiguanli* (micro-management) and *weitouzi* (micro-investment); to cultural consumption, with *weidianying* (micro-movies), *weixiaoshuo* (micro-fiction), and other *weimeiti* (micro-media). The miniaturization of online platforms, services, and content has become the most recurring feature experienced by Chinese digital media users. A typical day for a Chinese Internet user might begin by checking mentions and updates on one's microblogging accounts, perhaps accompanied by micro-movies and micro-novels watched and read while commuting, and constantly interspersed by micro-messages sent to friends and colleagues through mobile apps.

As local technology writers observe, Chinese digital media could be said to have entered a "micro-era" (*weishidai* 微时代) of mobility and miniaturization. While software development in Euro-American contexts is couched in buzzwords emphasizing the acts of sharing, networking, and personalization ("social," "participatory," "crowd," "smart," "instant," "personal"), the *wei* prefix of the Chinese micro-era summarizes a series of cultural patterns emerging from the local developments of digital media: decentralization, fragmentation, dispersion, and immediacy. Recurring descriptions of the *weishidai* portray it as a time in which the dissemination of information is sped up and made more effective by the shortness and immediacy of micro-sociality. In more utopian theorizations, the *weishidai* is envisioned as a technological revolution ushering in a new *weiwenhua* (micro-culture) of individuality, freedom, grassroots participation, and youth.

Regardless of the degree of enthusiasm with which its theorists embrace it, depictions of the *weishidai* agree in considering it more than a trivial development of local digital media and rather a shift in forms of engagement and participation with wide societal implications, some positive (such as spontaneous social actions and grassroots campaigns), others negative (such as rumors, personal attacks, and online crime). For these reasons, it is commonly argued, digital media in the *weishidai* should be monitored and regulated through ad hoc measures.

Quite tellingly, the term *weishidai* is also used in the title of a Chinese online drama series released in 2014 on the Tencent video platform. *Weishidai zhi lian* (*Love in the Micro-Era*) is centered on the stories of six *90hou* (born after 1990) characters negotiating romance through social networking platforms. The linkage between miniaturized digital media, younger generations, and romantic experiences emphasizes the pervasiveness of communication technologies in Chinese everyday life and the shift toward micro-social practices. Sending short messages and emoticons to personal contacts throughout the day, publishing microblog updates on personal pages, sharing *weishipin* (micro-videos) through WeChat, or watching *weidianying* (micro-movies) on video-streaming platforms, all become activities integrated in the rhythms of everyday life.

While the miniaturization of digital media might seem a radical break from the sociality allowed by desktop computers and fixed Internet connections, studies of communication in everyday life show how the diminutive size of messages does not necessarily imply emotional detachment or social distance. Instead, the micro-social practices in the *weishidai* allow digital media users to maintain emotional connections across daily routines and commutes and facilitate the organization of everyday activities with intimate others.

The idea of *weishidai* is just one of several imaginaries prophesizing the developments of communication technologies in China. Other technological imaginaries depict China as developing the Internet into a new, powerful driver of economic development (the "Internet Plus" promoted by current premier Li Keqiang), or as accelerating the balkanization of the Web through a nationalist stance on Internet governance (the propagandistic idea of *wangluo qiangguo* "strong Internet nation"). In contrast to these imaginaries, the concept of *weishidai* is much less prescriptive and seeks to summarize the contemporary configuration of communication technologies as they become increasingly ubiquitous, pervasive, and lightweight. Lightness has been identified as one of the main features of how communication technologies are taken up by users in their everyday lives. Digital media in the *weishidai* allow more dispersed and mobile practices of micro-sociality, and their diminutive size, dispersed across portable screens, enables new forms of engagement with the consumption and creation of content and leisure.

Gabriele de Seta

See also: *Egao* and Online Satire, China; Great Firewall, China

Further Reading

Chen, Yujie, and Haile Liu. 2012. "The Micro Era." *China Pictorial.* April 1. www.chinapictorial.com.cn/en/features/txt/2012-04/01/content_444412.htm. Accessed March 26, 2016.

Cheng, Chi, and Yakun Yang. 2013. "Chuantong Meiti Shishui 'Weishidai' [Traditional Media Test the Waters of the 'Micro-Era']." *Xinwen Qianshao.*

Ito, Mizuko. 2005. "Introduction: Personal, Portable, Pedestrian." In *Personal, Portable, Pedestrian: Mobile Phones in Japanese Life*. Ed. Mizuko Ito, Daisuke Okabe, and Misa Matsuda, 1–16. Cambridge, MA: MIT Press.

Miyata, Kakuko, Jeffrey Boase, Barry Wellman, and Ken'ichi Ikeda. 2005. "The Mobile-izing Japanese: Connecting to the Internet by PC and Webphone in Yamanashi." In *Personal, Portable, Pedestrian: Mobile Phones in Japanese Life*. Ed. Mizuko Ito, Daisuke Okabe, and Misa Matsuda, 143–164. Cambridge, MA: MIT Press.

Tao, Dongfeng. 2014. "Lijie Weishidai de Weiwenhua [Understanding the Micro-Culture of the Micro-Era]." *Jinrong Bolan*.

Voci, Paola. 2014. "Quasi-Documentary, Cellflix and Web Spoofs: Chinese Movies' Other Visual Pleasures." In *China's iGeneration: Cinema and Moving Image Culture for the Twenty-First Century*. Ed. Matthew D. Johnson, Keith B. Wagner, Tianqi Yu, and Luke Vulpiani, 45–55. New York: Bloomsbury.

Chapter 6: Sports

Introduction

Sports, in their many forms, play an important role in the daily lives and the culture of billions of people around the world. Most people believe that taking part in sports is an essential component of a well-rounded education. Children receive physical education in most societies, and many grow up to continue playing sports and engaging in physical activities as an amusing diversion and as a means to stay physically fit. Sports can be broadly defined to include everything from chess to soccer to mountain climbing; the category does not refer exclusively to competitive ball sports that are so popular for international audiences.

Physical activities like yoga, mountain climbing, or the martial arts of Japan, Korea, China, the Philippines, and other regions, do not necessarily involve competition (though they sometimes do) but are generally engaged in for the sake of the practitioner's physical, mental, and spiritual well-being. Activities like chess, on the other hand, involve the fiercest competition, but they do not generally involve the kind of physical exertion of more conventional sports. Taking part in these sports is extremely important, but watching them can be equally or even more important to sports fans of Asia and Oceania, as in other regions of the world.

In Asia and Oceania, the American observer will find some unfamiliar sports, like *jai alai*, a game similar in some ways to handball but played with a ball caught and thrown with a basket-like device. The sport's roots in modern-day Spain have led to its popularity in foreign colonies of Latin America and especially the Philippines. Cricket, long a befuddlement to American audiences, is also a relic of the days of colonialism and imperialism, and it continues to be extremely popular in former British colonies like present-day India, Pakistan, Bangladesh, Australia, and New Zealand. Similar in some ways to baseball, the rules of cricket, and its surrounding culture, have little appeal to most Americans in spite of the game's prevalence in the regions listed above, as well as South Africa, some Caribbean countries, and of course Great Britain and Ireland. In Central Asia, horsemanship, archery, and wrestling have long been valued skills from Mongolia to Kazakhstan and beyond, and even today these activities continue to be important among the peoples there who trace their roots to the nomadic herders of the grasslands and steppe. Americans are familiar with table tennis (ping-pong) and badminton, but in some countries of East and Southeast Asia, these sports are more than casual recreation activities, as they are in the United States, but rather draw huge crowds and fierce competition. Rugby and its variations are extremely popular in Australia and New Zealand, and these two countries consistently field some of the best teams in the world.

Other sports of Asia and Oceania will be more familiar to American audiences and participants, like soccer, baseball, and even American football. Soccer (or football to most people around the world) is increasingly important in Asia and Oceania, though most countries in this region do not compete on the highest levels of Europe and Latin America. Japan, South Korea, and increasingly Australia, however, are emerging as regional soccer powerhouses, while most other countries in the region favor other national sports at the expense of international competitiveness in soccer. Baseball is also naturally familiar to the American audience, and in the last hundred years it has sunk deep cultural roots into several regions of Asia, especially Taiwan and Japan. Golf has surged in popularity in Japan and more recently among the growing middle and upper classes of China. As a luxury activity, golf in Asia, as in the United States, has a rather exclusive niche and is a favorite activity of many Japanese, Korean, and Chinese elites. Surfing and skateboarding are popular pastimes in China, Japan, and other regions. Australia, New Zealand, and many Pacific islands have thriving surf communities that host world competitions and draw the most daring of athletes. China's Hainan Island has recently been the site of surfing competitions that have elevated that sport around China.

While some dismiss spectator sports as insubstantial and frothy cultural distractions reminiscent of gladiatorial competitions, for others, watching their favorite team or athletes compete on television or in person can be a hugely important experience. Sometimes a team that represents a local town, city, state, or country can receive almost religious devotion from its fans. Watching competitions can

X-League Football in Japan

Baseball was famously adopted by Japan in the late 19th century, and today, American football has also taken root there. The X-League is a popular American football league in Japan. The league has existed since 1971 and was initially called the Japan American Football League. It essentially parallels NCAA college football rules. Teams are promoted or demoted within four divisions based on their performance. The top division is X1 with 18 teams separated into the Eastern, Central, and Western divisions. The season has three stages. During Stage 1, teams play within their division. The top three teams from each division advance to the Super 9 (Stage 2). From there, four teams move on to the final stage, which decides the two teams playing in the Japan X Bowl. The winner then plays the collegiate champion for the national title in the Rice Bowl. Americans can play in the X-League, though teams are limited to four foreign players each.

Matthew B. Turetsky

take on a ritual aspect, and for some fans, their love for their favorite team or athlete can be as important as any other aspect of their proclaimed identity. In Australia, the cities of Sydney and Melbourne are fierce rivals in rugby and other sports, while domestic leagues for cricket, soccer, baseball, and other sports draw huge local crowds throughout the region.

In some regions, sports and other physical activities are a means of cultural expression. In the Himalayas, mountaineering has transformed dramatically from the colonial to the postcolonial era, as embodied by the Sherpas of the region, once employed by colonists as porters and in recent years distinguished mountaineers in their own right. In Mongolia, sports and the festivals connected to them are a way of keeping alive what many believe to be quintessential Mongolian identity. In Australia and New Zealand, participation by Aboriginal and Maori people, respectively, is also an important cultural practice. Aboriginal participation in soccer, cricket, and rugby, for example, like Maori participation, is a decision by the indigenous people to take part in the sports of the historical colonizers of their homelands. In Taiwan and Japan, baseball was embraced about a century ago by the local population and so enthusiastically so that now Japanese and Taiwanese players rank among the greatest in the world. Indeed, professional baseball players move regularly between the best teams of Japan and the United States.

From yoga to mountaineering to soccer, sports in Asia and Oceania play an enormous role in daily life and popular culture, and this chapter, while it does not cover all aspects of sports in this part of the world, provides some representative examples of the ways in which people experience them.

Jeremy A. Murray and Kathleen M. Nadeau

Further Reading

Cha, Victor D. 2011. *Beyond the Final Score: The Politics of Sport in Asia*. New York: Columbia University Press.

Markovits, Andrei S., and Lars Rensmann. 2010. *Gaming the World: How Sports Are Reshaping Global Politics and Culture*. Princeton, NJ: Princeton University Press.

Mills, James H. 2005. *Subaltern Sports: Politics and Sport in South Asia*. London: Anthem Press.

Younghan, Cho, and Charles Leary. 2014. *Modern Sports in Asia: Cultural Perspectives*. London: Routledge.

ANTARCTIC EXPEDITIONS AND SPORTS

Antarctica is the coldest, windiest, most inhospitable place on earth. It is not conducive to human habitation, but inhabit Antarctica they do, in small, isolated, station-based communities. Sporting and other recreational activities are part of the fabric of human habitation and, in the Antarctic, sports play an important role in the physical and social dynamic of close-knit, isolated communities. For most inhabitants of Antarctica, whether short or long term, sports consist of recreational and enjoyable diversions from daily work, but there are also those who engage in competitive and extreme sporting activities in the region. This latter category is much more rare, and most of the sporting activity on Antarctica builds camaraderie instead of encouraging intense competition.

There are two key factors that shape sporting activities in the great southland for most people living in the station-based communities of the region. Firstly, the physical environment (climate, weather, topography) is a determinant on what sports can be played, where they can be played, and when they can be played. Secondly, besides a few exceptional circumstances, the sheer isolation of Antarctica precludes overly competitive sports that may cause severe injury or social isolation within the community. Sports in the Antarctic, therefore, are constrained by acceptable sporting etiquette and rules of behavior that mitigate risk of physical or social injury.

The fact that there are two distinct seasons in Antarctica means that there are two distinct categories of sporting activities, relative to each season. The Antarctic summer season (generally between October and April) culminates with 24 hours of daylight and is conducive to outdoor recreation. The Antarctic winter season (generally between May and September) celebrates the midwinter solstice and 24 hours of darkness, affording only indoor sporting activities for those living in the region's stations. During the summer season, sporting activities can be team based or individual. Individual pursuits include Nordic skiing and trekking, both recreational activities that are combined with field training. These activities enable controlled movement within the Antarctic environment between stations and deep field locations, for scientific projects or other requirements outside the station boundaries.

Additionally, skiing, snowboarding, and similar pursuits are confined within station boundaries and are purely for physical and social well-being. Some individual sporting activities, such as weight lifting, gym training, and aerobics can be undertaken all year round and, in a closed communal environment, are similarly beneficial for both physical well-being and social interaction. On designated social occasions, such as Australia Day (January 26), competitive team events are organized. Outdoor games like cricket, touch football, and cross-country ski/running events (including the occasional marathon race) are organized on a semicompetitive basis with the emphasis being on the social interaction rather than any result.

For example, there is a traditional midwinter swim to celebrate the winter solstice. Outside temperatures are about –25°F (–32°C), and the water temperature a "mild" 28°F (–2°C). Before the swim, a hole must be hacked into ice that is six feet thick (two meters). But this activity is more about celebrating the occasion and the social participation rather than demonstrating any aquatic sporting prowess.

During the Antarctic winter, outdoor sporting activity is high risk and, for long periods of time, not possible. As a consequence, the sporting activity among the station-based population shifts to indoor recreation. Traditional "pub games" such as billiards, snooker, darts, and table tennis are played socially and competitively both on an inter- and intra-station basis. Other indoor sports such as rock-wall climbing, yoga, Pilates, and chess are also vigorously played throughout the year. Summer indoor sports such as volleyball and badminton are also played. Sporting facilities and equipment are provided on most stations and include modestly equipped gymnasiums, ski courses and ski equipment, mountain bikes, and a range of other low-risk sporting equipment.

Besides the communal sporting activities of the stations and their longer-term residents of Antarctica, there are also less common and more extreme sporting events that have become part of the Antarctic world. These sporting events see the arrival of very short-term visitors to Antarctica. The Antarctica Marathon, the 4 Deserts Race Series, and the Antarctic Ice Marathon are three such activities that see athletes visit Antarctica and some of its nearby islands for extreme displays of physical endurance and sporting ability.

The Antarctica Marathon and Half Marathon takes place annually in February or March and has been held 16 times at the time of this writing and is completely booked for the coming years. The marathon course follows a gravel road that connects the Antarctic stations of Russia, Chile, Uruguay, and China in a standard marathon distance of 26.2 miles. The Antarctic Ice Marathon and the Frozen Continent Half Marathon have similarly challenged runners since 2005. Organizers of the race explain that the Antarctic Ice Marathon was arranged so that runners could complete a marathon on all seven continents. The Antarctic Ice Marathon also includes a 100-kilometer run (about 62 miles) on Antarctica.

As the final 250-kilometer (155 miles) portion of the 4 Deserts Series Race, the Antarctica portion of the race has been held every other year. The other three desert races in this competition are Chile's Atacama, a Chinese portion of the Gobi, and an Egyptian portion of the Sahara. This race, with each portion more than five times the length of a marathon, is obviously an extreme endeavor, and a maximum of 200 runners are allowed to compete. Active for 13 years at the time of writing, some races host only a handful or a few dozen intrepid runners.

Besides these extreme sports, just visiting the Antarctic as a tourist often involves sporting activities, from kayaking to hiking to cross-country skiing and more. Tourists have been visiting Antarctica for decades, and in recent years, accessibility and improved safety have led to increasing numbers of visitors, now into the tens of thousands per year. Concern for the natural environment has led to strict regulations on outdoor activities in the Antarctic, including the proper disposal of waste and protection of wildlife. To date, most Antarctic tourism is restricted to ship-based activities, with limited and short visits on land for recreational activities including hikes and skiing. On land, only the station-based communities make Antarctica their home for longer periods.

Roger Knowles

See also: Sherpas and Himalayan Mountaineering

Further Reading

Australian Antarctic Division. www.antarctica.gov.au. Accessed March 26, 2016.

U.S. Antarctic Program External Panel of the National Science Foundation. 2006. "Antarctica Past and Present." www.nsf.gov/pubs/1997/antpanel/antpan05.pdf. Accessed March 26, 2016.

Walker, Gabrielle. 2013. *Antarctica: An Intimate Portrait of a Mysterious Continent.* New York: Houghton Mifflin Harcourt.

BASEBALL, JAPAN

Invented in America, baseball is "America's pastime" and has been among the most popular of sports there for over 150 years. Today, baseball has reached many countries and is quickly becoming a worldwide sport, giving professional baseball a wide range of diversity. The sport has gained a great following and popularity in many other countries, like Mexico, Cuba, Dominican Republic, and Brazil. What some might not realize is that baseball is not only America's pastime, nor is it a sport that has grabbed popularity just in the western hemisphere. Baseball in Japan has been a national pastime for over 100 years and a symbol of great pride for the Japanese. As in America, baseball has become a large part of Japanese culture and national identity.

Under the rule of the Meiji emperor (1852–1912), education in Japan underwent major reform. In 1872 the Meiji emperor implemented the Education Code of 1872; however, the code made no mention of physical fitness. One objective of the code was to introduce Western studies into the Japanese curriculum and hire teachers from the United States. W. Grey Dixon, an American educator in Japan, realized that students were often becoming sick due to the lack of any outdoor activities. Student education solely focused on the mind, and the body began to suffer. Another foreign teacher, William E. Griffis (1843–1928), also took notice of the health of the Meiji-era students. Together, Dixon and Griffis helped to develop and promote outdoor activity, which they called "outdoor games."

Set up in high school, the outdoor games consisted of military exercises. At first, the students did not take the outdoor games seriously, and teachers noticed that the students needed more; they needed to have activities they could train for and then compete in. By the early 1890s, it became clear that the outdoor games needed to include activities that promoted stamina and self-discipline, as well as athletic clubs to promote commitment from its members. These clubs would then compete on a collegiate level, and the victors would bring pride and a favorable reputation to their schools. The first sport to organize for collegiate competition

Baseball has been a very popular pastime and spectator sport in Japan for over a century. Here, fans in Sapporo, Hokkaido, support their local team, the Nippon-Ham Fighters in a 2010 image. (Paul Dymond/Alamy Stock Photo)

was crew, or rowing, due to its simplicity. Baseball, however, eventually won the hearts of students and the larger community by the late 1890s.

Of all the Western teachers that helped in the promoting of outdoor athletics and the introduction of baseball, Horace Wilson (1843–1927) would become the man of greatest recognition for Japanese baseball. In 1873 Wilson introduced baseball to the students at Kaisei-ko, now Tokyo University. Wilson had created a rulebook, and Kaisei-ko students began to master the game. When it came to competition, it was Ichiko, an elite preparatory school, that dominated in competition for the first 15 years. Ichiko was so good that they even challenged the Yokohama Athletic Club (YAC), a baseball club made up of American naval personnel, to an international match. The YAC declined the invitation due to an earlier event known as the "Imbrie Affair," which had taken place during a baseball game and had led to an American teacher being assaulted by angered students. But Ichiko would not let up and continued to invite the YAC to a competition every year.

Then on May 23, 1896, Ichiko and the YAC played the first official baseball game between American and Japanese teams. There were many American fans in the stands who heckled the Japanese players as they took the field. The Ichiko team was nervous during their warm-ups, but when the game started the heckling stopped, and Ichiko dominated the game. The final score was Ichiko 29, YAC 4. The American players, beaten at their own game, were in such awe that they issued a rematch, which Ichiko proudly accepted. The game took place on June 5, 1896, and the YAC recruited additional players. When the game was over, the results were about the same; Ichiko 32, YAC 9. On June 27, 1896, they played on Ichiko's home field, where Ichiko won again in humiliating fashion by a score of 22–6. Then on July 4, 1896, the YAC would have their victory with a final score of 14–12. There were 12 games played between Ichiko and YAC. Ichiko only lost two, with a total run count of 230–64. Ichiko earned the respect of the Americans and also of the world of baseball following these games. This brought great pride to their school, their community, and their country. As word traveled to the United States about Ichiko's domination of the YAC, Ichiko began receiving invitations to American college baseball tournaments. The first to send an invitation was Yale University. Ichiko brought such popularity to baseball in Japan that the athletic governing body for schools created a championship series that highlighted the best schools and players, and this continues to the present day.

Then in 1908, Reach Sporting Goods Company sponsored the first professional American team to visit Japan. The team, made up of players from the various professional teams, had no big-name players added to the roster and included some minor-league players. The American team played Keio University to a sold-out crowd of 6,000 spectators. Then in 1913, professional teams from America began to tour Japan. The first were the Chicago White Sox and the New York Giants, who played only two games. Reach Sporting Goods Company would sponsor two more tours through Japan in 1920 and 1922. In 1934 American baseball sent its biggest stars to Japan, with hopes to promote peace and prevent any fighting between the two countries. Players like Babe Ruth, Lou Gehrig, and Jimmie Fox were on the roster. They played 18 games to sellout crowds, which inspired executives to create their own professional baseball league in Japan.

Newspaper mogul Matsutaro Shoriki (1885–1969) took the lead in creating a semiprofessional baseball league by finding corporations to cover travel expenses. The league consisted of eight teams. On December 26, 1934, with Matsutaro heading the Yomiuri Giants, the league played for a championship trophy. It took two years for the league to become competitive, and it was not until 1937 that all eight teams finally formed. It was in 1937 that baseball in Japan found its first professional baseball league as players began to receive salaries. In 1936 the league played between 25 and 30 games, and by 1937, they were playing 100 games a season. After World War II, the teams played 140 games per season. In 1950 another league formed, the Pacific League, and the Japanese Professional League changed its name to the Central League. Schedules would change four times from the early 1950s to 1963 before they settled on a 130-game season in 1966.

In 1964 the first Japanese player made a breakthrough into Major League Baseball (MLB). Masanori Murakami (1944–) came to California to play baseball for the San Francisco Giants as a relief pitcher. His time in the MLB was cut short due to contract disputes with the Nankai Hawks. Masanori would return to Japan and never play baseball in the MLB again. Other Japanese players would make their way to America to play for MLB teams, but none made the impact on American baseball of Ichiro Suzuki (1973–). Ichiro signed a contract with the Seattle Mariners in 2001, making him the first Asian-born player to sign an MLB contract. In his astounding debut, Ichiro won the most votes for the All-Star game, the American League (AL) batting title, the Silver Slugger Award, the Gold Glove Award, and was elected both AL Rookie of the Year and AL Most Valuable Player. Ichiro still plays today and is on pace to become, in 2016, one of only 28 players to have over 3,000 hits in a career, securing his place in both the American Baseball Hall of Fame and the Japanese Baseball Hall of Fame.

Baseball in Japan is more than just a competition. It is also a spiritual activity for some Japanese players. According to some players and analysts, playing baseball is how they train their spirit. They wash their souls with a clean hit. They put their spirit into each throw of the baseball, contributing their spirit to the way of baseball. According to some popular and scholarly analyses of the game in both countries, many Japanese people play baseball differently from their American counterparts. In America, the game is played with aggression, and winning is essential. In Japan, teams play from a defensive standpoint. In America, a tie is viewed as a negative outcome for both teams in competition, yet, in Japan, a tie is considered by some to be just as favorable as a win: Not only does each team display mastery of the skills of baseball and competition, they have both saved face for their club, their town, and their sponsor. In Japan, baseball is a *ma-no* sport. *Ma-no* means an interval of time, a pause, a certain distance. The game is made of pauses in which the fans can think about the next move and a pick-off strategy used by the pitcher to stall while considering the next play. What truly separates the game of baseball in Japan is the success of a women's professional league.

In 2009, Kenichi Kakutani, president of the health-food company Wakasa Seikatsu, founded the women's professional league. The league consists of three teams playing 40 games each with a season of seven months (March to October).

American Baseball Players in Japan

American baseball players started joining Japan's Nippon Professional Baseball (NPB) league in the 1930s and more regularly in the 1960s. Players who did not thrive in American Major League Baseball (MLB) sometimes found success in Japan. Players were once recruited to Japan only in the twilight of their career, but Japanese scouts now monitor and sign players who alternate frequently between major- and minor-league play, often targeting power hitters. Since 1937 there have been 11 Most Valuable Players and six Japan Series MVPs from America. In 1979 Charlie Manuel, later a World Series-winning MLB manager, led the Kintetsu Buffaloes to a pennant title while winning the Pacific League Most Valuable Player Award. American managers and coaches have also worked in the NPB, like former Mets manager Bobby Valentine, who led the Chiba Lotte Mariners to a championship in 2005.

Matthew B. Turetsky

Japan is not the only country that hosts women's baseball leagues. Every other year, in August, countries take turns hosting the Women's Baseball World Cup (WBWC); Japan puts together an all-star team from their professional teams to compete. The sport of baseball, for women, is beginning to grow throughout the world, and with the additional stage of the WBWC and the continued support of Japanese fans, Japan hopes to expand the women's professional league.

Hector E. Lopez

See also: Baseball, Taiwan

Further Reading

Blenkinsopp, Alexander. 2002. "Asian Invasion: Baseball's Ambassadors." *Harvard International Review* 24, no. 1 (Spring).

Fitts, Robert K. 2013. *Banzai Babe Ruth Baseball, Espionage, and Assassination during the 1934 Tour of Japan.* Lincoln: University of Nebraska Press.

Ikei, Masaru. 2000. "Baseball, Besuboru, Yakyu: Comparing the American and Japanese Games." *Indiana Journal of Global Legal Studies* 8, no. 1.

Krieger, Daniel. 2012. "For Some Women, the Name of the Game Is Baseball." *New York Times.* www.nytimes.com/2012/03/20/sports/baseball/20iht-baseball20.html?_r=0. Accessed March 26, 2016.

Obojski, Robert. 1975. *The Rise of Japanese Baseball Power.* Radnor, PA: Chilton Books.

Roden, Donald. 1980. "Baseball and the Quest for National Dignity in Meiji Japan." *American Historical Review* 85, no. 3 (June): 511–534.

BASEBALL, TAIWAN

In Taiwan, the game of baseball is more than just an imported "American" sport. It is a colonial legacy that was planted and sunk deep roots during the 50-year Japanese occupation of the island from 1895 to 1945. Baseball in Taiwan has never thoroughly shed its Japanese heritage—even in the name of the game, still called by many in Taiwanese "*yagyu*" (from the Japanese *yakyū*), and in the Taiwanese-Japanese-English playground calls of "*picha*," "*si-tu-rii-ku*," and "*out-tow*."

The sport, well developed in Japanese schools by the 1890s, was imported to the new colony of Taiwan in 1897 and was initially played by colonial bureaucrats, bankers, and their sons in Taihoku (Taipei). After the end of World War I, when assimilationist (*dōka*) ideology began to carry the day—particularly considering the need to differentiate Japanese colonialism from the supposedly more violent Western brand—Taiwanese youth joined in this game as well.

In the early 1920s, the Nōkō Baseball Team, made up of Amis Aborigine boys, achieved great fame when they traveled to Japan in the summer of 1925 for a series of games against Japanese school teams. This tour was also described as "perfect Taiwan propaganda," meant to show off in the home islands the products of the "islandwide 'savage' education enterprise" that the colonial government was carrying out in Taiwan. In their travels that took them from Tokyo to Hiroshima, the team that the Japanese media referred to as "savage children" won four of their nine games, losing four and tying one, and earned wide praise for their "serious attitude and scientific strategies." Four of Nōkō's star players actually stayed on in Japan to play for Heian High School in Kyōto. They led Heian to the famed Kōshien High School Baseball Tournament in 1927 and 1928, and three of them went on to play and study at Hōsei University. These Aborigine men are remembered as pioneers among the many Taiwanese players who went on to fruitful collegiate and professional baseball careers in the "home islands" of Japan.

The most famous of all Taiwanese baseball traditions was that born at the Tainan District Jiayi Agriculture and Forestry Institute (abbreviated Kanō) in the late 1920s. Under the guidance of manager Kondō Hyōtarō, a former standout player who had toured the United States with his high school team, Kanō dominated 1930s Taiwan baseball. What made the Kanō team special was its triethnic composition; in 1931 its starting nine was made up of two Han Taiwanese, four Taiwan Aborigines, and three Japanese players. Kanō won the Taiwan championship, earning the right to play in the hallowed Kōshien High School Baseball Tournament held near Osaka four times between 1931 and 1936. The best of these, the 1931 squad, was the first team ever to qualify for Kōshien with Taiwanese players on its roster. Kanō placed second in the 23-team national tournament that year, their skills and intensity winning the hearts of the Japanese public. This team of Han, Aboriginal, and Japanese players "proved" to nationally minded Japanese, in an extremely visible fashion, the colonial assimilationist myth—that both Han and Aborigine Taiwanese were willing and able to take part alongside Japanese in the cultural rituals of the Japanese state.

Participation in Japan's national game—which would soon become Taiwan's as well—allowed Taiwanese people to prove and live their acculturation into the colonial order at the very moment that Taiwanese baseball successes worked to subvert it. Taiwanese subjects could use baseball skills and customs taught by the Japanese to appeal for equal treatment within the national framework that baseball represented in so many ways. The Taiwanese baseball community, through its many triumphs, was also able to use this arena to offer the final proof that the colonial enterprise that aimed to shackle the Taiwanese population in permanent subservience was bound to fail. Nevertheless, the 1931 Kanō team mentioned above is still a very popular nostalgic symbol today in Taiwan and Japan. The recent blockbuster film *Kano* (dir. Umin Boya, 2014), which attributes Taiwanese baseball success to values of discipline, dignity, and unity learned from the Japanese, won great popular praise in both countries.

In 1945, at the end of World War II, Taiwan was taken over by the Republic of China (ROC) government. It quickly embarked on a full program of "motherlandification," outlawing the use of Japanese language and the consumption of Japanese culture, with the exception of baseball. Under the Chinese Nationalist Party (KMT, Guomindang/Kuomintang), the game received little official support compared to basketball, soccer, and track and field. The Japanese influence on baseball was still strong though. Literally every baseball coach in Taiwan for the next three decades was an alumnus of colonial rule; the majority of them saw this work as continuing the culture and way of life that they had learned for decades as Japanese subjects.

Also, it was extremely common for Taiwanese baseball fans to have access to news-paper reports and magazines that were sent to "Free China" by their teachers, neighbors, and friends who had returned to Japan. These connections to Japan continued to matter after 1949, when the Chinese mainland came under rule by the People's Republic of China (PRC) and the ROC ruled only the one province of Taiwan (plus several small surrounding islands).

During the 1960s and 1970s, Taiwan's baseball connections with Japan were personified by longtime Yomiuri Giants' first baseman Oh Sadaharu (or in Chinese, Wang Zhenzhi). The finest baseball player in Japanese baseball history, Oh was the son of a Chinese father and a Japanese mother. The mutual Taiwanese–mainlander suspicion and resentment that had built over the first two decades of KMT rule of Taiwan could be transcended by Oh's dual ethnic status as a Chinese Japanese as well as by his brilliant accomplishments and gentle, cultured manner. Oh visited Taiwan several times, and, even though he was not Taiwanese, by the 1980s and 1990s he had become an important symbol of Taiwan's baseball culture, its ties to Japan, and also the accomplishments of Chinese sojourners abroad. In 2009 Oh said he received the "greatest honor of his life" when the ROC government awarded him the Order of Brilliant Star with Grand Cordon.

Taiwan was perhaps best known around the world during the 1970s and 1980s for its incredible Little League baseball program. Their 12-year-olds won 10 Little League World Series titles between 1969 and 1981 and 17 in the 28-year period from 1969 to 1996. Taiwan's teenage representatives also won 17 Senior League world championships (ages 13–16) between 1972 and 1992, and 17 more Big League world championships (ages 16–18) between 1974 and 1996. The Nation-alist government insisted that these yearly triumphs proved their national strength and ability to recapture mainland China from the Communists; they even gloated via huge loudspeakers off the coast of Fujian Province in 1969, "Mainland compa-triots, the ROC youth baseball team's world championship is the [Chinese] nation's greatest sporting accomplishment in history and is the result of a superior educa-tional system. Just think, what kind of lives are your children living now?"

For decades, the finest of these players produced in Taiwan's Little League system went on to play professionally in Japan; this changed in 1990 with the establishment of Taiwan's own Chinese Professional Baseball League. The CPBL achieved great popularity and cultural relevance by the mid-1990s. Since that time, however, it has been set back by repeated game-throwing scandals, the rise of the competing Taiwan Major League (1997–2002), and by American Major League Baseball's (MLB) success in recruiting many of Taiwan's best players to play pro-fessionally in North America. Taiwanese players like Chien-Ming Wang, Wei-Yin Chen, and Hong-Chih Kuo have excelled in MLB but at the cost of the decline of the professional game in Taiwan.

Alongside Taiwan's decline at the Little League level, baseball over the last two decades has become a much less central part of Taiwanese identity. Taiwan contin-ues to be a regular host of the Baseball World Cup (now called the WBSC Premier 12), but today the game and its "Japanese" roots are perhaps valued most for their ability to distinguish Taiwan linguistically, culturally, socially, and politically from the superpower PRC and the powerful threat it represents on the Asian mainland just 90 miles away.

Andrew D. Morris

See also: Baseball, Japan

Further Reading

Hsieh, Shih-yuan 謝仕淵. 2012. *'Guoqiu' dansheng qianji: Rizhi shiqi Taiwan bangqiushi* 「國球」誕生前記：日治時期臺灣棒球史 [A Record of the "National Game" before Its Birth: The History of Taiwanese Baseball under Japanese Rule]. Tainan 台南: Guoli Taiwan lishi bowuguan 國立台灣歷史博物館.

Hsieh, Shih-yuan 謝仕淵, and Hsieh Chia-fen 謝佳芬. 2003. *Taiwan bangqiu yibainian* 台灣棒球一百年 [One Hundred Years of Baseball in Taiwan]. Taibei 台北: Guoshi chubanshe 果實出版社.

Morris, Andrew D. 2010. *Colonial Project, National Game: A History of Baseball in Taiwan.* Berkeley: University of California Press. (Portions used in this essay by permission of University of California Press.)

Morris, Andrew D. 2015. "Oh Sadaharu / Wang Zhenzhi and the Possibility of Chineseness in 1960s Taiwan." In *Japanese Taiwan: Colonial Rule and Its Contested Legacy.* Ed. Andrew D. Morris, 155–170. London: Bloomsbury Academic.

Reaves, Joseph A. 2002. *Taking in a Game: A History of Baseball in Asia.* Lincoln: University of Nebraska Press.

Sundeen, Joseph Timothy. 2001. "A 'Kid's Game'? Little League Baseball and National Identity in Taiwan." *Journal of Sport & Social Issues* 25, no. 3 (August): 251–265.

Yu, Junwei. 2007. *Playing in Isolation: A History of Baseball in Taiwan.* Lincoln: University of Nebraska Press.

BASKETBALL, PHILIPPINES

Basketball has evolved from a physical education program implemented inside recreation centers to one of the most celebrated spectator sports in the world. Since the 1970s, basketball has grown into a major sporting event with a following that immensely surpasses those who play the game. In the Philippines, a national survey indicates that 73.5 percent of the total population 18 years old and above watch basketball, both as live spectators and television viewers. From plush stadiums in Metro Manila to the makeshift courts in the countryside, no game appears to have captivated a nation more and appealed to Filipinos of different socioeconomic backgrounds than basketball.

Filipinos were first exposed to basketball as spectators during the American colonial period. They acquired the fundamentals of the game while witnessing military personnel from the United States shoot hoops for leisure. Playing the game benefited American soldiers because it helped curb vices and impart the values of courage, discipline, and patriotism. When Young Men's Christian Association (YMCA) missionaries came as military chaplains to the Philippines, they fostered interest in basketball among the locals. Engrossed bystanders soon began to applaud local players as some Filipinos learned to play the game.

Basketball eventually found a niche in Philippine schools in 1910. Since its introduction as part of the physical education curriculum of public schools, many students became interested. In particular, women with no previous exposure to any sport were encouraged to play, and women's basketball became one of the greatest crowd drawers during the Manila Carnival's National Athletic Championship from 1911 to 1913. However, this development proved to be controversial when some sectors viewed the sport as unsuitable for women owing to its physical nature. Basketball was also branded a game for weaklings because of the strong interest and support it drew from women, which in turn discouraged male athletes from playing the game. In the ensuing years, the popularity of basketball particularly among students and urban workers waned with the emergence of volleyball and the sustained mass appeal of baseball.

In 1924 basketball earned a new lease on life when it was included as a major part of the newly established National Collegiate Athletic Association (NCAA). By then, it had transformed into a man's game. The sport attracted college students and became the biggest crowd drawer in a multisport, interschool tournament that was slowly gaining national repute. The country's top colleges and universities soon took up the mantle of promoting the game, which further revived the public's interest in basketball. As a result, it was proposed that the sport be included as an official event in national interscholastic tournaments due to its increasing popularity at the elementary and secondary levels as well as in many interprovincial competitions. Women have remained involved as avid supporters and distinguished sports analysts, but actually few have played the game. Colleges continue to field women's basketball teams, but volleyball has been seen as more attuned to females and deemed more acceptable to the general public as a women's sport.

Philippine Boxing, Manny Pacquiao

Manny Pacquiao, or Emmanuel Dapidran Pacquiao, has been the world boxing champion in an astounding eight weight divisions, the only fighter to hold this distinction. He was born in Kibawe, Bukidnon, Philippines, on December 17, 1978. His single mother was not able to adequately provide for her six children, and Pacquiao left home for Manila at age 14 in search of better opportunities. In Manila, Manny found his way to a gym, where he was taken in and trained as a boxer; he quickly excelled. Pacquiao was the world's No. 1 lightweight boxer from 2009 until 2012, when he was knocked out in Las Vegas by Juan Manuel Marquez. Pacquiao won 10 world titles and the lineal championship in four different weight classes. He is also a prominent figure in Philippine politics, in spite of his controversial statements criticizing same-sex marriage. In 2015, *Forbes* magazine listed him as the second-highest-paid athlete in the world.

Kathleen M. Nadeau and Jeremy A. Murray

At the international level, Philippine national teams began to establish a strong following when they won 9 of the 10 Far Eastern Games championships. The 1936 Berlin Olympics also provided a venue for the Philippines, only two years removed at that time from obtaining autonomy from the United States through the establishment of a commonwealth government, to earn international acclaim. The country's relative success at the event was replicated almost 20 years later, when it won the bronze medal in the 1954 World Basketball Championships in Rio de Janeiro, Brazil, recording its most important achievement in international competitions. This series of triumphs enabled the Philippines, still a fledgling nation-state at that time, to gain international recognition. These victories in basketball likewise promoted unity among the Filipino people. The strong nationalist sentiment that came with each win virtually transformed the entire country into a big cheering squad. Furthermore, basketball, particularly in the postwar era, was viewed as a way of reaffirming the Philippines' status as a nation-state. Fresh from obtaining independence as a republic from the United States, the hardwood court afforded Filipinos a platform to showcase their abilities as athletes and prove that freedom from colonial rule was opportune and well deserved. For Filipinos who experienced the atrocities of war, basketball offered an opportunity to, in a sense, exact cathartic revenge on their perceived erstwhile persecutors, an observation reminiscent of the vitriolic heckling in postwar football matches between European nations and West Germany. To some fans, the sport has turned into a "full-fledged social affair," an event where the glitterati go to see and be seen. Apart from its economic and social rewards, basketball's accessibility has been an undeniable factor in its appeal and successful embedment in Philippine society. The game requires fewer players, less space, and less equipment than other major sports, such as baseball and football. Also, people don't have to reside near a gymnasium or a public court to play basketball; they can build makeshift hoops.

As succeeding generations became more immersed in playing and watching basketball, its hold on society was enhanced to the point that it is now unthinkable for many Filipinos to dissociate their lives completely from the game. Under martial law, Ferdinand Marcos' policies, most notably the exercise of strict control over the nation's broadcast and print media, proved a catalyst for reinforcing basketball's esteemed position in Philippine culture. There were only a few television channels, and the cronies of Marcos had a monopoly of ownership over all of them. Political debate and messages of dissent were strongly discouraged. The few local productions that weren't banned tended to be variety shows, musicals filled with love songs, and the emergent Philippine Basketball Association (PBA), the commercial league of professional basketball players. The government's de facto imposition of basketball on the Philippine masses ensured that the sport permeated every level of society, so much so that a survey conducted by the Manila-based Social Weather Station (SWS) many years after the demise of the Marcos regime found that 83 percent of men and 64 percent of women named basketball their favorite sport to watch, and 58 percent of men called it their favorite sport to play.

Basketball has been more than just a national pastime for Filipinos; it has become a social norm, a right of passage particularly for young boys. When boys reach adolescence, they are afforded privileges. Their parents allow them to stray away from their homes and roam their neighborhoods relatively unfettered, getting into trouble but also acquiring skills on how to conduct themselves as men. Inevitably, these boys end up playing basketball, first in their own neighborhood but then branching out to compete against other kids from other areas. Basketball signals their entry into a larger public sphere. Even people who do not play the game end up being impacted by basketball. For instance, some Filipinos disclosed that they learned to count by keeping a score sheet during televised games for their parents. For popular players who ventured into other fields like business and politics after hanging up their jerseys, the sport became their ticket to a successful profession or career away from basketball.

Enrique Niño P. Leviste

See also: Baseball, Japan; Baseball, Taiwan

Further Reading

Antolihao, Lou A. 2010. "Rooting for the Underdog: Spectatorship and Subalternity in Philippine Basketball." *Philippine Studies* 58, 449–80.

Bartholomew, Rafe. 2010. *Pacific Rims.* New York: New American Library.

Naismith, James. 1941. *Basketball: Its Origins and Development.* New York: Association Press.

Pope, Steven W. 1995. "An Army of Athletes: Playing Fields, Battlefields, and the American Military Sporting Experience." *Journal of Military History* 59, 435–56.

Sandoval, Gerardo A., and Ricardo G. Abad. 1997. "Sports and the Filipino: A Love Affair." *Social Weather Bulletin* 97, 3–4.

CRICKET

Cricket is a "manly sport." So wrote Lord Denning, Master of the Rolls, in the seminal 1977 nuisance judgment *Miller v. Jackson*, a case in which his Lordship was slightly less anxious than was plaintiff Mrs. Miller at the prospect of white-stitched crimson-leather-bound asteroids (that is, cricket balls) being "hit for six" into the Miller family garden (and possibly a window or two).

Like other bat-and-ball games, the aim of cricket is for the fielding team to get the batting team "out." To this end, the bowler bowls the ball overarm along the "crease," a 22-yard rectangular area. The ball must bounce once before the targeted "wicket," a wooden structure comprising three vertical sticks, or "stumps," which hold aloft two smaller horizontal sticks, or "bails." Hit the wicket and "howzat!" cries the fielding team in joy! (The difficult matter of "sticky wickets" we leave for another day.) The batsman guards the wicket with a cricket bat, held downwards, and seeks to score points, "runs," by striking the ball (preferably as far as Mrs. Miller's garden) and then running back and forth along the crease. Two batsmen are in play at any one time, standing at either end of the crease, and so alternate the batting. Hitting the ball beyond the "boundary" (the edge of the playing field) earns six runs, or four, if the ball touches the ground first.

The rules are all rather complicated and nobody fully understands them all, though it is common knowledge that if it rains you can win a "test match," a match played over several days. The game originated in England a very long time ago and is played in many former British colonies, all of which delight at sticking it to the old imperial overlord by "beating 'em at their own game"—something they are rather good at.

There are numerous national and international competitions, followed by avid fans around the world. The International Cricket Council (ICC, originally and not insignificantly named the "Imperial Cricket Conference" at its 1909 founding until a later name change) is the governing body of the sport, and it administers a variety of competition with over 100 members. Matches are played in various formats, which include the longer-form test matches, the one-day matches, and the newer "Twenty20" format, which is a shortened version consisting of 20 "overs," something akin to a baseball inning.

The powerhouse teams in international play include England, as one might expect, but other countries often best the game's creators, including and especially the former colonies of Australia and India. South Africa, Pakistan, Bangladesh, and the West Indies also consistently perform very well in international play. The sport, while often perceived by Americans with confusion (when perceived at all), is in fact the focus of intense followers. While it may seem priggish or elitist to the outsider, it draws populist passions from fans in all walks of life. The complex historical relations between the most competitive nations can add fuel to the burning rivalries and heighten the stakes of major competitions.

The "Barmy Army," so named by the Australian media, follow the English team to its international competitions. India has the "Swami Army" or "Bharat Army," who also follow their team. Cricket is also shared by diasporic communities, and Indians around the world watch cricket in person when their team visits their adopted countries. Watching their team on television is also a way to connect to home.

Australia and England play a special competition known as the Ashes, a joking reference to the remains of English cricket, allegorically cremated following a defeat by the Australians in 1882. In response, the English vowed to reclaim the "ashes," and they became the prize of a regular competition between the two countries. The Ashes competition is held at least every four years, either in England or Australia. The two sides are historically well matched, since at the time of writing, each has won 32 of the Ashes tournaments, with four draws.

More important than the rules and the complex stipulations of international competition is how the game is described on radio, a comforting, soothing experience that accompanies the eternal summers of childhood in Albion where the sun shines on the meadow and time stands still. "In summertime village cricket is the delight of everyone." So said his Lordship, and who am I to disagree.

William Langran

See also: Regional and Unique Sports; Soccer

Further Reading

Astill, James. 2013. *The Great Tamasha: Cricket, Corruption, and the Turbulent Rise of Modern India*. New York: St. Martin's.

Eastaway, Robert. 1993. *Cricket Explained*. New York: St. Martin's Griffin.

Major, John. 2009. *More Than a Game: Cricket's Early Years*. New York: Harper Perennial.

Wilson, James. 2011. "The Delight of Everyone: James Wilson Considers Lord Denning's Most Perfectly Crafted Judgment." *New Law Journal*. September 23. www.newlaw journal.co.uk/nlj/content/delight-everyone. Accessed September 18, 2015.

HORSE RACING, PHILIPPINES

Horse racing in the Philippines dates back about 200 years to the Spanish colonial era, when it was a social event for the prominent and wealthy Filipino, Spanish, and English families of Manila. "Fun runs" were held along the streets of Manila on holidays, with the Spanish governor of the Philippines and top church functionaries frequently in attendance. The riders were often the owners of the horses themselves, using the occasion to display their horsemanship and compete for tokens such as watches and medals.

Given the cost of maintaining horses for pleasure, racing was primarily a pastime of the rich. So it was the social elite of the day that founded the Manila Jockey Club (MJC) in 1867 as a social club to provide an organizational structure that would arrange the regular holding of races, keep statistical records, and perform other necessary functions pertaining to the formal conduct of the sport. This makes MJC the first and oldest racing club in the country, and the first in Southeast Asia. Its establishment marked the start of formal horse racing in the country, with rules of the sport and organized wagering. A temporary racetrack was first built in Santa Mesa; later a permanent clubhouse and track, the San Lazaro Hippodrome, was constructed in Tayuman in the 1930s by architect Juan Nakpil in the geometric art deco style fashionable at the time.

With a change in ownership in the mid-1990s, a modern facility worth over 1 billion pesos was erected in Carmona, Cavite—the San Lazaro Leisure Park (SLLP). The old San Lazaro Hippodrome was torn down to give way to real-estate developments such as a mall and residential condominiums. Upon the advent of the American colonial regime, the Americans further developed the sport and established legalized betting, which opened the sport up to a wider audience. In June 1937, American and Filipino sportsmen organized the Santa Ana Turf Club, which later became the Philippine Racing Club Inc. (PRC) and built its Santa Ana Park (SAP) racecourse on 25 hectares in Makati, near Santa Ana, Manila.

Over the years, other racetracks were built in Pasay City and Batangas, but of those, only MJC and PRC survived. For decades, the races were held on alternate weeks at the two tracks, at first three days a week, then four, five, and, from 2008 to 2012, six days a week, in order to boost revenue. In January 2009, PRC transferred its racetrack operations to a 70-hectare property in Naic, Cavite, also at a cost of over 1 billion pesos. Its old site in Makati is now being developed into a joint-venture residential-shopping-entertainment project.

In February 2013, a third racing club—Metro Manila Turf Club (MMTC)—was established and its racetrack, Metroturf Racecourse, was opened. The facility is located on a 40-hectare property straddling the towns of Malvar and Tanauan in Batangas.

The sport of horse racing is supervised and regulated by the Philippine Racing Commission (Philracom), founded in 1974, an agency under the Office of the President (OP), while the betting aspect of the sport is regulated by another OP agency, the Games and Amusements Board (GAB). The sport, as conducted in the Philippines, is thoroughbred flat racing on dirt, in which horses gallop around an oval-shaped racetrack surfaced with sand for predetermined distances—from 900-meter sprints to 2,050-meter races. There are no turf racetracks in the Philippines.

Thoroughbreds were imported time and again into the country for military and civilian use during the Spanish and American colonial periods, but these horses did not thrive. Most Philippine racing was conducted with *nativo* (native) horses. Some of these were descended from Javanese ponies brought over in early times, because horses are not native to the Philippines; evidence for this is in the fact that local plants are unsuitable for forage. Thoroughbreds for the sport were imported into the country again beginning in the 1960s.

In the Philippines' tropical climate, race meetings are held year-round, unlike in temperate and desert countries where there are racing seasons. From 2008 to 2012, the six-day race week ran from Tuesday to Sunday, usually with 8 races from Tuesday to Thursday, 9 on Friday, and from 11 to 13 on weekends. There are no races held on Good Friday, Christmas Day, New Year's Day, All Saints' Day, and Independence Day. With the advent of MMTC, two race days each week are allotted to each of the three racing clubs and rotated among them to achieve as equitable a balance of weekdays and weekends as possible.

According to Philracom (2015) statistics, there are around 2,000 registered racehorses, nearly 500 horse owners, and over 5,000 direct and indirect employees in the racing and breeding industries. Among them are jockeys, racehorse trainers, exercise riders, grooms, grooms' helpers and jockeys' helpers, equine veterinarians, farriers, and those who work in racetrack administration, operations, supervision, and on the breeding farms located mostly in and near Lipa, Batangas.

The services offered by the three racing clubs—MJC, PRC, and MMTC—in addition to the conduct of races, are bet-collection and payoff through a computerized pari-mutuel wagering system. The clubs have a popular menu of betting options that attract an estimated 100,000 or more racing fans of all social classes. Racing has been grossing an average of 8 billion pesos annually since 2002 in betting turnover, with about 73 percent of that amount available as dividends, while the rest go to taxes (almost 10 percent) and for horse prizes and racing club shares (8.5 percent according to their franchise laws, which are enacted by Congress). Because the racetracks, now in Cavite and Batangas, are inaccessible to their mostly

Manila-based racing fans, over 90 percent of bets are now placed at around 350 off-track betting stations (OTBs) mostly in Luzon, with fans watching live coverage of the races over cable television.

The horses that compete belong to private individuals. Some of these horse owners have banded into common-interest groups, of which there are now three— the Metropolitan Association of Race Horse Owners (MARHO), founded 1974; the Philippine Thoroughbred Owners and Breeders Organization (Philtobo), established 1991; and the Klub Don Juan de Manila, set up in 2002. These three horse owners' groups maintain their own funds and hold their own activities, such as racing festivals, but when necessary they unite into a collective informally called "the Tri-Org" to find solutions to pressing industry issues.

The jockeys are organized under the New Philippine Jockeys Association (NPJA), and the trainers under the Philippine Race Horse Trainers Association (PRHTA). Other industry workers such as grooms do not have their own formal organizations but tend to raise their concerns as loose collectives when necessary.

The clients or customers of horse racing are termed "bettors," "racing fans," or "aficionados," and, a term of their own coinage, *bayang karerista*—"racing nation." There are no formal organizations but informal groups that communicate largely through the Internet, and over the years, because of influential members, sometimes even stage their own sponsored racing festivals.

Racing in the country today is a billion-peso industry. Beyond being a sport or a business, it has given rise to a community that over nearly 200 years has developed a distinct culture and corresponding norms, practices, and even its own argot or slang (*salitang karera*). An estimated 6 billion pesos has been invested in infrastructure, bloodstock, real estate for racetracks and ranches, OTBs, and other related economic activities. The industry makes heavy and regular use of mass communication, notably broadcast, to air live racing coverage and to disseminate other information necessary to bettors and viewers—the betting matrix and race results and dividends—over cable television.

In addition, news stories and columns in both English and Pilipino are carried in broadsheets, tabloids, and magazines and occasionally on television programs. Recent technological advances have also made horse racing a feature on the Internet, with the rise of racing blogs and forums that disseminate racing tips, news, and gossip. Text messaging using cellular phones is also heavily used to share information such as race schedules, lineups (list of entries), betting tips, and race results. Social media also plays a role in connecting the *bayang karerista* or "racing nation." The races are broadcast live over cable television via providers such as Destiny Cable and Sky Cable in the Metro Manila area. Other cable providers may opt to pick up the free-to-air signal; thus, racing may be watched all over the country. The races may also be viewed via the Internet using video-streaming technology over the websites and Facebook pages of PRC, MJC, and Philracom; YouTube; and fan websites such as Manila Horsepower.

While the GAB monitors the betting aspect, Philracom supervises and regulates the conduct of the sport and also licenses racing clubs, horse owners, racing officials, jockeys, trainers, and grooms. As part of its mandate, Philracom uses at least 60 percent, often more, of its roughly 80 to 100 million peso annual budget to sponsor the races by way of additional horse prizes (in addition to that percentage coming from the betting pool and from sponsors). As a result, major races with big prize money, called "stakes races," are an eagerly awaited tradition among racing aficionados, such as the Triple Crown series for elite three-year-olds.

Another government agency that supports horse racing as part of its charter is the Philippine Charity Sweepstakes Office (PCSO). Its two annual flagship races are the Silver Cup and highly prestigious Presidential Gold Cup, the longest continuously held sports event in Philippine history. The Philippine Amusement and Gaming Corporation (PAGCOR) also occasionally sponsors races as a corporate entity. Private corporate sponsors also support horse-racing events in exchange for media values. Horse racing has always enjoyed steady, if not strong, government support because it remits an average of 1 billion pesos a year in direct taxes to the national treasury, not counting the amount from indirect taxes.

Jenny Ortuoste

See also: Lottery Show, Philippines (Chapter 4: Television and Radio)

Further Reading

Feleo, A. B., ed. 1997. *The Manila Jockey Club: 130 Years of Horseracing in Southeast Asia.* Manila, PH: Manila Jockey Club.
Philippine Racing Commission. www.philracom.gov.ph.

MARTIAL ARTS, CHINA

The Chinese martial arts, typically termed *wushu* in China and known colloquially in the West as kung fu, include a large number of boxing, wrestling, weapons, health, ritual, and performance disciplines that reflect the country's complex social development. Students of Chinese history have noted accounts of wrestling, fencing, striking, and archery dating from the late Bronze Age. Nevertheless, almost all of the modern Chinese martial arts have their antecedents in the Qing or Ming dynasties and underwent a process of adaptation during the politically tumultuous 20th century. These changes included the shift away from small, lineage-based teaching structures to open public schools, the transformation of the martial arts from professional skills to voluntary recreational activities, and lastly a concerted effort to associate them with themes of cultural continuity and nationalism. China's many local fighting traditions have come to be understood as a vast repository of traditional physical culture and national identity.

Since the 1970s, these practices have grown increasingly popular. Systems such as Taijiquan and Wing Chun have become some of the most recognizable and popular contemporary martial arts styles. This spread owes much to their frequent appearance in action films, television programs, video games, and novels. While often seen as an aspect of "traditional culture," these practices, in their current state, are very much a product of China's modernization process and subsequent engagement with global market forces.

The earliest surviving manuals of detailed martial arts instruction date to the Ming dynasty. Examples of this literature include a chapter on boxing as a form of military training included by General Qi Jiguang in his *New Treatise of Military Efficiency*, a work on pole fighting entitled *Sword Classic* by General Yu Dayou and Cheng Zhongyou's *Techniques for After Farming Pastime*.

Yet many of the most popular martial arts systems practiced today trace their origins to the later Qing dynasty. While self-defense methods existed throughout this period, they grew in popularity during the second half of the dynasty as political instability escalated. During this era, the martial arts were frequently seen as a way of securing one's livelihood, either as a soldier, security guard, instructor, opera performer, traveling patent medicine salesman, yamen runner, enforcer, or criminal. They were also associated with rural areas, where peasants turned to them as a method of militia training and recreation to relieve the monotony of village life.

Increased disorder during the 19th century led to more individuals being introduced to the martial arts through the expansion of the local militia system and as a result of the rise of rural banditry. Martial artists were also involved in a number of uprisings, including the Eight Trigram Rebellion (1813), the Taiping Rebellion (1850–1864), and most notably the Boxer Uprising (1899–1901).

Douglas Wile has argued that psychological insecurity stemming both from the breakdown of the political order and increased imperialism encouraged some individuals to turn to the martial arts (particularly Taijiquan) as a source of cultural pride. Unfortunately, the disastrous results of the Boxer Uprising damaged the popularity of the Chinese martial arts. The reliance on invulnerability magic and spirit possession by Shandong's poor peasant fighters convinced many modernizers that the martial arts had no place in modern Chinese society.

Social attitudes toward the martial arts began to change after the 1911 Xinhai Revolution. Reformers within the martial arts community argued that boxing could be purified of its rural associations and backward superstitions. It might then become a suitable form of physical exercise for educated middle-class individuals, a demographic that had previously had little to do with these practices.

The best known of these efforts during the 1920s was the Jingwu Athletic Association (founded in 1910). This group harnessed the power of the media and advertising to construct the first national martial arts brand. Its various chapters introduced tens of thousands of individuals to a modernized vision of the Chinese martial arts, focusing on the twin goals of physical fitness and "national salvation." Building on the prior success of this movement, the ruling Guomindang Party later created the Central Guoshu Institute to officially promote a unified and modernized vision of the Chinese martial arts. The Guoshu Movement tended to be more statist in its aims. It also sought to use the martial arts as a means of strengthening Chinese nationalism and resisting foreign aggression.

The 1949 victory of the Communist Party had serious repercussions for the traditional martial arts. These schools typically drew their strength from specific groups in local communities, such as lineage associations, political factions, labor unions, or secret societies. Communist social reforms systematically dismantled these institutions, leaving no social space for the traditional martial arts to exist. A number of practitioners joined state-sponsored athletic training programs or universities that supported the creation of a new vision of the Chinese martial arts, termed *wushu*. This included the creation of new types of individual displays (both armed and unarmed), called *taolu*, and a unified system of kickboxing known as *sanda*.

Centuries of Chinese migration resulted in the establishment of strong martial arts traditions in Taiwan, Hong Kong, Singapore, Malaysia, and eventually the West. Many of these overseas communities received a fresh influx of mainland immigrants following the Communist victory in 1949. These populations developed martial traditions that represent older folk systems as well as the rationalized modern styles of the Republican period, leading to a division in the sorts of arts emphasized in the PRC and the diaspora. Following the end of the Cultural

Shaolin Temple

The Shaolin Monastery, located in Dengfeng County of Henan Province, is one of China's most famous Buddhist temples. It is associated with the creation of Chan Buddhism and is said to be the spiritual home of the traditional Chinese martial arts.

Built by Emperor Xiaowen of the Northern Wei dynasty at the end of the fifth century CE, Shaolin was initially known as a center of Buddhist scholarship. The first hint of the temple's association with martial practices emerged in 621 when a number of its personnel aided Li Shimin's (600–649) efforts to establish the Tang dynasty by defeating a small contingent of troops loyal to a rival warlord.

Nevertheless, it was during the second half of the Ming dynasty (1368–1644) that the monastery achieved national fame for its martial excellence. During this era, the Shaolin monks, known for their pole-fighting skills, contributed a monastic army to help combat the incursions of pirate bands harassing the country's coastlines. Their success further increased the temple's reputation, and Shaolin fighting techniques were discussed in a number of martial arts manuals from the late Ming and Qing (1644–1911) eras.

The Shaolin Temple has been destroyed and rebuilt multiple times in its long history. Most famously, it was burned by a local warlord in 1641 (prior to the Qing invasion) and again in 1928. Its monks faced further persecution during the Cultural Revolution (1966–1976). However, Jet Li's hugely popular 1982 film *The Shaolin Temple* renewed the Chinese public's interest in the monastery and paved the way for its current revitalization. Today Shaolin is once again a center of Chan practice and martial arts instruction. It has also become one of the most popular tourist destinations in China.

Benjamin N. Judkins

Revolution (1966–1976), various traditional folk styles began to reemerge on the mainland. Likewise, *wushu* schools have since been established around the globe.

It is impossible to understand the global success of the Chinese martial arts without carefully considering the role of the media. Jin Yong, a writer of *wuxia* or "martial hero" novels, is perhaps the most widely read modern Chinese author. Likewise, Bruce Lee's rise to superstardom following the release of *Enter the Dragon* (1973) elevated the global visibility of the Chinese martial arts. This created the potential for them to become an accepted aspect of Western consumer culture. Jet Li's appearance in *The Shaolin Temple* (1982) helped to spark renewed interest in these practices across the PRC. The continued popularity of martial arts films, novels, comic books, and video games all point to the enduring effect that these fighting styles have had on both Chinese and global popular culture.

Benjamin N. Judkins

See also: Martial Arts, Japan

Further Reading

Henning, Stanley E. 2003. "The Martial Arts in Chinese Physical Culture, 1865–1965." In *Martial Arts in the Modern World.* Ed. Thomas A. Green and Joseph R. Svinth, 13–36. London: Praeger.

Hsu, Adam. 2006. *Lone Sword against the Cold Sky: Principles and Practice of Traditional Kung Fu.* Santa Cruz, CA: Plum Publications.

Kennedy, Brian, and Elizabeth Guo. 2005. *Chinese Martial Arts Training Manuals.* Berkeley, CA: Blue Snake Books.

Lorge, Peter. 2012. *Chinese Martial Arts: From Antiquity to the Twenty-First Century.* New York: Cambridge University Press.

Wile, Douglas. 1996. *Lost Tai-Chi Classics from the Late Ching Dynasty.* Albany, NY: SUNY Press.

MARTIAL ARTS, JAPAN

The martial arts in Japan have a long and illustrious history on both the main islands of Japan as well as the island of Okinawa. There are dozens of forms or systems of Japanese martial arts, which are performed with and without weapons. In historical terms, Japanese martial arts are separated into two distinct periods. Those in the first period include martial arts before the Meiji Restoration in 1868 and are known as *koryu* or *kobudo*, translated as "old style" or "old martial arts" respectively. They mostly came about during the Edo or Tokugawa Period (1603–1868), when Japan was under the Tokugawa Shogunate. The old style was built on and motivated by centuries of warfare and became the foundation for the newer styles of martial arts, the *gendai budo* or *shinbudo.*

The three emphases of the old style were, in order of importance, combat, discipline, and morality. Old martial arts were a way of organizing men into a fighting force that would be fierce on the battlefield. This is evident in the strict emphasis on structure and discipline. In the early days of martial arts in Japan, they were not practiced for leisure, nor were they practiced for physical fitness, though both of these are motivators for the newer forms of martial arts. The old martial arts were not intended to be practiced by the lower classes and were restricted to use by the samurai, or warrior classes, for use in warfare.

These martial arts styles also incorporated the cultivation of the mind and spirit. This relates back to the idea of discipline and the enforcement of a strict code of conduct and ethics upon those who were to use the martial arts. At the core of each martial art was the development and cultivation of human character, and this cultivation replaced more conventional aspects of education. Training in martial arts was also intended to instill loyalty, imbuing the practitioner with a devotion and love of country or region that would lead them to fight and die for their cause. In many ways, the Japanese martial arts were parallel to the Spartan training program, *agoge*, of classical Greece, which molded young men into the warriors of that culture. Many belief systems were incorporated into the ethos of Japanese martial arts, including Daoism (Taoism), Zen (Chan) Buddhism, Confucianism, and others. This comes as no surprise as those philosophies emphasize self-development, discipline, respect, honor, virtue, and focus, thus making them an easy transition into a martial art. In the past century, the philosophical and ethical dimensions of the Japanese martial arts are perhaps best captured in the popular book by Inazo Nitobe, *Bushido: The Soul of Japan*, written in English and published in 1899 and later translated into Japanese.

Koryu, or "old style," was an all-encompassing style that focused on many different weapon styles. *Bojutsu*, or "staff technique," canonized a tradition of fighting with a staff that had been practiced for centuries and taught that the staff was to be considered as an extension of one's limbs. *Jittejutsu*, "*jitte* technique," focused on the safe disarmament and submission of opponents who would often be carrying swords. This technique involved the use of a small iron baton, or *jitte*, and was more practical for use in law enforcement than on the battlefield. *Kenjutsu*, or "technique of the sword," is the general term for all the disciplines that involved swordsmanship. This has largely been replaced by kendo, or "the way of the sword." *Kenjutsu* is sometimes portrayed as the quintessential historical art of Japanese culture, embodied in the samurai. There are countless methods to learn that are encompassed within the art of the sword, such as the way to draw the sword, wield it, and return it to its scabbard.

Kyujutsu, or the "art of archery," is also significant within the Japanese martial arts. While popular perception of the Japanese martial arts places great emphasis on the samurai sword, the use and technique of a bow was often much more vital on the battlefield than sword fighting. The course of many battles before the Meiji Restoration was determined by skill with a bow and especially drawing a bow on horseback. Mounted archery is an extremely difficult art to master, and it was often a more valuable art on the battlefield than was swordsmanship.

Naginatajutsu, or "art of the *naginata*," refers to the fighting methods of the *naginata*, a hybrid of a sword and a spear. This weapon was often used against cavalry, and in hand-to-hand combat it provided an advantage over a normal sword. To the uninitiated, the *naginata* is an unwieldy weapon, but in recent years it has developed within a sporting context that is especially popular today among Japanese women. The *naginata* has developed a feminine cultural affiliation as the weapon of choice for women defending the home, and this affiliation continues in the predominance of women in *naginata* competitions today. *Sojutsu*, or "art of the spear," is important to both Japanese history and mythology. The spear requires less training than do other arts, such as the sword and the bow, and was a common weapon for more inexperienced warriors. *Tantojutsu*, or "art of the *tanto*," refers to the methods of wielding what can most easily be described as a knife, and the art was often practiced against longer weapons. This art has easily translated to the modern age where knife fighting has become more popular for defense in close quarters.

The only martial art that was practiced without a weapon was jujitsu, also known today as jujitsu) or "the gentle/yielding art," which would become increasingly popular as time went on and be practiced by a wider variety of people, not just warriors. This martial art focused more on throwing, grappling, breaking of joints, and closing the distance between two fighters. Its name, the "yielding method," was in contrast to the striking systems of fighting, such as Korean tae kwon do and Japanese karate, which both place an emphasis upon kicks and striking, respectively. Yielding to an opponent's momentum and channeling that force to subdue the opponent earned jujitsu its name. Karate, or "empty hand" style, is a striking system developed on Okinawa and became popular in Japan in the 20th century. It gained popularity around the world in the latter half of the 20th century, popularized in film and television shows.

Many of these arts are still taught as part of a revitalized curriculum. The modern martial arts that *koryu* has been adapted into are not hugely different from the ancient systems. The modern arts merely place more focus upon the development of character and virtue, and they are no longer meant for battlefield training. Modern martial arts tend to focus more upon the sporting aspect, similar to boxing today and the Ultimate Fighting Championship (UFC).

Two of the prominent modern martial arts are jujitsu and judo. Both of these arts involve hand-to-hand combat instead of a focus on weaponry. Jigoro Kano (1860–1938) was the founder of the modern concept of judo ("yielding/gentle way"), and his two principles that would form the basis of judo practice were "minimal effort, maximum efficiency" and "softness controls hardness." Both of these are related to the idea that if one's opponent is larger and stronger, fighting on the basis of strength and resistance will always end in defeat, but if one can fight with balance and the diverting of force, then a bigger and stronger opponent can be defeated. This becomes the basis of many of the submissions and choke holds, for example, the "triangle choke" in which a judo practitioner can cut off oxygen to the opponent's air supply with one's legs while blocking punches with one's arms. Judo would develop into many different martial arts, such as sambo and Brazilian jujitsu, which spread to other countries and began among other things—a thriving scene in sport martial arts, self-defense schools, the UFC, and other mixed martial

Sumo

Sumo is a competitive wrestling sport that is highly revered in Japanese culture. Sumo originated in Japan, which is the only country where it is practiced as a sport. Sumo incorporates many elements of the Japanese Shinto faith, and some of these rituals still take place in sumo today. Before every sumo match, the wrestlers (*rikishi*), often large or obese individuals, communicate their respect for their opponent and for the tradition of sumo through these rituals. In the competition itself, the two wrestlers try to do one of two things: force the opponent out of a circular ring or force the opponent to touch the ground with any body part other than his feet.

Whereas the martial arts developed in the late Edo or Tokugawa period of Japan and were more affected by that militarized era and the philosophies Daoism and Confucianism, sumo was more affected by the indigenous Japanese Shinto religion, and its strict traditions continue to govern the sport. Even in modern times, these traditions have endured, shaping not only the wrestling matches but also strict regimentation of the lives of the wrestlers outside of the ring and the status of the sport in Japanese society. Sumo was never seen as useful for war or battle but was always a religious or traditional activity that was sponsored and staged as entertainment by emperors or other influential people.

Connor J. Gahre

arts leagues. Brazilian jujitsu was developed in part by the Gracie family in 20th-century Brazil, and it became hugely popular in Brazil and around the world. This would, in turn, influence the creation of the UFC near the end of the 20th century.

Out of this rich tradition of martial training and self-cultivation, the Japanese martial arts have developed into countless schools and practitioners in Japan and around the world. From karate and judo to sumo and aikido and many other systems, millions of practitioners have been influenced by the huge popularity of the Japanese martial arts. Like yoga, the Japanese martial arts have developed into a physical, spiritual, and mental discipline, adapting to a world that seeks this type of activity as a ritual, a diversion, or just a pastime that engages and trains the mind and body.

Connor J. Gahre

See also: Martial Arts, China; Yoga

Further Reading

Craig, Darrell Max. 1995. *Japan's Ultimate Martial Art: Jujitsu before 1882.* Tokyo: Tuttle Publishing.
Hall, David A. 2012. *Encyclopedia of Japanese Martial Arts.* New York: Kodansha USA.
Nitobe, Inazo. 2012 [1899]. *Bushido: The Soul of Japan.* New York: Kodansha USA.

Skoss, Diane. 1997. *Koryu Bujtusu: Classical Warrior Traditions of Japan*. Warren, NJ: Koryu Books.

Suino, Nicklaus. 2006 [1996]. *Training Secrets of the Japanese Martial Arts: Budo Mind and Body*. Boston: Weatherhill.

MONGOLIAN SPORTS

The three traditional Mongolian sports of wrestling, archery, and horseback riding originated as practice for hunts or as military training. Physical exercise and endurance were vital in the preparation of the Mongolian armies, although pleasure and entertainment were also part of the attraction of such athletics. The contests in these three sports were often informal, but the annual Naadam festivals, which originated in the 17th century, were more organized and the most renowned. Convened in summer during the height of the milking of mares, Naadam involved considerable rituals relating to shamanism and Buddhism. The scattering of mare's milk, as an offering to the ancestors, heaven, and the gods, initiated the events. The powerful Buddhist monasteries added to the ritualistic nature of the games because some monks participated in the contests.

At the present time, the national Naadam is held in July in the capital city of Ulaan Baatar, but regional and local Naadams are convened at various times in the summer. These athletic events serve as a valuable link between the glorious Mongolian past and the less grandiose present.

Twentieth-century politics influenced the three sports and Naadam. The socialist state, which took power in 1921, eliminated rituals and religious expressions and mandated that the national Naadam be held on July 11, the date of the Socialists' success in overcoming opposition and establishing a new system. Politics and the military supplanted rituals and religion. Parades of soldiers, weapons, and politically favored groups, including workers, children, and bands, preceded the entrance to the stadium, the new venue for the contests of wrestling and archery but not horseback riding.

The postsocialist Naadams, after 1990, have severed politics from the celebrations and sports. Parades in Sükhbaatar, the central venue in the capital city of Ulaan Baatar, persist, but the martial element of the socialist period has been excised. A group in crisp and colorful costumes is the principal constituent in the parade before the actual arrival in the stadium for wrestling and archery and a nearby location for the finish line of the horse race.

Horses and horse racing were the major assets and skills that contributed to the Mongolians' astonishing success in the 13th century in creating the largest contiguous land empire in world history. The Mongolians cherished their horses for the mobility they offered herders in rounding up animals after they had grazed in areas a distance away from the encampments. In addition, the mobility of the steeds provided a tactical advantage in battle, and horses allegedly also transported shamans to heaven.

Mongolian boys and girls ride horses, with or without saddles, at an early age, often before the age of 15, and the Naadam horse race is limited to children. Over the past few years, Mongolians have become concerned over the injuries children have sustained in these races, leading to calls for greater safety measures.

The bow and arrow were invaluable assets in Mongolian combat. The ability to shoot while riding at full speed and the far greater range of the Mongolian bow and arrow than any contemporaneous bows and arrows offered a tremendous advantage during the expansion of the Mongolian Empire. Foreign travelers observed that children were taught to shoot at a very young age. Although guns, rifles, and other weapons have superseded bows and arrows, the Mongolians still value skill in archery and include it as one of the sports in the Naadam festivities. Male archers aim at a target about 250 feet away while women shoot arrows at a site about 200 feet in the distance. The contestants use traditional bows, integrating the event with the past.

Wrestling is the most popular and sophisticated sport in the Naadam. These contests stretched back at the very least to Chinggis Khan's (Genghis Khan, 1167–1227) era. Women also participated in such competitions, and Khutulun, daughter of one of Chinggis Khan's great-grandsons, was renowned as a champion wrestler and defeated numerous prospective suitors who wagered hundreds or thousands of horses to best and then marry her. Modern Naadam wrestling matches are limited to men.

Wrestlers in the Naadam celebrations follow prescribed rituals that often captivate the audience. Their clothing is clearly specified, which includes cloth shorts and the upturned boots that Mongolians favor, and ensures that the men's upper torso is not covered. They also wear a hat and a ceremonial scarf known as a *khadag*, which they doff before their matches. All the wrestlers circle the field clockwise and then scatter mare's milk for the gods. When their match is announced, both wrestlers flap their arms like birds (in the manner of the Garuda, an Indian mythical bird) and dance in a circular direction. The winner of the match also performs the Garuda dance at the end of the contest. The victor must compel his opponent to touch the earth with his knee, elbow, or torso, although the palms may touch the ground without a penalty. He can trip up the other combatant, but the kickboxing techniques of punching and kicking are prohibited. Wrestlers are ranked based on their success, starting with "falcon" and ending with "titan" as the greatest competitor.

The Naadam victor is considered to be the national champion and is accorded considerable status and monetary rewards. The popularity of wrestling resulted in the construction of a special stadium dedicated to the sport in Ulaan Baatar. Perhaps even more intriguing, a wrestler named Badmaanyambuugiin Bat-Erdene has been in the Parliament since 2004 and received 41.97 percent of the votes when he ran for president in 2013, a possible indication of the status enjoyed by wrestlers.

Following in Khutulun's steps, a few Mongolian women take part in freestyle wrestling but not in the Mongolian form. In fact, Soronzonboldyn Battseteg (1990) won a bronze medal in the 63 kilogram wrestling competition in the London Olympics in 2012.

Wrestling has also translated into interest and success in the Japanese sports of sumo and judo. As early as the 1980s, several Mongolians arrived in Japan to study and compete in sumo. By 2003 Dolgorsüren Dagvadorj (1985) reached the highest rank of *yokozuna*, and the Japanese lionized him, although a brawl outside the ring and what turned out to be false accusations of match fixing somewhat tarnished his image. Before his retirement, he earned tens of millions of dollars and burnished his image by founding the Asashōryū Foundation, which provides support for the Mongolian Olympic team and for Mongolian college students in Japan and Mongolia. Three more Mongolians have received the highest ranking in sumo and have received much media attention in both Japan and Mongolia. In judo, Mongolians received a gold medal and a silver medal in the 2008 Olympics and silver and bronze medals in the 2012 Olympics. Such successes have generated more and more participation in the sport.

By and large, the sports the Mongolians currently play, as well as the international contests in which they have excelled, require little equipment and relatively modest kinds of training facilities. For example, they won gold and silver medals in boxing in the 2008 Olympics and silver and bronze medals in boxing and a bronze medal in wrestling in the 2012 Olympics. The athletics in which ordinary Mongolians take part also require only rudimentary resources. They enjoy basketball, volleyball, table tennis, boxing, wrestling, karate, and kickboxing, all of which can be played in almost any venue. Physical education was an essential element of instruction under the socialist system and is still valued, although the available funding is limited.

Morris Rossabi

See also: Uyghur Sports

Further Reading

May, Timothy. 2007. *The Mongol Art of War: Chinggis Khan and the Mongol Military System.* Yardley, PA: Westholme.
Rossabi, Morris. 1994. "All the Khan's Horses." *Natural History* 103: 48–57.
Serruys, Henry. 1974. *Kumiss Ceremonies and Horse Racing: Three Mongolian Texts.* Wiesbaden, DE: Otto Harrassowitz.

PUBLIC-SQUARE DANCING, CHINA

Chinese public-square dancing (*guangchangwu* 广场舞) is a popular exercise routine among middle-aged and elderly people in the morning and evening and happens in public squares, parks, plazas, and other spaces around China's cities. It should be noted that this has no relation to the "square dancing" of American popularity, in which a square-like diagram is imagined on the floor and certain choreographed routines are danced to American country music; rather, this is dancing in the *public squares* of China, or public-square dancing. The practice involves synchronized low-impact dancing, usually by a group of middle-aged women, to amplified music in a public space.

This mass hobby appeared and attained great popularity in China in the mid-1990s when the privatization reforms caused hundreds of thousands of urban workers to be laid off or forced into retirement from state-run enterprises. Thus, a growing legion of women, who have been known to some as the "dancing grannies," began organizing and practicing their own choreographed dance with a variety of styles for the benefit of their health and self-fulfillment. The popularity of public-square dancing seems unstoppable throughout the country because of its low cost and very low requirements for participation.

According to a China Central Television (CCTV) news report of November 2013, it has been estimated that there are over 100 million regular practitioners of the dance in China, most of whom are women aged from 40 to 65. However, entering into the 2010s, public-square dancing has been subjected to some negative evaluations due to the related noise issue. Besides complaints and arguments about the practice, nearby residents of some gathering points have reacted more violently to the amplified music that accompanies the dancing. These altercations have frequently occupied the headlines related to public-square dancing on social media. As a direct consequence, the Chinese government issued a set of standardized routines to regulate public-square dancing in the spring of 2015. But this move failed to please either side and faced widespread criticism. Behind the increasingly acute conflicts between the dancing grannies and local residents, the real challenge for Chinese society is how to introduce alternative entertainment and ensure enough open spaces for the activities of aging people within a crowded setting.

Guangchangwu has roots in both ancient and modern Chinese history. Group dance has been a typical ritual for important celebrations and agricultural occasions since ancient times. In the modern period, several traditional forms, such as *yangge* (秧歌), have been adapted by the Chinese Communist Party as an efficient propaganda tool for promoting communist ideology. The practice in this form reached its peak during the Cultural Revolution (1966–1976), while most of today's dancing grannies were still in their teens and young adulthood. Therefore, when many of them suffered from career disappointment and the perceived emptiness of the spiritual world in the mid-1990s, public-square dancing unsurprisingly became the best way to relieve boredom, keep fit, and revive positive memories of the old days. In addition, the activity also provides a lively social platform. With similar life experiences, participants easily find like-minded friends and share the same generational topics of conversation and similar concerns.

Most public-square dancing groups are voluntary and self-organized. All they require is a sufficient place and some basic audio equipment. Squares and public spaces near markets or close to home are the favorite choices for the dancing grannies, so that they can bargain for fresh vegetables in the morning and take care of their grandchildren in the early evening. The dancers organize themselves into rank. The proficient dancers usually stay in the front and center, while beginners are in the back where they can watch the leaders and learn the moves. The groups use a variety of accompaniment music for practice. Some groups like Western pop songs or even waltzes, but most choose contemporary Chinese popular songs or

"Red Songs" (*hongge* 红歌), older hits with revolutionary themes from the Mao period (1949–1976). Dancing groups' members normally wear all kinds of exercise clothing, but some more advanced groups wear matching costumes and use props to attract more public attention.

Despite helping elderly people to keep in good health, dispel loneliness, and expand their social circles, *guangchangwu's* noise pollution disturbs some nearby residents. With the rapid growth of the participants' numbers, a large dancing group would often be divided into several small ones for different levels of dancers. In other cases, when experienced dancers become dissatisfied with the current leadership in their group and have enough followers, they split off and form their own groups, sometimes practicing right next to each other. As a result, multiple sound sources play together in a narrow space, especially early in the morning and late in the evening when working people might be trying to sleep. Furthermore, different groups dancing in the same area often consider themselves to be in competition, which always causes serious rivalry for the best spaces and louder amplification. In response, local residents occasionally adopt more extreme measures to demonstrate their disapproval of the amplified noise. A Beijing man fired a shotgun into the air in order to chase off dancing groups near his home in 2013. In the city of Wuhan, angry neighbors dumped feces from the upper floors onto a troupe of dancing grannies below. And in Wenzhou, residents pooled US$42,300 to purchase their own sound system to blare warnings to dancers about violating noise pollution laws. In addition, the dancers also drew complaints because they blocked sidewalks, parking lots, and building entrances.

The Chinese government reacted to these increasingly fierce complaints and incidents by issuing 12 standard or model dancing routines in March 2015. Two Chinese government agencies, the State General Administration of Sports and the Ministry of Culture, designed and guided the development of these model routines and announced that trained instructors would be hired to introduce them around the country. The government's official media outlet, Xinhua News Agency, explained on the same day that the new routines would help make public-square dancing a unified and scientific activity that generates positive energy.

However, the regulatory step was clearly unwelcome. Local residents complained that it did nothing to relieve or solve the noise problem. And the dancers preferred to keep the right to choose their own routines and clearly felt unhappy about the government's involvement. As some news sources pointed out, many of the dancers had no other outlets, and the real dilemma of Chinese society was the lack of other social opportunities for the elderly population. Only an increase of public sports venues would satisfy urban residents' need for fitness routines such as public-square dancing, but under the current urbanization process and population growth, public spaces are still limited and scarce.

Jingqiu Zhang

See also: Chinese Alternative Music Scenes (Chapter 1: Popular Music)

Further Reading

BBC News. 2013. "Dancing Grannies Raise a Ruckus." *China* blog. December 12. www.bbc.com/news/blogs-china-blog-25330651. Accessed September 26 2015.

Jacobs, Andrew. 2015. "China Puts a Hitch in the Step of 'Dancing Grannies.'" *New York Times*. March 24. http://sinosphere.blogs.nytimes.com/2015/03/24/china-seeks-to-impose-its-own-routine-on-public-dancing/?_r=2. Accessed September 25, 2015.

Sheehan, Matt. 2015. "Wrath of Dancing Grandmothers Forces Chinese Government to Backtrack." *World Post*. March 26. www.huffingtonpost.com/2015/03/25/china-grandmother-line-dancing_n_6938894.html. Accessed September 26, 2015.

REGIONAL AND UNIQUE SPORTS

Many of the sports of Asia and Oceania are wholly unfamiliar to most Americans or Europeans, while others may be familiar but in a different way. Field hockey, polo, and table tennis are three examples of sports in this latter category, with which we may be familiar but which hold a very different place in the cultures of Asia and Oceania. Field hockey and polo, for example, are rough-and-tumble sports in some parts of Asia and have none of the gender specificity or elitism that are often associated with them in the West. Table tennis, badminton, and other sports are played around the world, but in Asia the sports have an especially strong culture of heated competition at the elite level, which most in the West would be unfamiliar with. Sports like *buzkashi* ("goat dragging"), *kabaddi*, or *pacu jawi* ("push ahead cow") may be completely new to the reader. This brief entry can only serve to touch on a few of the fascinating and diverse regional and unique sporting activities of this enormous part of the world, with special attention to those not examined elsewhere in this volume.

In the United States, when people think about sports like badminton and table tennis (ping-pong), it is often in the context of casual fun at a picnic or in a rec room. But in Asia and Oceania, these two sports have a much more serious following. While table tennis originated as an after-dinner amusement in the West in the late 19th century, it has since developed into a sport of supreme athleticism and dizzying speed. Played like tennis but as if in miniature on a table with a small net, the game, when competitive, is extremely fast moving and involves long-range play and minute calculations. In the spring of 1971, when Beijing and Washington had no official diplomatic relations, a complex Cold War geopolitical environment led to an American table-tennis delegation being invited to the People's Republic of China. This turned out to be the eve of Sino-U.S. rapprochement, or warming relations. "Ping-pong diplomacy," as it came to be known, reflected a gradual thaw in the Sino-U.S. relationship, influenced in part by a shared hostility and wariness toward the Soviet Union. Table tennis officially became an Olympic sport in 1988, and it has since then been spectacularly dominated by players from the People's Republic of China (PRC) with occasional strong showings from other countries, like Japan and South Korea.

Badminton is similar in some ways to tennis but is played with a shuttlecock, or plastic half-sphere with feathers extending from it, and launched across a slightly

Pacu jawi or "Mud Cow Racing" is a visually striking rural pastime of Indonesia. Now a sport, the activity grew out of the practice of demonstrating the animal's worth before a sale by running it in front of prospective buyers. Here, a jockey runs his team in West Sumatra, Indonesia. (Rodney Ee)

higher net. Unlike in tennis and table tennis, the shuttlecock is never meant to intentionally touch the ground, and if this occurs in bounds on an individual or team's side, this means the loss of the point. As in table tennis, the PRC is a dominant force in the badminton world, but other countries, like India, Japan, Malaysia, South Korea, Indonesia, and Thailand, also consistently perform well in international competition.

Bandy is similar in many ways to ice hockey. Played on ice, but with a ball rather than a puck, bandy is in fact a precursor of hockey. Bandy developed earlier than hockey, and a variant of bandy, known as rink bandy, is more similar to hockey. Bandy is generally played on a much larger ice field with 11 players to a side, all of whom play with sticks, as in hockey, except for the goalkeeper who does not use a stick. While Scandinavian countries like Sweden, Finland, and Norway dominate the official world championships, along with Russia, Central Asian countries like Kazakhstan and Kyrgyzstan have very strong bandy cultures, and they perform relatively well on the international stage.

Jai alai is similar in some ways to handball but is played with a basket-like device. During play, the ball, or *pelota*, can reach amazing speeds of up to 200 miles per hour, making this a potentially hazardous sport indeed! Originating in Basque country in Spain, and with a name that means "merry festival" in Basque, this sport is very popular in the Philippines though with a checkered past that includes Spanish colonialism and more recently, illegal gambling. The sport also has strong followings in Latin America, the United States, and of course in Spain.

Sepak takraw is a popular sport whose alternate name of "kick volleyball" may give the reader some sense of what the game looks like. Played over a net similar to that of volleyball with a rattan ball, players can use body parts similar to in soccer—the legs, chest, and head. This game is similar to the popular Brazilian game footvolley. The sport has adherents around the world but is most popular in Southeast Asian countries, like Laos, Vietnam, Malaysia, Thailand, and the Philippines. In Myanmar (Burma), *chinlone* has some similarities to *sepak takraw*, and yet it defies easy categorization, since it is part sport and part dance, with no winners or losers. A Western viewer might be reminded of hacky sack, perhaps, or the common exercise of soccer players honing their ball-handling skills by juggling a ball with their legs, chest, and head. Similarly, *chinlone* players juggle a ball using their feet, with players approaching the middle of a circle to wow their companions with a dazzling solo display of skill. Sometimes a barker calls out moves and entertains a gathered crowd with color commentary.

For an American reader, reference to the sport of polo may bring to mind the upper crust of American and English society, engaged in equestrian showmanship between breaks for tea or champagne. But polo and its variants look quite different in other parts of the world. The sport originated in India, and variations of it remain popular there and throughout Central Asia to the north. In Central Asia, *buzkashi*, or "goat dragging" is in many ways similar to polo, but instead of knocking a ball toward the opponent's goal, a goat carcass is dragged toward the opponent's side of the field. This rowdy sport, also known as *kokpar*, is a far cry from polo as we may know it, but it is in fact similar in many ways and hugely popular in most countries of Central Asia, where it has a long history and is the national sport of Afghanistan.

Field hockey is another sport that may be familiar to an American or European reader but in a different context. When Americans refer to "hockey," they generally mean ice hockey, which is far more popular in North America, but throughout much of the world, "hockey" refers to field hockey, and "ice hockey" requires the modifier. In South Asia, for example, field hockey is enormously popular and is the national sport of Pakistan as well as being extremely important in India. In the United States, field hockey is far more popular as a women's sport, particularly at the high school and college level, but in this the Americans are the exception. Throughout most of the world, participation in field hockey between men and women is relatively balanced. In India and Pakistan, the men's field hockey teams are very successful in international competition, whereas the Australian women are among the sport's best. South Korea, the PRC, and Malaysia are also strong international competitors in field hockey.

Pacu jawi, literally "push ahead cow" in the Minangkabau people's dialect of Sumatra in Indonesia, is also referred to as "mud-cow racing" in English. This remarkable sport features a jockey standing with each foot on a simple wooden frame attached to two separate bulls standing side by side. The jockey stands with each hand holding one of the animals' tails. The beasts are spurred on across a muddy field at maximum possible speed, sometimes with the encouragement of the jockey biting the bulls' tails! The winner is the jockey-bull team that runs across the field in the fastest time and the straightest line. The sport began as a postharvest diversion but also served to demonstrate the strength and vitality of bulls by their sellers. Today at many *pacu jawi* competitions, the races are followed by the sale of the animals. The sport has spread to some parts of mainland Southeast Asia in slightly different forms.

Kabaddi is the national sport of Bangladesh and is also very popular in India and Pakistan. The sport has spread throughout the world in various forms and today has enthusiastic followings in various regions, including Iran, England, Nepal, Malaysia, and others. An American viewer watching a *kabaddi* match might be reminded of a game of high-speed, and sometime ferocious, capture the flag or tag. One player at a time, a "raider," runs into the opposing team's field and tries to tag members of the other team and return to her or his side. If the tagged player is unable to prevent the raider from returning to his or her own side (and this can include a fierce wrestling match in the effort to restrain the raider), then the tagged player is out and a point is won for the raider's side. A noteworthy aspect of the game is that the raider is only allowed one breath to do this—repeating a chant of "*kabaddi, kabaddi, kabaddi*" indicates to the referee that the raider has not inhaled—and if he or she inhales before returning, then the raider is out and no point is won.

There are many forms of martial arts practiced around the world, and in Asia and Oceania the practices are especially diverse and plentiful. *Muay thai*, also known as Thai kickboxing, has become popular around the world. Added to the usual fist striking of boxing, elbows, shins, and knees are also used to strike opponents, and clinching or grappling is an added dimension. *Let whay* or *lethwei* is also known as Burmese kickboxing and is similar in many ways to *muay thai*. *Pradal serey* or *kun khmer* is the Cambodian form that is similar to *muay thai* and *let whay*, and in Laos, *muay lao* is the local form. Local martial arts forms make up sports and recreation in many other parts of Asia and Oceania. Chinese and Japanese martial arts are certainly global phenomena, as is Korea's tae kwon do, all of which can be found practiced by people around the world.

Dragon-boat racing is a team paddling sport with a long history in China, related to the Duanwu Festival, which falls around the summer solstice every year. One observance of this festival has traditionally been dragon-boat racing, and today, the Duanwu holiday is sometimes called the Dragon Boat Festival. The dragon boat generally includes about 20 people rowing, with one person steering in the rear and one drumming the rhythm of the paddles at the front of the long and narrow boat. A dragon head and tail adorn the boat. With the creation in 1991 of the International Dragon Boat Federation, which now has over 60 member countries, the sport has gone global, with adherents around the world, from Canada to Norway to Australia, and of course to China and Hong Kong.

Surfing originated in the islands of Polynesia in the South Pacific. On Tahiti, Hawai'i, Samoa, and Tonga, the indigenous people were observed by visitors as early as the 18th century riding waves into the shore on planks. In the late 19th and early 20th century, surfing moved from Hawai'i to California, and modern surfing was born. Today surfing is extremely popular in many parts of the world but perhaps nowhere more so than in Australia, where some of the most extreme conditions can be found to challenge the expert and intrepid surfer. The beaches of Southeast Asia, Japan, Taiwan, and China have seen an increase in surfing recently. Taiwan's subtropical neighbor, Hainan Island, has become a popular destination for both amateur and professional surfers. Surfing was born in the Pacific, and it continues to thrive there.

These are just a few of the many regional and unique sports of Asia and Oceania. Many of the sports common around the world are also popular in these regions, but the colorful and thrilling world of regional sports and physical activities is worth further explorations by the reader and the curious traveler.

Jeremy A. Murray

See also: Martial Arts, China; Martial Arts, Japan; Mongolian Sports

Further Reading

Abrisketa, Olatz Gonzalez. 2013. *Basque Pelota: A Ritual, an Aesthetic.* Reno, NV: Center for Basque Studies.

Azoy, G. Whitney. 2012 [2003]. *Buzkashi: Game and Power in Afghanistan*, 3rd ed. Long Grove, IL: Waveland Press.

Cho, Younhan, and Charles Leary. 2014. *Modern Sports in Asia: Cultural Perspectives.* London: Routledge.

Sen, Ronojoy. 2015. *Nation at Play: A History of Sport in India.* New York: Columbia University Press.

RUGBY AND AUSTRALIA-RULES FOOTBALL

Rugby is one of several hugely popular world sports classified generally as a kind of football. Other major sports in the football category are American (or gridiron) football and soccer, the latter of which people in most other countries refer to simply as "football" without any other qualifier. While increasingly popular in the United States, rugby football (or what we will call just "rugby" here) is not nearly as popular as its American football and soccer counterparts.

Rugby and several of its variations are hugely popular in Australia and New Zealand as well as some of the other island nations of Oceania. Like cricket, rugby's popularity is another legacy of British colonial occupation of the region, and rugby continues to be important to the sports world of Great Britain and Ireland today. Rugby has several derivative games, most importantly, rugby *league* (sometimes simply referred to as "league") and rugby *union* (generally the game referred to simply as "rugby"). A quite distinctive game known as Australian-rules football (or Australian football, or "Aussie rules") may appear similar to rugby to a foreign viewer, but it is something quite different, as will be noted below.

In both rugby league and rugby union, the ball is advanced down the field with a player carrying it, having the option to throw the ball backwards or sideways, but not forwards, to a teammate. The ball is then touched down in the opponent's in-goal area for points (a try), something like a touchdown in the end zone of American football.

Rugby union and rugby league diverged in the 19th century due to disputes between professional and amateur players. The rules gradually began to diverge in an attempt by rugby league adherents to make the game more exciting and to draw in larger crowds. Rugby league is easier to understand for Americans due to its relative similarity to American football, and rugby union's more complex and strategy-based play makes it more difficult to follow, and in some ways, a slower game.

One main difference between the two games is that in rugby union, when a player is tackled, the ball is contested in what can become a "ruck" when a number of players pile onto the recently tackled player and the ball to try to gain possession in a physical contest that can be quite rough. In rugby league, however, when a player is taken down, the team of the tackled player maintains possession of the ball, and play is usually quickly resumed, something like a downed ball in American football. As in American football, in rugby league, the team with possession is allowed a limited number of such tackles in their attempt to score. While in American football, a team gets four downs in their attempt to score, in rugby league, a team gets six tackles by the opponent per possession in their attempt to reach the opponent's goal line. Also distinguishing the games, rugby union is played with 15 players per side, while rugby league has 13 per side; a try is awarded five points and a penalty kick or drop goal (a dropkicked ball) through the uprights is three points in rugby league; while these scoring instances are awarded four points for a try, two points for a penalty kick, and one point for a drop goal in rugby league. Today rugby union is much more common and popular worldwide, and Australia is the only country where rugby league is more popular than rugby union. Historically, the two versions of the game have split along class lines as well.

Australian-rules football is a test of endurance like few other sports. It is played in four 20-minute quarters, on an oval field that can be as long as 185 meters (over 200 yards, or twice an American football field) and as wide as 155 meters (about 170 yards), between two teams of 22 players on each side, with 18 on the field for each side at any given time. The remarkably large field already distinguishes Aussie rules from any other game. Unlike either variation of rugby, in Aussie rules there is no throwing of the ball to pass between teammates, but you can "handpass" or "handball" the ball, or hit it with a clenched fist out of your own hand, thus launching it to a teammate. The ball is carried up the field, as sometimes is the case in rugby, but it must be bounced every 15 meters. Scoring is achieved by kicking the ball through the middle posts, something like the uprights in rugby or American football, but with simply two posts and no bottom bar. This type of scoring earns six points. Hitting one of the posts with the ball, kicking a ball through the middle posts after having it deflected, or kicking a ball through one of the middle posts and one of the secondary or behind posts, all are called a "behind" and they earn one point each.

"Marking" the ball is a kind of passing in Aussie-rules football, and it is accomplished by kicking the ball in the air at least 15 meters up the field and having a teammate catch it. Play is then temporarily stopped while the team that successfully accomplished the mark is given a free kick after a short time to regroup. To an American audience, this might look something like a rush offense in American football after a long reception, as players hustle up the field before the restart. The "spectacular mark" or "specky" as it is informally known in Australia, is an eye-popping aspect of an Aussie-rules match in which the teammate on the receiving end of a mark launches high in the air to make the catch, often vaulting off the back of a player on the opposing team! In American football, a rough parallel could be drawn to a receiver "going across the middle" to make an exceptional leaping catch. Both are bold and dangerous moves, but both are also indeed spectacular, and they are crowd favorites. The Australian Football League (AFL) is a wildly popular spectator sport in Australia. Women's leagues of both rugby union and Aussie rules are also rising in popularity in Australia, and women's rugby has seen a rapid increase in popularity all around the world, especially since the 1990s.

Rugby union is very popular in both New Zealand and Australia, and both rugby league and Aussie rules are extremely popular in Australia. At the time of writing (September 2015) New Zealand and Australia hold the No. 1 one and No. 3 spots, respectively, in rugby union's world rankings, and the No. 1 and No. 2 spots, respectively, in rugby league's world rankings. The New Zealanders had a banner year indeed for rugby play in 2015. Their rugby union team is known as the All Blacks, and their rugby league team is known as the Kiwis. The All Blacks have long performed a *haka* (a celebratory or war dance in the tradition of the indigenous Maori people) known as the *Ka Mate* before international matches,

Maori Haka

Haka is the traditional war dance of the indigenous Maori community in New Zealand. It is a ritual posturing dance consisting of vigorous foot-stamping, chest-pounding, and tongue-protruding gestures accompanied by rhythmic body movement and singing ancestral songs. Song compositions often include genealogical history and narratives about epic feats as well as improvisations that deal with the present. *Haka*, originally, was used as a war cry but also for other ceremonial occasions. At the end of the 19th century, the "native" Maori soccer team first used the *haka* war cry to begin their football or soccer games against opponents. By the beginning of the 20th century, the New Zealand rugby team picked up this tradition of dancing and singing the *haka* in local and international arenas. The *haka*, today, is the internationally loved and ferocious war cry of New Zealand contact sports games.

Kathleen M. Nadeau

reminiscent of the way Maori warriors would perform a *haka* before a battle to demonstrate their strength and intimidate their opponent.

Some other teams from Oceania on the world rankings of rugby union are Fiji, Tonga, and Samoa, all coming in the top 13 national teams in September 2015, in spite of their relatively small populations. In rugby league, Samoa, Papua New Guinea, Fiji, Tonga, and the Cook Islands all rank in the top 20. The popularity of both forms of rugby throughout Oceania is clear in these rankings.

Jeremy A. Murray

See also: Sports Fanaticism, Australia

Further Reading

Andrews, Malcolm. 1995. *The A-Z of Rugby League*. Auckland, AU: Hodder Moa Beckett.

Biscombe, Tony, and Peter Drewett. 2009. *Rugby: Steps to Success*. Champaign, IL: Human Kinetics.

Coventry, James. 2015. *Time and Space: The Tactics That Shaped Australian Rules and the Players and Coaches Who Mastered Them*. Sydney, AU: ABC Books/HarperCollins Australia.

Richards, Huw. 2007. *A Game for Hooligans: The History of Rugby Union*. Edinburgh, UK: Mainstream Publishing.

SHERPAS AND HIMALAYAN MOUNTAINEERING

High-altitude mountaineering is one of the most dangerous sports in the world. Hundreds of people die every year in falls from great heights, in blinding storms, and especially—in terms of numbers—in avalanches. Yet thousands more are drawn by the combination of risky adventure and stunning natural beauty to attempt to climb the highest mountains on earth.

The idea of trying to climb high and dangerous mountains emerged first in Europe in the 19th century as part of various projects of the modernizing world. Some of these projects were scientific, including an interest in learning about the capacity of the human body to survive in extreme environments and an interest in measuring and exploring the remote areas of the planet. But some of these projects were part of a negative reaction to modernization, a desire to get away from a society that was becoming more urbanized and technologized and to recover a more direct relationship with nature.

There are only 14 mountains in the world over 8,000 meters high (a meter is a little over three feet; 8,000 meters is over 26,000 feet), and all of them are located in the Himalayan range, or its western extension, the Karakorams. Eight of these are located in Nepal, including the highest of all, Mount Everest, which tops off at 29,018 feet.

The first attempts to climb Mount Everest took place in the 1920s and 1930s, led by British army officers. They took with them large numbers of local men as "coolies" to carry their gear and provide the support labor for the expeditions. The "coolies" at first were drawn from a variety of local ethnic groups, including

Sherpas from the Solu-Khumbu region of Nepal, but over the course of the early expeditions the Sherpas distinguished themselves from the other groups as being particularly good at this kind of work and also particularly congenial to work with. Eventually only Sherpas were chosen for expedition work, and thus began the link between Sherpa ethnicity and Himalayan climbing that continues to this day.

The Everest expeditions of the 1920s and 1930s all failed, and mountaineering was more or less suspended in the 1940s as a result of World War II. Expeditions began again in the 1950s. In 1950 Annapurna in central Nepal became the first peak over 8,000 meters ever to be climbed. There were several more attempts on Everest, and finally in May 1953, a New Zealander named Edmund Hillary and a Sherpa named Tenzing Norgay reached the summit. The British press went wild, and Hillary, Tenzing, and "the Sherpas" in general became world famous almost overnight.

After the "conquest" of Everest, Himalayan mountaineering continued to evolve. The Sherpas became increasingly skilled and increasingly specialized in the technical high-altitude climbing that is associated with the name of "Sherpa." For the most part, the low-altitude portering work is now left to members of other ethnic groups in the region.

In the 1970s the feminist movement reverberated throughout the world, and the decade saw the influx of significant numbers of women into the previously all-male world of mountaineering. They not only came, they conquered. In 1975

Edmund Hillary and Tenzing Norgay Sherpa, the first two people to reach the summit of Mount Everest, the highest mountain in the world. May 1953. (AP Images)

(which was the official United Nations International Women's Year), Junko Tabei headed an all-women's Japanese expedition and reached the top of Mount Everest from the south side, while Phantog, a Tibetan woman, was part of a mixed-gender expedition and reached the top via the previously unclimbed north side. A number of Sherpa women also became involved in mountaineering at that time, including Pasang Lhamu Sherpa who was the first Sherpa woman to reach the summit of Everest but died on the way down.

The 1980s saw the beginning of another transformation of the sport: the development of commercial mountaineering. From the very beginning in the 19th century, mountaineering was a sport of amateurs, not in the sense of climbers being unskilled and inexperienced but in the sense of expeditions being organized purely for the pleasure of the participants and not for commercial motives. Starting in the 1980s, some Western climbers started businesses in which they offered to guide anyone to the top who wanted to go and had the money to pay for it. The price was very steep (currently about $250,000 per person), but the concept turned out to be extraordinarily popular, and these commercially organized expeditions have now virtually taken over Mount Everest.

The impact of this shift has been enormous. Although statistics are not available for the numbers of people on the mountain at any one time, the numbers have clearly multiplied many times over, such that, for example, there is now a two-hour wait in a queue below the summit in order to get one's turn to step up on the top. And of course with more climbers there is more gear to be carried and more Sherpas needed to assist. One effect of the growth of numbers of people has been, not surprisingly, the growth of numbers of fatalities, with the Sherpas being disproportionately affected. In 2014 there was an avalanche that killed 16 Sherpas (and no Westerners); in 2015 the 8.1 magnitude Nepal earthquake set off an avalanche on Everest that killed at least 20 people, including 10 Sherpas, 5 international climbers, and 5 unidentified individuals. While people have always died in avalanches in the Himalayas, the numbers of fatalities are rising as there are, many would argue, simply too many people on the mountain.

Recent years have also seen a rise in conflict on the mountains, and this too appears to be related at least in part to commercialization. That is, with too many groups and too many people on the mountain, and with only a relatively narrow corridor of approach to the summit, people start getting in each other's way. There have been attempts to rationalize relations between the various commercial groups, but at the same time there are old-fashioned noncommercial expeditions on the mountain that are not party to the agreements among the commercial expeditions. An infamous incident in 2013 appears to be an outcome of one such situation, in which several European climbers in a private expedition were felt to have interfered with a Sherpa group fixing ropes on behalf of the commercial groups on a very dangerous ice face. The Sherpas became very angry with the Europeans, and some rocks were thrown, although in the end no one suffered more than minor cuts and bruises.

It is important to realize that most Sherpa people are not actually "Sherpas" in the sense of being employed in high-altitude climbing. For these other Sherpas, the majority, mountaineering has also been important but in different ways. For one thing, the money earned in mountaineering has benefited not only the climbing Sherpas but also their whole families and, indirectly, their communities. In addition, there has been (for better and for worse) a massive influx of tourists to the Sherpa region, which is on the main route to Mount Everest. Sherpas have taken advantage of that as well, building lodges, restaurants, and teahouses to service the tourist industry.

And then there is education. After the Hillary-Tenzing success on Everest, Hillary decided to devote his life to working on behalf of the Sherpa community. He created a nonprofit organization called the Himalayan Trust and set about building schools and hospitals in the Sherpa area as well as endowing scholarships for promising young Sherpa men and women to go on to high school and higher education. The Sherpas were quick to take advantage of these opportunities too, and there are now many Sherpas in professions including medicine, dentistry, finance, filmmaking, and natural resource management.

Sherry B. Ortner

See also: Antarctic Expeditions and Sports

Further Reading

Blum, Arlene. 1980. *Annapurna: A Woman's Place*. San Francisco: Sierra Club Books.

Fisher, James F. 1990. *Sherpas: Reflections on Change in Himalayan Nepal*. Berkeley: University of California Press.

Krakauer, Jon. 1997. *Into Thin Air: A Personal Account of the Mount Everest Disaster.* New York: Villard.

Ortner, Sherry B. 1999. *Life and Death on Mt. Everest: Sherpas and Himalayan Mountaineering*. Princeton, NJ: Princeton University Press.

SOCCER

Soccer, the most popular sport on the planet, is widely played and watched throughout East Asia, South Asia, and Oceania. The Japanese and Chinese women's national teams have consistently succeeded in the World Cup finals, with Japan winning the 2011 World Cup. Though Asian and Oceanic nations have not reached the top tier of world soccer in men's competition, there are many competitive leagues supported by passionate fans. Together, South Korea and Japan hosted the men's 2002 World Cup, the biggest sporting event in the world, held once every four years. The South Korean men made it to the semifinal, the furthest into the competition an Asian nation has ever gone.

China

A number of 20th-century Chinese leaders have been soccer players and fans. In his early twenties, Mao Zedong (1893–1976) played goalkeeper at a teachers' college in his native Hunan Province. Deng Xiaoping (1904–1997) described watching games together with Zhou Enlai (1898–1976), and while paramount leader of China, at 90 years old, Deng had World Cup matches recorded to be watched in his free time. China's current president Xi Jinping, a fan of the game, explained his three wishes for the growth of soccer in the nation. First, to qualify for a men's World Cup (China qualified for the 2002 men's World Cup but failed to score); second, to host a World Cup; and finally, to win the World Cup. President Xi did not, however, put a time line on his wishes.

Xi's push for success in the men's game has led to plans to separate China's soccer association from its national sports administration in order to give more autonomy to the association. There is to be an expansion of programs to promote young people's involvement in soccer, an uphill battle, since talented Chinese athletes have traditionally been more likely to pursue individual sports. The plan also calls for an oversight board to monitor professional leagues, ensuring strict enforcement of rules concerning the match fixing that has plagued the professional game. China's professional leagues have struggled with corruption over the years, but the real-estate moguls who have invested heavily in the sport have recently been working to clean it up. China's Super League is now competitive in Asian soccer, importing foreign stars and coaches, including the famous Brazilian coach Luiz Felipe Scolari. The Chinese club Guangzhou has won the Chinese Super League four years in a row, playing Japanese League champions, Gamba Osaka, in 2015 for the Asian Champions League semifinal. Guangzhou invested US$130 million from 2010 to 2015, spending on foreign stars, including Brazilian international Paulinho; from the English premier club, Tottenham Hotspur; and former Real Madrid striker Robinho.

Japan

Japan, a power in the women's game, has qualified for the last five men's World Cups and has won the Asian Cup four times. Japan also advanced to the second round of the World Cup in 2010 in South Africa and while hosting with South Korea in 2002.

The Japanese men's national team includes many players enjoying success internationally, with five currently in the Bundesliga (the top Germapn league), two in Serie A (the top Italian league), and two in the English Premier League (the top English league). The biggest star may be Shinji Kagawa, who played with superclub Manchester United in the Premier League before moving to Borussia Dortmund in the Bundesliga, where he scored 28 goals. Now playing with Leicester City in the English Premier League, Shinji Okazaki scored the most goals of any Japanese player while playing in the Bundesliga for Stuttgart and FSV Mainz. Okazaki is currently the top active goal scorer for the national team. Keisuke Honda and Shunsuke Nakamora are other notable Japanese superstars.

The term *sakkā*, which comes from "soccer," is more commonly used than *futtobōru*, from "football," in Japan. The JFA's (Japanese Football Association) Japanese name is Nippon Sakkā Kyōkai. Japan's top tier of professional soccer is the J-League (launched in 1993). There is also the L-League for women in Japan, which, although not professional, is the most competitive women's soccer league in Japan with multiple divisions. After defeating the United States to win the final of the 2011 World Cup, the Japanese women's national team has continued to have one of the world's strongest programs. In 2015 the Japanese women's national team finished as runners-up to the United States in the World Cup and as of 2015 were ranked fourth in the world.

Australia

As in the United States, the Australian game is not "football" but "soccer," which helps to differentiate it from Australian-rules football. A number of Australian men's stars have excelled in Europe, including Tim Cahill and Harry Kewell, with Mile Jedinak an up-and-coming star with the Premier League's Crystal Palace. Many others have also had success in the top tiers of the European leagues. This professional success has not translated to victories in the men's World Cup, however, where Australia, though an often dangerous and surprising opponent, has never advanced past the Round of 16. The men's national team, nicknamed the Socceroos, did win the 2015 Asian Cup with record-breaking attendances and viewership. The Socceroos also qualified for the 2014 World Cup in Brazil, where Tim Cahill was recognized for scoring one of the tournament's most memorable goals. The Australian women, nicknamed the Matildas (from the song "Waltzing Matilda"), have found greater World Cup success, three times making a run to the quarterfinals. Australia's semiprofessional W-League, established in 2008, is the top tier of the women's game, and the A-League, established in 2005, is the top tier for men's soccer.

South Korea

The top tier of South Korean men's soccer is the K-League, with the K-League Classic as the top division. The league was formed in 1983 as the Korean Super League and changed its name to the K-League in 1998. To better develop its national talent, the league limits the number of foreign players allowed on each team and also the number that can be on the field at one time. Women's soccer in South Korea has not had the success of neighboring China and Japan.

In the men's game, Son Heung Min plays for Tottenham in the English Premier League and Chung Yong Lee with Crystal Palace. Both players are having success, and a rivalry now exists, followed by millions in South Korea when their teams compete. The players are friends off the field and both are members of the national team. South Korea's men's national team is perhaps the strongest in Asia, consistently good, with a fourth-place finish in 2002.

North Korea

The DPR Korea League is the highest league in the North Korean soccer system. The men's national team qualified for the 2010 World Cup but did not make it out of the group stage. The North Koreans, however, achieved a historic success in the 1966 World Cup. The North Korean men stunned powerful Italy then went on to lose to Portugal in the quarterfinals after being up 3–0 early in the match. The North Korean women's national team made it to the quarterfinals in the 2007 World Cup, but they were disqualified from the 2015 competition for using performance-enhancing drugs.

India, Pakistan, and Bangladesh

India's professional I-League was founded in 2007, and in 2013 a separate top league, the Super League, was formed. India will host the 2017 FIFA Under-17 World Cup (automatically qualifying as hosts). In the 1930s, 1940s, and 1950s, the Indian National team insisted on playing barefoot, and this prompted FIFA to establish a rule in 1948 banning barefoot play. Although India qualified for the 1950 World Cup in Brazil, they did not make the trip and there were rumors (likely unfounded) that this was because they would not be permitted to play barefoot. Although soccer is popular in India, it is surpassed by cricket, and the newly established professional leagues have not yet produced players of the caliber that would bring success in World Cup qualifying. The popularity of soccer as a women's sport is slowly taking hold but still lags far behind powers such as China and Japan.

Bangladesh's professional B-League has been known as the Bangladesh Premier League since 2009. Soccer was traditionally the most popular sport in Bangladesh, but now, as in India and Pakistan, cricket has overtaken soccer. Despite widespread cultural resistance to the participation of women, the 2010 South Asian Games, hosted in Dhaka, Bangladesh, featured women's soccer as one of the events, and Bangladesh now has an under-19 women's national team.

Although soccer is popular in Pakistan, professional leagues and the national team have not had much success. The Pakistani Premier League is the current professional league in the country, and players of Pakistani heritage have found success overseas, with Etzaz Hussain, born in Norway of Pakistani parents, featuring as a young star for FC Molde, in Norway. Hussain is the first player of Pakistani origin to play in a major European club competition.

Soccer is a hugely popular sport in many countries across Asia and Oceania. And yet, in an area representing the majority of the world's population and some of its richest countries and biggest economies, rarely does any nation crack FIFA's top 50 rankings of the men's game. Africa, on the other hand, has 11 nations in the world's top 50. On the other hand, the women's game, which has met great success with Japan, China, and Australia among the world's best, still faces contradictions in other regions as women are kept from the game due in part to social and cultural biases related to gender.

In the men's game, there are various reasons given for the competitive disparity—for example, nations such as India, which has a comparatively underfunded professional league, do not allow players of dual nationality to join the national team. This policy disqualifies Indian-born dual-national players competing at a high level in European leagues. Guam (an island nation of less than 200,000 people that does allow dual nationals, many of whom compete in the more competitive MLS, Major League Soccer, in the United States) can therefore compete with much larger nations, recently defeating India, a nation of more than a billion people, in a match. Other reasons cited are the desperate search, in nations such as China, for instant success—leading to a cyclical hiring and firing of star coaches, intended to lead the men's team to World Cup success rather than patiently developing the youth system.

Star men's players such as Japan's Shinji Okazaki describe how the "culture and history of soccer is still short—insufficient even, I think, if you're talking about having a proper go at the World Cup," but "Asia is getting stronger, and the level of the Asian Cup is going up incredibly" (Kerr 2015).

Timothy I. Murray and Aaron R. Murray

See also: Rugby and Australian-Rules Football

Further Reading

Cho, Younghan. 2014. *Football in Asia: History, Culture, and Business*. Abingdon, UK: Routledge.

Economist. 2014. "The Party's Goal." December 13. www.economist.com/news/china /21636097-football-long-national-shame-becomes-compulsory-school-partys-goal ?fsrc=email_to_a_friend. Accessed March 26, 2016.

Foer, Franklin. 2010. *How Soccer Explains the World: An Unlikely Theory of Globalization*. New York: Harper.

Galeano, Eduardo. 2013. *Soccer in Sun and Shadow*. London: Nation Books.

Kerr, Jack. 2015. "Football in Asia: Improving, but Still Trailing Far Behind Africa." *The Guardian*. February 4. www.theguardian.com/football/blog/2015/feb/05/football-in -asia-improving-but-still-trailing-far-behind-africa. Accessed March 26, 2016.

Light, Richard, and Wataru Yasaki. 2003. "Breaking the Mould: J League Soccer, Community and Education in Japan." *Football Studies* 6: 37–50.

SPORTS FANATICISM, AUSTRALIA

"The Melbourne Cup is the Australasian National Day. It would be difficult to overstate its importance. . . . I can call to mind no specialized annual day, in any country, whose approach fires the whole land with a conflagration of conversation and preparation and anticipation and jubilation. No day save this one; but this one does it" (Twain 1897, 355).

Though more than 100 years old, Mark Twain's quote continues to speak to the perception of Australia as a country—and especially Melbourne as a city—that is fanatical about sport. While it is perhaps hyperbolic to say that sport means more to Australians than it does to those in all other countries, it is also true to say that since Australia was invaded and then colonized by the British, sport has become intertwined with national and local identities and is a significant area of popular culture and obsession.

The cultural fascination of the new Australians with sports became evident early, with cricket and horse racing quickly becoming prominent sites of intense public discussion and spectatorship. Both were sports of the empire, brought over by the British, and both were drawing significant crowds to events in the second half of the 1800s. The team game of cricket soon afforded the chance of competition between the Australians and the British, and it became a critical part of Australian nationalism even before the federation of Australia in 1901. But while cricket administrators in England sought to limit crowds and the development of a spectator culture around the game, those involved in the game in Australia encouraged public interest and viewing of contests. As a result, cricket crowds at most games were soon significantly bigger in Australia than in England. The crowds also tended to be considerably more diverse, with many men from all classes attending games and a number of women also coming to view the spectacle.

The popularity of cricket continued to grow after Federation in 1901, and soon the captaincy of the Australian team was spoken of (in a manner that was only half joking) as the second most important job in Australia after the prime minister. Australians' passion for cricket helped those associated with the game become household names. The radio commentator Alan McGilvray (1909–1996), for example, became known to many as the "Voice of Summer." The perceived importance of cricketing knowledge as central to Australian identity was so great that the most important debate over Australia's recent citizenship test was over whether to include a question on Australia's most famous cricketer, Don Bradman (1908–2001). The considerable importance of cricket to many Australians also enabled the Australian media baron Kerry Packer (1937–2005) to revolutionize the game. Indeed, the one-day version of cricket that Packer funded succeeded in part because so many people watched the games on the Australian television channel that he then owned (Channel 9).

Horse racing also became a national spectacle, though here the focus was turned inward rather than to the international stage. With Australia's wide geographical expanses, horses became a central aspect of daily life for many new Australians, and they were celebrated in literature, poems, art, and racing. So popular was the spectacle of horse racing that major races were frequently declared public holidays in towns and cities. The Melbourne Cup was the paradigmatic example of this, as noted by Twain above. Established in 1861, it has been a public holiday for those in the state of Victoria since 1877, with more than 100,000 spectators frequently gathering in the area around the Flemington racing course to view the proceedings. The Melbourne Cup soon became the biggest horse race in Australia, becoming known, with some justification, as "the race that stops a nation."

That Melbourne became the Australian center of horse racing, rather than the older Australian city of Sydney, was due in part to the Victorian gold rush that began in the 1850s. Before the gold rush—arguably the largest in history—Melbourne was a small frontier town. After the rush, Melbourne had grown into a major modern metropolis peopled by citizens from around the world. The wealth generated by the gold funded very generous prizes for horse races and other sporting events.

Many who had journeyed to Melbourne were politically and socially progressive, and successful strike action in 1856 led to a maximum eight-hour working day for many men, while female factory workers were also granted an eight-hour working day in 1873. With Australia approaching full employment for men during the 1870s, the colonies, and Melbourne in particular, were known as the "Working Man's Paradise," while factory and shop work for women also abounded. This fed into an associated leisure culture where many sports and other popular entertainments flourished, and Melbourne became known around the world as a city that was mad about sports.

The sport that became most synonymous with Melbourne was Australian-Rules football. Formally codified in 1859, it is unique in that it is the only major spectator sport in the world that developed at the same time as the city in which it was founded. Australian-Rules football (or Aussie rules) is similar in some ways to rugby and soccer, but it is a distinctive game in its own right and is played on an oval-shaped field with 18 players per side. Initially played in parks and gardens—as a spectacle that any passerby could see—the game was soon embraced by people from all classes and most notably was strongly supported by many women as well as men. Indeed, women made up an estimated 30 to 50 percent of typical paying crowds from as early as the 1880s and onward. There was even a moral panic over the way some women used their hatpins as weapons against errant umpires and players from the opposing team!

In the 1880s, a new word was developed to denote the passionate supporters of this new sport: "barrackers." As is often the case, the etymology of the term is contested, but it referred to the yelling of spectators, with "barrack" meaning to shout out derisively. Over time the meaning of "barrackers" evolved to primarily refer to the followers of a team. Nevertheless, the passions of supporters did not diminish, and by the early 1900s, the people of Melbourne were sustaining two semiprofessional competitions composed of about 20 clubs based around the city. The so-called "mania" of Melbournians for Australian-Rules football was so great that everyone—regardless of class, race, religion, or sex—was expected to follow a team. For much of the year "footy," as the game was termed, vied with Melbourne's notoriously changeable weather as the main topic of general conversation, and the game came to be referred to as the city's inner language.

The culture was inclusive in that most people were generally welcomed as supporters. However, those who did not want to converse or think about footy found all the talk about the game oppressive. In 1967 two Melbourne journalists who cared little for the game raised the notion of an "antifootball" group. They were startled to receive hundreds of letters supporting the idea, and the "Anti-Football League" was formed. Both an act of protest and a humorous response to the frustration of being continually expected to care and talk about a sport, the Anti-Football League quickly gained more members than the most popular Australian-Rules football club. The League remains active, although in a more limited capacity than in its first decade. Yet the fervor for Australian-Rules football continued, and the game remains the most-watched sport in Australia with a national (professional)

Australian Football League that evolved out of one of the Melbourne competitions (and half of the teams are still based in Melbourne).

In two Australian states, however, Rugby League, not Australian-Rules football, became the dominant football code. Although Rugby League does not shape the popular culture of Sydney and Brisbane to the same extent that Australian-Rules football shapes life in Melbourne, the three annual Rugby League State of Origin contests between New South Wales and Queensland tend to generate the most passionate and largest sporting crowds seen in Australia. It is worth noting, though, that the biggest Rugby League crowds have come when State of Origin matches have been played in Melbourne.

Another football code, association football (or soccer), has also been the site of significant fan passions in Australia. Although this form of football has been played in Australia for at least 130 years, it has still tended to be seen as a foreign culture and is most commonly referred to as "soccer" rather than football, as in North America. This game has enjoyed periods of mass popularity, often associated with waves of migration from areas of the world where it is the dominant football code. At other times, it has been a place where first- and second-generation migrants gather to follow games with an intense zeal. Followers of soccer from the 1970s to 1990s, for instance, would experience worlds of Australian ethnicity that many other citizens were unaware of. A distrustful mainstream media and general public focused on the violent clashes that sometimes erupted between different groups of migrant supporters, whereas violence within Australian-Rules football and Rugby League crowds tended to go unreported. More recently, those governing soccer have implemented a controversial policy of "de-ethnicization" (banning, for example, both club names that point to an "ethnic" identity and the use of flags and symbols from other countries) in an attempt to broaden the game's appeal beyond the migrant communities that have largely grown the game in Australia.

Matthew Klugman

See also: Rugby and Australian-Rules Football; Soccer

Further Reading

Cashman, Richard, and Rob Hess, eds. 2011. *Sport History and Australian Culture: Passionate Pursuits*. Petersham, AU: Walla Walla Press.

Klugman, Matthew. 2011. "'Football Is a Fever Disease Like Recurrent Malaria and Evidently Incurable': Passion, Place and the Emergence of an Australian Anti-Football League." *The International Journal of the History of Sport* 28, no. 10: 1426–1446.

Twain, Mark. 1897. *Following the Equator*. Hartford, CT: The American Publishing Company.

UYGHUR SPORTS

Uyghur sports are divided into three interrelated categories—children's games, traditional competitions, and Western-style sports—all of which are played primarily by men and boys. From wrestling to forms of stickball, from "goat-pulling" on horseback to "rabbit-pulling" on sleds, Uyghur traditional sports are part of the weave of everyday life from youth to old age. Over the past two decades, the increase in formal education in the Uyghur homeland of Southern Xinjiang, coupled with the spread of television and Internet media, has led to a greater popularity of Western sports, such as soccer, basketball, and boxing. Despite the recent overlay of Western sports, the traditional games and competitions of rural Uyghur life continue to play an important, yet diminishing, role in Uyghur masculinity.

A prominent feature of Uyghur children's games is that everyday objects are turned into tools of play. The team sport known variously as *chukchuk-kaltek*, *gaga*, or *walley* (hereafter *walley*) that is played universally by Uyghur young men from Ghulja (Yinning 尹宁) to Khotan (Hetian 和田), employs locally produced items—two sticks—and a sophisticated set of rules similar to baseball. It centers on a small "home" circle in the dirt called a *koyla* that has a small hole in the middle of it. Into this hole, players diagonally insert a small stick made of mulberry or apricot wood. This small stick (approximately six inches in length) is then hit with a bigger stick, which is often made out of a softer wood such as poplar—the hitting end of the larger stick is shaped slightly like a paddle.

The main actions in the game are first smacking the small stick, making it bounce into the air, and then slapping it away into the field of play where defenders are waiting to catch it with a hat or with their bare hands. If the stick lands, the opposing team tries to throw the small stick to hit the big stick, which is now lying in the *koyla*. If the defender fails to hit it, the original hitter is given an opportunity to hit the small stick again from wherever it lands. If the defender cannot catch the stick after the second hit, he is punished. He is forced to run with the little stick back to the *koyla* yelling the word "*walley*" with a single breath.

Walley is often played by a mix of boys and young adults ranging between the ages of 7 to 20. As with many traditional Uyghur sports, winning is not as closely related with the number of points accrued. Instead, winning has to do with the pride that comes from making a player from the other team yell *walley* all the way to the *koyla* while a player from the opposing team goads him with the stick. Like many Uyghur group activities, the pride that comes from performing well, as well as the shame that comes from being defeated, is an essential aspect in the performance of masculinity.

Two of the most important traditional Uyghur adult sports also revolve around a performance of masculinity. For instance, Uyghur wrestlers use their arm strength and upper body to throw their opponents onto the ground. Each wrestler maintains a hold on the other wrestler's belt. It is important that neither of the wrestlers attempt any "tricks" such as tripping or kicking. Even grabbing the arm of the opponent is considered "lady-like." The key to wrestling well is not just winning but also losing with dignity.

Another important traditional sport among Uyghur men is *oglaq-tatish* (*buzkashi* in Farsi). The game features a competition between two teams mounted on horses and wrestling over a headless young goat. The aim of the game is to hoist the goat into an elevated goal. The best players usually ride the fastest and strongest horses. They often build a social reputation around their passion for the game; although they may not be very wealthy, they will spend the majority of their income on the care of their horse and set aside long amounts of time in preparation for the game.

In most rural settings, this game was traditionally set up as a competition between villages or neighborhoods. In the winter, kids sometimes mimic the game of the adults by taking sleds out onto the ice on frozen ponds and "pulling" a dead rabbit in team competitions between neighborhoods. As the rural countryside is developing under China's Open Up the West policy, the sport is also changing in other ways. In places such as Hotan and Kashgar prefectures, many wealthy participants in the sport are now sourcing their horses in international locations such as Russia and Turkmenistan. These horses can cost anywhere from US$30,000 to $100,000. The sport is thus becoming a source of conspicuous consumption for a few local elites and less a source of village pride. Yet despite these changes, the danger and raw masculine energy of the sport remains constant.

Over the past two decades, Western sports such as soccer, basketball, and boxing have also come to the Uyghur countryside. Soccer in particular has developed

Buzkashi, or "goat dragging," is a very popular sport in northwestern China's Xinjiang region, as well as throughout other parts of central Asia. It is the national sport of Afghanistan, and while rules vary, it basically looks like a rougher version of polo, with two sides dragging a goat or calf carcass from one side of a field to the other, as opposed to hitting a ball with a mallet. Here Tajik horsemen compete in a 2015 match in Xinjiang. (Xinhua/Jiang Wenyao)

a large following among Uyghurs due to the relative accessibility of the game. Many of them follow their favorite teams in Europe, watching Uyghur-language broadcasts of the games on Xinjiang provincial television channels. Over the past few years, a Uyghur team was established as part of a third-tier Chinese league. But because the regional government is extremely fearful of large groups of Uyghurs gathering in urban settings (government experts refer to mass spectator sports as a potential training ground for terrorism), the team was disbanded in 2014. While it lasted, it consistently broke the record for the largest audience for a soccer team in China with a regular attendance of over 50,000 at home games.

Basketball was first popularized in the mid-1990s after Adiljan (the first Uyghur member of the national team) became the star on the Chinese team in the Barcelona Olympics. A few years later, boxing was popularized in the figure of Abdushikur. Seemingly out of nowhere, he became the first Uyghur boxing king of China, winning the national championship for a couple years straight in the late 1990s. He was followed quickly by Abdurahman Ablakim, who won the East Asia Cup and then became the first Chinese boxer to qualify for the Sydney Olympics in 2000.

Since that time there have been many Uyghur boxers and basketball stars, but none is more famous than Shiralijan, an athlete who trained first as a boxer and then transitioned to basketball. His fame reached its peak when he took the Xinjiang team, the Flying Tigers, to the Chinese Basketball Association championships in 2014. At the end of game four of the championship round, he pumped his fist to the hostile Beijing crowd that had been chanting racial epithets at him during his entire performance. The image of his defiance went viral on the Uyghur Internet, becoming a meme with hundreds of social media users posting similar pictures.

As many scholars have noted, sports and spectatorship are one way in which people—in this case Uyghur men—perform their identity. Whether in the countryside or in the city, Uyghurs find a sense of themselves in their performance of sport.

Darren Byler and Parhat Ablat

See also: Horse Racing, Philippines; Mongolian Sports

Further Reading

Byler, Darren. 2014a. "Shiralijan's Fist and Xinjiang Spirit." *Beijing Cream.* April 4. https://beigewind.wordpress.com/2014/04/04/shiralijans-fist-and-xinjiang-spirit. Accessed May 18, 2015.

Byler, Darren. 2014b. "Baseball in Xinjiang and the Documentary 'Diamond in the Dunes.'" *Beijing Cream.* September 2. https://beigewind.wordpress.com/2014/09/02/baseball-in-xinjiang-and-the-documentary-diamond-in-the-dunes. Accessed May 18, 2015.

Byler, Darren. 2015. "Uyghur Kids and Their 'Dream from the Heart.'" *Beijing Cream.* January 30. http://beijingcream.com/2015/01/dfxj-uyghur-kids-and-their-dream-from-the-heart. Accessed May 18, 2015.

WEIQI (SURROUNDING CHESS), CHINA

Weiqi is the Chinese name for a classic board game for two players using black and white game pieces. The deceptively simple course of the game involves each player taking turns placing one stone at a time, with black always going first, with the ultimate purpose of surrounding as much territory as possible. With a history of more than 4,000 years, the game certainly predates its Western chess counterpart in any of its forms (the earliest predecessor of which dates to Gupta India and the sixth century CE) and has changed very little since antiquity. It spread first to Japan and Korea then finally Europe, the Americas, and other countries in the East. With it has traveled Chinese philosophy and an opportunity to bridge political divides.

Weiqi was the preserve of the scholar class in China until the 1700s. Our forefathers may have invented the game by placing black and white pieces in a square drawn on the ground. The legend of *weiqi*'s invention by the ancient Chinese ruler Yao of the third millennium BCE emphasizes the educational meaning of this game; it is said that Yao invented *weiqi* to educate his rather witless son. Ban Gu (32–92 CE), a first-century Chinese historian, remarked of *weiqi* that its board was the image of the universe, with rules that govern the empire, thus the game started to have cultural significance.

During the Six Dynasties period (222–589 CE) or Period of Disunity, people gave *weiqi* other names, such as "hand talking" and "forgetting sadness." By the time of the Tang dynasty (618–906 CE), *weiqi* had become a kind of art that was seen as a miniature version of the cosmos. The center of the board resembles the Supreme Ultimate (*Taiji*), and the black and white pieces symbolize *yin* and *yang* (the two opposing principles in nature). It contains endless variations just like heaven and earth. In a 1368 text by scholar Zhang Ni called *The Classic of Weiqi in Thirteen Chapters*, the game is outlined as follows: "Vast numbers of things began from one. In the way of *weiqi*, there are 360 crosses plus one. 'One' refers to the source of all things, from which other things are derived. Three hundred and sixty are the degrees for circling the earth. The board is then divided into four parts, signaling the four seasons. Each corner has 90 crosses, which means 90 days. The peripheral 72 crosses refer to *hou* (a period of five days). The 360 in *weiqi* is distributed equally for yin and yang, in black and white" (author's translation).

While this grand description may exaggerate the importance of *weiqi*, it indicates that it is more than just a trial of strength between two players.

No definite conclusion has been reached on when *weiqi* was invented. Among different theories the most popular one is that the ancient ruler Yao invented it, while others suggest that it originated from trigram and divination rituals.

The word *weiqi* firstly appeared in *Huai Nan Zi*, a seminal Chinese philosophy book written in about 150 BCE. This book mainly focuses on Daoist (Taoist) theory, and in the first extant mention of *weiqi*, it compares the game to swordplay, in that they both are all about nature. It is said that the invention of *weiqi* has something to do with Qizi (ca. 1100 BCE), who was an eminent master of divination, celestial phenomena observation, and calendar making. His philosophical thinking paved the foundation for the origin of not only *weiqi*, but also the *Yijing* (also known as the *Zhou Yi* or *I Ching*), the most important book of Chinese traditional philosophy). The guidelines for the rules of *weiqi* are based on simple celestial and natural phenomena. *Weiqi* boards and pieces were the tools used for celestial phenomena observation and divination. Another early reference to *weiqi* is in the *Zuo Commentary* (*Zuo Zhuan*), a classic Chinese history covering the period between 722 BCE to 468 BCE, which refers to the *weiqi* player holding a stone piece and not being able to decide where to play the piece. The text asks how his indecisiveness can ever bring victory. Confucius also mentioned *weiqi* in the compilation of his teachings known as the *Analects* (*Lunyu*), in which he says that the people go about their daily routines wondering about the meaning of life. He says that at least they can play *weiqi*, which itself has some significance.

This shows that at that time there was already a leisure class. This provided a basis for developing *weiqi*. In the *Mencius*, another philosophy text named for Confucius's most famous student, it described a strong *weiqi* player, Yiqiu, as being a well-known *weiqi* player in the country. This indicates that at that time, in the fourth and third centuries BCE, there were already national *weiqi* masters.

Weiqi did not enjoy high social status in the early Han dynasty (202 BCE–220 CE). However, things began to change after the prominent historian Ban Gu associated *weiqi* with Daoist teachings, noting that the black pieces were to the white pieces as yin is to yang. Interest in *weiqi* was sparked in the court, and by the time of the late Han dynasty it had spread through the nation. Scholars devoted themselves to habits such as *weiqi* to avoid military service; and in return, *weiqi* was further developed as an independent intellectual challenge.

The first golden age of *weiqi* came soon after the Han-era publication of the *weiqi* rhapsody, *Weiqi fu*, by Ma Rong (79–166 CE), and the establishment of the *Weiqi* Ministry in the government. The Weiqi Ministry was the first official *weiqi* organization and was in charge of managing players and recording games. Meanwhile, *weiqi* was officially announced as one of the Chinese Arts, and a complete grading system was established.

The booming economics in the Tang dynasty (618–906) made it fertile ground for *weiqi* to grow. It was said that every single person in Chang'an (today Xi'an), the capital city of the Tang, knew how to play. A large number of *weiqi*-related ideas emerged, such as reciting verses in turns to create spontaneous poetry. Three generations later, *weiqi* was involved in the bureaucratic system: there were *weiqi* experts whose work was to play the emperor and *weiqi* masters who taught in the royal court. In the Song dynasty (960–1279), *weiqi* continued to attract more popularity. Many Song emperors were loyal fans, and the educated elites gathered regularly to play *weiqi* and compose poems about the game. What was once a court activity became more widely known.

Emperors in the Ming dynasty (1368–1644) banned *weiqi* many times in order to combat moral decline, but as most of them were *weiqi* lovers themselves, the prohibition was ineffective and the prosperity of commerce allowed it to flourish. By the middle of the dynasty, there were already three *weiqi* groups in the empire, and at the same time, many *weiqi* manuals were produced, such as the *Four Stones Manual* and the *Endgame Manual*. In the Qing dynasty (1644–1911), *weiqi* became less popular in the royal court and started to become popular in literati and folk classes. From the manuals of *weiqi* players such as Huang Longshi, Xu Xingyou, Liang Weijin, Shi Ding'an, and Fan Xiping, *weiqi* skill had already reached its highest level in ancient China.

Although playing *weiqi* requires few resources, its development depends on the prosperity of the people. In the late-Qing period, the Chinese economy declined amid foreign invasions and domestic rebellions. Because of social unrest, there were no national *weiqi* organizations or tournaments. *Weiqi* players could not even fill their bellies. They could only live by gambling, which greatly limited the level of professional players. In 1909 a Japanese professional came to China and defeated all of China's famous players. This shocked the Chinese *weiqi* society and at the same time forced China to rethink its *weiqi* tradition. First, China canceled the previous *weiqi* rules. Second, influenced by Japan, Chinese *weiqi* players started to pay attention to the opening, endgame, and whole-board thinking instead of just focusing on fighting. Many players such as Gu Shuiru and Wu Qingyuan (Go Seigen) went to Japan to study. Prior to the 1940s, with the exception of Wu Qingyuan, Chinese *weiqi* players were much weaker than the Japanese.

After 1949 and the founding of the People's Republic of China, *weiqi* entered a new era. With the support of government, the Beijing Weiqi Club was set up. It has been formally acknowledged as a national sport event since 1956. In 1962 the China Weiqi Association was founded. In 1964 China published the "China *Weiqi* Player Dan-System Regulation." From then *weiqi* had formal organizations and a competition system. At the same time, communication between China and Japan became more frequent.

In the chaos of the Cultural Revolution, which began in 1966, *weiqi* was criticized as part of the "four olds," (old culture, old customs, old habits, old ideas), and nobody dared to play. In 1973, as the Cultural Revolution wound down, the national *weiqi* competition recovered; then in 1976 a Chinese team defeated Japan for the first time in a friendly match, in which Chinese player Nie Weiping won six games out of seven. In 1985 the friendly match was renamed the Sino-Japan Weiqi Match. China won the first three sessions, which symbolized the recovery of Chinese *weiqi* as a sport.

At the same time that Chinese players regained world-class form, the Japanese went ahead with research on *weiqi* culture and helped to spread the game to Western countries. In March 2016, *weiqi* made global news when Google's computer program AlphaGo defeated the *weiqi* world champion, South Korean Lee Sedol. The man-versus-machine headline has provided *weiqi* with a recent surge of worldwide interest in the game. Today more than 60 countries have official organizations and take part in the annual World Amateur Weiqi Championship.

In Europe and America, there are about 10 professional *weiqi* players and 200,000 active amateur players. It can be said that whether as sport, art, or culture, in the 21st century, *weiqi* will continue moving into a new realm.

To learn more about *weiqi*, see the following websites:

- Many young Westerners play *weiqi* after watching this anime series: Hikaru No Go. www.youtube.com/watch?v=F6D8_vZ4zJk&list=PLy6qUnpsApbr DNbLrr_KiV5aqQmNqW9ie
- The most comprehensive *weiqi* library: Sensei's Library. http://senseis.xmp.net.
- A lively 15-minute film introducing the basic rules of *weiqi*: https://www. youtube.com/watch?v=6P0IxBlR9hE
- The three best online *weiqi* servers: www.gokgs.com; www.tygembaduk. com; http://pandanet-igs.com/communities/pandanet.

Yuanbo Zhang

See also: Video Games, China (Chapter 7: Video Games)

Further Reading

Moskowitz, Marc. 2013. *Go Nation: Chinese Masculinities and the Game of Weiqi in China.* Berkeley: University of California.

Ng Jun Sen. 2016. "Interest in Weiqi Peaks after Computer Beats Top Player." *AsiaOne.* March 20. http://news.asiaone.com/news/singapore/interest-weiqi-peaks-after-computer -beats-top-player. Accessed March 26, 2016.

Shotwell, Peter. 2003. *Go! More Than a Game.* Boston: Tuttle Publishing.

Toshiro, Kageyama. 1996. *Lessons in the Fundamentals of Go.* Santa Monica, CA: Kiseido Publishing Co.

Zhang, Ni. 1368. *The Classic of Weiqi in Thirteen Chapters.* Beijing: National Library of China.

YOGA

The practice of yoga is a physical, mental, and spiritual discipline originating in India over 5,000 years ago. While there are many disagreements among scholars and practitioners of yoga over its meaning and origins, taking a look at the literal translation of the word "yoga" offers us a concrete starting point in defining this ambiguous discipline. The word "yoga" means "to yoke" (as in connecting two animals with a harness or yoke in order to pull a plow or cart) in the ancient Indic language of Sanskrit. Yoga is therefore generally described as the act of unifying the mind with the body, with yoga serving like a yoke as the connection between these two.

The history and origins of yoga remain contested due to the fact that the teachings of yoga were transmitted orally, from teacher to student. While there may have been some early records of certain teachings, these would have been written on palm leaves or thin paper, which were eventually lost or destroyed. This makes uncovering the earliest foundations of yoga a very challenging and perhaps impossible task for the scholar. Among texts that still exist, the word "yoga" was first mentioned in the *Rig Veda*, a sacred Indian text written in Sanskrit, composed in the second millennium BCE. The *Rig Veda* (also rendered *Rigveda*) is a collection of hymns and is widely considered to be the oldest and most important of the Vedic texts.

Scholars and teachers of yoga alike have claimed different legacies and lineages of yoga. Among the most prominent was Patanjali, an Indian sage who lived in the fourth and fifth centuries CE. Patanjali's *Yoga Sutras* is generally believed to be the first compendium of yoga. The word *sutra* literally means either "thread" or "rule" in Sanskrit, and Patanjali's text consists of brief statements on yoga and more general philosophy. The text seems to have been widely circulated and translated in its early years but then saw little popularity for about 1,000 years until its rediscovery in the late 19th and early 20th centuries. In the past century, many practitioners of yoga as we know it today found their inspiration in Patanjali's *Yoga Sutras*.

In its earliest forms, the physical aspect of yoga was developed as a means to enhance meditation. The practice known today as hatha yoga (literally "forceful yoga") emphasizes the physical discipline of the practice, which in turn prepares the practitioner for meditation. This vigorous physical discipline, then, was actually meant to help the practitioner sit still. Through a series of poses, the practitioner could calm the muscles, nervous system, and the mind through dedication to this practice.

Today there are many schools of yoga, with various types of yoga being created just in the past 20 years. Although the true foundations of yoga are ambiguous, many scholars say that yoga as we know it today was founded by Tirumalai Krishnamacharya (1888–1989), considered the grandfather of yoga. Krishnamacharya was a yoga teacher and healer and also a scholar of Indian philosophy who shared his teachings in his books. He brought together yoga teachings with ayurvedic medicine and traditional Indian philosophy. Many students of yoga believe that almost every school of yoga in the world stems from Krishnamacharya's teachings. He was also known as the "teacher of teachers," having also taught B. K. S. Iyengar and Pattahbi Jois, who became two of the world's prominent yoga teachers and went on to create their own schools of yoga.

Bellur Krishnamachar Sundaraja Iyengar (1918–2014) studied under Tirumalai Krishnamacharya, who was also his brother-in-law. Iyengar later created his own school of yoga, and this is known today as Iyengar yoga. Iyengar elaborated on Krishnamacharya's method by approaching the yoga poses scientifically. A progressive approach was developed from simple to difficult poses, and he categorized each pose by its effects on the nervous system: purifying, pacifying, stimulating, nourishing, and cleansing. The school of Iyengar is alignment-based yoga with great attention to detail, and props like blocks and straps are generally provided for precision in the practitioner's alignment. The famous violinist Yehudi Menuin (1916–1999) became a student of Iyengar and later invited him to North America, which popularized the practice of yoga almost immediately. In 1965 Iyengar wrote *Light on Yoga*, which became an international best seller, considered by some to be the "bible of yoga."

K. Pattabhi Jois (1915–2009) also studied under Tirumalai Krishnamacharya along with Iyengar. Jois later developed the practice of ashtanga yoga. Ashtanga derived its name from Patanjali's *Yoga Sutras*, noted above, and literally means "eight-limbed yoga," referring to the eight limbs or aspects of yoga as compiled by Patanjali. Ashtanga yoga became hugely popular in the West, including among celebrities. Jois opened his own school of yoga, The Ashtanga Institute, in Mysore, India. Ashtanga yoga is quite different from the precise and deliberate practice of Iyengar Yoga. It involves a fast-paced sequence of yoga poses that are sometimes held for long periods while controlling the breath.

Besides these foundational figures, there are many other fascinating individuals who have been a part of the development of yoga both in India and around the world. In the 1890s, a Hindu monk known as Swami Vivekananda (born Narendranath Dutta, 1863–1902) toured the United States and Great Britain, lecturing on spirituality and captivated his audiences. Like Jois, he also interpreted Patanjali's *Yoga Sutras*, but unlike Krishnamacharya, Jois, and Iyengar, he emphasized yoga without the vigorous physical practice, instead emphasizing meditation, visualization, and breath work. Rabindranath Tagore (1861–1941) also spread teachings of Indian spirituality through the 19th and 20th centuries.

Another remarkable figure who served to further popularize yoga was Indra Devi (born Eugenie Peterson, 1899–2002). Born in Latvia, she was inspired by Tagore's writings and traveled to India to become one of Krishnamacharya's students. A truly global figure, Devi traveled to China in the 1930s and taught yoga classes to many students, including China's first lady, Song Meiling (Madame Chiang Kai-shek). Devi also taught in many other countries, including Mexico, Argentina, and perhaps most famously, she taught yoga to some of the biggest stars of Hollywood in the 1940s and 1950s, like Greta Garbo and Gloria Swanson. Devi notably taught a form of yoga that was separate from the religious dimension that some had incorporated into their practice, and in this way, made yoga something that could perhaps be more easily introduced to many other cultures.

In recent decades, many schools of yoga and variations on the practice have been introduced, such as yoga for various physical ailments like arthritis. Research has shown the positive effects of yoga and meditation on both the physical and psychological health of practitioners. Some teachers and practitioners of yoga incorporate a practice designed to help cope with depression and posttraumatic stress disorder (PTSD). In the past few years, advocates of yoga's health benefits have encouraged the adoption of yoga in schools. This initially encountered resistance from parents who were concerned that their children would be indoctrinated with the tenets of Hinduism, but informed educators could point to the legacy of teachers like Indra Devi to demonstrate that yoga could still provide profound benefits without the religious or spiritual dimension.

Along with yoga's increasing popularity around the world, there has also been a commercialization of yoga, as it has become a multibillion-dollar industry. With accessories and other products from yoga mats to hair bands and pants, yoga is used to sell any number of must-have commodities, despite the simplicity and austerity of the practice's roots. As the number of yoga practitioners increases and its many forms proliferate, its popularity seems assured for decades and perhaps centuries to come.

Katherine M. Jakovich

See also: Regional and Unique Sports

Further Reading

Bryant, Edwin F. 2009. *The Yoga Sutras of Patanjali*. New York: North Point Press.
Devi, Indra. 2002. *Yoga for You*. Layton, UT: Gibbs Smith.
Iyengar, B. K. S. 1995 [1979]. *Light on Yoga*, rev. ed. New York: Schocken.
Syman, Stefanie. 2010. *The Subtle Body: The Story of Yoga in America*. New York: Farrar, Straus and Giroux.

Chapter 7: Video Games

Introduction

At the time of writing, over a billion people spend at least an hour a day playing video games. This is a remarkable figure to consider. Popular culture, especially for young people, often involves playing video games of various kinds. Broadly defined, video games are simply any electronic games that involve human interaction and visual (video) feedback on any kind of device that displays feedback to the user. Playing video games, or gaming, is wildly popular, and while the pastime got off to a slow start with various prototypes and experiments in the mid-20th century, in the 1970s, and more definitively by the 1980s, many different platforms emerged to make video games a common hobby and source of entertainment around the world.

For those who came of age in the 1980s, thinking about video games may conjure images of arcade-style games, booths in noisy public spaces where one or two users insert a few coins and play a limited game. Jumping ahead to the time of

Indonesian Video Games

Gaming in Indonesia, as elsewhere in the world, is largely the product of global gaming industries. The games are largely imported, but there exists a growing network of locally produced online games catering specifically to Indonesian audiences. *Nusantara Online* (*The Online Archipelago*) is a massively multiplayer online role-playing game (MMORPG) that started in 2006 by a group of college students at the Bandung Institute of Technology (ITB) in West Java. Its creators were critical of foreign cultural influences in Indonesia as a result of the importation of foreign television, films, and games. They created a game to promote Indonesian national identity by basing the narrative content of *Nusantara Online* on a massive database of Indonesian historical content. Players choose an avatar—priest, warrior, archer, magician, or assassin—and embark on a series of missions drawn from precolonial Indonesian history, namely the kingdoms of Majapahit, Sriwijaya, and Pajajaran. While *Nusantara Online* has yet to outsell most imported games, the desire to create more locally generated gaming content marks a shift in the gaming industry in Indonesia. Local and international game developers are aware of the potential for huge growth in the Indonesian market.

Megan Robin Hewitt

writing, today the video-game world is hugely diverse, and games are more commonly played on personal computers or on specialized game consoles in the home. In many regions of Asia, the Internet café is also an extremely popular place for video games, somewhat reminiscent of video-game arcades of the past.

Today, video games can be very simple puzzle games like *Candy Crush Saga*, generally played on a cell phone to pass the time; but they can also be spectacularly complex "massively multiplayer online role-playing games" (MMORPG) like *World of Warcraft*. Playing video games can involve anything from dipping into your cell phone at the bus stop for a few rounds of a puzzle game or ferociously competing with faceless opponents around the world in a role-playing game that keeps you glued to your seat for hours, or in extreme cases, even days.

In Asia and Oceania, as in other parts of the world, video-game culture has taken hold among a significant part of the population and has come to define much of the identity of its most devoted adherents. This subculture of new media is somewhat vaguely defined, but it has become closely connected with various Internet platforms and naturally thus involves games and gamers that are played largely online. These involve the conventional video games like *Quake*, *World of Warcraft*, *Halo*, and others, but also more immersive games that include augmented reality or artificial reality. In these latter forms of gaming, the player has an avatar representation of her or himself in the cyberspace of the game, and this avatar can go about ordinary activities, from educational projects to simple daily chores. *Sims* and *Second Life* draw huge followings, and they give rise to the debate of whether these seemingly social interactions are not, in fact, taking the gamers out of the real world and into more asocial environments online.

Further, in many conventional video games, extreme violence is commonplace, including the disturbingly prevalent episodes of sexism and dehumanizing sexual violence. While there is a substantial community of female gamers in Asia, the preponderance of gamers both at home and in Internet cafés are male. Critics of the gaming world contend that the regularity of violence, disturbing imagery, and almost institutionalized sexism and dehumanization of women within the games has led to a subculture that is desensitized to, or worse, accepting of, the kind of imagery depicted in the games. Scandals surrounding these and other negative portrayals of video gaming have done little to dissuade the massive numbers of video-game enthusiasts.

Another dubious aspect of video games in Asia is the phenomenon known as "gold farming," in which one participant goes through the sometimes exhausting process of progressing a video-game avatar to a certain stage of a game and then sells that avatar to someone else who did not want to bother with the lower stages of the game. Much gold farming takes place within the People's Republic of China (PRC), in spite of a ban on the practice. Chinese gamers make it their daily work to kill monsters, collect virtual points, or do whatever else is involved in a particular game, and then they advertise the avatar that they have advanced to a certain level. Millions of U.S. dollars are spent every year for these services, and the illegality of the practice means that it is carried out similarly to any illicit practice, and some label this sweatshop work and exploitative.

Japanese Video Games

Japan has long been one of the most important video-gaming countries. Some of today's most popular video-game companies originated in Japan and are still based there. In the early history of video gaming, Japan's Nintendo and Sega gaming systems were among the most popular all around the world. Taito and Namco are among Japan's many other prominent video-game producers. Video gaming in Japan followed the course of much of the rest of the world, from arcade-style games to home console games, and now increasingly to mobile gaming, especially on cell phones. In fact, at the time of writing, Japan comprises the world's largest market for mobile games. As one of the earliest gaming cultures, and host of many of the industry's pioneers, Japan continues to be an important leader in global video-game culture today.

Jeremy A. Murray

E-sports, or multiplayer video-game tournaments, are especially popular in the PRC, South Korea, Japan, and Taiwan. Professional gamers from these regions, especially South Korea, consistently perform very well in these huge competitions, such as the League of Legends World Championship, that draw millions of viewers. The prizes for the winning individuals or teams include trophies and huge cash rewards, sometimes as much as a million U.S. dollars. These global competitions host gamers from all around the world, but in recent years it seems that especially competitors from the above-mentioned regions seem to dominate the upper echelons of play. A culture of fans and regimented training in South Korea reflects a greater infrastructure that supports e-sports in a way perhaps unfamiliar to a foreign observer.

While some might be puzzled by the categorization of video games as a sport, like including chess or checkers, there are those who would defend gaming as not only a sport but an educational, productive, and even healthy choice. Puzzle games and so-called brain-training games have surged in popularity. Some educators have begun experimenting with various kinds of video games in the classroom. The massive appeal of video games is undeniable, and their hold in Asia and Oceania represents a crucial component of popular culture in these regions.

Jeremy A. Murray and Kathleen M. Nadeau

Further Reading

Barboza, David. 2005. "Ogre to Slay? Outsource It to Chinese." *New York Times*. December 9. http://www.nytimes.com/2005/12/09/technology/ogre-to-slay-outsource-it-to-chinese.html. Accessed March 26, 2016.

Groen, Andrew. 2013. "Why Gamers in Asia Are the World's Best eSport Athletes." *PC World*. May 14.

Owen, Phil. 2015. *WTF Is Wrong with Video Games?: How a Multi-Billion-Dollar Creative Industry Refuses to Grow Up*. Seattle: Amazon Digital Services, Inc.

Wolf, Mark J. P., ed. 2008. *The Video Game Explosion: A History from PONG to PlayStation and Beyond*. Westport, CT: Greenwood Press.

GAMING, PHILIPPINES

The industry of video gaming is strong and has grown despite economic challenges. However, piracy, a practice defined by *Black's Law Dictionary* as the "unauthorized and illegal reproduction or distribution of materials protected by rights," presents a major hindrance to this industry's sustained success. The case of the Philippines, a country that possesses one of the fastest-growing economies in Southeast Asia, attests to this conundrum. Video gaming is prevalent in the country, yet the prohibitive cost of legitimately acquiring hardware (consoles, hand-held devices, and computers) and software (CDs, DVDs, Blu-rays) has motivated many gamers to seek alternative, often illegal sources of these goods. As a result, the distribution of cheap, illegal copies of video games, an undeniably lucrative venture, has proliferated. The emergence of an underground economy that supports and benefits from piracy has made it difficult for government authorities to put a stop to this illegal activity. When one considers how vast and deeply entrenched the piracy network has become, questions as to why current legislation criminalizing the aforementioned has been ineffective somehow become moot. Other notable factors that have contributed to the prevalence of piracy in the Philippines include the dearth of resources for and the lack of interest in tackling the problem, the lack of education and institutional support within the nation, and the lenient application of laws by the courts and police.

According to a Business Software Alliance-International Data Group (BSA-IDG) study on global piracy, software piracy in the Philippines declined from 71 percent in 2005 to 69 percent in 2008. Financial losses due to piracy, however, rose from $76 million to $212 million during the same time period. It also estimates that a 10-point reduction of the 71 percent piracy rate in 2005 would have produced an additional $32 million in tax revenues and $623 million to the economy. These numbers are important because news about these disturbing losses engenders a climate of ambivalence among companies that intend to invest in the Philippines. Weak intellectual property rights enforcement strongly discourages the strengthening of international trade partnerships between the Philippines and other countries and impairs its economic status. Potential investors are also bound to suffer substantial losses if this predicament remains preponderant. Furthermore, copyright holders are not recognized for their creative work. Protecting the creator's economic incentives counts as one of the major tenets of intellectual property law. If creators of video games fail to earn just compensation for their work, the dissemination of new ideas and innovations in the future will be effectively curtailed.

To combat piracy and protect the copyrights and patents of creators and authors, the Philippine government passed its own set of property laws. Specifically, the Intellectual Property Code was ratified on June 6, 1997, and amended on March 28, 2001. It established the Intellectual Property Office (IPO) and authorized this agency to carry out statutes and punish violators of the code. Addressing copy-right infringement comprises one of the major provisions. Penalties include the seizure of products that have been subjected to infringement, the forfeiture of all property involved in the infringement, and the imposition of substantial administrative fines. The individuals who crafted the code drew insight from and incorporated provisions from the Berne Convention, intellectual property laws from the United States, and the Trade-Related Aspects of Intellectual Property Rights (TRIPS). The Berne Convention for the Protection of Literary and Artistic Works, an international agreement that covers "every production in the literary, scientific and artistic domain, whatever the mode of expression," rests on two foundational principles. First, member countries are obligated to provide works of nationals from other Berne member countries the same protections afforded the works of local authors. Second, member countries are expected to meet a minimum set of criteria when they craft their copyright laws. Berne adherents are also expected to award authors "exclusive rights to make and authorize translation, reproduction, public performance, and adaptation of their works." Expanding upon the Berne provisions, the TRIPS agreement included "protection for computer programs as literary works" and the "original selection or arrangement of databases." Unlike the Berne agreement, it outlines a "more extensive [set of] civil and criminal enforcement obligations."

The Philippine government has identified several obstacles to sustaining initiatives against piracy. Based on Jennifer Kim Vitale's study of video-game piracy in the country, the lack of coherence and cohesiveness in government actions resulting from the presence of different mandates for enhancing the intellectual property system constitutes one of the significant stumbling blocks. Also, the absence of reliable records on enforcement and prosecution contributes to the lack of transparency in operations and the insufficiency of data that inform strategic and tactical operations and policy making. Public awareness and knowledge on how to address the piracy problem has likewise been low. This is further reinforced by the shortage of institutional and personnel support from the intellectual property (IP) community. Furthermore, corruption, organized crime, and other political factors have reinforced such deficiencies.

At the level of the household, piracy has afforded many families a sustainable livelihood. Thus, involvement in illicit activities has become a matter of survival rather than of right or wrong. Eliminating piracy, in other words, would deny people job opportunities that promise a steady source of income. For individuals who cannot afford to purchase video-game hardware and software at legitimate prices because doing so would take away a huge percentage of their annual income, cheap and relatively accessible pirated software has been a viable option. In 2008 the National Statistics Office (NSO) reported that the average family income in 2006 was P173,000 or roughly US$3,700. Hence, it becomes evident that a video game that would sell for $60 in the United States (with an average family income between $50,000 and $60,000) would be too expensive for gamers in the Philippines.

Providing further motivation to the local piracy industry is the underground sub-culture that has developed and entrenched itself over time. Individuals who supply illegal copies of video games and their clients observe an unwritten code of honor. Akin to legitimate exchanges involving business partners, deals and agreements are kept, payments are made on time, and obligations between transacting parties are fulfilled. The local piracy industry further boasts of a robust network that extends overseas as smuggling of pirated goods into the Philippines has become prevalent. In fact, considerable amounts of pirated gaming paraphernalia have been circulating via underground yet established "trade routes." This development has made it more cumbersome for authorities to stifle illegal operations. Conflicting interests of the video-gaming industry with regard to the defense of intellectual property rights has also motivated activities that endorse piracy. By providing gamers with "legitimate" channels to discover game secrets or leaks, a marketing ploy to boost sales, the video-game industry has indirectly urged gamers to hack technological protection measures (TPMS) of video games.

Finally, Vitale maintains that the sponsorship of piracy by wealthy and well-connected Filipinos undermines efforts to eradicate illicit activities. In fact, stall owners of pirated goods are well organized and are believed to enjoy ample protection from enforcement authorities. It is also believed that they have developed an intricate communication system that warns them of impending raids.

Enrique Niño P. Leviste

See also: Mobile Phones, Philippines (Chapter 5: Internet and Social Media); Social Media, Philippines (Chapter 5: Internet and Social Media)

Further Reading

Sumo, Ryan. 2008. "Piracy and the Underground Economy." *The Escapist.* June 15. www .escapistmagazine.com/articles/view/video-games/issues/issue_158/5045-Piracy-and -the-Underground-Economy. Accessed May 26, 2015.
Vitale, Jennifer Kim. 2010. "Video Game Piracy in the Philippines: A Narrowly Tailored Analysis of the Video Game Industry & Subculture." *Pace International Law Review* 22: 297–329.

VIDEO GAMES, AUSTRALIA AND NEW ZEALAND

Video games are now both a form of mass-media popular entertainment and also an art form, with the soundtrack for the DICE award-winning PlayStation3 game *Journey* (2012) nominated for a Grammy Award in 2013. A recent annual survey by the Interactive Games and Entertainment Association revealed that gaming is now a mainstream activity in Australian households, showing the profile of the average Australian gamer to be a 32-year-old male who plays games for two hours daily, and that 47 percent of Australian women also play video games. Award-winning video-game journalist Jason Hill started the popular Fairfax Media newspaper syndicated weblog *Screen Play*, an Australian game news and review site that ran from 2006 to 2014. The video-game-review television show *Good Game*, hosted by Bajo and Hex, has also screened on ABC Television since 2006, providing current video-game reviews and news.

Game players may be seen as "casual," "hardcore" gamers, and new players (also known as "noobs," short for "newbie"), with both hardcore and casual gamers also comprising a large online community, and with perennial discourse topics including whether violence in games causes violence in real life; ethical issues and so-called "moral panics" around sexism and misogyny (such as the 2014 "Gamergate" controversy), ageism, racism, and religious discrimination in games; and whether video games are an art form or not. In the subgenre of "serious games," a controversial independent video game *Escape from Woomera* was developed in Australia in 2003–2004 and depicted asylum-seeker refugees held by the Australian government in an illegal-immigration mandatory detention facility. Also controversially, until the implementation of an R18+ rating in 2013, Australia's highest available rating classification for video games was MA15+, meaning that various adult-market video games either required modification before release or were refused classification. Notably, the first video-game transmedia "adaptation" of J. R. R. Tolkien's novel *The Hobbit* (1937) was developed by Australian company Beam Software and published in 1982 by Melbourne House, becoming a best-selling computer game.

Historically, popular video games in Australia and New Zealand, in general, have been similar to those in the United States and United Kingdom. The NPD Group Inc. tracks video-game retail sales across the various available Australian (i.e., PAL, as opposed to NTSC television format) territory game platforms, namely PlayStation3, Xbox360, Wii, PlayStation4, Windows/Mac computer games, Nintendo DualScreen, Nintendo 3DS, XboxOne, Wii U, PlayStation2, PlayStation Portable, PlayStation Vita, DOS, GameBoy Advance, Xbox, and GameCube. The best-selling games in certain of these platforms (in terms of retail sales revenue) as tracked by NPD Group are as follows. The top 10 PlayStation3 games include: *Grand Theft Auto V*; *Call of Duty: Black Ops, Modern Warfare 3*, and *Black Ops II*; *Gran Turismo 5*; *Red Dead Redemption*; *Call of Duty: Ghosts*; *Battlefield 3*; *The Last of Us*; and *Elder Scrolls V: Skyrim*. Similarly, on Xbox360, the top 10 titles include *Grand Theft Auto V*; *Call of Duty: Black Ops I and II*; *Halo: Reach*; *Call of Duty: Modern Warfare 3*; *Halo 4*; *Elder Scrolls V: Skyrim*; *Red Dead Redemption*; *Battlefield 3*; and *Call of Duty: Ghosts*. On Nintendo Wii, the top 10 games are *Fit Plus*; *New Super Mario Bros. Wii*; *Mario Kart Wii*; *Donkey Kong Country Returns*; *Super Mario Galaxy 2*; *Wii Sports Resort*; *Skylanders Giants*; *Skylanders: Spyro's Adventure*; *Just Dance 2*; and *Just Dance*. On PlayStation4, the top-selling titles have included *Call of Duty: Advanced Warfare*; *Grand Theft Auto V*; *Watch Dogs*; *FIFA 15*; *Destiny*; *Far Cry 4*; *The Last of Us*; *Call Of Duty: Ghosts*; *Assassin's Creed: Unity*; and *Assassin's Creed IV: Black Flag*.

These most popular PlayStation4 titles listed above also reveal an older, more adult target market compared to the Nintendo Wii console; the list also indicates the popularity of soccer (e.g., *FIFA*) games in the Australian/New Zealand game market and also on television, particularly on the Special Broadcasting Service (SBS-TV), which caters to Australians of ethnic, including European, descent and

Video games continue to be very popular in Australia and New Zealand, as they are throughout Oceania, Asia, and the world. Here, gamers at the 2015 EB Games Expo in Sydney, Australia, play *Street Fighter V*. For some people, video gaming has become a serious competitive activity, with national and international competitions bringing huge prizes and large global audiences. (mjmediabox/Alamy Stock Photo)

culture, among whom soccer (aka "football") is traditionally popular. On Windows/Mac, the best-selling titles include *Starcraft II: Wings of Liberty*; *Diablo III*; *The Sims 3*; *World of Warcraft: Cataclysm*; *The Sims 3: Pets*; *The Sims 3: Ambitions Expansion Pack*; *The Sims 3: Late Night Expansion Pack*; *Starcraft II: Heart of the Swarm Expansion Pack*; *WoW: Mists of Pandaria Expansion Pack*; and *The Elder Scrolls Online*. The popular computer game (combined Windows/Mac) titles list above reveals the tendency of computer gamers (as opposed to console game players) to prefer role-playing games (RPGs) such as the *Starcraft*, *Diablo*, and *WoW* games, and also "life-simulation" games (e.g., *The Sims* sequels and expansions). Both computer-screen resolutions and combination keyboard/mouse game control systems can lend themselves better to RPGs and simulations, where more complex game inputs may be required and more onscreen detail is desirable, noting also that many console gamers also have HD or Ultra-HD television sets. On Nintendo DS, the most popular titles are *Pokemon White*, *Pokemon Black*, *and Pokemon Soulsilver*; *Mario Kart DS*; *New Super Mario Bros DS*; *Pokemon HeartGold*, *Pokemon Black*, *and Pokemon White Version 2*; *Moshi Monsters: Moshling Zoo*; and *Art Academy*.

These popular Nintendo DS games above indicate the success of the Pokemon transmedia story world (spanning across games, movies, television, comics, and other media) and also the general skew toward a younger audience of the Nintendo

DS platform, including also the painting and drawing training game *Art Academy*. In the older DOS games domain, the popular titles have historically included *20,000 Leagues under the Sea*; *Death Rally*; *Sam and Max Hit the Road*; *Leisure Suit Larry*; *Sport of Kings*; *Rome*; *Winter Sports*; *Amazon*; *Police Quest II*; and *Worms United*. These older DOS (disk operating system) games also reveal some popular titles from the 1980s and 1990s, including various "graphical text adventure game" series such as *Police Quest* and *Leisure Suit Larry*. *Sam and Max Hit the Road* was a cult comedy classic from LucasArts based on the comic, and it could also be argued the *Worms* series gameplay later evolved into similar action-strategy-style games such as *Angry Birds*.

Some famous games developed in Australia include *Ty the Tasmanian Tiger*, developed by Krome Studios (EA Games, 2002); *Looney Tunes: Acme Arsenal*, developed by Redtribe (Warner Bros Interactive, 2007); and *Fruit Ninja* (Halfbrick Studios, 2010). Game developers who have created Australian Football League (aka AFL, or Australian-rules football games) on various game platforms include Beam Software, Electronic Arts, Wicked Witch Software, Big Ant Studios, and IR Gurus (aka Transmission Games).

J. T. Velikovsky

See also: Popular Transmedia, Australia (Chapter 5: Internet and Social Media); Social Media, Australia (Chapter 5: Internet and Social Media)

Further Reading

Australian Interactive Games & Entertainment Association. www.igea.net. Accessed March 26, 2016.

Game Connect Asia Pacific (Australian-region annual game developer conference). http://gcap.com.au. Accessed March 26, 2016.

Jenkins, H. 2004. *First Person: New Media as Story, Performance, and Game*. Cambridge, MA: MIT Press.

NPD Group's Games Market Research (Australia/New Zealand). www.thenpdgroup.com.au/wps/portal/npd/au/industry-expertise/video-games. Accessed March 26, 2016.

Tsumea (Australia and New Zealand game developer news website). www.tsumea.com. Accessed March 26, 2016.

VIDEO GAMES, CHINA

The Chinese video-game market, encompassing PC, mobile, and console-based gaming, is an increasingly important part of the global game industry. Despite many complex regulations, including bans and censorship, as well as concerns about piracy and intellectual property rights, the market has grown by leaps and bounds since the introduction of home console systems in the late 1980s. Revenues from the Chinese market are, as of 2015, second only to those of North America. The game industry in China is increasingly important within both East Asian and global contexts.

Early home console systems of the 1980s, such as the Nintendo Entertainment System (NES), were rarely found in China, largely due to their astronomical price. However, from 1987, Chinese companies began making third-party machines (popularly known as "clones") that could play copies of original releases. These systems, such as the NES clone produced by Little Tyrant (Xiao Bawang 小霸王), were far less expensive than legitimate consoles, and the game cartridges often included multiple games. These systems remained popular in China (as well as Hong Kong and Taiwan) until the early 2000s, particularly clones of the NES, Super Nintendo, and Sega Genesis.

The Chinese government was very concerned about the impact playing video games had on children. In 2000 the Ministry of Culture announced a ban on the sale of consoles, despite the small market share claimed by legitimate systems, citing concerns over the physical and mental well-being of children. This made it technically illegal for companies like Sony and Microsoft to sell their PlayStation or Xbox systems in China, but such systems were imported and sold illegally. This was actually a "gray market" environment, as the ban was not strongly enforced. In contrast to black markets, which require some degree of secrecy, gray-market transactions take place quite openly. Consumers in major cities such as Shanghai and Beijing were able to purchase legitimate games and systems, often imported from Hong Kong, Macau, or Taiwan. While many people imagine China as a land of cheap and perhaps pirated goods, the prices for such gray-market goods often met or exceeded prices in Japan, North America, or Europe. However, consoles were often sold with many pirated games already installed.

Despite the ban, not all systems remained illegal. Beginning in 2003, Nintendo, under the brand iQue, has produced and sold China-specific "plug-and-play" systems that do not require the purchase of separate games. The iQue DS, a handheld platform, is a Nintendo DS with Chinese-region settings. Nevertheless, cloned systems (such as the "Vii") remained very popular—and much cheaper—alternatives to even these legal consoles.

In early 2014, the State Council announced that it was lifting the ban on console sales in the Shanghai Free Trade Zone, which had been created the previous year. This meant that consoles such as the Sony PlayStation4 and the Microsoft Xbox One could legally and freely be sold in Shanghai. But because these consoles were, in fact, available previously, the expected demand is not particularly high. According to some researchers, most console gamers in China have modified systems that can play pirated games, few are willing to pay retail prices for packaged games (downloading pirated copies instead), and they are often unable to utilize online features and networks due to controls on the Chinese Internet and company-supported systems.

Another reason the lifting of the console ban may not have as large an impact as some people speculate is that PC gaming remains the most important market sector in China, with nearly $15 billion in revenues during 2014. While the kinds of games people play are very similar to other markets, the locations where people play PC games are often quite different. Beginning in the late 1990s, Internet cafés (wangba 网吧) began to appear in China due to the expense of personal computers and Internet connections. These days, although computer ownership and Internet access have increased dramatically over the past decade, some game players continue to frequent cafés. This means that for subscription-based gaming services, Chinese players tend to pay on an hour-to-hour basis, versus a monthly subscription, as is common elsewhere.

One of the most popular types of games in China is the massively multiplayer online role-playing game (MMORPG), where players create an avatar, kill enemies, and complete quests, all in a persistent world (one that continues even when the player logs off). Presently, domestic Chinese game companies, such as Tencent, NetEase, Shanda, Perfect World, and Kingsoft, dominate the domestic market, but many foreign games—particularly games from Korean and U.S. developers—have enjoyed broad popularity. One of the best examples is Blizzard Entertainment's *World of Warcraft* (*WoW*). Because MMORPGs and other online games require ongoing support, the relationship of foreign developers to the Chinese market is different from that for games that can be played offline. Foreign companies must partner with a Chinese company, which handles localization (translation of the game into Chinese), technical support, and interactions with the Chinese government.

MMORPGs have also been the focus of sustained government regulation. In 2006, citing fears of addiction, the government insisted that game companies implement a timer system to limit the amount of access minors would have to online games. Government ministries have also required changes to games, such as removing skeleton enemies in *WoW* in 2007, again citing concerns over appropriateness of content for the Chinese market. However, similar content often appears in domestically produced Chinese MMORPGs, leading to speculation that such regulations have an economic motive. Regulation is further complicated by the fact that two government ministries—the Ministry of Culture (MoC) and the General Association of Press and Publication (GAPP)—often disagree on issues of censorship and regulation. This means that companies often receive conflicting messages, creating confusion for developers and irritation among players. For instance, an expansion to *WoW* was approved by the MoC in 2009, only to have GAPP announce several months later that the game was operating illegally and needed to be halted. These announcements often have less to do with the games themselves and more to do with an internal power struggle within the Chinese government.

Despite such regulation issues, expansion into the burgeoning Chinese market has been a high priority for foreign companies. But Chinese players also comprise an important and sometimes problematic part of in-game economies, particularly in "real money transactions" (RMT), or the purchase of digital goods for actual currency. The most well-known examples are found in MMORPGs, such as *WoW*. Popularly known as "gold farming" (known in Chinese as *daG* 打, G meaning "gold"), workers (known as "gold farmers") collect in-game currency and items to be sold to other players, usually in the West, for actual real-world currency. In an alternative method, workers create powerful in-game avatars, which are then sold to players. Many game operators expressly ban these kinds of transactions in their game, but RMTs have proven difficult to regulate. They also create tension between Chinese and foreign players, who often believe all Chinese players must be gold farmers.

Despite the challenges posed by operating within China, domestic and foreign companies are eager to expand in one of the world's most profitable and fastest-growing markets. In addition to the robust PC gaming sector, mobile games (played on phones) are developing quickly. In a global context, the Chinese market is no longer secondary to other East Asian countries but a vital part of the global industry.

Maggie Greene

See also: Internet Addiction, China (Chapter 5: Internet and Social Media)

Further Reading

Jin, Ge. *Gold Farmers*. www.chinesegoldfarmers.com. Accessed May 31, 2015.

Lindtner, Silvia, and Marcella Szablewicz. 2011. "China's Many Internets: Participation and Digital Game Play across a Changing Technology Landscape." In *Online Society in China: Creating, Celebrating, and Instrumentalising the Online Carnival*. Ed. David Kurt Herold and Peter Marolt, 89–105. New York: Routledge.

Nardi, Bonnie, and Yong Ming Kow. 2010. "Digital Imaginaries: How We Know What We (Think We) Know about Chinese Gold Farming." *First Mind* 15, no. 6 (June). http://firstmonday.org/ojs/index.php/fm/article/view/3035/2566. Accessed May 31, 2015.

Niko Partners. http://nikopartners.com. Accessed May 31, 2015.

VIDEO GAMES, SOUTH KOREA

Video games have a vastly different public perception in South Korea than in many other countries. Video games in Western countries are often seen as primarily a hobby. In many ways video games are indeed a passive leisure activity in the consciousness of the general public and are even seen as a childish and immature activity. In South Korea, however, video games have recently taken on a cultural status that is generally perceived to be far more socially legitimate and prominent.

Some of this discrepancy can be traced to macroeconomics and political developments throughout the region in recent years. In the late 1990s, there was a currency collapse in Thailand, which had major regional repercussions. South Korean banks were bankrolling large and aggressive business expansion, which led to nonperforming loans, and Kia (South Korea's third-largest auto manufacturer) was compelled to ask for emergency loans to prevent bankruptcy. South Korean currency began plummeting against the U.S. dollar. In response to the crisis, the South Korean government made infrastructure, including telecommunications and the Internet, a priority, as this was an emerging market that could be used to generate more capital and thus avoid a recession. As a result, much of the youth of the time were involved in a telecom boom, and an ancillary result was their attraction to playing video games online, sometimes at the expense of traditional outdoor sports.

In response to this trend toward online gaming and other video games, the government itself created the Korea e-Sports Association. Now the phenomenon that was e-sports had official backing, and from the national government no less, which aided in increasing e-sports' popularity with many South Korean citizens. This, however, does not mean that everyone was invested in these gaming forums. It is still a niche market, but it is growing much faster than in the United States. Perhaps as a direct result of this political and economic investment, video games in South Korea have become more socially acceptable in the eyes of the general public. For example, gaming in South Korea is much more popular among women, and women are included in video-game conventions. In fact, for young people, many dates take place in Internet cafés, with the couple playing video games. In general terms, playing video games is not stigmatized as childish or antisocial in the way it is in the United States and many other regions. In the United States, many politicians of both the left and right have come out against the playing of video games as dangerous to the youth and the moral fabric of society. In the realm of politics, the government has certainly not supported video gaming the way South Korea's government has.

While the perception of video games as a hobby does persist in South Korea, gamers are not seen in that way by those who are involved in the professional gaming community. The life of a professional or extremely avid video-game player is often spent practicing, with few breaks for anything else. In order to be competitive in televised video-game tournaments, the reality of daily life entails playing video games through the entire day until early the following morning. These tournaments require a kind of endurance as well, as they are still a physical activity. Certain games require hundreds of clicks a minute and superb hand-eye coordination. Quick decision making in rapidly changing circumstances is also required. Many hours go into training in order to be successful in these tournaments, as only a few top-placing teams or individuals actually win prize money. Many teenagers and young adults, especially males, have to work to break into the top teams that qualify. There are 12 top teams that can support the many hours of practicing.

Of course, this infrastructural emphasis from the government and social legitimacy, as well as the media and the common perception of gaming, has brought negative as well as positive results. In the United States, it is perhaps the negative perception of video games that tends to make the issue of gaming addiction relatively rare. In the United States, the media and government officials treat video games as an immature activity that needs to be moderated so that individuals can live fulfilling lives. While this opens a debate, the stigmatization of gaming has doubtless served to quietly limit the amount of gaming addiction in the United States. This is very different in South Korea. With so many video-game tournaments, and with winners being placed on pedestals, the enthusiasm surrounding the culture has infused young people with the desire for that fame and prominence. Playing video games professionally is seen as much more attainable than being a professional in sports or popular music, for example. It is estimated that South Korea has the highest rates of video-game addiction in the world and that children are increasingly showing signs of video-game addiction. Further, South Korea has been home to many tragic incidents in which deaths have resulted from excessive gaming; the deaths sometimes occur from the player never ceasing to play, or neglecting a family member or loved one, or even gamers committing murder in order to satisfy their appetite to play or compete.

This startling trend has been confronted in various ways. Many treatment centers have opened to specifically treat addiction to video games, and they focus on "detoxing" the addict and having them engage in other recreational activities. Recently there has been debate and discussion by the government that examines the incentivizing of the playing of video games in the first place, and this includes the possibility of placing a kind of curfew upon video games in order to curb addiction. Such measures have apparently only made things worse in many cases, as games are played during the day instead of studying, and many children use their parents' gaming or e-mail accounts to access games. These are some of the problems of attempting to dissuade citizens from engaging in the activity or even merely moderating the excesses of gaming. The issue is born from government support as well as media depictions of gaming.

When discussing the phenomenon of video games in South Korea, there are a few games that are especially prominent. The most important game in the country is *StarCraft* and its sequels, created by Blizzard Entertainment, based in Orange County. *StarCraft* and *StarCraft II* are science-fiction real-time strategy games (RTS) that entail the player controlling units of soldiers on a battlefield and attempting to eliminate the enemy team. The player can play as three different species (Terran, Zerg, Protoss), each of which has countless unique units as well as structures to build and create. *League of Legends* is a popular team-based multiplayer brawl game where players control a single unit and use that unit's abilities to eliminate other players or teams of players. *Defense of the Ancients* (DotA) is the game that inspired the gameplay in *League of Legends*, and it and its sequel have a very strong following in South Korea. These games are some of the most popular professionally played games in South Korea, and the tournaments for them often occur in large venues throughout the country. For example, the world championship was held in a stadium that was built for the World Cup, when South Korea hosted that event in 2002. Many other games are popular as well. *World of Warcraft*, the famous massively multiplayer online (MMO) video game, was also developed by Blizzard Entertainment. Other popular games include *Counter-Strike* and it various spin-offs, created by Valve. This is a first-person shooter multiplayer game and is extremely popular among professional gamers around the world. The Battlefield series, made by Dice Entertainment, is another first-person shooter game that focuses on larger teams and a realistic military experience.

Many other competitive gaming scenes in other countries have been influenced by the success in South Korea. In the United States, only recently has *StarCraft II* become popular among competitive players, and this was directly influenced by the Korean phenomenon that has made *StarCraft* competitions into a must-see event among the gaming enthusiast public.

Connor J. Gahre

See also: Internet Addiction, China (Chapter 5: Internet and Social Media)

Further Reading

Groom, Nelson. 2014. "Online Gaming Is South Korea's Most Popular Drug." *Vice*. January 16. http://www.vice.com/read/online-gaming-is-south-koreas-most-popular-drug. Accessed March 26, 2016.

Heo, Jongho, Juhwan Oh, S. V. Subramanian, Yoon Kim, and Ichiro Kawachi. 2014. "Addictive Internet Use among Korean Adolescents: A National Survey." *PLoS One* 9, no. 2: e87819. doi: 10.1371/journal.pone.0087819.

Levy, Karine. 2014. "In South Korea, Competitive Video Games Are Almost as Popular as Soccer." *Business Insider*. October 19. http://www.businessinsider.com/e-sports-are -popular-in-south-korea-2014-10. Accessed March 26, 2016.

Mozur, Paul. 2014. "For South Korea, E-Sports Is National Pastime." *New York Times*. October 19. http://www.nytimes.com/2014/10/20/technology/league-of-legends-south-korea -epicenter-esports.html. Accessed March 26, 2016.

Rousse-Marquet, Jennifer. 2013. "Online Gaming: An Integral Part of the South-Korean Culture." *INA Global*. June 20. http://www.inaglobal.fr/en/video-games/article/online -gaming-integral-part-south-korean-culture. Accessed March 26, 2016.

Chapter 8: Fashion and Couture

Introduction

Fashion in Asia and Oceania represents a fusion of different styles, colors, and images. Local designers are setting new fashion trends that spread from fashion hubs such as Tokyo, Seoul, and Shanghai to other fashion-conscious centers locally and abroad. K-fashion and indie pop fashion continue to shape and be shaped by youth cultures everywhere in Southeast Asia and around the world. Local fashion designers living in Newmarket, New Zealand; Hong Kong, China; and Dhaka, Bangladesh experiment with new dressmaking techniques, such as gluing instead of sewing, and innovative clothing styles that combine traditional and modern elements often in uniquely local and futuristic ways. Muslim veiling trends, especially among the younger generations today, often boast highly fashionable and cheerful designs and sexy styles. Local designers are also opening new clothing lines through blogging hubs, attracting fashion-conscious consumers everywhere, instantaneously, online.

K-pop Fashion

Korean popular music artists have become associated with fashion to an extent unmatched by other Korean celebrities. Bold fashion choices and access to new markets has increased cooperation between major international designers and K-pop stars. Jeremy Scott, the lead designer for Moschino, has worked extensively with the members of 2NE1, especially the girl group's leader, CL, whom he calls his muse. Nicola Formichetti, creative director of Diesel, has worked with the stylistic trendsetter G-Dragon, front man of the boy group Big Bang. The bold fashion choices and distinctive image of the artists managed by YG Entertainment, including 2NE1 and Big Bang, has now gained a Korean institutional tie to the major conglomerate Samsung with the 2015 launch of a new brand, Nona9on, by Samsung's textile/fashion branch, Cheil Industries. This brand may be able to achieve a dominant position in K-pop fashion, much of which is currently sold piecemeal through small Internet pop-ups with limited selections. YG also has a cosmetics brand, Moonshot. K-pop stars are increasingly frequent guests on the side of the couture runway in Europe as well as at the ever-growing Seoul Fashion Week held each fall. Their visages also grace the covers and fashion spreads in almost every edition of the fashion magazines in Korea, including Korean editions of *Vogue*, *Céci*, *Nylon*, *Allure*, *Bazaar*, and so on.

CedarBough T. Saeji

The new millennial rise of China and India, ascending now on par with Singapore, Taiwan, Japan, and South Korea, have decentered and transformed the way people think about fashion in relation to the global economy. No longer are apparent and leading world centers of high fashion based predominantly in the United States (New York City) and European Union (Paris), rather, today, they are everywhere multiplying and emerging, especially out of Asia and Oceania. Local fashion and apparel industries in the culturally and historically diverse contexts of these two magnificent world regions, like everywhere else, are strongly influenced by consumers' spending power. The speed of the Internet continues to increase capital flows, creative interactions, production, employment, wages, and the buying power of individual spenders, which, in turn, largely drives local fashion industries.

However, the current prosperity brought by globalization distributes wealth unevenly into the 21st century. Local income disparities between the rich and poor, arguably, have grown wider in most of the countries of Southeast Asia as well as in India and China. Designer clothes manufactured in China and Indonesia are intended for wealthier clientele of leading local elite families and foreign consumers in overseas markets that inflate prices well beyond the means of the local seamstresses and tailors who made them. The Philippines, Indonesia, and China are currently among the largest mass producers of textile apparels for fashion industries around the world. Fashionable adornments, bodily modifications, and new clothing styles often have as much to do with local religious affiliations, governmental ordinances, markets, and consumers as with the export and sale of locally manufactured and produced goods and apparels.

The clothes that people choose to wear in their home, workplaces, and public spaces often depend on the occasion and their own individual or family pooled income, social standing, and status in the family and community in which they live. Their choice of clothing may be strongly influenced by changing and prevailing religious doctrines or political beliefs, as in the case of local Indonesian and Bangladeshi majority Muslim populations, where females may display their sexuality discretely and subtly or hide it altogether in spaces outside the home.

Another example is South Asia, where local majority Hindus may or may not dress according to their caste and type of work they do. In places like the Philippines, T-shirts and jeans are widely worn not only because they are popular and affordable for everyone but, more importantly, because uniformity in dress discourages competitive dressing in a predominately Roman Catholic country, where the line separating church and state is not always clear.

Compared to Asia, Australia and New Zealand are more heavily influenced by fashion trends in the United States and Europe. As in the United States, local people can choose from a wide selection of different fashions, styles, and price ranges. Local fashion industries in both countries have become highly competitive in the international fashion scene. Retailers in Australia have outsourced their new clothing designs and manufacturing productions to Indonesia, China, and Vietnam, where local laborers are paid less and profit margins are higher. New Zealand has broadened its trading ties beyond Oceania and the United States to include China and the European Union countries. Their fashions are infused with a conscious appreciation of local cultural identities and pluralism, jettisoning them into international fame.

This chapter includes rich and detailed discussions on topics as varied as Islamic and Japanese youth fashions, Philippine and Nepali national attires, henna and tattooing, and body modifications and beauty pageants. Readers will be introduced by way of these examples to the wonderfully visual and delightful world of changing fashion trends and seemingly timeless styles.

Kathleen M. Nadeau and Jeremy A. Murray

Further Reading

Dharwadker, Vinay, and Donna L. Halper. 2007. "South and Southeast Asia: Fashion and Appearance." In *The Greenwood Encyclopedia of World Popular Culture, Volume 6: Asia and Pacific Oceania.* Ed. Gary Xu and Vinay Dharwadker, 69–90. Westport, CT: Greenwood Press.

Fernandes, Clinton, ed. 2008. *Hot Spot: Asia and Oceania.* Westport, CT: Greenwood Press.

Xiao, Hui. 2007. "East Asia and Oceania: Fashion and Appearance." In *The Greenwood Encyclopedia of World Popular Culture, Volume 6: Asia and Pacific Oceania.* Ed. Gary Xu and Vinay Dharwadker, 59–68. Westport, CT: Greenwood Press.

BEAUTY PAGEANTS, PHILIPPINES

Beauty pageants first appeared in the Philippines in 1908, 10 years after American occupation began, as the military rulers searched for an expedient public-relations tool to ingratiate themselves to the native population. Having almost freed themselves from over 300 years of Spanish rule, the Filipinos lost 220,000 of their compatriots to the Americans as they attempted to defeat a second colonization, to no avail. In 1908, six years after the end of the Philippine-American War, the American junta of the new colony was desperate to earn any form of goodwill from their new subjects.

Navy captain George T. Langhorne came up with the idea to produce a colonial Filipino version of the World Fair. It was to be bankrolled by prominent moneyed members of Filipino Spanish and American colonial society. Governor General James F. Smith supported the idea, thus paving the way for the Manila Carnival, which, according to its slogans at the time was a festival of fun with three main purposes: revelry, industrial expansion, and political harmony. The pinnacle event was to be the search for the King and Queen of the Manila Carnival.

Such a competition was the perfect venue by which the Filipino-Spanish mestizo elite would be able to once again demonstrate their superiority over the native and mostly peasant Filipino population, as only the prominent and wealthy were eligible to compete. Many contestants and winners were even close relatives of revolutionary heroes and founders of the future Republic of the Philippines. Most of the candidates made sure to market their knowledge of Spanish art and culture. As America entrenched its rule over time, contestants highlighted their skills in speaking English and knowledge of American culture to set themselves ahead of the pack.

The winners entered the contests via ballots, which were sold to the public, thus allowing only the moneyed and influential to participate. The inaugural beauty contest in 1908 reflected pervading societal racism: a King and Queen of the West would be crowned, as well as a King and Queen for the East. American Marjorie Colton was crowned Queen of the Occident, with Colonel George T. Langhorne himself as her king. The first ever Filipina crowned Queen of the Orient was Pura Garcia Villanueva of Iloilo province. Manuel Gomez was crowned King of the Orient.

The remaining contestants were declared maids of honor and courtiers, of course divided according to their race. Consequently, newspaper accounts documented differing treatments of the Western and Eastern crown holders, with the Filipino kings and queens receiving unfair treatment from carnival authorities themselves. One account even reported the King and Queen of the Orient being charged for tickets to the carnival. Such incidents possibly discouraged the organizers from crowning two sets of winners, as this practice was only repeated in 1920, when the Queen of the Occident title was resurrected so it could be awarded to Virginia Randolph Harrison, the daughter of the governor general of the Philippines, Francis Burton Harrison.

The pattern set by the Queen of the Manila Carnival would be replicated across the Philippine archipelago, from small towns to major cities, paving the way for the creation of the new title Miss Philippines in 1926. At this point, politics had entered the pageant dynamics, with local leaders such as mayors and governors intervening if not directly choosing their own representatives to the national competition. Such a candidate was Anita Noble of Batangas Province, who competed after the provincial governor unilaterally crowned her Miss Batangas. Noble would go on to be crowned the first-ever Miss Philippines, alongside the final Queen of the Manila Carnival, Socorro Henson of Pampanga.

Miss Noble's life as Miss Philippines perhaps represents the level of agency afforded women as a result of winning. Upon her return to Batangas, she received a hero's welcome and was involved in various public events merging entertainment and politics. She went on to marry Juan Nakpil, a graduate of Harvard University, whose bloodline directly linked him to the Filipino Revolution against Spain. His father was Julio Nakpil, a hero of the Filipino-Spanish War, while his mother was no less than Gregoria de Jesus, herself one of the women fighters against Spain whose first husband had been Andres Bonifacio, the father of the Filipino Revolution.

If political expediency benefiting American empire was to give rise to the Manila Carnival and its beauty pageant, it was the Filipinos' pathway to eventual independence from America that led to its eventual end. Three years after the birth of the Commonwealth of the Philippines, Filipinos once again began tasting the flavor of freedom, lessening their appetite for American-sponsored fare such as the Manila Carnival, leading to its demise in 1939.

The Filipinos resurrected the Miss Philippines pageant, crowning Miss Teresita Sanchez on April 26, 1952, a few years after Americans finally granted the Philippines full independence after World War II, with Manila as the worst-bombed location next to Warsaw, Poland. This manifestation of the pageant hewed closer to its contemporary versions, with the usual cast of sponsors ranging from swimsuit makers (Catalina), airlines (Pan Am), film companies (Universal), and cigarette factories.

If politicians intervened in the results of the pageant from 1908 to 1939, in 1952 the pageant was in itself owned by the City of Manila, more specifically Arsenio Lacson, its newly elected mayor, who was quick to wield his influence over Manila's powerful elite. It was Lacson who attached the pageant to a social justice platform in the form of advocacy for Boys' Town and Girls' Home, which tended to impoverished youth.

Mayor Lacson and the City of Manila also owned the franchise to the city pageant, Miss Manila. In 1953, 20-year-old Norma Jimenez won the crown, earning the right to represent Manila in the national pageant. But the losing candidate was not going down without a fight. She met face to face with Mayor Lacson himself to make her case for a reconsideration of the decision. Her name was Imelda Romualdez of Tacloban City. Ms. Romualdez was persistent and indefatigable in her appeal, as recounted by the mayor's wife, Mrs. Luz Lacson, who considered her "a pest." Romualdez's charm would work on the mayor, who relented by creating a special title for Romualdez, Muse of Manila. Jimenez would go on to compete in Miss Philippines 1953, losing to eventual winner Christina Galang of Tarlac. Imelda Romualdez's fame as Muse of Manila earned the admiration of a young senator from Ilocos Norte named Ferdinand Marcos, who proposed to her after a two-week courtship. Together, Ferdinand and Imelda Romualdez Marcos would rule and pillage the Philippines from 1965 to 1986.

In 1963, 20-year-old Gemma Guerrero Cruz of Manila's most elite won the title Miss Philippines and the right to represent the country for the first time in the Miss International pageant in the United States. Cruz's mother was the respected journalist and historian Carmen Nakpil Guerrero, whose brother was the Philippine ambassador to the Court of St. James in England, the esteemed writer Leon Maria Guerrero. On her father's side, she was a great-niece of the Filipino national hero Jose Rizal, who was assassinated by the Spaniards. Cruz's patriotic pedigree further elevated the status of beauty pageants in the nation, demonstrating their efficacy and respectability as platforms for women to demonstrate their excellence.

Cruz did not disappoint in her role as the first-ever representative to the 1964 Miss International pageant in Long Beach, California, where she won the title. Her winning answer to the question as to why she wanted to win the competition and what she would do with the $10,000 cash prize: " . . . I want to win this contest, but not for myself, but for my country. And I'm going to donate the money to Boys' Town. I will build a house for them, the children who sleep in the streets of Manila." With that answer, Guerrero Cruz linked feminist patriotism, entertainment, and political savvy, in stark opposition to the image of women propagated in one of *Billboard*'s top-selling songs of 1964, Roy Orbison's "Pretty Woman."

Upon her return to Manila, Cruz received a ticker-tape parade befitting a war hero. She had put not only the Filipino woman but also the Philippines itself on the world stage. The crown was monumental enough to serve as a proxy for the defeat at the hands of foreign domination. Here was a nation twice colonized, sending a young woman to battle to demonstrate her agency, beauty, and intelligence, and she proved herself above all her counterparts. Indeed, the Miss International 1964 crown proved to be the reentry of the Philippines onto the world stage as a viable nation, and it took a 20-year-old student to claim the metaphorical victory.

The 1960s saw the birth of commercial beauty titles, with Miss Caltex as the most prominent. Franchised and sponsored by the California Texas Oil Company, Miss Caltex required candidates to travel the Philippines while promoting the corporation and soliciting votes from the public. Winners received a cash contract as the public face of Caltex and a trip around the world donated by Air France. By the time the last Miss Caltex was crowned in 1970, the cash prize had doubled and included a brand-new car.

In 1965 former Muse of Manila Imelda Romualdez stood beside her husband, Ferdinand Marcos, as he took the oath as president of the Philippines. Their approach to power was entrenched in creating a public image of the Philippines as a nation of beauty and prosperity despite the massive poverty that was a result of the lack of international recovery efforts at the end of World War II. (America had left its former colony without support for reconstruction, unlike Europe, which benefitted from the Marshall Plan.) Beauty pageants thus became a favored tool to distract the population from endemic corruption and other societal problems. Newly crowned queens were utilized to promote the rulers of the state. With poverty widespread and opportunities for women few, they remained one of the few outlets for women to gain some form of economic agency. But not all competitors were complacent and complicit; Miss World Philippines 1972 Margarita "Maita" Gomez joined the Communist armed movement fighting the Marcos dictatorship. Gomez took up arms and went into hiding until the Marcoses fell out of power in 1986. Thereafter, she continued her advocacy for social justice, especially for women. She passed away in her sleep on July 12, 2012.

To this day, beauty pageants continue to serve many functions, from political tools to commercial marketing campaigns. They continue to attract multitudes of Filipino women, who bring with them, even before beauty, the pragmatic intelligence of working with what little society offers them to gain the place they deserve in effecting individual and sometimes social change. With winners that range from the daughter of an American general to the great-niece of a national hero to a communist insurgent, at minimum, beauty pageants remain a platform for the diverse struggles and dreams of the Filipino woman.

Francis Tanglao-Aguas

See also: National Attire, Philippines

Further Reading

Castro, Alex R. 2014a. *Aro Katimyas Da! A Memory Album of Titled Kapampangan Beauties.* Angeles City, PH: Holy Angel University Press.
Castro, Alex R. 2014b. "Manila Carnivals 1908–1939: A Pictorial History of the Greatest Annual Event in the Orient." manilacarnivals.blogspot.com. Accessed March 26, 2016.
Torre, Ricky. 2013. "Remembering the Year of Gemma." www.rappler.com. Accessed March 26, 2016.

BODY MODIFICATION

Body modification is a broad category that can include anything from foot binding to tattoos to earrings. Any intentional changes to the anatomy fall into this broad category. Body modification is undertaken for any number of reasons, which have historically included rites of passage, aesthetics, or perceived physical attractiveness, and individual self-expression. The choice to undergo body modification can be a result of social or cultural norms or it can be in direct contravention of social norms. This broad definition is a good place to start, since in Asia and Oceania, body modification has a long history and, currently, diverse manifestations.

Perhaps the most well-known historical example of body modification in Asia is the Chinese tradition of foot binding. This practice began among elite women in the Song dynasty (960–1279) and was most likely begun for aesthetic reasons, in order to achieve an impossibly small, feminine foot, considered attractive in this time. The practice was finally banned in the early 20th century by China's Manchu rulers of the Qing dynasty (1644–1911). It is noteworthy that the Mongol rulers of the Yuan (1279–1368) and the Manchu rulers of the Qing did not engage in foot binding, and the women in these and many other ethnic minority groups in China never adopted the practice. It was mainly a practice of the majority Han Chinese, and by the 19th century, it had become widespread not only among elites but also among China's lower classes as a means to marry young women into higher-status families. This is obviously an extreme example of body modification, since the arch of the foot was broken through a complex procedure of binding the foot in tight cloth wrappings, and the four smaller toes were folded down around the largest. The procedure was extremely painful and made it difficult for women to walk.

Another extreme example of body modification is found among the women of the Kayan Lahwi tribe in Myanmar (Burma) and northern Thailand, who appear to have extremely long necks, stretched by coiled brass rings. In this practice, young girls are adorned with brass coils around their necks that are gradually increased throughout their lives, pushing the clavicle or collarbone down and giving the appearance of an elongated neck. As with foot binding, this practice is generally believe to be related to aesthetics or the perceived physical beauty of the women who undergo this modification. The practice continues among some women in these groups today.

Ritual tattooing and cutting of the body has been a common practice among cultural groups around the world throughout history, and some groups continue these practices today in various forms. In Papua New Guinea, for example, the skin-cutting ritual of the Kaningara tribe is an important rite of passage for young men. Unlike the above two examples of body modification, this one is reserved exclusively for men. In fact, it is designed to reinforce the maleness of the individual undergoing the ritual and to separate him from his mother's care and her ancestral line. Tattooing has long represented a rite of passage in many other cultures. Famously, the indigenous Maori of New Zealand have engaged in the ritual of *ta moko*, which is loosely termed tattooing but traditionally involves cutting and inking, not just the inking of a tattoo. These tattoos are often prominent facial decorations and are seen among cultural groups throughout Asia. The Li women of the highlands of China's Hainan Island, for example, have traditionally used facial tattoos to mark their rite of passage into married life. Today, some Maori people still choose to adopt the *ta moko*, which sometimes involves the more traditional cutting and inking of the skin but can also be done by nonpurists with a modern tattoo machine. The revival of the *ta moko* in recent decades has spread beyond the Maori community, leading some to question its cultural importance when divorced from the ritual significance of the Maori practice. Tattooing is popular around the world, although throughout Japanese history it has been taboo. In Japan, as in China, criminals and slaves were traditionally marked with tattoos, sometimes on their faces. In Japan's Tokugawa era (1603–1867), members of the *yakuza*, an organized crime syndicate still in existence, began to practice full-body tattooing as a membership ritual, and this practice continues today. For these reasons, while some young people in Japan choose tattoos, it is still considered taboo to have tattoos that are visible in public.

Some forms of body modification found in Asia and Oceania are also not uncommon in the United States. Plastic surgery is familiar to American observers, from facial alterations to breast implants or even buttock and calf enhancements. Artificial tanning or bleaching of the skin, body-hair removal, tattooing, and body piercings are also common in the United States as well as in Asia and Oceania. Some manifestations of these practices, however, are different, based on differing and overlapping aesthetics of beauty in the different regions. Deep artificial tanning, for example, is found to be attractive among some Americans, and it is also a part of some kinds of Japanese street fashion, particularly the *ganguro* style.

On the other hand, having very light skin has been historically favored by the elites of many regions in Asia, including India and China. In India, some consider fairer skin to be a sign of higher status within the caste system. In China, women who see light skin as a marker of beauty and status often favor as pale a complexion as possible. In south China and in Southeast Asia, where labor outdoors naturally means darker skin for some, pale skin is sometimes seen as a marker of leisure as well. With a premium placed on pale skin for both beauty and status, products and medical procedures cater to this aesthetic, especially for women, but not without controversy. Some observers assert that skin-whitening products can have dangerous long-term effects, including stripping the skin of its natural pigmentation and healthy composition. Facial scarves, umbrellas, and other sun blockers are also popular among Chinese women, and some at the beach even choose full-body coverings that also include a product nicknamed the "facekini," which covers the entire face like a ski mask.

Double eyelid surgery, or East Asian blepharoplasty, is a procedure in which the single eyelid is surgically converted to a double eyelid, meaning a crease is added to the eyelid. The epicanthic fold at the inner eye is also sometimes removed as part of this procedure. Controversies surround this elective procedure, since some critics claim that those who undergo the surgery are trying to adhere to a white or Western standard of beauty. Many disagree, and regardless of criticism, it is a very popular procedure in Taiwan, South Korea, Japan, and increasingly in the People's Republic of China. While aesthetics are the main impetus behind this surgery, some assert that the reason for the procedure is to increase job prospects in a society that values this appearance. As with everything from breast enhancement to foot binding, questions and controversies surrounding these body modifications lead us to think not only about the individual who elects to undergo them, but more significantly to consider the culture and the social pressures exerted on that individual to make that choice.

Jeremy A. Murray

See also: Henna

Further Reading

Chow, Kat. 2014a. "Is Beauty in the Eye(lid) of the Beholder?" *NPR CodeSwitch: Frontiers of Race, Culture and Ethnicity.* November 17. http://www.npr.org/sections/codeswitch/2014/11/17/363841262/is-beauty-in-the-eye-lid-of-the-beholder. Accessed March 26, 2016.

Chow, Kat. 2014b. "The Many Stories behind Double Eyelid Surgery." *NPR CodeSwitch: Frontiers of Race, Culture and Ethnicity.* November 18. http://www.npr.org/sections/codeswitch/2014/11/18/364670361/the-many-stories-behind-the-double-eyelid-surgery. Accessed March 26, 2016.

Tan, David. 2012. "Who's the Fairest of Them All?" *Asian Scientist Magazine.* September 18. http://www.asianscientist.com/2012/09/features/skin-whitening-products-asia-2012/. Accessed March 26, 2016.

Krutak, Lars (tattoo anthropologist). http://larskrutak.com. Accessed March 26, 2016.

Krutak, Lars. "Making Boys into Men: The Skin-Cutting Ritual of the Kaningara Tribe of Papua New Guinea" http://larskrutak.com/making-boys-into-men-the-skin-cutting-ritual-of-the-kaningara-tribe-of-papua-new-guinea. Accessed March 26, 2016.

HENNA

Hands and feet intricately patterned with ornate reddish-brown henna body-art patterns, or *mehndi*, the Hindu word for henna, is an iconic symbol of South Asian womanhood. A bride's hennaed hands and feet are often the dramatic centerpiece of an emotionally charged Bollywood drama or a lush fashion magazine display of bridal sarís. Families throughout the Middle East, the Arabian Peninsula, South and Southeast Asia often choose to have a lavish "Night of the Henna" party for the bride prior to her wedding. The bride sits unmoving for several hours while a family member or artist applies henna in fashionable patterns. Though henna body art is associated in Western perception with Hindu Indian brides, the practice originated in premonotheistic cultures, and the primary carrier has been Islam. Jewish, Christian, Sikh, and Zoroastrian women also have a Night of the Henna tradition in the regions where henna grows naturally and is widely used culturally. The history of henna is rich and complex; henna is part of many cultural traditions, including traditions other than ornamenting the bride.

Henna, *lawsonia inermis*, is a small tree that grows in tropical semiarid zones. The plant can tolerate long droughts and poor soil but cannot survive frost. Though henna grows in many frost-free areas, most commercially cultivated henna is presently grown in the Sojat region of India. The leaves of henna are dried, pulverized, and mixed with a mildly acidic liquid to create a green paste that will stain skin, fingernails, and hair reddish brown. Henna probably grew in North Africa during the late Neolithic, based on the land area that would have had suitable climate during the Ice Age and the genetic diversity of henna in the region. Over the centuries, birds spread henna from North Africa to other regions by consuming the berries prior to migration and eliminating seeds when they paused along rivers and oases, and people spread the practices of henna through cultural dispersion.

Humans independently discovered henna more than once and in more than one location. The most common use of henna is to mask the appearance of aging by dying gray hair. Men and women hennaed their hair to cover gray in ancient Egypt (Fletcher 2002). There is evidence of markings consistent with henna body art on the hands and feet of Bronze Age Minoan and Ugaritic marriageable young women in the eastern Mediterranean (Cartwright-Jones 2006). During the Roman period, writers recorded that Syrian, Palestinian, and Persian people were using henna as hair dye and body art. These pre-Islamic henna traditions extended into the Arabian Peninsula, where they were later incorporated into Muslim social celebrations: marriage, Eids, celebration, and sacrifice. The Night of the Henna evolved from the earlier henna traditions of fertile women. Smaller henna parties for the groom paralleled the bride's party; henna was applied to the extended family or the whole wedding party to celebrate a wedding.

The fundamental uses of henna from East Africa, the Middle East, and the Arabian Peninsula were carried across the Indian Ocean on coastal trade routes to South Asia prior to the Common Era, particularly to the western coast of India. Trade and cultural contact associated with the spread of Islam beginning in the seventh century CE, as well as intermarriage through conversion and colonization, spread henna use farther into Malaysia, the Philippines, and the western coast of Australia. These cultural migrations included the henna traditions incorporated into Muslim culture. Persian traditions of highly ornamental henna entered northern India through alliances during the Mughal dynasties. Noble women from politically influential families brought their beautification techniques into the South Asian royal harems, interchanging techniques and traditions of red body cosmetics from southern and eastern India and dark henna with complex henna work from Persia and Arabia.

In the 19th century, the Night of the Henna was practiced primarily in Muslim households in South Asia, rather than in Hindu households. India originally had diverse local traditions for weddings that have diminished with the popularization of the northwest cultural wedding style. The Hindu adaptation of the Night of the Henna was gradual; by the late 20th century, it had become the fashion of the increasingly popular pan-Indian wedding style. As elaborate as the Night of the Henna is, other henna practices are not, and never were, sacred religious rituals. Henna has always been a family celebration, even though the celebration may be part of a religious holiday. Henna is not applied by clergy in a sacred space. Henna is most often applied by family members at home, or, if budget permits and taste requires, by a beauty professional in a salon.

The traditional vivid red body-art markings on eastern and southern Indian women and in Indian paintings through the 19th century were done with *alta*, *kumkum*, and *lac* rather than henna. *Alta* is a ruby body paint made from betel leaf. *Kumkum* is a red-orange powdered cosmetic made from alkalized turmeric. *Lac* is a vivid red shellac body paint made from *Laccifer lacca* secretions. These auspicious bright-red body cosmetics have been used in South Asia to ornament both men and women for over 2,000 years and were used as part of the essential daily toilette as well as for weddings, religious holidays, and social events. Early images of Hindu goddesses, particularly Durga and Lakshmi, had vivid red hand markings rather than the rust color of henna. These red body-art cosmetics remain in use in southern and eastern India but have diminished in popularity in the last few decades due to the popularization of henna, which tends to be rust colored, or with added chemicals, black. Chemical red, orange, and fuchsia cosmetics have replaced the traditional auspicious red cosmetic formulas.

The traditional bridal artists in India were *Nai*, the barbering caste, but *mehndi* training courses and competitions are now available to prepare any person to compete for a part of the lucrative body-art market. Henna artistry allows a woman to earn money when other avenues of education and income might be viewed as unsuitable. Henna artists use their cell phones to book appointments, show photographs of their work, and carry on a full schedule of henna work while remaining secluded, if their families so require. Other henna artists work in salons or markets, and both female and male artists earn a living through henna. Women and men who have limited options for earning a living, but who have a steady hand with drawing and a companionable personality, have good prospects for earning an income through henna. Henna art prices often triple prior to holidays; people who can do stylish and innovative patterns work late into the night for Eids (Muslim festivals), Diwali (the Hindu festival of light), and Karva Chauth (the Hindu fast for the married woman).

In the late 20th century, improvements in milling practices in the South Asian henna industry produced henna powders that facilitated more complex artwork. Before improved henna processing techniques were available, artists either used fresh henna leaves ground into pulp or sifted coarsely ground henna powder through cloth, mixing a workable paste with a mildly acidic liquid. These basic henna pastes were applied with pins, twigs, or wires and manipulated into simple patterns. When milk packaged in plastic bags became available in the South Asian markets, women adapted a technique similar to applying fancy icing to a cake; they rolled the milk bag plastic into cones and filled the cones with henna paste. This allowed them to quickly apply more ornate patterns. The fine henna lines were sealed to the skin by dabbing lemon juice and sugar onto the pattern. Plastic cones facilitated increasingly vivid, intricate patterns and raised henna from the realm of household folk art into a fashionable art form. Around the turn of the 21st century, artists added glitter, sequins, thickened nail polish, and dyes to their henna to achieve more color and dazzle.

When the South Asian cosmetic producers began adding para-phenylenediamine black dye to henna hair-dye products, women found this "black henna" produced a fast, black body marking if it was applied to skin. This highly concentrated chemical hair dye was adapted into henna body art, and the practice of applying "black henna" temporary tattoos or "outline black" henna became widespread by the late 1990s. The allergic reactions caused by the para-phenylenediamine black dye were not understood at first and only later connected to serious blistering and injuries. "Black henna" created with para-phenylenediamine has become fashionable throughout the areas where henna is traditional.

"Black henna" migrated into Western popular culture in the late 1990s. Because henna body art was not well understood in the West and was conflated with tattooing, "black henna" temporary tattoos emerged as popular souvenirs for people who wished to have an exotic tattoo without the commitment of permanent ink. Artists working in areas of tourism in South and Southeast Asia offered "black henna" temporary tattoos to vacationers eager for a bold tattoo that would disappear after they returned home. Because the skin reaction from "black henna" is delayed by 3 to 30 days, often appearing after the visitor returned home, the artists and their clients did not understand that painting para-phenylenediamine "black henna" on skin causes severe injuries. This delay has meant that injuries from "black henna" continue today.

Catherine Cartwright-Jones

See also: Body Modification

Further Reading

Boubaya, A., H. Hannachi, N. Marzougui, T. Triki, F. Guasmi, and A. Ferchichi. 2013. "Genetic Diversity Assessment of Lawsonia Inermis Germplasm in Tunisian Coastal Oases by ISSR and RAPD markers." *Dendrology* 69: 31–39.
Cartwright-Jones, C. 2006. *Developing Guidelines on Henna: A Geographical Approach.* MA thesis, Kent State University, 122–146.
Fletcher, J. 2002. "Ancient Egyptian Hair and Wig, the Ostracon." *The Journal of the Egyptian Study Society* 13, no. 2 (Summer).
Lestringant, G. G., A. Bener, and P. M. Frossard. 1999. "Cutaneous Reactions to Henna and Associated Additives." *The British Journal of Dermatology* 141, no. 3: 598–600.
Pasricha, J. S., R. Gupta, and S. Panjwani. 1980. "Contact Dermatitis to Henna (Lawsonia)." *Contact Dermatitis* 6, no. 4: 288–289.

HIJABERS (ISLAMIC VEILING IN INDONESIA AND BANGLADESH)

Indonesia

A contemporary fashion trend for Indonesian Islamic women is to wear a headscarf or veil. The wearing of the veil has become a popular public statement of their cultural and religious identity and individuality. In the mid-20th century, mainly only older women returning from Mecca wore the veil to show their milestone pilgrimage status. Most young people, especially teenagers, wore uniforms to school and, outside of the classroom, they wore Western-style clothing such as blue jeans and T-shirts. Back then, this was a symbol of rebellion against the establishment, much to the consternation of their more conservative parents. By the late 1980s and 1990s, the popularity of Western clothing styles began to wane as some Islamic women began donning the veil. Many of these earlier women wore a headscarf to protest against some of the negative effects of "Western" capitalism on local social life. They were disturbed by the quandary of the rich getting richer while the poor were increasing in numbers and getting poorer. Also, so-called "bad Western values," such as the rise of prostitution, exploitation of the poor, and even the poor preying on each other in desperation for their own advantage, were disturbing and contradictory of the traditional Indonesian value of caring for the less fortunate as a community.

By the arrival of the new millennium, especially after the terrorist bombings of September 11, 2001, and the subsequent United States-led invasion of Iraq, condemned by much of the international community, many more Muslim women in Indonesia began veiling themselves in solidarity with the suffering of their Muslim brothers and sisters in the Middle East. The interesting twist of this new fashionable Indonesian style is that it is being creatively and playfully localized as women are decorating the head coverings so that they are more attractive and eye-catching. Of course, this is counterproductive to the original purpose of wearing a hijab, which is generally understood to be modesty and propriety. Among some young Indonesian Muslim women, the so-called "jilboobs," there is even a style of veiling and covering the body so that the curves of their figures are clear under their tight clothing. The term "jilboob" is used derisively by the local Muslim majority, who do not approve of the trend of these young people, who are rebelling against those calling for every female Muslim to wear a veil. There are Facebook groups related to this trend that harass women found on the social networking site, or on other social media, having photos of themselves in tight clothes. The pressure of the Islamic movement toward the more conservative Saudi Arabian style is increasing. Nowadays, along with these rebellious trends, more women are becoming increasingly conservative and covering their faces with black veils and wearing a one-piece long black dress.

Bangladesh

In Bangladesh today, the younger generation of women are covering themselves in fashionably beautiful clothing styles. Wearing soft- and bright-colored veils; lipstick; tight-fitting knickers, jeans, or nicely cuffed loose-fitting pants; and fancy shoes, this newer generation of women enjoy the freedom to choose different veiling styles and fashionable clothing while adhering to their religious and cultural values and principles. The wearing of the Muslim veil in Bangladesh, however, is a relatively new phenomenon, encouraged, in part, by the millions of returning migrant workers, especially from the Gulf States. Around the beginning of the new millennium, it was not uncommon to see women walking around the cities and towns of Bangladesh cloaked completely in burqa-veils. During this period there were many heated debates, locally, over the question of veiling, so much so that in 2010 the Supreme Court ruled against forcing women to wear veils as being a "flagrant abuse of their basic human rights." Traditionally, Bangladeshi women have worn the sari and *shalwar kamees* (light, loose-fitted trousers).

Bordered by India in the north and the Bay of Bengal to the south, the culture of Bangladesh has long been influenced by Hinduism and Islam. One of Bangladeshis' greatest national heroes today is a Hindu scholar and novelist, Rabindranath

Tagore (1861–1941), who fought for national independence from British colonialism. After Eastern Bengal, now called Bangladesh, gained independence in 1941, it was initially part of what became East Pakistan. It was considered to be the agricultural hub of the nation, while West Pakistan, what we now call simply Pakistan, was its industrial center. The Bengalis of East Pakistan were agitating for independence from West Pakistan. They felt that they were being neglected by the central government when it came to regional funding matters. In 1971 West Pakistan invaded East Pakistan to quell the independence movement, which brought about a bloody civil war. India supported the Bengalis, who won their independence and broke away from Pakistan to become the newly independent nation of Bangladesh.

Kathleen M. Nadeau

See also: Sari

Further Reading

Nadeau, Kathleen, and Sangita Rayamajhi. 2013. *Women's Roles in Asia*. Santa Barbara, CA: Greenwood Press.

Purnamasari, Ratna Dewi. 2013. "The Rise of Muslim Fashion Industry in Indonesia." *Jakarta Globe*, Blogs, Cultural Musings. June 4. http://jakartaglobe.beritasatu.com/blogs/the-rise-of-the-muslim-fashion-industry-in-indonesia. Accessed March 26, 2016.

Saikia, Yasmin. 2011. *Women, War, and the Making of Bangladesh, Remembering 1971*. Durham, NC: Duke University Press.

Tasnim, Zaarrin. 2014. "Modest Fashion: The Rise of the Hijab Culture." August 24. http://dhakainsider.com/lifestyle/modest-fashion-the-rise-of-the-hijab-culture. Accessed September 13, 2015.

NATIONAL ATTIRE, PHILIPPINES

The *terno* is a dress for women characterized by unique stiff sleeves likened to standing butterfly wings about to take flight. The sleeves arch gracefully about two inches above the shoulder and hang midway to the elbow or shorter. *Ternos* come in all lengths, although traditionally they are floor length and even sport trains. They are dressy even as they vary for daytime and evening functions.

Terno means "matching." The word originally confirmed that an upper garment (called *camisa*) made of net-like textile had been dyed to match the separate skirt (called *saya*) of densely woven fabric such as brocade. It also referred to matching embellishments, usually appliqué and embroidery, throughout the ensemble.

The style evolved from the earlier *traje de mestiza*, literally "garb of those with mixed parentage," those who were not offspring of a Spanish mother and father when the Philippines was part of the Spanish Empire. (*Mestizar* means to cross breeds, usually of animals.) Like the *terno*, its antecedent went through different modes but was typified in the 1890s by a bell skirt of velvet or silk, a sheer blouse of naturally off-white threads having voluminous sleeves with dainty lacelike embroidery, and a kerchief. When Europe's fashionable tunic and chemise reached the Philippines in the early 1900s during the American colonial era, the new, slim silhouette acquired a following, and the *terno* overtook the *traje*.

The early *terno* was worn with a *pañuelo*, a stiffly starched and folded kerchief in the same fabric as the blouse; it covered the shoulders up to where the sleeves stand and positioned its triangular apex at the center of the wearer's back. The carefully folded kerchief is often described as resembling an orchid and was held in place with a front brooch. Native *sinamay* from banana-leaf thread and *piña* woven from wild pineapple-leaf thread were popular fabrics for the stiff *camisa* and *pañuelo*. During the 1920s, *cañamazo* or *babarahin* cloth from Switzerland, which was finer than native weaves, became a favored alternative.

The *camisa* had three pieces. Each of the two sleeves was shaped by pleating it at the top of the armhole when sewing it to the blouse. The waist-long blouse proper was shaped by front and back tucks kept in place with straight pins. Pins also closed the blouse down the front. One had to be dainty or risk getting pricked. Pins were removed and stitching undone before the garment was laundered. Pieces of a *camisa*—and the *pañuelo*—were stored flat and heavily starched. They were reassembled each time for wearing.

Eventually a single fabric was used when the *terno* became one piece with a zipper, strongly influenced by the Western evening gown. In the 1930s and 1940s, sleeves were attached by hook-and-eye or snaps so that a dress could be worn two ways. In 1947 women began to wear the *terno* without what was sometimes considered the cumbersome *pañuelo*.

In the 1960s, the *terno* jacket (with butterfly sleeves) was made to wear over an evening gown or dress; in more recent times, versions have been made to team with pants. It is not unusual for a *terno* to be elaborately decorated with beadwork, appliqué, painting, woodblock printing, and embroidery. Some *ternos* are walking exhibits of masterful handiwork.

The *barong Tagalog* is a long-sleeved shirt worn untucked. The term literally means "upper garment of the Tagalog," the Tagalog being an ethnolinguistic group living in what is today's Metro Manila and the adjacent provinces of Bulacan, Laguna, and Batangas. The shirt was originally designed for men. Its fabrics were transparent, thin, and the natural off-white color of common native-loomed fabrics. It is claimed that the sheerness prevented a rebellious wearer from concealing a weapon during Spanish colonial times.

The *barong* is best known for exuberant embroidery on the *pechera*, the area around the front button opening that runs from the neckline to midchest or lower. The *barong*'s length has varied, even reaching below the knee. Western shirt fashion influences its collar and cuffs, which can be standing, ruffled, or pointed.

In the 1950s and 1960s, the *barong* became an increasingly acceptable office attire alternative instead of a Western shirt and necktie or a business suit. A short-sleeve *barong* with pockets evolved. The office *barong* is made in nontransparent fabrics that do not require ironing or steaming. As a uniform, the *barong* may even sport a company's logo. During the 1960s, when Pierre Cardin opened a shop in the Ermita district of Manila City, his Italian head tailor, Giovanni Sana, began experimenting with trimming the *barong*'s silhouette, adapting it to bell-bottom pants then in mode. He also popularized the *barong* dress and the *barong* blouse for women, which remain popular.

The formal *barong* is customarily still sewn of native hand-loomed fabrics, but there are variations made from diverse cloths and ornamentations, some styled by celebrated visual artists. Today the *barong* comes in all colors. A thin, white cotton undershirt was traditionally worn with the off-white *barong* of native hand-loomed material. But today, full lining that matches or complements the *barong's* color is common.

When an event's dress code specifies Filipiniana, it means guests should wear the national attire because the occasion is special. Kindergarten and grade-school boys graduate wearing a *barong*, usually unembellished and shiny. Beauty queens, including little girls, and key participants in traditional Roman Catholic fiesta rituals such as Flores de Mayo, Santacruzan, and Easter Sunday Salubong often wear a *terno* or a *barong*. A Filipiniana-themed wedding is aspirational across social strata, even for Filipinos residing overseas. The Philippine president's annual State of the Nation speech is attended by legislators and their spouses in what has become an much-anticipated fashion event featuring national attire.

Investment in a *terno* or *barong* can be significant when it is custom designed by a celebrated Philippine fashion house or bespoke by an exclusive tailor, fully hand-embroidered with exquisite cutwork and heavily beaded, or embellished with myriad glass crystals. For those with a practical bent or a limited budget, there are ready-to-wear versions in a variety of price ranges at department stores, dry-goods sections of public markets, and clothing rentals catering to weddings and town fiesta balls. Wearing a *terno* or a *barong Tagalog* makes Filipinos feel Filipino.

Felice Prudente Sta. Maria

See also: Beauty Pageants, Philippines

Further Reading

Alejo-Hila, Ma. Corazon, Mitzi Marie Aguilar-Reyes, and Anita Feleo. 2008. *Garment of Honor, Garment of Identity*. Manila, PH: EN Barong Filipino.

Bernal, Salvador F., and Georgina R. Encanto. 1992. *Patterns for the Filipino Dress: From the Traje de Mestiza to the Terno (1890s–1960s)*. Manila, PH: Cultural Center of the Philippines.

De la Torre, Visitacion. 1968. *The Barong Tagalog: The Philippines' National Wear.* Quezon City: University of the Philippines Press.

Moreno, Jose. 1990. *Kasalan*. Manila, PH: J. Moreno.

Ramos, Barge. 2007. *Pinoy Dressing: Weaving Culture into Fashion*. Mandaluyong City, PH: Anvil Publishing.

SARI

Sari is a single length of untailored cloth, approximately 5.5 meters (about 18 feet) long and 1 meter (about 3 feet) in width worn by women primarily of India, Nepal, Bangladesh, Sri Lanka, and Pakistan. The fabric is woven into an infinite variety of textures, colors, and designs out of yarns of cotton, silk, a mixture of cotton and silk, chiffons, and tissues, to name only a few. The word "sari" is derived from Sanskrit, meaning a piece of cloth.

The origin of the sari can be traced back to the Indus Valley civilization that existed between 2800 and 1800 BCE. During this time, the female priests wore long pieces of cloth draped around them or parted at the legs for easy movement. The long piece of cloth worn thus can be seen in all the religious arts and paintings of the time. This form of wearing the long piece of cloth was practiced by women then and still is by the temple dancers in India. The Hindu myths tell tales of women clad in saris, either long ones that reached the ankles or shorter knee-length versions, of saris whose ends were used as veils to enhance the beauty of their hairstyles, or to cover the upper part of their bodies, since bodices were not worn in many instances. The religious epic *Mahabharata* narrates the tale of Draupadi, the wife of the five Pandava princes, who was prevented from being disrobed of her sari by Lord Krishna. This episode in *Mahabharata* is termed "Draupadi's *Vastraharan.*" The reference here to the disrobing of Draupadi's sari is to state how the sari has always been part of a woman's attire in the South Asian context, except that it has gone through several changes and modifications over the centuries. Ancient Sanskrit and Tamil poetry and literature also describe the beauty of these flowing saris.

The sari is a garment made of a single piece of cloth, usually about 18 feet long and 3 feet wide. There are dozens of ways to drape a sari, and they can come in countless colors and patterns. The sari is popularly worn by women of South Asia, and this image shows a woman in Rajasthan, India, wearing a bright sari. (Vikram Raghuvanshi/iStockphoto.com)

The sari is considered part of the cultural heritage of India, Nepal, Sri Lanka, and Bangladesh, a tradition to be followed and respected. Saris are often worn as part of rituals, during religious ceremonies, weddings, festivals, or other celebratory gatherings. Saris, in their resplendent colors, textures, and intricate patterns, are a significant part of the bridal trousseau in wealthy families. They are also part of traditional religious requirements, where women sit down to perform *pujas*, or acts of worship, or other rituals in a sari. Any traditional family would expect their newlywed daughter-in-law, in the early days of her marriage, to walk around the house and do the daily chores of cooking and serving and meeting the family members wearing a sari. It is a mark of distinction, a dignified identity of a woman, a sign of respectability.

The sari is an aspect of cultural heritage, but within the context of modernization and globalization, it is treated more as a sophisticated accessory one cannot do without. At the same time, it is also seen as something that cannot be worn every day as part of the daily wear. This is especially true of the wealthier class. This is because with the increasing need for mobility for women working outside the home, the sari is often considered a hindrance, especially by the younger generation. The need for a matching underskirt, a blouse to go with it, and the high level of maintenance the sari calls for is something that the younger generation can do without. Therefore, saris are worn on special occasions by the younger generation, and there is an extra effort made to spend more on the sari to make it look more glamorous, together with the stylish blouse, which in fact turns out to be more expensive than what a simple working-class woman would spend for her daily-wear sari. For women from the less-wealthy social strata, like factory workers and domestic workers, coarsely woven cotton saris are the most comfortable and affordable daily wear.

There are distinct varieties of saris worn by women of South Asia. India, the largest country in Asia with regional diversity, boasts of varieties of saris, with each design, pattern, and texture idiosyncratic of the state or region that produces it. Some of the well-known types of saris are the Banarasi saris, woven in silk and gold brocades. These are often part of wealthy bridal trousseaus and are in very high demand during the wedding season. Since they are very heavy in texture, with intricate patterns and Zari work (very fine embroidery), they are expensive and not worn on a daily basis but only on festive occasions. The patterns, which are usually of flowers, leaves, architectural designs, and Mughal patterns, lend sophistication to the saris. Many of the more expensive ones have gold and silver threads woven into the *pallu* (the part that is draped over the shoulder) of the sari. It derives its name from the city Varanasi (Banaras), where it was originally made. Another attractive feature of this sari is the colorful dyeing of the silk fabrics. The other renowned type of sari is the Kanjivaram sari, which can be said to be the South Indian counterpart of the Banarasi sari. It is also known as Kanchipuram sari, taking its name from the little town of Kanchipuram, in Tamil Nadu, South India. These saris are more conservative in design, woven out of rich silk yarns with gold and intricately patterned brocade for its border.

Then there are the famous handloom cotton saris, dyed, embroidered, hand painted, or in machine-produced prints. Like other types of saris, cotton saris too come in a variety of price ranges. But cotton saris, because of the simplicity of the yarn, and because the cotton threads are much cheaper than the silk ones and therefore very affordable, are worn by the less-affluent members of society. But in the summer, cotton and handloom saris are considered excellent to ward off the heat. Thus, in these handloom saris, aesthetics and comfort are blended to make them more expensive and, therefore, also worn by the wealthier class.

The Jamdani sari from Bangladesh is another beautiful fabric of handwoven finest muslin with beautiful floral prints and little geometric patterns of varied colors carrying the heritage of Bengal. It derives its name, Jamdani, from the technique of weaving. They are mainly woven out of cotton yarns, or silk, or a mixture of silk and cotton. When they were custom designed for royalty and other nobility in the past, the silk and cotton threads were woven with metal threads of gold and silver and were therefore very expensive.

The Dhaka weaves of Nepal are another famous fabric woven by hand out of cotton threads. The fabric takes its name from the unique design, "Dhaka patterns," which are neither floral nor abstract but are rather geometric in shape, with the designs almost similar to the Jamdani saris of Bangladesh. Not only saris, but also shawls, scarves, and other clothes are made out of these Dhaka weaves in Nepal.

The saris come in different colors: plain single-colored saris, or a single color with plain or blended and brocaded borders. Saris are produced in a combination of colors, stark contrasts, subtle hues, psychedelic patterns, you name the color and there is a sari in that hue. The weavers usually take days to complete one sari, especially the brocaded silk yarns. But now that women have started working outside the home, taking up positions in offices and traveling as part of their jobs, there has been an increase in mass production of inexpensive saris made of cotton, synthetic nylon georgette, and polyester yarns. These saris are very easy to manage and maintain on a daily basis, requiring very little or no ironing, no starches during washing, and are easy to fold and stack. Since the majority of women in South Asia prefer to wear saris to work, especially those who are midcareer, a daily change of saris becomes a necessity. Therefore, affordable and easy maintenance takes priority.

Draping a sari is an art. It is a certain relationship that a woman develops with the sari. Selecting a sari to suit the wearer, her complexion, her figure, or a certain occasion is in itself tricky. There are more than 80 ways to drape a sari. Wrapping one end of the sari, tucking the end into the underskirt, making a few pleats with the remaining length, tucking the pleats in between the waist and the tightly tied underskirt, then draping the remaining part after the pleats over the shoulder—this is an elaborate exercise that is mastered with practice. With the sari and the underskirt also comes the elaborately designed, tailored, and embroidered cotton or silk blouse or the short coat worn on the upper part of the body. This blouse can also be of plain cotton or silk to match or contrast the colors of the sari. The combination sari, blouse, and draping is part of the art of sari wearing and brings the sari to life. When the woman pleats her sari and drapes it over her shoulder, she has to make sure that the prints and embroideries are visible, and the pleating and the draping has to be done so that the designs and colors are elaborately displayed. Moreover, the draping also depends upon the fashion of the times; the country, region, religion, ethnicity, and wealth of the wearer; the texture, print, and embroidery of the fabric; and the occasion for which the sari is being worn. Therefore, wearing a sari is indeed an art.

Many corporations, including some airlines of India, Nepal, and Bangladesh, have uniforms for their employees, and the sari is one such uniform for women.

Saris worn as uniforms are usually made by machine, mass produced, and easy to wear on a daily basis. In such instances, the saris are considered formalwear and are draped very professionally for ease of mobility.

Today, in spite of the vast selection of saris worn in Asia and around the world, machine-made synthetic saris with a variety of theme prints and unique patterns have become very popular. This is also due to the need for efficiency and ease and mainly to cater to the demands of working women. Handwoven, heavily brocaded saris, which were very popular a few decades ago, have been replaced by such machine-produced saris, to the distress of weavers and their industry. Nevertheless, beautiful handwoven silk, chiffon, and cotton saris are still sought after in order to grace festive occasions.

Sangita Rayamajhi

See also: Henna

Further Reading

Askari, Nasreen. 1991. *Uncut Cloth: Saris, Shawls, and Sashes*. London: Merrell Holberton.

Gillow, John, and Nicholas Barnard. 1991. *Traditional Indian Textiles*. London: Thames and Hudson.

Lynton, Linda. 2002. *The Sari: Styles, Patterns, History, Techniques*. New York: Thames & Hudson.

Patil, Vimla. 2012. "The Origin of the Saree." *eSamskriti*. www.esamskriti.com/essay-chapters/THE-ORIGIN-OF-THE-SAREE-1.aspx. Accessed March 26, 2016.

"The Saree: The Very Essence of Womanhood." 2013. www.dollsofindia.com. Accessed March 26, 2016.

YOUTH FASHION, JAPAN

From the late 1990s onward, Japanese youth fashion has been a strong influence on global style, inspiring not just the street looks of teenagers worldwide but also the runway collections of prestigious designers in Paris and New York. Unique Japanese subcultures such as Harajuku Girls, Gothic-Lolita, and Gyaru have thousands of followers in distant lands, while youth-oriented Japanese brands such as A Bathing Ape and Evisu have clothed hip-hop royalty. Most intriguingly, Japanese youth fashion has changed long-held stereotypes about Japan: teenage style is celebrated for its freedom and creativity, strongly contrasting the country's alleged preference for rigidity and conformity.

Despite the industry's current success, Japanese companies only began to sell clothing specifically to teenagers in the early 1960s. From the prewar period up to the first two decades after the war, youth were expected to dress each day in their student uniforms and then adopt appropriate work attire upon employment. Most young men could be found in their plain black *tsume-eri* (or *gakuran*) outfits and owned a single set of bland clothing for playing with friends. Young women, meanwhile, sewed their own dresses from surplus materials using patterns provided

Japanese youth fashion includes a broad spectrum of dress, ranging from the mainstream to the more specific subcultures of Harajuku girls, Gothic-Lolita, and Gyaru. This 2014 image shows an anime cosplayer (costume player) in Gothic-Lolita attire at the Thai-Japan Anime and Music Festival 4 in Bangkok, Thailand. (Tofudevil/Dreamstime.com)

in fashion magazines. Adults fiercely discriminated against any teens daring to wear their own distinct styles, such as the Hawaiian shirts and MacArthur sunglasses of the *Apure* (from the French *après-guerre*) in the late 1950s, the cabana-boy outfits of the Sun Tribe (*Taiyō-zoku*) of the late 1950s, and the leather jackets on the Thunder Tribe (*kaminari-zoku*) motorcycle gangs of the early 1960s.

The ready-to-wear fashion market for youth began in earnest around 1964, first with men. The brand VAN Jacket debuted a line of clothing based on the American Ivy League collegiate look, and new magazines like *Men's Club* and *Heibon Punch* spread these styles to the baby-boomer generation, who had just reached college age. This was a controversial business move at the time. Tabloids incessantly complained about the immorality of VAN selling clothing to youth, and police arrested hundreds of teens dressed in "Ivy" clothing on the streets of Ginza from 1964 to 1965, believing them to be delinquents. This tension eventually resolved, however, and by the end of the 1960s, young men could choose between Ivy clothing, European-influenced "continental" (*konchi*) style, and more radically, hippie looks copied from the United States.

Women, on the other hand, continued to make their own clothing until the early 1970s, when two magazines *An•An* and *Non•no* appeared in the market to champion ready-to-wear fashions. Domestic jeans brands also became a hit with both sexes, with a record 45 million pairs sold in 1973. Society had some doubts about women in denim, but these were laid to rest after the 1977 "Jeans Controversy" (*jīpan ronsō*), when a young woman successfully fought for the right to wear jeans in the classroom against a pedantic American professor at an Osaka university. Society generally came to see fashion as an extension of the wider rise in youth consumerism, and with the exception of obvious working-class delinquent looks, teens had freedom to indulge in fashion styles as long as they abandoned them upon graduation from college.

By the end of the 1970s, the Harajuku neighborhood in Tokyo had become the national center of Japanese youth fashion. The area rose to prominence when rock-and-roll clothing shop Cream Soda kicked off a craze for retro 1950s American style. Teens from around the country descended upon Harajuku, with boys in slicked-back ducktail hairstyles and girls in ponytails and poodle skirts. A Sunday "pedestrian paradise" in Yoyogi Park attracted related groups such as the rock-and-roll–loving greaser Rollers Tribe and the pastel kung-fu disco-loving Bamboo Shoot Tribe (*takenoko-zoku*), both of which danced in groups around a boombox.

The preppie craze of the early 1980s further boosted Harajuku's cachet, as "traditional" clothing shops such as Beams and Crew's attracted wealthy teens through importing prestigious Anglo-American looks. By 1985 Harajuku's narrow street Takeshita-doori hosted dozens and dozens of tiny shops catering to youth, and the tree-lined Omotesandō-doori offered luxury boutiques of foreign brands. Surprisingly, teens could afford these luxury garments, including avant-garde domestic brands such as Yohji Yamamoto and Comme des Garçons, thanks to the bubble economy of the late 1980s putting unprecedented amounts of money in their pockets.

Harajuku's fortunes went down with the bubble economy, but the neighborhood reemerged as the center of Japanese casual street fashion in the mid-1990s. For women, dabbling in French casual looks escalated into complicated multilayer ensembles in an almost hallucinatory mix of colors and absurd piles of accessories. The "street snap" magazine *FRUiTS* amped up this arty style: Women who wanted to be shot for the magazine started wearing more and more extreme outfits to impress the photographers and beat out peers. *FRUiTS*'s international distribution then spread word of this unique look overseas, and this made the word "Harajuku" synonymous with an intense form of fashion expression. This culminated in American singer Gwen Stefani producing a 2004 single called "Harajuku Girls" and creating a clothing line called Harajuku Lovers in homage to the neighborhood.

On the menswear side, the Ura-Harajuku area became famous in the 1990s as the birthplace of street fashion brands A Bathing Ape (Bape), Undercover, Head Porter, and Goodenough. Famous for their limited edition T-shirts, the brands became prize bounty for the cultural cognoscenti in New York, London, and Paris. The Ura-Harajuku guru Hiroshi Fujiwara pioneered techniques such as limiting supply, hiding stores, and eschewing advertising to drive consumer interest, which later informed the marketing of global brand Nike (where Fujiwara worked as a consultant). Bape became the go-to brand for the hip-hop community in the mid-2000s, while the punk-inspired Undercover impressed the high-end fashion community with its unsettling runway shows in Paris.

In the 1990s, Harajuku's neighboring district Shibuya also became a major fashion center. The *kogyaru*—young women with light-brown hair, fake tans, heavy makeup, and hiked-up miniskirts—set the country's style agenda for most of the decade. Originally a look associated with elite private-school students, the *gyaru* style changed dramatically at the end of the 1990s when working-class teens from outside of Tokyo co-opted it. Their distortion became known as *ganguro*—nearly pitch-black faces with white eye makeup, colored streaks in the hair, and dangerously high heels—and kicked off a moral panic about extreme dress, casual prostitution, and improper hygiene.

In the 21st century, the overall decline in consumer spending and the shrinking youth population has dulled the edge of Japanese fashion. Teens with smaller budgets have come to rely on basic clothes from mass retailer UNIQLO, foreign fast-fashion importers Forever 21 and H&M, and low-priced provincial clothier Shimamura. There are only a handful of new subcultures: for example, the Gothic-Lolita girls who wear over-the-top black lacey dresses and hang out on weekends near Harajuku station. The *gyaru* subculture lived on but dropped the nightmarish *ganguro* look to settle into a demure style of blond hair, heavy eye makeup, and pleasant apparel.

The Japanese youth fashion market may have lost steam compared to the 1990s, but the economies of Tokyo neighborhoods of Harajuku, Shibuya, Omotesandō, Daikanyama, and Kōenji still revolve around selling clothing to teenagers, as do the dozens of youth fashion areas in cities around the country. "Select shops," boutiques targeting youth, like Beams, United Arrows, Ships, Tomorrowland, and Journal Standard, have hundreds of shops. Even after two decades of economic stagnation, Japanese youth fashion is a significant market in its own right, and it is recognized more and more as a creative force in the global fashion ecosystem.

W. David Marx

See also: K-pop (Chapter 1: Popular Music)

Further Reading

Evers, Izumi, and Patrick Macias. 2010. *Japanese Schoolgirl Inferno: Tokyo Teen Fashion Subculture Handbook*. San Francisco, CA: Chronicle Books.
Kawamura, Yuniya. 2012. *Fashioning Japanese Subcultures*. London: Bloomsbury Academic.
Keet, Philomena, and Yuri Manabe. 2007. *Tokyo Look Book*. New York: Kodansha USA.
Mabuchi, Kōsuke. 1989. *"Zoku"-tachi no Sengoshi* [The Post-War History of the Tribes]. Tokyo: Sanseido.
Marx, W. David. 2015. *Ametora: How Japan Saved American Style*. New York: Basic Books.

Appendix: Top Ten Lists

MUSIC

Top Ten All-Time Songs for Asia

Rank	Song	Singer/Writer
1	"Sukiyaki" (Japan)	Hachidai Nakamura/ Rokusuke Ei
2	"Leum mai long" ("Won't Forget") (Thailand)	Traditional folk song
3	"Shima uta" ("Island Song") (Japan)	Kazufumi Miyazawa
4	"Yue liang dai biao wo de xin" ("The Moon Represents My Heart") (China)	Weng Ching-hsi/Sun Yi
5	"Rasa sayang" ("Loving Feeling") (Malaysia)	Traditional folk song
6	"Hana" ("Flower") (Japan)	Shoukichi Kina
7	"Bengawan solo" ("Solo River") (Indonesia)	Gesang
8	"Arirang" (Korea)	Traditional folk song
9	"Chnam oun dop pram muay" ("I'm Sixteen") (Cambodia)	Ros Sereysothea/traditional
10	"Deng zhe ni hui lai" ("I Wait for Your Return") (China)	Chen Re Jin/Yen Huan

"Paul Fisher's Top Ten Greatest Songs Ever from Asia." April 20, 2015. Farsidemusic.wordpress.com.

Top Ten Most-Viewed K-pop Videos around the World (October 2015)

Rank	Song	Singer(s)
1	"Verbal Jint (I)"	Taeyon
2	"Ooh Ahh"	Twice (girl group)
3	"Twenty-Three"	IU (Lee Ji-eun)
4	"4 Walls"	f(x) (girl group)
5	"No Makeup"	Zion T (Kim Hae-sol)
6	"A Million Pieces"	Kyuhyun
7	"You Don't Know Me"	Soyou & Brother Su
8	"Insane"	Ailee
9	"Way Back Home"	BToB (boy group)
10	"Oh My Girl"	SeungHee

"Billboard's Most Viewed K-Pop Videos around the World for October 2015." Billboard.com.

Top Ten All-Time Songs for New Zealand

Rank	Song	Singer/Writer
1	"Nature"	Fourmyula/Wayne Mason
2	"Don't Dream It's Over"	Crowded House/Neil Finn
3	"Loyal"	Dave Dobbyn
4	"Counting the Beat"	Swingers/Phil Judd et al.
5	"Six Months in a Leaky Boat"	Split Enz/Tim Finn
6	"Sway"	Bic Runga
7	"Slice of Heaven"	Dave Dobbyn with Herbs
8	"Victoria"	Dance Exponents/Jordan Luck
9	"She Speeds"	Straightjacket Fits/Shayne Carter
10	"April Sun in Cuba"	Dragon/Paul Hewson, Mark Hunter

"APRA Top 11 New Zealand Songs of All Time." Sergent.com.au.

Top Ten All-Time Songs for Australia

Rank	Song	Singer/Band
1	"True Blue"	John Williamson
2	"Down Under"	Men at Work/Colin Hay
3	"Still Call Australia Home"	Peter Allen
4	"Khe Sanh"	Cold Chisel
5	"Great Southern Land"	Icehouse
6	"Beds Are Burning"	Midnight Oil
7	"You're the Voice"	John Farnham
8	"Sounds of Then"	GANGgajang
9	"Better Be Home Soon"	Crowded House (Australian/New Zealand)
10	"For the Working-Class Man"	Jimmy Barnes

Duncan, Kate. "Australian Geographic's Top Classic Aussie Songs." January 27, 2001. Australian Geographic.com.au.

Top Ten Best-Selling Albums Performed by Australian/New Zealand Artists

Rank	Album	Artist/Band
1	Back in Black	AC/DC (Australian)
2	Savage Garden	Savage Garden (Australian)
3	Don't Ask	Tina Arena (Australian)
4	Innocent Eyes	Delta Goodrem (Australian)
5	Recurring Dream	Crowded House (Australian/New Zealand)
6	How Bizzare	Lorde, Ella Yelich O'Connor (New Zealand)
7	Supersystem	The Feelers (New Zealand)
8	Drive	Big Runga (New Zealand)

(continued)

Rank	Album	Artist/Band
9	*What to Do with Daylight*	Brooke Fraser (New Zealand)
10	*The Crusader*	Scribe, Malo Laufutu (New Zealand)

"Australian Recording Industry Association." Aria.com.au.
"Top Ten Kiwi Music Successes of the Past Ten Years." February 7, 2009. Nzherald.co.nz.

LITERATURE

Top Ten All-Time Novels of Asia

Rank	Title	Author	Year
1	*The Dream of the Red Chamber*	Cao Xueqin	1791
2	*A Fine Balance*	Rohinton Mistry	1995
3	*Rashomon*	Ryūnosuke Akutagawa	1915
4	*The Thousand Nights and One Night*	Anonymous	1706
5	*Heat and Dust*	Ruth Prawer Jhabvala	1975
6	*All about H. Hatterr*	G. V. Desani	1948
7	*The Wind-Up Bird Chronicle*	Haruki Murakami	1994
8	*Spring Snow*	Yukio Mishima	1969–1971
9	*Midnight's Children*	Salman Rushdie	1980
10	*The God of Small Things*	Arundhati Roy	1997

"Ten Best Asian Novels of All Time." Telegraph.co.uk.

Top Ten Best-Selling Books in Australia (2015)

Rank	Title	Author	Publisher/Year
1	*American Sniper*	Chris Kyle et al.	HarperCollins, 2014
2	*The Girl on the Train*	Paula Hawkins	DoubleDay, 2015
3	*14th Deadly Sin*	James Patterson	Century, 2015
4	*Family Food*	Pete Evans	Plum, 2014
5	*Mightier than the Sword*	Jeffrey Archer	MacMillan, 2015
6	*Prodigal Son*	Danielle Steele	Bantam, 2015
7	*Going Paleo*	Pete Evans and N. T. Gedgaudas	Plum, 2015
8	*That Sugar Book*	Damon Gameau	MacMillan, 2015
9	*The Happy Cookbook*	Lola Berry	Plum, 2013
10	*Still Alice*	Lisa Genova	Simon & Schuster, 2010

"Top Ten Best Selling Books in Australia." September 1, 2015. *Sydney Morning Herald*. Smh.com.au.

Top Ten Books by New Zealand Authors (2000–2009)

Rank	Title	Author	Publisher/Year
1	*Mister Pip*	Lloyd Jones	Dial Press, 2007
2	*Blindsight*	Maurice Gee	Penguin, 2005
3	*The Vintner's Luck*	Elizabeth Knox	MacMillan, 2000
4	*Tu*	Patricia Grace	Ateneo de Manila University Press, 2005
5	*Tarzan Presley*	Nigel Cox	Victoria University Press, 2004
6	*My Name was Judas*	C. K. Stead	Vintage, 2006
7	*Stonedogs*	Craig Marriner	Vintage, 2001
8	*The Book of the Film of the Story of My Life*	William Brandt	Grand Central Publishing, 2007
9	*Novel about my Wife*	Emily Perkins	Bloomsbury, USA, 2008
10	*The 10PM Question*	Kate DeGoldi	Candlewick Press, 2008

"Top Ten New Zealand Books of the Decade." December 31, 2009. Nzherald.co.nz.

FILM

Top Ten All-Time Asian Films

Rank	Title	Year	Director (Country)
1	*Tokyo Story*	1953	Ozu Yasujiro (Japan)
2	*Rashomon*	1950	Kurosawa Akira (Japan)
3	*In the Mood for Love*	2000	Wong Kar Wai (Hong Kong)
4	*The Apu Trilogy*	1955	Satyajit Ray (India)
5	*A City of Sadness*	1989	Hou Hsiao-hsien (Taiwan)
6	*Seven Samurai*	1954	Kurosawa Akira (Japan)
7	*A Brighter Summer Day*	1991	Edward Yang (Taiwan)
8	*Still Life*	2006	Jia Zhangke (China)
9	*The Housemaid*	1960	Kim Ki-young (South Korea)
10	*Close-Up*	1990	Abbas Kiarostami (Iran)

"Busan Festival Proposes Ranking of Best-Ever Asian Films. Korea's Busan Asian Cinema 100 List." Variety.com.

Top Ten Most Popular Movies at the Australian Box Office

Rank	Title	Release Date	Genre
1	*Crocodile Dundee*	1986	Romantic comedy adventure
2	*Australia*	2008	Historical melodrama
3	*Babe*	1995	Family

(continued)

Rank	Title	Release Date	Genre
4	*Happy Feet*	2006	Musical comedy
5	*Moulin Rouge*	2006	Musical romance
6	*The Great Gatsby*	2013	Romance drama
7	*Crocodile Dundee II*	1988	Romance comedy adventure
8	*Strictly Ballroom*	1992	Musical comedy
9	*Red Dog*	2011	Adventure comedy
10	*The Dish*	2000	Historical drama

"Top 100 Australian Feature Films of All Time, Ranked by Reported Gross Australian Box Office." January 2011. www.screenaustralia.gov.au/research/statistics/boxofficeaustraliatop100.aspx.

Top Ten All-Time Films of Australia

Rank	Title	Year
1	*The Adventures of Priscilla, Queen of the Desert*	1994
2	*Rabbit-Proof Fence*	2002
3	*Moulin Rouge*	2001
4	*Wolf Creek*	2005
5	*Muriel's Wedding*	1994
6	*Crocodile Dundee*	1986
7	*Dark City*	1998
8	*Dead Calm*	1989
9	*Romper Stomper*	1992
10	*Strictly Ballroom*	1992

"25 Best Australian Movies Ever." Stuff.tv.

Top Ten All-Time Films of New Zealand

Rank	Title	Year	Director
1	*Once Were Warriors*	1994	Lee Tamahori
2	*Boy*	2010	Taika Waititi
3	*Whale Rider*	2002	Niki Caro
4	*Goodbye Park Pie*	1981	Geoff Murphy
5	*Heavenly Creatures*	1994	Peter Jackson
6	*The Piano*	1993	Jane Campion
7	*In My Father's Den*	2004	Brad McGann
8	*Utu*	1983	Geoff Murphy
9	*Smash Palace*	1981	Roger Donaldson
10	*The Quiet Earth*	1986	Geoff Murphy

"Best Kiwi Films of All Time." Movies-interactives.co.nz.

TELEVISION AND RADIO

Top Ten Best Asian Television Shows (2014)

Rank	Title	Genre	Country
1	*Fall in Love with Me*	Drama	Taiwan
2	*My Love from Another Star*	Drama	Korea
3	*Love Myself or You?*	Drama	Taiwan
4	*Mischievous Kiss: Love in Tokyo*	Drama	Tokyo
5	*No Game, No Life*	Manga adaptation	Japan
6	*Mysterious Summer*	Drama	Japan
7	*Secret Love Affair*	Drama	Japan
8	*Roommate*	Drama	Korea
9	*ST: Scientific Task Force*	Detective story	Japan
10	*Discovery of Romance*	Drama	Korea

Tseng, Ada. "Top Ten Hit TV Shows of 2014." December 30, 2014. Myxfinity.com.

Top Ten Most Popular TV Shows in India (2015)

Rank	Title	Channel
1	*Sath nibhana sathiya*	Star Plus
2	*Meri ashiqul tumse hi*	Colors
3	*Kumkum bhagya*	Zee
4	*Sasurai simar ka*	Colors
5	*Ye hai mohabbatein*	Star Plus
6	*Chakravartin ashok samrat*	Colors
7	*Ye rishta kya kehlata hai*	Star Plus
8	*Tarak mehta ka ooitah Chashma*	SAB
9	*Udaan*	Colors
10	*Jodha akbar*	Zee

"Top Ten Most Popular Indian TV Serial of 2015." July 15, 2015. Topwebsitelists.com.

Top Ten Best-Ever Korean Dramas

Rank	Title	Released
1	*Boys over Flower*	2009
2	*Secret Garden*	2010
3	*The Heirs*	2013
4	*My Love from the Star*	2013
5	*Rooftop Prince*	2012
6	*The First Shop of Coffee Prince*	2007
7	*Moon Embracing Moon*	2012
8	*Full House*	2004

(continued)

Rank	Title	Released
9	*Dream High*	2011
10	*You're Beautiful*	2009

"Top Ten Best Korean Drama." The10bestreview.com.

Top Ten Best-Ever Australian TV Shows

Rank	Title	Released
1	*Offspring*	2010
2	*Hey Hey It's Saturday*	1986
3	*Young Talent Time*	1971
4	*Neighbors*	2000
5	*Home and Away*	1994
6	*Kath and Kim*	2002
7	*Prisoner: The Original*	1979
8	*A Country Practice*	1985
9	*Heartbreak High*	1994
10	*Secret Life of Us*	2001

"The Top 10 Australian TV Shows, Ever. Entertainment." March 19, 2015. Mamamia.com.au.

Top Ten Best-Ever New Zealand Comedy Series

Rank	Title	Released
1	*A Week of It*, "Series One, Episode Three"	1977
2	*Gliding On*, "No Smoke without Fire"	1981
3	*The Best of Billy T. James Collection*	1992
4	*Funny Business*, excerpts	1988–1991 (excerpts)
5	*The Top Twins*, "Highland Games"	2000
6	*Eating Media Lunch* "Best of (Episode)"	2006
7	*Pulp Sport*, "Series Seven, Episode One"	2009
8	*bro'Town*, "The Weakest Link"	2004
9	*The Jaquie Diaries*, "Brown Sweat (Episode Three)"	2008
10	*Seven Days*, "Series One, Episode Three"	2008

"Top 10 NZ Comedy Series." NZonscreen.com.

INTERNET AND SOCIAL MEDIA

Top Ten Countries/Regions with Best Internet Coverage in Asia

Rank	Country	Percentage of Internet Penetration
1	Taiwan	64%
2	Hong Kong	61%

(continued)

Rank	Country	Percentage of Internet Penetration
3	Singapore	59%
4	Australia	57%
5	New Zealand	57%
6	Malaysia	53%
7	China	46%
8	Maldives	44%
9	Thailand	36%
10	Philippines	32%

"Social Media Usage in Asia Pacific—Statistics and Trends." Go-globe.com.

Top Ten Asia Pacific Facebook Users by Country

Rank	Country	Percentage of Online Population
1	Indonesia	96%
2	Vietnam	94%
3	Malaysia	94%
4	Philippines	94%
5	Thailand	93%
6	India	93%
7	Hong Kong	93%
8	Taiwan	91%
9	Singapore	91%
10	Australia	78%

"Social Media Usage in Asia Pacific—Statistics and Trends." Go-globe.com.

Top Ten Chinese Social Media Sites

Rank	Name	Western Counterpart
1	Sina Weibo	Twitter of China
2	Tencent Weibo	Retweeting; also like Facebook
3	Renren	Schoolyard, reconnecting friends
4	PengYou	Facebook-like site
5	QQ	Instant messaging
6	Douban	Similar to MySpace
7	Diandian	Tumblr of China
8	Youku	Video site
9	WeChat	Mobile voice/text app
10	Jiepang	Location-mobile networking service

"Ten Chinese Social Media Sites You Should be Following." March 27, 2013. Synthesio.com.

SPORTS

Top Ten Most Popular Asian Sports Stars

Rank	Name	Sport	Country
1	Manny Pacquiao	Boxing	Philippines
2	Masahiro Tanaka	Baseball	Japan
3	Li Na	Tennis	China
4	Viktor Ahn (Ahn Hyun-soo)	Speed skating	Russia (native, South Korea)
5	Jeremy Lin	Basketball	Taiwan
6	Kei Nishikori	Tennis	Japan
7	Hyun-jin Ryu	Baseball	South Korea
8	Kumar Sangakkara	Cricket	Sri Lanka
9	Shinji Okazaki	Soccer	Japan
10	Inbee Park	Golf	South Korea

Chi, Samuel. "Ten Biggest Asian Sports Stars, A Look at the Biggest Asian Names in the World Sport Today." August 28, 2014. Thediplomat.com.

Top Ten Australian Athletes of All Time

Rank	Name	Sport
1	Don Bradman	Baseball
2	Herb Elliott	Running
3	Rod Laver	Tennis
4	Margaret Court	Tennis
5	Heather McKay	Tennis
6	Dawn Fraser	Swimming
7	Ken Rosewall	Tennis
8	Betty Cuthbert	Running
9	Peter Thomson	Golf
10	Mark Ellis	Football (soccer)

"Top 10 Greatest Australian Athletes of All Time." Sporteology.com.

Top Ten New Zealand Athletes of All Time

Rank	Name	Sport
1	Valerie Adams	Shot put
2	Peter Snell	Running
3	Yvette Williams	Long jump
4	Murray Halberg	Running
5	Ian Ferguson	Rowing
6	Jack Lovelock	Running

(continued)

Rank	Name	Sport
7	Malcolm Champion	Swimming
8	John Walker	Running
9	Danyon Loader	Swimming
10	Barbara Kendall	Boardsailing

"New Zealand's Greatest Ever Athletes." Nz.sports.yahoo.com.

VIDEO GAMES

Top Ten Best Asian Characters in Video Games

Rank	Name	Characteristic
1	Lau Chan	Fighter, father figure
2	Knives Chau	Fighter, female
3	Ada Wong	Bad girl, gunslinger
4	Ryo Hazuki	Fighter, dude
5	Inspector "Tequila" Yuen	Gun-busting detective
6	Chell	Fighter, female
7	Ghost	Fighter, dude
8	Faith	Smart female
9	Chun Li	Street fighter, female
10	Wei Shen	Undercover cop, male

Hester, Larry. "The 10 Best Asian Characters in Video Games." Complex.com.

Top Ten Japanese Best-Selling Video Games of All Time

Rank	Name	Copies
1	Pokemon (Red, Blue, Green) for Gameboy	7.8 million
2	Super Mario Brothers for Famicon	6.8 million
3	Super Mario Brothers for Nintendo	6.3 million
4	Pokemon (Gold, Silver) for Gameboy	6.1 million
5	Pokemon (Diamond, Pearl) Nintendo	5.8 million
6	Pokemon (Black, White) Nintendo	5.45 million
7	Pokemon (Ruby, Sapphire) Gameboy	5.4 million
8	Animal Crossing: Wild World, Nintendo	5.25 million
9	Brain Age 2: More Brain Training, Nintendo	5.1 million
10	Monster Hunter Portable 3rd for PlayStation	4.7 million

"Japan's 30 Best Selling Video Games of All Time." En.rocketnews24.com.

FASHION

Top Ten Asian Supermodels (2015)

Rank	Name	Country
1	Tao Okamoto	Japan
2	Liu Wen	China
3	Godfrey Gao	Taiwan/Canada
4	Sui He	China
5	Fei Fei Sun	China
6	Xiao Wen Ju	China
7	Du Juan	China
8	Ming Xi	China
9	Shu Pei	China
10	Zhao Lei	China

Arogundade, Ben. "Enter the East: The World's Top 10 Asian Fashion Models." Arogundade.com.

Top Ten Asian Fashion Designers, Models, and Actresses (2013)

Rank	Name	Role
1	Zhang Ziyi	Actress
2	Fan Bingbing	Actress/singer/producer
3	Alexander Wang	Designer
4	Liu Wen	Model
5	Rinko Kikuchi	Actress
6	Carol Lim	Designer
7	Ji Hye Park	Model
8	Eunice Lee	Designer
9	Rita Fukushima	Model/actress
10	Humberto Leon	Designer

Jacques, Renee. "Asian Style Icons: Designers, Models & Actresses Dominating the Fashion Industry." June 19, 2013. Huffingtonpost.com.

Top Ten Most Influential Asian Fashion Blogs

Rank	Title	Blogger	Country
1	Pony's Makeup	Pony (Park Hye Min)	Korea
2	Ulimali	Uli Chan	Singapore
3	P.O. Box Style	Ploy Chava	Thailand
4	Dreachong	Andrea Chong	Singapore
5	Style from Tokyo	Rei Shito	Japan
6	Break My Style	Laureen Uy	Philippines

(continued)

Rank	Title	Blogger	Country
7	*Emily's Anthology*	Emily Quak	Malaysia
8	*Tina Loves*	Tina Leung	Hong Kong
9	*Belluspuera*	Velda Tan	Singapore
10	*Bagaholidboy*	Alvin Cher	Singapore

"Be," 10 Asian Bloggers That Have Gone International." Asia.be.com.

Top Ten Australian Fashion Designers (2015)

Rank	Name (Label)
1	(Nicky and Simone Zimmerman)
2	Ramon Martin and Ryan Lobo (Tome NYC)
3	Kym Ellery (Ellery)
4	(Sass and Bide)
5	Camilla Freeman Topper (Camilla & Marc)
6	(Michael Lo Sordo)
7	Becky Cooper (Bec & Bridge)
8	Lace Aficionados (Lover)
9	Toni Maticevski (Maticevski)
10	Dion Lee

Schmidt, Chantelle. "The Fashion Spot: The Top 10 Australian Fashion Designers to Know." March 15, 2015. Thefashionspot.com.

Top Ten New Zealand Fashion Designers (2015)

Rank	Name (Label)
1	Elizabeth and Neville Findlay (Zambesi)
2	Deborah Calder (Storm)
3	Sara Munro (Company of Strangers)
4	(Karen Walker)
5	(Trelise Cooper)
6	Denise L'Estrange Corbet and Francis Hooper (World)
7	(Adrienne Whitewood)
8	Kirsha Witcher (Salasai)
9	Danielle Burkhart (My Boyfriend's Back)
10	Rowan Anderson (Working Style)

"New Zealand, the Best Art, Food, Culture, Travel: Top 10 New Zealand Fashion Designers You Should Know." Theculturetrip.com.

Selected Bibliography

Abelmann, Nancy. 2003. *The Melodrama of Mobility: Women, Talk, and Class in Contemporary South Korea*. Honolulu: University of Hawai'i Press.

Armstrong, Charles K. 2003. "The Cultural Cold War in Korea, 1945–1950." *The Journal of Korean Studies* 62, no. 1: 71–99.

Askari, Nasreen. 1991. *Uncut Cloth: Saris, Shawls, and Sashes*. London: Merrell Holberton.

Aung San Suu Kyi. 1991. *Freedom from Fear and Other Writings*. New York: Penguin Books.

Barboza, David. 2005. "Ogre to Slay? Outsource It to Chinese." *New York Times*. December 9. http://www.nytimes.com/2005/12/09/technology/ogre-to-slay-outsource-it-to-chinese.html. Accessed March 26, 2016.

Baulch, Emma. 2007. *Making Scenes: Reggae, Punk, and Death Metal in 1990s Bali*. Durham, NC: Duke University Press.

Bax, Trent. 2014. *Youth and Internet Addiction in China*. New York: Routledge.

Blenkinsopp, Alexander. 2002. "Asian Invasion: Baseball's Ambassadors." *Harvard International Review* 24, no. 1 (Spring).

Blythe, Martin. 1994. *Naming the Other: Images of the Maori in New Zealand Film and Television*. Metuchen, NZ: The Scarecrow Press.

Booth, Gregory, and Bradley Shope, eds. 2014. *More than Bollywood, Studies in Indian Pop Music*. New York: Oxford University Press.

Brenner, Robin E. 2007. *Understanding Manga and Anime*. Westport, CT: Libraries Unlimited.

Cashman, Richard, and Rob Hess, eds. 2011. *Sport History and Australian Culture: Passionate Pursuits*. Petersham, AU: Walla Walla Press.

Cha, Victor D. 2011. *Beyond the Final Score: The Politics of Sport in Asia*. New York: Columbia University Press.

Chi, Pang Yuan, and David Der Wei Wang, eds. 2000. *Chinese Literature in the Second Half of a Modern Century: A Critical Survey*. Bloomington: Indiana University Press.

Cho, Younghan. 2014. *Football in Asia: History, Culture, and Business*. Abingdon, UK: Routledge.

Coventry, James 2015. *Time and Space: The Tactics That Shaped Australian Rules and the Players and Coaches Who Mastered Them*. Sydney: ABC Books/HarperCollins Australia.

Cui, Litang, and Michael H. Prosser. 2014. *Social Media in Asia*. Dörzbach, Germany: Dignity Press.

DeNardis, Laura. 2014. *The Global War for Internet Governance*. New Haven, CT: Yale University Press.

Dương, Lan. 2007. "Long-Legged Girls and the Transnational Circuits of Vietnamese Popular Culture." In *Transnational Feminism in Media and Cinema*. Ed. Katarzyna Marciniak, Áine O'Healy, and Anikó Imre, 163–184. New York: Palgrave Macmillan Press.

Dwyer, Ralph, and Christopher Pinney, eds. 2001. *The History, Politics and Consumption of Public Culture in India*. New Delhi: Oxford University Press.

Endeshaw, Assafa. 2004. "Internet Regulation in China: The Never-ending Cat and Mouse Game." *Information & Communications Technology Law* 13, no. 1: 41–57.

Farquhar, Mary, and Zhang Yingjin. 2010. *Chinese Film Stars*. London: Routledge.

Fernandes, Clinton, ed. 2008. *Hot Spot: Asia and Oceania*. Westport, CT: Greenwood Press.

Fuhr, Michael. 2016. *Globalization and Popular Music in South Korea: Sounding Out K-Pop*. New York: Routledge.

Gajarawala, Toral Jatin. 2012. *Untouchable Fictions: Literary Realism and the Crisis of Caste*. New York: Fordham University Press.

Hartley, L., and P. Schiaffini, eds. 2008. *Modern Tibetan Literature and Social Change*. Durham, NC: Duke University Press.

Hocking, Scott, and Bill Collins, eds. 2006. *100 Greatest Films of Australian Cinema*. Richmond, AU: Scribal Publishing.

Hong, Euny. 2014. *The Birth of Korean Cool: How One Nation Is Conquering the World through Pop Culture*. New York: Picador.

Howard, Keith. 2006. *Korean Pop Music: Riding the Wave*. Folkestone, UK: Global Oriental.

Hsu, Adam. 2006. *Lone Sword against the Cold Sky: Principles and Practice of Traditional Kung Fu*. Santa Cruz, CA: Plum Publications.

Jackson, Kym. 2012. *The Hollywood Survival Guide: For Aussie Actors*. Sydney, AU: Perfict Books.

Kawamura, Yuniya. 2012. *Fashioning Japanese Subcultures*. London: Bloomsbury Academic.

Keane, Michael, and Albert Moran. 2009. *Television across Asia: TV Industries, Programme Formats and Globalisation*. London: Routledge.

Kim, Cheehyung. 2012. "Total, Thus Broken: *Chuch'e Sasang* and North Korea's Terrain of Subjectivity." *The Journal of Korean Studies* 17, no. 1: 69–96.

Kim, Kyung Hyun, and Youngmin Choe, eds. 2014. *The Korean Popular Culture Reader*. Durham, NC: Duke University Press.

Kitley, Philip. 2000. *Television, Nation, and Culture in Indonesia*. Athens, OH: Ohio University Press.

Kurosawa, Akira. 1983. *Something Like an Autobiography*. New York: Vintage Books.

Lal, Vinay, and Ashis Nandy. 2007. *Fingerprinting Popular Culture: The Mythic and the Iconic in Indian Cinema*. New Delhi: Oxford University Press India.

Lie, John. 2015. *K-pop: Popular Music, Cultural Amnesia, and Economic Innovation in South Korea*. Los Angeles: University of California Press.

Manabe, Noriko. 2015. *The Revolution Will Not Be Televised: Protest Music after Fukushima*. New York: Oxford University Press.

Markovits, Andrei S., and Lars Rensmann. 2010. *Gaming the World: How Sports Are Reshaping Global Politics and Culture*. Princeton, NJ: Princeton University Press.

Martens, Emiel. 2012. "Maori on the Silver Screen: The Evolution of Indigenous Feature Filmmaking in Aotearoa/New Zealand." *International Journal of Critical Indigenous Studies* 5, no. 1 (October): 1–30.

Mehta, Nalin. 2015. *Behind a Billion Screens: What Television Tells Us about Modern India*. Noida, IN: HarperCollins India.

Mills, James H. 2005. *Subaltern Sports: Politics and Sport in South Asia*. London: Anthem Press.

Moran, Albert, and Chris Keating. 2009. *The A to Z of Australian Radio and Television*. Lanham, MD: Scarecrow Press (Rowman & Littlefield).

Morris, Andrew D. 2010. *Colonial Project, National Game: A History of Baseball in Taiwan.* Berkeley: University of California Press.

Moskowitz, Marc L. 2010. *Cries of Joy, Songs of Sorrow: Chinese Pop Music and Its Cultural Connotations.* Honolulu: University of Hawai'i Press.

Nadeau, Kathleen, and Sangita Rayamajhi. 2013. *Women's Roles in Asia.* Santa Barbara, CA: Greenwood Press.

Ortner, Sherry B. 1999. *Life and Death on Mt. Everest: Sherpas and Himalayan Mountaineering.* Princeton, NJ: Princeton University Press.

Pertierra, Raul. 2012. *The New Media, Society and Politics in the Philippines.* Berlin, Germany: Friedrich-Ebert-Stiftung.

Robinson, Luke. 2013. *Independent Chinese Documentary: From the Studio to the Street.* New York: Palgrave Macmillan.

Saikia, Yasmin. 2011. *Women, War, and the Making of Bangladesh, Remembering 1971.* Durham, NC: Duke University Press.

Sandoval, Gerardo A., and Ricardo G. Abad. 1997. "Sports and the Filipino: A Love Affair." *Social Weather Bulletin* 97: 3–4.

Schwartz, Ronald, and Robert Barnett, eds. 2003. *Tibetan Modernities: Notes from the Field on Social and Cultural Change.* Leiden, NL: Brill.

Shotwell, Peter. 2003. *Go! More Than a Game.* Boston: Tuttle Publishing.

Sionil, F. Jose. 1984. *Mass: A Novel.* Sydney, AU: George Allen & Unwin.

Strecher, Matthew. 2014. *The Forbidden Worlds of Haruki Murakami.* Minneapolis: University of Minnesota Press.

Tan, David. 2012. "Who's the Fairest of Them All?" *Asian Scientist Magazine.* September 18. http://www.asianscientist.com/2012/09/features/skin-whitening-products-asia-2012/. Accessed March 26, 2016.

Tharoor, Shashi. 1989. *The Great Indian Novel.* New York: Arcade Publishing.

Toer, Pramoedya Ananta. 1975. *This Earth of Mankind.* New York: Penguin Books.

Wallis, Cara. 2011. "New Media Practices in China: Youth Patterns, Processes, and Politics." *International Journal of Communication* 5: 406–436.

Wang, David Der-wei, and Carlos Rojas, eds. 2007. *Writing Taiwan: A New Literary History.* Durham, NC: Duke University Press.

Wicks, James. 2014. *Transnational Representations: The State of Taiwan Film in the 1960s and 1970s.* Hong Kong: Hong Kong University Press.

Willnat, Lars, and Annette Aw. 2014. *Social Media, Culture and Politics in Asia.* Frankfurt, Germany: Peter Lang Publishing.

Wolf, Mark J. P., ed. 2008. *The Video Game Explosion: A History from PONG to PlayStation and Beyond.* Westport, CT: Greenwood Press.

Xu, Gary, and Vinay Dharwadker, eds. 2007. *The Greenwood Encyclopedia of World Popular Culture, Volume 6: Asia and Pacific Oceania.* Westport, CT: Greenwood Press.

Yadava, Mukesh. 2014. "Domesticating Shakespeare: A Study of Indian Adaptation of Shakespeare in Popular Culture." *European Journal of English Language and Literature Studies* 2, no. 3 (September): 48–58.

Yang, Guobin. 2015. *China's Contested Internet.* Copenhagen, DK: Nordic Institute of Asian Studies.

Younghan, Cho, and Charles Leary. 2014. *Modern Sports in Asia: Cultural Perspectives.* London: Routledge.

Zhang, Rui. 2008. *The Cinema of Feng Xiaogang: Commercialization and Censorship in Chinese Cinema after 1989.* Hong Kong: Hong Kong University Press.

Zhu, Ying, and Stanley Rosen, eds. 2010. *Art, Politics, and Commerce in Chinese Cinema.* Hong Kong: Hong Kong University Press.

Zhu, Ying. 2012. *Two Billion Eyes: The Story of China Central Television.* New York: The New Press.

Zhu, Ying. 2008. *Television in Post-Reform China: Serial Dramas, Confucian Leadership and the Global Television Market.* New York: Routledge.

About the Editors and Contributors

Editors

Kathleen M. Nadeau is a professor of anthropology at California State University, San Bernardino. She authored *Liberation Theology in the Philippines: Faith in a Revolution* (Praeger) and *The History of the Philippines* (Greenwood). Nadeau coauthored, with Sangita Rayamajhi, *Women's Roles in Asia* (Greenwood). Her coedited collections, with Jonathan Lee, include *Encyclopedia of Asian American Folklore and Folklife* (ABC-CLIO); a special issue of *Amerasia: Asian American Folklore: Passages and Practices* 39, no. 2 (2013); and *Asian American Identities and Practices: Folkloric Expressions in Everyday Life*. Her work has appeared in *Critical Anthropology*, *Human Organization*, *Journal for Scientific Study of Religion*, *Geografiska Annaler*, *Philippine Quarterly of Culture and Society*, and *Urban Anthropology*, among other scholarly journals and books. Nadeau's current research focuses on faith and community resilience to climate change in the Philippines.

Jeremy A. Murray is an assistant professor of Chinese history at California State University, San Bernardino. His research focuses mainly on the history of Hainan Island in the 20th century. He has also published work on Chinese history in film and memory, including the portrayals of World War II through mainstream Chinese cinema, and has also written on Chinese legal history and the South China Sea. His forthcoming book, *China's Lonely Revolution: The Local Communists' Struggle for Survival on Hainan Island*, is based on the history of the Chinese Communist revolution as experienced from the marginalized perspective of Hainan Island.

Contributors

Parhat Ablat is an independent scholar and consultant. He captained and coached Xinjiang University's baseball team, featured in the documentary *Diamond in the Dunes* (2014).

Elise Anderson is a doctoral candidate in Central Asian Studies at Indiana University, pursuing a degree in both Folklore and Ethnomusicology, and Area Studies.

Myrtati Dyah Artaria completed her doctorate at Arizona State University and is a lecturer with the Department of Anthropology at the Universitas Airlangga in Indonesia.

E. Taylor Atkins is Presidential Teaching Professor in the Department of History at Northern Illinois University in DeKalb, Illinois.

Sangita Babu is an associate professor at SBR College in Berhampur University, Odisha, India.

Joi Barrios is a poet and literature scholar teaching at University of California, Berkeley. In 1998 she was among 100 women chosen as Weavers of History for the Philippine Centennial.

Emily Baum completed her doctorate in Chinese history at University of California, San Diego, and is an assistant professor of history at the University of California, Irvine.

Deanna Bibler studies anthropology at California State University, San Bernardino.

Robin E. Brenner is Teen Librarian at the Brookline Public Library in Massachusetts. She has served on multiple awards committees. She is the editor-in-chief of the graphic novel review website noflyingnotights.com.

Roger J. Bresnahan is Professor of Literature at Michigan State University, specializing in the literature and history of the Philippines and Southeast Asia.

Cherish Aileen A. Brillon is an associate professor in the Department of Communication at Far Eastern University in Manila, Philippines.

Jason Brown-Galindo is a California State University of San Bernardino graduate in history, focusing on Middle Eastern and East Asian cultures.

Darren Byler completed his MA in East Asian Studies at Columbia University and is currently a doctoral candidate in anthropology at the University of Washington.

Jessica Carniel is a lecturer in Humanities at the University of Southern Queensland. Her broad research interests include Australian Studies and Cultural Studies.

Catherine Cartwright-Jones completed her doctoral research work on henna in the Geography Department of Kent State University (2015) and contributed numerous articles to *The Oxford Encyclopedia of Islam and Women* (2013).

Angie C. Chau (周安琪) is a postdoctoral teaching scholar of modern Chinese literature and film at Arizona State University.

Siyu Chen is a doctoral candidate in the Department of Cultural Studies and Oriental Languages at the University of Oslo.

Desmond Cheung teaches East Asian History at Portland State University, Oregon.

Gabriele de Seta is a postdoctoral fellow at the Institute of Ethnology, Academia Sinica, in Taipei, Taiwan. His research interests include digital media use and practices of vernacular creativity in everyday life.

Yangdon Dhondup is a research associate at the School of Oriental and African Studies, University of London.

Lan Duong is an associate professor in the Department of Media and Cultural Studies at the University of California, Riverside.

Joshua L. Freeman completed his masters in Uyghur literature at Xinjiang Normal University and is currently a doctoral candidate at Harvard University.

Brandon Fryman is an adjunct professor of anthropology at the University of La Verne, focusing on human rights, social justice, sustainable development, program evaluation, needs assessment, and agency.

Jojo M. Fung, SJ, is an assistant professor of Contextual Theology at the East Pastoral Institute and the Asian Theology Program at the Loyola School of Theology, Manila, Philippines.

Connor J. Gahre completed his bachelor's with a double major in history and political science at California State University, San Bernardino.

Howard Goldblatt is a translator of Chinese literature, notably the works of Huang Chunming and Mo Yan, and he was Research Professor of Chinese at the University of Notre Dame.

Haomin Gong is an assistant professor of Chinese at Case Western Reserve University in Cleveland, Ohio.

Maggie Greene is a modern Chinese historian and assistant professor of history at Montana State University in Bozeman, Montana.

Isabelle Henrion-Dourcy is an anthropologist at Université Laval (Québec) whose research focuses on Tibetan performing arts, especially drama and folk-song genres, and Tibetan media, mostly television and Internet.

Megan Robin Hewitt is a doctoral candidate in South and Southeast Asian Studies at the University of California, Berkeley, with research interests in cultural movements of Indonesia.

Shan Huang is a doctoral student in anthropology at Stanford University, and his work concerns cultural politics in contemporary China.

Katherine M. Jakovich is an adjunct instructor of yoga in the Department of Kinesiology at California State University, San Bernardino.

Benjamin N. Judkins holds a doctoral degree in Political Science from Columbia University and is a founding editor of the interdisciplinary academic journal *Martial Arts Studies*.

Paul Kendall is a lecturer in Chinese Studies at the University of Westminster. His research explores the relationship between space, music, and sound in urban China.

Nyla Ali Khan is a faculty member at the University of Oklahoma. Her research focuses on the culture and politics of her homeland, Jammu and Kashmir, and she is the author, most recently, of *The Life of a Kashmiri Woman: Dialectic of Resistance and Accommodation* (2014).

Cheehyung Harrison Kim is Korea Foundation Assistant Professor of History at the University of Missouri's Department of History.

Love Kindstrand is a doctoral student at the University of Chicago interested in temporalities of crisis and hope and spaces of dissent and autonomy.

Li Cho Kiu is a doctoral candidate in sociology, National University of Singapore. His work examines the celebrity politics and governance of attention in China.

Matthew Klugman is an Australian Research Council DECRA Fellow at the Institute of Sport, Exercise and Active Living, Victoria University, Melbourne, Australia.

Roger Knowles is the manager of the Australian Antarctic Division's Supply Management Group in Hobart, Tasmania (40°S) and Antarctica (66°S).

William Langran is an international lawyer and holds degrees in Chinese Languages and History (SOAS), International Relations (Cambridge), and Law (Cornell Law School).

Jun Lei is a doctoral candidate in comparative literature at University of California, San Diego.

Enrique Niño P. Leviste is an assistant professor of sociology and anthropology at the Ateneo de Manila University, Quezon City, Philippines.

Perry Link is Chancellorial Chair for Innovation in Teaching Across Disciplines at the University of California, Riverside.

Monica Liu is a PhD candidate in the Department of Sociology at University of California, San Diego, and research associate at the UC-Fudan Center on Contemporary China.

Hector E. Lopez is a master's student in history at California State University, San Bernardino.

Susannah Malkan is an assistant professor and chair of the Department of Sociology at S. K. Somaiya College, and her research focuses on the Hindi film industry.

Noriko Manabe is an assistant professor in musicology at Princeton University, specializing in music and social movements in Japan.

Emiel Martens is an assistant professor in media studies at the University of Amsterdam, the Netherlands.

W. David Marx is author of *Ametora: How Japan Saved American Style* (2015) as well as editor-in-chief of a web journal on Japanese culture, Neojaponisme.com.

Karline McLain is an associate professor of South Asian Religion, Chair of the Religious Studies Department at Bucknell University, and author of *India's Immortal Comic Books: Gods, Kings, and Other Heroes* (2009).

Patit Paban Mishra is an emeritus professor of history at Sambalpur University in Odisha, India.

Ryan Moran is a visiting assistant professor at University of California, Riverside. He is currently working on a manuscript on the history of life insurance in modern Japan.

Andrew D. Morris is a professor of modern Chinese and Taiwanese history at California Polytechnic State University, San Luis Obispo.

Aaron R. Murray studied history and education at SUNY Binghamton, New York University, and Bard College.

Timothy I. Murray studied history at SUNY Albany and law at Atlanta's John Marshall Law School.

Sherry B. Ortner is a distinguished professor of anthropology at University of California, Los Angeles, and has conducted extensive fieldwork with the Sherpas of Nepal.

Jenny Ortuoste holds a doctoral degree in Communication from the University of the Philippines-Diliman and writes opinion and horse-racing columns for the Philippine daily newspaper *The Standard.*

Protima Pandey is a public interest lawyer in northern California (www.baylegal .org). She is licensed to practice law in California and India.

Marco Pellitteri (PhD) is JSPS Research Fellow, Kobe University. His current research is on Japanese pop cultures in Europe. He is the author of *The Dragon and the Dazzle: Models, Strategies, and Identities of Japanese Imagination* (2010).

Dechen Pemba graduated from the University College London and is editor of the website High Peaks Pure Earth (http://highpeakspureearth.com), which monitors and translates Tibetan news and blogs.

Lourdes M. Portus is a professor at the College of Mass Communication, University of the Philippines. She currently serves as Special Assistant to the President.

Stephen Prince is a professor of cinema at Virginia Tech. A former president of the Society for Cinema and Media Studies, he is the author of numerous books on film history and criticism. His audio commentaries can be heard on the DVD and Blu-ray editions of Akira Kurosawa's films.

Felicidad A. Prudente is a professor of ethnomusicology at the University of the Philippines.

Sangita Rayamajhi is a professor of Literature and Gender and Sexuality Studies with the Asian University for Women, Bangladesh.

Françoise Robin is a professor of Tibetan Studies at the Institut National des Langues et Civilisations Orientales in Paris. She specializes in Tibetan cinema and literature.

Luke Robinson is a lecturer in Film Studies in the Department of Media and Film, University of Sussex, U.K. He is the author of *Independent Chinese Documentary: From the Studio to the Street* (2013).

Morris Rossabi is a distinguished professor of history at Columbia University, writing and teaching about Mongolian history.

CedarBough T. Saeji is an assistant professor of Korean Studies at Hankuk University of Foreign Studies in the Republic of Korea. Her research focuses on cultural heritage, folk theater, dance, and media.

Felice Prudente Sta. Maria writes nonfiction about Philippine culture, including topics such as foods, fabrics, and transformative events. A recipient of the Southeast Asian Write Award, she is a Philippine National Museum trustee and a member of Ayala Museum's Board of Advisors.

Stefan Schutt is a former research program leader and current honorary fellow within the Centre for Cultural Diversity and Wellbeing at Victoria University in Melbourne. His research focuses on people's everyday use of technology.

Flair Donglai Shi is a graduate student at University College London. He specializes in world literatures and Asian studies.

Alka Singh teaches English at Dr. Ram Manohar Lohiya National Law University, Lucknow. Her publications include *Gender Roles in the Postmodern World* (2014) and *Postmodernism: Texts and Contexts* (2014).

Ravindra Pratap Singh teaches English at University of Lucknow. His publications include *Flea Market and Other Plays* (2014), *Ecologue*, and *When Brancho Flies*.

Daniel A. Stolp studied history and education at California State University, San Bernardino.

Matthew C. Strecher is a professor of Japanese literature and culture at Sophia University in Tokyo, and he is the author, most recently, of *The Forbidden Worlds of Haruki Murakami* (2014).

Shreerekha Subramanian is an associate professor of humanities and the first recipient of the Marilyn Mieszkuc Professorship of Women's Studies at University of Houston-Clear Lake.

Barbara Sum completed her bachelor of science degree in Anthropology at California State University, San Bernardino.

Sejal Sutaria is a research associate at the University of Exeter and specializes in 20th-century postcolonial Anglophone literature, international modernisms, and human rights.

Francis Tanglao-Aguas is an associate professor of Asian American Studies, Africana Studies, and Theater at the College of William and Mary in Virginia.

Sindhu Sara Thomas is an assistant professor with the Department of English at Somaiya College, Mumbai, India.

Sylvia Tiwon is an associate professor of South and Southeast Asian Studies at the University of California, Berkeley.

Matthew B. Turetsky teaches in the Berlin Central School district (Berlin, NY), and he studied psychology and education at SUNY New Paltz and CUNY Hunter.

J. T. Velikovsky is a Narratology scholar, Transmedia (movies, games, television) writer-director-producer, and story analyst for major movie studios, funding organizations, and the Australian Writers Guild.

James Wicks is an associate professor of literature and film studies at Point Loma Nazarene University in San Diego, California.

Yidi Wu is a doctoral candidate in history at the University of California, Irvine. She has conducted oral history interviews with Chinese college students of the 1950s for her dissertation and incorporates documentaries in her teaching.

Kyejung R. Yang is an instructor of anthropology at De Anza College. She received a doctorate from University of Illinois at Urbana-Champaign. Her research interests include Korean popular cultures, globalization, and the negotiation of Korean identity.

Lijun Yang is a professor of sociology at South China University of Technology, Guangzhou, China.

Yiyi Yin is a graduate student in the Critical Studies Division of the School of Cinematic Arts at the University of Southern California.

Jingqiu Zhang earned an interdisciplinary master's degree in the College of Social and Behavioral Sciences at California State University, San Bernardino, where he also earned his bachelor's degree in History.

Yuanbo Zhang is an anthropology graduate of London School of Economics and Political Science and a five-*dan* amateur *weiqi* player in Hangzhou, China.

Index

Page numbers in **bold** indicate the location of main entries.